REGISTER OF
SEAMEN'S PROTECTION CERTIFICATES
FROM THE
PROVIDENCE, RHODE ISLAND
CUSTOM DISTRICT
1796–1870

From the Custom House Papers
in the Rhode Island Historical Society

CLEARFIELD COMPANY

Published for Clearfield Company by
Genealogical Publishing Co., Inc.
Baltimore, Maryland, 1995

ISBN 9780806345345

INTRODUCTION

In response to the impressment of American seamen by British ships, Congress passed an *Act for the Relief and Protection of American Seamen* in 1796. The Act required customs collectors to maintain a record of all United States citizens serving on United States vessels. Each seaman, once registered with the customs collector, was given a Seaman's Protection Certificate. These certificates vouched for the citizenship of the individual and included identifying information such as height, complexion, place of birth, and, in some cases, eye and hair color. The intention of these certificates was to discourage impressment.

The Rhode Island Historical Society has six volumes of "Register of Protections Granted to American Seamen" from 1796–1870. These registers are part of the United States Custom House Papers housed in the Manuscript Division of the Rhode Island Historical Society Library at 121 Hope Street, Providence, Rhode Island. The volumes contain the seaman's name, age, height, place of birth, and color of complexion.

The Custom House Papers for Providence came into the collections of the Rhode Island Historical Society in two groups, ten years apart. In 1802, the U.S. Treasury Department gave to the Society records stored at the Providence Custom House. In 1912, former Senator Jesse Metcalf rescued records on the verge of being destroyed by the National Archives in Washington and presented them to the Society.

This book was produced from a typescript of a handwritten card index created for the registers. In the mid 1980s, Christine Lamar, Reference Librarian at the Society, coordinated the effort to type this index. All information had been transferred from the original volumes to the card index, except for height.

This volume is in alphabetical order by surname and includes the date of certification, age, complexion, place of birth, and the book and page number the information appears on in the original volume. There are several asterisk notations throughout the index. Some note that names are out of order. Others explain that a yellow complexion refers to a mulatto complexion.

Some names in this index lack a volume and page reference. Instead, the citation refers to Newport, Rhode Island, sworn statements and birth certificates. These loose documents cannot be located in the providence Custom House Papers at this time but were available when the card index was created.

Maureen Taylor, Rhode Island Historical Society

REGISTER OF SEAMEN'S PROTECTION

NAME	DATE OF CERTIFICATION	AGE	COMPLEXION	PLACE OF BIRTH	BOOK	PAGE
Abbersoue, John	May 11, 1809	20	dark	Hartford, Conn.	4	1
Abbey, Edward	Dec. 20, 1796	41	black	N. Prov., R.I.	1	6
Abbey, Edward	Apr. 1, 1800	49	black	Prov., R.I.	2	1
[Abbey] Abbe, Henry	May 2, 1799	21	light	Windham, Conn.	2	1
Abbey, Obadiah	May 17, 1819	34	dark	Endfield, Conn.	4	2
Abbott, Charles Henry	Sept. 13, 1849	17	light	Cranston, R.I.	5	3
Abbott, Israel	Dec. 15, 1800	23	dark	Coventry, R.I.	2	32
? Abbot, Jonathan	Apr. 22, 1797	25	dark	Prov., R.I.	1	6
Abbott Joseph W.	Dec. 18, 1847	16	light	Belfast, Me.	5	2
Abbott, Nathaniel	July 5, 1828	26	light	Saco, Me.	4	3
Abbott, Nathaniel D.	May 29, 1827	19	light	Prov., R.I.	4	3
Abbott, Thomas B.	Dec. 30, 1822	17	light	Prov., R.I.	4	3
** Abeley, Constantine	Aug. 25, 1845	22	dark	Boston, Ma.	5	2
Abell, Robert	Jan. 9, 1806	23	dark	Rehoboth, Ma.	3	68
Aborn, Caesar	Apr. 7, 1797	35	blk/face	Pawtuxet, R.I.	1	6
Aborn, Caesar	Aug. 27, 1804	38	black	Newport, R.I.	3	1
Aborn, Lewis S.P.	May 7, 1821	15	light	Prov., R.I.	4	3
Aborn, Peleg	May 24, 1800	21	light	Cranston, R.I.	2	1
Aborn, Samuel B.	Dec. 8, 1823	17	dark	Prov., R.I.	4	3
Aborn, Thomas Henry	May 18, 1818	18	light	Warwick, R.I.	4	2
Aborn, Wanton	Dec. 18, 1827	22	yellow*	Prov., R.I.	4	3
Aborn, William W.	Oct. 13, 1835	21	dark	Cranston, R.I.	5	1
Acherson, William	Jan. 9, 1845	19	light	New York, N.Y.	5	2
Acherson, William	Aug. 20, 1845	20	light	New York, N.Y.	5	2
[Ackley] Akeley, William	May 19, 1798	26	dark	Boston, Ma.	2	1
Ackworth William F.	Dec. 16, 1841	28	dark	Balt., Md.	5	2
Adams, Adolphus	Aug. 16, 1854	25	light	Charleston, S.C.	5	3
Adams, Alfred	Nov. 11, 1831	23	light	So. Kingston, R.I.	5	1
Adams, Benj. Dexter	May 26, 1853	24	light	Bellingham, Ma.	5	3
Adams, Charles	Oct. 2, 1844	23	light	Charlestown, S.C.	5	2
Adams, Charles	Mar. 15, 1849	20	light	Hadley, Ma.	5	3
Adams, Frederick	Dec. 14, 1847	21	light	Hampden, Me.	5	2

*Mulatto

**Abbot, Wescott   Nov. 25, 1807   13   light   Warwick, R.I.   4   1

REGISTER OF SEAMEN'S PROTECTION

NAME	DATE OF CERTIFICATION	AGE	COMPLEXION	PLACE OF BIRTH	BOOK	PAGE
Adams, George	Mar. 29, 1851	24	dark	Boston, Ma.	5	3
Adams, George	July 28, 1803	22	black	Hartford, Conn.	2	32
Adams, George W.	Dec. 5, 1859	32	dark	New York, N.Y.	6	1
Adams, George Wyllys	June 18, 1832	17	dark	Charlestown, Ma.	5	1
Adams, James	Apr. 20, 1807	21	dark	Sharon, N.H.	4	1
Adams, John	Dec. 30, 1820	33	black	Warwick, R.I.	4	2
Adams, John	May 10, 1828	24	ruddy	So. Kingstown, RI	4	3
Adams, John	Mar. 3, 1848	35	yellow	Balt., Md.	5	2
Adams, John N.	July 17, 1833	23	black	New Bedford, Ma.	5	1
Adams, John Quincy	June 5, 1843	18	black	Prov., R.I.	5	2
Adams, Moses	Nov. 25, 1797	26	light	Preston, Conn.	1	6
Adams, Thomas	Dec. 22, 1797	30	dark	Boston, Ma.	1	6
Adams, Thomas	July 7, 1809	12	dark	Prov., R.I.	4	1
Adams, Thomas	Mar. 9, 1846	25	dark	New York, N.Y.	5	2
Adams, William	Sept. 5, 1801	26	light	Barrington, R.I.	2	32
Adams, William B.	Sept. 20, 1834	20	light	Brandywine, Del.	5	1
Adams, William R.	Sept. 6, 1862	28	dark	Boston, Ma.	6	1
Adamson John S.	Nov. 2, 1848	38	light	Whitby, Great Britain	5	2
Adamson, William T.	July 23, 1841	22	light	New York, N.Y.	5	2
Addington, Henry	July 1, 1844	19	light	Edgartown, Md.	5	2
Addison, John S.	Dec. 6, 1809	20	light	Prov., R.I.	4	1
Aikins, Francis H.	Mar. 4, 1840	23	light	Dartmouth, Ma.	5	1
Aiken, Samuel	Mar. 9, 1832	27	dark	Phila., Pa.	5	1
Ailsworth, William P.	Sept. 26, 1826	18	light	No. Kingstown, RI	4	3
Albert, Dwellay	Oct. 2, 1821	18	dark	Tiverton, R.I.	4	3
Albert, John	Oct. 13, 1834	29	black	Newport, R.I.	5	1
Albertson, Peter	Aug. 17, 1844	20	light	Boston, Ma.	5	2
Albro, Benjamian	1798 to 1799	Sept. 28, 1780		Newport, R.I.	* -	-
Albro, Esek	Mar. 13, 1816	21	light	Prov., R.I.	4	2
Albro, George	Aug. 5, 1803	23	dark	Newport, R.I.	2	32
Albro, James	1798 to 1799	June 1, 1773		Newport, R.I.	* -	-
Alden, James	Mar. 27, 1811	25	light	Rehoboth, Ma.	4	1
Aldrich, Allen	Dec. 5, 1861	16	dark	Prov., R.I.	6	1
Aldrich, Edward	June 4, 1819	19	light	Prov., R.I.	4	2

*Newport, R. I.

REGISTER OF SEAMEN'S PROTECTION

NAME	DATE OF CERTIFICATION	AGE	COMPLEXION	PLACE OF BIRTH	BOOK	PAGE
Aldrich, Ezra	1798 to 1799	Apr. 17, 1776		Richmond, Ma.	*--	--
Aldrich, John	Mar. 8, 1850	22	dark	Oxford, Ma.	5	3
Aldrich, Lanford B.	Mar. 20, 1834	24	dark	Upton, Ma.	5	1
Aldrich, Lyman	Dec. 11, 1827	21	light	Smithfield, R.I.	4	3
Aldrich, Marcus	Dec. 8, 1804	22	dark	Glocester, R.I.	3	2
Aldrich, Rufus	Dec. 21, 1796	16	light	Mendon, Ma.	1	6
Aldrich, Rufus	Apr. 23, 1800	19	dark	Mendon, Ma.	2	1
Aldrich, Rufus B.	Feb. 19, 1806	16	light	Cumberland, R.I.	3	68
Aldrich, Whipple	Nov. 11, 1803	21	light	Prov., R.I.	2	45
Aldrich, William Derilley	Sept. 27, 1842	15	light	St. Mary's, Ga.	5	2
Aldrich, Wm. H.	Apr. 10, 1849	28	light	No. Prov., R.I.	5	3
Aldrich, William H.	Nov. 22, 1849	18	light	Prov., R.I.	5	3
Alers, John G.	Apr. 8, 1840	31	light	Brake Oldenburg, Ger.	5	2
Alexander, Andrew J.	Jan. 19, 1847	17	fair	Smithfield, R.I.	5	2
Alexander, Edward	Mar. 27, 1857	26	mulatto	Phila., Pa.	5	4
Alexander, James C.	July 22, 1836	24	dark	Phila., Pa.	5	1
Alexander, John	Aug. 18, 1815	23	black	Tiverton, R.I.	4	2
Alexander, Lance	July 30, 1803	18	dark	Prov., R.I.	2	32
Alexander, William	Mar. 23, 1805	20	dark	New York, N.Y.	3	2
Alexander, William F.	May 18, 1867	23	dark	Killingly, Conn.	6	1
Alexander, William H.	Nov. 11, 1803	21	light	Prov., R.I.	2	45
Alford, Edward	Mar. 7, 1805	25	dark	Boston, Ma.	3	2
Alger, William	Apr. 26, 1800	27	dark	Prov., R.I.	2	1
Allardice, James	Mar. 8, 1853	30	light	Balti., Md.	5	3
Allen, Adam	Dec. 20, 1806	15	black	Barrington, R.I.	4	1
Allen, Alfred	Dec. 2, 1859	25	light	New York, N.Y.	6	1
Allen, Bariah	June 27, 1821	36	dark	Portsmouth, R.I.	4	3
Allen, Barnet	Oct. 12, 1861	48	dark	Bristol, R.I.	6	1
Allen, Benjamin	Feb. 11, 1828	29	dark	Nantucket, Ma.	4	3
Allen, Benjamin	Dec. 3, 1835	21	light	Bristol, R.I.	5	1
Allen, Caleb	Jan. 4, 1826	22	light	No. Kingstown, R.I.	4	3
Allen, Caleb	Nov. 10, 1826	23	light	E. Greenwich, R.I.	4	3
Allen, Caleb W.	Feb. 24, 1812	32	light	Tolland, Conn.	4	2

*Newport, R. I.

NAME	DATE OF CERTIFICATION	AGE	COMPLEXION	PLACE OF BIRTH	BOOK	PAG
Allen, Carlton	Sept. 13, 1803	16	light	Portsmouth, R.I.	2	45
Allen, Charles	Jan. 10, 1851	38	light	Dover, N.H.	5	3
Allen, Charles R.	Nov. 19, 1845	28	fair	Phila., Pa.	5	2
Allen, Charles	Aug. 24, 1846	25	light	Phila., Pa.	5	2
Allen, Chester	Oct. 11, 1810	22	light	Windham, Conn.	4	1
Allen, Christopher	Feb. 13, 1821	31	light	No. Kingstown, R.I.	-	-
sworn statement of Ray G. Allen in Custom House Papers.						
Allen, Christopher	Feb. 27, 1823	34	light	No. Kingstown, R.I.	4	3
Allen, Curry	Nov. 1, 1833	21	black	Barrington, R.I.	5	1
Allen, David	Oct. 16, 1811	21	light	Wardsborough, VT.	4	2
Allen, Dexter B.	July 19, 1839	18	light	No. Prov., R.I.	5	1
Allen, Edmund W.	May 21, 1834	33	light	Hallowell, Me.	5	1
Allen, Elisha	1798 to 1799	Aug. 18, 1780		Wesport, Ma.	* -	-
Allen, Ezra S.	June 24, 1841	21	light	Barrington, R.I.	5	2
** Allen, Fayett	Mar. 24, 1797	14	light	Prov., R.I.	1	6
Allen, George	June 19, 1797	15	dark	Prov., R.I.	1	6
Allen, George	Dec. 15, 1800	21	light	Prov., R.I.	2	32
Allen, George	Aug. 20, 1803	22	dark	Prov., R.I.	2	32
Allen, George	Dec. 19, 1842	14	light	Prov., R.I.	5	2
Allen, George W.	Nov. 8, 1799	22	light	Tolland, Conn.	2	1
Allen, George W.	Apr. 5, 1815	21	light	Taunton, Ma.	4	2
Allen, George W. F.	Nov. 5, 1841	17	light	Prov., R.I.	5	2
Allen, George W. T.	Oct. 26, 1849	39	dark	No. Kingstown, R.I.	5	3
Allen, Gershom	Oct. 11, 1803	23	light	Harwick, Ma.	2	45
Allen, Henry	Nov. 10, 1803	18	light	Amsterdam, N.Y.	2	45
Allen, Henry	Nov. 30, 1804	18	light	Portsmouth, R.I.	3	2
Allen, Henry A.	June 14, 1836	24	light	No. Prov., R.I.	5	1
Allen, Henry M.	Feb. 28, 1849	16	light	Rehoboth, Ma.	5	3
Allen, Herman	Nov. 11, 1803	19	light	Rehoboth, Ma.	2	45
Allen, Herman	Dec. 19, 1800	16	dark	Rehoboth, Ma.	2	32
Allen, Hezekiah	Apr. 27, 1803	22	light	Fairfield, Conn.	2	32
Allen, Jack	Oct. 21, 1801	19	black	Barrington, R.I.	2	32
Allen, James	Apr. 3, 1800	47	dark	Prov., R.I.	2	1
Allen, James	Nov. 5, 1804	18	light	Rehoboth, Ma.	3	1
**Allen, George	Feb. 13, 1805	46	dark	New Castle, Del.	3	2

*Newport, R. I.

REGISTER OF SEAMEN'S PROTECTION

NAME	DATE OF CERTIFICATION	AGE	COMPLEXION	PLACE OF BIRTH	BOOK	PAGE
Allen, James	July 19, 1806	20	light	Rehoboth, Ma.	3	10
Allen, James	May 3, 1843	18	light	Barrington, R.I.	5	2
Allen, James	Nov. 11, 1852	30	mulatto	No. Kingstown, R.I.	5	3
Allen, James F.	Oct. 20, 1841	17	light	Prov., R.I.	5	2
Allen, Jeremiah	July 30, 1804	14	light	Washington, N.C.	3	1
Allen, Jeremiah	June 7, 1805	15	light	Washington, N.C.	3	2
Allen, John	May 8, 1799	22	light	E. Greenwich, R.I.	2	1
Allen, John	Apr. 24, 1849	30	dark	New York, N.Y.	5	3
Allen, Joesph	July 10, 1805	26	dark	Boston, Ma.	3	68
Allen, Joseph	Sept. 9, 1808	19	light	Newport, R.I.	4	1
Allen, Joseph	Jan. 30, 1811	21	light	Newport, R.I.	4	1
Allen, Joseph	Nov. 2, 1848	24	dark	So. Kingstown, R.I.	5	2
Allen, Joseph Cooke	May 30, 1803	20	light	Prov., R.I.	2	32
Allen, Joseph K.	Oct. 5, 1829	17	light	Barrington, R.I.	5	1
Allen, Joseph K.	March 26, 1841	28	light	Barrington, R.I.	5	2
Allen, Joseph W.	Oct. 10, 1833	25	dark	Auburn, N.Y.	5	1
Allen, Joshua, Jr.	Oct. 20, 1818	18	light	Rochester, Ma.	4	2
Allen, Lewis	June 12, 1832	16	light	Prov., R.I.	5	1
Allen, Matthew	Sept. 23, 1796	21	light	Barrington, R.I.	1	3
Allen, Noah P.	May 31, 1809	19	light	Rehoboth, Ma.	4	1
Allen, Noble	December 9, 1835	43	dark	Rehoboth, Ma.	5	1
Allen, Paschal	Mar. 11, 1831	22	dark	Barrington, R.I.	5	1
Allen, Peter	Nov. 27, 1835	23	black	Dover, Del.	5	1
Allen, Philip	1798 to 1799	May 14, 1770		Westport, Ma.	*-	-
Allen, Philip	Aug. 3, 1805	20	dark	Wiseasset, Me.	3	68
Allen, Preston	Oct. 29, 1824	24	light	Attleboro, Ma.	4	3
Allen, Robert	Oct. 11, 1797	11	light	Warwick, R.I.	1	6
Allen, Russell W.	Sept. 16, 1806	13	light	Prov., R.I.	3	10
Allen, Samuel	Aug. 10, 1796	22	dark	Swansea, Ma.	1	1
Allen, Samuel	1798 to 1799	Sept. 27, 1777		So. Kingstown, R.I.	-	-
Allen, Samuel S.	June 13, 1810	15	light	Prov., R.I.	4	1
Allen, Samuel S.	Nov. 28, 1820	23	light	Prov., R.I.	4	2
Allen, Samuel S.	Dec. 7, 1838	24	mulatto	E. Greenwich, R.I.	5	1

*Newport, R. I.

NAME	DATE OF CERTIFICATION	AGE	COMPLEXION	PLACE OF BIRTH	BOOK	PAGE
Allen, Stephen	July 7, 1845	17	dark	W. Greenwich, R.I.	5	2
Allen, Sylvester	Jan. 29, 1799	21	light	Barrington, R.I.	2	1
Allen, Thomas	Apr. 16, 1806	18	brown	Warwick, R.I.	3	68
Allen, Thomas	July 13, 1807	21	yellow*	E. Greenwich, R.I.	4	1
Allen, Tower	Mar. 28, 1810	21	black	Barrington, R.I.	4	1
Allen, Tower	Dec. 13, 1806	19	black	Barrington, R.I.	4	1
Allen, Welcome	Mar. 4, 1797	24	light	Cumberland, R.I.	1	6
Allen, Welcome	Oct. 14, 1807	22	light	Pomfret, Conn.	4	1
Allen, Weston	Nov. 4, 1806	13	light	Rochester, Ma.	4	1
Allen, Wheaton	Oct. 3, 1826	20	dark	Seekonk, Ma.	4	3
Allen, Wiley Caleb	Oct. 2, 1798	18	light	Tolland, Conn.	2	1
Allen, William	June 27, 1810	25	black	Phila., Pa.	4	1
Allen, William	Dec. 16, 1830	26	light	Alexandria, D.C.	5	1
Allen, William	June 28, 1852	21	dark	New York, N.Y.	5	3
Allen, William	Aug. 30, 1852	36	mulatto	No. Kingston, R.I.	5	3
Allen, William, Jr.	Apr. 24, 1804	29	light	Harwick, Ma.	3	1
Allen, William H.	June 4, 1838	17	light	Warwick, R.I.	5	1
Allen, William H., Jr.	Oct. 13, 1845	20	light	Providence, R.I.	5	2
Allen, William S.	Apr. 24, 1834	29	dark	Calvert, Md.	5	1
Allin, Ira Richard	Mar. 2, 1821 b. 2.24.1806		light	Barrington, R.I.	-	--
Son of Ira Allin of Barrington; birth certificate in Custom House Papers.						
Allin, James	Oct. 26, 1812	21	light	Portsmouth, R.I.	4	2
Allin, John	June 29, 1857	21	dark	New Bedford, Ma.	5	4
Allin, Shearjashub B.	Oct. 23, 1809	24	light	Barrington, R.I.	4	1
Allison, Robert	Dec. 9, 1803	24	light	Princeton, N.J.	2	24
?Allot, Jonathan	Apr. 22, 1797	25	dark	Providence, R.I.	1	6
Allyn, Henry W.	May 16, 1857	20	light	Onondaga Co., N.Y.	5	4
Allyn, Jonathan	May 4, 1810	16	light	Norton, Ma.	4	1
Almy, Daniel	1798-1799		Apr. 29, 1782	Norwich, Conn.	-	--
Almy, Jesse	Oct. 25, 1809	23	black	Newport, R.I.	4	1
Almy, Joseph, Jr.	Nov. 11, 1852	17	light	Smithfield, R.I.	5	3
Almy, Samuel	Aug. 3, 1796	23	light	Tiverton, R.I.	1	1
Almy, Serril	Mar. 12, 1811	20	light	Providence, R.I.	4	1
Almy, Williams	June 24, 1841	19	light	Providence, R.I.	5	2
Alvin, George	Jan. 23, 1849	24	light	New Orleans, La.	5	2
Almy, Williams	Nov. 11, 1852	20	light	Smithfield, R.I.	5	3

*mulatto

NAME	DATE OF CERTIFICATION	AGE	COMPLEXION	PLACE OF BIRTH	BOOK	PAGE
Amay, James	Nov. 28, 1820	28	black	Providence, R.I.	4	2
Ambros[e], John	May 30, 1804	30	yellow*	New York, N.Y.	3	1
Ambrose, John	June 23, 1806	34	Yellow	New York, N.Y.	3	68
Ambrose, John	Dec. 18, 1809	37	yellow*	New York, N.Y.	4	1
Ambrose, Robert	1798-1799	July 24, 1768		Newport, R.I.	*-	--
Ames, David	Apr. 20, 1818	20	dark	Prospect, Ma. [Me.]	4	2
Ames, James B.	July 19, 1827	20	light	Providence, R.I.	4	3
Ames, John C.	Dec. 18, 1851	22	sandy	Lincolnsville, Me.	5	3
Ames, Simeon	Sept. 2, 1803	22	light	Groton, Ma.	2	45
Ames, Simeon	July 27, 1799	18	light	Groton, Ma.	2	1
Ames, Wilber	Aug. 30, 1826	22	light	Killingly, Conn.	4	3
Amesbury, Joseph H.	Nov. 24, 1841	18	light	No. Prov., R.I.	5	2
Ammidou, Stephen	Dec. 8, 1804	24	dark	Mendon, Ma.	3	2
Amsburg, Daniel S.	May 21, 1821	24	dark	Providence, R.I.	4	3
Amsbury, Eleagro W.	Dec. 6, 1828	25	light	Providence, R.I.	4	3
Amsbury, Homer	July 8, 1822	21	dark	Petersham, Ma.	4	3
Amsbury, William	June 15, 1836	20	light	NO. Prov., R.I.	5	1
**Amsbury, JOhn G.	Nov. 21, 1854	19	dark	Providence, R.I.	5	3
Anderson, Andrew	July 14, 1819	28	light	Plymouth, Ma.	4	2
Anderson, Andrew	Dec. 11, 1849	18	light	New York, N.Y.	5	3
Anderson, Alexander	Feb. 23, 1852	24	dark	Boston, Ma.	5	3
Anderson, Alexander	Feb. 23, 1852	25	light	New York, N.Y.	5	3
Anderson, Charles	Oct. 31, 1834	21	light	New York, N.Y.	5	1
Anderson, Isaac J.	Sept. 17, 1847	18	light	Baltimore, Md.	5	2
Anderson,'James	May 2, 1801	40	black	Exeter, R.I.	2	32
Anderson, John	Oct. 26, 1835	23	light	Portsmouth, N.H.	5	1
Anderson, John	Nov. 2, 1844	28	light	Portland, Me.	5	2
Anderson, John	Feb. 28, 1849	23	light	New York, N.Y.	5	3
Anderson, John	Nov. 25, 1854	21	light	New York, N.Y.	5	4
Anderson, Philip	Feb. 7, 1812	24	black	Kent County, Md.	4	2
Anderson, Richard	June 16, 1862	28	light	Boston, Ma,	6	1
Anderson, Robert	Apr. 8, 1857	21	light	Providence, R.I.	5	4
Anderson, Silvester	Oct. 22, 1803	18	light	Coventry, R.I.	2	45
Anderson, Stephen	July 7, 1798	22	light	New York, NY	2	1
Andre, Josephus	Apr. 8, 1852	39	dark	Baltimore, Md.	5	3
Andrews, Asa A.	Feb, 7, 1849	25	light	Foster, R.I.	5	3

*mulatto   *Newport, R. I.

**out of order

NAME	DATE OF CERTIFICATION	AGE	COMPLEXION	PLACE OF BIRTH	BOOK	PAGE
Andrews, Charles	May 2, 1799	25	light	E. Greenwich, R.I.	2	1
Andrew[s], Charles	Sept. 11, 1804	30	light	Coventry, R.I.	3	1
Andrews, Charles P.	May 22, 1839	17	light	E. Greewich, R.I.	5	1
Andrews, Daniel P.	Jan. 4, 1849	21	light	Blackstone, Ma.	5	2
Andrews, Ebenezer, Jr.	Jan. 22, 1847	22	florid	Providence, R.I.	5	2
Andrews, George W.	June 18, 1841	18	light	E. Greenwich, R.I.	5	2
Andrews, George W.	May 26, 1846	22	fair	E. Greenwich, R.I.	5	2
Andrews, James	Aug. 7, 1845	19	dark	Phila., Pa.	5	2
Andrews, Jesse	Dec. 4, 1798	32	light	Warwick, R.I.	2	1
Andrews, John	Nov. 30, 1803	21	light	E. Greenwich, R.I.	2	45
Andrew[s], John	Oct. 24, 1849	47	light	Coventry, R.I.	5	3
Andrews, Jonathan	July 1, 1797	30	dark	E. Greenwich, R.I.	1	6
Andrews, Joseph	May, 20, 1821	27	dark	Dighton, Ma.	4	3
Andrews, Joseph	Oct. 9, 1848	31	light	Eastport, Me.	5	2
Andrews, Lyman	Dec. 4, 1851	22	dark	Smithfield, R.I.	5	3
Andrews, Merrett	May 30, 1849	45	light	Coventry, R.I.	5	3
Andrews, Nathaniel	May 15, 1802	24	dark	Glocester, R.I.	2	32
Andrews, Nathaniel	Mar. 27, 1805	20	light	Taunton, Ma.	3	2
Andrews, Samuel	Jan. 13, 1837	33	light	Plymouth, Ma.	5	1
Andrews, Seth	July 1, 1801	16	light	Cranston, R.I.	2	32
Andrews, Seth	Mar. 24, 1815	29	light	Dighton, Ma.	4	2
Andrews, Silvester	Aug. 16, 1805	20	light	Coventry, R.I.	3	68
Andrews, Silvester	Jan. 2, 1810	24	light	Coventry, R.I.	4	1
Andrews, Thomas	Mar. 5, 1804	19	light	W. Greenwich, R.I.	3	1
Andrews, Thomas	Nov. 19, 1849	27	light	Providence, R.I.	5	3
Andrews, Vernon W.	Mar. 26, 1864	26	light	Coventry, R.I.	6	1
Andrews, Whipple	Dec. 19, 1800	40	light	E. Greenwich, R.I.	2	32
Andrews, William	May 18, 1809	21	light	Cranston, R.I.	4	1
Andrews, William	Dec. 9, 1819	21	light	Taunton, Ma.	4	2
Andrews, William, Jr.	Dec. 22, 1817	18	light	Dighton, Ma.	4	2
Andrews, Zeplianiak	July 26, 1809	21	brown	Providence, R.I.	4	1
Andros, Samuel	Sept. 28, 1850	22	light	Portland, Me.	5	3
Angelis, Charles	Feb. 23, 1852	16	dark	Portland, Me.	5	3
Angel, James	Sept. 3, 1811	20	light	Providence, R.I.	4	2
Angell, Charles	May 20, 1839	22	light	No. Prov., R.I.	5	1
Angell, Daniel	Apr. 24, 1854	24	light	Johnston, R.I.	5	3
Angell, Fenner	Mar. 9, 1854	19	light	Johnston, R.I.	5	3

NAME	DATE OF CERTIFICATION	AGE	COMPLEXION	PLACE OF BIRTH	BOOK	PAGE
Angell, George F.	Aug. 26, 1845	23	light	No. Prov., R.I.	5	2
Angell, Henry R.	May 30, 1849	19	light	No. Prov., R.I.	5	3
Angell, Israel	Aug. 17, 1810	18	light	Scituate, R.I.	4	1
Angell, James	Mar. 4, 1818	21	brown	Providence, R.I.	4	2
Angell, James, Jr.	Nov. 24, 1806	17	light	Providence, R.I.	4	1
Angell, Jessee	Nov. 23, 1798	19	dark	No. Prov., R.I.	2	1
Angell, John	Dec. 30, 1819	22	black	Johnston, R.I.	4	2
Angell, Joseph F.B.	Feb. 26, 1825	21	light	Providence, RI	4	3
Angell, Richard A.	Nov. 30, 1849	21	light	Smithfield, R.I.	5	3
Angell, Shadrach	Nov. 29, 1824	23	light	Smithfield, R.I.	4	3
Angell, Sylvanus R.	Sept. 14, 1849	18	light	Providence, R.I.	5	3
Angell, Theodore S.	Apr. 8, 1834	17	light	Providence, R.I.	5	1
Angell, Thomas B.	May 25, 1816	21	light	Providence, R.I.	4	2
Angell, Tristam H.	Sept. 1, 1849	27	light	Seekonk, Ma.	5	3
Angell, William E.	Nov. 1, 1836	16	light	Foster, R.I.	5	1
Anness, Arthur F.	Dec. 8, 1828	22	light	Providence, R.I.	4	3
Annis, Ebenezer	Nov. 6, 1813	34	light	Cape Ann, Ma.	4	2
Annis, Olney	May 17, 1830	22	light	Providence, R.I.	5	1
Annis, Thomas	May 10, 1799	18	dark	Baltimore, Md.	2	1
Ansow, John	Aug. 23, 1800	19	light	Providence, R.I.	2	1
Anthony, Daniel, Jr.	July 3, 1798	27	light	Smithfield, R.I.	2	1
Anthony, Edward G.	May 28, 1859	15	dark c.	Warwick, R.I.	6	1
Anthony, Edward G.	May 8, 1868	24	medium	Warwick, R.I.	6	1
Anthony, Henry A.	Mar. 16, 1868	17	light	Charlestown, R.I.	6	1
Anthony, James	Mar. 30, 1805	36	dark	Warwick, R.I.	3	2
Anthony, James	Apr. 13, 1818	36	dark	Warwick, R.I.	3	2
Anthony, James S.	Nov. 23, 1838	26	black	Charlestown, R.I.	5	1
Anthony, John	Sept. 6, 1803	28	dark	Warwick, R.I.	2	45
Anthony, Joseph	Oct. 29, 1803	13	light	Providence, R.I.	2	45
Anthony, Joseph	Apr. 29, 1806	16	light	Providence, R.I.	3	68

NAME	DATE OF CERTIFICATION	AGE	COMPLEXION	PLACE OF BIRTH	BOOK	PAGE
Anthony, Joseph	Oct. 9, 1849	25	dark	New Bedford, Ma.	5	3
Anthony, Joseph	Oct. 19, 1849	24	light	New Bedford, Ma.	5	3
Anthony, Joseph	Dec. 14, 1849	24	dark	New Bedford, Ma.	5	3
Anthony, Joseph T.	Dec. 6, 1814	20	dark	Providence, R.I.	4	2
Anthony, Mark	Jan. 7, 1804	19	dark	Newport, R.I.	3	1
Anthony, Pearse	1798 to 1799	Jan. 7, 1771		Portsmouth, R.I.	** -	-
Anthony, Prince	Dec. 1, 1800	20	black	New York, N.Y.	2	32
Anthony, Samuel	Sept. 10, 1811	18	light	Scituate, R.I.	4	2
Anthony, Solomon	Nov. 14, 1809	22	yellow*	Burrilville, R.I.	4	1
Anthony, Virgil	Oct. 26, 1849	14	light	Providence, R.I.	5	3
Anthony, William	1798 to 1799	Jan. 10, 1774		Newport, R.I.	** -	-
Anthony, William	July 15, 1803	16	dark	Providence, R.I.	2	32
Anthony, William	Apr. 29, 1797	22	dark	No. Prov., R.I.	1	6
Anthony, William	Oct. 27, 1835	18	mulatto	Smithfield, R.I.	5	1
Anthony, Wm. Henry	Dec. 20, 1842	19	dark	Providence, R.I.	5	2
Anthone, Frank	Oct. 7, 1854	21	dark	New York, N.Y.	5	3
Aplin, Joseph	Oct. 21, 1803	18	light	Providence, R.I.	2	45
Aplin, Stephen A., Jr.	Apr. 21, 1809	20	brown	Providence, R.I.	4	1
Appleby, Joshua	1798 to 1799	Dec. 5, 1770		----	** -	-
Armington, Abel	June 16, 1798	19	dark	Rehoboth, Ma.	2	1
Armington, Abel	Sept. 19, 1796	16	dark	Rehoboth, Ma.	1	3
Armington, Alfred	Mar. 15, 1811	16	light	Rehoboth, Ma.	4	1
Armington, Alverin	Apr. 3, 1820	18	light	Seekonk, Ma.	4	2
Armington, Ambrose	Feb. 13, 1801	19	light	Rehoboth, Ma.	2	32
Armington, Asa, Jr.	June 1, 1809	18	dark	Rehoboth, Ma.	4	1
Armington, Benjamin	Sept. 22, 1796	24	light	Rehoboth, Ma.	1	3
Armington, Charles	Sept. 28, 1829	25	dark	Seekonk, Ma.	5	1
Armington, Daniel	Apr. 11, 1815	23	light	Barrington, R.I.	4	2
Armington, Edward	Sept. 27, 1825	17	dark	Seekonk, Ma.	4	3
Armington, George W.	Nov. 28, 1832	16	light	Oxford, Ma.	5	1
Armington, Harvey	Mar. 2, 1810	17	light	Barrington, R.I.	4	1
Armington, Horace W.	Sept. 25, 1827	22	dark	Seekonk, Ma.	4	3
Armington, James G.	Mar. 6, 1815	24	dark	Barrington, R.I.	4	2
Armington, John	Mar. 4, 1797	21	light	Rehoboth, Ma.	1	6
Armington, John, Jr.	Sept. 23, 1796	20	dark	Rehoboth, Ma.	1	3
Armington, John P.	Mar. 31, 1819	19	light	Seekonk, Ma.	4	2
Armington, Joseph, 2nd.	Mar. 7, 1815	19	light	Barrington, R.I.	4	2

*mulatto   **Newport, R.I.

NAME	DATE OF CERTIFICATION	AGE	COMPLEXION	PLACE OF BIRTH	BOOK	PAGE
Armington, Levi J.	June 14, 1836	23	dark	No. Prov., R.I.	5	1
Armington, Russell	May 29, 1818	24	light	No. Prov., R.I.	4	2
Armington, Walker	Sept. 21, 1796	25	dark	Rehoboth, Ma.	1	3
Armington, William	Dec. 12, 1797	23	light	Rehoboth, Ma.	1	6
Armstrong, Carroll	Nov. 5, 1859	41	Fair	Alexandria, Va.	6	1
Armstrong, Clovis	June 25, 1836	18	light	Gloucester, R.I.	5	1
Armstrong, William	Oct. 19, 1812	35	black	Phila., Pa.	4	2
Arnam, Richard V.	July 17, 1806	24	light	Cumberland, R.I.	3	10
Arnest, Benjamin N.	May 31, 1844	24	dark	Balti., Md.	5	2
Arnold, Almon W.	Dec. 27, 1853	22	light	Cranston, R.I.	5	3
Arnold, Artemas	Mar. 9, 1815	20	light	Scituate, R.I.	4	2
Arnold, Arthur F.	May 9, 1810	15	fair	Foster, R.I.	4	1
Arnold, Augustus	Nov. 28, 1796	18	light	Warwick, R.I.	1	6
Arnold, Benedict	July 26, 1797	20	dark	Warwick, R.I.	1	6
Arnold, Benedick	1798 to 1799	June 4, 1770		Warren, R.I.	**-	-
Arnold, Caesar	Jan. 19, 1802	24	black	Smithfield, R.I.	2	32
Arnold, Caleb	Aug. 25, 1845	17	fair	No. Prov.,R.I.	5	2
Arnold, Christopher W.	Nov. 3, 1840	19	light	Warwick, R.I.	5	2
Arnold, Cornelius	Nov. 17, 1849	19	light	Providence, R.I.	5	3
Arnold, Daniel	July 27, 1799	24	light	Scituate, R.I.	2	1
Arnold, David	Dec. 5, 1796	18	dark	Warwick, R.I.	1	6
Arnold, David	Dec. 12, 1797	19	dark	Warwick, R.I.	1	6
Arnold, David	Nov. 14, 1807	18	Yellow*	Plainfield, Conn.	4	1
Arnold, Edwin W.	Oct. 15, 1860	16	dark	Warwick, R.I.	6	1
Arnold, Elijah Z.	Mar. 22, 1817	19	light	Smithfield, R.I.	4	2
Arnold, Elisha	Dec. 10, 1817	44	light	Coventry, R.I.	4	2
Arnold, Francis B.	Aug. 10, 1839	22	light	Springfield, Ma.	5	1
Arnold, George	Mar. 4, 1797	21	dark	Coventry, R.I.	1	6
Arnold, George	Feb. 17, 1800	18	dark	Warwick, R.I.	2	1
Arnold, George B.	June 12, 1800	23	dark	Warwick, R.I.	2	1
Arnold, George Brown	Oct. 31, 1799	22	dark	Warwick, R.I.	2	1
Arnold, George F.	Oct. 19, 1835	13	light	Providence, R.I.	5	1
Arnold, George G.	Apr. 6, 1815	19	light	Warwick, R.I.	4	2
Arnold, Isaac Allington	Jan. 23, 1797	18	light	E. Greenwich, R.I.	1	6
Arnold, Isaac Allington	Nov. 7, 1796	16	light	E. Greenwich, R.I.	1	6&5
Arnold, Israel	May 15, 1807	22	light	Cranston, R.I.	4	1

*mulatto
**Newport, R.I.

NAME	DATE OF CERTIFICATION	AGE	COMPLEXION	PLACE OF BIRTH	BOOK	PAGE
Arnold, Israel	Dec. 14, 1830	16	light	Warwick, R.I.	5	1
Arnold, James	Dec. 9, 1825	29	mulatto	Smithfield, R.I.	4	3
Arnold, James B.	May 30, 1849	38	light	Smithfield, R.I.	5	3
Arnold, John	July 23, 1801	22	light	Newport, R.I.	2	32
Arnold, John, Jr.	Mar. 4, 1805	17	light	Cranston, R.I.	3	2
Arnold, John F.	Oct. 18, 1849	22	light	Warwick, R.I.	5	3
Arnold, John R.	Nov. 6, 1828	22	light	Smithfield, R.I.	4	3
Arnold, John W.	July 17, 1839	22	light	Warwick, R.I.	5	1
Arnold, Joseph	Mar. 14, 1810	21	dark	Cranston, R.I.	4	1
Arnold, Joseph W.	Feb. 10, 1849	24	light	Providence, R.I.	5	3
Arnold, Josiah	Aug. 24, 1796	25	dark	Warwick, R.I.	1	1
Arnold, Lewis L.M.	May 26, 1851	18	dark	Providence, R.I.	5	3
Arnold, Moses	Nov. 16, 1803	20	light	Cranston, R.I.	2	45
Arnold, Moses	May 4, 1810	21	black	E. Greenwich, R.I.	4	1
Arnold, Nathaniel	Apr. 16, 1800	18	dark	Warwick, R.I.	2	1
Arnold, Nathaniel	May 14, 1811	17	dark	Warwick, R.I.	4	2
Arnold, Obadiah	Mar. 13, 1810	18	fair	Foster, R.I.	4	1
Arnold, Oliver	Mar. 25, 1815	19	light	E. Greenwich, R.I.	4	2
Arnold, Peleg R.	Nov. 18, 1818	32	dark	Cranston, R.I.	4	2
Arnold, Pero	Jan. 2, 1804	20	yellow*	Smithfield, R.I.	3	1
Arnold, Pero	July 14, 1806	21	yellow	Providence, R.I.	3	68
Arnold, Pero	Feb. 24, 1813	26	yellow*	Providence, R.I.	4	2
Arnold, Reuben	Aug. 1, 1801	17	light	E. Greenwich, R.I.	2	32
Arnold, Reuben M.	Dec. 3, 1821	22	light	Glocester, R.I.	-	-
Nov. 3, 1799 son of George W. and Sophia Arnold. Birth certificate in Custom House Papers.						
Arnold, Rufus	Nov. 5, 1805	20	light	Cumberland, R.I.	3	68
Arnold, Samuel	Nov. 8, 1800	22	dark	Cumberland, R.I.	2	32
Arnold, Samuel	Apr. 15, 1818	17	ruddy	Warwick, R.I.	4	2
Arnold, Seth	July 24, 1811	23	light	Smithfield, R.I.	4	2
Arnold, Simon	1798 to 1799	July 25, 1756		Newport, R.I.	**-	-
Arnold Sion H.	Mar. 16, 1843	19	light	Cranston, R.I.	5	2
Arnold, Smith	Dec. 1, 1800	27	dark	Smithfield, R.I.	2	32
Arnold, Stephen	Nov. 14, 1800	18	light	Warwick, R.I.	2	32
Arnold, Stephen	Nov. 11, 1822	17	dark	Coventry, R.I.	4	3

*mulatto
**Newport, R.I.

REGISTER OF SEAMEN'S PROTECTION

NAME	DATE OF CERTIFICATION	AGE	COMPLEXION	PLACE OF BIRTH	BOOK	PAGE
Arnold, Thomas	Mar. 8, 1799	20	dark	Warwick, R.I.	2	1
Arnold, Thomas, Jr.	Mar. 29, 1817	37	light	Warwick, R.I.	4	2
Arnold, Thomas P.	Sept. 13, 1796	18	light	E. Greenwich, R.I.	1	2
Arnold, Welcome	Dec. 9, 1800	19	dark	Warwick, R.I.	2	32
Arnold, Welcome	Oct. 2, 1801	24	dark	Providence, R.I.	2	32
Arnold, Welcome	Oct. 29, 1824	16	dark	Providence, R.I.	4	3
Arnold, William	Sept. 15, 1809	17	light	Providence, R.I.	4	1
Arnold, William	May 8, 1810	22	light	Cumberland, R.I.	4	1
Arnold, William	Dec. 27, 1822	14	fair	E. Greenwich, R.I.	4	3
Arnold, William	July 31, 1837	18	light	Duchess Co., No.East, NY	5	1
Arnold, William W.	June 7, 1815	18	light	Cranston, R.I.	4	2
Arnold, Ziba	Mar. 10, 1801	21	dark	Cumberland, R.I.	2	32
Arnslom, William	Aug. 10, 1852	21	light	Albany, N.Y.	5	3
Arthur, John	Apr. 7, 1852	17	light	Bristol, R.I.	5	3
Arthur, Wm. A.	Dec. 15, 1854	30	light	Eastport, Me.	5	4
Asbry, Matil	Oct. 17, 1834	26	black	New York, N.Y.	5	1
Ash, William	June 28, 1832	23	mulatto	Dedham, Ma.	5	1
Ash, William	June 23, 1841	19	light	No. Providence, R.I.	5	2
Ash, William	Mar. 14, 1842	19	light	No. Providence, R.I.	5	2
Asher, John	Mar. 10, 1843	47	mulatto	Durham, Conn.	5	2
Ashton, Joshua	July 31, 1818	22	light	Providence, R.I.	4	2
Atherbow, Watson	June 27, 1827	21	dark	Attleboro, Ma.	4	3
Atkins, David	Feb. 14, 1862	28	light	Poughkeepsie, N.Y.	6	1
Atkins, John	June 6, 1804	17	light	Norfolk, Va.	3	1
Atkins, Silas	Apr. 15, 1835	22	dark	Wilmington, N.C.	5	1
Atkinson, Henry	Feb. 4, 1834	30	black	Norwich, Conn.	5	1
Atkinson, John	Apr. 24, 1805	27	dark	Campton, Pa.	3	2
Atset, Joseph	May 4, 1810	45	dark	Old Town, Ma. [Me.]	4	1
Atset, Joseph, Jr.	Mar. 28, 1810	17	brown	Wilmington, N.C.	4	1
Attaquin, Soloman	Aug. 27, 1796	32	dark	Plymouth, Ma.	1	1
Atwater, John	Mar. 22, 1815	15	light	New Haven, Conn.	4	2
Atwood, Benj. W.	Mar. 23, 1857	33	fair	Provincetown, Ma.	5	4
Atwood, Henry	Mar. 30, 1843	18	light	Warwick, R.I.	5	2
Atwood, Jeremiah	May 9, 1807	17	light	Cranston, R.I.	4	1

REGISTER OF SEAMEN'S PROTECTION

NAME	DATE OF CERTIFICATION	AGE	COMPLEXION	PLACE OF BIRTH	BOOK	PAG
Atwood, Preseroed?	Nov. 14, 1809	18	light	Dighton, Ma.	4	1
Atwood, Thomas	May 9, 1807	60	light	Cranston, R.I.	4	1
Atwood, William	Dec. 5, 1837	17	light	Providence, R.I.	5	1
Atwood, William	Nov. 8, 1843	23	dark	Boston, Ma.	5	2
Auboyneau, Paul L.A.	Nov. 6, 1804	25	light	Petit Frou? San Domingo [Haiti]	3	2
Austin, Benajah	Oct. 12, 1844	22	light	No. Kingston, R.I.	5	2
Austin, Benjamin	Nov. 3, 1819	22	light	No. Kingston, R.I.	4	2
Austin, Charles E.	Oct. 31, 1832	21	light	Waterford, Conn.	5	1
Austin, Clark	Sept. 6, 1864	21	Medium	So. Kingston, R.I.	6	1
Austin, Daniel	1798 to 1799	Year 1768		Jameston, R.I.	* -	-
Austin, David	Aug. 17, 1824	22	dark	Newport, R.I.	4	3
Austin, Esek W.	Mar. 24, 1831	26	light	No. Kingston, R.I.	5	1
Austin, Ezekiel	Nov. 20, 1807	19	light	E. Greenwich, R.I.	4	1
Austin, George H.	Jan. 3, 1821	21	light	Newport, R.I.	4	3
Austin, John	Aug. 2, 1850	19	light	New York, N.Y.	5	3
Austin, John F.	Sept. 24, 1861	24	light	Wickford, R.I.	6	1
Austin, Joseph	Aug. 8, 1846	19	light	Ipswich, N.H.	5	2
Austin, Nathaniel S.	June 23, 1841	20	light	Cranston, R.I.	5	2
Austin, Peter	1798 to 1799	Feb. 19, 1783		Newport, R.I.	* -	-
Austin, Peter	Oct. 8, 1817	34	light	Newport, R.I.	4	2
Austin, Russell	Oct. 19, 1797	22	dark	No. Kingstown, R.I.	1	6
Austin, Thurston	July 20, 1804	21	light	No. Kingstown, R.I.	3	1
Austin, Thurston	Oct. 5, 1804	22	light	No. Kingstown, R.I.	3	1
Austin, William	July 3, 1807	21	light	Coventry, R.I.	4	1
Avery, Elisha	Aug. 5, 1805	25	light	New London, Conn.	3	68
Avery, Isaac	May 17, 1809	28	black	Preston, Conn.	4	1
Avery, Levi	Nov. 23, 1818	20	dark	Sandwich, Ma.	4	2
Avery, Thomas J.	Feb. 21, 1810	20	black	Somers, Conn.	4	1
Avery, William B.	Aug. 6, 1859	18	fair	Providence, R.I.	6	1
Axum, James	Nov. 22, 1799	28	black	Phila., Pa.	2	1
Aylsowrth, John, Jr.	Oct. 12, 1799	16	light	E. Greenwich, R.I.	2	1
Aylesworth, Thomas	May 17, 1797	27	dark	E. Greenwich, R.I.	1	6
Ayrault, Newport	Aug. 10, 1798	50	black	Newport, R.I.	2	1
Ayres, John W.	Sept. 28, 1850	19	dark	Salem, Conn.	5	3
Ayres, William	July 6, 1833	26	light	Roxbury, Ma.	5	1

*Newport, R. I.

REGISTER OF SEAMEN'S PROTECTION

NAME	DATE OF CERTIFICATION	AGE	COMPLEXION	PLACE OF BIRTH	BOOK	PAGE
Babcock, Asa	May 24, 1808	21	brown	Westerly, R.I.	4	5
Babcock, Bradford	1798 to 1799	May 4, 1781		Dighton, Ma.	* -	-
Babcock, Bradford Waite	1798 to 1799	May 4, 1782		Dighton, Ma.	* -	-
Babcock, Charles H.	Nov. 25, 1859	19	dark	Hopkinton, R.I.	6	2
Babcock, Daniel P.	July 24, 1837	28	---	So. Kingstown, R.I.	5	8
Babcock, George W.	Sept. 7, 1843	27	light	Attleboro, Ma.	5	9
Babcock, Henry	Mar. 5, 1806	46	black	Hopkinton, R.I.	3	72A
Babcock, James	Dec. 22, 1805	19	black	Providence, R.I.	3	72A
Babcock, Levi Ide	Apr. 10, 1834	18	light	Providence, R.I.	5	7
Babcock, Oliver	Mar. 23, 1822	29	light	Westerly, R.I.	4	9
Babcock, Samuel	May 24, 1861	24	dark	Arcadia, R.I.	6	2
Babcock, Tristain	Feb. 18, 1805	36	yellow*	So. Kingstown, R.I.	3	50
Babcock, William	Mar. 31, 1828	37	dark	Westfield, Ma.	4	10
Babcock, William N.	June 29, 1833	21	light	No. Kingstown, R.I.	5	7
Babson, George	Dec. 7, 1832	28	light	Boston, Ma.	5	6
Back, Thomas	Nov. 3, 1862	24	light	Boston, Ma.	6	2
Backet, William	Sept. 10, 1847	24	black	Harwich, Ma.	5	11
Backus, Charles	Dec. 10, 1806	18	yellowish	Norwich, Conn.	4	5
Backus, George W.	June 20, 1818	18	light	Norwick, Conn.	4	8
Backus, Luther D.	Dec. 18, 1824	17	dark	Newport, R.I.	4	9
Backus, Richard	Jan. 25, 1830	18	light	So. Kingstown, R.I.	5	6
Bacon, Abel F.	Dec. 9, 1807	17	light	Barnstable, Ma.	4	5
Bacon, Abel F.	Dec. 7, 1811	21	light	Barnstable, Ma.	4	6
Bacon, Elias	May 3, 1797	22	light	Wrentham, Ma.	1	21
Bacon, Elijah	1798 to 1799	July 20, 1772		Providence, R.I.	* -	-
Bacon, Isaiah	Mar. 18, 1797	32	light	Providence, R.I.	1	7
Bacon, Jakes	Aug. 15, 1815	28	light	Barnstable, Ma.	4	7
Bacon, John	May 7, 1813	17	light	Providence, R.I.	4	7
Bacon, John	Aug. 16, 1831	26	light	Boston, Ma.	5	6
Bacon, Sylvester	Apr. 26, 1811	17	light	Barnstable, Ma.	4	6
Bacon, William	May 12, 1815	15	light	Providence, R.I.	4	7
Badger, Henry	Nov. 9, 1850	21	light	Plymouth, Me.	5	12
Badin, John	Oct. 30, 1800	22	dark	Alexandria, Va.	2	25
Bagley, Joseph	Oct. 16, 1855	23	light	Westerly, R.I.	5	91
Bagley, Marain	Jan. 1, 1805	18	dark	Chatham, Conn.	3	50

*mulatto
*Newport, R. I.

REGISTER OF SEAMEN'S PROTECTION

NAME	DATE OF CERTIFICATION	AGE	COMPLEXION	PLACE OF BIRTH	BOOK	PAGE
Bailey, Aaron	July 11, 1818	22	dark	Boston, Ma.	4	8
Bailey, Adam	Dec. 12, 1803	20	yellow*	So. Kingstown, R.I.	2	22
Bailey, Adam	May 13, 1806	20	yellow*	Groton, Conn.	3	74
Bailey, Albert P.	Sept. 28, 1840	16	light	Providence, R.I.	5	9
Bailey, Caleb W.	Sept. 6, 1849	20	dark	Warwick, R.I.	5	12
Bailey, Charles	Dec. 17, 1844	38	black	Indian River, Del.	5	10
Bailey, Frederick	May 30, 1806	23	dark	Little Compton, R.I.	3	78
Bailey, Frederick	Jan. 2, 1861	18	dark	Burrillville, R.I.	6	2
Bailey, George	Aug. 17, 1801	19	light	Salem, Ma.	2	33
Bailey, Gideon	May 17, 1797	26	dark	E. Greenwich, R.I.	1	21
Bailey, Ira F.	July 2, 1858	20	dark	Greenbush (?), Me.	6	2
Bailey, Israel	May 7, 1800	23	light	Maidshore, Vt.	2	25
Bailey, Noah B.	Aug. 13, 1846	33	light	Middletown, Conn.	5	10
Bailey, Simeon Allyn	Nov. 24, 1826	19	light	Groton, Conn.	4	10
Bailey, William	May 22, 1855	25	black	Norfolk, Va.	5	91
Baker, Allen	May 9, 1815	22	light	Dennis, Ma.	4	7
Baker, Amos C.	Apr. 2, 1828	27	light	Harwich, Ma.	4	10
Baker, Benajah	Oct. 26, 1803	19	light	Rehoboth, Ma.	2	44
Baker, Bradick	Nov. 20, 1818	21	dark	Falmouth, Ma.	4	8
Baker, Caleb	Oct. 11, 1803	26	dark	Cranston, R.I.	2	44
Baker, Caleb	May 2, 1805	26	dark	Warwick, R.I.	3	58
Baker, Caleb	July 14, 1806	27	dark	Cranston, R.I.	3	78
Baker, Caleb Hill	Sept. 24, 1819	20	dark	Warren, R.I.	4	8
Baker, Calvin	June 27, 1849	29	dark	Dennis, Ma.	5	11
Baker, Charles	Dec. 8, 1832	21	light	Somerset, Ma.	5	6
Baker, David	Nov. 5, 1852	18	light	Warren, R.I.	5	13
Baker, Ebenezer	July 27, 1820	19	light	Yarmouth, Ma.	4	8
Baker, Edward	Oct. 3, 1801	20	dark	Upton, Ma.	2	33
Baker, Elijah	Aug. 30, 1834	49	light	Dennis, Ma.	5	7
Baker, Elijah	Mar. 10, 1842	25	light	Yarmouth, Ma.	5	9
Baker, Freeman	Apr. 13, 1855	44	light	New Bedford, Ma.	5	91
Baker, Freeman R.	May 2, 1821	18	light	Dennis, Ma.	4	9
Baker, Geo. B.	Dec. 9, 1848	19	fair	Swanzea, Ma.	5	11
Baker, Henry	Mar. 3, 1797	20	dark	Warwick, R.I.	1	7
Baker, Hiram	Jan. 2, 1818	18	dark	Yarmouth, Ma.	4	7

*mulatto

NAME	DATE OF CERTIFICATION	AGE	COMPLEXION	PLACE OF BIRTH	BOOK	PAGE
Baker, Isaac	Oct. 27, 1804	15	light	Falmouth, Ma.	3	49
Baker, Jehial	Mar. 28, 1815	18	light	Yarmouth, Ma.	4	7
Baker, Jeremiah	July 19, 1806	14	light	Barrington, R.I.	3	78
Baker, John	Sept. 30, 1796	24	dark	Cranston, R.I.	2	4
Baker, John	Oct. 31, 1800	18	dark	Smithfield, R.I.	2	25
Baker, John H.	Apr. 12, 1858	21	dark	Monravia, N.Y.	6	2
Baker, Johnthan	Dec. 15, 1847	46	dark	Yarmouth, Ma.	5	11
Baker, Joseph	Oct. 30, 1800	27	light	Yarmouth, Ma.	2	25
Baker, Joseph	June 6, 1820	20	light	Seekonk, Ma.	4	8
Baker, Joseph	Mar. 25, 1848	19	dark	Orvington, Me.	5	11
Baker, Joseph L.	Mar. 24, 1857	16	light	New Bedford, Mass.	5	91
Baker, Judah, Jr.	Oct. 24, 1849	20	light	Dennis, Ma.	5	12
Baker, Morris	May 1, 1821	22	light	Yarmouth, Ma.	4	9
*Baker, Moses	1798 to 1799	Sept. 26, 1786		Somerset, Ma.	*-	-
Baker, Nathaniel	Jan. 29, 1798	13	light	Providence, R.I.	1	25
Baker, Nathaniel	July 25, 1801	21	dark	Providence, R.I.	2	33
Baker, Phillip	Sept. 23, 1864	37	light	New Bedford, Ma.	6	2
Baker, Samuel	Aug. 8, 1808	17	dark	Providence, R.I.	4	5
Baker, Samuel	July 2, 1811	20	dark	Providence, R.I.	4	6
Baker, Samuel	Aug. 23, 1822	34	light	Dennis, Ma.	4	9
Baker, Thatcher	Apr. 5, 1819	20	light	Yarmouth, Ma.	4	8
Baker, Thomas	Nov. 16, 1803	23	dark	Liberty Co., Ga.	2	49
Baker, Timothy	Sept. 26, 1829	19	dark	Yarmouth, Ma.	5	6
Baker, Tristam	Oct. 7, 1819	21	light	Yarmouth, Ma.	4	8
Baker, William	Sept. 7, 1799	17	dark	No. Kingstown, R.I.	2	2
Baker, William, Jr.	May 13, 1809	21	dark	Providence, R.I.	4	5
Baker, Zadock	Nov. 21, 1833	19	light	Dennis, Ma.	5	7
Baker, Zadock	Sept. 12, 1843	29	light	Dennis, Ma.	5	9
Baker, Zebulon	Jan. 8, 1830	20	light	Yarmouth, Ma.	5	6
Balch, James R.	Dec. 5, 1817	16	light	Westport, Ma.	4	7
Baldwin, Abraham S.	Jan. 16, 1851	42	light	Bloomfield, N.J.	5	13
Baldwin, Geo. D.	Apr. 18, 1855	19	light	New Haven, Conn.	5	91
Baldwin, John H.	July 1, 1844	25	dark	Sullivan Co., N.Y.	5	10
Ball, Barsil	Nov. 8, 1843	21	light	New Shoreham, R.I.	5	10
Ball, Bartlett	Oct. 27, 1835	20	light	New Shoreham, R.I. (Block Island)	5	7

*Moses Baker of Tiverton, R.I.
**Newport, R. I.

REGISTER OF SEAMEN'S PROTECTION

NAME	DATE OF CERTIFICATION	AGE	COMPLEXION	PLACE OF BIRTH	BOOK	PAGE
Ball, Edward	Nov. 24, 1849	21	light	Springfield, Ma.	5	12
Ball, Gideon	1798 to 1799	Mar. 12, 1796		Block Island, R.I.	-	-
Ball, Jonathan S.	Mar. 27, 1834	21	light	New Shoreham,(B.I.)R.I.	5	7
Ball, Nicholas	Apr. 23, 1844	15	light	New Shoreham,(B.I.)R.I.	5	10
Ball, Simon R.	Mar. 28, 1834	19	light	New Shoreham,(B.I.)R.I.	5	7
Ballard, George	May, 3, 1844	23	light	Boston, Ma.	5	10
Ballou, Chas. S.	June 15, 1855	18	light	Wrentham, Ma.	5	91
Ballou, Darius	Jan. 27, 1807	22	florid	Glocester, R.I.	4	5
Ballou, Francis	June 15, 1842	19	light	Kirkland, N.Y.	5	9
Ballou, George	Apr. 7, 1854	22	dark	Smithfield, R.I.	5	13
Ballou, John C.	June 18, 1861	36	dark	Providence, R.I.	6	2
Ballou. Nahum	Apr. 2, 1798	24	dark	Cumberland, R.I.	1&2	25&2
[Ballou],Bellue,Prosper	Nov. 5, 1799	17	light	Cumberland, R.I.	2	25
Ballou, Seth T.	Sept. 28, 1830	17	light	Rehoboth, Ma.	5	6
Ballou, William	Mar. 7, 1855	32	light	Norwich, N.Y.	5	91
Ballou, Wm. R.	May 30, 1849	33	light	Burrillville	5	11
Balter, Thomas	May 27, 1830	35	dark	Boston, Ma.	5	6
Barnfield, James Tillard	Aug. 18, 1803	17	light	New York, N.Y.	2	44
Banks, John	Aug. 9, 1834	22	black	Edenton, N.C.	5	7
Baptist, John	Sept. 25, 1834	56	dark	New Orleans, La.	5	7
Bar, Robert	Mar. 10, 1853	22	dark	Boston, Ma.	5	13
Barber, Alfred	June 28, 1822	23	dk. Yellow	Norwich, Conn.	4	9
Barber, James	Dec. 26, 1800	20	light	Newport, R.I.	2	33
Barber, James	Feb. 21, 1806	24	light	Newport, R.I.	3	72A
Barber, John	Sept. 20, 1799	21	black	Charlestown, R.I.	2	2
Barber, John	July 15, 1800	21	black	Charlestown, R.I.	2	25
Barber, Joseph A.	Nov. 29, 1820	20	light	Tiverton, R.I.	4	8
Barber, Simon	July 17, 1804	24	black	Exeter, R.I.	3	4
Barber, William	Dec. 16, 1824	15	dark	Norwich, Conn.	4	9
Barber, Wm. H.	Feb. 27, 1851	21	light	New Haven, Conn.	5	13
Bardeen, Robert	Mar. 16, 1799	22	light	Middleboro, Ma.	2	2
Barker, Alexander	1798-1799	Oct. 4, 1787		Middletown, R.I.	* -	-
Barker, Henry	Oct. 15, 1850	36	light	Newport, R.I.	5	12
Barker, Jabez	1798-1799	Apr. 5, 1782		Dartmouth, Ma.	* -	-
Barker, James M.	Dec. 7, 1832	16	light	Providence, R.I.	5	6
Barker, Jeremiah B.	Apr. 5, 1809	20	light	Providence, R.I.	4	5

*Newport, R. I.

REGISTER OF SEAMEN'S PROTECTION

NAME		DATE OF CERTIFICATION	AGE	COMPLEXION	PLACE OF BIRTH	BOOK	PAGE
Barker,	John D.	Dec. 16, 1837	37	dark	Boston, Ma.	5	8
Barker,	Joseph	1798-1799	Nov. 20, 1762		Middletown, R.I.	** -	-
Barker,	Peleg	May 9, 1797	23	light	Newport, R.I.	1	21
Barker,	Peter	Nov. 10, 1804	18	light	New York, N.Y.	3	50
Barker,	Richard	June 7, 1821	22	brown	Boston, Ma.	4	9
Barker,	Thomas	Mar. 28, 1827	23	brown	Falmouth, England	4	10
Barker,	William	1798-1799	May 6, 1781		Dighton, Ma.	** -	-
Barker,	William Cyrus	Aug. 31, 1849	24	light	Providence, R.I.	5	12
Barlow,	Allen	Nov. 4, 1820	21	brown	Rochester, Ma.	4	8
Barlow,	James C.	Nov. 11, 1850	18	light	Gardiner, Me.	5	12
Barlow,	Otis W.	Nov. 11, 1850	20	light	Newport, R.I.	5	12
Barlow,	Reuben W.	Mar. 5, 1840	17	dark	Sandwich, Ma.	5	8
Barlow,	Reuben W.	Oct. 8, 1841	17	light	Sandwich, Ma.	5	9
Barnaby,	Ambrose	Nov. 30, 1849	46	light	Warren, R.I.	5	12
Barnard,	Adonijah	Aug. 8, 1812	21	light	Simsbury, Conn.	4	7
Barnard,	John S.	Nov. 10, 1849	31	light	Providence, R.I.	5	12
Barnard,	Kingston	May 14, 1798	27	black	Charleston, S.C.	2	2
Barnes,	Edward	July 31, 1854	18	yellow	Phila., Pa.	5	91
Barnes,	Fred N.	Mar. 3, 1856	24	light	Hardwick, Ma.	5	91
Barnes,	Henry	Feb. 11, 1853	26	light	Providence, R.I.	5	13
Barnes,	Henry L.	Dec. 30, 1852	17	light	Smithfield, R.I.	5	13
Barnes,	John	June 16, 1855	18	light	Norwalk, Conn.	5	91
Barnes,	Lysander	July 13, 1840	36	dark	Brookfield, Ma.	5	9
Barnes,	Robert	Sept. 26, 1796	21	light	Charleston, S.C.	1	3
Barnes,	Samuel	May 23, 1806	22	light	Guilford, Vt.	3	74
Barnes,	Thomas	Oct. 18, 1860	24	fair	New York, N.Y.	6	2
Barnes,	William	June 1, 1837	39	light	Norfolk, Va.	5	8
Barnes,	William	Aug. 7, 1841	43	dark	New York, N.Y.	5	9
Barney,	Charles	Oct. 12, 1807	20	yellow*	Swansea, Ma.	4	5
Barney,	Charles G.	Apr. 15, 1833	17	dark	Seekonk, Ma.	5	6
Barney,	Charles H.	Apr. 25, 1857	26	light	Taunton, Ma.	5	92
Barney,	Emery	Sept. 27, 1854	19	light	Columbus, Ohio	5	91
Barney,	Franklin S.	July 23, 1853	19	dark	Taunton, Ma.	5	13
Barney,	Jack	Dec. 1, 1800	22	black	New York, N.Y.	2	25

*mulatto
**Newport, R. I.

REGISTER OF SEAMEN'S PROTECTION

Page 20

NAME	DATE OF CERTIFICATION	AGE	COMPLEXION	PLACE OF BIRTH	BOOK	PAGE
[Barney]Berny, James	May 24, 1800	21	dark	Providence, R.I.	2	25
Barney, James O.	Aug. 7, 1852	20	light	Baton Rouge, La.	5	13
Barney, James D.	Aug. 9, 1810	15	light	Providence, R.I.	4	6
Barney, Jeremiah	May 3, 1799	23	light	Rehoboth, Ma.	2	2
Barney, Josephus	Jan. 8, 1827	18	light	Swansea, Ma.	4	10
Barney, Orrin	June 19, 1857	23	fair	Portsmouth, N.H.	5	92
Barney, Samuel	Mar. 22, 1805	17	black	Swansea, Ma.	3	58
Barney, Samuel	Mar. 19, 1806	18	black	Swansea, Ma.	3	74
Barney, Wanton	July 16, 1824	25	light	Coventry, R.I.	4	9
Barney, Washington	Mar. 29, 1851	21	black	Boston, Ma.	5	13
Barney, William	Nov. 1, 1800	28	light	Rehoboth, Ma.	2	25
Barnstead, George T.	Jan. 26, 1860	29	fair	Eastport, Me.	6	2
Baron, Lewis	May 16, 1836	27	light	New Orleans, La.	5	7
Barr, Jacob	Mar. 7, 1831	19	light	Phila., Pa.	5	6
Barr, William P.	Mar. 19, 1855	17	light	Providence, R.I.	5	91
Barritt, Joseph	Oct. 21, 1820	19	light	Thompson, Conn.	4	8
Barrett,* William	June 30, 1832	21	dark	New Castle, Del.	5	6
Barron, John	Sept. 13, 1809	23	brown	New York, N.Y.	4	6
[Barron] Barrow, John C.	May 5, 1846	47	fair	Boston, Ma.	5	10
Barrows, Sampson	Mar. 15, 1845	29	mulatto	High Co., N.C.	5	10
Barrus, Charles	Mar. 27, 1866	42	dark	Boston, Ma.	6	2
Barry, Samuel	1798-1799	Aug. 21, 1780		Westerly, R.I.	*** -	-
Barry, Edward	Oct. 30, 1804	46	dark	Phila., Pa.	3	49
Barry, William	Oct. 26, 1839	46	black	Portsmouth, N.H.	5	8
Barry, William	Feb. 26, 1846	19	black	New York, N.Y.	5	10
Barsautee, John	Oct. 3, 1855	54	fair	Portsmouth, N.H.	5	91
Barsett, Thomas	Apr. 2, 1805	22	yellow**	Groton, Conn.	3	58
Barstow, [Bastow] Geo.	Oct. 12, 1803	18	dark	Providence, R.I.	2	44
Barstow, Paris	Jan. 6, 1830	14	light	Providence, R.I.	5	6
Barstow, Robert	Mar. 20, 1815	18	light	Hanover, Ma.	4	7
Barter, Darius	June 24, 1863	17	light	St. George, Me.	6	2
Barter, Thomas	June 24, 1863	44	light	St. George, Me.	6	2
Bartholick, Pontillas	Jan. 20, 1801	24	light	Warwick, R.I.	2	33
Bartholick, Pontillas	Dec. 6, 1805	27	light	Warwick, R.I.	3	72A

*possibly Bassett
**mulatto

NAME	DATE OF CERTIFICATION	AGE	COMPLEXION	PLACE OF BIRTH	BOOK	PAGE
Bartholick, Steward*	Jan. 19, 1801	31	light	Warwick, R.I.	2	33
Bartholick, Stewart*	July 9, 1806	37	light	Warwick, R.I.	3	78
Bartlett, Edward	Nov. 29, 1848	24	light	Lynn, N.H.	5	11
Bartlett, Jencks	Aug. 2, 1848	26	dark	Smithfield, R.I.	5	11
Bartlett, Nathaniel P.	Feb. 24, 1827	14	dark	Providence, R.I.	4	10
Bartlett, William	Apr. 6, 1854	20	light	New York, N.Y.	5	13
Bartley, Francis	Oct. 20, 1851	23	light	Sag Harbor, N.Y.	5	13
Bartling, William H.	Feb. 16, 1857	20	light	Phila., Pa.	5	91
Barton, Albert G.	July 8, 1831	17	dark	Providence, R.I.	5	6
Barton, Anthony	Dec. 20, 1797	24	black	Warwick, R.I.	1	21
Barton, Anthony	May 27, 1806	32	black	Warwick, R.I.	3	78
Barton, George W.	July 16, 1804	29	dark	Providence, R.I.	3	4
Barton, Henry	May 2, 1803	22	dark	Providence, R.I.	2	33
Barton, Henry	Mar. 16, 1809	26	light	Providence, R.I.	4	5
Barton, John	Nov. 12, 1836	31	mulatto	Dorchester Co., Md.	5	8
Barton, Rufus	Sept. 15, 1803	39	light	Warwick, R.I.	2	44
Barton, Rufus	Oct. 22, 1803	17	light	Warren, R.I.	2	44
Barton, Samuel	Nov. 20, 1821	21	dark	Warren, R.I.	-	--
Sworn statement of George Hoar in the Custom House Papers. Apr. 20, 1800.						
Barton, Samuel H.	Dec. 9, 1815	18	light	Swansea, Ma.	4	7
Barton, Seth W.	July 9, 1822	20	freckled	Warren, R.I.	4	9
Barton, Thomas	Dec. 2, 1850	20	dark	New York, N.Y.	5	12
Barton, William	Apr. 13, 1865	25	light	Melrose, N.Y.	6	2
Bassett, John	July 8, 1808	24	black	Boston, Ma.	4	5
Bassett, Samuel	Nov. 22, 1805	19	light	Rochester, Ma.	3	72A
Bassett,**William	June 30, 1832	21	dark	New Castle, Del.	5	6
Basten, Martin	June 7, 1849	27	black	Boston, Ma.	5	11
Basto, George	Mar. 13, 1807	21	light	Providence, R.I.	4	5
Bastow, James	Dec. 4, 1818	25	dark	Providence, R.I.	4	8
Batchelar, Henry W.	Feb. 1, 1841	16	light	Providence, R.I.	5	9
Bateman, William A.	Oct. 26, 1849	18	light	E. Greenwich, R.I.	5	12
Bates, Arnold	Feb. 7, 1832	15	light	Warwick, R.I.	5	6
Bates, Arnold P.	Dec. 22, 1840	19	light	Scituate, R.I.	5	9
Bates, Benjamin	Dec. 16, 1805	41	light	Abington, Ma.	3	72A

*same person[t? d?]

**Possibly Barrett

NAME	DATE OF CERTIFICATION	AGE	COMPLEXION	PLACE OF BIRTH	BOOK	PAGE
Bates, Benoui?	Nov. 19, 1828	22	mulatto	Warwick, R.I.	4	10
Bates, James	June 15, 1832	26	light	Abraccam, N.J.	5	6
Bates, Jeremiah	Mar. 14, 1812	21	yellow	Warwick, R.I.	4	6
Bates, Jonathan	Oct. 24, 1796	16	light	Exeter, R.I.	1	7,4
Bates, Joseph	Oct. 29, 1800	22	dark	No. Kinstown, R.I.	2	25
Bates, Merritt	Apr. 11, 1798	31	dark	New Bedford, Ma.	1&2*	25&2*
Bates, Merritt	Feb. 23, 1805	36	light	New Bedford, Ma.	3	50
Bates, Rubin	Dec. 9, 1803	16	dark	Attleboro, Ma.	2	22
Bates, Sampson	June 12, 1818	21	yellow	Warwick, R.I.	4	8
Bates, Spenoer	Dec. 16, 1797	15	dark	Exeter, R.I.	1	21
Bates, Spensar	Sept. 9, 1801	18	dark	Exeter, R.I.	2	33
Bates, William	Sept. 10, 1857	28	dark	New Haven, Conn.	6	2
Bates, William P.	June 2, 1838	25	dark	Bristol, R.I.	5	8
Batey, John	Dec. 30, 1865	30	dark	Whitehall, N.Y.	6	2
Bathe, William	Oct. 4, 1841	28	ruddy	Phila., Pa.	5	9
Batt, James	Oct. 16, 1804	26	light	Petersburgh, Va.	3	49
Battel, Martin	Sept. 29, 1849	20	light	Brooklyn, N.Y.	5	12
Battey, Isaac S.	Aug. 31, 1849	31	dark	Providence, R.I.	5	12
Battey, John	Sept. 6, 1832	24	dark	Salem, Ma.	5	6
Baxter, Ansell	May 10, 1819	40	light	Yarmouth, Ma.	4	8
Baxter, Arvin	May 17, 1819	15	light	Barnstable, Ma.	4	8
Baxter, Benjamin	Sept. 13, 1819	37	dark	Dennis, Ma.	4	8
Baxter, Benjamin	Jan. 3. 1827	21	light	Dennis, Ma.	4	10
Baxter, David	Dec. 21, 1819	29	dark	Yarmouth, Ma.	4	8
Baxter, David, Jr.	Dec. 28, 1830	17	freckled	Barnstable, Ma.	5	6
Baxter, Franklin	Nov. 29, 1820	30	light	Yarmouth, Ma.	4	8
Baxter, Franklin	Nov. 27, 1837	50	light	Yarmouth, Ma.	5	8
Baxter, Henry	Sept. 27, 1805	20	dark	Springfield, Ma.	3	72
Baxter, Hiram B.	Nov. 18, 1825	25	light	Yarmouth, Ma.	4	9
Baxter, John	May 23, 1835	18	light	Thomaston, Me.	5	7
Baxter, Joseph	May 11, 1819	52	light	Yarmouth, Ma.	4	8
Baxter, Samuel M.	June 12, 1849	34	light	Smithfield, R.I.	5	11
Baxter, Seth	Jan. 19, 1818	21	light	Harwich, Ma.	4	7
Baxter, Warren	Dec. 21, 1819	25	dark	Yarmouth, Ma.	4	8
Baxter, William	May 17, 1819	27	dark	Yarmouth, Ma.	4	8
Baxter, William	Mar. 16, 1831	18	light	Barnstable, Ma.	5	6

*Book 1 page 25, Book 2 page 2.

REGISTER OF SEAMEN'S PROTECTION

NAME	DATE OF CERTIFICATION	AGE	COMPLEXION	PLACE OF BIRTH	BOOK	PAGE
Baxter, William	May 13, 1837	26	black	Phila., Pa.	5	8
Baxter, William	July 31, 1837	21	light	Troy, N.Y.	5	8
Baxter, Zadock	May 13, 1822	34	light	Yarmouth, Ma.	4	9
Baxter, Zenus	Apr. 25, 1820	22	light	Yarmouth, Ma.	4	8
Baxter, Zenas	Nov. 9. 1843	42	light	Barnstable, Ma.	5	10
Bayard, Augustus	Oct. 30, 1852	22	black	Providence, R.I.	5	13
Bayley, Richard	Oct. 6, 1801	29	black	New York, N.Y.	2	33
Baylies, Francis	Dec. 22, 1817	14	dark	Taunton, Ma.	4	7
Bazzil, Francis	Nov. 6, 1805	16	light	Providence, R.I.	3	72
Beach, Horace H.	Aug. 2, 1850	19	light	Milton, N.Y.	5	12
Beach, James	Sept. 12, 1804	23	light	Reading, Conn.	3	4
Beals, Comfort	Mar. 29, 1811	26	light	Abbington, Ma.	4	6
Bean, Benson	Feb. 24, 1849	25	light	Barrington, R.I.	5	11
Bean, Ulyses	May 17, 1819	22	dark	Barnstable, Ma.	4	8
Beardsley, Samuel H.	July 13, 1849	22	light	New York, N.Y.	5	11
Beaty, John	Nov. 30, 1835	28	light	Newburyport, Ma.	5	7
Beaumont, John P.	Mar. 13, 1827	28	dark	Grafton, N.H.	4	10
Bebee, Allen	Mar. 25, 1828	24	light	Warren, R.I.	4	10
Bechet, William	Sept. 7, 1852	28	black	New York, N.Y.	5	13
Beckford, John N.C.	Oct. 29, 1839	32	dark	Providence, R.I.	5	8
Beckwith, George	June 29, 1833	25	yellow	New London, Conn.	5	6
Beckwith, Henry	Aug. 27, 1859	22	dark	Providence, R.I.	6	2
Beckwith, Joseph L.(?)	Mar. 17, 1865	30	dark	No. Prov., R.I.	6	2
Beckwith, Thomas	Sept. 30, 1835	31	dark	New York, N.Y.	5	7
Beebe, Albert	Oct. 8, 1861	26	dark	Foster, R.I.	6	2
Beebe, Allen	1798-1799	Mar. 31, 1784		Cambridge, Ma.	* -	--
Beebe, Orson W.	May 19, 1838	18	dark	Providence, R.I.	5	8
Beebe, Samuel	1798-1799	Apr. 11, 1780		Newport, R.I.	* -	--
Begand, Peter	Aug. 5, 1805	36	dark	Nantes, France	3	58
Begle, Ransom	Aug. 15, 1839	19	light	Phila., Pa.	5	8
Belcher, Ransom	Jan. 11, 1800	19	light	Wrentham, Ma.	2	25
Belding, Daniel	Dec. 23, 1817	28	light	Yarmouth, Ma.	4	7
Belknap, Isaac B.	Oct. 29, 1849	19	light	Seekonk, Ma.	5	12
Bell, George W.	Mar. 24, 1843	24	mulatto	Washington, D.C.	5	9
Bell, Isaac W.	July 17, 1839	27	dark	Boston, Ma.	5	8
Bell, James	Mar. 3, 1835	29	dark	New York, N.Y.	5	7

*Newport, R. I.

NAME	DATE OF CERTIFICATION	AGE	COMPLEXION	PLACE OF BIRTH	BOOK	PAGE
Bell, John	Nov. 14, 1842	18	dark	Boston, Ma.	5	9
Bell, Thomas	Aug. 11, 1858	20	light	Johnson, R.I.	6	2
Bell, William	Nov. 14, 1842	22	light	Boston, Ma.	5	9
Bellows, Daniel S.	Sept. 24, 1849	22	light	Smithfield, R.I.	5	12
Belsi, John	Nov. 14, 1842	21	light	Genesses, N.Y.	5	9
Bemis, Daniel W.	Aug. 11, 1838	38	light	Boston, Ma.	5	8
Bemis, George	Oct. 14, 1840	19	dark	Boston, Ma.	5	9
Bemiss, William B.	Sept. 24, 1805	23	light	Providence, R.I.	3	72
Benchley, Nathan	Apr. 14, 1806	20	light	Smithfield, R.I.	3	74
Benchley, William S.	Aug. 17, 1824	22	dark	Smithfield, R.I.	4	9
Benham, Peter C.	Sept. 6, 1864	29	dark	Groton, Conn.	6	2
Benjamin, Lyman	Nov. 20, 1832	20	black	Hebron, Conn.	5	6
Benjamans, Samuel	Jan. 19, 1811	25	light	Exeter, R.I.	4	6
Bennar, Wm. R.	Sept. 19, 1856	39	dark	Wilmington, Del.	5	91
Bennast, Joseph	Dec. 18, 1850	20	dark	New Orleans, La.	5	12
Benner, Alexander	Mar. 7, 1853	22	light	Salem, Ma.	5	13
Bennett, Asa	July 12, 1803	20	dark	Warwick, R.I.	2	33
Bennett, Asa	Oct. 29, 1849	27	light	Cranston, R.I.	5	12
Bennett, Belia	Sept. 1, 1836	19	dark	Sterling, Conn.	5	7
Bennett, Benjamin	Dec. 28, 1822	32	dark	E. Greenwich, R.I.	4	9
Bennett, Charles	June 21, 1824	23	dark	Sandwich, Ma.	4	9
Bennett, Chas. B.	Nov. 20, 1841	48	black	Flemington, N.J.	5	9
Bennett, Dan[L] S.	Mar. 28, 1855	30	fair	Cranston, R.I.	5	91
Bennett, Ezra	Nov. 2, 1803	28	light	Scituate, R.I.	2	44
Bennett, Ezra	Aug. 10, 1808	33	florid	Scituate, R.I.	4	5
Bennett, George	Aug. 31, 1809	19	light	Cheshire, Ma.	4	6
Bennett, John	Apr. 10, 1798	20	dark	County Kent, R.I.	1&2*	25&2*
Bennett, John	Aug. 24, 1804	20	light	Providence, R.I.	3	4
Bennett, John	June 27, 1800	21	dark	Warwick, R.I.	2	25
Bennett, John	Aug. 27, 1806	21	light	Providence, R.I.	3	78
Bennett, Joseph	Dec. 16, 1803	36	light	Smithfield, R.I.	2	22
Bennett, Joseph, Jr.	Aug. 23, 1821	17	light	Cumberland, R.I.	4	9
Bennett, Leonard W.	Sept. 6, 1849	26	light	Foster, R.I.	5	12
Bennett, Pardon	1798-1799	Jan. 31, 1768		Tiverton, R.I.	** -	--
Bennett, Pardon W.	Apr. 2, 1810	20	dark	Sterling, Conn.	4	6
Bennett, Russell	May 5, 1809	17	light	Warwick, R.I.	4	5

*Book 1 page 25, Book 2 page 2
**Newport, R.I.

REGISTER OF SEAMEN'S PROTECTION

NAME	DATE OF CERTIFICATION	AGE	COMPLEXION	PLACE OF BIRTH	BOOK	PAGE
Bennett, Samuel W.	Mar. 10, 1832	24	light	New York, N.Y.	5	6
Bennett, Stephen	Dec. 20, 1799	23	dark	Warwick, R.I.	2	25
Bennett, Stephen H.	Dec. 23, 1823	25	light	Newport, R.I.	4	9
Bennett, Timothy	Dec. 16, 1797	20	light	Cumberland, R.I.	1	21
Bennett, Thomas	Apr. 26, 1800	24	dark	Warwick, R.I.	2	25
Bennett, William F.	Jan. 25, 1798	36	light	London, England	1	25
Bennett, Zeblam	July 15, 1854	18	light	Coventry, R.I.	5	91
Benson, Abraham	Nov. 29, 1821	21	yellow	Seekonk, Ma.	4	9
Benson, Arffee?	Sept. 5, 1803	34	black	Newport, R.I.	2	44
Benson, Edward	Jan. 25, 1858	27	yellow	Providence, R.I.	6	2
Banson, Edward A.	Mar. 18, 1852	22	mulatto	Providence, R.I.	5	13
Benson, George	May 17, 1836	28	black	Hudson, N.Y.	5	7
Benson, James R.	Jan. 6, 1819	16	light	Providence, R.I.	4	8
Benson, John	Nov. 24, 1798	23	dark	Scituate, Ma.	2	2
Benson, John	Aug. 21, 1840	29	light	Gorham, Me.	5	9
Benson, John C.	Aug. 12, 1805	13	light	Newport, R.I.	3	72
Benson, Martin, Jr.	Aug. 10, 1811	25	light	Newport, R.I.	4	6
Benson, William B.	July 2, 1810	15	light	Providence, R.I.	4	6
Bent, Jacob	Oct. 18, 1858	25	dark	Charlestown, R.I.	6	2
Bentley, Benjamin	May 3, 1797	19	light	E. Greenwich, R.I.	1	21
Bentley, John	Mar. 4, 1797	17	light	E. Greenwich, R.I.	1	7
Bentley, Nathaniel	1798-1799	Apr. 17, 1782		Taunton, Ma.	* -	--
Bentley, Simon W.	Dec. 28, 1822	19	light	E. Greenwich, R.I.	4	9
Bentley, Thomas	1798-1799	Sept. 8, 1775		Warwick, R.I.	* -	--
Bentley, William	Sept. 26, 1805	21	dark	Warwick, R.I.	3	72
Bentley, William	June 17, 1806	22	brown	Warwick, R.I.	3	78
Benton, Charles Henry	Aug. 3, 1852	33	light	Mobile Co., Ala.	5	13
Benton, Daniel	Aug. 30, 1822	29	black	Plainfield, Conn.	4	9
Benton, Frederic	Aug. 2, 1806	27	light	Hamburgh, Germany	3	78
Benton, Wm. H.	June 28, 1849	28	light	Boston, Ma.	5	11
Bernard, Kingston	May 1, 1799	29	black	Charleston, S.C.	2	2
Berry, Allen	May 8, 1826	21	light	Yarmouth, Ma.	4	10
Berry, Chas. E.	Dec. 20, 1848	19	fair	Prospect, Me.	5	11
Berry, David, Jr.	Dec. 17, 1818	17	ruddy	Brewster, Ma.	4	8
Berry, Ebenezer	Dec. 15, 1847	32	dark	Yarmouth, Ma.	5	11
Berry, Edwin P.	May 13, 1856	35	dark	Westerly, R.I.	5	91

*Newport, R.I.

Page 26

REGISTER OF SEAMEN'S PROTECTION

NAME	DATE OF CERTIFICATION	AGE	COMPLEXION	PLACE OF BIRTH	BOOK	PAGE
[Barry]Berry, Freeman	Oct. 9, 1834	26	dark	Yarmouth, Ma.	5	7
Berry, Isaac	Oct. 10, 1821	23	light	Yarmouth, Ma.	4	9
Berry, James	July 13, 1803	23	dark	Providence, R.I.	2	44
Berry, James	Mar. 27, 1799	20	dark	Providence, R.I.	2	2
[Berry]Berrey, John	Oct. 2, 1801	22	dark	New York, N.Y.	2	33
Berry, John Henry	June 24, 1847	28	colored	Jamaica, N.Y.	5	10
Berry, Nicholas Q?	Dec. 18, 1850	23	light	Prospect, Me.q	5	12
Berry, Samuel	Apr. 4, 1839	26	black	Providence, R.I.	5	8
Berry, Samuel	Mar. 12, 1842	29	black	New York, N.Y.	5	9
Beswick, Horatio	Dec. 29, 1846	24	fair	Salem, Ma.	5	10
Betts, [Burnet]Burril	Jan. 4, 1838	28	light	Wilton, Conn.	5	8
Beverly, Charles	Sept. 16, 1803	15	light	Providence, R.I.	2	44
Beverly, Frank	June 6, 1853	23	light	Providence, R.I.	5	13
Beverly, Stephen, Jr.	Dec. 24, 1818	19	light	Providence, R.I.	4	8
Beverly, William	Nov. 22, 1836	24	light	Providence, R.I.	5	8
Bezely, John	Mar. 4, 1839	25	light	Providence, R.I.	5	8
Beckford, James	Oct. 4, 1854	22	light	Winstead, Conn.	5	91
Bicknall, Asa	Oct. 30, 1805	16	light	Barrington, R.I.	3	72
Bicknell, Asa	Nov. 7, 1823	25	light	Providence, R.I.	4	9
Bicknell, Henry	Dec. 28, 1822	19	brown	Cumberland, R.I.	4	9
Bicknell, Howland V.	Aug. 28, 1849	38	light	No. Kingston, R.I.	5	12
Bicknall, Jeffery	Nov. 19, 1796	24	black	Mansfield, Conn.	1	7
Bicknall, John	Nov. 1, 1826	21	light	Exeter, R.I.	4	10
Bicknall, John	Sept. 17, 1853	20	dark	Pawtuxet, R.I.	5	13
Biekcum, Charles B.	Dec. 26, 1827	19	light	Haverhill, Ma.	4	10
Bigelow, Francis	July 16, 1810	22	light	Framingham, Ma.	4	6
Bigelow, James, Jr.	Nov. 29, 1830	25	light	Nantucket, Ma.	5	6
Bigelow, Jonathan	June 9, 1804	23	light	Hartford, Conn.	3	3
Bigelow, Lewis	Apr. 12, 1854	22	light	Boston, Ma.	5	91
Bigelow, William B.	Oct. 24, 1823	17	light	Providence, R.I.	4	9
Billings, Alphonse C.	Apr. 22, 1815	18	light	Providence, R.I.	4	7
Billings, Asa	Feb. 4, 1797	23	dark	Norwich, Conn.	1	7
Billings, Elknah	July 16, 1804	21	light	Canton, Ma.	3	4
Billings, Henry A.	Mar. 1, 1849	21	light	Sharon, Ma.	5	11
Billings, John	May 14, 1800	20	light	Providence, R.I.	2	25
Billings, John R.	May 18, 1809	17	light	Providence, R.I.	4	5

REGISTER OF SEAMEN'S PROTECTION

NAME	DATE OF CERTIFICATION	AGE	COMPLEXION	PLACE OF BIRTH	BOOK	PAGE
Billingslea, William	Sept. 9, 1825	21	dark	Hartford, C'. Md.	4	9
Billington, John	1798-1799	Apr. 7, 1782		So. Kingston, R.I.	* -	--
Billson, Samuel	July 30, 1839	19	light	Taunton, Ma.	5	8
Bimton, Barney	Sept. 19, 1843	33	black	Plainfield, Conn.	5	9
Bingham, John	Sept. 28, 1847	19	dark	New York, N.Y.	5	11
Binns, James	May 20, 1851	21	dark	Richmond, Va.	5	13
Bintom, John	Nov. 13, 1829	22	black	Plainfield, Conn.	5	6
Binton, Patrick	Nov. 1, 1812	23	black	Plainfield, Conn.	4	7
Birch, Thomas	May 30, 1842	20	light	New York, N.Y.	5	9
Bird, James	Apr. 22, 1797	25	light	Providence, R.I.	1	21
Bird, James	Sept. 4, 1813	18	light	Providence, R.I.	4	7
Bird, John	Aug. 27, 1803	33	light	Ann Arundel, Md.	2	44
Bird, Joshua W.	Oct. 27, 1801	22	light	Staten Island, N.Y.	2	33
Bird, Samuel	July 22, 1816	18	light	Providence, R.I.	4	7
Bird, William	Apr. 8, 1818	16	light	Providence, R.I.	4	8
Bishop, Albert E.	May 18, 1867	21	light	Newburyport, Ma.	6	2
Bishop, Comfort, Jr.	Dec. 8, 1809	23	brown	Rehoboth, Ma.	4	6
Bishop, Henry	Mar. 23, 1805	21	dark	Providence, R.I.	3	58
Bishop, Norman	May 14, 1802	21	dark	Attleboro, Ma.	2	33
Bishop, Nathaniel	Aug. 15, 1803	19	dark	Rehoboth, Ma.	2	44
Bishop, Nathaniel	Dec. 25, 1800	17	dark	Rehoboth, Ma.	2	33
Bishop, Lemuel	Dec. 14, 1803	30	light	Attleboro, Ma.	2	49
Bishop, Lemuel	May 23, 1800	28	light	Attleboro, Ma.	2	25
Bishop, Thomas	Dec. 12, 1809	25	brown	Rehoboth, Ma.	4	6
Bishop, William	Dec. 19, 1818	19	light	Johnsbury, Vt.	4	8
Bishop, William	Feb. 19, 1845	25	light	Portland, Me.	5	10
Bissell, Charles	Oct. 20, 1796	17	light	Preston, Conn.	1	7&4
Bissell, John	1798-1799	Nov. 10, 1780		No. Kingston, R.I.	* -	--
Bistow, John H.	Mar. 9, 1809	31	light	suppose R.I.	4	5
On board the British Frigate Amplrion.						
Black, Jacob	Feb. 21, 1844	21	dark	No. Prov., R.I.	5	10
Black, James	Sept. 7, 1815	29	light	Warwick, R.I.	4	7
Blackman, Burrel H.	Oct. 24, 1843	23	dark	Scituate, R.I.	5	9
Blado, Abraham	July 28, 1860	28	mulatto	Stamford, Conn.	6	2
Blagdon, Jos. M.	Sept. 26, 1850	25	dark	Sullivan[Sallwein], Me.	5	12
Blair, Benjamin	July 27, 1799	17	light	E. Greenwich, R.I.	2	2
Blair, David A.	Apr. 24, 1815	27	light	E. Greenwich, R.I.	4	7

*Newport, R. I.

NAME	DATE OF CERTIFICATION	AGE	COMPLEXION	PLACE OF BIRTH	BOOK	PAGE
Blair, James	Oct. 7, 1807	25	light	Rutland, Ma.	4	5
Blair, John	Oct. 10, 1808	24	**light**	**Rutland**, Ma.	4	5
Blake, Franklin	Mar. 2, 1859	23	light	Stockton, Me.	6	2
Blake, John	Feb. 19, 1810	23	black	Phila., Pa.	4	6
Blake, Nicholas	Aug. 3, 1801	22	dark	Portland, Me. [Ma.]	2	33
Blake, William	Apr. 8, 1816	37	black	Providence, R.I.	4	7
Blake, William	Mar. 17, 1848	37	dark	Boston, Ma.	5	41
Blake, William	Dec. 18, 1850	21	light	Dennis, Ma.	5	12
Blanchard, Andrew G.	Mar,. 16, 1852	21	dark	Cumberland, Me.	5	13
Blanchard, Emory	Aug. 3., 1849	29	dark	Petersham, Ma.	5	12
Blanchard, Seth	Nov. 13, 1800	21	light	Charleston, Ma.	2	25
Blanchard, William	July 7, 1840	24	light	Warwick, R.I.	5	8
Blanchard, William	Oct. 29, 1849	35	dark	Warwick, R.I.	5	12
Blanding, Franklin	Mar. 14, 1809	19	light	Rehoboth, Ma.	4	5
Blanding, James	Oct. 23, 1804	23	light	Rehoboth, Ma.	3	49
Blanding, Robert	June 23, 1809	17	light	Rehoboth, Ma.	4	6
Blanding, Thomas J.	Aug. 30, 1849	26	light	Providence, R.I.	5	12
Blankinship, James	Oct. 19, 1810	15	light	Rochester, Ma.	4	6
Blankinship, Joseph	Oct. 17, 1804	18	light	Rochester, Ma.	3	49
Bley, Isaac	Sept. 3, 1811	21	light	Middleborough, Ma.	4	6
Blinn, James M.	Dec. 2, 1803	18	dark	Providence, R.I.	2	49
Bliss, James L., Jr.	June 16, 1864	24	light	Fall River, Ma.	6	2
Blinn, Joseph T.	Aug. 4, 1837	17	light	Providence, R.I.	5	8
Blish, Sylvester	Dec. 19, 1821	17	light	Barnstable, Ma.	4	9
Bliss, Daniel	July 13, 1807	21	yellowish	Warwick, R.I.	4	5
Bliss, Daniel	Sept. 1, 1809	23	yellow	Warwick, R.I.	4	6
Bliss, Isaiah	Mar. 6, 1827	17	dark	Yarmouth, Ma.	4	10
Bliss, James P.	Aug. 14, 1840	17	dark	Providence, R.I.	5	9
Bliss, Jacob, Jr.	Aug. 19, 1815	20	light	Springfield, Ma.	4	7
Bliss, Jermiah C.	Feb. 10, 1849	32	dark	Newport, R.I.	5	11
Bliss, Obadiah	Nov. 29, 1848	17	yellow	Warwick, R.I.	5	11
Bliss, Timothy	Jan. 30, 1849	36	light	Yarmouth, Ma.	5	11
Bliss, Wanton	Dec. 4, 1809	21	yellow	Warwick, R.I.	4	6
Bliss, William	Aug. 27, 1810	24	light	Rehoboth, Ma.	4	6
Bliven, Isaac R.	Dec. 16, 1800	18	light	Providence, R.I.	2	33
Bliven, James	1798-1799		Nov. 20, 1761	Westerly, R.I.	* -	--

Luke Bliven of Newport swears the above to be true. Yr. 1799

| Blodgett, Samuel, C. | Jan. 1, 1800 | 19 | light | Providence, R.I. | 2 | 25 |

*Newport, R.I.

NAME	DATE OF CERTIFICATION	AGE	COMPLEXION	PLACE OF BIRTH	BOOK	PAGE
Blois, Charles	Sept. 25, 1804	23	light	Albany, N.Y.	3	49
Bloss, Job	May 17, 1804	22	dark	Glocester, R.I.	3	3
Bodace, Albert Martin *	Nov. 10, 1852	53	mulatto	Providence, R.I.	5	13
Bogman, Benjamin	Aug. 1, 1801	20	light	Providence, R.I.	2	33
Bogman, Benjamin	Nov. 11, 1803	20	light	Providence, R.I.	3	46
Bogman, Edward	Oct. 31, 1796	15	light	Providence, R.I.	1	7&5
Bogman, Jacob	Nov. 15, 1803	26	light	Providence, R.I.	2	46
Bogman, James	Sept. 26, 1804	19	light	Providence, R.I.	3	49
Bogman, William	Sept. 30, 1806	19	light	Providence, R.I.	3	28
Bois, William S.	Feb. 4, 1834	25	black	Boston, Ma.	5	7
Boles, William	Oct. 30, 1807	19	light	Rochester, Ma.	4	5
Bolitho John	July 23, 1804	42	dark	Boston, Ma.	3	4
Bolls, George	Mar. 5, 1804	20	dark	Providence, R.I.	3	3
Boltwood, Joseph P.	Aug. 28, 1826	17	light	Lempeter, N.H.	4	10
Boman, Alfred	June 9, 1854	33	black	Brookhaven, N.Y.	5	91
Bonel, Thomas	Feb. 20, 1844	26	dark	Baltimore, Md.	5	10
Bonn, Henry	Apr. 4, 1809	19	light	Warwick, R.I.	4	5
Bonn, John Henry	Mar. 8, 1819	25	light	Warwick, R.I.	4	7
Bonsall, Thomas	June 12, 1820	32	light	Mendon, Ma.	4	8
Booker, James	Aug. 24, 1796	18	light	New York, N.Y.	1	1
Boorom, Isaac, Jr.	Nov. 25, 1814	15	light	Providence, R.I.	4	7
Boose, James	Mar. 13, 1818	28	yellow	Providence, R.I.	4	7
Booth, Liman	Aug. 4, 1837	27	mulatto	Williamstown, Ma.	5	8
Booth, Thomas	Aug. 4, 1796	20	dark	E. Greenwich, R.I.	1	1
Bootman, Charles	Nov. 9, 1813	21	black	Chelsea, Ma.	4	7
Boozes, Charles	Dec. 11, 1810	22	yellow	Providence, R.I.	4	6
Booze, Charles	July 14, 1803	15	black	Providence, R.I.	2	44
Borden, George	Oct. 17, 1833	26	black	Fairfield, Conn.	5	7
Borden, George G.	June 11, 1860	16	light	Fall River, Ma.	6	2
Borden, John	May 25, 1815	16	light	Troy, Ma.	4	7
Borden, John	Mar. 5, 1849	20	fair	Dublin, N.H.	5	11
Borden, William	Mar. 5, 1849	22	light	Dublin, N.H.	5	11
Bordot, Alexander	Nov. 23, 1808	22	dark	Island of St. Peters	4	5
Borland, John L.	July 10, 1804	16	light	Swansea, Ma.	3	4
Bosley, John	July 10, 1805	24	dark	Baltimore, R.I.	3	58
Boss, Perry	Apr. 23, 1811	16	dark	So. Kingstown, R.I.	4	6
Boss, William A.	Apr. 12, 1830	17	light	Scituate, R.I.	5	6
*Boden, Samuel	Oct. 29, 1830	22	light	Marblehead, Ma.	5	6

REGISTER OF SEAMEN'S PROTECTION

NAME	DATE OF CERTIFICATION	AGE	COMPLEXION	PLACE OF BIRTH	BOOK	PAGE
Bosworth, Asa H.	Mar. 22, 1855	19	light	Swansea, Ma.	5	91
Bosworth, Edward	Aug. 24, 1815	14	brown	Providence, R.I.	4	7
Bosworth, George H.	Nov. 4, 1829	16	light	Providence, R.I.	5	6
Bosworth, Hezekiah F.	Apr. 2, 1840	45	light	Lenox, Ma.	5	8
Bosworth, Joseph	1798-1799	June 3, 1771		Barrington, R.I.	** -	--
Bosworth, Nehemiah	Nov. 27, 1843	31	light	Plympton, Ma.	5	10
Bosworth, Smith	Oct. 27, 1845	22	fair	Providence, R.I.	5	10
Bourke, Joseph	May 19, 1810	16	yellow	Newport, R.I.	4	6
Bourn, Abraham O.	July 8, 1822	20	light	Rehoboth, Ma.	4	9
Bourn, Allen	July 3, 1807	26	dark	Rochester, Ma.	4	5
Boyrn, David	Oct. 25, 1803	22	dark	Falmouth, Ma.	2	44
Bourr, John	Oct. 3, 1831	39	black	Newport, R.I.	5	6
Bourn, Roswell	Oct. 9, 1826	19	light	Attleborough, Ma.	4	10
Bourn, Wilder	Aug. 20, 1827	26	light	Rehoboth, Ma.	4	10
Boutow, Nathan	Dec. 28, 1844	22	dark	No. Salem, N.Y.	5	10
Bonec[Bovec], Francis	June 13, 1834	23	dark	New Orleans, La.	5	7
Bowdish, John	Aug. 7, 1811	23	brown	Dartmouth, Ma.	4	6
Bowden, Benjamin A.	Apr. 26, 1839	30	dark	Marblehead, Ma.	5	8
*** Boden, Samuel	Oct. 29, 1830	22	light	Marblehead, Ma.	5	6
Bowden, Jason A.	June 12, 1861	19	dark	Cumberland, R.I.	6	2
Bowdoin, Hazard	Mar. 18, 1809	32	dark	Scituate, R.I.	4	5
Bowdon, Albiou	Dec. 19, 1854	28	light	Addison, Me.	5	91
Bowel, John	Nov. 17, 1803	45	black	Africa	2	49
Bowen, Amos	July 8, 1815	16	dark	Rehoboth, Ma.	4	7
Bowen, Augustus G.	Apr. 28, 1846	24	fair	Coventry, R.I.	5	10
Bowen, Benjamin	Aug. 10, 1803	25	light	Providence, R.I.	2	44
Bowen, Benjamin	Nov. 28, 1797	14	light	Providence, R.I.	1	21
Bowen, Benjamin	Feb. 5, 1801	17	light	Providence, R.I.	2	33
Bowen, Benjamin	Apr. 30, 1803	19	light	Providence, R.I.	2	33
Bowen, Benjamim	Apr. 10, 1798	21	light	Providence, R.I.	1&2*	25&2
Bowen, Charles	Dec. 17, 1799	19	light	Johnston, R.I.	2	25
Bowen, Charles	Aug. 9, 1845	21	dark	Providence, R.I.	5	10
Bowen, Charles B.	Mar. 19, 1852	29	light	Providence, R.I.	5	13
Bowen, Daniel	Sept. 23, 1796	28	dark	Rehoboth, Ma.	1	3
Bowen, Elihsa F.	Aug. 19, 1824	22	dark	Coventry, R.I.	4	9
Bowen, Enoch	May 6, 1815	21	light	Rehoboth, Ma.	4	7
Bowen, Ephraim	May 18, 1830	27	light	Rehoboth, Ma.	5	6

*Book 1, page 25, Book 2, page 2.
**Newport, R. I.
*** misfiled

REGISTER OF SEAMEN'S PROTECTION

NAME	DATE OF CERTIFICATION	AGE	COMPLEXION	PLACE OF BIRTH	BOOK	PAGE
Bowen, Ezra	May 27, 1856	19	light	Providence, R.I.	5	91
Bowen, George	Sept. 17, 1806	22	brown	Rehoboth, Ma.	3	28
Bowen, George	Jan. 4, 1823	18	brown	Providence, R.I.	4	9
Bowen, Hail	Nov. 13, 1821	27	light	Warren, R.I.	4	9
Bowen, Henry	June 9, 1804	16	light	Providence, R.I.	3	3
Bowen, Henry	Dec. 21, 1840	28	light	Dighton, Ma.	5	9
Bowen, Isaac	Nov. 18, 1797	15	light	No. Providence, R.I.	1	21
Bowen, Isaac	Feb. 27, 1849	23	light	Providence, R.I.	5	11
Bowen, James	May 30, 1815	22	brown	Seekonk, Ma.	4	7
Bowen, Jeremiah	1798-1799	April 3, 1773		Dighton, Ma.	* -	--
Bowen, Jeremiah	Feb. 24, 1851	25	light	Warren, R.I.	5	13
Bowen, John Greene	Jan. 2, 1821	21	light	Warren, R.I.	-	--

DOB.Feb. 18, 1799. Son of Martin & Nancy Bowen. Birth certificate in Custom House Papers.

NAME	DATE OF CERTIFICATION	AGE	COMPLEXION	PLACE OF BIRTH	BOOK	PAGE
Bowen, Jonathan	Apr. 18, 1855	27	light	Rehoboth, Ma.	5	91
Bowen, Joseph	July 17, 1805	17	light	Providence, R.I.	3	58
Bowen, Joseph	Dec. 30, 1823	28	dark	Seekonk, Ma.	4	9
Bowen, Nathan	Sept. 2, 1801	18	dark	Bristol, R.I.	2	33
Bowen, Nelson W.	Oct. 7, 1833	19	dark	Norton, Ma.	5	7
Bowen, Nelson W.	Aug. 30, 1834	20	dark	Norton, Ma.	5	7
Bowen, Nicholas W.	Mar. 6, 1820	14	light	Seekonk, Ma.	4	8
Bowen, Obadiah	July 29, 1815	24	brown	Dighton, Ma.	4	7
Bowen, Oliver	Sept. 12, 1804	19	light	Coventry, R.I.	3	4
Bowen, Ole. E.	Mar. 17, 1845	47	light	Sweden	5	10
Bowen, Pardon M.	Aug. 29, 1849	23	light	Rehoboth, Ma.	5	12
Bowen, Pomp	Jan. 29, 1798	49	black	Cape Mount, Africa	1	25
Bowen, Pompey	July 27, 1801	55	black	Providence, R.I.	2	33
Bowen, Primus	June 21, 1815	22	black	Providence, R.I.	4	7
Bowen, Richard	Aug. 15, 1797	21	light	Coventry, R.I.	1	21
Bowen, Ruben	1798-1799	Mar. 11, 1777		Warren, R.I.	-	--
Bowen, Ruben	Nov. 28, 1796	16	light	Glocester, R.I.	1	7
Bowen, Samuel	Dec. 19, 1797	15	dark	Providence, R.I.	1	21
Bowen, Samuel	Apr. 7, 1804	22	light	Providence, R.I.	3	3
Bowen, Seril	Sept. 5, 1796	15	light	Glocester, R.I.	1	2
Bowen, Sylvester	Aug. 8, 1806	17	light	Barrington, R.I.	3	78
Bowen, Timothy	Dec. 27, 1797	25	dark	Rehoboth, Ma.	1	21
Bowen, William	May 8, 1822	17	black	Providence, R.I.	4	9
Bowen, William	Nov. 18, 1825	22	light	Warwick, R.I.	4	9

*Newport, R. I.

NAME	DATE OF CERTIFICATION	AGE	COMPLEXION	PLACE OF BIRTH	BOOK	PAGE
Bowen, William	Apr. 27, 1826	23	light	Warwick, R.I.	4	10
Bowen, William	Dec. 16, 1847	13	light	Newport, R.I.	5	11
Bowers, Alfred	Oct. 9, 1810	23	light	Rehoboth, Ma.	4	6
Bowers, David O.M.	Oct. 29, 1849	20	light	Co. of Glenn, Ga.	5	12
Bowers, Edward C.	July 8, 1824	15	dark	Middletown, Conn.	4	9
Bowers, George H.	Sept. 19, 1844	19	light	Fredonia, Ga.	5	10
Bowers, Isaac	Oct. 25, 1805	21	dark	Providence, R.I.	3	72
Bowers, Jerathmel	Dec. 7, 1807	15	light	Somerset, Ma.	4	5
Bowers, John	Nov. 9, 1797	20	dark	Rehoboth, Ma.	1	21
Bowers, John	Dec. 14, 1825	50	mulatto	Dighton, Ma.	4	9
Bowers, John	Nov. 1, 1843	23	light	Providence, R.I.	5	9
Bowers, John C.	May 23, 1823	21	light	Thompson, Conn.	4	9
Bowers, Joseph	Mar. 15, 1797	23	dark	Rehoboth, Ma.	1	7
Bowers, Lemuel	Sept. 17, 1800	21	dark	Rehoboth, Ma.	2	25
Bowers, Nathan I.	Oct. 19, 1843	23	dark	Pawtucket, Ma.	5	9
Bowers, Sam L W.	Nov. 21, 1849	17	light	Providence, R.I.	5	12
Bowers, Silvester	May 8, 1799	22	light	Rehoboth, Ma.	2	2
Bowers, Wanton O.	Jan. 29, 1828	21	dark	Bristol, R.I.	4	10
Bowers, William	July 22, 1816	15	light	Providence, R.I.	4	7
Bowers, William	Sept. 5, 1817	17	light	Providence, R.I.	4	7
Bowers, William A.	Dec. 4, 1820	25	light	Somerset, Ma.	4	8
Bowers, Wm. D.	Apr. 11, 1852	16	light	Providence, R.I.	5	13
Bowers, William Lloyd	Nov. 11, 1840	14	light	Providence, R.I.	5	9
Bowler, Samuel B.	Oct. 21, 1812	14	light	Providence, R.I.	4	7
Bowles, Charles	Mar. 2, 1811	46	yellow	Hanover, Ma.	4	6
Bowman, William	Oct. 29, 1804	23	dark	Pomfret, Conn.	3	49
Bowmer, Eleaser	Oct. 16, 1824	18	light	Troy, Ma.	4	9
Boxall, James	Nov. 9, 1846	24	fair	Providence, R.I.	5	10
Boyce, William	Mar. 11, 1815	20	light	Seekonk, Ma.	4	7
Boyd, Andrew W.	Apr. 7, 1817	19	light	Providence, R.I.	4	7
Boyd, James W.	Nov. 12, 1841	25	Indian	Boston, Ma.	5	9
Boyd, John	Aug. 29, 1845	24	dark	Bristol, Me.	5	10
Boyd, Thomas A.	Mar. 18, 1815	20	dark	E. Greenwich, R.I.	4	7
Boyd, William	July 31, 1854	22	light	Boston, Ma.	5	91
Boyd, William	Apr. 1, 1858	24	dark	Taunton, Ma.	6	2
Boyer, Joseph S.	May 21, 1833	23	light	New York, N.Y.	5	6
Boyle, James H.	Oct. 20, 1845	19	light	New York, N.Y.	5	10

REGISTER OF SEAMEN'S PROTECTION

NAME	DATE OF CERTIFICATION	AGE	COMPLEXION	PLACE OF BIRTH	BOOK	PAGE
Boyle, Thomas	Aug. 21, 1858	21	light	Salem, Ma.	6	2
Boyln, Lawrence	Aug. 1, 1850	20	light	New York, N.Y.	5	12
Bracket, Levi	Oct. 2, 1844	18	light	Lyndon, VT,	5	10
Bradfield, Echo	Dec. 7, 1811	21	yellow	No. Kingstown, R.I.	4	6
Bradford, Alonzo	May 24, 1856	25	fair	Warwick, R.I.	5	91
Bradford, Benjamin S.	June 12, 1844	18	dark	So. Kingston, R.I.	5	10
Bradford, George S.	Sept. 8, 1856	18	fair	Bangor, Me.	5	91
Bradford, Henry	Feb. 7, 1798	16	light	Providence, R.I.	1	25
Bradford, Henry	June 16, 1852	24	mulatto	Providence, R.I.	5	13
Bradford, James	Apr. 22, 1807	17	light	Colrain, Ma.	4	5
Bradford, James	May 9, 1808	18	light	Colrain, Ma.	4	5
Bradford, Joel	May 7, 1806	27	light	Rehoboth, Ma.	3	74
Bradford, John	Dec. 22, 1797	17	dark	Stonington, Conn.	1	21
Bradford, Jonathan	Sept. 8, 1803	16	light	Guilford, Vt.	2	44
Bradford, Lemuel	1798-1799	May 26, 1780		Bristol, R.I.	* -	--
Bradford, Southard	Sept. 20, 1837	31	dark	Plymouth, Ma.	5	8
Bradford, William	Apr. 10, 1848	30	light	Providence, R.I.	5	11
Bradley, George	Mar. 1, 1867	24	dark	Providence, R.I.	6	2
Bradley, Henry	Dec. 22, 1823	21	light	New Haven, Conn.	4	9
Bradley, John	Aug. 5, 1837	27	freckled	New York, N.Y.	5	8
Bradley, John	Dec. 30, 1850	32	light	Salem, Ma.	5	12
Bradley, Schuyler	Mar. 20, 1806	19	light	New Haven, Conn.	3	74
Bradley, William	Oct. 3, 1807	33	brown	Somerset, Ma.	4	5
Brady, James	Oct. 14, 1844	24	light	New York, N.Y.	5	10
Bradshaw, James	Oct. 16, 1841	20	light	Providence, R.I.	5	9
Brady, John	Dec. 8, 1852	42	light	Cambridge, Ma.	5	13
Braley, Martin	Nov. 23, 1841	19	dark	Rochester, Ma.	5	9
Bramon, William R.	May 1, 1839	28	light	So. Kingstown, R.I.	5	8
Bran, Amos	May 22, 1827	20	brown	Coventry, R.I.	4	10
Branan, Edward	Mar. 3, 1848	32	light	New York, N.Y.	5	11
Branch, Daniel	June 6, 1843	19	light	Pawtucket, Ma.	5	9
Branch, Daniel	Dec. 4, 1850	25	light	Attleboro, Ma.	5	12
Branch, James	Aug. 24, 1846	18	fair	Providence, R.I.	5	10
Branch, Joseph	June 6, 1843	21	light	Pawtucket, Ma.	5	9
Branch, Levi	Apr. 29, 1806	18	light	Lisbon, Conn.	3	74
Brand, Samuel B.	July 25, 1836	21	light	Westerly, R.I.	5	7
Branfield, Charles	Oct. 2, 1804	26	black	Phila., PA.	3	49

*Newport, R. I.

NAME	DATE OF CERTIFICATION	AGE	COMPLEXION	PLACE OF BIRTH	BOOK	PAGE
Brant, Hosiah	Dec. 5, 1855	23	light	W. Greenwich, R.I.	5	91
Brant, John	Dec. 10, 1804	17	light	New York, N.Y.	3	50
Brassbridge, Otis	July 19, 1841	21	light	Strafford, N.H.	5	9
Brastow, Frank	Dec. 24, 1852	19	light	Providence, R.I.	5	13
Brastow, Henry B.	Mar. 18, 1844	15	light	Providence, R.I.	5	10
Bray, Crowell	Jan. 19, 1818	21	light	Yarmouth, Ma.	4	7
Bray, Edmund	Dec. 15, 1819	25	light	Yarmouth, Ma.	4	8
Bray, John G.	Mar. 20, 1845	27	black	Providence, R.I.	5	10
Brayton, David	Jan. 7, 1804	45	light	Rehoboth, Ma.	3	3
Brayton, Stephen	July 11, 1806	18	black	Smithfield, R.I.	3	78
Brayton, Thomas	1798-1799	Dec. 30, 1796		Tiverton, R.I.	* -	--
Brayton, William	Feb. 25, 1823	21	yellow	Rehoboth, Ma.	4	9
Brazier, William	June 5, 1832	22	sandy	Phila., Pa.	5	6
Breese, John Walbone	1798-1799	Dec. 12, 1778		Newport, R.I.	* -	--
Frances Walbone swears the above to be true.						
Breese?, Lewis	Dec. 27, 1854	22	light	New York, N.Y.	5	91
Brennan, Mark	July 15, 1854	17	light	Cumberland, R.I.	5	91
Brent, George	Sept. 2, 1864	20	black	New London, Conn.	6	2
Brenton, George T.	Apr. 1, 1825	23	black	Providence, R.I.	4	9
Brewster, Benjamin	Apr. 22, 1809	29	brown	Scituate, Ma.	4	5
Brickley, Anson P.	Mar. 31, 1825	18	light	Providence, R.I.	4	9
Bridges, George	Mar. 25, 1835	21	light	New York, N.Y.	5	7
Brien, John	Sept. 7, 1853	21	dark	Providence, R.I.	5	13
Briggs, Albert C.	Oct. 18, 1861	30	dark	Foster, R.I.	6	2
Briggs, Alpheus	Oct. 12, 1818	16	light	Rochester, Ma.	4	8
Briggs, Andrew	Apr. 24, 1857	28	dark	Berkley, Ma.	5	92
Briggs, Benjamin Gorton	Apr. 21, 1801	20	dark	Warwick, R.I.	2	33
Briggs, Benjamin G.	Sept. 6, 1803	23	dark	Warwick, R.I.	2	44
Briggs, Byron	June 12, 1855	22	light	E. Greenwich, R.I.	5	91
Briggs, Byron	Aug. 15, 1870	37	light	E. Greenwich, R.I.	6	2
Briggs, Charles	May 30, 1835	22	light	No. Providence, R.I.	5	7
Briggs, Charles	Dec. 19, 1859	23	dark	Franklin, Conn.	6	2
Briggs, Charles A.	Nov. 20, 1839	28	light	Nantucket, Ma.	5	8
Briggs, Daniel	Jan. 5, 1833	15	dark	Smithfield, R.I.	5	6
Briggs, Daniel	Apr. 22, 1839	17	light	Cranston, R.I.	5	8
Briggs, Daniel E.	Sept. 8, 1855	36	dark	Coventry, R.I.	5	91
Briggs, David	June 26, 1798	23	dark	Warwick, R.I.	2	2

*Newport, R. I.

NAME	DATE OF CERTIFICATION	AGE	COMPLEXION	PLACE OF BIRTH	BOOK	PAGE
Briggs, David	Feb. 1, 1812	38	dark	Warwick, R.I.	4	6
Briggs, David	June 1, 1825	23	light	Dartmouth, Ma.	4	9
Briggs, David L.	July 12, 1856	23	fair	------- Mass.	5	91
Briggs, Edward J.	Oct. 20, 1845	26	light	Brooklyn, N.Y.	5	10
Briggs, Elijah	May 26, 1815	23	light	Providence, R.I.	4	7
Briggs, Erastus B.	Oct. 8, 1849	29	light	Sterling, Conn.	5	12
Briggs, George	Oct. 24, 1820	52	light	Freetown, Ma.	4	8
Briggs, George W.	Oct. 22, 1849	21	light	Coventry, R.I.	5	12
Briggs, Henry	Aug. 27, 1859	27	light	New Bedford, Ma.	6	2
Briggs, Henry A.	Mar. 18, 1844	26	light	Phila., Pa.	5	10
Briggs, Israel	Nov. 2, 1810	24	brown	Wareham, Ma.	4	6
Briggs, Israel P.	Dec. 10, 1819	17	light	NO. Prov., R.I.	4	8
Briggs, Jabes D.	Dec. 13, 1825	27	dark	Rochester, Ma.	4	9
Briggs, James	Aug. 19, 1845	24	dark	Warwick, R.I.	-	--
Briggs, Job	Sept. 25, 1804	17	dark	Warwick, R.I.	3	4
Briggs, John	Nov. 30, 1799	23	light	Coventry, R.I.	2	25
Briggs, John	Dec. 21, 1810	21	light	Attleboro, Ma.	4	6
Briggs, John H.	Oct. 19, 1849	24	light	Coventry, R.I.	5	12
Briggs, Jonathan T.	Oct. 24, 1849	25	light	Coventry, R.I.	5	12
Briggs, Joseph	Aug. 12, 1846	46	dark	Harwich, Ma.	5	10
Briggs, Miller	Oct. 17, 1803	22	light	Warwick, R.I.	2	44
Briggs, Miller	Jan. 2, 1804	23	dark	Warwick, R.I.	3	3
Briggs, Nathan	June 12, 1815	20	light	W. Greenwich, R.I.	4	7
Briggs, Paul	Nov. 4, 1818	20	light	Wareham, Ma.	4	8
Briggs, Peirce	Nov. 8, 1797	17	light	Warwick, R.I.	1	21
Briggs, Peleg	Dec. 13, 1817	16	ruddy	Boston, Ma.	4	7
Briggs, Ray S.	Mar. 20, 1835	22	light	South Kingstown, R.I.	5	7
Briggs, Samuel	May 18, 1805	16	dark	Warwick, R.I.	3	58
Briggs, Stukely B.	Nov. 8, 1843	26	light	No. Kingstown, R.I.	5	10
Briggs, Sylvester	Dec. 24, 1852	34	dark	Dighton, Ma.	5	13
Briggs, Tisdale, Jr.	Apr. 17, 1838	19	dark	Dighton, Ma.	5	8
Briggs, Washington	Oct. 18, 1844	18	dark	Berkley, Ma.	5	10
Briggs, Willard	June 26, 1847	18	dark	Warwick, R.I.	5	11
Briggs, William A.	June 15, 1842	18	light	Coventry, R.I.	5	9
Brightman, Peter	Jan. 2, 1835	21	black	Tiverton, R.I.	5	7
Brightman, Thomas G.	May 1, 1799	25	dark	Portsmouth, R.I.	2	2
Brindley, Cato	Jan. 16, 1804	27	black	Newport, R.I.	3	3

NAME	DATE OF CERTIFICATION	AGE	COMPLEXION	PLACE OF BIRTH	BOOK	PAGE
Brinckly, George	Dec. 10, 1838	37	black	Phila., Pa.	5	8
Brintley, George	Mar. 15, 1828	26	black	Warwick, R.I.	4	10
Brintom, Ed	Feb. 7, 1818	30	black	Plainfield, Conn.	4	7
Bristol, Ebenezer	Oct. 23, 1838	20	black	Providence, R.I.	5	8
Bristol, Ira	Mar. 28, 1836	23	black	Trenton, N.J.	5	7
Britney, William	May 15, 1867	26	Medium	Eastport, Me.	6	2
Britten, William *	1798-1799			Settled in Newport, R.I. on or Before Sept. 3, 1783		
Broad, James	Aug. 5, 1837	23	light	New York, N.Y.	5	8
Brockenbury, Wm.	Aug. 21, 1845	45	black	Portsmouth, N.H.	5	10
Broderick, Thomas	Nov. 1, 1799	36	dark	Cork, Ireland	2	2
Brotley [brumbley], John	Nov. 2, 1804	23	light	Stonington, Conn.	3	50
Brookfield, George	Jan. 1, 1805	20	light	Boston, Ma.	3	50
Brooks, Alanzo	Sept. 7, 1810	27	light	Concord, Ma.	4	6
Brooks, Charles	Mar. 7, 1849	20	light	Providence, R.I.	5	11
Brooks, Charles	Feb. 16, 1857	31	light	Burlington, N.J.	5	91
Brooks, James	Mar. 28, 1837	27	black	Boston, Ma.	5	8
Brooks, James F.	Feb. 14, 1837	24	light	Phila., Pa.	5	8
Brooks, Thomas	Aug. 3, 1805	19	dark	Newcastle, Del.	3	58
Brophey, Daniel	Oct. 14, 1844	16	light	Portland, Me.	5	10
Brotherson, William	Mar. 8, 1831	20	light	New Bedford, Ma.	5	6
Brown, Allen	Apr. 4, 1799	18	dark	Barrington, R.I.	2	2
Brown, Alonso	Mar. 28, 1833	24	dark	Worcester, Ma.	5	6
Brown, Anson P.	Feb. 2, 1854	18	light	Providence, R.I.	5	13
Brown, Arthur F.	Feb. 25, 1831	31	light	Providence, R.I.	5	6
Brown, Arthur Fenner	Sept. 25, 1817	17	light	Providence, R.I.	4	7
Brown, Arnold	Aug. 5, 1803	23	light	Cumberland, R.I.	2	44
Brown, Arnold	Dec. 27, 1806	27	light	Cumberland, R.I.	4	5
Brown, Arnold	Mar. 22, 1800	21	light	Cumberland, R.I.	2	25
Brown, Asa	Dec. 20, 1810	18	light	Woodstock, Conn.	4	6
Brown, Benjamin	Aug. 23, 1800	23	light	Milford, Ma.	2	25
Brown, Benjamin	Oct. 7, 1820	18	light	Providence, R.I.	4	8
Brown, Benjamin	Nov. 4, 1843	16	mulatto	Providence, R.I.	5	10
Brown, Benjamin D.	Aug. 17, 1858	21	light	Providence, R.I.	6	2
Brown, Benowy	June 25, 1818	18	light	No. Prov., R.I.	4	8
Brown, Billy	Sept. 10, 1796	18	light	Attleboro, Ma.	1	2
Brown, Billy	Apr. 5, 1797	18	light	Attleboro, Ma.	1	7
Brown, Boston	----------	28	black	Africa	1	21
Brown, Charles	Mar. 23, 1827	19	mulatto	Providence, R.I.	4	10

REGISTER OF SEAMEN'S PROTECTION

NAME	DATE OF CERTIFICATION	AGE	COMPLEXION	PLACE OF BIRTH	BOOK	PAGE
Brown, Charles	Dec. 10, 1840	21	yellow	Providence, R.I.	5	9
Brown, Charles	June 3, 1858	22	light	New York, N.Y.	6	2
Brown, Charles D.	Mar. 26, 1841	26	dark	New York, N.Y.	5	9
Brown, Charles E.	Apr. 27, 1841	29	light	Harlem, N.Y.	5	9
Brown, Charles U.	July 12, 1848	24	black	Baltimore, Md.	5	11
Brown, Christopher	June 17, 1835	31	dark	Smithfield, R.I.	5	7
Brown, Clark	Mar. 3, 1820	25	black	Barrington, R.I.	4	8
Brown, Clarke	July 6, 1818	23	light	East Greenwich, R.I.	4	8
Brown, Colrill D.	Oct. 7, 1833	19	light	Johnston, R.I.	5	7
Brown, Cupid	June 21, 1815	20	black	So. Kingstown, R.I.	4	7
Brown, Daniel	Oct. 20, 1801	33	dark	Marblehead, Ma.	2	33
Brown, Daniel	Feb. 28, 1804	22	dark	Warwick, R.I.	3	3
Brown, David	Nov. 6, 1828	30	ruddy	Smithfield, R.I.	4	10
Brown, David O.	Oct. 21, 1844	17	black	Providence, R.I.	5	10
Brown, Davis	Mar. 22, 1815	21	light	Providence, R.I.	4	7
Brown, Dexter	Nov. 16, 1804	19	light	Rehoboth, Ma.	3	50
Brown, Dexter	Oct. 4, 1806	21	dark	Rehoboth, Ma.	3&4*	28&5*
Brown, Edward	Mar. 22, 1797	13	light	Providence, R.I.	1	7
Brown, Edward	Nov. 5, 1833	31	black	Troy, Ma.	5	7
Brown, Edward, Jr.	1798-1799	Apr. 8, 1769		Newport, R.I.	**_	--
Brown, Edward G.	Oct. 23, 1819	24	light	Newport, R.I.	4	8
Brown, Edwin T.	June 20, 1839	19	black	So. Kingstown, R.I.	5	8
Brown, Edwin T.	Nov. 28, 1849	31	black	So. Kingstown, R.I.	5	12
Brown, Elisha, Jr.	May 9, 1799	15	dark	Providence, R.I.	2	2
Brown, Elisha	Aug. 31, 1849	26	dark	Warwick, R.I.	5	12
Brown, Ezekiel B.	Apr. 6, 1841	19	light	Cumberland, R.I.	5	9
Brown, Fenner	July 20, 1805	13	light	Cumberland, R.I.	3	58
Brown, Gardner	Oct. 11, 1824	19	dark	Swansea, Ma.	4	9
Brown, George	Feb. 7, 1798	16	light	E. Greenwich, R.I.	1	25
Brown, George	1798-1799	Nov. 10, 1779		Westerly, R.I.	**-	--
Brown, George	Sept. 18, 1805	27	dark	Baltimore, Md.	3	72
Brown, George	Mar. 12, 1833	15	black	Providence, R.I.	5	6
Brown, George	Nov. 9, 1848	24	light	Salem, Ma.	5	11
Brown, George W.	Feb. 3, 1853	22	light	Brookhaven, N.Y.	5	13

*Book 3, page 28. Book 4, page 5.

** Newport, R. I.

NAME	DATE OF CERTIFICATION	AGE	COMPLEXION	PLACE OF BIRTH	BOOK	PAGE
Brown, Henry	July 19, 1804	17	black	New York, N.Y.	3	4
Brown, Henry	Dec. 5, 1804	17	black	New York, N.Y.	3	50
Brown, Henry	Aug. 7, 1806	18	light	E. Greenwich, R.I.	3	78
Brown, Henry	May 1, 1809	23	black	Stonington, Conn.	4	5
Brown, Henry	Mar. 19, 1819	19	black	Barrington, R.I.	4	8
Brown, Henry	Nov. 24, 1828	19	ruddy	Providence, R.I.	4	10
Brown, Henry B.	Mar. 13, 1816	16	light	Smithfield, R.I.	4	7
Brown, Henry F.	Nov. 21, 1828	23	black	So. Kingstown, R.I.	4	10
Brown, Henry O.	May 10, 1840	16	black	Sterling, Conn.	5	8
Brown, Hezekiah	May 16, 1805	24	light	Scituate, R.I.	3	58
Brown, Hiram	Nov. 18, 1841	32	light	Turner, Me.	5	9
Brown, Ira	May 14, 1811	19	black	Dudley, Ma.	4	6
Brown, Ira	July 21, 1818	25	black	Providence, R.I.	4	8
Brown, Isaac	July 27, 1819	22	light	Providence, R.I.	-	--
Brown, Isaac T.	May 17, 1833	19	dark	Providence, R.I.	5	6
Brown, Isaiah S.	June 27, 1826	27	light	Rehoboth, Ma.	4	10
Brown, James	Dec. 28, 1797	13	black	Providence, R.I.	1	25
Brown, James	Apr. 14, 1798	31	dark	Providence, R.I.	1&2*	25&2*
Brown, James	Dec. 14, 1798	16	black	Providence, R.I.	2	2
Brown, James	Dec. 13, 1800	20	black	Providence, R.I.	2	25
Brown, James	Feb. 10, 1804	21	black	Providence, R.I.	3	3
Brown, James	Dec. 31, 1806	23	dark	Ashford, Conn.	4	5
Brown, James	May 13, 1809	30	black	Providence, R.I.	4	5
Brown, James	Oct. 6, 1810	27	black	Providence, R.I.	4	6
Brown, James	Nov. 20, 1810	23	dark	Providence, R.I.	4	6
Brown, James	Aug. 2, 1817	21	light	No. Prov., R.I.	4	7
Brown, James	Dec. 28, 1820	22	black	Warwick, R.I.	4	8
Brown, James	Sept. 6, 1832	17	light	Hartford, Conn.	5	6
Brown, James	May 14, 1834	14	light	Providence, R.I.	5	7
Brown, James Mar	Mar. 22, 1851	34	dark	Oxford, Ma.	5	13
Brown, James A.	June 11, 1849	31	light	Smithfield, R.I.	5	11
Brown, James E.	Oct. 15, 1835	23	light	No. Kingstown, R.I.	5	7
Brown, James H.	Nov. 3, 1820	16	dark	Providence, R.I.	4	8
Brown, James Noice	Mar. 23, 1798	19	light	Providence, R.I.	1	25

*Book 1, page 25. Book 2, page 2.

REGISTER OF SEAMEN'S PROTECTION

NAME	DATE OF CERTIFICATION	AGE	COMPLEXION	PLACE OF BIRTH	BOOK	PAGE
Brown, James T.	Nov. 30, 1803	21	black	Providence, R.I.	2	49
Brown, James W.	Aug. 30, 1825	22	light	Rehoboth, Ma.	4	9
Brown, James W.	June 9, 1842	17	dark	------, Va.	5	9
Brown, Jeremiah	Nov. 25, 1796	18	light	No. Prov., R.I.	1	7
Brown, Jeremiah	Jan. 7, 1807	18	light	Providence, R.I.	4	5
Brown, Jeremiah	May 22, 1809	23	black	So. Kingston, R.I.	4	6
Brown, Job	Mar. 4, 1812	23	florid	Warwick, R.I.	4	6
Brown, John	Sept. 29, 1796	18	dark	Rehoboth, Ma.	1	3
Brown, John	Mar. 24, 1797	21	light	Warwick, R.I.	1	7
Brown, John	Aug. 24, 1799	17	light	Warren, R.I.	2	2
Brown, John	Nov. 30, 1803	20	dark	Rehoboth, Ma.	2	49
Brown, John	July 25, 1804	18	light	Attleboro, Ma.	3	4
Brown, John	Jan. 12, 1804	20	light	Providence, R.I.	3	3
Brown, John	Sept. 24, 1805	18	light	Attleboro, Ma.	3	72
Brown, John	Oct. 26, 1805	20	black	Baltimore, Md.	3	72
Brown, John	Nov. 20, 1805	35	dark	Somerset, Ma.	3	72A
Brown, John	Apr. 22, 1807	33	light	Newport, R.I.	4	5
Brown, John	Oct. 20, 1809	22	black	New York, N.Y.	4	6
Brown, John	Aug. 29, 1815	28	light	Boston, Ma.	4	7
Brown, John	Aug. 2, 1825	32	light	Smithfield, Ma.	4	9
Brown, John	Sept. 21, 1837	43	yellow	New Castle, Del.	5	8
Brown, John	Sept. 29, 1837	23	dark	New Orleans, La.	5	8
Brown, John	Apr. 4, 1839	34	dark	Salem, Ma.	5	8
Brown, John	Feb. 20, 1844	24	light	No. Prov., R.I.	5	10
Brown, John	Nov. 19, 1845	23	dark	Phila., Pa.	5	10
Brown, John	July 27, 1848	22	dark	Stonington, Conn.	5	11
Brown, John	Aug. 5, 1850	17	light	New York, N.Y.	5	12
Brown, John	July 10, 1852	34	light	New York, N.Y.	5	13
Brown, John	Nov. 5, 1852	22	mulatto	Providence, R.I.	5	13
Brown, John	Nov. 16, 1853	22	light	Eastport, Me.	5	13
Brown, John	Nov. 5, 1855	28	mulatto	Colchester, Conn.	5	91
Brown, John	June 16, 1856	27	fair	Calais, Me.	5	91
Brown, John, Jr.	Sept. 4, 1813	18	light	Somerset, Ma.	4	7
Brown, John B.	July 17, 1839	28	black	Providence, R.I.	5	8
Brown, John C.	Mar. 30, 1861	21	light	Buffalo, N.Y.	6	2
Brown, John F.	Mar. 3, 1849	23	light	Seekonk, Ma.	5	11
Brown, John H.	Mar. 23, 1808	18	dark	Providence, R.I.	4	5
Brown, John	Nov. 5, 1805	22	light	Providence, R.I.	3	72

REGISTER OF SEAMEN'S PROTECTION

Page 40

NAME	DATE OF CERTIFICATION	AGE	COMPLEXION	PLACE OF BIRTH	BOOK	PAGE
Brown, John P.	Dec. 5, 1820	16	light	Providence, R.I.	4	8
Brown, John Thomas	Feb. 12, 1799	20	light	Cambridge, Ma.	2	2
Brown, Jonathan	Oct. 18, 1797	24	light	Rehoboth, Ma.	1	21
Brown, Jonathan, 2nd	Feb. 3, 1812	19	dark	Dartmouth, Ma.	4	6
Brown, Joseph	May 23, 1797	28	black	Chester, Pa.	1	21
Brown, Joseph	1798-1799	July 9, 1770		Westport, Ma.	* -	--
Brown, Joseph	Sept. 16, 1803	25	black	Stonington, Conn.	2	44
Brown, Joseph	Aug. 22, 1804	22	black	Westerly, R.I.	3	4
Brown, Joseph	Jan. 31, 1828	18	black	Cranston, R.I.	4	10
Brown, Joseph	June 1, 1835	41	dark	Boston, Ma.	5	7
Brown, Joseph	Sept. 28, 1838	21	light	New York, N.Y.	5	8
Brown, Joseph	Feb. 3, 1853	21	light	Brookhaven, N.Y.	5	13
Brown, Joseph, Jr.	Oct. 26, 1839	35	dark	Islip, N.Y.	5	8
Brown, Joseph R.	Nov. 2, 1819	19	-----	Providence, R.I.	4	8
Brown, Joseph R.	June 27, 1844	42	light	Salem, Ma.	5	10
Brown, Joseph R.C.	Nov. 27, 1849	20	light	No. Kingston, R.I.	5	12
Brown, Josiah	July 16, 1821	19	black	Cranston, R.I.	4	9
Brown, Kingsley	Jan. 4, 1826	17	light	No. Kingstown, R.I.	4	10
Brown, Levi B.	June 16, 1858	25	fair	Providence, R.I.	6	2
Brown, Martin, Jr.	Feb. 8, 1832	32	light	Barrington, R.I.	5	6
Brown, Nathan, Jr.	Feb. 9, 1797	16	dark	No. Kingstown, R.I.	1	7
Brown, Nathan Wood	Dec. 29, 1823	16	light	Swansea, Ma.	4	9
Brown, Nathaniel	Nov. 11, 1820	27	light	Newport, R.I.	4	8
Brown, Nicholas	June 3, 1797	35	black	Portland, Me.	1	21
Brown, Nicholas	Oct. 23, 1810	17	dark	Rehoboth, Ma.	4	6
Brown, Nicholas	Mar. 13, 1818	51	yellow	Portland, Ma.	4	7
Brown, Noah	May 18, 1798	16	black	Providence, R.I.	2	2
Brown, Noah	June 7, 1806	24	black	Providence, R.I.	3	78
Brown, Obadiah	Apr. 4, 1797	18	light	Providence, R.I.	1	7
Brown, Obadiah S.	Apr. 11, 1806	11	light	Providence, R.I.	3	74
Brown, Obadiah S.	July 28, 1819	24	light	Providence, R.I.	4	8
Brown, Oliver	Aug. 17, 1797	28	dark	Rehoboth, Ma.	1	21
Brown, Oliver	July 12, 1839	26	light	Hempstead, N.Y.	5	8
Brown, Oliver M.	Nov. 20, 1841	18	light	Aleborough, Me.	5	9
Brown, Parson	Aug. 6, 1846	29	black	Norfolk, Va.	5	10
Brown, Peleg R.	Aug. 14, 1834	19	light	Warren, R.I.	5	7
Brown, Peter	May 13, 1799	17	light	Providence, R.I.	2	2

*Newport, R. I.

REGISTER OF SEAMEN'S PROTECTION

NAME	DATE OF CERTIFICATION	AGE	COMPLEXION	PLACE OF BIRTH	BOOK	PAGE
Brown, Peter M.	June 2, 1806	20	light	Providence, R.I.	3	78
Brown, Philip	Nov. 3, 1853	30	light	New Bedford, Ma.	5	13
Brown, Philip	Jan. 23, 1854	30	light	New Bedford, Ma.	5	13
Brown, Prince	Sept. 15, 1803	45	black	Newburyport, Ma.	2	44
Brown, Prince	Aug. 21, 1832	48	black	No. Kingstown, R.I.	5	6
Brown, Reuben	Aug. 15, 1810	17	black	Barrington, R.I.	4	6
Brown, Richard	Apr. 28, 1797	20	light	Providence, R.I.	1	21
Brown, Russell	Nov. 9, 1796	24	light	Barrington, R.I.	1	7&5
Brown, Russell	July 21, 1841	19	light	Warren, R.I.	5	9
Brown, Sabin	June 11, 1849	38	light	Smithfield, R.I.	5	11
Brown, Samuel	Dec. 27, 1797	30	light	Newport, R.I.	1	25
Brown, Samuel	June 23, 1821	32	brown	Falmouth, Ma.	4	9
Brown, Samuel	Oct. 27, 1845	38	mulatto	Boston, Ma.	5	10
Brown, Samuel	Jan. 1, 1855	47	mulatto	Boston, Ma.	5	91
Borwn, Samuel, Jr.	Jan. 2, 1805	22	dark	Westerly, R.I.	3	50
Brown, Samuel A.	Sept. 28, 1844	17	light	Smithfield, R.I.	5	10
Brown, Samuel G.	Oct. 18, 1833	23	black	Boston, Ma.	5	7
Brown, Seth	Jan. 24, 1810	27	dark	Cambridge, Ma.	4	6
Brown, Simon	1798-1799	Sept. 22, 1778		Dighton, Ma.	** -	--
Brown, Sisson	Aug. 28, 1804	17	light	E. Greenwich, R.I.	3	4
Brown, Sylvester	Apr. 7, 1804	16	light	Providence, R.I.	3	3
Brown, Thomas	Sept. 29, 1804	19	yellow*	No. Kingstown, R.I.	3	49
Brown, Thomas	Oct. 15, 1832	24	light	New York, N.Y.	5	6
Brown, Thomas	July 7, 1835	32	dark	New Orleans, La.	5	7
Brown, Thomas	Sept. 1, 1842	23	light	Nantucket, Ma.	5	9
Brown, Thomas H.	May 17, 1867	38	fair	Worcester, Ma.	6	2
Brown, Timothy	Oct. 23, 1837	21	black	Sterling, Conn.	5	8
Brown, Whipple	Mar. 27, 1810	19	dark	Attleboro, Ma.	4	6
Brown, William	Oct. 29, 1803	19	light	Bristol, R.I.	2	44
Brown, William	Mar. 5, 1805	20	black	New York, N.Y.	3	50
Brown, William	Aug. 12, 1806	22	light	New York, N.Y.	3	78
Brown, William	Sept. 8, 1815	18	brown	Providence, R.I.	4	7
Brown, William	June 7, 1825	18	light	Norwalk, Conn.	4	9
Brown, William	Sept. 8, 1836	26	dark	Providence, R.I.	5	7
Brown, William	Dec. 23, 1837	22	light	New York, N.Y.	5	8
Brown, William	Dec. 1, 1838	29	light	Dover, N.H.	5	8

*mulatto
**Newport, R. I.

REGISTER OF SEAMEN'S PROTECTION

NAME	DATE OF CERTIFICATION	AGE	COMPLEXION	PLACE OF BIRTH	BOOK	PAGE
Brown, William	Feb. 23, 1852	22	light	New York, N.Y.	5	13
Brown, Wm. A.	Jan. 30, 1849	22	light	Providence, R.I.	5	11
Brown, Wm. E.	June 27, 1854	28	light	Pawtucket, R.I.	5	91
Brown, William H.	Aug. 28, 1806	21	light	Somerset, Ma.	3	28
Brown, William H.	Aug. 29, 1806	23	light	No. Kingstown, R.I.	3	28
Brown, Wm. Henry	Mar. 14, 1843	19	light	Providence, R.I.	5	9
Brown, Wm. S.	1798-1799	Mar. 5, 1784		New York, N.Y.	* -	--
Brown, William T.	June 25, 1861	16	light	Norwich, Conn.	6	2
Brown, William W.	June 16, 1858	28	dark	Providence, R.I.	6	2
Brownell, Artemas	June 15, 1801	23	light	Little Compton, R.I.	2	33
Brownell, George	1798-1799	Oct. 12, 1778		Portsmouth, R.I.	* -	--
Brownell, James	Nov. 13, 1849	24	light	Newport, R.I.	5	12
Brownell, Joseph	June 25, 1836	18	dark	Little Compton, R.I.	5	7
Brownell, Loring Richmond	Sept. 30, 1796	26	light	Little Compton, R.I.	2	4
Brownell, Putnam	Aug. 15, 1798	22	light	Little Compton, R.I.	2	2
Brownell, Stephen J.	Apr. 25, 1844	38	light	Rutland, Ma.	5	10
Brownell, Sylvester	July 3, 1824	39	light	Westport, Ma.	4	9
Brownell, Thomas	Mar. 26, 1800	22	light	Newport, R.I.	2	25
Brownell, Uriah	Mar. 24, 1831	18	dark	Westport, Ma.	5	6
Browning, Borden	1798-1799	Aug. 5, 1774		Portsmouth, R.I.	* -	--
Browning, Dennis	1798-1799	Aug. 14, 1775		Little Compton, R.I.	* -	--
Browning, Ezekiel H.	Sept. 25, 1849	24	light	So. Kingston, R.I.	5	12
Browning, George W.	Sept. 25, 1849	20	light	So. Kingston, R.I.	5	12
Browning, James	Mar. 5, 1858	49	black	So. Kingston, R.I.	6	2
Browning, John G.	July 13, 1824	22	light	No. Kingstown, R.I.	4	9
Browning, Stephen P.	May 23, 1821	18	light	Rutland, Ma.	4	9
Brownson, Willis	Oct. 23, 1820	20	light	Hartford, Conn.	4	8
Bruce, Edward	Nov. 24, 1806	13	light	Providence, R.I.	4	5
Bruce, Jeremiah	May 30, 1820	23	brown	Providence, R.I.	4	8
Brunson, Hillyer	Mar. 30, 1836	19	ruddy	Hartford, Conn.	5	7
Brushell, David	June 3, 1811	20	yellow	Plainfield, Conn.	4	6
Bryan, Alexander	Sept. 10, 1857	67	yellow C.	Prince William, Va.	6	2
Bryan, Walker	Feb. 2, 1854	24	mulatto	Providence, R.I.	5	13
Bryant, Augustus	Dec. 15, 1854	17	light	Boston, Ma.	5	91
Bryant, Joseph	Aug. 2, 1854	20	fair	Providence, R.I.	5	91
Bryant, Wm. I.	Sept. 3, 1842	16	light	No. Prov., R.I.	5	9
Bryant, John	Nov. 29, 1848	27	dark	Medbury, N.H.	5	11

*Newport, R.I.

REGISTER OF SEAMEN'S PROTECTION

NAME	DATE OF CERTIFICATION	AGE	COMPLEXION	PLACE OF BIRTH	BOOK	PAGE
Bryer, William	Dec. 15, 1830	25	dark	Newport, R.I.	5	6
Buck, Bowman H.	Mar. 19, 1846	19	fair	Princeton, N.J.	5	10
Buck, Joshua	Sept. 2, 1801	21	dark	Hampshire, Ma.	2	33
Buck, Richard	Mar. 25, 1809	20	light	Killingly, Conn.	4	5
Buckley, William	May 26, 1851	21	light	Hillsdale, N.Y.	5	13
Buckley, William C.	July 23, 1833	20	light	Rochester, N.Y.	5	7
Bucklin, Asa	Mar. 13, 1797	21	light	Rohoboth, Ma.	1	7
Bucklin, Asa	Apr. 7, 1815	37	light	Seekonk, Ma.	4	7
Bucklin, Daniel	Oct. 29, 1849	25	dark	Seekonk, Ma.	5	12
Bucklin, David	July 16, 1804	18	light	Rehoboth, Ma.	3	4
Bucklin, Earl	Aug. 12, 1808	21	light	Rehoboth, Ma.	4	5
Bucklin, Edward	Mar. 23, 1801	18	dark	Rehoboth, Ma.	2	33
Bucklin, Edward	July 16, 1804	21	dark	Rehoboth, Ma.	3	4
Bucklin, George	Dec. 9, 1799	32	dark	Providence, R.I.	2	25
Bucklin, Isaac H.	Aug. 15, 1836	18	light	Seekonk, Ma.	5	7
Bucklin, James, Jr.	Dec, 9, 1830	28	ruddy	Seekonk, Ma.	5	6
Bucklin, James 3rd.	June 9, 1826	26	light	Seekonk, Ma.	4	10
Bucklin, John	Jan. 4, 1819	18	light	Seekonk, Ma.	4	8
Bucklin, John	July 10, 1837	25	black	NO. Prov., R.I.	5	8
Bucklin, Joseph	Aug. 3, 1807	19	dark	Rehoboth, Ma.	4	5
Bucklin, Otis	Mar. 15, 1797	26	dark	Rehoboth, Ma.	1	7
Bucklin, Otis	July 20, 1803	31	dark	Rehoboth, Ma.	2	44
Bucklin, Otis	Sept. 11, 1833	18	light	Seekonk, Ma.	5	7
Bucklin, Richard Luther	Jan. 17, 1826	14	dark	Seekonk, Ma.	4	10
Bucklin, Samuel	Jan. 3, 1824	20	light	Seekonk, Ma.	4	9
Bucklin, Samuel	June 9, 1826	22	light	Seekonk, Ma.	4	10
Bucklin, Samuel S.F.	Oct. 21, 1833	14	light	Concord, Ma.	5	7
Bucklin, Thomas	Apr. 26, 1806	36	black	Roshester, Va.	3	74
Bucklin, William	Sept. 11, 1833	17	light	Seekonk, Ma.	5	7
Bucklin, William	Nov. 12, 1841	19	light	Seekonk, Ma.	5	9
Bucklin, William	July 29, 1845	22	dark	Providence, R.I.	5	10
Budlong, James E.	Nov. 24, 1819	19	light	Providence, R.I.	4	8
Budlong, John S.	May 4, 1821	23	light	Cranston, R.I.	4	9
Budlong, Philip	Mar. 3, 1812	23	light	Warwich, R.I.	4	6
Budlong, Pierce	Mar. 17, 1828	24	light	Warwick, R.I.	4	10
Buffington, Alfred S. Jr.	Mar. 6, 1849	16	light	Providence, R.I.	5	11
Buffington, John	Feb. 9, 1816	18	dark	Providence, R.I.	4	7
Buffington, John E.	July 10, 1854	17	light	Middletown, R.I.	5	91

NAME	DATE OF CERTIFICATION	AGE	COMPLEXION	PLACE OF BIRTH	BOOK	PAGE
Buffum, Samuel H.	Sept. 28, 1855	27	light	Providence, R.I.	5	91
Buffum, Wm. H.	June 21, 1856	14	dark	Providence, R.I.	5	91
Buffum, William H.	Sept. 22, 1859	18	fair	Providence, R.I.	6	2
Buley, Henry	June 14, 1852	36	mulatto	Milton, Del.	5	13
Bullard, Horatio	Jan. 1, 1833	23	light	Sturbridge, Ma.	5	6
Bullard, Jonathan	Dec. 16, 1803	21	light	Rehoboth, Ma.	2	22
Bullock, Cyrus	Mar. 8, 1806	19	light	Rehoboth, Ma.	3	72A
Bullock, Daniel E.	May 15, 1835	24	light	No. Kingstown, R.I.	5	7
Bullock, Esra	Oct. 16, 1826	18	light	Rehoboth, Ma.	4	10
Bullock, Ezra	May 5, 1855	47	light	Rehoboth, Ma.	5	91
Bullock, Israel	Oct. 22, 1796	17	dark	Rehoboth, Ma.	1	7&4
Bullock, Jabez	Aug. 31, 1849	22	light	NO. Kingston, R.I.	5	12
Bullock, John	Feb. 7, 1798	16	light	Providence, R.I.	1	25
Bullock, John H.	Aug. 31, 1849	34	light	No. Kingston, R.I.	5	12
Bullock, Levi	Jan. 19, 1856	57	fair	Northport, Me.	5	91
Bullock, William	Nov. 26, 1856	20	fair	Lincolnville, Me.	5	91
Bullock, Wm. F.	Nov. 15, 1851	22	dark	Bristol, R.I.	5	13
Bunker, Frances	Oct. 30, 1804	25	black	Phila., Pa.	3	49
Bunker, Necholas	June 22, 1838	21	light	Albany, N.Y.	5	8
Bunnel, Henry	Oct. 5, 1831	19	light	Southington, Conn.	5	6
Bunsley, Samuel S.	Aug. 5, 1840	22	light	Morris Co., N.J.	5	9
Bunsley, John W. S.	Aug. 5, 1840	23	light	Springfield, Ma.	5	9
Buntin, Joseph C.	Nov. 12, 1835	23	light	Concorc, N.H.	5	7
Burbanks, Caleb	Jan. 11, 1849	28	fair	Providence, R.I.	5	11
Burbank, Thomas	May 7, 1831	26	dark	Freetown, Ma.	5	6
Burbidge George	Sept. 17, 1847	28	light	Savannah, Ga.	5	11
Burten, William	Aug. 11, 1801	17	light	Stonigton, Conn.	2	33
Burden George C.	Aug. 25, 1835	25	dark	Troy, Ma.	5	7
Burdick, Benjamin	1798-1799		May 4, 1778	Newport, R.I.	* -	--
Huling Burdick swears the above to be true.						
Burdick, Charles H.	Oct. 29, 1849	21	dark	Hopkinton, R.I.	5	12
Burdick, George	1798-1799		Mar. 16, 1774	Newport, R.I.	-	--
Burdick, Huling	1798-1799		Jan. 23, 1772	Newport, R.I.	* -	--
Benjamin Burdick swears the above to be true.						
Burdick, John	May 7, 1797	24	light	Hopkinton, R.I.	1	21
[Burdick]Burdock, John	Aug. 28, 1806	18	light	Baltimore, Md.	3	28
Burdick, John M.	Nov. 9, 1803	30	light	Hopkinton, R.I.	2	46
Burdick, Perry	Sept. 5, 1826	15	dark	Charlestown, R.I.	4	10
*Newport, R.I.						

REGISTER OF SEAMEN'S PROTECTION

NAME	DATE OF CERTIFICATION	AGE	COMPLEXION	PLACE OF BIRTH	BOOK	PAGE
Burdick, Stephen	July 27, 1819	22	light	Plainfield, Conn.	4	8
Burdick, William	Nov. 5, 1814	21	light	Hopkinton, R.I.	4	7
Burdick, William	July 20, 1821	14	dark	Newport, R.I.	--	
Sworn statement of Charles Devens of Newport, in the Custom House Papers. Oct. 1808						
Burdick, Wm. W.	Nov. 7, 1851	21	light	Hopkinton, R.I.	5	13
Burges, Jonathan	July 16, 1819	20	light	-----------	4	8
Burgess, Thomas J.	Mar. 22, 1845	23	light	Wayne, Me.	5	10
Burgess, William	Jan. 11, 1853	23	light	New York, N.Y.	5	13
Burke, Burrows A.	Apr. 12, 1815	18	light	Providence, R.I.	4	7
Burke, Charles S.	Apr. 11, 1859	30	fair	Chicago, Ill.	6	2
Burke, Edmund	Nov. 5, 1796	21	dark	Warwick, R.I.	1	7&5
Burke, Edward	Nov. 5, 1796	23	light	Warwick, R.I.	1	7
Burke, George	Aug. 6, 1849	26	black	Wayneshro, Pa.	5	11
Burke, James J.	Nov. 13, 1852	18	light	Boston, Ma.	5	13
Burke, Joseph	Nov. 5, 1851	23	light	Veesville, N.Y.	5	13
Burke, Reuben	May 16, 1799	22	light	Warwick, R.I.	2	2
Burke, William	Apr. 23, 1859	19	dark	New Bedford, Ma.	6	2
Burket, John	Apr. 20, 1797	18	dark	Johnston, R.I.	1	7
Burket, Nevin	Nov. 16, 1835	22	black	Baltimore, Md.	5	7
Burlingame, Amos	Aug. 17, 1796	18	light	Warwick, R.I.	1	1
Burlingame, George	Feb. 26, 1849	31	fair	Cumberland, R.I.	5	11
Burlingame, Hiram	Feb. 16, 1857	28	fair	Burrillville, R.I.	5	91
*Burlingham, Joshua, Jr.	June 13, 1821	24	light	Norwich, N.Y.	4	9
Burlingame, Moses	June 13, 1836	16	light	Smithfield, R.I.	5	7
Burlingame, Nehemiah	Nov. 8, 1830	23	ruddy	No. Kingstown, R.I.	5	6
Burlingame, Rufus	Sept. 7, 1805	20	light	No. Kingstown, R.I.	3	72
Burlingame, William	Nov. 12, 1796	28	light	Providence, R.I.	1	5&7
Burlingame, William	Dec. 2, 1799	33	light	Providence, R.I.	2	25
Burlingham, William	Aug. 11, 1804	19	light	Warwick, R.I.	3	4
Burne, William	Mar. 21, 1809	22	dark	Charleston, S.C.	4	5
Burneston, Caleb	Apr. 11, 1835	38	light	Baltimore, Md.	5	7
Burnham, Joseph, Jr.	June 26, 1830	23	light	Portland, Me.	5	6
Burnham, William	May 12, 1830	23	light	Providence, R.I.	5	6
Burns, Francis	1798-1799	May 15, 1785		Fredrickburg, Va.	-	--
Burns, John	Mar. 7, 1853	21	light	New York, N.Y.	5	13
Burns, Thomas	Mar. 21, 1804	20	dark	Charleston, S.C.	3	3
Burns, William	Dec. 2, 1841	18	dark	New York, N.Y.	5	9
Burr, Benjamin	Oct. 11, 1799	18	light	Rehoboth, Ma.	2	2

NAME	DATE OF CERTIFICATION	AGE	COMPLEXION	PLACE OF BIRTH	BOOK	PAGE
Burr, Damon	Nov. 19, 1796	25	black	Charleston, S.C.	1	7
Burr, David	Aug. 4, 1803	19	light	Providence, R.I.	2	44
Burr, David T.	July 15, 1841	15	light	Providence, R.I.	5	9
Burr, David T.	Aug. 21, 1847	22	fair	Providence, R.I.	5	11
Burr, Edward	Nov. 3, 1856	26	light	Brewer, Me.	5	91
Burr, George	July 15, 1806	14	light	Providence, R.I.	3	78
Burr, Henry Tenbroeck	June 9, 1844	15	light	Providence, R.I.	5	10
Burr, Isaiah	June 9, 1798	28	light	Warren, R.I.	2	2
Burr, Olney	Mar. 4, 1797	23	dark	Providence, R.I.	1	7
Burrell, Aaron	Dec. 20, 1849	28	mulatto	Stonington, Conn.	5	12
Burrill, Benjamin	Aug. 22, 1832	20	ruddy	Hartford, Conn.	5	6
Burrill, Cato	Nov. 19, 1796	26	black	Newport, R.I.	1	7
Burrill, Charles	June 11, 1808	23	light	Providence, R.I.	4	5
Burrill, Richard	Nov. 22, 1822	22	Black	Providence, R.I.	4	9
Burrill, Samuel	Nov. 27, 1832	33	dark	Newburyport, Ma.	5	6
Burroughs, Austin S.	Aug. 20, 1853	32	light	Providence, R.I.	5	13
*Burrows, Charles	Mar. 25, 1835	25	brown	New York, N.Y.	5	7
Burroughs, Chas. H.	Feb. 26, 1849	27	light	Providence, R.I.	5	11
Burroughs, David A.	Aug. 4, 1841	13	light	Stonington, Conn.	5	9
Burrough, Edward S.	Dec. 8, 1832	17	dark	Providence, R.I.	5	6
*Burrows, Frank	April 4, 1849	26	dark	New Orleans, La.	5	11
Burroughs, Isaac	Oct. 29, 1803	14	light	Freetown, Ma.	2	44
Burrough, James	Jan. 7, 1806	19	dark	Providence, R.I.	3	72A
Burrough, James	Dec. 28, 1807	20	dark	Providence, R.I.	4	5
Burroughs, Jesse	June 4, 1851	19	dark	Stonington, Conn.	5	13
Burroughs, John	Oct. 31, 1803	20	light	Providence, R.I.	2	44
Burroughs, John	June 4, 1851	21	dark	Stonington, Conn.	5	13
Burroughs, John	May 15, 1862	25	dark	Salisbury, Md.	6	2
Burroughs, John W.	Apr. 15, 1851	17	light	Taunton, Ma.	5	13
Burroughs, William	May 10, 1809	17	light	Boston, Ma.	4	5
Burrows, Smith	Nov. 21, 1849	20	light	Providence, R.I.	5	12
Burrows, Thomas	Mar. 30, 1857	22	light	Carlton, La.	5	92
Burrows, William	July 10, 1824	28	light	Hamburg, Germany	4	9
Burt, Aaron	Oct. 21, 1835	18	light	Providence, R.I.	5	7
Burt, George A.	Nov. 26, 1862	15	dark	Fall River, Ma.	6	2
Burt, Henry	Feb. 27, 1827	15	ruddy	Newport, R.I.	4	10
Burt, Leander P.	Feb. 5, 1849	22	light	Fall River, Ma.	5	11

*out of order

REGISTER OF SEAMEN'S PROTECTION

NAME	DATE OF CERTIFICATION	AGE	COMPLEXION	PLACE OF BIRTH	BOOK	PAGE
Burt, Lloyd B.	Apr. 29, 1807	30	dark	Woodstock, Conn.	4	5
Burt, Stephen P.	Feb. 25, 1823	23	ruddy	Taunton, Ma.	4	9
Burt, William	Oct. 13, 1804	16	black	Falmouth, Ma.	3	49
Burtins, James M.	July 30, 1839	28	dark	Baltimore, Md.	5	8
Burton, Albert W.	Aug. 5, 1850	19	light	Foster, R.I.	5	12
Burton, Charles	Apr. 9, 1864	28	light	Boston, Ma.	6	2
Burton(?), Charles L.	Nov. 18, 1844	16	light	Providence, R.I.	5	10
Burton, Edward F.	Nov. 29, 1848	29	mulatto	New Haven, Conn..	5	11
Burton, Francis	Nov. 26, 1849	21	light	Smithfield, R.I.	5	12
Burton, Henry	Jan. 2, 1805	24	dark	Providence, R.I.	3	50
Burton, Joseph	Apr. 17, 1805	21	light	Cranston, R.I.	3	58
Burton, Joseph	Aug. 2, 1805	23	light	Cranston, R.I.	3	58
Burton, Nicholas	May 1, 1818	32	black	Providence, R.I.	4	8
Burton, Solomon	Feb. 14, 1806	20	black	Warwick, R.I.	3	72A
Burton, William H.	Apr. 16, 1863	21	dark	Westchester, Pa.	6	2
Bushee, David	Oct. 24, 1854	23	light	New York, N.Y.	5	91
Butched, John	Aug. 26, 1841	25	light	New York, N.Y.	5	9
Butcher, James	May 3, 1806	25	black	Tarrytown, N.Y.	3	74
Butler, Carnelins	Sept. 25, 1821	40	light	Edgartown, Ma.	4	9
Bulter, Easton	Oct. 12, 1820	23	light	Yarmouth, Ma.	4	8
Bulter, Edward	Dec. 5, 1801	15	light	Falmouth, Ma.	2	33
Bulter, Edwin	Apr. 27, 1822	23	light	New York, N.Y.	4	9
Bulter, Emanuel	Oct. 28, 1803	14	black	Providence, R.I.	2	44
Bulter, Fortune	July 22, 1805	29	black	Deerfield, N.H.	3	58
Bulter, Fortune	May 12, 1806	30	black	Nottingham, N.H.	3	74
Butler, George	May 8, 1811	20	black	Providence, R.I.	4	6
Butler, John	Oct. 3, 1803	22	dark	Freetown, Ma.	2	44
Butler, John	Oct. 30, 1804	25	black	Glastonbury, Conn.	3	50
Butler, John H.	Sept. 29, 1847	21	yellow	Baltimore, Md.	5	11
Bulter, Joseph	Nov. 7, 1797	23	dark	Freetown, Ma.	1	21
Butler, Joseph, Jr.	Nov. 17, 1828	22	dark	Providence, R.I.	4	10
Butler, Peter	July 31, 1837	37	---	Buckingham, Pa.	5	8
Butler, Richard	Oct. 30, 1804	37	black	Cape Cepers, Africa	3	49
Butler, Thomas	Oct. 12, 1803	32	light	Freetown, Ma.	2	44
Butler, Thomas	Aug. 28, 1809	19	black	Providence, R.I.	4	6
Butler, William	Jan. 24, 1848	19	yellow	Baltimore, Md.	5	11
Butman, Avery	May 30, 1842	22	light	Killingly, Conn.	5	9

NAME	DATE OF CERTIFICATION	AGE	COMPLEXION	PLACE OF BIRTH	BOOK	PAGE
Butman, John	Oct. 11, 1799	22	dark	Tewkesbury, Ma.	2	2
Butman, Joseph	Aug. 15, 1800	21	dark	Lancaster, Ma.	2	25
Butman, Zebulon	Apr. 4, 1797	22	dark	Dracut, Ma.	1	7
Butts, Albert	June 4, 1844	17	light	Providence, R.I.	5	10
Butts, Benjamin	Apr. 19, 1817	18	ruddy	Providence, R.I.	-	--
Butts, George	July 9, 1821	21	dark	Warren, R.I.	--	--
Son of George & Avis Butts. Birth Certificate in Custom House Papers. DOB: Sept. 20, 1800.						
Butts, Gideon	Mar. 15, 1839	24	light	Fall River, Ma.	5	8
Butts, James E.	Sept. 13, 1811	18	light	Providence, R.I	4	6
Butts, John	----			July 3, 1772 Tiverton, R.I.	** -	--
Butts, Joseph B.	July 21, 1809	13	light	Providence, R.I.	4	6
Butts, Samuel W.	Apr. 23, 1849	46	light	Providence, R.I.	5	11
Butts, Wm. D.	Jan. 6, 1849	16	light	Providence, R.I.	5	11
Buxton, John P.	Oct. 22, 1818	21	light	No. Yarmouth, Ma.	4	8
Buzzard, Gershom W.	Nov. 14, 1803	21	light	Newton, Ma.	2	46
Buzzell, Hezekiah	Sept. 23, 1848	20	light	Lincolnsville, Me.	5	11
Byndless, Robert	Sept. 29, 1849	20	yellow	Phila., Pa.	5	12
?Byne, Henry	Mar. 6, 1797	21	light	Boston, Ma.	1	7
Byrns, John S.	Apr. 2, 1849	34	dark	New Orleans, La.	5	11
?Bysse, Henry	Mar. 6, 1797	21	light	Boston, Ma.	1	7
Cady, Barzillai F.	Sept. 26, 1817	19	dark	Killingly, Conn.	4	13
Cady, Benjamin	July 25, 1820	25	light	Killingly, Conn.	4	14
Cady, Frederick	Aug. 20, 1847	22	fair	Providence, R.I.	5	17
Cady, John C.	Dec. 12, 1818	20	light	Killingly, Conn.	4	13
Cady, Joseph W.	June 12, 1849	27	dark	Warwick, R.I.	5	18
Cady, William A.	May 15, 1838	16	light	Providence, R.I.	5	15
Caesar, Caleb	Jan. 2, 1823	23	yellow*	No. Prov., R.I.	4	14
Cafferty, John	June 23, 1841	16	light	Albany, N.Y.	5	16
Cahoon, Asa	Oct. 28, 1797	18	light	Providence, R.I.	1	31
Cahoone, Crosby	Mar. 24, 1863	18	light	Harwick, Ma.	6	3
Cahoone, Ebenezer	June 12, 1844	21	dark	Harwick, Ma.	5	17
Cahoone, William	June 22, 1854	21	light	Cumberland, R.I.	5	20
Callahan, James	Mar. 10, 1853	24	light	New York, N.Y.	5	20
Callaghan, Joseph	July 17, 1804	22	light	Baltimore, Md.	3	6
Cameron, Elnathan	Oct. 31, 1846	14	fair	Providence, R.I.	5	17
Cameron, John	Apr. 30, 1835	37	light	Philadelphia, Pa.	5	15
Cameron, William	Sept. 19, 1831	28	light	Sterlingshire, Scotland	5	14

*mulatto
**Newport, R.I.

NAME	DATE OF CERTIFICATION	AGE	COMPLEXION	PLACE OF BIRTH	BOOK	PAGE
Cameron, Wm. R.	Nov. 21, 1849	15	light	Providence, R.I.	5	18
Campbell, Alexander	Mar. 9, 1804	20	light	Marsfield, Conn.	3	5
Campbell, Daniel	Mar. 25, 1850	26	sandy	New York, N.Y.	5	19
Campbell, Edward	Dec. 24, 1830	38	light	Phila., Pa.	5	14
Campbell, George S.	May 10, 1833	22	light	---, Pa.	5	14
Campbell, James	June 18, 1844	19	light	Middletown, R.I.	5	17
Campbell, James	Sept. 30, 1850	25	light	Providence, R.I.	5	19
Campbell, James	Feb. 23, 1859	27	light	Phila., Pa.	6	3
Campbell, John	Feb. 7, 1849	21	fair	No. Prov., R.I.	5	18
Campbell, Robert	Dec. 20, 1848	25	fair	Salem, Ma.	5	18
Campbell, Robert	Aug. 15, 1851	21	dark	Fall River, Ma.	5	19
Cammel, Samuel	Dec. 26, 1804	22	dark	Norfolk, Va.	3	52
Campbell, William	Sept. 8, 1853	20	light	Troy, N.Y.	5	20
Campbell, William	Aug. 17, 1855	24	light	Toledo, Ohio	5	20
Camson, Thomas	May 12, 1834	24	light	Norfolk, Va.	5	15
Canada, James Brown	Aug. 24, 1799	21	light	Providence, R.I.	2	3
Canada, Prince	June 3, 1805	22	black	Rehoboth, Ma.	3	53
Cane, James	May 26, 1830	34	light	Brooklyn, N.Y.	5	14
Canfield, James	Dec. 12, 1845	20	fair	New York, N.Y.	5	17
Cann, Horace	Aug. 22, 1854	20	yellow	New Haven, Conn.	5	20
Cannon, George	June 2, 1831	27	black	Philadelphia, Pa.	5	14
Cannon, Philip	June 22, 1798	27	dark	Rush, Ireland	2	3
Canterman, John T.	Sept. 10, 1850	32	light	New York, N.Y.	5	19
Capchollar, Antoine	Oct. 18, 1841	21	dark	New Orleans, La.	5	16
Capen, Paul	Mar. 24, 1859	47	light	Thomaston, Me.	6	3
Cappers, Daniel H.	Nov. 9, 1850	19	light	Bangor, Me.	5	19
Capron, Christoper	Apr. 29, 1807	46	dark	Newport, R.I.	4	11
Capron, Leonard	Apr. 23, 1807	19	light	E. Greenwich, R.I.	4	11
Capron, Leonard	Nov. 15, 1819	33	light	E. Greenwich, R.I.	4	13
Capron, Nelson Mason	Dec. 27, 1852	18	light	Smithfield, R.I.	5	19
Capron, Oliver	Oct. 11, 1799	18	light	E. Greenwich, R.I.	2	3
Capron, Oliver	Dec. 13, 1800	20	dark	E. Greenwich, R.I.	2	27
Capron, Ovliver	Jan. 16, 1806	26	light	E. Greenwich, R.I.	3	61
Capron, William	Apr. 5, 1815	23	light	Nantucket, Ma.	4	13
Capron, William	May 16, 1839	18	light	Cumberland, R.I.	5	16
Capwell, Amos	Apr. 1, 1805	19	dark	Coventry, R.I.	3	53
Capwell, Amos	Dec. 23, 1809	24	dark	Coventry, R.I.	4	11

NAME	DATE OF CERTIFICATION	AGE	COMPLEXION	PLACE OF BIRTH	BOOK	PAGE
Capwell, Jabez Greene	Apr. 8, 1797	22	dark	Coventry, R.I.	1	8
Capwell, Thurston **	Nov. 19, 1849	22	light	W. Greenwich, R.I.	5	18
Card, Ezra	Mar. 20, 1799	20	dark	Warwick, R.I.	2	3
Card, George H.	Oct. 15, 1827	22	light	Cranston, R.I.	4	15
Card, Israel	Jan. 12, 1807	27	light	Warwick, R.I.	4	11
Card, Israel	Mar. 19, 1812	28	brown	Warwick, R.I.	4	12
Card, Johathan	1798-1799		Feb. 7, 1779	Charleston, S.C.	* -	--
Ray Card of Charlestown, R.I. swears the above to be true.						
Card, Jonathan, Jr.	June 9, 1804	18	light	Plainfield, Conn.	3	5
Card, Nathaniel	July 15, 1803	21	light	Warwick, R.I.	2	40
Card, Nathaniel	Dec. 31, 1799	18	light	Warwick, R.I.	2	27
Card, Perry G.	Mar. 10, 1847	22	dark	Charlestown, R.I.	5	17
Card, Ray	1798-1799		Aug. 15, 1780	So. Kingston, R.I.	* -	--
Jonathan Card of Charlestown, R.I. swears the above to be true.						
Card, Russell	June 2, 1849	21	light	E. Greenwich, R.I.	5	18
Card, Samuel	1798-1799		May 14, 1770	So. Kingston, R.I.	* -	--
Card, Sands	1798-1799		May 14, 1770	So. Kingston, R.I.	* -	--
Card, Stephen	Oct. 18, 1803	20	light	Rehoboth, Ma.	3	5
Card, Thomas	Feb. 11, 1855	25	light	Providence, R.I.	5	20
Card, Uriah	Nov. 22, 1849	28	light	Newport, R.I.	5	18
Card, William	1798-1799		Aug. 15, 1779	Stonington, Conn.	* -	--
Card, William	Feb. 6, 1804	20	light	Rehoboth, Ma.	3	5
Card, William, Jr.	June 22, 1807	21	brown	Warwick, R.I.	4	11
Carder, Elisha	Aug. 20, 1800	21	black	Warwick, R.I.	2	27
Carder, Elisha	Mar. 1, 1805	27	black	Colchester, Conn.	3	52
Carder, George W.	May 2, 1825	21	light	Killingly, Conn.	4	14
Carder, James B.	Jan. 16, 1849	19	dark	Warwick, R.I.	5	18
Carder, Joseph	Sept. 13, 1796	27	dark	Warwick, R.I.	1	2
Carey, James G.	May 25, 1852	18	light	Providence, R.I.	5	19
Carey, John	Mar. 31, 1809	23	light	Alexandria, Va.	4	11
Carey, John M.	Sept. 7, 1859	27	dark	Newburyport, Ma.	6	3
Carlile, Christopher M.	Oct. 23, 1829	15	light	Providence, R.I.	5	14
Carman, Henry	Dec. 30, 1845	28	dark	New York, N.Y.	5	17
Carmichael, Henry. E.	Dec. 28, 1846	19	fair	Newport, R.I.	5	17
Carnes, Phillip	Apr. 24, 1839	22	light	New York, N.Y.	5	15
Carney, John Osear	Mar. 10, 1852	22	light	Richmond, Me.	5	19
*Newport, R. I.						
**Car, William	Apr. 10, 1834	18	light	Killingly, Conn.	5	15

NAME	DATE OF CERTIFICATION	AGE	COMPLEXION	PLACE OF BIRTH	BOOK	PAGE
Carney, Thomas M.	June 10, 1841	21	light	Harlem, N.Y.	5	16
Carpenter, Anthony	Mar. 24, 1798	23	light	Cranston, R.I.	1	31
Carpenter, Benjamin G.	Mar. 18, 1829	14	light	Providence, R.I.	5	14
Carpenter, Benjamin R.	Feb. 3, 1841	19	light	Providence, R.I.	5	16
Carpenter, Caleb A.	Mar. 28, 1856	18	light	Rehoboth, Ma.	5	44
Carpenter, Calvin	June 25, 1811	15	light	Rehoboth, Ma.	4	12
Carpenter, Chas. H.	Oct. 17, 1855	22	fair	Lewistown, Del.	5	20
Carpenter, Christopher Smith	May 28, 1798	24	light	Voluntown, Conn.	2	3
Carpenter, Colenel J.	Oct. 18, 1849	40	light	E. Greenwich, R.I.	5	18
Carpenter, Cyrel	Mar. 22, 1805	19	light	Rehoboth, Ma.	3	52
Carpenter, Francis	Jan. 1, 1798	15	dark	No. Kingstown, R.I.	1	31
Carpenter, George	Nov. 25, 1814	35	light	Cranston, R.I.	4	12
Carpenter, George	June 5, 1835	15	light	Warwick, R.I.	5	15
Carpenter, George H.	Nov. 17, 1849	29	light	Rehoboth, Ma.	5	18
Carpenter, George R.	Aug. 18, 1824	17	light	Warwick, R.I.	4	14
Carpenter, Harry [Harvey]	Nov. 30, 1799	21	light	Cranston, R.I.	2	3
Carpenter, Hopkins	Dec. 3, 1796	25	dark	Cranston, R.I.	1	8
Carpenter, Ira	Mar. 15, 1849	21	light	Syracuze, N.Y.	5	18
Carpenter, Jesse	Feb. 23, 1849	48	light	Hartford, Pa.	5	18
Carpenter, John	July 2, 1804	16	dark	New York, N.Y.	3	6
Carpenter, John, Jr.	Mar. 5, 1806	15	light	Providence, R.I.	3	65
Carpenter, John, Jr.	Sept. 8, 1810	20	dark	Providence, R.I.	4	12
Carpenter, John C.	Sept. 3, 1832	16	light	Newport, R.I.	5	14
Carpenter, Lemuel G.	Oct. 23, 1829	16	light	Rehoboth, Ma.	4	14
Carpenter, Luther N.	June 10, 1833	26	dark	Rehoboth, Ma.	5	14
Carpenter, Nathan	Apr. 8, 1797	18	dark	Rehoboth, Ma.	1	8
Carpenter, Nathaniel	Apr. 21, 1801	20	light	Rehoboth, Ma.	2	27
Carpenter, Nathaniel	Aug. 28, 1804	23	dark	Rehoboth, Ma.	3	6
Carpenter, Nathaniel, Jr.	Mar. 5, 1805	20	light	Cranston, R.I.	3	52
Carpenter, Oliver	June 11, 1832	18	light	No. Kingston, R.I.	5	14
Carpenter, Pardon	Mar. 10, 1829	26	light	Hopkinton, R.I.	5	14
Carpenter, Peleg A.	OCT. 31, 1853	18	light	Newport, R.I.	5	20
Carpenter, Peter	Oct. 17, 1803	16	light	Rehoboth, Ma.	2	40
Carpenter, Peter	June 13, 1804	17	light	Rehoboth, Ma.	3	5
Carpenter, Richard	Dec. 17, 1803	18	dark	Rehoboth, Ma.	2	23
Carpenter, Russell	Oct. 4, 1809	21	dark	Cranston, R.I.	4	11

NAME	DATE OF CERTIFICATION	AGE	COMPLEXION	PLACE OF BIRTH	BOOK	PAGE
Carpenter, Samuel	1798-1799	June 21, 1782		No. Kingston, R.I.	* -	--
Carpenter, Thomas	Oct. 29, 1804	24	dark	Glocester, R.I.	3	6
Carpenter, Thomas	Mar. 29, 1856	19	light	Lanesville, Ma.	5	44
Carpenter, William	Sept. 17, 1806	17	light	So. Kingston, R.I.	3	32
Carpenter, William L.	Aug. 10, 1822	21	light	Foster, R.I.	4	14
Carr, Benjamin	June 24, 1839	21	light	E. Greenwich, R.I.	5	16
Carr, Caleb, 3rd	Apr. 23, 1824	20	light	Warren, R.I.	4	14
Carr, George C.	July 10, 1845	35	dark	Warren, R.I.	5	17
Carr, George C.	Mar. 29, 1851	41	dark	Warren, R.I.	5	19
Carr, James	Jan. 19, 1821	21	light	Rehoboth, Ma.	-	--

Sworn statement of Hannah Blake of Bristol in The Custom House Papers.

NAME	DATE OF CERTIFICATION	AGE	COMPLEXION	PLACE OF BIRTH	BOOK	PAGE
Carr, James	Nov. 28, 1844	17	light	Providence, R.I.	5	17
Carr, James	Sept. 26, 1850	20	light	Belfast, Me.	5	19
Carr, James	Apr. 24, 1854	22	light	Blackstone, Ma.	5	20
Carr, John	July 8, 1797	21	dark	Baltimore, Md.	1	8
Carr, John	1798-1799	Sept. 11, 1782		Newport, R.I.	* -	--

Samuel Carr swears the above to be true.

NAME	DATE OF CERTIFICATION	AGE	COMPLEXION	PLACE OF BIRTH	BOOK	PAGE
Car[r], John	Dec. 31, 1823	23	dark	North Kingstown, R.I.	4	14
Carr, John	Jan. 2, 1857	21	light	Fall River, Ma.	5	44
Carr, Joseph	Feb. 25, 1850	26	light	Marion, Pa.	5	19
Carr, Lindsey [Lyndesey]	Nov. 26, 1799	22	light	Coventry, R.I.	2	3
Carr, Martin	Feb. 20, 1845	19	light	Boston, Ma.	5	17
Carr, Robert	July 15, 1797	22	dark	Newton, Ma.	1	8
Carr, Robin	Sept. 26, 1803	28	black	Jamestown, R.I.	2	40
Carr, Robin	Aug. 28, 1807	32	black	Newport, R.I.	4	11
Carr, Samuel	Oct. 6, 1848	20	light	Cranston, R.I.	5	18
Carr, Samuel	Sept. 10, 1855	35	dark	So. Kingston, R.I.	5	20
Carr, Sayles	Nov. 18, 1798	29	light	Warwick, R.I.	1	31
Carr, Sayles	June 27, 1801	33	light	Warwick, R.I.	2	27
Carr, Stephen	1798-1799	Sept. 20, 1780		Warren, R.I.	* -	--
Carr, Thomas	Oct. 12, 1798	21	light	Baltimore, Md.	2	3
Carr, Turner, Jr.	Nov. 20, 1849	25	light	Warren, R.I.	5	19
** Car, William	Apr. 10, 1834	18	light	Killingly, Conn.	5	15
Carrier, Omri	Nov. 26, 1828	19	light	Providence, R.I.	4	15
Carrington, David W.	Mar. 9, 1858	20	light	Cleveland, Ohio	6	3
Carrington, Edward	Dec. 3, 1796	21	light	New Haven, Conn.	1	8
Carrique, Edward T.	May 25, 1829	18	light	Shoreham, Vt.	5	14
Carroll, Cornelius	Apr. 8, 1841	26	light	Phila., Pa.	5	16

*Newport, R. I.
**Misfiled

Page   53

NAME	DATE OF CERTIFICATION	AGE	COMPLEXION	PLACE OF BIRTH	BOOK	PAGE
Carroll, Thomas	June 22, 1854	22	dark	Smithfield, R.I.	5	20
Carrygan, Richard T.	Oct. 5, 1841	28	light	Nantucket, Ma.	5	16
Carson, James O.	Sept. 30, 1864	21	dark	Sag Harbour, N.Y.	6	3
Carter, Alexander	Oct. 10, 1821	16	light	Troy [Fall River], Ma.	-	--
Sworn statement of Mary Carter of Troy in the Custom House Papers. DOB-Feb. 20, 1805						
Carter, Alexander	Feb. 3, 1841	35	light	Pawtucket, Ma.	5	16
Carter, Alexander	Mar. 21, 1848	37	light	No. Prov., R.I.	5	17
Carter, Charles	July 19, 1817	20	black	Newport, R.I.	4	13
Carter, Charles	May 24, 1851	22	light	New York, N.Y.	5	19
Carter, David L.	Aug. 2, 1827	30	light	Colchester, Conn.	4	14
Carter, Edward	Feb. 17, 1835	24	light	Norwich, Conn.	5	15
Carter, Edward H.	1798-1799	Sept. 7, 1782		Newport, R.I.	** -	--
James Carter swears the above to be true.						
Carter, Frank	Sept. 25, 1850	19	light	Mobile, Ala.	5	19
Carter, Henry	May 8, 1807	27	light	Providence, R.I.	4	11
Carter, Hiram	June 29, 1836	25	light	Troy, Ma.	5	15
Carter, James	Apr. 8, 1800	20	light	Providence, R.I.	2	27
Carter, James	Mar. 11, 1805	24	light	Providence, R.I.	3	52
Carter, James	Apr. 11, 1807	27	light	Providence, R.I.	4	11
Carter, John	Feb. 8, 1798	20	light	Voluntown, Conn.	1	31
Carter, John	Nov. 20, 1811	28	brown	Provincetown, Ma.	4	12
Carter, John	Sept. 17, 1853	26	light	New York, N.Y.	5	20
Carter, John W.	May 14, 1851	28	light	Randolph, N.Y.	5	19
Carter, Samuel	1798-1799	Aug. 31, 1780		Newport, R.I.	**-	--
Robert Carter swears the above to be true.						
Carter, Thomas	Mar. 8, 1853	26	light	New York, N.Y.	5	20
Carter, William	Aug. 8, 1811	22	dark	Palmer, Ma.	4	12
Cartwright, Edward	1798-1799	June 18, 1787		Block Island, R.I.	** -	--
Cartwright, Simeon B.	Mar. 7, 1815	17	light	Dighton, Ma.	4	12
Carver, Thaddeus	Nov. 30, 1847	23	light	Vinalhaven, Me.	5	17
Carver, Wm. S.	Nov. 20, 1841	18	light	Vinalhaven, Me.	5	16
Cary, James	Mar. 27, 1835	27	light	Portland, Me.	5	15
Cary, John	Oct. 28, 1818	14	light	Cranston, R.I.	4	13
Cary, Nathaniel	May 8, 1820	33	dark	Shrewsbury, Ma.	4	14
Cary, Thomas S.	Mar. 2, 1811	19	light	Windham, Conn.	4	12
Cary, William	May 27, 1825	22	light	Cranston, R.I.	4	14
Cary, William	Feb. 23, 1828	45	yellow*	Smithfield, R.I.	4	15
Case, Alexander W.	Nov. 13, 1839	25	light	Warwick, R.I.	5	16

*mulatto
** Newport, R. I.

NAME	DATE OF CERTIFICATION	AGE	COMPLEXION	PLACE OF BIRTH	BOOK	PAGE
Case, Jacob	Sept. 27, 1854	20	dark	Eastport, Me.	5	20
Case, Joseph	Apr. 18, 1797	30	Blackface	So. Kingstown, R.I.	1	8
Case, Thomas	Apr. 12, 1821	30	black	So. Kingstown, R.I.	4	14
Casey, Walter	June 12, 1804	18	black	E. Greenwich, R.I.	3	5
Casey, Walter	Oct. 25, 1805	20	black	E. Greenwich, R.I.	3	61
Casman, Robert	Dec. 24, 1834	37	black	Brooklyn, N.Y.	5	15
Cassie, William	Apr. 5, 1841	18	light	Eastport, Me.	5	16
Castue, Raymond Castelew in Arnold's V. R.	1798-1799	Aug. 21, 1783		Little Compton, R.I.	**-	--
Caswell, Daniel, Jr.	Oct. 28, 1815	17	light	Duxbury, Ma.	4	13
Caswell, John	Dec. 3, 1814	21	light	Swansea, Ma.	4	12
Caswell, Philip	1798-1799	Oct. 24, 1766		Newport, R.I.	**-	--
Cathcart, Charles G.	Mar. 15, 1815	21	dark	Nantucket, Ma.	4	12
Caughlin, Cornelius	Jan. 13, 1846	24	fair	New Castle, Del.	5	17
Caulkins[Calkins], James	June 5, 1800	24	light	Edenton, N.C.	2	27
Cavalier, Dan'l James	June 11, 1849	41	dark Indian	New York, N.Y.	5	18
Cavalier, Edward Lewis	June 11, 1849	12	dark	Tiverton, R.I.	5	18
Ceasar, Daniel	Sept. 6, 1842	26	dark	No. Prov., R.I.	5	16
Ceasar, James	Jan. 17, 1855	47	mulatto	Albany, N.Y.	5	20
Ceasar, Sampson	Sept. 14, 1811	20	yellow*	Johnston, R.I.	4	12
Ceasar, Sampson	Jan. 8, 1810	18	yellow*	Johnston, R.I.	4	11
Ceasar, Samuel	Mar. 13, 1801	24	black	Johnston, R.I.	2	27
Ceasar, William	Apr. 6, 1801	21	black	Johnston, R.I.	2	27
Ceasar, William	Dec. 8, 1804	23	yellow*	Johnston, R.I.	3	52
Ceasar, William	Nov. 17, 1828	21	yellow*	No. Prov., R.I.	4	15
Cezar, Jere	July 31, 1837	30	dark	No. Prov., R.I.	5	15
Center, Edward	Dec. 18, 1800	17	light	Newport, R.I.	2	27
Center, Jeremiah	Sept. 6, 1803	29	brown	Woburn, Ma.	2	40
Cerney, John	Dec. 23, 1806	14	light	Hyde County, N.C.	4	11
Chace, Abner	July 9, 1839	25	light	Newport, R.I.	5	16
Chace, Allen, Jr.	Oct. 1, 1831	22	sandy	Freetown, Ma.	5	14
Chace, Alonzo	Apr. 23, 1832	26	light	Walpole, Ma.	5	14
Chace, Andrew C.	Dec. 4, 1833	24	dark	Coventry, R.I.	-	--
Chace, Benjamin D.	Aug. 31, 1849	28	florid	Swansea, Ma.	5	18
Chace, Caleb B.	Sept. 12, 1842	23	dark	Providence, R.I.	5	12
Chace, Charles	Nov. 5, 1805	16	light	Harwich, Ma.	3	61
Chace, Charles M.	Aug. 20, 1827	21	light	Warren, R.I.	4	14
Chace, Daniel	Dec. 22, 1797	17	light	Providence, R.I.	1	31

*mulatto   **Newport, R. I.

NAME	DATE OF CERTIFICATION	AGE	COMPLEXION	PLACE OF BIRTH	BOOK	PAGE
Chace, Daniel	Aug. 14, 1813	26	brown	Freetown, Ma.	4	12
Chace, David	Nov. 5, 1845	21	fair	Swansea, Ma.	5	17
Chace, Edward	Nov. 13, 1828	28	light	Warren, R.I.	4	15
Chace, Davis	Sept. 18, 1826	22	light	Dennis, Ma.	4	14
Cahce, Elisha	Oct. 27, 1801	24	light	Swansea, Ma.	2	27
Chace, Henry	Sept 21, 1809	20	light	Freetown, Ma.	4	11
Chace, Henry	Feb. 16, 1821	23	dk. Yellow*	Warwick, R.I.	4	14
Chace, Jabez	Mar. 19, 1819	21	light	Swansea, Ma.	4	13
Chace, Jacob	Nov. 30, 1803	15	dark	Swansea, Ma.	2	23
Chace, Jacob A.	May 1, 1821	29	dark	Swanswa, Ma.	4	14
Chace, James	Oct. 23, 1824	22	dark	Troy [Fall River], Ma.	4	14
Chace, John	June 2, 1800	16	dark	Providence, R.I.	2	27
Chace, John B.	Oct. 24, 1803	21	light	Providence, R.I.	2	40
Chace, John H.	Nov. 29, 1824	14	light	Warren, R.I.	4	14
Chace, Joseph	Apr. 4, 1804	16	light	Glocester, R.I.	3	5
Chace, Joseph	Dec. 24, 1806	19	light	Glocester, R.I.	4	11
Chace, Joseph	Aug. 28, 1815	26	light	Glocester, R.I.	4	13
Chace, Mark	1798-1799	Sept. 29, 1782		Swansea, Ma.	** -	--
Chace, Maxwell	Feb. 27, 1843	44	light	Warren, R.I.	5	17
Chace, Nathan B.	Mar. 5, 1855	25	fair	Coventry, R.I.	5	20
Chace, Nathaniel	July 1, 1803	41	dark	Harwich, Ma.	2	40
Chace, Noah	1798-1799	Aug. 14, 1787		Freetown, Ma.	** -	--
Chace, Richard S.	Oct. 16, 1827	18	dark	Swansea, Ma.	4	15
Chace, Robert	Aug. 13, 1828	15	dark	Camden, Me.	4	15
Chace, Russell P.	June 11, 1849	34	dark	Johnston, R.I.	5	18
Chace, Stephen	1798-1799	May 3, 1769		Somerset, Ma.	** -	--
Chace, Stephen	Sept. 12, 1801	19	dark	Smithfield, R.I.	2	27
Chace, Sterry G.	Feb. 9, 1849	30	light	Coventry, R.I.	5	18
Chace, Thomas	Aug. 1, 1801	19	light	Providence, R.I.	2	27
Chace, William Stillwell	Sept. 7, 1849	18	light	Providence, R.I.	5	18
Chace, William T.	Mar. 2, 1852	33	sandy	New Bedford, Ma.	5	19
Chace, William W.	Apr. 26, 1838	18	dark	Providence, R.I.	5	15
Chadbourne, Theodore	Jan. 4, 1865	18	light	Edgecomb, Me.	6	3
Chadwick, Edmund	June 10, 1805	23	light	Falmouth, Ma.	3	53
Chadwick, Joseph	June 16, 1821	22	light	Bradford, Ma.	-	--

Birth certificate in the Custom House Papers. DOB Sept. 3, 1799.

Chadwick, Thomas	1798-1799	Sept. 6, 1768		Newport, R.I.	** -	--

Jonathan Chadwick swears the above to be true.

*mulatto   **Newport, R. I.

NAME	DATE OF CERTIFICATION	AGE	COMPLEXION	PLACE OF BIRTH	BOOK	PAGE
Chaffee, Asa	Mar. 27, 1815	18	dark	Seekonk, Ma.	4	13
Chaffee, Daniel K., Jr.	Feb. 9, 1849	21	dark	Providence, R.I.	5	18
Chaffee, Hale	Nov. 24, 1809	22	brown	Swansea, Ma.	4	11
Chaffee, Josiah	Apr. 3, 1822	19	light	Woodstock, Conn.	4	14
Chaffee, Nathan M.	Aug. 24, 1849	37	light	Providence, R.I.	5	18
Chafee, Russell	Dec. 28, 1819	24	light	Rehoboth, Ma.	4	13
Chafee, Stephen	Nov. 1, 1828	19	light	Woodstock, Conn.	4	15
Chafee, William	Oct. 31, 1796	31	light	Rehoboth, Ma.	1	8&5
Chally, John	Oct. 20, 1797	28	light	Providence, R.I.	1	8
Chaloner, Charles	Jan. 16, 1804	32	black	Newport, R.I.	3	5
Chaloner, Francis	Dec. 13, 1806	27	black	Newport, R.I.	4	11
Chambers, Dublin	Dec. 29, 1809	15	black	Charleston, S.C.	4	11
Chambers, George	Aug. 15, 1832	52	black	Dover, Del.	5	14
Chambers, Harvey R.	Mar. 18, 1825	14	light	Providence, R.I.	4	14
Chambers, James, Jr.	July 9, 1817	18	light	Providence, R.I.	4	13
Chambers, James, H.	Nov. 13, 1840	19	light	Providence, R.I.	5	16
Chambers, Joseph	Jan. 21, 1818	16	light	Providence, R.I.	4	13
Chambers, Reuben B.	June 10, 1819	16	dark	West Haddam, Conn.	4	13
Chambers, Samuel	July 20, 1820	12	light	Providence, R.I.	4	14
Chambers, Wanton	Sept. 1, 1849	23	light	Providence, R.I.	5	18
Chambers, William J.	Mar. 15, 1855	19	light	Providence, R.I.	5	20
Champlin, Alex H.	Mar. 3, 1849	20	light	No. Prov., R.I.	5	18
Champlin, Fred	Oct. 17, 1861	25	dark	Old Lyme, Conn.	6	3
Champlin, Henry, Jr.	Apr. 28, 1852	19	light	Warren, R.I.	5	19
Champlin,,John	Apr. 9, 1810	23	dark	So. Kingston, R.I.	4	11
Champlin, John	Dec. 13, 1819	25	light	Norwich, Conn.	4	13
Champlin, John	Feb. 29, 1837	19	dark	Smithfield, R.I.	5	15
Champlin, John	Oct. 17, 1861	24	dark	Old Lyme, Conn.	6	3
Champlin, John K.	May 29, 1823	27	ruddy	So. Kingston, R.I.	4	14
Champlin, Orlando	Oct. 25, 1849	29	light	New London, Conn.	5	18
Champlin, Primus	Oct. 29, 1801	21	black	Manvil, Conn.	2	40
Champlin, W.H.H.	Dec. 24, 1858	18	mulatto	Providence R.I.	6	3
Champlin, Watson	May 20, 1811	27	dark	Exeter, R.I.	4	12
Champlin, William	June 16, 1815	21	light	So. Kingston, R.I.	4	13
Champlin, William	Oct. 18, 1849	40	light	Exeter, R.I.	5	18
Champney, Samuel	May 27, 1830	28	light	Boston, Ma.	5	14
Chandler, Benjamin T.	Apr. 15, 1833	18	black	Providence, R.I.	5	14

REGISTER OF SEAMEN'S PROTECTION

NAME	DATE OF CERTIFICATION	AGE	COMPLEXION	PLACE OF BIRTH	BOOK	PAGE
Chandler, Norman	June 14, 1811	21	light	Northbury[Northborough?], Ma.[4]		[12]
Chandler, William	Sept. 6, 1817	13	dark	Providence, R.I.	4	13
Chandler, William H.	June 26, 1849	31	light	Promfret, Conn.	5	18
Channing, Henry	1798-1799	Sept. 24, 1784		Newport, R.I.	* -	--
Chaples, Charles	Sept. 10, 1861	25	light	St. George, Me.	6	3
Chapman, Amos	Dec. 15, 1815	30	light	Scituate, R.I.	4	13
Chapman, Syria	Nov. 10, 1823	24	light	Cranston, R.I.	4	14
Chapman, William R.	Mar. 27, 1815	19	light	Cranston, R.I.	4	13
Chappell, Scranton	1798-1799	Dec. 14, 1750		So. Kingston, R.I.	* -	--
Chappell, Scranton	1798-1799	Jan. 25, 1780		So. Kingston, R.I.	* -	--
Chappell, Simon	1798-1799	Apr. 17, 1782		Newport, R.I.	* -	--
Cahppotin, Leon	Jan. 16, 1824	19	light	Boston, Ma.	4	14
Chard, James J.	Sept. 6, 1842	22	dark	New York, N.Y.	5	16
Cahrles, William	June 22, 1836	19	dark	New Orleans, La.	5	15
Chase, Abner	1798-1799	Mar. 13, 1771		Nantucket, Ma.	* -	--
Chase, Charles	Mar. 14, 1815	19	light	Somerset, Ma.	4	12
Chase, Ezra, Jr.	1798-1799	Sept. 12, 1778		Swansea, Ma.	* -	--
Chase, George	Jan. 18, 1860	31	dark	New Bedford, Ma.	6	3
Chase, Hail	Dec. 29, 1830	23	light	Swansea, Ma.	5	14
Chase, Holder	June 23, 1810	25	light	Portsmouth, R.I.	4	12
Chase, James	Mar. 18, 1825	16	dark	Portsmouth, R.I.	4	14
Chase, Jason	Apr. 24, 1804	28	light	Harwich, Ma.	3	5
Chase, Jencks	July 13, 1804	20	light	Swansea, Ma.	3	6
Chase, John, Jr.	Nov. 4, 1809	22	light	Clairmont, N.H.	4	11
Chase, Jonathan	July 12, 1819	32	dark	Edgecombe, Me.	4	13
Chase, Matthew	1798-1799	Aug. 7, 1776		Swansea, Ma.	* -	--
Chase, Neri	Mar. 7, 1815	21	dark	Harwich, Ma.	4	12
Chase, Peleg	Nov. 30, 1801	23	light	Swansea, Ma.	2	40
Chase, Philip	Feb. 14, 1806	19	dark	Swansea, Ma.	3	61
Chase, Remark	June 7, 1834	17	dark	Harwich, Ma.	5	15
Chase, Richard	1798-1799	July 18, 1778		Harwich, Ma.	* -	--
Chase, Weston	1798-1799	Dec. 16, 1780		Somerset, Ma.	* -	--
Chatman, Pero	June 27, 1809	22	black	Exeter, R.I.	4	11
Chatterton, Isaac	July 12, 1831	26	light	Duchess Co., N.Y.	5	14
Chedel, Daniel	Dec. 10, 1814	19	light	Providence, R.I.	4	12
Chedel, George	Mar. 7, 1857	57	fair	Pomfret, Vt.	5	44
Chedel, John, Jr.	Dec. 14, 1816	23	dark	Providence, R.I.	4	13

*Newport, R.I.

REGISTER OF SEAMEN'S PROTECTION

Page 58

NAME	DATE OF CERTIFICATION	AGE	COMPLEXION	PLACE OF BIRTH	BOOK	PAGE
Cheese, Henry	Oct. 30, 1833	41	black	Warwick, R.I.	5	14
Cheese, James	Nov. 1, 1828	21	black	Warwick, R.I.	4	15
Chenevard, William	June, 26, 1819	16	light	Hartford, Conn.	4	13
Cheney, James	Jan. 18, 1856	20	light	Portland, Me.	5	44
Cherris, David	Nov. 14, 1803	26	light	Salem, Ma.	2	48
Chesley, William P.	Nov. 5, 1844	21	light	Londonderry, N.H.	5	17
Chetto, Francis	Oct. 13, 1828	19	yellow*	So. Kingston, R.I.	4	15
Chickering, Zachariah	Jan. 11, 1816	20	light	Andover, Ma.	4	13
Child, Adam	Nov. 7, 1805	34	black	Newport, R.I.	3	61
Child, George Son of Hail and Almy Child. Birth certificate in Custom House Papers.	Apr. 14, 1821	18	light	Warren, R.I.	-	--
Child, James	May 13, 1822	15	light	Warren, R.I.	4	14
Child, James	June 27, 1825	19	light	Warren, R.I.	4	14
Child, Jered	Jan. 4, 1805	24	dark	Pomfret, Conn.	3	52
Child, Nathan Son of Hail and Almy Child. Birth certificate in Custom House Papers. DOB Jan. 21, 1799	Mar. 23, 1821	22	light	Warren, R.I.	-	--
Child, Samuel C.	Nov. 24, 1843	21	dark	Baltimore, Md.	5	17
Child, Samuel S.	June 3, 1806	18	dark	Woodstock, Conn.	3	65
Childs, Benjamin	Nov. 3, 1826	17	light	No. Kingston, R.I.	4	14
Childs, Robert	Sept. 16, 1847	19	dark	Baltimore, Md.	5	17
Childs, William	Aug. 26, 1807	21	light	Falmouth, Ma.	4	11
Chillson, George	Nov. 7, 1806	21	light	Providence, R.I.	4	11
Chipman, Allen W.	Jan. 2, 1835	19	dark	Warwick, R.I.	5	15
Chippey, Moses	Oct. 16, 1837	23	black	Phila., Pa.	5	15
Choate, John James	June 7, 1833	22	dark	Gloucester, Ma.	5	14
Christianson, Christian H.	Sept. 15, 1826	30	light	Arrondall, Norway	4	14
Christie, Alexander	Nov. 18, 1797	25	dark	Boston, Ma.	1	31
Christophers, Cato	Apr. 11, 1809	23	black	East Haddam, Conn.	4	11
Christopher, William	Sept. 12, 1845	29	dark	New York, N.Y.	5	17
Church, Benjamin	1798-1799	Oct. 5, 1775		Newport, R.I. **	-	--
Church, Benjamin B.	Sept. 8, 1800	25	dark	Newport, R.I.	2	27
Church, Charles	Apr. 19, 1819	24	light	Charlestown, R.I.	4	13
Church, Charles	June 26, 1841	36	light	Providence, R.I.	5	16
Church, James	Sept. 15, 1799	25	light	Providence, R.I.	2	3
Church, Jeremiah	July 27, 1803	17	black	Providence, R.I.	2	40
Church, John	Sept. 3, 1796	20	dark	No. Prov., R.I.	1	2
Church, Joseph	Dec. 21, 1825	21	ruddy	Charlestown, R.I.	4	14
Church, Luke	Nov. 26, 1828	26	dark	Charlestown, R.I.	4	15

*mulatto   **Newport, R.I.

NAME	DATE OF CERTIFICATION	AGE	COMPLEXION	PLACE OF BIRTH	BOOK	PAGE
Church, Nathaniel	May 10, 1800	31	dark	Little Compton, R.I.	2	27
Church, Prince	Feb. 26, 1839	20	black	Providence, R.I.	5	15
Church, Sherman	Apr. 2, 1841	16	light	Derby, Conn.	5	16
Church, Thomas	Dec. 1, 1806	21	yellow*	Dartmouth, Ma.	4	11
Church, Thomas L.	June 24, 1836	38	dark	Fairfield, Conn.	5	15
Church, William, Jr.	Oct. 2, 1819	19	light	Providence, R.I.	4	13
Church, Wm. 2d	June 28, 1841	36	light	Bristol, R.I.	5	16
Clark, Benjamin	Mar. 29, 1853	20	light	Providence, R.I.	5	20
Clark, Charles	Sept. 12, 1821	26	light	Hopkinton, R.I.	4	14
Clark, Charles G.	April 1, 1850	29	dark	Bristol, R.I.	5	19
Clark, Daniel	Dec. 21, 1796	27	dark	Sudbury, Ma.	1	8
Clark, Daneil	Dec. 2, 1805	17	dark	Hudson, N.Y.	3	61
Clark, Daniel	June 5, 1857	18	light	Providence, R.I.	5	44
Clark, Eli	Mar. 11, 1797	29	dark	Phila., Pa.	1	8
Clark, George	Dec. 8, 1810	20	yellow*	Newport, R.I.	4	12
Clark, George	Dec. 9, 1812	19	light	Warren, R.I.	4	12
Clark, George L.	July 16, 1841	17	dark	Providence, R.I.	5	16
Clark, James	Oct. 12, 1818	30	dark	Harwich, Ma.	4	13
Clark, James	Nov. 22, 1833	23	black	New York, N.Y.	5	14
Clark, James	Nov. 27, 1854	23	fair	Providence, R.I.	5	20
Clark, James	Sept. 26, 1857	23	light	Phila., Pa.	6	3
Clark, John	Nov. 12, 1796	25	dark	Newburyport, Ma.	1	8
Clark, John	Feb. 27, 1798	30	dark	Baltimore, Md.	1	31
Clark, John	Sept. 2, 1856	24	fair	----	5	44
Clark, John	Mar. 30, 1857	24	dark	New Orleans, La.	5	44
Clark, John C.	Oct. 8, 1849	20	light	Providence, R.I.	5	18
Clark, John J.	Nov. 5, 1849	30	dark	Bristol, R.I.	5	18
Clark, John L.	May 24, 1822	17	dark	Providence, R.I.	4	14
Clark, Jonathan	Oct. 8, 1831	21	dark	Seekonk, Ma.	5	14
Clark, Joseph	May 1, 1799	25	dark	Smithfield, R.I.	2	3
Clark, Joseph	June 5, 1843	37	black	Salem, N.J.	5	17
Clark, Joseph	Oct. 8, 1858	28	florid	Salem, Ma.	6	3
Clark, Jupiter	July 16, 1818	29	black	Ashford, Conn.	4	12
Clark, Lafayett	Apr. 23, 1855	20	light	Belfast, Me.	5	20
Clark, Leonard A.	May 29, 1856	21	dark	Wrentham, Ma.	5	44
Clark, Mark	Dec. 5, 1857	29	black	Rahway, N.J.	6	3
Clark, Michael	Aug. 15, 1865	22	light	New Haven, Conn.	6	3

*mulatto

NAME	DATE OF CERTIFICATION	AGE	COMPLEXION	PLACE OF BIRTH	BOOK	PAGE
** Clark, Richard	May 31, 1805	14	dark	Baltimore, Md.	3	53
Clark, Solomon, Jr.	Aug. 9, 1809	25	light	West Hampton, Ma.	4	11
Clark, Stephen	Sept. 29, 1797	21	light	Plainfield, Conn.	1	8
Clark, Thomas	May 24, 1804	25	light	No. Hampton, N.H.	3	5
Clark, Thomas	July 8, 1845	29	ruddy	New York, N.Y.	5	17
Clark, William	Mar. 1, 1797	19	light	No. Kingston, R.I.	1	8
Clark, William	July 20, 1805	36	dark	Baltimore, Md.	3	53
Clark, William	Dec. 16, 1829	22	light	So. Kingston, R.I.	5	14
Clark, William	Nov. 20, 1844	40	dark	New Shoreham, R.I.	5	17
Clark, William H.	Dec. 13, 1832	15	light	Providence, R.I.	5	14
Clark, Willis	Oct. 12, 1820	14	ruddy	Kingston, N.Y.	4	14
Clarke, Abel Marsh	1798-1799	Apr. 27, 1780		Newport, R.I.	* -	--
Clarke, Ambrose W.	Feb. 4, 1853	20	dark	Cumberlanc, R.I.	5	20
Clarke, Andrew	March 29, 1856	23	dark	Smithfield, R.I.	5	44
Clarke, Benjamin	1798-1799	Aug. 11, 1774		Portsmouth, R.I.	*-	--

Joseph Clarke of Newport, R.I. Swears the above to be true.

NAME	DATE OF CERTIFICATION	AGE	COMPLEXION	PLACE OF BIRTH	BOOK	PAGE
Clarke, Braman	Feb. 23, 1822	18	light	Providence, R.I.	4	14
Clarke, Charles	Mar. 8, 1853	21	light	Boston, Ma.	5	20
Clarke, Edward J.	Feb. 11, 1850	21	light	Norwich, Conn.	5	19
Clarke, Ephraim	June 6, 1838	29	dark	Phila., Pa.	5	15
Clarke, Grinnell	Dec. 22, 1827	22	light	Newport, R.I.	4	15
Clarke, Henry	1798-1799	Oct. 9, 1772		Newport, R.I.	*-	--
Clarke, Henry B.	Feb. 11, 1850	22	light	Cranston, R.I.	5	19
Clarke, James B.	Oct. 2, 1822	17	light	Providence, R.I.	4	14
Clarke, Jesse	July 22, 1836	38	dark	Freetown, Ma.	5	15
Clarke, John	June 12, 1815	21	fresh	Johnston, R.I.	4	13
Clarke, John	July 3, 1804	23	black	So. Kingston, R.I.	3	6
Clarke, John	Mar. 17, 1851	23	light	Manchester, N.H.	5	19
Clarke, John U.	July 16, 1855	19	light	Westerly, R.I.	5	20
Clarke, Joseph	1798-1799	Aug. 12, 1769		Newport, R.I.	*-	--
Clarke, Joseph T.	Aug. 12, 1837	30	light	Newport, R.I.	5	15
Clarke, Joshua	Aug. 31, 1849	28	light	No. Kingston, R.I.	5	18
Clarke, Lathan	1798-1799	Aug. 31, 1774		Middletown, R.I.	*-	--
Clarke, Nicholas	Nov. 30, 1839	22	light	So. Kingston, R.I.	5	16
Clarke, Riley	Apr. 3, 1820	25	light	Middletown, Conn.	4	14
**Clark, Robert	Feb. 3, 1801	22	light	New York, N.Y.	2	27
Clarke, Samuel	1798-1799	Oct. 9, 1780		Providence, R.I.	*-	--

** out of order.

*Newport, R. I.

NAME	DATE OF CERTIFICATION	AGE	COMPLEXION	PLACE OF BIRTH	BOOK	PAGE
Clarke, Samuel	Aug. 14, 1819?	20	light	Brewster, Ma.	4	13
Clarke, Samuel, Jr.	May 12, 1828	16	light	Bath, Me.	4	15
Clarke, Thomas	Nov. 27, 1797	22	light	Providence, R.I.	1	31
Clarke, William	June 16, 1798	23	dark	Providence, R.I.	2	3
Clarke, William	May 21, 1833	33	dark	West Cambridge, Ma.	5	14
Clarke, William	Feb. 26, 1850	26	dark	New York,N.Y.	5	19
Clarke, William H.	May 18, 1821	13	dark	Bristol, R.I.	-	--

Sworn statement of Benjamin Tilley of Bristol in The Custom House Papers. DOB-Mar. 19, 1808

NAME	DATE OF CERTIFICATION	AGE	COMPLEXION	PLACE OF BIRTH	BOOK	PAGE
Clarke, William N.	Nov. 30, 1849	49	light	Richmond, R.I.	5	19
Clason, Jacob	July 21, 1804	22	light	Hampton, Va.	3	6
Cleary, Wm. C.	May 29, 1855	28	light	Charlestown, Ma.	5	20
Cleavland, Albert	Aug. 31, 1849	44	light	Franklin, Ma.	5	18
Cleavland, John Rawson	July 30, 1804	22	light	Providence, R.I.	3	6
Cleavland, Seth	Sept. 14, 1798	18	light	Providence, R.I.	2	3
Cleavland, Seth, Jr.	Apr. 15, 1819	14	light	Providence, R.I.	4	13
Clegg, John W.	Dec. 22, 1823	21	light	Chelsea, Conn. [Norwich]	4	14
Clement, Alonzo F.	Aug. 5, 1864	21	light	Sandwich, Ma.	6	3
Clement, Henry	June 13, 1834	19	light	Norton, Ma.	5	15
Clement, Laprelate	Mar. 17, 1835	17	light	Norton, Ma.	5	15
Clements, Calvin	Jan. 26, 1854	18	light	Glocester, Ma.	5	20
Clements, John H.	Feb. 15, 1854	19	light	Ponobscot, Ma.	5	20
Clendening, Robert	Dec. 27, 1854	31	light	Baltimore, Md.	. 5	20
Clerier, Samuel W.	Aug. 9, 1855	24	light	Belfast, Me.	5	20
Cleveland, John Rawson	Apr. 10, 1798	16	light	Providence, R.I.	1&2	31&3*
Cleveland, Seth	Nov. 25, 1797	18	light	Providence, R.I.	1	31
Cleveland, Seth	Dec. 18, 1799	19	light	Providence, R.I.	2	3
Cleveland, Seth	Aug. 6, 1806	26	light	Providence. R.I.	3	32
Clifford, Abraham S.	Oct. 22, 1796	21	dark	Providence, R.I.	1	8&4
Clifford, Abraham Smith	Nov. 5, 1803	27	dark	Providence, R.I.	2	40
Clifford, Benjamin P.	July 22, 1848	14	dark	Searsport, Me.	5	18
Clifford, Henry E.	July 22, 1848	19	light	Searsport, Me.	5	18
Clifford, Joseph P.	Aug. 9, 1815	17	light	Providence, R.I.	4	13
Clifford, William	Oct. 11, 1805	40	black	Phila., Pa.	3	53
Clifton, Dennis	Nov. 11, 1818	19	light	Rochester, Ma.	4	13
Clough, James	Nov. 2, 1844	20	light	Topsham, Me.	5	17
Clough, Joseph J.	Nov. 2, 1841	22	dark	Sangersville, Me.	5	16
Coats, John	July 22, 1803	23	dark	Phila., Pa.	2	40

*Book 1, page 31. Book 2, page 3.

NAME	DATE OF CERTIFICATION	AGE	COMPLEXION	PLACE OF BIRTH	BOOK	PAGE
Coats, Luther	Oct. 2, 1801	16	dark	Northampton, Ma.	2	27
Cobb, Andrew P.	Aug. 1, 1864	18	light	Weir Village, Ma.	6	3
Cobb, Edward	Mar. 16, 1842	30	light	Boston, Ma.	5	16
Cobber, Henry	Feb. 24, 1845	31	light	Brunswick, Me.	5	17
Coburn, Cornwell	Mar. 12, 1834	26	black	Dracut, Ma.	5	15
Cockrane, Alexander	July 3, 1843	27	light	Eastport, Me.	5	17
Cochran, James	Oct. 1, 1831	23	light	Baltimore, Md.	5	14
Cochran, James B.	Sept. 2, 1839	27	light	No. Providence, R.I.	5	16
Codding, Caleb	Nov. 4, 1809	30	florid	Taunton, Ma.	4	11
Codling, John	Mar. 15, 1853	23	light	New York, N.Y.	5	20
Codner, John	Mar. 24, 1810	20	brown	Coventry, R.I.	4	11
Cody, Samuel	Oct. 31, 1796	21	dark	Hopkinton, Ma.	1	8&5
Coe, Edwin W.	Apr. 24, 1841	34	light	Prescott, Me.	5	16
Coffin, Brown, Jr.	June 30, 1810	20	light	Nantucket, Ma.	4	12
Coffin, Elisha	1798-1799	Nov. 26, 1779		Nantucket, Ma.	* -	--
Coffin, Elisha	Nov. 28, 1797	39	dark	Nantucket, Ma.	1	31
Coffin, John I.	Mar. 8, 1854	21	light	Springfield, Ma.	5	20
Coffin, Peleg	Apr. 6, 1815	19	light	Yarmouth, Ma.	4	13
Coffin, William	June 18, 1814	24	light	Edgartown, Ma.	4	12
Coggeshall, Charles S.	July 12, 1809	19	light	Providence. R.I.	4	11
Coggeshall, David	Sept. 26, 1796	18	dark	Warwick, R.I.	1	3
Coggeshall, David	Oct. 4, 1798	25	dark	E. Greenwich, R.I.	2	3
Coggeshall, Freegift	Mar. 21, 1815	18	light	Milford, Conn.	4	13
Coggeshall, George	Dec. 9, 1803	24	dark	E. Greenwich, R.I.	2	23
Coggeshall, George P.	June 21, 1804	19	light	Newport, R.I.	3	6
Coggeshall, George R.	July 23, 1841	15	dark	Providence, R.I	5	16
Coggeshall, Joseph	Aug. 16, 1803	23	light	Warwick, R.I.	2	40
Coggeshall, Pearce	Jan. 2, 1798	30	dark	Warwick, R.I.	1	31
Coggeshall, Royal	Aug. 23, 1831	29	light	E. Greenwich, R.I.	5	14
Cogshall, Thomas	Sept. 18, 1832	18	dark	Warwick, R.I.	5	14
Coghill, Daniel	June 11, 1851	26	light	Providence, R.I	5	19
Coghill, Thomas	Nov. 30, 1853	25	light	Providence, R.I.	5	20
Cogswell, Rowland	Mar. 1, 1834	36	dark	Warwick, R.I.	5	15
Coit, John, Jr.	1798-1799	Aug. 7, 1781		Newport, R.I.	* -	--
Colbey, John D.	Oct. 29, 1827	20	dark	Berkley, Ma.	4	15
Colburn, Eben	Apr. 10, 1834	29	light	Yarmouth, Ma.	5	15
Colcard, William D.	June 6, 1838	18	dark	Prospect, Me.	5	15

*Newport, R. I.

NAME	DATE OF CERTIFICATION	AGE	COMPLEXION	PLACE OF BIRTH	BOOK	PAGE
Cole, Allin or Allen	Oct. 12, 1796	25	light	Rehoboth, Ma.	1	4
Cole, Allen	Mar. 15, 1852	28	black	Washington, D.C.	5	19
Cole, Edmund	Dec. 2, 1852	34	light	Warren, R.I.	5	19
Cole, George	May 5, 1815	16	dark	Providence, R.I.	4	13
Cole, George A.	Dec. 15, 1827	18	light	Scituate, R.I.	4	15
Cole, Jacob	July 21, 1803	30	dark	Boston, Ma.	2	40
Cole, Jacob	Apr. 2, 1798	25	dark	Boston, Ma.	1&2	31&3*
Cole, James	July 2, 1817	21	light	Providence, R.I.	4	13
Cole, James	Dec. 15, 1853	19	light	Eastport, Me.	5	20
Cole, John	Dec. 31, 1799	16	light	Worcester, Conn.	2	27
Cole, John	Oct. 19, 1821	16	light	Rochester, Ma.	4	14
Cole, John G.	Oct, 24, 1849	33	light	Boston, Ma.	5	18
Cole, John H.	Aug. 31, 1849	24	light	Warwick, R.I.	5	18
Cole, Lockwood	Sept. 12, 1796	26	dark	Warwick, R.I.	1	2
Cole, Nathaniel	Nov. 30, 1799	16	light	Warwick, R.I.	2	3
Cole, Samuel	Aug. 28, 1807	37	light	Phila., Pa.	4	11
Cole, Soloman	Dec. 22, 1830	17	black	No. Prov., R.I.	5	14
Cole, William	Nov. 13, 1809	18	dark	Cranston, R.I.	4	11
Cole, Wm. N.	June 25, 1844	19	dark	Seekonk, Ma.	5	17
Cole, William W.	Jan. 13, 1855	23	light	Bucksport, Me,	5	20
Coleman, Benjamin	Oct. 31, 1796	40	light	Nantucket, Ma.	1	8&5
Coleman, Ebenezer T.	Dec. 5, 1833	16	light	Falmouth, Ma.	5	15
Coleman, Jesse B.	Aug. 12, 1840	19	light	Providence, R.I.	5	16
Coleman, Nathaniel	May 31, 1797	19	light	Nine Partners, N.Y.	1	8
Coleman, Peter	May 14, 1811	21	black	Albany, N.Y.	4	12
Coleman, Solomon	Dec. 16, 1803	19	dark	Coventry, Conn.	2	48
Colgem, Edward	Oct. 9, 1850	41	dark	Providence, R.I.	5	19
Collier, John	Nov. 15, 1847	27	black	Somersett Co., Md.	5	17
Collingwood, John H.	Jan. 5, 1858	18	light	Cranston, R.I.	6	3
Collins, Alpheus	Jan. 25, 1830	29	light	Warwick, R.I.	5	14
Collins, Benjamin	July 19, 1845	23	dark	Coventry, R.I.	5	17
Collins, Benjamin	Sept. 15, 1825	25	dark	Southboro, Ma.	4	14
Collins, Caleb	Mar. 13, 1811	23	light	E. Greenwich, R.I.	4	12
Collins, Daniel	Dec. 10, 1812	17	light	Providence, R.I.	4	12
Collins, George	Mar. 11, 1815	20	light	Cranston, R.I.	4	12
Collins, Henry	Nov. 24, 1830	21	light	Newport, R.I.	5	14
Collins, James	June 6, 1853	22	light	Fall River, Ma.	5	20

*Book 1, page 31. Book 2, page 3.

NAME	DATE OF CERTIFICATION	AGE	COMPLEXION	PLACE OF BIRTH	BOOK	PAGE
Collins, James	Nov. 9, 1846	27	fair	Louisvill, Ky.	5	17
Collins, James W.	Aug. 21, 1840	24	dark	Tiverton, R.I.	5	16
Collins, Jeremiah	Dec. 21, 1805	25	Cranston, R.I.		3	61
Collins, John	Mar. 18, 1851	21	light	Eastport, Me.	5	19
Collins, John	Sept. 27, 1843	23	dark	New York, N.Y.	5	17
Collins, Joseph	Nov. 14, 1835	45	mulatto	New York, N.Y.	5	15
Collins, Rufus	Dec. 6, 1805	23	dark	Scituate, R.I.	3	61
Collins, Samuel	June 5, 1798	17	light	Newport, R.I.	2	3
Collins, Tillinghast	Apr. 10, 1798	25	dark	Cranston, R.I.	1&2	31&3
Collins, Tillinghast	Apr. 18, 1807	34	light	Cranston, R.I.	4	11
Collins, William	July 19, 1853	30	light	Providence, R.I.	5	20
Collins, William	Nov. 1, 1836	33	dark	Boston, Ma.	5	15
Colman, William	June 8, 1799	28	black	Rehoboth, Ma.	2	3
Colson, Joseph	Nov. 7, 1836	21	light	Bucksport, Me.	5	15
Colson, Josiah	Sept. 28, 1858	30	fair	Calais, Me.	6	3
Colstone, David	Oct. 23, 1855	20	florid	Phila., Pa.	5	20
Colvin, Carpenter	Sept. 12, 1801	19	dark	Scituate, R.I.	2	27
Colvin, Colonel S.	Mar. 28, 1848	25	dark	Coventry, R.I.	5	17
Colvin, Dennis	Nov. 5, 1849	23	light	Coventry, R.I.	5	18
Colvin, James, Jr.	Nov. 26, 1849	39	light	Scituate, R.I.	5	18
Colvin, Nehemiah	May 26, 1835	21	light	Providence, R.I.	5	15
Colwell, Cyrus	June 28, 1823	17	light	Glocester, R.I.	4	14
Comee, Benjamin	June 2, 1797	23	dark	Cambridge, Ma.	1	8
Cimmins, James	July 13, 1805	24	dark	Baltimore, Md.	3	53
Comstock, Benjamin W.	June 17, 1850	42	light	Provdence, R.I.	5	19
Comstock, Charles	Nov. 30, 1841	18	light	Webster, Ma.	5	16
Comstock, Ephrain	Mar. 16, 1812	16	light	Providence, R.I.	4	12
Comstock, John	Dec. 23, 1796	20	light	Smithfield, R.I.	1	8
Comstock, John	Nov. 10, 1841	17	light	Burrillville, R.I.	5	16
Comstock, John S.	Aug. 20, 1841	19	light	New London, Conn.	5	16
Comstock, Richard W.	Oct. 22, 1850	17	dark	Providence, R.I.	5	19
Comstock, Samuel	Oct. 11, 1810	31	light	Warren, R.I.	4	12
Comstock, Sylvester	Mar. 12, 1853	16	light	Cumberland, R.I.	5	20
Comstock, Tristam B.	July 2, 1845	17	light	Coventry, R.I.	5	17
Comstock, William	Mar. 7, 1806	18	light	No. Prov., R.I.	3	65
Comstock, William	Dec. 10, 1823	17	dark	Dedham, Ma.	4	14
Condy, Samuel A.	Sept. 11, 1811	19	light	Boston, Ma.	4	12

*Book 1, page 31. Book 2, page 3.

NAME	DATE OF CERTIFICATION	AGE	COMPLEXION	PLACE OF BIRTH	BOOK	PAGE
Condy, Thomas H., Jr.	July 17, 1810	19	dark	Warwick, R.I.	4	12
Condy, Thomas Hollis	Dec. 2, 1796	38	dark	Boston, Ma.	1	8
Cone, Giles	Oct. 27, 1804	25	dark	Haddam, Conn.	3	6
Cone, Giles	Oct. 26, 1805	25	dark	Haddam, Conn.	3	61
Cone, John	Mar. 24, 1810	25	yellow*	Norwich, Conn.	4	11
Cone, Joshua	Nov. 1, 1803	22	dark	Weathersfield, Conn.	2	40
Congdon, Alsbury	Oct. 23, 1801	19	black	So. Kingstown, R.I.	2	27
Congdon, Benjamin	Mar. 7, 1804	21	yellow*	No. Kingstown, R.I.	3	5
Congdon, Bristol	Dec. 10, 1799	19	black	Charlestown, R.I.	2	3
Congdon, Bristol	May 18, 1815	33	black	Charlestown, R.I.	4	13
Congdon, Cato	Mar. 16, 1799	17	black	No. Kingstown, R.I.	2	3
Congdon, Cato	Apr. 1, 1812	27	black	No. Kingstown, R.I.	4	12
Congdon, Cuff	July 10, 1803	19	black	No. Kingstown, R.I.	2	40
Congdon, George	Jan. 26, 1819	19	fresh	No. Kingstown, R.I.	4	13
Congdon, George	Mar. 3, 1835	20	black	NO. Kingston, R.I.	5	15
Congdon, Henry	July 20, 1816	19	fresh	Exeter, R.I.	4	13
Congdon, Henry	Oct. 23, 1829	26	light	Providence, R.I.	-	--
Congdon, Hodge	June 13, 1810	33	black	Charlestown, R.I.	4	11
Congdon, Isaac	Mar. 4, 1840	35	dark	New Bedford, Ma.	5	16
Congdon, Isaac	Dec. 14, 1844	29	light	New Bedford, Ma.	5	17
Congdon, John	Feb. 22, 1812	21	brown	W. Greenwich, R.I.	4	12
Congdon, John B.	Mar. 23, 1805	19	light	Exeter, R.I.	3	52
Congdon, Jonathan	Jan. 14, 1812	21	brown	Exeter, R.I.	4	12
Congdon, Neptune	Mar. 18, 1806	38	yellow	Charlestown, R.I.	3	65
Congdon, Samuel C.	Mar. 16, 1836	26	black	Providence, R.I.	5	15
Congdon, Thomas	Nov. 7, 1801	19	black	Charlestown, R.I.	2	40
Congdon, Thomas H.	Aug. 13, 1833	18	black	Providence, R.I.	5	14
Congdon, William	May 5, 1815	16	light	Providence, R.I.	4	13
Congdon, William G.	Nov. 9, 1839	22	light	So. Kingstown, R.I.	5	16
Couger, William	June 18, 1811	17	dark	Norwich, Conn.	4	12
Conklin, George B.	Dec. 8, 1828	24	light	Templeton, Ma.	4	15
Conners, Charles	June 7, 1819	19	light	Boston, Ma.	4	13
Connoly, Francis	Mar. 7, 1853	20	light	New York, N.Y.	5	20
Connor, John	Feb. 14, 1852	25	light	Troy, N.Y.	5	19
Conner, Peter O.	Nov. 24, 1857	21	fair	New Orleans, La.	6	3
Conners, Matthew	Sept. 10, 1866	27	dark	Providence, R.I.	6	3
Conover, Samuel	Nov. 29, 1848	44	mulatto	Shrewsbury, N.J.	5	18

*mulatto

NAME	DATE OF CERTIFICATION	AGE	COMPLEXION	PLACE OF BIRTH	BOOK	PAGE
Cook, Amasa	Oct. 21, 1818	20	light	Franklin, Ma.	4	13
Cook, Benoui	Mar. 22, 1800	19	light	Scituate, R.I.	2	27
Cook, Borden	Mar. 24, 1827	23	light	Tiverton, R.I.	4	14
Cook, Bradford	1798-1799	June 15, 1780		Little Compton, R.I. *** -	--
Cook, Christopher	Aug. 21, 1824	27	light	Foster, R.I.	4	14
Cook, Daniel	1798-1799	Nov. 17, 1774		Tiverton, R.I. *** -	--
Cook, Daniel L.	Aug. 9, 1842	21	light	Warwick, R.I.	5	16
Cook, Easton	1798-1799	Sept. 11, 1778		Tiverton, R.I. *** -	--
Cook, Ebenzer	1798-1799	Oct. 30, 1767		New Bedford, Ma. *** -	--
Cook, Edward	June 4, 1800	23	dark	Providence, R.I.	2	27
Cook, Edward	Mar. 21, 1871	34	dark	Providence, R.I.	6	3
Cook, George	1798-1799	June 6, 1773		Portsmouth, R.I.	-	--
Cook, George	Mar. 18, 1825	22	light	Tiverton, R.I.	4	14
Cook, Isaac N.	Oct. 29, 1835	19	light	Templeton, Ma.	5	15
Cook, Isaac N.	Jan. 6, 1843	26	light	Cumberland, R.I.	5	17
Cook, Oliver Warner	1798-1799	--	---	Tiverton, R.I. *** -	--
Cook, Stephen	Nov. 29, 1828	23	light	Tiverton, R.I.	4	15
Cook, Stephen J.	June 18, 1862	26	dark	Tiverton, R.I.	6	3
Cook, William	June 17, 1796	28	dark	Tiverton, R.I.	1	8
Cook, William	May 2, 1827	31	dark	Tiverton, R.I.	4	14
Cook, William	June 2, 1830	38	dark	Cheraw, S.C.	5	14
Cook, William H.	Sept. 28, 1855	28	fair	New Bedford, Ma.	5	20
Cooke, Albert R.	Dec. 9, 1836	17	light	Providence, R.I.	5	15
Cooke, Daniel S.	Nov. 16, 1803	14	dark	Providence, R.I.	2	23
Cooke, Edward	Mar. 11, 1809	33	yellow*	Providence, R.I.	4	11
Cooke, James F.	Nov. 17, 1847	21	light	Cumberland, R.I.	5	17
Cooke, Jeremiah Olney	Aug. 4, 1802	18	light	Providence, R.I.	2	40
Cooke, John Alphonso	Mar. 17,1824	16	light	Portsmouth, R.I.	4	14
Cooke, Joseph C.	Dec. 5, 1836	24	light	Glocester, R.I.	5	15
Cooke, Lyndon A.	Apr. 3, 1817	20	light	Warwick, R.I.	4	13
Cooke, Nicholas, Jr.	Oct. 31, 1803	23	dark	Providence, R.I.	2	40
Cooke, Nicholas K	Apr. 15, 1818	17	light	Coventry, R.I.	4	13
Cooke, Parker	Sept. 11, 1822	20	brown	Troy, Ma. [Fall River]	4	14
Cooke, Thomas D.	Mar. 18, 1815	20	light	Tiverton, R.I.	4	12
Cooley, Chauncey, Jr.	Oct. 8, 1806	15	light	E. Windsor, Conn.	3&4	32&11**

*mulatto

**Book 3, page 32. Book 4, page 11.

***Newport, R. I.

NAME	DATE OF CERTIFICATION	AGE	COMPLEXION	PLACE OF BIRTH	BOOK	PAGE
Cooley, Isaac B.	Oct. 1, 1832	20	light	W. Springfield, Ma.	5	14
Cooley, John	Nov. 13, 1826	36	light	Springfield, Ma.	4	14
Cooley, Lyman	Mar. 22, 1815	17	light	E. Windsor, Conn.	4	13
Cooley, Richard	July 12, 1819	19	light	Norfolk, Va.	4	13
Coombs, Charles A.	June 2, 1849	16	light	Islesboro, Me.	5	18
Coombs, Edwin	July 14, 1856	18	fair	Islesboro, Me.	5	44
Coombs, George H.	Dec. 22, 1849	19	dark	Islesboro, Me.	5	19
Coombs, Pearce	Nov. 22, 1805	31	light	Wareham, Ma.	3	61
Coombs, Samuel	Feb. 16, 1857	22	light	Rockway, N.Y.	5	44
Coombs, Wm. R.	Dec. 22, 1849	49	light	Islesboro, Me.	5	19
Cooper, Daniel	May 17, 1867	25	black	Salem, Ma.	6	3
Cooper, Elliot	Jan. 7, 1818	33	light	Thompson, Conn.	4	13
Cooper, George	May 14, 1798	37	dark	Newport, R.I.	2	3
Cooper, Horace N.	Mar. 5, 1849	25	light	Seekonk, Ma.	5	18
Cooper, Isaac	June 7, 1798	36	black	Norfolk, Va.	2	3
Cooper, James	Sept. 1, 1804	19	black	New York, N.Y.	3	6
Cooper, John	Sept. 30, 1796	22	dark	Portsmouth, N.H.	2	4
Cooper, John	Feb. 1 1798	21	light	Newport, R.I.	1	31
Cooper, John	Dec. 27, 1797	22	dark	New York, N.Y.	1	31
Cooper, John	Feb. 14, 1837	27	light	Phila., Pa.	5	15
Cooper, John, Jr.	Feb. 15, 1806	20	dark	Norfolk, Va.	3	61
Cooper, Larkin A.	Apr. 26, 1850	16	light	Killingly, Conn.	5	19
Cooper, Nathaniel	Oct. 26, 1803	23	light	Rehoboth, Ma.	2	40
Cooper, Philip	Oct. 12, 1820	18	yellow*	Freetown, Ma.	4	14
Cooper, Robert	May 28, 1855	30	light	Baltimore, Md.	5	20
Cooper, Samuel	Nov. 9, 1797	21	dark	Plainfield, Conn.	1	31
Cooper, Samuel Philips	May 20, 1818	17	light	Boston, Ma.	4	13
Cooper, Thomas	Jan. 7, 1851	26	dark	Phila., Pa.	5	19
Cooti, John	Aug. 20, 1842	18	light	Phila., Pa.	5	16
Copeland, Henry M.	Dec. 29, 1846	19	fair	Westfield, Ma.	5	17
Corbatt, Robert	Nov. 12, 1796	48	dark	Cohaset, Ma.	1	8&5
Corbett, James	Aug. 6, 1796	20	light	Bridgewater, Ma.	1	1
Cordra, Celathel	June 14, 1800	20	dark	Somerset, Md.	2	27
Cordra, Celathel	Apr. 25, 1806	24	light	Vienna, Md.	3	65
Corey, Allen	June 6, 1806	16	light	E. Greenwich, R.I.	3	65
Corey, Allen	Sept. 23, 1805	14	light	E. Greenwich, R.I.	3	53

*mulatto

NAME	DATE OF CERTIFICATION	AGE	COMPLEXION	PLACE OF BIRTH	BOOK	PAGE
Corey, Alvin	Oct. 15, 1850	20	light	Scituate, R.I.	5	19
Corey, Benjamin	Dec. 19, 1812	23	light	Providence, R.I.	4	12
Corey, Benjamin C.	Mar. 17, 1815	23	light	No. Kingstown,' R.I.	4	12
Corey, Caleb	Nov. 9, 1797	18	dark	E. Greenwich, R.I.	1	31
Corey, Charles	June 3, 1853	23	light	Phila., Pa.	5	20
Corey, Charles E.	July 29, 1837	18	dark	No. Kingston, R.I.	5	15
Corey, Daniel	Apr. 17, 1815	18	dark	Providence, R.I.	4	13
Corey, Ebenezer H., Jr.	Oct. 10, 1806	19	dark	E. Greenwich, R.I.	4	11
Corey, Greene	June 19, 1811	15	light	Newport, R.I.	4	12
Corey, John	1798-1799	May 10, 1775		Portsmouth, R.I.	*** -	--
**Cory, Mason	Dec. 4, 1833	18	light	Hampton, Conn.	5	14
**Cory, Thomas	Aug. 21, 1835	21	light	Plainfield, Conn.	5	15
Cork, Hercules	Nov. 21, 1854	56	black	Montogomery Co., Md.	5	20
Cornelius, Benjamin	Dec. 12, 1845	25	dark	New York, N.Y.	5	17
Cornell, Anthony	1798-1799	Nov. 6, 1780		---	*** -	--
Cornell, Benjamin	Oct. 24, 1849	31	dark	Coventry, R.I.	5	18
Cornell, Edward Perry	Sept. 29, 1826	19	light	Newport, R.I.	4	14
Cornell, Edwin	Mar. 29, 1828	15	light	Somerset, Ma.	4	15
Cornell, George	1798-1799	July 17, 1779		Portsmouth, R.I.	*** -	--
Cornell, George W.	July 21, 1845	17	fair	New York, N.Y.	5	17
Cornell, Harvey	Oct. 29, 1849	22	dark	Abbington, Pa.	5	18
Cornell, Isaac	Dec. 4, 1833	29	dark	Providence, R.I.	5	14
Cornell, Jeremiah	Mar. 30, 1811	23	light	E. Greenwich, R.I.	4	12
Cornell, Jeremiah B.	Nov. 18, 1835	21	dark	E. Greenwich, R.I.	5	15
Cornell, Oliver	Mar. 13, 1816	21	light	Middletown, R.I.	4	13
Cornell, Oliver, Jr.	Mar. 25, 1812	19	light	Glocester, R.I.	4	12
Cornell, Phillip	Nov. 14, 1803	30	light	Scituate, R.I.	2	48
Cornell, Stephen	Nov. 14, 1803	21	light	Scituate, R.I.	2	48
Cornell, Stephen M.	Dec. 28, 1838	27	light	Cumberland, Me.	5	15
Cornel[l], William	Aug. 1, 1801	22	dark	E. Greenwich, R.I.	2	27
Cornell, William F.	Oct. 18, 1858	23	light	Providence, R.I.	6	3
Cornet, Isaac	Aug. 7, 1833	35	Indian	Plymouth, Ma.	5	14
Cornish, James	Nov. 17, 1836	22	black	Dorchester Co., Md.	5	15
Cornish, Joseph	Jan. 26, 1836	17	black	Warwick, R.I.	5	15
Corp[Corpe], Dean	Oct. 26, 1799	25	light	Warwick, R.I.	2	3

** out of order
***Newport, R.I.

NAME	DATE OF CERTIFICATION	AGE	COMPLEXION	PLACE OF BIRTH	BOOK	PAGE
Corp, Thomas	Mar. 10, 1840	17	light	Providence, R.I. ---	5	16
Corps, Stephen	May 17, 1797	29	light	Providence, R.I.	1	8
Corser, Benjamin, Jr.	Mar. 26, 1841	16	light	New York, N.Y.	5	16
Corsey, Nathaniel	Sept. 12, 1861	35	--	Baltimore, Md.	6	3
Cortney, Dennis	June 5, 1838	29	light	Edgartown, Ma.	5	15
Corwin, Benjamin G.	May 31, 1851	31	light	Riverhead, N.Y.	5	19
Cory, Ebenzer	Nov. 14, 1803	15	dark	E. Greenwich, R.I.	2	48
Cory, Gilbert	Nov. 8, 1810	18	light	Tiverton, R.I.	4	12
Cory, Joseph	June 1, 1809	20	light	Providence, R.I.	4	11
Cory, Mason	Dec. 4, 1833	18	light	Hampton, Conn.	5	14
Cory, Thomas	Aug. 21, 1835	21	light	Plainfield, Conn.	5	15
Corzon, Benjamin	June 1, 1835	20	dark	Boston, Ma.	5	15
Cosgrove, Michael	Aug. 1, 1842	18	light	Boston, Ma.	5	16
Cossy, Henry	Nov. 6, 1837	21	black	Hartford, Conn.	5	15
Costello, Michael	Mar. 5, 1862	21	light	Eastport, Me.	6	3
Coster, Joseph D.	Sept. 29, 1831	17	light	Providence, R.I.	5	14
Costley, John	Sept. 10, 1850	26	dark	Eastport, Me.	5	19
Coswell, William	Nov. 12, 1835	23	dark	Merdith, N.H.	5	15
Cottingham, Robert	Apr. 26, 1850	21	light	Newtown, Md.	5	19
Cotton, Benjamin R.	May 4, 1829	24	light	Freetown, Ma.	5	14
Cotton, Geo. B.	Oct. 1, 1844	22	light	Seekonk, Ma.	5	17
Cotton, John J.	June 5, 1838	23	light	Boston, Ma.	5	15
Cotton, Sylvanus P.	Mar. 13, 1815	17	light	Nantucket, Ma.	4	12
Cottrell, Jesse	Oct. 25, 1823	22	dark	Jamestown, R.I.	4	14
Cottrell,, Pero	Mar. 28, 1797	27	black	Exeter, R.I.	1	8
Cottrell, Samuel A.	Oct. 31, 1833	19	dark	So. Kingston, R.I.	5	14
Couillard, Uriah	Dec. 26, 1823	14	light	Frankfort, Me.	4	14
Courtis, William, Jr.	Sept. 7, 1803	28	light	Marblehead, Ma.	2	40
Courtney, James	Sept. 6, 1858	23	fair	Fall River, Ma.	6	3
Cousins, Abraham	Mar. 12, 1853	22	light	Brooklin, Me.	5	20
Couts, Thomas	Mar. 16, 1857	43	light	New Bedford, Ma.	5	44
Covell, Joseph S.	May 20, 1839	21	light	No. Provi., R.I.	5	16
Covell, Thomas Supposed to be foreign.	Mar. 24, 1810	45	light	Wellfleet, Ma.	4	11
Cowan, William	July 6, 1858	21	light	Dist. of Columbia	6	3
Coward, William	June 3, 1805	21	light	Washington, N.C.	3	53
Cowdrey, Thomas	APR. 7, 1840	54	light	Norwich, Conn.	5	16

NAME	DATE OF CERTIFICATION	AGE	COMPLEXION	PLACE OF BIRTH	BOOK	PAGE
Cowan, Wm. L.	July 20, 1852	27	dark	Cleveland, Ohio	5	19
Cowell, Thomas	Apr. 19, 1836	21	light	Seekonk, Ma.	5	15
Cowell, Thomas	Sept. 3, 1846	29	dark	London, Great Britain	5	17
Cowen, William	June 24, 1839	19	light	Eastport, Me.	5	16
Cowing, Seth Williams	Feb. 2, 1850	21	light	Dighton, Ma.	5	19
Cox, Andrew	Oct. 29, 1852	20	light	Wilmington, N.C.	5	19
Coy, John B.	June 12, 1819	14	light	Providence, R.I.	4	13
Coy, Samuel A.	Dec. 18, 1805	15	light	Providence, R.I.	3	61
Coyle, John	Feb. 19, 1859	25	light	Boston, Ma.	6	3
Coyle, Lawrence	Oct. 6, 1848	17	light	Taunton, Ma.	5	18
Coyle, Thomas	Jan. 19, 1854	18	fair	Plymouth, Ma.	5	20
Cozzens, Charles, Jr.	Oct. 2, 1828	22	light	Newport, R.I.	4	15
Cozzens, George	Mar. 8, 1805	18	light	Providence, R.I.	3	52
Cozzens, Henry	Apr. 20, 1799	17	light	Newport, R.I.	2	3
Cozzens, Henry P.	Oct. 12, 1807	38	light	Middletown, R.I.	4	11
Cozzens, John	1798-1799	Sept. 26, 1791		Newport, R.I.	* -	--
Benjamin Cozzens of Newport, R.I. swears the above to be true.						
Cozzens, Joseph, Jr.	1798-1799	Mar. 14, 1782		Newport, R.I.	* -	--
Cozzens, Lewis	Mar. 3, 1804	18	black	Providence, R.I.	3	5
Cozzens, Nathaniel W.	Jan. 10, 1810	20	dark	Providence, R.I.	4	11
Cozzens, Nathaniel W.	Mar. 6, 1812	23	dark	Providence, R.I.	4	12
Cozzens, Peter	1798-1799	Nov. 1, 1782		No. Kingston, R.I.	* -	--
Joseph Cozzens swears the above to be true.						
Cozzens, Robert	June 29, 1833	21	light	Newport, R.I.	5	14
Cozzens, Robert	Apr. 5, 1844	29	light	Newport, R.I.	5	17
Cozzens, Samuel	Nov. 18, 1850	24	light	Brookville, Me.	5	19
Cozzens, Stephen	Dec. 4, 1797	19	dark	Providence, R.I.	1	31
Cozzens, William	July 29, 1800	16	black	Providence, R.I.	2	27
Cozzens, William	Oct. 21, 1801	18	black	Providence, R.I.	2	27
Cozzens, William	Oct. 29, 1803	18	black	Providence, R.I.	2	40
Cozzens, William	Apr. 11, 1809	25	black	Providence, R.I.	4	11
Crabtree, Alfred	Sept. 11, 1830	20	light	Hancock, Me.	5	14
Cracken, Collin M.	Aug. 22, 1803	16	dark	Phila., Pa.	2	40
Craft, Cyrus L.	Nov. 11, 1853	41	light	Providence, R.I.	5	20
Craft, James	Mar. 17, 1845	20	florid	New York, N.Y.	-	--
Craft, John	Mar. 10, 1829	31	light	Newport, R.I.	5	14
Craft, Samuel	Nov. 25, 1805	47	black	Lexington, Ma.	3	61

*Newport, R.I.

REGISTER OF SEAMEN'S PROTECTION

NAME	DATE OF CERTIFICATION	AGE	COMPLEXION	PLACE OF BIRTH	BOOK	PAGE
Craig, Sylvester	Feb. 13, 1849	25	dark	Lyme, N.H.	5	18
Craine, Edwin	Nov. 21, 1853	25	florid	Stoughton, Ma.	5	20
Cram, John	Feb. 25, 1857	22	fair	Sanford, Me.	5	44
Cram, William	June 9, 1841	27	light	Weare, N.H.	5	16
Crandall, Alfred	May 26, 1851	21	light	Warwick, R.I.	5	19
Crandall, Amos	July 24, 1805	21	dark	Westerly, R.I.	3	53
Crandell, Benjamin	Dec. 9, 1825	28	dark	Providence, R.I.	4	14
Crandal[l], Gardner	Dec. 10, 1804	19	light	Westerly, R.I.	3	52
Crandall, James	Nov. 19, 1849	26	light	Hopkinton, R.I.	5	18
Crandall, John	Sept. 18, 1811	24	light	Providence. R.I.	4	12
Crandall, Joseph	Mar. 4, 1807	17	light	Providence, R.I.	4	11
Crandall, Joseph, Jr.	June 16, 1815	44	light	Westerly, R.I.	4	13
Crandall, Joseph D.	July 24, 1849	18	dark	Hopkinton, R.I.	5	18
Crandall, Lemuel	Apr. 4, 1814	18	light	Providence, R.I.	4	12
Crandall, Sanford	Oct. 29, 1849	24	light	Westford, N.Y.	5	18
Crandall, William W.	Oct. 10, 1812	20	light	Providence, R.I.	4	12
Crane, Joseph	Sept. 13, 1796	30	dark	Braintree, Ma.	1	2
Crank, Joseph	June 27, 1825	37	mulatto	Troy[Fall River], Ma.	4	14
Cranska, Franklin	Aug. 19, 1856	31	dark	Patterson, N.J.	5	44
Cranston, Charles G.	Apr. 3, 1848	22	light	Providence, R.I.	5	18
Cranston, John L.	July 29, 1839	39	dark	Kensington, Pa.	5	16
Cranston, Samuel	Mar. 2, 1810	20	light	No. Kingstoxn, R.I.	4	11
Cranston, Thomas	June 2, 1819	22	light	Warren, R.I.	4	13
Crapo, Abraham	Nov. 27, 1799	29	dark	Rochester, Ma.	2	3
Crapo, Ezra B.	Oct. 18, 1817	19	light	Middleboro, Ma.	4	13
Crapon, Amos A.	Apr. 10, 1848	26	light	Providence, R.I.	5	18
Crapon, Christopher	Jan. 2, 1798	37	dark	Newport, R.I.	1	31
Crapon, Daniel	Nov. 9, 1850	18	light	Smithfield, R.I.	5	19
Crapon, George W.	July 31, 1809	14	dark	Providence, R.I.	4	11
Crapon, Henry	May 13, 1819	19	dark	Providence, R.I.	4	13
Crapon, Jonathan	Nov. 28, 1797	24	dark	Newport, R.I.	1	31
Crapon, Oliver	July 7, 1798	17	light	E. Greenwich, R.I.	2	3
Crapon, Samuel	June 16, 1815	14	light	Providence, R.I.	4	13
Crapon, Samuel A.	Sept. 7, 1842	23	light	Providence, R.I.	5	16
Crapon, Thomas	Oct. 22, 1796	34	light	Newport, R.I.	1	8&4
Crapon, Thomas, Jr.	Aug. 28, 1812	15	light	Providence, R.I.	4	12
Crapon, William	Oct. 14, 1803	18	dark	Providence, R.I.	2	40

REGISTER OF SEAMEN'S PROTECTION

Page 72

NAME	DATE OF CERTIFICATION	AGE	COMPLEXION	PLACE OF BIRTH	BOOK	PAGE
Crause, George	Nov. 13, 1847	22	fair	Boston, Ma.	5	17
Crawford, Charles	May 7, 1828	17	yellow*	Providence, R.I.	4	15
Crawford, Henry W.	Sept. 16, 1863	29	dark	New York, N.Y.	6	3
Crawford, Montgomery copy granted Jan. 2, 1861	Oct. 14, 1854	16	light	No. Prov., R.I.	5	20
Crawford, Samuel	May 15, 1799	20	black	Providence, R.I.	2	3
Crawford, Samuel	Dec. 21, 1803	24	yellow*	Providence, R.I.	2	23
Creed, Phillip	Sept. 10, 1866	22	light	Providence, R.I.	6	3
Crehore, Samuel	Oct. 11, 1810	22	light	Dorchester, Ma.	4	12
Creigton, George	Sept. 9, 1853	25	light	Providence, R.I.	5	20
Crerar, David S.	Mar. 16, 1852	21	sandy	Eastport, Me.	5	19
Crins, John P.	Feb. 27, 1849	23	light	Providence, R.I.	5	18
Crins, Sindamys	Nov. 9, 1841	19	dark	Providence, R.I.	5	16
Crispin, John	June 22, 1854	30	dark	Providence, R.I.	5	20
Croak, David	May 4, 1805	19	dark	Castine, Me.	3	53
Crocker, George	Nov. 27, 1835	35	light	Troy, Ma.	5	15
Crombie, George	Apr. 13, 1853	25	light	New York, N.Y.	5	20
Cromby, John	Mar. 20, 1850	27	dark	Somerset, Ma.	5	19
Cromwell, Robert	Nov. 19, 1811	35	black	New York, N.Y.	4	12
Crook, Daniel	July 29, 1841	21	black	Morristown, N.J.	5	16
Crosby, George	Nov. 23, 1804	22	light	Boston, Ma.	3	52
Crosby, John P.	Nov. 7, 1825	20	light	Portsmouth, N.H.	4	14
Crosby, Martin	Nov. 2, 1801	21	light	New York, N.Y.	2	40
Crosby, Philander	May 11, 1839	20	freckled	Hampton, Me.	5	16
Crosby, Richard	Feb. 16, 1853	33	light	Mystic, Conn.	5	20
Crosby, William	Oct. 26, 1843	21	light	Coventry, R.I.	5	17
Crosley, Thomas	1798-1799	July 8, 1771		Phila., Pa.	** -	--
Cross, Samuel	Apr. 22, 1797	21	dark	Providence, R.I.	1	8
Crossman, Simon	Nov. 2, 1804	29	light	Taunton, Ma.	3	6
Crow, Benjamin	July 11, 1806	32	florid	Colerain, Ireland	3	65
Crouch, Charles	Dec. 24, 1855	35	dark	New York, N.Y.	5	44
Crowell, Alfred	May 13, 1863	45	dark	Yarmouth, Ma.	6	3
Crowell, Benjamin	Nov. 12, 1831	18	light	Yarmouth, Ma.	5	14
Crowell, Benjamin F.	Jan. 22, 1844	23	dark	Providence, R.I.	5	17
Crowell, David A.	Sept. 16, 1863	22	dark	Harwick, Ma.	6	3
Crowell, Ezra	Dec. 18, 1823	20	ruddy	Yarmouth, Ma.	4	14
Crowell, Hiram S.	Feb. 24, 1851	17	light	Warren, R.I.	5	19
Crowell, Isaac	Oct. 19, 1818	24	dark	Yarmouth, Ma.	4	13

*mulatto   **Newport, R.I.

NAME	DATE OF CERTIFICATION	AGE	COMPLEXION	PLACE OF BIRTH	BOOK	PAGE
Crowell, James	Nov. 1, 1817	21	black	Falmouth, Ma.	4	13
Crowell, John	Dec. 12, 1838	30	light	Southhold, N.Y.	5	15
Crowell, Peter	Dec. 3, 1833	25	light	Dennis, Ma.	5	14
Crowell, Samuel	Nov. 15, 1799	25	dark	Wrentham, Ma.	2	3
Crowell, Sears	Mar. 29, 1815	19	light	Yarmouth, Ma.	4	13
Crowell, Sheldon	Oct. 24, 1849	41	light	Yarmouth, Ma.	5	18
Crowell, Shubael	Apr. 9, 1831	26	light	New Bedford, Ma.	5	14
Crowell, William L.	July 15, 1862	25	light	Dennis, Ma.	6	3
Crowley, Augusta	Aug. 21, 1866	18	light	Addison, Me.	6	3
Crowley, David	July 16, 1850	21	light	Boston, Ma.	5	19
Crowley, John	Nov. 15, 1841	17	light	Providence, R.I.	-	--
Crowningshield, Wm. H.	Oct. 10, 1844	19	light	No. Prov., R.I.	5	17
Cruff, Darius	July 8, 1806	26	light	E. Greenwich, R.I.	3	65
Crumble, Alexander	Mar. 30, 1853	32	light	Providence, R.I.	5	20
Crumell, Robert	Feb. 20, 1804	36	black	New York, N.Y.	3	5
Crutch, George	Aug. 14, 1801	17	light	Charleston, S.C.	2	27
Cudworth, Darius	Aug. 21, 1829	40	dark	Berkley, Ma.	5	14
Cuffee, Samuel	Dec. 18, 1822	22	yellow*	Westport, Ma.	4	14
Culp, Nelson	Sept. 26, 1843	22	dark	Floral, N.Y.	5	17
Cumbea, Jonathan	Mar. 6, 1807	23	brown	Woodstock, Conn.	4	11
Cummings, Anthony	June 4, 1805	21	dark	Dighton, Ma.	3	53
Cummings, George	Mar. 9, 1854	23	light	New Bedford, Ma.	5	20
Cummings, James	Oct. 19, 1805	25	light	New York, N.Y.	3	53
Cummings, James	Mar. 25, 1809	25	yellow*	Boston, Ma.	4	11
Cummings, James	Dec. 23, 1856	18	light	Lowell, Ma.	5	44
**Cumin, John R.	June 4, 1844	27	light	New Bedford, Ma.	5	17
Cummings, Joseph	Nov. 14, 1803	24	light	Milton, Ma.	2	48
Cummings, Richard	May 7, 1832	19	black	Phila., Pa.	5	14
Cummings, Samuel	Sept. 23, 1806	25	black	Petersham, Ma.	3	32
Cummins, William C.	June 21, 1850	29	dark	Providence, R.I.	5	19
Cundall, John	Mar. 9, 1804	23	light	Newport, R.I.	3	5
Cunha, Jonade	June 29, 1857	18	dark	New Bedford, Ma.	5	44
Cuniv, Raymond Joseph	Feb. 23, 1852	23	dark	Norfolk, Va.	5	19
Cunningham, James	Apr. 23, 1852	21	dark	Albany, N.Y.	5	19

*mulatto

**name out of order should be after Cumbea, Jonathan.

NAME	DATE OF CERTIFICATION	AGE	COMPLEXION	PLACE OF BIRTH	BOOK	PAGE
Cunningham, John	Sept. 25, 1855	45	florid	New York,N.Y.	5	20
Cunningham, Michael	Mar. 28, 1848	18	dark	No. Prov., R.I.	5	17
Curien, Nicholas	May 1, 1806	18	light	No. Prov., R.I.	3	65
Curu, John	Dec. 26, 1800	25	dark	Charleston, S.C.	2	27
Curren, Patrick	Aug. 8, 1846	21	fair	Machias, Me.	5	17
Curry, Daniel	Sept. 26, 1857	26	fair	Calais, Me.	6	3
Curry, Henry	May 7, 1856	38	black	Milford, Del.	5	44
Currie, Horace	Aug. 16, 1812	19	dark	Providence, R.I.	4	12
Currie, James	Feb. 8, 1805	19	dark	Providence, R.I.	3	52
Currie, James	Aug. 1, 1842	18	light	Providence, R.I.	5	16
Currie, James	Apr. 20, 1799	45	light	Providence, R.I.	2	3
Currie, Robert	June 23, 1826	23	light	Providence, R.I.	4	14
Currie, Samuel, Jr.	May 6, 1806	18	light	Providence, R.I.	3	65
Currie, Samuel, Jr.	June 29, 1821	19	light	Providence, R.I.	4	14
Currie, William	Aug. 10, 1822	16	light	Providence, R.I.	4	14
Curry, Westly	Aug. 14, 1841	25	black	Milford, Del.	5	16
Curtis, Benjamin	July 20, 1803	24	dark	Boston, Ma.	2	40
Curtis, Daniel B.	Feb. 25, 1847	30	light	Providence, R.I.	5	17
Curtis, Eri	Dec. 3, 1825	24	light	Burrillville, R.I.	4	14
Curtis, George Earle	May 29, 1851	18	light	Providence, R.I.	5	19
Curtis, James	July 19, 1841	24	dark	Floyd, N.Y.	5	16
Curtis, Joseph W.	May 19, 1819	25	light	Shrewsbury, Ma.	4	13
Curtis, Gebina, 2d	June 13, 1811	23	light	Sharon, Vt.	4	12
Cushing, Chauncey	Apr. 26, 1810	20	dark	Rehoboth, Ma.	4	12
Cushing, Daniel	Dec. 29, 1806	17	brown	New Haven, Conn.	4	11
Cushing, Daniel Cook	Feb. 28, 1804	21	light	Providence, R.I.	3	5
Cushing, George R.	Sept. 21, 1866	18	light	Pembroke, Me.	6	3
Cushing, George W.	Mar. 28, 1800	22	light	Providence, R.I.	2	27
Cushing, Henry I.	May 19, 1846	26	dark	Providence, R.I.	5	17
Cushing, William	Oct. 22, 1804	19	light	Rehoboth, Ma.	3	6
Cushman, Allarton	June 1, 1809	18	light	Attleboro, Ma.	4	11
Curtis, Benjamin	Oct. 3, 1809	16	dark	Royalton, Vt.	4	11
Cutler, Ebenzer	Dec. 7, 1804	27	light	New York, N.Y.	3	52
Cutler, Prince	Feb. 27, 1805	16	black	Boston, Ma.	3	52
Cutter, Aaron	May 24, 1839	25	light	W. Cambridge, Ma.	25	16
Cutter, Benjamin	May 29, 1848	26	dark	Stonington, Conn.	5	18
Cutter, John	May 30, 1797	18	light	Newport, R.I.	1	8

REGISTER OF SEAMEN'S PROTECTION

NAME	DATE OF CERTIFICATION	AGE	COMPLEXION	PLACE OF BIRTH	BOOK	PAGE
Cutter, John	May 3, 1806	27	light	Newport, R.I.	3	65
Cutts, William	Dec. 21, 1825	21	light	Hallowell, Me.	4	14
Dacay, John C.	May 28, 1855	26	light	Fall River, Ma.	5	24
Daggett, Benjamin	May 12, 1807	44	light	Attleboro, Ma.	4	16
Daggett, Benjamin	Mar. 22, 1815	18	light	Rehoboth, Ma.	4	17
Daggett, Daniel	Oct. 12, 1816	22	light	Seekonk, Ma.	4	17
Daggett, Edward	Oct. 31, 1803	23	light	Rehoboth, Ma.	2	41
Daggett, Edward	May 24, 1804	23	light	Rehoboth, Ma.	3	7
Daggett, Elijah	Mar. 26, 1824	27	dark	Edgartown, Ma.	4	17
Daggett, Gilbert	Jan. 22, 1807	16	light	Rehoboth, Ma.	4	16
Daggett, Henry	Dec. 17, 1803	22	dark	Rehoboth, Ma.	2	43
Daggett, James	Oct. 22, 1803	43	light	Rehoboth, Ma.	2	41
Daggett, Mayhew	Oct. 26, 1803	22	dark	Attleboro, Ma.	2	41
Daggett, Nathan	Dec. 28, 1804	19	light	Providence, R.I.	3	8
Daggett, Preston	June, 4, 1804	20	light	Rehoboth, Ma.	3	7
Daggett, Robert, Jr.	Apr. 19, 1809	16	light	Rehoboth, Ma.	4	16
Daggett, Timothy	Dec. 24, 1817	15	light	Seekonk, Ma.	4	17
Daggett, William	June 2, 1819	20	light	Seekonk, Ma.	4	17
Daggett, William H.	Oct. 9, 1824	15	light	Providence, R.I.	4	17
Dailey, Amos	May 28, 1821	21	Yellow*	Warwick, R.I.	4	17
Dailey, Benjamin	Mar. 15, 1852	27	mulatto	Warwick, R.I.	5	23
Dailey, Daniel D.	Dec. 8, 1804	14	light	Providence, R.I.	3	8
Dailey, Daniel D.	Feb. 8, 1808	17	light	Providence, R.I.	4	16
Dailey, Daniel D.	Oct. 29, 1810	20	brown	Providence, R.I.	4	16
Dailey, Joseph	Mar. 14, 1801	30	black	Warwick, R.I.	2	4
Dailey, Joseph	Nov. 17, 1853	22	dark	Warwick, R.I.	5	24
Dailey, Samuel	Mar. 28, 1827	25	mulatto	Warwick, R.I.	4	17
Dailey, Wm. I.	Dec. 17, 1855	21	light	Boston, Ma.	5	24
Daily, James	Apr. 13, 1807	17	yellow*	Brooklyn, Conn.	4	16
Daily, Jeremiah P.	Aug. 11, 1845	25	yellow	Smithfield, R.I.	5	22
Daley, Jacob	Dec. 15, 1810	19	yellow*	Warwick, R.I.	4	16
Daley, James	June 18, 1806	19	yellow*	Foster, R.I.	3	59
Daley, Sylvester	Mar. 15, 1811	18	black	Foster, R.I.	4	16
Dayley, James	Jan. 2, 1798	24	yellow*	Warwick, R.I.	1	9
Dalton, Peter	Aug. 20, 1804	19	light	Coventry, R.I.	3	7
Dame, Herbert T.	Aug. 11, 1846	20	dark	London, N.H.	5	22

*mulatto

NAME	DATE OF CERTIFICATION	AGE	COMPLEXION	PLACE OF BIRTH	BOOK	PAGE
Damon, James S.	Nov. 1, 1849	40	light	Scituate, Ma.	5	23
Dana, Jonathan G.	Apr. 20, 1813	18	light	Providence, R.I.	4	17
Dana, Thomas G.	June 28, 1849	26	light	Providence, R.I.	5	23
Danford, Jacob	June 16, 1834	35	black	Shrewbury, Ma.	5	21
Danforth, Charles	June 7, 1816	19	fresh	Norton, Ma.	4	17
Danforth, Horatio	O t. 31, 1799	20	light	Providence, R.I.	2	4
Danforth, James	Oct. 3, 1837	19	light	Providence, R.I.	5	21
Danforth, Nathaniel	Nov. 12, 1840	29	light	Paris, N.Y.	5	22
Danforth, Samuel	Nov. 19, 1813	14	light	Providence, R.I.	4	17
Daniels, Benjamin F.	June 18, 1841	21	light	Franklin, Ma.	5	22
Daniels, Henry	Oct. 12, 1833	26	light	New London, Conn.	5	21
Daniels, Joseph	Feb. 12, 1806	21	yellow*	Phila., Pa.	3	60
Daniels, Joseph	May 24, 1833	40	mulatto	Newport, R.I.	5	21
Daniels, Joseph	June 6, 1854	22	light	Bangor, Me.	5	24
Daniels, Lewis	May 9, 1850	20	light	Mendon, Ma.	5	23
Daniels, Nathan	May 17, 1822	20	light	Mendon, Ma.	4	17
Daniels, Peter	July 22, 1834	23	dark	Dennis, Ma.	5	21
Daniels, Thomas	June 1, 1805	19	light	Norwich, Conn.	3	8
Daniels, William	Jan. 16, 1850	21	light	New York, N.Y.	5	23
Dardiff, Nicholas	June 10, 1857	31	dark	Staten Island, N.Y.	5	24
Darling, Frank	Apr. 1, 1865	24	light	E. Greenwich, R.I.	6	4
Darling, George	Dec. 7, 1835	29	dark	Norfolk, Va.	5	21
Darling, George H.	July 22, 1825	19	light**	Hebron, Conn.	4	17
Darling, John	1798-1799	Feb. 17, 1783		Bristol, R.I.	* * *-	--
Darling, Lewis	July 31, 1837	19	dark	Smithfield, R.I.	5	21
Darling, Samuel B.	Mar. 2, 1849	20	light	Providence, R.I.	5	23
Dashiell, Alexander	Apr. 8, 1819	34	light	Baltimore, Md.	4	17
Daskam, Charles	Oct. 22, 1834	24	light	New York, N.Y.	5	21
Davenport, Josiah	Oct. 7, 1796	24	light	(Little Compton)Seconnett	1	9&4
Davis, Alfred	July 12, 1826	23	ruddy	New London, Conn.	4	17
Davis, Arnold	Mar. 28, 1817	18	ruddy	Tiverton, R.I.	4	17
Davis, Benjamin	June 15, 1804	19	light	Little Compton, R.I.	3	7
Davis, Benjamin	June 17, 1805	20	light	Little Compton, R.I.	3	8
Davis, Benjamin	Oct. 28, 1825	23	light	Truro, Ma.	4	17
Davis, Charles W.	May 20, 1851	28	light	Providence, R.I.	5	23
Davis, Daniel	Apr. 25, 1826	20	light	Foster, R.I.	4	17
Davis, Elisha	1798-1799	Apr. 28, 1775		Freetown	***-	--

*mulatto
Freckled also.   * Newport, R.I.

REGISTER OF SEAMEN'S PROTECTION

NAME	DATE OF CERTIFICATION	AGE	COMPLEXION	PLACE OF BIRTH	BOOK	PAGE
Davis, Francis	Aug. 22, 1854	27	yellow	New Haven, Conn.	5	24
Davis, Frederick E.	June 8, 1860	18	light	Providence, R.I.	6	4
Davis, George	Aug. 29, 1839	28	brown	Phila., Pa.	5	22
Davis, George B.	Apr. 7, 1809	18	dark	Providence, R.I.	4	16
Davis, George S.	Jan. 26, 1860	33	fair	Brooklyn, N.Y.	6	4
Davis, Henry	July 31, 1854	22	light	Brooklyn, N.Y.	5	24
Davis, Isiah S.	Oct. 16, 1854	21	light	Beaufort, N.C.	5	24
Davis, Israel 2d	Nov. 25, 1809	21	dark	Providence, R.I.	4	16
Davis, James	1798-1799	Apr. 19, 1779		Coventry, R.I.	** -	--
Davis, James	Nov. 9, 1803	24	light	Bristol, R.I.	2	41
Davis, James	Nov. 1, 1839	42	light	Boston, Ma.	5	22
Davis, James	June 7, 1849	28	light	Roxbury, Ma.	5	23
Davis, James M.	Apr. 15, 1856	25	light	New Bedford, Ma.	5	24
Davis, Jeremiah A.	May 12, 1856	28	fair	Warwick, R.I.	5	24
Davis, Jesse	June 16, 1815	16	light	Providence, R.I.	4	17
Davis, Job	May 22, 1798	37	light	Newport, R.I.	2	4
Davis, Job	Dec. 22, 1809	48	light	Newport, R.I.	4	16
Davis, John	May 18, 1799	17	dark	Taunton, Ma.	2	4
Davis, John	May 17, 1800	18	dark	Taunton, Ma.	2	4
Davis, John	July 7, 1801	21	light	Ipswitch, Ma.	2	4
Davis, John	June 9, 1804	18	dark	Boston, Ma.	3	7
Davis, John	July 31, 1805	24	light	Coventry, R.I.	3	8
Davis, John	May 16, 1809	23	black	Phila., R.I.	4	16
Davis, John	June 12, 1811	39	black	Providence, R.I.	4	16
Davis, John	July 9, 1839	30	light	New Castle, Me.	5	22
Davis, John	Dec. 13, 1850	37	dark	Stockholm, Sweden	5	23
Davis, John	Mar. 17, 1857	21	fair	Phila., Pa.	5	24
Davis, John G.	Oct. 4, 1806	16	light	Providence, R.I.	3&4	59&16*
Davis, John P.	July 1, 1844	32	light	Phila., Pa.	5	22
Davis, Joshua	1798-1799	May 8, 1782		Rehoboth, Ma.	** -	--
Davis, King	Nov. 19, 1804	28	black	New York, N.Y.	3	7
Davis, Mason	1798-1799	Oct. 27, 1772		Westport, Ma.	** -	--
Davis, Mathew W.	Nov. 30, 1849	21	light	Rehoboth, Ma.	5	23
Davis, Moses	Apr. 26, 1806	21	brown	Edentown, N.C.	3	59
Davis, Nathaniel	Feb. 12, 1799	20	light	Berkley, Ma.	2	4
Davis, Nathaniel	July 11, 1801	25	black	New York, N.Y.	2	4
Davis, Peter A.	Nov. 12, 1840	24	light	Milford, Del.	5	22

*Book 3, page 59; book 4, page 16.
**Newport, R.I.

REGISTER OF SEAMEN'S PROTECTION

NAME	DATE OF CERTIFICATION	AGE	COMPLEXION	PLACE OF BIRTH	BOOK	PAGE
Davis, Richard	Oct. 28, 1816	18	ruddy	Freetown, Ma.	4	17
Davis, Richard Y.	Apr. 3, 1839	20	light	Boston, Ma.	5	22
Davis, Samuel	July 21, 1810	43	light	Newport, R.I.	4	16
Davis, Seth	May 22, 1798	61	light	Barnstable, Ma.	2	4
Davis, Shubael	Oct. 13, 1809	15	light	Falmouth, Ma.	4	16
Davis, Simon	Apr. 14, 1798	19	dark	Newport, R.I.	1&2	9&4*
Davis, Stephen H.	Aug. 31, 1849	21	light	Providence, R.I.	5	23
Davis, Thomas	Apr. 3, 1804	32	black	New York, N.Y.	3	7
Davis, Thomas	May 26, 1809	16	light	Providence, R.I.	4	16
Davis, Thomas	Sept. 8, 1812	19	light	Providence, R.I.	4	16
Davis, Thomas	May 12, 1829	41	light	Providence, R.I.	5	21
Davis, Thomas	Nov. 6, 1848	27	dark	Providence, R.I.	5	23
Davis, Wanton	July 31, 1805	22	light	Coventry, R.I.	3	8
Davis, William	June 17, 1797	24	light	Trenton, N.J.	1	9
Davis, William	Dec. 15, 1798	28	black	Long Island, N.Y.	2	4
Davis, William	1798-1799	Apr. 15, 1778		Westport, Ma.	** -	--
Davis, William	1798-1799	Oct. 24, 1779		No. Kingston, R.I.	** -	--
Davis, William	Sept. 30, 1809	18	light	Falmouth, Ma.	4	16
Davis, William	Aug. 28, 1821	21	black	No. Kingstown, R.I.	4	17
Davis, William	Aug. 30, 1836	23	dark	New Haven, Conn.	5	21
Davis, William	Oct. 14, 1844	19	dark	Charlestown, N.C.	5	22
Davis, William	Jan. 10, 1849	23	light	Phila., Pa.	5	23
Davis, William G.	Oct. 29, 1849	24	light	New York, N.Y.	5	23
Davison, George	Apr. 23, 1852	26	light	Calais, Me.	5	23
Davison, John	Dec. 10, 1851	24	light	Charleston, S.C.	5	23
Davol, George	1798-1799	Nov. 14, 1778		Tiverton, R.I.	** -	--
Davol, Nathan	Oct. 30, 1801	23	light	Freetown, Ma.	2	41
Davol, Preserve	1798-1799	Oct. 22, 1772		Tiverton, R.I.	** -	--
Davol, Stephen	1798-1799	May 8, 1766		Dartmouth, Ma.	-	--
Davoll, William	May 19, 1827	19	light	Bristol, R.I.	4	17
Dawes, William	Aug. 12, 1841	37	light	Dorchester, Ma.	5	22
Dawley, Daniel	Dec. 1, 1848	21	dark	Exeter, R.I.	5	23
Dawley, Nicholas T.	1798-1799			Jamestown, R.I.	** -	--
Dawson, John	May 27, 1815	19	light	Marblehead, Ma.	4	17
Day, Celvin	Aug. 4, 1825	21	dark	Plainfield, Conn.	4	17
Day, Harvey	June 28, 1836	34	dark	W. Springfield, Ma.	5	21
Day, Jacob	Mar. 21, 1836	18	black	Phila., Pa.	5	21

*Book 1, page 9; book 2, page 4.
** Newport, R.I.

NAME	DATE OF CERTIFICATION	AGE	COMPLEXION	PLACE OF BIRTH	BOOK	PAGE
Day, John	Jan. 3, 1838	38	light	Salem, Ma.	5	21
Day, John	Aug. 13, 1853	29	fair	Boston, Ma.	5	24
Day, John B.	Dec. 12, 1838	25	10	Freeport, Me.	5	22
Day, Robert	May 23, 1835	23	light	Lubec, Me.	5	21
Dayton, Geo. W.	Apr. 2, 1849	20	light	New London, Conn.	5	23
Dayton, Henry	Mar. 9, 1815	17	light	Newport, R.I. ?*	4	17
Dayton, Lewis	May 21, 1803	20	light	Providence, R.I.	2	14
Dayton, William	Nov. 30, 1821	39	light	Newport, R.I.	4	17
Dean, David	Oct. 30, 1819	22	light	Lebanon, Conn.	4	17
Dean, Edwin	Mar. 30, 1863	19	dark	Lincolnville, Me.	6	4
Dean, Elijah	Nov. 27, 1840	33	light	Westmoreland, N.H.	5	22
Dean, George B.	Oct. 24, 1849	44	light	Providence, R.I.	5	23
Dean, John Naturalized in ? Ma.	Aug. 31, 1849	27	light	Clithers, Great Britian	5	23
Dean, John Edward	June 3, 1853	21	dark	Berkley, Ma.	5	24
Dean, Miles S.	Jan. 4, 1823	25	light	Taunton, Ma.	4	17
Dean, Rufus	Sept. 25, 1848	17	light	Princetonville, Me.	5	23
Dean, Samuel	Nov. 28, 1849	33	dark	Burrillville, R.I.	5	23
Dean, Thomas	July 12, 1799	30	black	Dighton, Ma.	2	4
Deas, Hugh T.	Aug. 7, 1846	13	dark	Marion Co., S.C.	5	22
Deathe, Thomas	May 17, 1805	18	dark	No. Kingstown, R.I.	3	8
Deaull, William	Oct. 16, 1804	22	light	Camptown, Pa.	3	7
Deaves, John	Apr. 12, 1806	20	light	New York, N.Y.	3	59
Decatur, Oliver	Aug. 10, 1835	25	mulatto	Phila., Pa.	5	21
Decker, Christian	Mar. 30, 1852	25	light	New York, N.Y.	5	23
Decoster, Samuel	June 10, 1806	22	black	Salem, Ma.	3	59
Dedrick, Albert C.	Oct. 8, 1849	18	light	Warwick, R.I.	5	23
Daddrick, Hammond	Mar. 30, 1836	19	dark	Catskill, N.Y.	5	21
Dedrick, William	Mar. 19, 1805	17	light	Newport, R.I.	3	8
Dee, David	July 29, 1837	21	light	Providence, R.I.	5	21
Dee, Samuel	June 10, 1831	21	light	Saybrook, Conn.	5	21
Dee, William	June 10, 1831	25	light	Saybrook, Conn.	5	21
Degue, Petre	Apr. 23, 1832	36	light	New Orleans, La.	5	21
DeLahoyde, Thomas M.	Nov. 24, 1848	20	light	New York, N.Y.	5	49
?Delamare, Samuel	Aug. 27, 1840	22	light	Wiscasset, Me.	5	22
Delancy, James	Feb. 18, 1867	19	light	Troy, N.Y.	6	4
Deland, Daniel B.	Sept. 1, ----	19	light	Candor, N.Y.	5	22

*perhaps Providence.

NAME	DATE OF CERTIFICATION	AGE	COMPLEXION	PLACE OF BIRTH	BOOK	PAGE
Delano, Alfred N.	Feb. 26, 1853	20	dark	Lynn, Ma.	5	23
Delano, Charles	Oct. 20, 1818	18	light	Rochester, Ma.	4	17
Delano, James	Oct. 14, 1809	20	light	Rochester, Ma.	4	16
Delano, Rufus K.	Mar. 3, 1848	39	dark	Providence, R.I.	5	23
Delaware, John	Sept. 11, 1839	24	black	Bristol, R.I.	5	22
Deleny, James	May 19, 1851	24	dark	Bangor, Me.	5	23
Delong, Elias E.	Nov. 18, 1831	22	light	New York, N.Y.	5	21
Dely, William	May 16, 1853	30	dark	Boston, Ma.	5	24
Deming, DeWitt Clinton	June 5, 1857	15	fair	Tivoli, N.Y.	5	24
Deming, Morris, Jr.	Aug. 11, 1827	20	dark	Hartford, Conn.	4	18
Demous, David	May 14, 1806	17	yellow*	Tiverton, R.I.	3	59
Demoranvell, John	May 15, 1832	17	light	Providence, R.I.	5	21
Denise, Joseph L.	May 8, 1806	14	dark	New York, N.Y.	3	59
Denison, Ambrose	June 10, 1831	18	light	Saybrook, Conn.	5	21
Denison, John	Feb. 1, 1841	20	light	New London, Conn.	5	22
Dennis, Avery	Oct. 23, 1835	26	black	Hudson, N.Y.	5	21
Dennis, Avery	Mar. 5, 1841	26	black	Worcester, Ma.	5	22
Dennis, Fortune	Sept. 23, 1805	24	black	Providence, R.I.	3	60
Dennis, Henry	Nov. 26, 1832	23	light	Bristol, R.I.	5	21
Dennis, Hozea	Mar. 15, 1809	22	dark	Charlton, Ma.	4	16
Dennis, Noah	Sept. 17, 1805	18	black	Providence, R.I.	3	60
Dennis, Noah	June 21, 1817	31	black	Providence, R.I.	4	17
Dennison, Edgar	May 6, 1854	21	light	Stonington, Conn.	5	24
Dennison, Gilbert	Mar. 29, 1842	19	copper-color	Hopkinton, R.I.	5	22
Denny, James G.	June 13, 1850	24	dark	New York, N.Y.	5	24
Denny, Obediah	Jan. 12, 1855	24	light	Manchester, N.H.	5	24
Derby, Joseph (Darby)	July 22, 1803	49	dark	Boston, Ma.	2	41
Derly, Joseph	Dec. 10, 1853	19	light	Wickford, R.I.	5	24
Derrickson, Moses	Mar. 29, 1856	42	mulatto	Phila., Pa.	5	24
Devereaux, Horace	Apr. 14, 1853	16	light	Prospect, Me.	5	23
Devine, Charles	June 15, 1853	20	dark	Boston, Ma.	5	24
Devine, Frank	July 16, 1855	19	light	Smithfield, R.I.	5	24
Devuall, James	Aug. 28, 1807	22	light	Providence, R.I.	4	16
Devol, Joseph	Oct. 9, 1798	25	light	Tiverton, R.I.	2	4
Devol, Royal	Oct. 28, 1829	27	light	Portsmouth, R.I.	5	21
Dewal, James	July 20, 1797	37	dark	Providence, R.I.	1	9
Dewall, James	Feb. 16, 1803	15	light	Providence, R.I.	2	41

*mulatto

REGISTER OF SEAMEN'S PROTECTION

NAME	DATE OF CERTIFICATION	AGE	COMPLEXION	PLACE OF BIRTH	BOOK	PAGE
Dewey, James	Sept. 19, 1803	21	dark	So. Kingstown, R.I.	2	41
Dewey, John E.	Dec. 18, 1819	26	dark	So. Kingstown, 'R.I.	4	17
Dewiers, William	Mar. 9, 1804	32	dark	Providence, R.I.	3	7
DeWires, John	Dec. 20, 1797	32	dark	Providence, R.I.	1	9
DeWires, William	Nov. 24, 1798	28	light	Providence, R.I.	2	4
DeWyers, William	Oct. 24, 1801	29	dark	Providence, R.I.	2	4
D'Wolf, Levi, Jr.	Jan. 20, 1821	--	light	Bristol, R.I.	-	--
Sworn statement of William Manchester of Bristol in Custom House Papers. DOBNov. 24, 1801.						
D'Wolf, Samuel J.	June 6, 1846	24	light	Boston, Ma.	5	22
Dexter, Abner	Oct. 15, 1811	19	dark	Rochester, Ma.	4	16
Dexter, Alexander	July 30, 1803	18	dark	E. Greenwich, R.I.	2	41
Dexter, Benjamin	Nov. 14, 1802	19	dark	Rochester, Ma.	2	41
Dexter, Benjamin F.	Mar. 20, 1815	25	light	Killingly, Conn.	4	17
Dexter, Charles	Oct. 22, 1803	21	light	Rochester, Ma.	2	41
Dexter, Edward A.	Apr. 2, 1852	21	sandy	Cumberland, R.I.	5	23
Dexter, Gregory	Nov. 7, 1797	18	light	Cumberland, R.I.	1	9
Dexter, Henry H.	July 21, 1823	22	light	Providence, R.I.	4	17
Dexter, Horace	Oct. 10, 1844	19	dark	Cumberland, R.I.	5	22
Dexter, Jacob C.	Dec. 19, 1817	26	yellow*	Hartford, Conn.	4	17
Dexter, James A.	Oct. 28, 1845	28	dark	NO. Prov., R.I.	5	22
Dexter, John Willard	Oct. 29, 1804	21	light	Grafton, Ma.	3	7
Dexter, Joseph D.	Jan. 25, 1854	19	light	Seekonk, Ma.	5	24
Dexter, Obed D.	Dec. 24, 1855	27	light	Fairhaven, Ma.	5	24
Dexter, Samuel	Nov. 5, 1799	18	light	Walpole, Ma.	2	4
Dexter, Samuel P.	Dec. 21, 1829	21	dark	Newburyport, Ma.	5	21
Dexter, Slater	June 8, 1843	16	dark	NO. Prov., R.I.	5	22
Dibden, Wyett	Apr. 24, 1800	19	dark	Providence, R.I.	2	4
Dickason, James D.	June 6, 1798	36	light	Phila., Pa.	2	4
Dickey, George	Apr. 8, 1816	15	light	Providence, R.I.	4	17
Dickey, Robert	July 7, 1797	25	dark	Providence, R.I.	1	9
Dickey, Robert	1798-1799	Jan. 26, 1773		Providence, R.I.	** -	--
Dickson, Robert	Nov. 11, 1803	24	light	Baltimore, Md.	2	43
Digans, Abel	May 14, 1810	21	yellow	Stonington, Conn.	4	16
Diggs, Francis	May 14, 1856	32	yellow	Bristol, R.I.	5	24
Dill, Nathan	May 22, 1855	20	dark	Freedom, Me.	5	24
Dill, Thomas	May 22, 1855	17	dark	Freedom, Me.	5	24
Dillibur, James C., Jr.	Nov. 24, 1828	20	light	Providence, R.I.	4	18
Dilliangham, Moses	July 18, 1825	23	light	Brewster, Ma.	4	17

*mulatto
**Newport, R.I.

REGISTER OF SEAMEN'S PROTECTION

NAME	DATE OF CERTIFICATION	AGE	COMPLEXION	PLACE OF BIRTH	BOOK	PAGE
Dillings, Thomas	Oct. 2, 1801	16	dark	Providence, R.I.	2	4
Dillman, Peter	May 19, 1840	42	light	Baltimore, Md.	5	22
Dillon, Benjamin	Apr. 8, 1857	22	fair	Providence, R.I.	5	24
Dillon, Daniel	Apr. 7, 1851	27	light	New York, N.Y.	5	23
Dillon, Richard	May 12, 1810	16	light	Scituate, R.I.	4	16
Dillon, Thomas	Jan. 5, 1843	22	light	New York, N.Y.	5	22
Diman, Charles	Feb. 27, 1804	26	black	Nantuckett, Ma.	3	7
Dimeunt, John	Apr. 15, 1808	28	yellow	Coventry, R.I.	4	16
Dimock, Ebenezer	Oct. 13, 1803	16	light	Falmouth, Ma.	2	41
Dimond, Jonathan	Oct. 6, 1801	22	black	E. Greenwich, R.I.	2	4
Dingle, John	May 7, 1856	20	yellow	Indian River, Del.	5	24
Dinham, Charles G.	Sept. 18, 1834	18	light	Bath, Me.	5	21
Dinsey, Henry	Mar. 13, 1833	21	black	Providence, R.I.	5	21
Dinsmore, Elam	July 9, 1832	22	light	Anson, Me.	5	21
Disley, H. George	Jan. 8, 1849	25	light	Proivdence, R.I.	5	23
Disley, Paul F.	July 18, 1839	17	light	Providence, R.I.	5	22
Disley, William S.	Dec. 12, 1837	20	dark	Providence, R.I.	5	21
Dix, Comfort	June 4, 1811	27	light	Sturbridge, Ma.	4	16
Dixon, Thomas	Jan. 2, 1798	21	light	E. Greenwich, R.I.	1	9
Doane, Charles	June 11, 1838	24	dark	Portland, Me.	5	21
Doane, Francis C.	May 26, 1831	27	light	Eastham, Ma.	5	21
Doane, Reuben	Mar. 9, 1805	28	dark	Eastham, Ma.	3	8
Dobson, Edmund Naturalized Sept. 1829.	Mar. 13, 1830	36	light	Baccles, England	5	21
Dockerill, John	July 15, 1834	21	light	Portland, Me.	5	21
Dodd, Henry R.	Jan. 1, 1855	39	light	Salem, Ma.	5	24
Dodge, Edwin, Jr.	Nov. 30, 1820	24	light	Poughkeepsie, N.Y.	4	17
Dodge, Gideon O.	Apr. 3, 1847	18	fair	New Shoreham, R.I.	5	22
Dodge, John C.	Feb. 21, 1812	14	dark	Providence, R.I.	4	16
Dodge, Nehemiah, Jr.	July 10, 1819	17	light	Providence, R.I.	4	17
Dodge, Noah	Oct. 19, 1846	18	dark	Newport, R.I.	5	22
Dodge, Olney	Feb. 24, 1849	25	sandy	Smithfield, R.I.	5	23
Dodge, Samuel G.	Oct. 11, 1817	13	dark	Providence, R.I.	4	17
Dodge, William	July 29, 1864	25	dark	Boston, Ma.	6	4
Dods, George, Jr.	Mar. 19, 1805	14	light	Providence, R.I.	3	8
Dods, George D.	Oct. 6, 1809	18	dark	Providence, R.I.	4	16
D'Oliver, George	Mar. 21, 1840	17	dark	Marblehead, Ma.	5	22
D'Oliver, Thomas	July 10, 1803	27	dark	Boston, Ma.	2	41

REGISTER OF SEAMEN'S PROTECTION

NAME	DATE OF CERTIFICATION	AGE	COMPLEXION	PLACE OF BIRTH	BOOK	PAGE
D'Oliver, Thomas J.	Sept. 6, 1836	28	light	Portsmouth, N.H.	5	21
Donahue, Cornelius	Aug. 26, 1851	23	light	Providence, R.I.	5	23
Donahue, James	Aug. 21, 1858	21	florid	New York, N.Y.	6	4
Donaldson, James K.	Oct. 25, 1822	18	light	New York, N.Y.	4	17
Donaldson, Talman	Nov. 14, 1820	19	light	New York, N.Y.	4	17
Donnal, James	June 21, 1845	23	light	New York, N.Y.	5	22
Donnell, John O.	July 15, 1854	20	light	Cumberland, RI.	5	24
Donnison, James	Aug. 22, 1803	21	light	Providence, R.I.	2	41
Donnison, James	Oct. 27, 1800	18	light	Providence, R.I.	2	4
Dooley, Michael	Dec. 19, 1865	25	light	Gloucester, Ma.	6	4
Doore, Daniel	May 7, 1831	18	light	Dover, N.H.	5	21
Doran, Charles	Sept. 11, 1866	28	light	Westport, Ma.	6	4
Doran, Joseph	Sept. 6, 1858	23	fair	Boston, Ma.	6	4
Doran, Thomas Shiels	Dec. 19, 1850	40	light	Meath, Ireland	5	23
Naturalized in Boston, June 11, 1847.						
Doran, John	Aug. 21, 1854	22	dark	Rochester, N.Y.	5	24
Dorøs, Charles	July 10, 1832	20	black	No. Prov., R.I.	5	21
Dorons, William	Sept. 19, 1833	29	black	Providence, R.I.	5	21
Doten, Amasa	July 30, 1841	27	dark	Plymouth, Ma.	5	22
Dotten, Amasa	Nov. 28, 1849	28	light	Eastport, Me.	5	23
Doty, Edward	Oct. 27, 1840	20	light	New York, N.Y.	5	22
Doty, William M.	Sept. 25, 1829	21	dark	Providence, R.I.	5	21
Doud, George	Jan. 14, 1824	18	light	Warwick, R.I.	4	17
Douglass, Andrew M.	Oct. 14, 1863	28	light	Nantucket, Ma.	6	4
Douglass, Barnabas N.	Oct. 28, 1809	18	brown	Middleboro, Ma.	4	16
Douglas, Edward	Feb. 10, 1835	28	light	Jamaica, N.Y.	5	21
Douglas, James, Jr.	Apr. 15, 1833	21	light	So. Kingston, R.I.	5	21
Douglass, James, Jr.	May 26, 1835	22	light	So. Kingston, R.I.	5	21
Douglas, John	Oct. 27, 1813	21	black	Richmond, Va.	4	17
Douglas, John	Sept. 20, 1834	18	light	So. Kingston, R.I.	5	21
Douglass, Peter	Nov. 21, 1804	16	yellow*	Plainfield, Conn.	3	7
Douglass, Randall	June 7, 1805	23	dark	No. Kingstown, R.I.	3	8
Douglass, Robert	July 29, 1843	20	dark	Gouldsboro, Me.	5	22
Douglas, William	Oct. 28, 1803	27	black	New Shoreham, R.I.	2	41
Douglas, William	Oct. 26, 1837	23	dark	So. Kingston, R.I.	5	21
Dough, John	Aug. 12, 1815	22	light	Carrituck, N.C.	4	17
Doull, Daniel	June 16, 1856	25	dark	Providence, R.I.	5	24
Douglas, Edward	Mar. 22, 1821	19	dark	Newport, R.I.	-	--
Sworn statement of Josias Lawton of Newport, in Customs House Papers. year of birth 1802.						

*mulatto

REGISTER OF SEAMEN'S PROTECTION

NAME	DATE OF CERTIFICATION	AGE	COMPLEXION	PLACE OF BIRTH	BOOK	PAGE
Douville, Lowrey	Oct. 17, 1799	13	dark	Warwick, R.I.	2	4
Douville, Charles Lowrey	Nov. 12, 1803	18	dark	Warwick, R.I.	2	43
Douville, Lowery C.	Mar. 7, 1806	20	dark	Warwick, R.I.	3	59
Douville, C. Lowrey	Aug. 9, 1808	22	dark	Warwick, R.I.	4	16
Douville, Samuel Jospeh	Sept. 5, 1803	15	dark	Warwick, R.I.	2	41
Douville, Samuel	Sept. 24, 1805	17	dark	Warwick, R.I.	3	60
Douville, Samuel J.	Oct. 17, 1807	19	dark	Warwick, R.I.	4	16
Dow, George W.	Apr. 14, 1853	19	dark	Prospect, Me.	5	23
Dow, Henry	Oct. 10, 1810	22	light	Hampton, Ma.	4	16
Dow, William	Oct. 23, 1849	33	light	Wiscasset, Me.	5	23
Dowd, Aaron	July 13, 1804	17	dark	Warwick, R.I.	3	7
Dowd, Benjamin	July 29, 1809	20	dark	Warwick, R.I.	4	16
Dowd, Benjamin	May 17, 1811	22	dark	Warwick, R.I.	4	16
Dowd, George W.	Nov. 18, 1834	22	light	Baltimore, Md.	5	21
Dowd, Isaac	Sept. 25, 1834	37	light	Warwick, R.I.	5	21
Dowd, Warren	Oct. 23, 1820	18	brown	Warwick, R.I.	4	17
Dower, Julius C.	Mar. 27, 1806	42	dark	Providence, R.I.	4	16
Downing, Chas. H.	June 20, 1855	21	light	New Haven, Conn.	5	24
Downing, Joseph	Nov. 16, 1804	21	dark	Brooklyn, Conn.	3	7
Downs, James	July 19, 1841	16	dark	Frankfort, Me.	5	22
Downs, Marcus	Dec. 18, 1847	22	light	Frankfort, Me.	5	22
Downs, William B.	May 15, 1811	19	light	Norwich, Conn.	4	16
Downs, Williamson	Jan. 3, 1850	32	dark	Frankfort, Me.	5	23
Downy, Nathan	May 26, 1831	27	light	Harwich, Ma.	5	21
Doyle, James	Aug. 17, 1853	22	light	Boston, Ma.	5	24
Doyle, John	July 30, 1806	47	light	Calverston, Ireland	3	59
Doyle, Martin	Mar. 22, 1849	27	light	Boston, Ma.	5	23
Doyle, William F.	Sept. 1, 1860	30	dark	Phila., Pa.	6	4
Drake, Lewis	Sept. 21, 1803	22	light	Easton, Ma. 1	2	41
Drake, Otis	Aug. 24, 1799	21	light	Taunton, Ma.	2	4
Draper, Jonathan G.	June 12, 1819	18	light	Providence, R.I.	4	17
Dresser, Benjamin F.	Oct. 16, 1811	21	dark	Thompson, Conn.	4	16
Dresser, Jacob, Jr.	Oct. 13, 1807	27	light	Thompson, Conn.	4	16
Drew, Charles	May 12, 1800	19	light	Boston, Ma.	2	4
Dring, John	1798-1799	Nov. 4, 1774		Little Compton, R.I. *	-	--
Drinkwater, Alonzo J.	Dec. 17, 1856	21	light	Northport, Me.	5	24
Drinkwater, Elbridge	Sept. 23, 1848	38	light	Northport, Me.	5	23

*Newport, R.I.

REGISTER OF SEAMEN'S PROTECTION

NAME	DATE OF CERTIFICATION	AGE	COMPLEXION	PLACE OF BIRTH	BOOK	PAGE
Driscoll, John	Sept. 16, 1847	32	dark	Watertown, Ma.	5	22
Driscoll, John	Feb. 19, 1867	18	light	Newport, R.I.	6	4
Driver, Henry O.	Sept. 4, 1855	21	light	Newark, N.J.	5	24
Drody, Thomas	Apr. 3, 1815	22	light	Sandwich, Ma.	4	17
Drown, John J.*	Dec. 29, 1809	21	light	Barrignton, R.I.	4	16
Drown, Jonathan J.**	Dec. 29, 1809	21	light	Barrington, R.I.	4	16
Drummond, Charles	Nov. 30, 1849	21	light	New York, N.Y.	5	23
Drummond, Geo. W.	July 3, 1848	25	black	Philadelphia, Pa.	5	23
Drummond, James	Jan. 30, 1855	23	light	Smithfield, R.I.	5	24
Drury, William G.	Apr. 4, 1827	23	light	Marblehead, Ma.	4	17
Duckhem, William	Apr. 28, 1841	321	brown	Phila., Pa.	5	22
Dudley, George N.	Dec. 28, 1857	25	light	Douglas, Ma.	6	4
Dudley, Samuel C.	June 12, 1810	25	light	Roxbury, Ma.	4	16
Duffee, Samuel	Aug. 12, 1809	24	florid	Chester, N.H.	4	16
Dugan, Charles A.	Mar. 8, 1839	19	light	Boston, Ma.	5	22
Duggan, James M.	Aug. 24, 1848	32	dark	Boston, Ma.	5	23
Duhamel, Joseph	Aug. 28, 1849	32	dark	Champlain, N.Y.	5	23
Duke, Oliver	Mar. 3, 1857	22	dark	Milbury, Ma.	5	24
Dumonte, William	Jan. 20, 1844	21	dark	Lubec, Me.	5	22
Duley, George W.H.	Nov. 12, 1840	30	light	New York, N.Y.	5	22
Dunbar, James	Oct. 27, 1840	25	light	New York, N.Y.	5	22
Dunbar, John	May 24, 1808	14	dark	Westerly, R.I.	4	16
Dunbar, Joseph A.	Oct. 10, 1857	48	black	Providence, R.I.	6	4
?Duncan, Andrew N.	Sept. 5, 1801	24	dark	Boston, Ma.	?	4
Duncan, John	Sept. 28, 1848	26	light	Erie, Pa.	5	23
Duncan, John	Apr. 13, 1853	22	light	New York,N.Y.	5	23
Dunham, Daniel	May 5, 1815	19	light	Providence, R.I.	4	17
Dunham, William	1798-1799	Nov. 3, 1783		Newport, R.I.	* -	--
Barbara Dunham swears the above to be true.						
Dunlap, John	Oct. 2, 1852	29	light	Buffalo, N.Y.	5	23
Dunley, Wm.	Apr. 2, 1853	35	light	New York, N.Y.	5	23
Dunn, Benjamin, Jr.	June 1, 1820	19	ruddy	Providence, R.I.	4	17
Dunn, Edward	Nov. 11, 1850	17	light	Warwick, R.I.	5	23
Dunn, Henry M.	Aug. 13, 1834	21	light	Albany, N.Y.	5	21
Dunn, John	Oct. 5, 1852	23	dark	New York, N.Y.	5	23

*see: Drown, Jonathan J.

*In margin "this ought to be John J. Drown".
**Newport, R.I.

NAME	DATE OF CERTIFICATION	AGE	COMPLEXION	PLACE OF BIRTH	BOOK	PAGE
Dunn, John	July 22, 1859	21	dark	Boston, Ma.	6	4
Dunn, William R.	Oct. 29, 1805	20	light	Phila., Pa.	3	60
Dunwell, Henry A.	June 5, 1833	16	dark	Providence, R.I.	5	21
Dunwell, John	Mar. 24, 1798	28	light	Providence, R.I.	1	9
Dunwell, John, 2d	July 19, 1815	21	light	Providence, R.I.	4	17
Dunwell, Samuel	July 7, 1797	23	dark	Providence, R.I.	1	9
Dunwell, Samuel	May 12, 1802	28	dark	Providence, R.I.	2	41
Dunwell, Samuel	Oct. 27, 1803	29	dark	Providence, R.I.	2	41
Dunwell, Samuel	May 16, 1803	16	dark	Newport, R.I.	2	41
Dunwell, Samuel	Mar. 8, 1805	18	dark	Newport, R.I.	3	8
Dunwell, Samuel	Apr. 11, 1806	32	light	Providence, R.I.	3	59
Dunwell, Samuel	Apr. 24, 1809	21	dark	Newport, R.I.	4	16
Dunwell, William	1798-1799	Mar. 21, 1807		Newport, R.I.	* * -	--
Dunwell, William	Dec. 7, 1799	19	light	Newport, R.I.	2	4
Dunwell, William	Oct. 10, 1828	14	light	Providence, R.I.	4	18
Duparr, Charles	June 26, 1830	19	dark	Salem, Ma.	5	21
Durancy, Thomas	Oct. 9, 1856	22	fair	Brooklyn, N.Y.	5	24
Durant [Durrant], Dan'l	Aug. 17, 1803	29	light	Falmouth, Ma.	2	41
Durfee, Benjamin Son of Thomas Durfee.	1798-1799	Dec. 25, 1802		Troy, ?	* * -	--
Durfee, Charles	May 3, 1799	18	black	Tiverton, R.I.	2	4
Durfee, Charles	Aug. 4, 1806	25	black	Tiverton, R.I.	3	59
Durfee, Corey Benjamin Durfee of Tiverton, R.I.	1798-1799	Mar. 5, 1785 Swears the above to be true.		Tiverton, R.I.	* * -	--
Durfee, Edward	Dec. 5, 1796	20	light	Worcester, Ma.	1	9
Durfee, George	Oct. 13, 1845	28	ruddy	Lubec, Me.	5	22
Durfee, Guilford H.	Oct. 30, 1827	25	light	Tiverton, R.I.	4	18
Durfee, James	Dec. 6, 1825	19	ruddy	Tiverton, R.I.	4	17
Durfee, Jonathan	Jan. 5, 1798	17	dark	Tiverton, R.I.	1	9
Durfee, Joseph	1798-1799	Jan. 5, 1771		Tiverton, R.I.	* * -	--
Durfee, Simeon	Mar. 11, 1797	24	black	Tiverton, R.I.	1	9
Durfee, Simeon	Jan. 5, 1798	25	yellow*	Tiverton, R.I.	1	9
Durfee, William	1798-1799	June 15, 1778		Tiverton, R.I.	* * -	--
Durfee, William, 2d	Apr. 14, 1818	19	dark	Tiverton, R.I.	4	17
Durfee, William H.	Mar. 29, 1821	16	light	Tiverton, R.I.	4	17
Durham, John	Oct. 4, 1852	16	light	Champlain, N.Y.	5	23
Durham, Wing	1798-1799	Feb. 9, 1780		Plainfield, Conn.	* * -	--
Duroy, Walter A.	June 18, 1864	23	dark	Fall River, Ma.	6	4

*mulatto
**Newport, R.I.

REGISTER OF SEAMEN'S PROTECTION

NAME	DATE OF CERTIFICATION	AGE	COMPLEXION	PLACE OF BIRTH	BOOK	PAGE
Duval, Lorenzo G.	Oct. 11, 1844	17	light	Scituate, R.I.	5	22
Dutch, John C.	Jan. 11, 1847	26	fair	Epping, N.H.	5	22
[Dwyer]Dwires, William	Nov. 14, 1798	28	light	Providence,R.I.	2	4
Dwight, Darius	Oct. 13, 1807	25	light	Thompson, Conn.	4	16
Dwignt, Joseph H.	Dec. 22, 1849	20	light	Commington, Ma.	5	23
Dwignt, George	Jan. 4, 1823	20	light	Wethersfield, Conn.	4	17
Dyall, John	Apr. 18, 1846	26	light	Eastport, Me.	5	22
Dyer, Aaron	Mar. 12, 1830	30	dark	Middletown, R.I.	5	21
Dyer, Adam	Aug. 5, 1811	25	light	Provincetown, Ma.	4	16
Dyer, Albert F.	Oct. 11, 1830	26	light	Providence, R.I.	5	21
Dyer, Albert Richmond	Sept. 24, 1844	16	light	Providence, R.I.	5	22
Dyer, Ezekiel, Jr.	Oct. 11, 1844	27	dark	Bridgewater, Ma.	5	22
Dyer, Fortune	Dec. 13, 1822	30	black	No. Kingstown, R.I.	4	17
Dyer, George	Aug. 25, 1841	45	dark	Chatham, Ma.	5	22
Dyer, George	Sept. 24, 1844	19	light	Kingston, R.I.	5	22
Dyer, Isaac	Sept. 27, 1803	22	yellow*	So. Kingstown, R.I.	2	41
Dyer, Isaac	June 17, 1801	19	black	So. Kingstown, R.I.	2	4
Dyer, Jabez	Nov. 11, 1803	20	light	Windham, Conn.	2	43
Dyer, Jabez	May 28, 1798	15	light	Windham, Conn.	2	4
Dyer, Lucius	Aug. 17, 1811	23	dark	Windham, Conn.	4	16
Dyer, Thomas	Nov. 9, 1812	30	dark	Cranston, R.I.	4	16
Eagan, Barton	July 27, 1840	18	light	Boston, Ma.	5	25
Eager, Nathan	July 12, 1826?	26	dark	Warwick, Ma.	4	21
Eames, David	Mar. 15, 1815	21	light	Providence, R.I.	4	21
Eames, John Costen	Aug. 1, 1854	49	light	Providence, R.I.	5	26
Eames, William	Oct. 2, 1844	24	dark	Charleston, S.C.	5	25
Earl, James	July 15, 1854	17	light	Cranston, R.I.	5	26
** Earl, John	May 17, 1804	26	light	Portsmouth, R.I.	3	9
Earle, Albert	Mar. 12, 1850	29	light	Smithfield, R.I.	5	26
Earle, Edward	Oct. 5, 1864	27	light	New York, N.Y.	6	5
Earle, George B.	Apr. 21, 1807	16	light	Providence, R.I.	4	21
Earle, John	Nov. 12, 1804	49	dark	Providence, R.I.	3	9
Earle, John	Sept. 7, 1805	28	light	Newport, R.I.	3	9
Earle, John T.	Feb. 1, 1798	17	light	Providence, R.I.	1	10
Earle, John T.	Aug. 9, 1803	21	dark	Providence, R.I.	2	5
Earle, William	Oct. 31, 1803	18	light	Providence, R.I.	2	5
Earle, William	Aug. 25, 1806	20	light	Providence, R.I.	3	20
** Earl, William	1798-1799	Feb. 17, 1778		Bristol, R.I. ***	-	--
** Earl, William	Apr. 20, 1853	38	dark	Eastport, Me.	5	26

*mulatto   *** Newport, R.I.

NAME	DATE OF CERTIFICATION	AGE	COMPLEXION	PLACE OF BIRTH	BOOK	PAGE
Easterbrooks, Martin	Dec. 24, 1830	28	light	Warren, R.I.	5	25
Easterbrooks, Martin	July 2, 1821	18	light	Warren, R.I.		DOB-Oct.
Son of William & Lois Easterbrooks. Birth certificate in the Custom House Papers. 10, 1802.
Eastman, George W.	Dec. 6, 1849	19	light	Pittston, Me.	5	26
Easton, Syphax	Dec. 30, 1809	24	black	Newport, R.I.	4	21
Eathforth, Samuel, Jr.	July 20, 1809	20	light	Providence, R.I.	4	21
Eathforth, William C.	Mar. 19, 1827	25	light	Providence, R.I.	4	21
Eaton, Caleb	July 1, 1847	24	fair	Calais, Me.	5	25
Eaton, Isaac I.	Mar. 10, 1797	23	light	Freetown, Ma.	1	10
Eaton, Joseph	Oct. 31, 1818	23	light	Newport, R.I.	4	21
Eaton, Joshua	Jan. 8, 1811	25	light	Reading, Ma.	4	21
Eaton, Theodore H.	July 27, 1846	19	fair	New Rochell, N.Y.	5	25
Ebby, Samson	June 19, 1810	19	yellow	Charlestown, R.I.	4	21
Ebby, Samuel	Mar. 28, 1811	21	yellow	So. Kingstown, R.I.	4	21
Eccles, John	July 30, 1839	18	light	Taunton, Ma.	5	25
Eccleston, Frederick	Oct. 16, 1841	16	light	Norridgwock, Me.	5	25
Eddy, Benjamin	Mar. 20, 1826	22	dark	Warren, R.I.	4	21
Eddy, Benjamin C.	Nov. 6, 1811	20	brown	Providence, R.I.	4	21
Eddy, Caleb	Dec. 7, 1797	32	light	Providence, R.I.	1	10
Eddy, Charles C.	Nov. 5, 1859	29	fair	Warren, R.I.	6	5
Eddy, Charles W.	Dec. 27, 1833	17	light	Providence, R.I.	5	25
Eddy, Daniel T.	Aug. 31, 1849	32	dark	Proivdence, R.I.	5	26
Eddy, Esek	Jan. 25, 1799	28	light	Glocester, R.I.	2	5
Eddy, Gardner	Oct. 18, 1817	19	light	Swansea, Ma.	4	21
Eddy, George	Aug. 5, 1805	32	dark	Smithfield, R.I.	3	9
Eddy, George	Oct. 27, 1849	36	light	Taunton, Ma.	5	26
Eddy, James	Nov. 20, 1833	19	light	Somerset, Ma.	5	25
Eddy, James	Nov. 10, 1848	19	light	Auburn, Me.	5	25
Eddy, John S.	July 29, 1799	19	light	Rehoboth, Ma.	2	5
Eddy, Jonathan	Sept. 28, 1804	32	light	Providence, R.I.	3	9
Eddy, L. William	Oct. 18, 1843	26	dark	Somerset, Ma.	5	25
Eddy, Sampson	Nov. 17, 1806	14	yellow	Chalestown, R.I.	4	21
Eddy, Samuel J.	Sept. 3, 1849	25	light	Newport, R.I.	5	26
Eddy, William	Mar. 31, 1800	21	light	Providence, R.I.	2	5
Eddy, William	Apr. 6, 1811	32	light	Providence, R.I.	4	21
Eddy, William	Oct. 19, 1843	27	dark	Somerset, Ma.	5	25
Eddy, William, 2d	May 29, 1817	17	light	Providence, R.I.	4	21
Eddy, William F.	May 13, 1856	21	light	Fall River, Ma.	5	26

REGISTER OF SEAMEN'S PROTECTION

NAME	DATE OF CERTIFICATION	AGE	COMPLEXION	PLACE OF BIRTH	BOOK	PAGE
Edes, Peter	Aug. 17, 1807	22	light	Boston, Ma.	4	21
Edgcomb, Frederick	Oct. 9, 1855	21	light	Bath, Me.	5	26
Edmonds, Benjamin	June 12, 1800	24	dark	Warwick, R.I.	2	5
Edmonds, John	Sept. 5, 1836	33	dark	Portsmouth, N.H.	5	25
Edson, Cyrus	Sept. 21, 1803	26	light	Middleboro, Ma.	2	5
Edson, Peter	Aug. 9, 1800	19	dark	Rehoboth, Ma.	2	5
Edwards, Benjamin J. [I?]	July 1, 1846	35	dark	Falmouth, Ma.	5	25
Edwards, Edward	Aug. 9, 1841	38	dark	Salem, Ma.	5	25
Edwards, Ichabod B.	Mar. 28, 1827	20	light	Chatham, Conn.	4	21
Edwards, Israel	Mar. 5, 1810	17	dark	Scituate, R.I.	4	21
Edwards, James	June 21, 1839	23	light	Phila., Pa.	5	25
Edwards, Samuel	Sept. 2, 1839	64	mulatto	Warren, R.I.	5	25
Edwards, Simon	Feb. 25, 1820	17	dark yel.	Barnstable, Ma.	4	21
Edwards, William	Nov. 13, 1811	17	yellow	Glocester, R.I.	4	21
Edwards, William	June 15, 1819	28	dark	Coventry, R.I.	4	21
Edwards, William	Mar. 22, 1837	25	dark	Boston, Ma.	5	25
Edwards, Zophas	Aug. 20, 1803	21	dark	New York, N.Y.	2	5
Egean, James	Aug. 22, 1843	24	light	New York, N.Y.	5	25
Eggleston, David M.	Feb. 17, 1835	21	light	Torrington, Conn.	5	25
Elwen[Eirven], John	Apr. 21, 1855	36	dark	Mount Holly, N.J.	5	26
Elder, Adam	Aug. 9, 1845	21	dark	Watertown, N.Y.	5	25
Elder, James [son of John]	Apr. 18, 1840	31	light	Baltimore, Md.	5	25
Elderkin, Bela	May 17, 1806	23	light	Windham, Conn.	3	9
Elderkin, William S.	Apr. 30, 1855	20	fair	Hartford, Conn.	5	26
Eldred, Benedict, Jr.	Dec. 20, 1819	17	light	So. Kingstown, R.I.	4	21
Eldred, Clark	Nov. 28, 1797	20	light	No. Kingstown, R.I.	1	10
Eldred, Henry	May 1, 1799	24	dark	Stonington, Conn.	2	5
Eldred, Robert, Jr.	Nov. 19, 1828	28	light	No. Kingstown, R.I.	4	22
Eldred, Rowland	May 31, 1803	21	dark	No. Kingstown, R.I.	2	5
Eldred, William	July 10, 1821	19	dark	Falmouth, Ma.	4	21
Eldredge, Edmund	May 7, 1827	23	dark	Chatham, Ma.	4	21
Eldredge, Ezra, Jr.	Nov. 13, 1819	21	light	Barnstable, R.I.	4	21
Eldredge, Isaac, Jr.	Mar. 7, 1815	21	light	Chatham, Ma.	4	21
[Eldridge]Eldredge, Jacob	June 6, 1806	17	black	Jamestown, R.I.	3	9
Eldredge, Jonathan	May 16, 1818	18	light	Chatham, Ma.	4	21
Eldrich, George	Nov. 20, 1805	17	black	Warwick, R.I.	3	9
Eldridge, Charles	Mar. 29, 1853	34	light	New York, N.Y.	5	26
Eldridge, Elnathan	Apr. 16, 1840	36	dark	Chatham, Ma.	5	25

**see ** on page 90 for balance of Eldredge's.

NAME	DATE OF CERTIFICATION	AGE	COMPLEXION	PLACE OF BIRTH	BOOK	PAGE
Eldridge, Ephraim	Oct. 24, 1829	22	light	Chatham, Ma.	5	25
Eldridge, Erastus	Dec. 19, 1855	21	dark	Harwich, Ma.	5	26
Eldridge, Jack	Apr. 18, 1807	21	black	Brookline, Conn.	4	21
Eldridge, James G.	Aug. 27, 1831	23	light	Ovington, Me.	5	25
** Eldredge, Robert M.	June 9, 1827	20	dark	Warwick, R.I.	4	21
** Eldredge, Robert M.	Apr. 13, 1831	23	Indian	Warwick, R.I.	5	25
** Eldredge, Stephen	Feb. 17, 1854	28	light	New London, Conn.	5	26
Eldridge, Joseph	Mar. 2, 1849	24	light	Seekonk, Ma.	5	26
Eldridge, Randall	Aug. 4, 1803	18	dark	No. Kingstown, R.I.	2	5
Eldridge, Stephen	Dec. 15, 1847	21	light	Yarmouth, Ma.	5	25
Eldridge, William	Feb. 24, 1842	23	light	Rochester, N.Y.	5	25
Ellenwood, James H.	Jan. 10, 1831	43	light	Portland, Me.	5	25
Ellery, Benjamin	Aug. 19, 1822	18	light	Newport, R.I.	4	21
Ellery, Eugene	Sept. 24, 1817	15	light	Newport, R.I.	4	21
Elless, John E.	Dec. 13, 1824	16	mulatto	Boston, Ma.	4	21
Elliot, Ambrose	Oct. 8, 1834	18	light	Thomaston, Me.	5	25
Elliot, Asael	Mar. 21, 1815	26	light	Taunton, Ma.	4	21
Elliot, John E.	July 17, 1840	18	light	Warren, R.I.	5	25
Elliot, Nathaniel, Jr.	Mar. 26, 1821	32	dark	Barrington, R.I.	4	21
Elliott, Elijah	Oct. 16, 1811	23	light	Thompson, Conn.	4	21
Ellis, Edward	Aug. 10, 1846	33	dark	Niagara, N.Y.	5	25
Ellis, Fortune	Nov. 7, 1836	25	black	Baltimore, Md.	5	25
Ellis, Gideon	Aug. 26, 1818	48	light	Sandwich, Ma.	4	21
Ellis, Henry, Jr.	Dec. 15, 1824	22	dark	Coventry, R.I.	4	21
Ellis, Henry W.	Oct. 8, 1842	14	light	Cranston, R.I.	5	25
Ellis, Henry W.	Aug. 31, 1849	22	light	Cranston, R.I.	5	26
Ellis, Jonathan	Mar. 15, 1815	16	light	Providence, R.I.	4	21
Ellis, Josephus	Aug. 26, 1818	18	brown	Sandwich, Ma.	4	21
Ellis, Nathan B.	June 21, 1824	19	dark	Sandwich, Ma.	4	21
Ellis, Samuel E.	Oct. 16, 1855	30	mulatto	Liston, Conn.	5	26
Ellis, Thomas	1798-1799	Aug. 12, 1779		Westerly, R.I.	* -	--
Ellis, Zebedee	June 3, 1797	20	light	Rochester, Ma.	1	10
Ellston, Robert M.	Aug. 31, 1849	23	black	New York, N.Y.	5	26
Elward, James	Dec. 9, 1841	14	light	Portland, Me.	5	25
Elward, Michael	Apr. 4, 1861	24	dark	Charlestown, Ma.	6	5
Emerson, Francis	June 24, 1841	19	light	Smithfield, R.I.	5	25
Emerson, Frederick	July 14, 1856	16	dark	Bucksport, Me.	5	26

*Newport, R. I.

REGISTER OF SEAMEN'S PROTECTION

NAME	DATE OF CERTIFICATION	AGE	COMPLEXION	PLACE OF BIRTH	BOOK	PAGE
Emerson, William	Aug. 15, 1857	26	dark	Northampton Co., Va.	6	5
Emerson, William H.	Oct. 31, 1846	17	fair	Cambridgeport, Ma.	5	25
Emery, Daniel	Jan. 23, 1822	19	light	Thomaston, Me.	4	21
Emmons, Wm. E.	Oct. 14, 1853	19	light	LongBranch, N.J.	5	26
Engalls, Benjamin	Nov. 8, 1803	21	dark	Rehoboth, Ma.	2	5
English, James	Apr. 16, 1849	43	light	Boston, Ma.	5	26
English, Samuel	Nov. 2, 1833	33	light	Norfolk, Va.	5	25
English, Sam'l, J.	Feb. 1, 1854	16	light	Providence, R.I.	5	26
?Enkles, Lewis	Sept. 15, 1804	23	dark	Hudson, N.Y.	3	9
Ennis, Christopher	Mar. 15, 1836	19	mulatto	Albany, N.Y.	5	25
Ennis, Joseph	Mar. 25, 1853	20	dark	New Orleans, La.	5	26
Ennis, Samuel	Sept. 27, 1820	18	light	Exeter, R.I.	4	21
Ennis, Thomas	May 5, 1800	20	dark	Baltimore, Md.	2	5
Enos, Benjamin	Sept. 27, 1836	27	black	Warwick, R.I.	5	25
Enos, Joseph	Oct. 22, 1849	24	dark	Old Town, Ma.	5	26
Enos, Joseph	Feb. 25, 1861	20	dark	Nantucket, Ma.	6	5
Ensley, John	Nov. 19, 1803	19	black	New York, N.Y.	2	5
Ensworth, Joseph B.	Nov. 19, 1804	21	dark	Canterbury, Conn.	3	9
Erwin, William	Mar. 11, 1833	33	light	Piermont, N.H.	5	25
Esenwair, Charles	Apr. 28, 1853	22	light	Albany, N.Y.	5	26
Essex, Benjamin	Dec. 22, 1853	21	light	Warwick, R.I.	5	26
Essex, Charles	July 5, 1844	18	dark	Richmond, R.I.	5	25
Essex, Henry	June 24, 1844	20	light	Warwick, R.I.	5	25
Essex, Huit	Jan. 2, 1810	22	dark	NO. Kingstown, R.I.	4	21
Essex, James	Dec. 4, 1849	28	dark	W. Greenwich, R.I.	5	26
Esten, Alonzo M.	Apr. 23, 1849	17	light	Smithfield, R.I.	5	26
Esten, Henry	Mar. 31, 1800	17	light	North Prov., R.I.	2	5
Esterling, Richard	Sept. 18, 1839	23	light	Alexandria, D.C.	5	25
Estey, John A.	July 21, 1820	21	light	Hartford, Conn.	4	21
Etchberger, James	June 7, 1839	38	dark	Baltimore, Md.	5	25
Etherington, John	May 6, 1797	32	dark	Newport, R.I.	1	10
Ethington, Thomas	Sept. 27, 1803	43	black	Phila., Pa.	2	5
Eustis, Edwin	May 22, 1855	21	light	Northampton, Ma.	5	26
Evans, Alfred	Dec. 11, 1816	18	fresh	Somerset, Ma.	4	21
Evans, Albert P.	Sept. 5, 1848	15	light	Providence, R.I.	5	25
Evans, Barak, M.	Aug. 30, 1805	21	light	Johnston, R.I.	3	9
Evans, Barak M.	July 28, 1809	25	light	Johnston, R.I.	4	21

NAME	DATE OF CERTIFICATION	AGE	COMPLEXION	PLACE OF BIRTH	BOOK	PAGE
Evans, David	Dec. 11, 1816	21	light	Somerset, Ma.	4	21
Evans, David	Dec. 26, 1845	28	fair	Newport, R.I.	5	25
Evans, Edward	Mar. 16, 1852	22	dark	Boston, Ma.	5	26
Evans, James	Dec. 2, 1859	21	light	Utica, N.Y.	6	5
Evans, John	Apr. 13, 1805	22	light	New Haven, Conn.	3	9
Evans, John	June 26, 1811	17	light	Somerset, Ma.	4	21
Evans, John	Jan. 26, 1847	25	fair	New York, N.Y.	5	25
Evans, Moses A.	Oct. 8, 1861	28	light	Glocester, R.I.	6	5
Evans, Wallace	Mar. 9, 1837	22	light	Baltimore, Md.	5	25
Evans, William	Nov. 28, 1815	27	dark	Harwich, Ma.	4	21
Evans, William	Nov. 19, 1845	23	light	New Orleans, La.	5	25
Evans, William	Dec. 5, 1859	26	dark	New York, N.Y.	6	5
Evans, William H.	July 22, 1839	21	dark	Boston, Ma.	5	25
Eveleth, William	July 11, 1815	19	dark	Providence, R.I.	4	21
Everett, Edward A.	Aug. 31, 1849	27	light	Providence, R.I.	5	26
Everly, John	Nov. 28, 1849	15	light	New York, N.Y.	5	26
Ewer, David	June 18, 1814	35	light	Barnstable, Ma.	4	21
Ewer, Henry R.	Feb. 8, 1847	30	fair	Sandwich, Ma.	5	25
Fairbanks, Edward R.	Mar. 5, 1844	16	light	Providence, R.I.	5	29
Fairchild, Pero	May 5, 1797	18	black	Providence, R.I.	1	11
Fairman, Roger	July 27, 1804	31	dark	Canterbury, Conn.	3	11
Fairweather, James	Nov. 2, 1827	19	mulatto	So. Kingstown, R.I.	4	24
Fairwell, William	Aug. 15, 1839	29	light	Rochester, Ma.	5	28
Fales, Harvey	Nov. 10, 1806	18	light	Wrentham, Ma.	4	23
Fales, John T.	Oct. 5, 1849	52	light	Attleboro, Ma.	5	30
Fales, Nath'l	Nov. 12, 1841	28	light	Taunton, Ma.	5	29
Fales, Timothy	Apr. 23, 1821	16	light	Taunton, Ma.	4	24
Fanning, George H.	Nov. 27, 1837	28	dark	Providence, R.I.	5	28
Fanning, John M.	Oct. 29, 1849	23	light	Griswold, Conn.	5	30
Fanning, Thomas	Aug. 21, 1844	21	dark	Phila., Pa.	5	29
Fanton, Joseph	Apr. 20, 1846	20	fair	Weston, Conn.	5	29
Farley, Benjamin	Feb. 6, 1849	18	dark	Providence, R.I.	5	29
Farley, John	Nov. 16, 1865	20	light	Calais, Me.	6	6
Farman, Charles	Mar. 28, 1854	33	yellow	New Bedford, Ma.	5	30
Farmer, Henry H.	Aug. 6, 1833	20	dark	Providence, R.I.	5	28
Farmer, Thomas	June 16, 1810	28	dark	Goffstown, N.H.	4	23
Farnham, Caleb, Jr.	Oct. 14, 1803	22	light	Uxbridge, Ma.	2	6

NAME	DATE OF CERTIFICATION	AGE	COMPLEXION	PLACE OF BIRTH	BOOK	PAGE
Farnam, Daniel H.	May 20, 1819	21	brown	Providence, R.I.	4	24
[Farnham]Farnam, David	May 25, 1804	18	dark	Lisbon, Conn.	3	11
Farnham, Elijah	Apr. 29, 1803	20	light	Hampton, Conn.	2	6
Farnham, John C.	May 31, 1823	22	dark	Woolwich, Me.	4	24
Farnum, Wm. M.	Nov. 17, 1849	37	light	Johnston, R.I.	5	30
Farny, Martin	Apr. 19, 1837	21	dark	New York, N.Y.	5	28
Farrell, James	Aug. 9, 1847	23	fair	Albany, N.Y.	5	29
Farrel, William	July 21, 1835	22	light	Freetown, Me.	5	28
Farren, John	Mar. 8, 1797	19	dark	Dingley, Ireland	1	11
Farrer, Ezra	Nov. 29, 1800	32	light	Upton, Ma.	2	6
Farrier, Arthur	Apr. 8, 1812	13	light	Providence, R.I.	4	23
Farier, Robert	June 17, 1797	13	dark	Providence, R.I	1	11
Farrier, William	Nov. 11, 1803	17	light	Providence, R.I.	2	22
Farrington, George	Oct. 18, 1806	35	light	Salisbury, Md.	4	23
Farris, David M.	Dec. 24, 1828	20	dark	Barnstable, Ma.	4	24
Farrow, Asa	Oct. 21, 1839	17	light	Killingly, Conn.	5	28
Fassett, Amariah	May 6, 1815	21	light	Dedham, Ma.	4	23
Faulkner, John B.	Mar. 9, 1826	21	light	Brooklyn, Conn.	4	24
Faulkner, William	Sept. 27, 1854	18	light	Eastport, Me.	5	30
Featherson, William T.	Oct. 21, 1834	24	light	Portland, Me.	5	28
Feeler, Peter	Jan. 3, 1846	27	yellow	New York	5	29
Fellows, Seth	Apr. 23, 1856	17	light	Lockport, N.Y.	5	30
Fenley, Thomas	Sept. 13, 1800	24	dark	Provincetown, Ma.	2	6
Fenner, Alpheus	Apr. 8, 1811	18	light	Johnston, R.I.	4	23
Fenner, Anthony B.	Mar. 24, 1846	36	dark	Warwick, R.I.	5	29
Fenner, Bowen	Apr. 17, 1805	22	light	Cranston, R.I.	3	11
Fenner, Charles	Aug. 11, 1796	23	dark	Cranston, R.I.	1	1
Fenner, Erastus L.	Aug. 13, 1845	17	dark	Providence, R.I.	5	29
Fenner, Henry	Sept. 13, 1815	19	brown	Providence, R.I.	4	23
Fenner, James, 2d	Jan. 1, 1823	23	light	Providence, R.I.	4	24
Fenner, John	Dec. 19, 1797	37	light	Johnston, R.I.	1	11
Fenner, Lou A.	Mar. 28, 1807	30	light	Cranston, R.I.	4	23
Fenner, Nathan B.	Aug. 31, 1848	33	light	Cranston, R.I.	5	29
Fenner, Pardon	July 28, 1800	24	dark	Cranston, R.I.	2	6
Fenner, Richard	Sept. 30, 1796	22	light	Coventry, R.I.	2	4
Fenner, Zephania B.	Oct. 14, 1807	16	light	Providence, R.I.	4	23
Fenton, Joseph	Sept. 25, 1801	21	light	Providence, R.I.	2	6

NAME	DATE OF CERTIFICATION	AGE	COMPLEXION	PLACE OF BIRTH	BOOK	PAGE
Ferera, Joseph	May 2, 1848	25	dark	Mobile, Ala.	5	29
Ferguson, John	Apr. 4, 1799	22	light	Charleston, S.C.	2	6
Fern, Edward	May 11, 1803	24	dark	Alexandria, Va.	2	6
Fernald, Oliver	Aug. 26, 1845	30	light	Lebanon, Me.	5	29
Fernald, Samuel C.	Mar. 2, 1846	17	fair	Boston, Ma.	5	29
Ferrier, William	Mar. 29, 1800	13	light	Providence, R.I.	2	6
Ferris, John	Mar. 10, 1798	26	light	Boston, Ma.	1	11
Field, Albert	Apr. 24, 1811	18	light	Providence, R.I.	4	23
Field, Benjamin	Feb. 27, 1796	21	light	Providence, R.I.	1	3
Field, Charles H.	June 26, 1861	14	dark	Hallowell, Me.	6	6
Field, George W.	Jan. 23, 1854	19	light	Johnston, R.I.	5	30
Field, Isaac	Mar. 28, 1810	15	light	Providence, R.I.	4	23
Field, James	Sept. 29, 1809	28	light	Charleston, S.C.	4	23
Field, John W.	Sept. 4, 1849	26	dark	Providence, R.I.	5	30
Field, John S.E.	Apr. 15, 1845	18	light	Pawtucket, Ma.[now RI]	5	29
Field, Lewis P.	Jan. 13, 1849	29	fair	Providence, R.I.	5	29
Field, Samuel	Dec. 21, 1805	13	light	Providence, R.I.	3	12
Field, Samuel H.	Nov. 16, 1810	18	dark	Providence, R.I.	4	23
Field, Thomas F.	Jan. 6, 1823	21	light	Cranston, R.I.	4	24
Field, William	Nov. 16, 1803	19	dark	Providence, R.I.	2	22
Finch, Oliver D.	Jan. 6, 1818	21	yellow	Brooklyn, Conn.	4	24
Finch, Stephen, Jr.	Mar. 16, 1809	19	yellow	Brookline, Conn.	4	23
Findley, John	Apr. 13, 1854	21	light	Smithfield, R.I.	5	30
Finemore, Alexander W.	Jan. 30, 1828	21	mulatto	Worcester, Ma.	4	24
Finney, George	Oct. 28, 1818	23	light	E. Greenwich, R.I.	4	24
Finnicks, Oliver J.	June 29, 1830	37	black	Dorset, Md.	5	28
Fish, Arthur	July 1, 1844	17	dark	Falmouth, Ma.	5	29
Fish, Charles D.	Nov. 23, 1840	37	light	Falmouth, Ma.	5	29
Fish, Consider	Oct. 13, 1803	17	light	Barnstable, Ma.	2	6
Fish, Francis	Oct. 27, 1804	20	light	Falmouth, Ma.	3	11
Fish, Stephen	Aug. 3, 1835	38	light	Kingston, Ma.	5	28
Fish, Theophilus	Oct. 25, 1796	32	light	Falmouth, Ma.	1	11&4
Fish, William	July 16, 1855	24	fair	Bangor, Me.	5	30
Fisher, Alpheus	June 30, 1841	17	light	No. Prov., R.I.	5	29
Fisher, Andrew S.	Mar. 7, 1839	23	light	Phila., Pa.	5	28
Fisher, Caleb M.	Nov. 28, 1821	17	light	Wrentham, Ma.	4	24
Fisher, Charles	Dec. 11, 1833	24	black	Taunton, Ma.	5	28

NAME	DATE OF CERTIFICATION	AGE	COMPLEXION	PLACE OF BIRTH	BOOK	PAGE
Fisher, Charles	Aug. 22, 1846	28	black	Taunton, Ma.	5	29
Fisher, George	Apr. 11, 1809	18	black	Providence,R.I.	4	23
Fisher, George A.	Nov. 1, 1803	23	dark	Rehoboth, Ma.	2	22
Fisher, George J.	Jan. 8, 1833	17	light	Cumberland, R.I.	5	28
Fisher, George U.	Dec. 24, 1852	17	light	Wrentham, Ma.	5	30
Fisher, George W.	June 16, 1832	15	light	Providence, R.I.	5	28
Fisher, Hammond	Jan. 4, 1800	17	dark	Wrentham, Ma.	2	6
Fisher, James	Aug. 10, 1840	35	light	Salem, Ma.	5	29
Fisher, James	Mar. 25, 1857	32	fair	Boston, Ma.	5	30
Fisher, John	Dec. 7, 1805	18	black	New Bedford, Ma.	3	12
Fisher, John	May 11,1858	25	light	Hartford, Conn.	6	6
Fisher, John Wm.	Mar. 28, 1856	18	dark	Providence, R.I.	5	30
Fisher, John R.	May 31, 1851	16	light	Providence, R.I.	5	30
Fisher, John R.	July 27, 1853	18	light	Providence, R.I.	5	30
Fisher, Justin T.	July 1, 1844	18	light	Falmouth, Ma.	5	29
Fisher, Lewis P.	Nov. 9, 1810	19	light	Wrentham, Ma.	4	23
Fisher, Obed	May 5, 1815	21	light	Dedham, Ma.	4	23
Fisher, Seth	May 16, 1839	16	light	Providence, R.I.	5	28
Fisher, Seth, Jr.	July 20, 1816	24	light	Providence, R.I.	4	23
Fisher, Thomas R.	Sept. 5, 1823	21	light	Wrentham, Ma.	4	24
Fisher, William	Dec. 7, 1838	30	light	Providence,R.I.	5	28
Fisher, William	Dec. 2, 1848	35	light	Nantucket, Ma.	5	29
Fisher, William	Aug. 11, 1858	29	dark	Barrington, R.I.	6	6
Fisher, William M.	Mar. 25, 1831	32	light	Bath, Me.	5	28
Fisk, Cyrus	June 7, 1816	29	dark	Waltham, Ma.	4	23
Fisk, Edmund	June 1, 1805	18	light	Johnston, R.I.	3	12
Fisk, Emory	Oct. 25, 1849	18	light	Cumberland, R.I.	5	30
Fisk, Jacob F.	Dec. 13, 1814	23	light	Dracut, Ma.	4	23
Fisk, Squire, Jr.	Nov. 12, 1803	19	dark	Cumberland, R.I.	2	22
Fitch, George B.	Feb. 8, 1844	23	light	Claremont, N.H.	5	29
Fitch, James	Oct. 4, 1800	17	black	Providence, R.I.	2	6
Fitch, Lucius	Aug. 27, 1803	17	light	Windham, Conn.	2	6
Fitch, Samuel	July 15, 1806	27	black	Windham, Conn.	3	12
Fitts, Emery	Aug. 5, 1851	23	dark	Worcester, Ma.	5	30
Flagg, Abraham	May 21, 1805	34	black	Newport, R.I.	3	11
Flamar, George	July 31, 1828	--	----	Fall River, Ma.	-	--

Married Dorothy S. Clark of Attleboro. By Rev. Benedict Record.

NAME	DATE OF CERTIFICATION	AGE	COMPLEXION	PLACE OF BIRTH	BOOK	PAGE
Flanigan, George	Mar. 3, 1857	19	fair	New York, N.Y.	5	30
Flanigan, Michael	June 9, 1856	17	light	Detroit, Michigan	5	30
Fleming, Darius	Sept. 8, 1857	19	light	Geneva, N.Y.	6	6
Fleming, Samuel	Sept. 7, 1859	36	black	Milford, Del.	6	6
Fletcher, Daniel	Apr. 1, 1835	16	black	Windham, Conn.	5	.28
Fletcher, Leroy E.	Aug. 22, 1862	18	light	Stockton, Me.	6	6
Fletcher, Thomas	Oct. 8, 1856	27	mulatto	Washington, D.C.	5	30
Fletcher, William C.	Nov. 19, 1838	34	mulatto	Plymouth, Ma.	5	28
Fliming, William	Nov. 18, 1797	28	light	Ireland	1	11
Flinn, William	Apr. 17, 1840	21	dark	New York, N.Y.	5	29
Flint, Daniel	Dec. 21, 1804	24	light	Wilmington, Ma.	3	11
Flint, Horace	Nov. 19, 1832	37	light	Manchester, Conn.	5	28
Flood, Thomas	Dec. 1, 1848	27	dark	Providence, R.I.	5	29
Flood, Thomas	Nov. 1, 1852	30	dark	Harwich, Ma.	5	30
Floyd, James	July 13, 1839	27	dark	Bath, Me.	5	28
Flynn, Charles	Feb. 15, 1860	28	fair	New York, N.Y.	6	6
Flynn, John	Oct. 27, 1804	17	light	Woodstock, Conn.	3	11
Flynn, John	May 20, 1807	20	light	Woodstock, Conn.	4	23
Flynn, John	Mar. 21, 1806	18	light	Woodstock, Conn.	3	12
Fobler, William	Aug. 6, 1810	44	black	Salem, Ma.	4	23
Foley, Michael	May 19, 1851	19	light	New York, N.Y.	5	30
Foley, Peter	Sept. 10, 1866	28	light	Boston, Ma.	6	6
Follet, John	Oct. 7, 1812	28	brown	Cumberland, R.I.	4	23
Follet, Layton J.	Dec. 30, 1816	21	light	Cumberland, R.I.	4	23
Follett, Luis	May 19, 1806	20	light	Attleboro, Ma.	3	12
Follett, Olney P.	Oct. 5, 1847	25	fair	Mendon, Ma.	5	29
Follett, Philip M.	June 11, 1848	22	light	Cumberland, R.I.	5	29
Follett, Samuel	June 26, 1847	21	fair	Swansea, Ma.	5	29
Follett, William C.	Aug. 3, 1850	18	light	No. Prov., R.I.	5	30
Follett, William Henry	Aug. 1, 1854	18	light	No. Prov., R.I.	5	30
Follow, Isaac	Feb. 20, 1812	25	yellow	Masshpee, Ma.	4	23
Fones, Christopher	1789-1799	Dec. 24, 1772		No. Kingston, R.I.	* -	--
Fones, Joseph	Oct. 22, 1849	26	light	No. Kingston, R.I.	5	30
Fones, William H.	June 25, 1835	21	light	No. Kingston, R.I.	5	28
Foote, Benjamin	Oct. 16, 1833	32	light	Bath, Me.	5	28
Foot, John Henry	Aug. 28, 1815	16	light	Providence, R.I.	4	23
Forbes?, Samuel	Aug. 13, 1847	19	dark	Eastport, Me.	5	29
Forbush, Reuben	Jan. 11, 1831	23	light	Stow, Ma.	5	28

*Newport, R.I.

REGISTER OF SEAMEN'S PROTECTION

NAME	DATE OF CERTIFICATION	AGE	COMPLEXION	PLACE OF BIRTH	BOOK	PAGE
Ford, Charles H.	May 23, 1858	17	dark	Providence, R.I.	6	6
Ford, Edward	July 13, 1841	25	mulatto	Baltimore, Md.	5	29
Ford, John	Mar. 13, 1847	21	light	New York City, N.Y.	5	29
Ford, William T.	Dec. 18, 1851	17	dark	Searsport, Me.	5	30
Formby, James	Dec. 26, 1866	26	dark	Providence, R.I.	6	6
Forrester, William	Nov. 4, 1833	17	dark	Cranston, R.I.	5	28
Fortune, Joseph	Apr. 10, 1835	22	dark	Norwich, Conn.	5	28
Fortune, Richard	Nov. 23, 1807	23	black	Plainfield, Conn.	4	23
Fosberg, John G.	Jan. 14, 1834	19	light	Boston, Ma.	5	28
Foss, Nason	Nov. 28, 1827	23	light	Brunswick, Me.	4	24
Foss, Thomas	Oct. 29, 1803	26	dark	Boston, Ma.	2	6
Fossett, James, Jr.	June 8, 1838	22	light	Bristol, Me.	5	28
Foster, Benjamin J.	May 8, 1820	18	dark	Providence, R.I.	4	24
Foster, Charles T.	June 2, 1837	24	light	Scituate, Ma.	5	28
Foster, George	June 2, 1820	25	yellow	Providence, R.I.	4	24
Foster, George	Sept. 6, 1826	21	light	Providence, R.I.	4	24
Foster, George	June 11, 1835	23	dark	Nantucket, Ma.	5	28
Foster, George	Oct. 19, 1842	38	light	Providence, R.I.	5	29
Foster, George W.	Oct. 8, 1817	15	light	Providence, R.I.	4	24
Foster, James	Mar. 9, 1798	27	dark	Providence, R.I.	1	11
Foster, James	Apr. 2, 1819	19	brown	Providence, R.I.	4	24
Foster, James, Jr.	Aug. 31, 1825	29	dark	Danvers, Ma.	4	24
Foster, James B.	Apr. 25, 1842	24	light	Providence, R.I.	5	29
Foster, James S.	Jan. 18, 1850	22	light	No. Prov., R.I.	5	30
Foster, Jpb	Dec. 12, 1801	30	dark	New York, N.Y.	2	6
Foster, John C.	Jan. 24, 1866	25	light	Jersey City, N.J.	6	6
Foster, John S.	May 15, 1841	30	light	Providence, R.I.	5	29
Foster, Joseph B.	May 12, 1815	17	light	Lynn, Ma.	4	23
Foster, Robert Watson	Dec. 20, 1822	25	light	New Castle, Great Britian	4	24
Foster, Samuel	July 17, 1844	25	dark	New York, N.Y.	5	29
Foster, Squire	Nov. 9, 1811	21	light	Rehoboth, Ma.	4	23
Foster, Theodore R.	Nov. 3, 1827	16	light	Foster, R.I.	4	24
Foster, William	Feb. 23, 1805	25	dark	Smithfield, R.I.	3	11
Foster, William	June 19, 1809	21	dark	Warwick, R.I.	4	23
Foster, William M.	Apr. 6, 1865	46	light	St. George, Me.	6	6
Fountain, John	Nov. 26, 1861	25	dark	Milford, Del.	6	6
Fowler, Christopher	Oct. 21, 1801	22	dark	No. Kingstown, R.I.	2	6

NAME	DATE OF CERTIFICATION	AGE	COMPLEXION	PLACE OF BIRTH	BOOK	PAGE
Fowler, Edward	Mar. 3, 1857	27	light	Williamsburg, N.Y.	5	30
Fowler, John H.	Sept. 13, 1858	15	light	No. Kingstown, R.I.	6	6
Fowler, Oliver W.	Oct. 16, 1839	22	dark	Preston, Conn.	5	28
Fowler, Orchard	Sept. 20, 1796	17	dark	Gilford, Conn.	1	3
Fowler, Samuel	Oct. 3, 1828	29	light	Newport, R.I.	4	24
Fowler, Samuel	Aug. 6, 1834	19	light	Jamestown, R.I.	5	28
Fowler, Samuel	Oct. 6, 1835	23	light	Newport, R.I.	5	28
Fowler, Samuel R.	Nov. 27, 1827	35	dark	Ipswich, Ma.	4	24
Fox, Charles	Aug. 26, 1815	16	dark	Providence, R.I.	4	23
Fox, George	Mar. 27, 1811	13	light	Providence, R.I.	4	23
Fox, George	Aug. 31, 1833	57	black	Phila., Pa.	5	28
Fox, Peter	Jan. 5, 1833	15	light	Phila., Pa.	5	28
Foy, Daniel	Oct. 15, 1844	23	light	Providence, R.I.	5	29
Foy, Thomas	July 8, 1809	19	yellow	Dighton, Ma.	4	23
Foy, Thomas	Apr. 23, 1812	22	yellow	Dighton, Ma.	4	23
Francheville, William	Nov. 6, 1834	20	light	Alexandria, D.C.	5	28
Francis, Edward	Oct. 6, 1818	20	black	New York, N.Y.	4	24
Francis, Henry	Aug. 4, 1806	31	light	Tiverton, R.I.	3	12
Francis, Henry	Mar. 25, 1826	15	mulatto	Providence, R.I.	4	24
Francis, Henry	Sept. 4, 1835	31	black	Warwick, R.I.	5	28
Francis, Jacob	Mar. 25, 1851	55	black	Greenbush, N.Y.	5	30
Francis, James J.	Aug. 16, 1854	20	black	Providence, R.I.	5	30
Francis, John	Aug. 29, 1803	21	black	Newport, R.I.	2	6
Francis, John	July 10, 1807	25	light	Boston, Ma.	4	23
Francis, John	Mar. 8, 1853	24	light	New York, N.Y.	5	30
Francis, Jospeh	Aug. 21, 1845	21	dark	New London, Conn.	5	29
Francis, Joseph	Oct. 10, 1849	25	dark	New Bedford, Ma.	5	30
Francis, Joseph	Oct. 20, 1849	24	yellow	New York, N.Y.	5	30
Francis, Nelson	May 16, 1833	22	mulatto	Boston, Ma.	5	28
Francis, Paul	Sept. 2, 1864	27	black	----, Fla.	6	6
Francis, Thomas	Dec. 27, 1816	29	black	Providence, R.I.	4	23
Francis, Thomas Graham	Oct. 13, 1863	32	dark	Providence, R.I.	6	6
Francis, Tobias	Oct. 12, 1853	22	black	Stony Brook, N.Y.	5	30
Francis, William	July 27, 1804	13	light	New York, N.Y.	3	11
Francis, William	Mar. 28, 1812	22	light	Providence, R.I.	4	23
Francis, William	Oct. 10, 1822	19	black	Kings County, N.Y.	4	24
Francis, William	Nov. 28, 1832	20	black	New Bedford, Ma.	5	28

NAME	DATE OF CERTIFICATION	AGE	COMPLEXION	PLACE OF BIRTH	BOOK	PAGE
Frank, John	Jan. 22, 1859	20	light	Phila., Pa.	6	6
Frank, William	Mar. 11, 1853	19	mulatto	New Orleans, La.	5	30
Franklin, Abraham	Oct. 7, 1841	21	mulatto	Johnston, R.I.	5	29
Franklin, Benjamin	Oct. 2, 1797	31	dark	Providence, R.I.	1	11
Franklin, George	Aug. 31, 1818	20	light	Nantucket, Ma.	4	24
Franklin, Henry T.	June 21, 1845	38	light	Middletown, Conn.	5	29
Franklin, James	June 4, 1798	28	dark	Providence, R.I.	2	6
Franklin, James	Feb. 16, 1857	23	light	New Haven, Conn.	5	30
Franklin, John	Mar. 26, 1857	23	light	Phila., Pa.	5	93
Franklin, Joseph	Oct. 20, 1849	22	dark	New York, N.Y.	5	30
Franklin, Robert M.	Feb. 22, 1826	17	dark	Newport, R.I.	4	24
Franklin, Silas S.	Dec. 15, 1825	13	light	Providence, R.I.	4	24
Franklin, Thomas	July 19, 1800	23	light	Scituate, R.I.	2	6
Franklin, Warren	July 27, 1844	22	light	Boston, Ma.	5	29
Franklin, Warren P.	Aug. 20, 1841	19	light	Boston, Ma.	5	29
Frasier, Isaiah	May 11, 1855	19	dark	New York, N.Y.	5	30
Frasier, Thomas	May 19, 1810	34	yellow	Somerset, Ma.	4	23
Frazer, Alex M.	Aug. 27, 1853	25	light	Northport, Me.	5	30
Frazer, Daniel	Nov. 27, 1849	26	light	Providence, R.I.	5	30
Frazier, George W.	Jan. 6, 1834	24	black	New York, N.Y.	5	28
Freden, Sweaney	June 7, 1799	26	light	Norfolk, Va.	2	6
Frederick, Alexander	Nov. 19, 1852	28	dark	Charleston, S.C.	5	30
Frederick, Folliot	Apr. 15, 1835	25	light	New Orleans, La.	5	28
Frederick, John P.	June 9, 1806	20	light	Newark, N.J.	3	12
Freebody, William	Oct. 4, 1819	21	yellow	Newport, R.I.	4	24
Freeborn, Joseph	1798-1799	June 22, 1779		Portsmouth, R.I.	* -	--
Freeborn, Stephen	1798-1799	Aug. 1 or Sept. 1, 1779		Portsmouth, R.I.--	--*
Freeman, Aaron	Mar. 29, 1819	26	black	Rehoboth, Ma.	4	24
Freeman, Alexander	Oct. 27, 1821	18	black	Westerly, R.I.	4	24
Freeman, Caesar	Sept. 15, 1806	21	black	Colchester, Conn.	3	12
Freeman, Charles	Oct. 4, 1805	41	dark	Attleboro, Ma.	3	12
Freeman, Charles	Aug. 6, 1831	21	light	Mendon, Ma.	5	28
Freeman, Charles	May 16, 1833	19	black	Fairfield, Conn.	5	28
Freeman, Edward	Dec, 29, 1845	45	black	New York, N.Y.	5	29
Freeman, Elias	Apr. 4, 1844	25	mulatto	Colchester, Conn.	5	29
Freeman, Henry F.	F. Nov. 11, 1850	18	light	Warwick, R.I.	5	30
Freeman, James	Oct. 14, 1828	17	black	Hartford, Conn.	4	24
Freeman, James	Feb. 1, 1854	17	black	Providence, R.I.	5	30

* Newport, R.I.

NAME	DATE OF CERTIFICATION	AGE	COMPLEXION	PLACE OF BIRTH	BOOK	PAGE
Freeman, James	Apr. 23, 1855	25	dark	New York, N.Y.	5	30
Freeman, James H.	July 13, 1824	27	light	Sandwich, Ma.	4	24
Freeman, Jebiel	July 11, 1822	21	black	Colchester, Conn.	4	24
Freeman, John	Sept. 25, 1804	21	dark	Cumberland, R.I.	3	11
Freeman, John	Mar. 23, 1805	27	black	Troy, N.Y.	3	11
Freeman, John	Aug. 11, 1810	15	brown	Alexandria, Va.	4	23
Freeman, John	Sept. 19, 1810	27	yellow	New York, N.Y.	4	23
Freeman, John	Jan. 6, 1834	23	black	Boston, Ma.	5	28
Freeman, Jonathan	June 12, 1809	26	black	Sharon, Conn.	4	23
Freeman, Joshua	Oct. 6, 1818	25	dark	Boston, Ma.	4	24
Freeman, Lawrence	Aug. 13, 1834	16	light	Providence, R.I.	5	28
Freeman, Merl	May 10, 1818	--	----	Of Attleboro	-	--
Married Nancy Albro of No. Proivdence. By Rev. Benedict Record.						
Freeman, Morris	Jan. 15, 1802	17	dark	Wrentham, Ma.	2	6
Freeman, Nero	Nov. 25, 1797	24	black	Groton, Conn.	1	11
Freeman, Peter	Aug. 13, 1810	27	black	Hartford, Conn.	4	23
Freeman, Richard	June 18, 1802	23	black	Attleboro, Ma.	2	6
Freeman, Samuel	June 2, 1817	19	dark	Cumberland, R.I.	4	24
Freeman, Silas	Nov. 9, 1842	29	black	Glastonbury, Conn.	5	29
Freeman, Thomas	Mar. 28, 1837	25	black	Plattsburg, N.Y.	5	28
Freeman, William	Nov. 8, 1826	--	----	of Attleboro	-	--
Married Mary Slocum of Valley Falls. By Bev. Benedict Record.						
Freeman, William	Dec. 13, 1856	23	mulatto	Providence, R.I.	5	30
Freeman, William H.	Mar. 19, 1830	23	black	Guilford, Conn.	5	28
French, Charles	Aug. 13, 1834	36	dark	Boston, Ma.	5	28
French, Cyrus	Aug. 16, 1813	19	light	Rehoboth, Ma.	4	23
French, Ebenezer	Nov. 21, 1832	24	light	Dunstable, Ma.	5	28
French, Edward	Dec. 15, 1823	17	light	Providence, R.I.	4	24
French, Edward A.	Sept. 17, 1845	24	light	Berkley, Ma.	5	29
French, Harvey	June 30, 1823	24	light	Seekonk, Ma.	4	24
French, John	Mar. 11, 1797	16	light	Stoughton, Ma.	1	11
French, John	May 31, 1837	46	light	Norfolk, Va.	5	28
French, Joseph	Dec. 15, 1817	20	dark	Providence, R.I.	4	24
French, Joseph S.	Nov. 2, 1847	22	dark	Berfley, Ma.	5	29
French, Nathaniel	Oct. 31, 1803	19	dark	Providence, R.I.	2	6
French, Robert	June 9, 1856	22	florid	Portland, Me.	5	30
French, Samuel	Dec. 29, 1829	20	light	Troy, Ma.	5	28
French, Thomas	Mar. 29, 1800	19	dark	Rehoboth, Ma.	2	6

REGISTER OF SEAMEN'S PROTECTION

NAME	DATE OF CERTIFICATION	AGE	COMPLEXION	PLACE OF BIRTH	BOOK	PAGE
French, Zachariah	Oct. 5, 1805	19	light	Rehoboth, Ma.	3	12
Frew, Peter	Nov. 10, 1846	24	ruddy	Eastport, Me.	5	29
Frewlay John	Apr. 23, 1857	19	light	Bristol, R.I.	5	93
Frier, George	July 18, 1850	25	light	New Orleans, La.	5	30
Frieze, George H.	Nov. 12, 1858	27	yellow	Wilmington, Del.	6	6
Frisbee, John L.L.	July 5, 1855	22	fair	Kittery, Me.	5	30
Fritz, Charles	Sept. 21, 1866	21	dark	New York, N.Y.	6	6
Frost, Jacob	Dec. 21, 1818	25	black	Cambridge, Ma.	4	24
Frost, John	Aug. 24, 1852	25	light	-----, N.Y.	5	30
Fry, Benjamin	Aug. 8, 1846	38	dark	Vasselborough, Me.	5	29
Fry, George	Oct. 28, 1805	18	black	Providence, R.I.	3	12
Fry, George	May 19, 1847	28	fair	Providence, R.I.	5	29
Fry, John E.	Nov. 4, 1853	25	florid	Andover, Ma.	5	30
Fry, Nathaniel	June 8, 1813	16	light	Taunton, Ma.	4	23
Fry, Noel	Dec. 27, 1822	23	yellow	No. Kingstown, R.I.	4	24
Fry, Peter	May 22, 1809	18	black	Exeter, R.I.	4	23
Fry, Samuel	Sept. 12, 1809	27	brown	W. Greenwich, R.I.	4	23
Fry, Thomas	Jan. 12, 1835	23	black	No. Kingston, R.I.	5	28
Fry, William	May 21, 1799	15	black	Providence,R.I.	2	6
Fry, William	Dec. 2, 1803	20	black	Providence, R.I.	2	22
Fry, William	June 20, 1797	36	black	E. Greenwich, R.I.	1	11
Fry, William A.	July 27, 1860	19	malatto	E. Greewich, R.I.	6	6
Fuller, Allen	Sept. 28, 1804	21	dark	Rehoboth, Ma.	3	11
Fuller, Andrew	Aug. 19, 1845	40	dark	Salem, Ma.	5	29
Fuller, Calvin	Mar. 6, 1850	22	dark	Dover, N.H.	5	30
Fuller, Clifford A.	Aug. 5, 1850	17	light	Foster, R.I.	5	30
Fuller, George N.	Nov. 9, 1847	37	dark	Cumberland, R.I.	5	29
Fuller, James	Jan. 9, 1798	25	black	Bedford, Ma.	1	11
Fuller, James	Nov. 9, 1841	23	dark	Killingly, Conn.	5	29
Fuller, John	Sept. 7, 1799	22	light	Cumberland, R.I.	2	6
Fuller, John C.	Nov. 28, 1834	25	light	Providence, R.I.	5	28
Fuller, Jonathan T.	Sept. 25, 1807	17	light	Providence, R.I.	4	23
Fuller, Joseph	Aug. 10, 1797	21	light	Cranston, R.I.	1	11
Fuller, Joseph	Dec. 21, 1805	22	light	No. Prov., R.I.	3	12
Fuller, Russell	May 27, 1797	25	light	Rehoboth, Ma.	1	11
Fuller, Zephaniah	July 7, 1801	18	light	Duxbury, Ma.	2	6
Furbush, William	Aug. 15, 1821	19	brown	Salisbury, Md.	4	24
Furlong, Edward	Aug. 6, 1855	18	dark	Providence, R.I.	5	30

NAME	DATE OF CERTIFICATION	AGE	COMPLEXION	PLACE OF BIRTH	BOOK	PAGE
Furrow, Joseph	Oct. 31, 1838	28	light	Killingly, Conn.	5	28
Gabard, John	1798-1799		Resided in Newport from 1783-1798		*-	--
Gabel, Daniel	Dec. 13, 1817	25	dark	Phila., Pa.	4	27
Gage, George R.	May 22, 1840	20	light	No. Prov., R.I.	5	32
Gage, George R.	Mar. 25, 1853	32	dark	No. Prov., R.I.	5	34
Galacar, George A.	July 21, 1841	18	light	No. Prov., R.I.	5	32
See: Golicar, George A. as spelled in Book 5, page 32.						
Galbreth, William	June 22, 1833	22	dark	Carlisle, Pa.	5	31
Gale, Calvin	Sept. 10, 1808	20	dark	Roxbury, Ma.	4	26
Gale, Martin	Oct. 9, 1828	36	black	Smithfield, R.I.	4	28
Galigan, James	Feb. 21, 1854	24	light	Bangor, Me.	5	34
Gallagher, James	Mar. 14, 1850	22	light	Providence, R.I.	5	33
Galloway, Isaiah	Oct. 4, 1849	23	dark yellow	Baltimore, Md.	5	33
Gallup, James	Sept. 20, 1808	21	light	Voluntown, Conn.	4	26
Gallup, Miner	June 26, 1854	24	light	? N.Y.	5	34
Galson, George	Jan. 10, 1851	26	dark	New Orleans, La.	5	33
Galum, Anthony	May 16, 1820	20	black	Newport, R.I.	4	27
Galvean, John	Oct. 18, 1841	20	light	New Orleans, La.	5	32
Gammons, Ephraim	June 18, 1844	38	light	Middleboro, Ma.	5	32
Gann, William	Nov. 2, 1803	25	light	Hookstown, Md.	2	38
Gano, Esek H.	Aug. 8, 1812	14	dark	Farankfort, Ky.	4	27
Gano, John S.	Oct. 20, 1803	16	light	Hudson, N.Y.	2	38
Gant, Francis	Dec. 4, 1830	51	light	Roxbury, Ma.	5	31
Garden, William	May 11, 1803	21	light	New York, N.Y.	2	38
Gardiner, Alfred S.	Oct. 3, 1866	26	medium	So. Kingstown, R.I.	6	7
Gardiner, Chas. H.	Mar. 9, 1854	17	dark	Warwick, R.I.	5	34
Gardiner, Dan'l A.	Mar. 9, 1854	18	dark	Warwick, R.I.	5	34
Gardiner, Dwight	Sept. 28, 1864	21	dark	NO. Stonington, Conn.	6	7
Gardiner, George	Feb. 25, 1837	22	black	Palmyra, Me.	5	31
Gardiner, Geo. H.	Mar. 5, 1849	24	light	So. Kingston, R.I.	5	33
Gardiner, Gorton	May 5, 1797	23	dark	Warwick, R.I.	1	12
Gardiner, Jeremiah B.	Sept. 10, 1849	19	light	So. Kingston, R.I.	5	33
Gardiner, John C.	Dec. 11, 1821	19	light	No. Kingston, R.I.	4	27
Gardiner, Nathaniel J.	Apr. 6, 1848	23	light	So. Kingston, R.I.	5	33
Gardiner, Nicholas B.	June 28, 1849	20	light	Scituate, R.I.	5	33
Gardiner, Oliver	Oct. 15, 1831	22	black	E. Greenwich, R.I.	5	31
Gardiner, Silas S.	Oct. 14, 1851	16	light	Bath, Me.	5	33
Gardiner, Thomas	May 31, 1851	20	light	New York, N.Y.	5	33

*Newport, R. I.

NAME		DATE OF CERTIFICATION	AGE	COMPLEXION	PLACE OF BIRTH	BOOK	PAGE
Gardner, Adam		May 23, 1806	25	yellow	Kingston, N.Y.	3	66
Gardner, Alfred		Aug. 26, 1815	12	brown	Newport, R.I.	4	27
Gardner, Amboy		Mar. 26, 1819	35	black	Middletown, R.I.	4	27
Gardner, Amos		Sept 30, 1843	23	mulatto	Boston, Ma.	5	32
Gardner, Augustus Mumford		Nov. 3, 1804	16	light	Warwick, R.I.	3	14
Gardner, Benj. W.		Oct. 27, 1849	23	light	So. Kingston, R.I.	5	33
Gardner, Cyrus		July 20?, 1804	16	dark yellow*	No. Kingstown, R.I.	3	13
Gardner, Cyrus		Apr. 11, 1809	23	yellowish	No. Kingstown, R.I.	4	26
Gardner, Daniel		Dec. 30, 1819	23	black	No. Kingstown, R.I.	4	27
Gardner, Edward		1798-1799	Nov. 18, 1778		So. Kingston	** -	--
Gardner, Edward C.		1798-1799	Nov. 8, 1778		So. Kingston	** -	--
Gardner, Edward		Nov. 7, 1836	18	light	Nantucket, Ma.	5	31
Gardner, Elisha		Sept. 15, 1804	24	light	So. Kingstown, R.I.	3	14
Gardner, Ephraim		Nov. 18, 1796	35	dark	So. Kingstown, R.I.	1	12
Gardner, Ephraim		Dec. 26, 1809	48	dark	So. Kingstown, R.I.	4	26
Gardner, Frank		1798-1799	Oct. 16, 1780		So. Kingston	** -	--
Gardner, George		Oct. 27, 1801	25	black	So. Kingstown, R.I.	2	38
Gardner, George G.		May 1, 1837	19	light	Bristol, R.I.	5	31
Gardner, George R.		July 13, 1840	18	light	Jamestown, R.I.	5	32
Gardner, George S.		Aug. 28, 1841	25	black	Palmyra, Me.	5	32
Gardner, Gideon		Nov. 15, 1796	32	dark	No. Kingstown,	1	12
Gardner, Gideon		Apr. 26, 1815	20	black	No. Kingstown, R.I.	4	27
Gardner, Hyman		1798-1799	Feb. 3, 1783		So. Kingston	** -	--

Amos Gardner of So. Kingston swears the above to be true.

NAME		DATE OF CERTIFICATION	AGE	COMPLEXION	PLACE OF BIRTH	BOOK	PAGE
Gardner, Isaac		Sept. 1, 1797	19	light	E. Greenwich, R.I.	1	12
Gardner, Isaac		Feb. 27, 1834	31	black	E. Greenwich, Conn.	5	31
Gardner, Jack		Nov. 9, 1796	28	black	No. Kingstown, R.I.	1	12&5
Gardner, James		Oct. 16, 1804	21	dark	Bridgewater, Ma.	3	14
Gardner, James		Dec. 15, 1809	47	black	So. Kingstown, R.I.	4	26
Gardner, James B.		Oct. 18, 1830	25	dark	Newport, R.I.	5	31
Gardner, Jeremiah		July 24, 1807	22	black	No. Kingstown, R.I.	4	26
Gardner, Jeremiah		Aug. 27, 1845	28	dark	Richmond, R.I.	5	33
Gardner, Jeremiah S.		July 11, 1827	22	dark	So. Kingstown, R.I.	4	28
Gardner, Jerome		May 26, 1830	33	light	Boston, Ma.	5	31

*mulatto
**Newport, R. I.

REGISTER OF SEAMEN'S PROTECTION

NAME	DATE OF CERTIFICATION	AGE	COMPLEXION	PLACE OF BIRTH	BOOK	PAGE
Gardner, John	1798-1799	Jan. 19, 1779		So. Kingston, R.I.	** -	--
Gardner, John	Sept. 29, 1803	19	black	No. Kingstown, R.I.	2	38
Gardner, John	Jan. 16, 1804	24	yellow*	Newport, R.I.	3	13
Gardner, John	Nov. 30, 1805	17	light	Exeter, R.I.	3	66
Gardner, John	Dec. 10, 1818	38	fresh	Warren, R.I.	4	27
Gardner, John	Dec. 12, 1821	19	light	No. Kingstown, R.I.	4	27
Gardner, John	Nov. 28, 1828	23	black	Newport, R.I.	4	28
Gardner, John	Dec. 12, 1833	18	dark	So. Kingston, R.I.	5	31
Gardner, John	Apr. 15, 1836	19	black	So. Kingston, R.I.	5	31
Gardner, John A.	July 21, 1844	19	light	Newport, R.I.	5	32
Gardner, John H.	Nov. 15, 1828	28	light	No. Kingstown, R.I.	4	28
Gardner, Jonathan	Jan. 31, 1823	29	dark	NO. Kingstown, R.I.	4	27
Gardner, Joseph	Nov. 19, 1801	14	dark	Warren, R.I.	2	38
Gardner, Joseph	Sept. 27, 1826	28	mulatto	Canterbury, Conn.	4	28
Gardner, Joseph	Oct. 1, 1844	17	light	No. Prov., R.I.	5	32
Gardner, Joseph W.	Mar. 7, 1815	18	light	No. Kingstown, R.I.	4	27
Gardner, Josiah	Aug. 10, 1822	39	fresh	No. Kingstown, R.I.	4	27
Gardner, Nathan	Apr. 14, 1810	25	brown	No. Kingstown, R.I.	4	26
Gardner, Nathaniel	Oct. 17, 1806	21	light	Providence, R.I.	4	26
Gardner, Nathaniel	Dec. 12, 1832	28	yellow	No. Kingston, R.I.	5	31
Gardner, Nicholas	Nov. 26, 1804	22	light	Warwick, R.I.	3	14
Gardner, Palmer	Apr. 3, 1804	21	dark	No. Kingstown, R.I.	3	13
Gardner, Peleg C.	Mar. 15, 1815	16	light	No. Kingstown, R.I.	4	27
Gardner, Peter	July 7, 1804	20	black	No. Kingstown, 'R.I.	3	13
Gardner, Pero	Oct. 24, 1818	25	black	E. Greenwich, R.I.	4	27
Gardner, Prince	Jan. 16, 1804	25	black	Newport, R.I.	3	13
Gardner, Robert	Aug. 26, 1797	17	light	So. Kingstown, R.I.	1	12
Gardner, Robert	Nov. 24, 1828	26	dark	So. Kingstown, R.I.	4	28
Gardner, Robert	1798-1799	Feb. 18, 1781		So. Kingstown, R.I.	** -	--

Amos Gardner of So. Kingstown swears the above to be true.

NAME	DATE OF CERTIFICATION	AGE	COMPLEXION	PLACE OF BIRTH	BOOK	PAGE
Gardner, Rodman	Sept. 9, 1836	21	dark	So. Kingston, R.I.	5	31
Gardner, Sam'l B.	Apr. 5, 1856	22	fair	E. Greenwich, R.I.	5	34
Gardner, Stephen	Aug. 13, 1807	23	black	So. Kingstown, R.I.	4	26
Gardner, Varnum S.	Oct. 18, 1849	22	light	Exeter, R.I.	5	33
Gardner, Wanton	Oct. 19, 1818	27	yellow	Providence, R.I.	4	27
Gardner, Willet C.	Dec. 24, 1816	21	dark	So. Kingstown, R.I.	4	27
Gardner, William A.	Oct. 29, 1849	24	dark	NO. Kingston, R.I.	5	33

*mulatto
**Newport, R. I.

NAME	DATE OF CERTIFICATION	AGE	COMPLEXION	PLACE OF BIRTH	BOOK	PAGE
Gardner, William C.	Nov. 11, 1840	23	light	No. Kingston, R.I.	5	32
Gardner, Wm. H.	Mar. 26, 1853	28	dark	Newport, 'R.I.	5	34
Gardner, Winsor	Nov. 19, 1806	18	black	E. Greenwich, R.I.	4	26
Garland, George	Nov. 19, 1853	22	light	Eastport, Me.	5	34
Garrison, William	Nov. 27, 1835	20	black	New York, N.Y.	5	31
Gaskill, Charles	Nov. 10, 1860	30	dark	Tuckerton, N.J.	6	7
Gasper, William	Mar. 24, 1831	29	light	New York, N.Y.	5	31
Gates, Horace	Mar. 23, 1855	24	light	No. Prov., R.I.	5	34
Gates, Stanton C.	Nov. 20, 1849	23	light	Richmond, R.I.	5	33
Gates, Thomas S.	Oct. 16, 1839	19	dark	Norwich, Conn.	5	32
Gatewood, Bennett P.	May 5, 1810	34	light	Parish of St. Geo., Va.	4	26
Gauson, Samuel	June 27, 1806	20	yellow	Windham, Conn.	3	66
Gavit, Samuel	Feb. 7, 1798	22	dark	So. Kingstown, R.I.	1	15
Gavitson, John	Aug. 19, 1839	22	light	Rochester, Ma.	5	32
Gavitt, Hazard	Sept. 30, 1846	17	fair	So. Kingston, R.I.	5	33
Gay, William	Mar. 6, 1843	23	light	New York, N.Y.	5	32
Gayton, Charles M.	Apr. 3, 1855	19	light	Fall River, Ma.	5	34
Gear, John C.	July 29, 1839	20	light	New London, Conn.	5	32
Gee, George	July 5, 1805	23	light	New York, N.Y.	3	66
George, A. Hender	Aug. 30, 1853	18	light	Camden, Me.	5	34
George, Prince	Dec. 29, 1797	25	black	Barnstable, Ma.	1	15
George, William	May 18, 1857	20	light	Providence, R.I.	5	34
Gerald, Stephen G.	Mar. 5, 1849	20	light	Providence, R.I.	5	33
German, James	Dec. 10, 1841	14	light	Providence, R.I.	5	32
Gibbings, William	Apr. 12, 1852	21	light	Bath, Me.	5	34
Gibbons, John	1798-1799	May 8, 1781		Norwich, Conn.	*-	--
Gibbons, Major	June 5, 1804	21	dark	Petersburgh, Va.	3	13
Gibbs, Abraham	Apr. 1, 1800	46	black	Charleston, S.C.	2	7
Gibbs, Caleb	Oct. 2, 1804	13	light	Providence, R.I.	3	14
Gibbs, Elisha	Oct. 10, 1806	16	light	Newport, R.I.	4	26

Gibbs, Henry of Somerset 1798-1799   Jan. 20, 1784 Tiverton, R.I.   *-   -•
  Wanton Chase of Somerset swears the same to be true. That Gibbs is of dark complexion,
   dark hair, dark eyes, small scar on left side of nose.

Gibbs, Henry	Feb. 21, 1810	15	yellow	Providence, R.I.	4	26
Gibbs, John	July 20, 1805	23	dark	Cecil Co., Md.	3	66
Gibbs, John F.	Sept. 27, 1805	25	light	Providence, R.I.	3	66
Gibbs, John Henry	Mar. 2, 1851	20	light	Somerset, Ma.	5	20

*Newport, R. I.

REGISTER OF SEAMEN'S PROTECTION

NAME	DATE OF CERTIFICATION	AGE	COMPLEXION	PLACE OF BIRTH	BOOK	PAGE
Gibbs, Josephus	Oct. 3, 1810	16	light	Wareham, Ma.	4	26
Gibbs, Stephen	Oct. 30, 1823	16	black	Providence, R.I.	4	28
Gibbs, Stephens	Oct. 11, 1809	23	light	Wareham, Ma.	4	26
Gibbs, Tabor	1798-1799	Aug. 28, 1772		Little Compton	* -	--
Gibbs, Theodore A.	Nov. 16, 1847	22	light	Hamilton, Ma.	5	33
Gibbs, Thomas	Oct. 2, 1804	11	light	Providence, R.I.	3	14
Gibbs, William	Nov. 29, 1848	28	mulatto	Phila., Pa.	5	33
Gibbs, William S.	Oct. 24, 1809	14	yellow	Providence, R.I.	4	26
Gibson, Francis	Mar. 4, 1845	34	dark	New York, N.Y.	5	32
Gibson, Hugh	Mar. 31, 1804	19	light	Congo River, Md.	3	13
Gibson, James	Apr. 19, 1864	35	dark	Wilmington, Del.	6	7
Gibson, Samuel	Apr. 6, 1812	27	black	New Haven, Conn.	4	27
Gibson, Thomas F.	Sept. 6, 1856	24	dark	Fall River, Ma.	5	34
[Giddings]Gidens, Phillip	Sept. 21, 1796	17	dark	Providence, R.I.	1	3
Gideon, Joseph	Apr. 11, 1797	29	dark	Rouen, France	1	12
Gidley, James	Sept. 8, 1801	20	light	Phila., Pa.	2	7
Gifford, Horatio C.	Feb. 15, 1855	22	fair	New Bedford, Ma.	5	34
Gifford, John	June 15, 1804	22	light	Providence, R.I.	3	13
Gifford, John	May 2, 1807	25	light	Providence, R.I.	4	26
Gifford, John	Sept. 12, 1820	21	dark	Falmouth, Ma.	4	27
Gifford, John L.	June 3, 1839	21	light	Tiverton, R.I.	5	32
Gifford, Joshua	Dec. 16, 1797	25	dark	Tiverton, R.I.	1	12 -
Gifford, Peleg	Apr. 22, 1797	20	light	Providence, R.I.	1	12
Gifford, Peleg	May 1, 1799	22	light	Providence, R.I.	2	7
Gifford, Peleg	Aug. 16, 1805	27	light	Providence, R.I.	3	66
Gifford, Peleg	Dec. 6, 1809	33	light	Providence, R.I.	4	26
Gifford, Thomas W.	Nov. 17, 1849	28	light	New Bedford, Ma.	5	33
Gifford, Wm. B.	Apr. 21, 1854	22	dark	Newport, R.I.	5	34
Gilbert, George	Dec. 29, 1810	28	black	Wethersfield, Conn.	4	26
Gilbert, Hiram	Dec. 12, 1837	26	black	Mayfield, N.Y.	5	32
Gilbert, John	Oct. 16, 1834	35	yellow	Exeter, R.I.	5	31
Gilbert, Nathan	Dec. 7, 1837	30	black	Mayfield, N.Y.	5	32

*Newport, R. I.

NAME	DATE OF CERTIFICATION	AGE	COMPLEXION	PLACE OF BIRTH	BOOK	PAGE
Gilchrist, William	Apr. 28, 1841	30	light	Johnstown, N.Y.	5	32
Gilhuly, Michael	Aug. 17, 1853	22	light	Providence, R.I.	5	34
Gillespie, George A.	Sept. 2, 1834	26	light	Phila., Pa.	5	31
Gilious, William	Feb. 4, 1797	33	black	Woodbridge, N.J.	1	12
Gillies, John	June 1, 1825	27	dark	Dartmouth, Ma.	4	28
Gillis, Archibald	Sept. 6, 1858	32	dark	Eastport, Me.	6	7
Gillman, Ira C.	Oct. 24, 1856	21	light	St. George, Me.	5	34
Gillman, Joseph	Dec. 29, 1800	28	dark	Newmarket, N.H.	2	7
Gilmore, Bartholemew K.	May 27, 1841	19	dark	Providence, R.I.	5	32
Gilmore, Elbridge G.	June 9, 1828	18	dark	Franklin, Ma.	4	28
Giton, Elisha	Nov. 7, 1845	28	colored	Providence, R.I.	5	33
Gladding, Benjamin, Jr.	Aug. 4, 1796	21	light	Providence, R.I.	1	1
Gladding, John	1798-1799	June 5 or 15, 1771		Newport, R.I.	*-	--
Gladding, John H.	Nov. 26, 1839	19	light	Providence, R.I.	5	32
Gladding, Nathaniel	1798-1799	Aug. 14, 1771		Dighton, Ma.	*-	--
Gladding, Samuel	Nov. 1, 1848	22	dark	Bristol, R.I.	5	33
Gladding, Solomon	1798-1799	June 7, 1772		Newport, R.I.	*-	--
Gladding, Soloman Edward	1798-1799	Feb. 19, 1801		Newport, R.I.	*-	--
Gladding, Thomas D.	Dec. 28, 1816	16	dark	Providence, R.I.	4	27
Gladding, Thomas D., Jr.	Nov. 7, 1849	24	dark	Providence, R.I.	5	33
Gladding, William B.	Oct. 11, 1841	16	dark	Providence, R.I.	5	32
Glasko, Alba	Mar. 16, 1851	20	mulatto	Pomfret, Conn.	5	33
Glazier, John, Jr.	1798-1799	Aug. 4, 1778		No. Kingstown, R.I.	*-	--

John Glazier of E. Greenwich swears the above to be true.

NAME	DATE OF CERTIFICATION	AGE	COMPLEXION	PLACE OF BIRTH	BOOK	PAGE
Gleason, Jonathan	Mar. 9, 1805	22	light	Heath, Ma.	3	14
Glidden, Charles R.	Aug. 21, 1846	22	fair	Freedom, Me.	5	33
Glover, John	July 17, 1834	26	light	Dover, N.H.	5	31
Goddard, Henry	1798-1799	July 7, 1762		Newport, R.I.	*-	--
Goddard, Solomon	1798-1799	Mar. 6, 1784		Newport, R.I.	*-	--
Godfrey, Christopher	Dec. 2, 1841	16	light	Providence, R.I.	5	32
Godfrey, Christopher C.	Nov. 20, 1818	21	light	Providence, R.I.	4	27
Godfrey, David	Dec. 16, 1818	19	dark	Chatham, Ma.	4	27
Godfrey, Elisha	May 8, 1819	29	light	Yarmouth, Ma.	4	27
Godfrey, George	Mar. 24, 1797	20	dark	E. Greenwich, R.I.	1	12
Godfrey, John	Aug. 17, 1801	20	dark	E. Greenwich, R.I.	2	7
Godfrey, John	Jan. 24, 1848	35	dark	Phila., Pa.	5	33
Godfrey, John	Feb. 15, 1850	48	light	Bristol, R.I.	5	33

*Newport, R. I.

REGISTER OF SEAMEN'S PROTECTION

NAME	DATE OF CERTIFICATION	AGE	COMPLEXION	PLACE OF BIRTH	BOOK	PAGE
Godfrey, John A.	Sept. 7, 1861	22	dark	Cumberland, R.I.	6	7
Godfrey, Joshaua, Jr.	Oct. 19, 1830	16	dark	Providence, R.I.	5	30
Godfrey, Samuel G.	Sept. 18, 1811	16	brown	Providence, R.I.	4	26
Godfrey, Samuel G.	Nov. 18, 1841	48	light	Providence, R.I.	5	32
Godfrey, William	1798-1799	Oct. 27, 1783		Taunton, Ma.	* _	--
Goff, Charles	Feb. 16, 1854	18	light	Rehoboth, Ma.	5	34
Goff, Chester	Dec. 16, 1837	26	dark	Boston, Ma.	5	32
Goff, Joseph	May 18, 1847	20	dark	No. Providence,R.I.	5	33
Goff, Nicholas	Dec. 6, 1796	30	light	Rehoboth, Ma.	1	12
Goff, Silvanns	Oct. 29, 1803	21	dark	Berkeley, Ma.	2	38
Goff, William	May 13, 1856	38	light	Monaghan, Ireland	5	34
Golden, George	Oct. 7, 1834	23	black	Baltimore, Md.	5	31
Golden, Thomas	Nov. 26, 1849	25	light	New York, N.Y.	5	33
Golicar, George A.	July 21, 1841	18	light	No. Prov., R.I.	5	32
Goller, Samuel	Dec. 23, 1796	37	dark	Peekskill, N.Y.	1	12
Gomer, Aaron	Apr. 30, 1799	16	black	Wethersfield, Conn.	2	7
Gomer, Edward	Aug. 16, 1803	23	black	Wethersfield, Conn.	2	38
Gonsolve, John, Jr.	Sept. 10, 1798	17	light	Providence, R.I.	2	7
Gonsolve, Joseph	Dec. 7, 1798	19	light	Providence, R.I.	2	7
Gonsolve, Samuel	Dec. 3, 1806	14	brown	Providence, R.I.	4	26
Gonsolve, William	Apr. 17, 1807	17	light	Providence, R.I.	4	26
Goodale, Samuel D.	May 13, 1834	17	light	W. Boylston, Ma.	5	31
Goodall, Joseph	Aug. 1, 1834	22	mulatto	Phila., Pa.	5	31
Goodnow, Stephen	Nov. 22, 1803	17	light	Sudbury, Ma.	2	38
Goodspeed, Charles	Aug. 25, 1845	23	dark	Glocester, R.I.	5	33
Goodspeed, Cyril	Apr. 24, 1811	17	light	Foster, R.I.	4	26
Goodwin, Thomas	Oct. 29, 1852	21	dark	Providence, R.I.	5	34
Gordon, Cudd	Mar. 26, 1800	19	black	So. Kingstown, R.I.	2	7
Gordon, Leonard R.	June 27, 1849	18	light	Cranston, R.I.	5	33
Gordon, Thomas	Aug. 17, 1855	21	fair	Warrenton, Fla.	5	34
Gorham, Edwin	Nov. 12, 1833	17	dark	Providence, R.I.	5	31
Gorham, John	Nov. 14, 1807	25	light	Falmouth, Ma.	4	26
Gorman, Henry	Dec. 9, 1848	21	sandy	Providence, R.I.	5	33

*Newport, R. I.

NAME	DATE OF CERTIFICATION	AGE	COMPLEXION	PLACE OF BIRTH	BOOK	PAGE
Gormly, James	July 12, 1845	19	dark	New London, Conn.	5	32
Gorman, John	Mar. 3, 1848	25	light	New York, N.Y.	5	33
Gorman, Michael	July 22, 1852	21	light	Providence, R.I.	5	34
Gorman, Thomas	Aug. 3, 1841	27	light	New York, N.Y.	5	32
Gorrie, William	Sept. 15, 1823	16	light	Lyman, Me.	4	28
Gorton, Anthony	Mar. 22, 1797	22	light	Warwick, R.I.	1	12
Gorton, Clarke	Nov. 15, 1797	18	light	Warwick, R.I.	1	12
Gorton, Daniel	May 25, 1799	23	light	Warwick, R.I.	2	7
Gorton, George	Aug. 18, 1807	15	light	Warwick, R.I.	4	26
Gorton, George	May 10, 1809	17	light	Warwick, R.I.	4	26
Gorton, Hale	Mar. 20, 1835	17	ruddy	Warwick, R.I.	5	31
Gorton, James W.	Nov. 15, 1806	16	light	Warwick, R.I.	4	26
Gorton, James W.	July 5, 1809	19	light	Warwick, R.I.	4	26
Gorton, Joel B.	Nov. 23, 1858	23	light	Warwick, R.I.	6	7
Gorton, John H.	May 7, 1810	21	dark	Warwick, R.I.	4	26
Gorton, Lowry J.[allman]	Nov. 2, 1820	22	ruddy	Warwick, R.I.	4	27
Gorton, Nathan	Sept. 6, 1803	19	light	Warwick, R.I.	2	38
Gorton, Richard	Jan. 14, 1836	49	black	Brooklyn, N.Y.	5	31
Gorton, Samuel	June 17, 1797	23	dark	Warwick, R.I.	1	12
Gorton, William H.	May 20, 1822	16	dark	Newport, R.I.	4	27
Gorton, Wm. K.	Mar. 31, 1855	28	light	Providence, R.I.	5	34
Gosedea, John	July 31, 1854	20	light	New Orleans, La.	5	34
Goslyn, John	May 12, 1845	20	light	Bristol, R.I.	5	32
Gosweling, William	Dec. 19, 1832	23	light	Princess Anne, Md.	5	31
Gould, Daniel	Nov. 14, 1803	25	light	Phila., Pa.	2	38
Gould, Elijah	Sept. 30, 1846	17	fair	So. Kingston, R.I.	5	33
Gould, Frederick	Dec. 1, 1853	20	light	Boston, Ma.	5	34
Gould, George H.	July 8, 1837	18	light	Providence, R.I.	5	31
Gould, John	May 23, 1805	22	light	?Patuxent, Md.	3	14
Gould, John	Sept. 23, 1836	23	light	New Bedford, Ma.	5	31
Gould, Robert	Nov. 11, 1835	19	black	Providence, R.I.	5	31
Gould, Thomas	1798-1799	July 27, 1778		So. Kingstown, R.I.	*-	--

NAME	DATE OF CERTIFICATION	AGE	COMPLEXION	PLACE OF BIRTH	BOOK	PAGE
Gould, William	June 11, 1807	26	light	Boston, Ma.	4	26
Gould, William	Dec. 3, 1828	20	light	Salem, Ma.	4	28
Gove, Albert P.	Apr. 1, 1850	20	light	Edgecomb, Me.	5	33
Gowdy, Charles	July 15, 1831	22	light	Suffield, Conn.	5	31
Gowing, John	Mar. 24, 1835	33	dark	New York, N.Y.	5	31
Grace, William	Mar. 5, 1862	25	dark	New York, N.Y.	6	7
Grady, Martin W.	June 15, 1841	24	light	Carver, Ma.	5	32
Grafton, Charles O.B.	Apr. 1, 1844	16	dark	Providence, R.I.	5	32
Grafton, Isaac P.	Jan. 21, 1818	21	light	Providence, R.I.	4	27
Grafton, Nathaniel	Sept. 6, 1803	16	dark	Providence, R.I.	2	38
Grafton, Nathaniel	July 24, 1820	30	dark	Providence, R.I.	4	27
Grafton, Samuel	Mar. 9, 1798	16	dark	Providence, R.I.	1	15
Graham, Alfred	Sept. 29, 1847	40	black	Brooklyn, N.Y.	5	33
Graham, George	Apr. 20, 1840	19	light	Wilmington, N.C.	5	32
Graham, Henry	Apr. 2, 1853	16	light	Providence, R.I.	5	34
Graham, James	Mar. 15, 1850	34	dark	Dumfermline, Scotland	5	33
Graham, Thomas	Oct. 10, 1800	21	black	Hartford, Conn.	2	7
Grainger, Benjamin	July 9, 1803	24	light	Providence, R.I.	2	38
Grainger, Joshua	Nov. 11, 1803	18	light	Providence. R.I.	2	38
Grainger, Joshua I.	Feb. 5, 1810	25	light	Providence, R.I.	4	26
Granger, Benjamin	July 30, 1804	24	dark	Providence, R.I.	3	13
Granger, Joshua Ingraham	Dec. 20, 1800	15	light	Providence, R.I.	2	7
Grandison, Abraham, Jr.	Dec. 23, 1829	22	light	Boston, Ma.	5	31
Grannell, Francis R.	Jan. 27, 1830	15	light	Eastport, Me.	5	31
Grannell, William	Aug. 18, 1797	20	dark	Georgetown, Md.	1	12
Grant, Albert	June 4, 1838	17	light	Barrington, R.I.	5	32
Grant, Cyrus	Aug. 23, 1796	23	dark	Wrentham, Ma.	1	1
Grant, Cyrus F.	Aug. 2, 1820	19	light	Attleboro, Ma.	4	27
Grant, Israel	June 7, 1828	18	dark	Warren, R.I.	4	28
Grant, Israel J.	Nov. 31, 1847	37	dark	Warren, R.I.	5	33
Grant, James	Dec. 31, 1822	26	light	Swansea, Ma.	4	27
Grant, Jeremiah D.	June 6, 1825	17	light	Bristol, R.I.	4	28
Grant, Lewis	Jan. 1, 1835	28	dark	Bristol, R.I.	5	31
Grant, Peter	Apr. 12, 1852	22	light	Bath, Me.	5	34

NAME	DATE OF CERTIFICATION	AGE	COMPLEXION	PLACE OF BIRTH	BOOK	PAGE
Grant, Richard	Feb. 22, 1853	25	mulatto	Eastport, Me.	5	34
Grant, Samuel	Sept. 5, 1831	24	light	Hancock, Me.	5	31
Grant, William	Sept. 25, 1834	43	dark	Portland, Me.	5	31
Graves, Gardner	1798-1799	May 25, 1773		Tiverton, R.I.	*-	--
Graves, John	May 20, 1807	20	brown	Scituate, R.I.	4	26
Graves, Joseph	Dec. 8, 1827	22	light	Wiscasset, Me.	4	28
Graves, Samuel	Nov. 1, 1806	27	light	Scituate, R.I.	4	26
Graves, William L.	Dec. 8, 1828	21	light	Salem, Ma.	4	28
Graves, Zephaniah, Jr.	June 11, 1797	16	light	Swansea, Ma.	1	12
Gray, Church	Oct. 22, 1807	21	light	Little Compton, R.I.	4	26
Gray, Edward of Tiverton, R.I.	1798-1799	year 1777		Bristol, R.I.	*-	--
Gray, D. Flint	Oct. 3, 1844	18	light	New York, N.Y.	5	32
Gray, David	May 5, 1810	22	light	Providence, R.I.	4	26
Gray, Franklin	May 3, 1844	19	light	Somerset, Ma.	5	32
Gray, George	Mar. 7, 1839	23	light	Phila., Pa.	5	32
Gray, Henry	May 3, 1826	19	light	Yarmouth, Ma.	4	28
Gray, Henry	July 9, 1839	22	light	Boston, Ma.	5	32
Gray, Henry J.	June 14, 1828	21	freckled	Portsmouth, N.H.	4	28
Gray, John	1798-1799	Sept. 1777		Tiverton, R.I.	*-	--
Gray, John	Nov. 12, 1835	45	black	Portsmouth, N.H.	5	31
Gray, John	Mar. 25, 1853	19	black	Boston, Ma.	5	34
Gray, John Smith	May 5, 1815	15	brown	Providence, R.I.	4	27
Gray, Joshua	May 3, 1826	26	light	Yarmouth, Ma.	4	28
Gray, Robert	Aug. 17, 1797	25	light	Worcester, Ma.	1	12
Gray, Thomas	May 27, 1805	17	light	Savannah, Ga.	3	14
Gray, William	Aug. 29, 1803	17	black	Baltimore, Md.	2	38
Grayson, John	Nov. 30, 1855	21	mulatto	Providence, R.I.	5	34
Grayson, Stephen	July 14, 1800	29	dark	Boston, Ma.	2	7
Grayson, Thomas	May 29, 1832	23	light	Providence, R.I.	5	31
Greatreaks, John	May 17, 1817	15	light	W. Haddam, Conn.	4	27
Greatreaks, William	July 26, 1809	23	dark	Providence, R.I.	4	26

*Newport, R. I.

NAME	DATE OF CERTIFICATION	AGE	COMPLEXION	PLACE OF BIRTH	BOOK	PAGE
Green, Caesar	June 10, 1797	23	black	Warwick, R.I.	1	12
Green, Caleb Car[r]	Sept. 26, 1796	27	light	Warwick, R.I.	1	3
Green, David	Aug. 27, 1804	24	dark	Stratham, N.H.	3	13
Green, Eldredge N.	Aug. 25, 1819	17	dark	Woodstock, Conn.	4	27
Green, George	Feb. 17, 1804	19	dark	Providence, R.I.	3	13
Green, Hawkins	1798-1799	Feb. 14, 1776		So. Kingstown, R.I.	** -	--
James Perry of S. K. swears the above to be true.						
Green, Ira C.	Nov. 3, 1856	25	fair	Norwich, Conn.	5	34
Green, James	Mar. 11, 1797	19	black	Warwick, R.I.	1	12
Green, James	Aug. 17, 1821	20	light	New Haven, Conn.	4	27
Green, John	Nov. 25, 1797	25	light	Warwick, R.I.	1	12
Green, John	1798-1799	Sept. 8, 1765		Warwick, R.I.	-	--
Green, John	Nov. 24, 1798	15	light	No. Kingstown, R.I.	2	7
Green, John	June 9, 1800	18	black	Providence, R.I.	2	7
Green, Joseph L.	Aug. 17, 1797	20	light	Warwick, R.I.	1	12
Green, Malachi	Sept. 29, 1797	32	dark	Warwick, R.I.	1	12
Green, Otis	June 3, 1797	20	light	Mendon, Ma.	1	12
Green, Peleg	Aug. 13, 1804	30	dark	Providence, R.I.	3	13
Green, Peter	July 12, 1817	25	black	Johnston, R.I.	4	27
Green, Rholly [Rhodes?]	Dec. 6, 1844	26	light	Coventry, R.I.	5	32
Green, Tobe	Aug. 9, 1798	20	black	Kent, R.I.	2	7
Green, Tobey	Mar. 27, 1805	27	black	Warwick, R.I.	3	14
Green, Uriah	Feb. 7, 1798	--	yellow*	Warwick, R.I.	1	15
Green, William	Jan. 12, 1831	22	light	Salem, Ma.	5	31
Greene, Abiel	Jan. 27, 1800	35	black	Bridgewater, Ma.	2	7
Greene, Alfred	Dec. 5, 1827	16	black	Providence, R.I.	4	28
Greene, Alexander	Aug. 21, 1858	22	florid	Nantucket, Ma.	6	7
Greene, Anthony H.	Oct. 15, 1833	22	light	Warwick, R.I.	5	31
Greene, Benjamin	Nov. 5, 1796	18	dark	Warwick, R.I.	1	12&5
Greene, Benjamin	Feb. 13, 1807	21	dark	Uxbridge, Ma.,	4	26
Greene, Benjamin D.	Nov. 24, 1804	34	light	Warwick, R.I.	3	14
Greene, Cato	Nov. 28, 1810	25	black	E. Greenwich, R.I.	4	26
Greene, Charles	Apr. 17, 1815	20	light	Warwick, R.I.	4	27
Greene, Charles H.	Jan. 17, 1842	16	light	Johnston, R.I.	5	32
Greene, Christopher	Mar. 29, 1805	25	black	Coventry, R.I.	3	14
Greene, Cyrus	Jan. 25, 1847	16	dark	Smithfield, R.I.	5	33
Greene, Daniel P.	Nov. 6, 1828	22	ruddy	Charlestown, R.I.	4	28

**Newport, R. I.
*mulatto

NAME	DATE OF CERTIFICATION	AGE	COMPLEXION	PLACE OF BIRTH	BOOK	PAGE
Greene, David	Dec. 20, 1797	30	black	Warwick, R.I.	1	15
Greene, David A.	Mar. 20, 1835	20	dark	Warwick, R.I.	5	31
Greene, Edgar	Sept. 9, 1822	15	light	Warwick, R.I.	4	27
Greene, Edward	Nov. 24, 1826	19	mulatto	Providence, R.I.	4	28
Greene, Eli	Oct. 16, 1804	20	light	Whitingham, Vt.	3	14
Greene, Franklin M.	May 23, 1823	20	light	New Bedford, Ma.	4	27
Greene, Frederick	Jan. 19, 1856	24	mulatto	Phila., Pa.	5	34
Greene, George	Mar. 24, 1820	32	yellow	Hartford, Conn.	4	27
Greene, George	Oct. 15, 1849	24	light	Rehoboth, Ma.	5	33
Greene, George B.	Sept. 9, 1842	24	dark	Richmond, R.I.	5	32
Greene, Godfrey	Sept. 13, 1796	28	light	Warwick, R.I.	1	2
Greene, Henry	Nov. 6, 1815	21	light	E. Greenwich, R.I.	4	27
Greene, Henry	Oct. 21, 1818	21	black	Providence, R.I.	4	27
Greene, Henry	Nov. 24, 1827	22	black	Providence, R.I.	4	28
Greene, Henry W.	Mar. 2, 1848	24	light	Topsham, Me.	5	33
Greene, Jacob C.	Sept. 15, 1801	22	light	Cranston, R.I.	2	38
Greene, James	May 19, 1804	19	light	Warwick, R.I.	3	13
Greene, James	Feb. 26, 1851	25	light	Providence, R.I.	5	33
Greene, Jared	Oct. 16, 1809	22	dark	Stafford, Conn.	4	26
Greene, Job	Dec. 20, 1797	18	black	E. Greenwich, R.I.	1	15
Greene, Job C.	Sept. 26, 1849	23	light	Charlestown, R.I.	5	33
Greene, John	Oct. 5, 1803	19	light	New York, N.Y.	2	38
Greene, John	m. Judith Tarr, Oct. 1812			Rev. Benedict Record		
Greene, John	Nov. 1, 1813	19	light	Providence, R.I.	4	27
Greene, John	Dec. 24, 1816	22	light	Barnstable, Ma.	4	27
Greene, John, Jr.	Dec. 28, 1818	17	black	Providence, R.I.	4	27
Greene, John C.	July 7, 1845	20	yellow	Coventry, R.I.	5	32
Greene, John W.	Mar. 16, 1825	16	ruddy	Warwick, R.I.	4	28
Greene, Joseph	Aug. 24, 1846	18	fair	Coventry, R.I.	5	33
Greene, Lewis Allen	Mar. 1, 1862	31	brown	Providence, R.I.	6	7
Greene, Malachi R.	Oct. 16, 1819	18	light	Woodstock, Conn.	4	27
Greene, Nathaniel	Dec. 9, 1807	18	light	Warwick, R.I.	4	26
Greene, Nathaniel	Apr. 9, 1834	22	black	Baltimore, Md.	5	31
Greene, Peris	Nov. 10, 1797	17	light	Mendon, Ma.	1	12

NAME	DATE OF CERTIFICATION	AGE	COMPLEXION	PLACE OF BIRTH	BOOK	PAGE
Greene, Peter	July 6, 1810	20	yellow	Warwick, R.I.	4	26
Greene, Philip	June 2, 1800	18	dark	Warwick, R.I.	2	7
Greene, Pomp	Feb. 22, 1805	27	black	Warwick, R.I	3	14
Greene, Pompey	Jan. 1, 1807	29	black	Warwick, R.I.	4	26
Greene, Richard W.	Aug. 6, 1811	20	light	Warwick, R.I.	4	26
Greene, Samuel	May 16, 1809	22	black	Cranston, R.I.	4	26
Greene, Seneca	June 15, 1804	22	dark	Warwick, R.I.	3	13
Greene, Simon Ray	May 16, 1818	26	ruddy	E. Greenwich, R.I.	4	27
Greene, Solomon	Dec. 4, 1827	31	mulatto	Providence, R.I.	4	28
Greene, Stephen C.	Oct. 6, 1807	28	light	Providence, R.I.	4	26
Greene, Thomas	Dec. 4, 1800	19	light	Providence, R.I.	2	7
Greene, Thomas	Dec. 20, 1800	30	dark	Coventry, R.I.	2	7
Greene, Thomas	Mar. 6, 1806	26	light	No. Providence, R.I.	3	66
Greene, Thomas	Oct. 2, 1807	27	light	No. Providence, R.I.	4	26
Greene, Thomas Rice	June 2, 1800	17	light	Warwick, R.I.	2	7
Greene, Thomas W.	Nov. 15, 1803	25	light	Coventry, R.I.	2	38
Greene, Toby	Oct. 15, 1796	18	black	Cranston, R.I.	1	12&4
Greene, William	May 16, 1799	26	dark	Providence, R.I.	2	7
Greene, William	Apr. 22, 1800	38	light	Providence, R.I.	2	7
Greene, William	June 11, 1808	45	light	Providence, R.I.	4	26
Greene, William H.	Oct. 22, 1828	17	light	Providence, R.I.	4	28
Greene, William M.	Sept. 16, 1815	16	light	Warwick, R.I.	4	27
Greene, William Warren	May 15, 1799	15	dark	Warwick, R.I.	2	7
Greene, William Warren	Mar. 22, 1824	18	brown	Warwick, R.I.	4	28
Greenhill, Diah	June 11, 1833	29	light	Promfret, Conn.	5	31
Greenlaw, James H.	Sept. 21, 1866	25	light	Pembroke, Me.	6	7
Greenleaf, John	Aug. 21, 1846	21	fair	Hartford, Conn.	5	33
Greenleaf, William	Jan. 22, 1844	25	dark	Providence, R.I.	5	32
Greenman, Edward	July 15, 1822	27	light	Hampton, Conn.	4	27
Greenman, Israel D.	Sept. 20, 1833	22	light	No. Kingston, R.I.	5	31
Greenman, William	1778-1700	Sept. 25, 1781		Newport, R.I.	* -	--
Greenman, William, Jr.	July 20, 1816	20	light	Steorntown, N.Y.	4	27
Greenough, Thomas	June 24, 1800	24	dark	Bradford, Ma.	2	7

*Newport, R. I.

NAME	DATE OF CERTIFICATION	AGE	COMPLEXION	PLACE OF BIRTH	BOOK	PAGE
Greenwood, Samuel S.	Nov. 9, 1846	24	fair	Hubbardston, Ma.	5	33
Gregory, Harry	June 17, 1859	21	light	New York, N.Y.	6	7
Gregory, John	Jan. 23, 1822	22	light	Camden, Me.	4	27
Gregory, William	Dec. 20, 1848	22	light	Eastport, Me.	5	33
Gridley, Rufus	Apr. 30, 1799	23	light	Roxbury, Ma.	2	7
Grier, John	Apr. 7, 1851	23	light	Phila., Pa.	5	33
Griffen, Adam	Aug. 8, 1806	26	yellow	Springfield, Ma.	3	66
Griffen, Allen	Mar. 26, 1821	13	black	Rye, N.Y.	4	27
Griffen, Ebenezer, Jr.	Dec. 3, 1828	20	light	Salem, Ma.	4	28
Griffin, Alexander	June 12, 1832	22	mulatto	Warren, R.I.	5	31
Griffin, Charles	Sept. 8, 1855	21	black	Providence, R.I.	5	34
Griffin, DeGrasse	Nov. 5, 1835	29	dark	Killingnorth, Conn.	5	31
Griffin, Moses	Oct. 25, 1809	24	yellow	Brunswick, Ma. or Me.?	4	26
Griffin, Stephen A.	May 16, 1834	16	light	Charlestown, R.I.	5	31
Griffiths, Griffith	July 13, 1852	25	light	Charleston, N.C.	5	33
Griffiths, James	Oct. 29, 1849	23	light	Foster, R.I.	5	33
Griffiths, John	Sept. 10, 1838	18	dark	New York, N.Y.	5	32
Griffiths, Lemuel	Sept 2, 1842	17	light	New York, N.Y.	5	32
Grimes, Alfred	Apr. 29, 1839	25	black	Providence, R.I.	5	32
Grimes, Michael	Aug. 17, 1857	25	light	Providence, R.I.	6	7
Grimes, Thomas	July 2, 1836	18	light	Baltimore, Md.	5	31
Grimley, James	May 17, 1867	21	light	Providence, R.I.	6	7
Grimshaw, Charles	June 5, 1833	20	light	Hartford, Conn.	5	31
Grinell, William T.	Mar. 31, 1862	21	dark	Tiverton, R.I.	6	7
Grinnell, Diah	Aug. 26, 1850	46	light	Pomfret, Conn.	5	33
Grinnell, John	Oct. 14, 1854	13	light	Providence, R.I.	5	34
Grinnell, Joseph	1798-1799		July 27, 1770	Little Compton, R.I.	*-	--

Oliver Grinnell his brother swears the above to be true.

NAME	DATE OF CERTIFICATION	AGE	COMPLEXION	PLACE OF BIRTH	BOOK	PAGE
Grinnell, Joseph	July 31, 1837	19	light	So. Kingston, R.I.	5	31
Grinnell, Joshua	June 25, 1836	19	light	Charlestown, R.I.	5	31
Grinnell, Lyman J.	May 29, 1832	24	light	So. Kingston, R.I.	5	31
Grinnell, Thomas E.	Aug. 12, 1818	32	dark	Providence, R.I.	4	27
Grinell, Warren	Nov. 11, 1841	18	light	Charlestown, R.I.	5	32
Grinnell, Wilson	June 23, 1801	19	light	Providence, R.I.	2	7

*Newport, R. I.

NAME	DATE OF CERTIFICATION	AGE	COMPLEXION	PLACE OF BIRTH	BOOK	PAGE
Gros, Peter Herbert	Aug. 28, 1797	30	dark	Dunkirk, France	1	12
Settled in America previous to September, 1783.						
Gross, John W.	Dec. 1, 1848	20	fair	Scituate, R.I.	5	33
Gross, William F.	June 21, 1845	19	dark	Allentown, Pa.	5	32
Grotos, John	Nov. 24, 1814	17	yellow	Plainfield, Conn.	4	27
Grosse, Amasa	Mar. 30, 1852	21	dark	Providence, R.I.	5	34
Grover, Charles	Apr. 20, 1860	21	fair	New York, N.Y.	6	7
Grover, Joseph	June 7, 1843	21	light	Dedham, Ma.	5	32
Grover, William J.	Nov. 15, 1844	24	light	Bowdoin, Me.	5	32
Grundy, Amos, Jr.	Jan. 9, 1845	38	dark	Marblehead, Ma.	5	32
Guard, John	Apr. 6, 1850	18	light	New York, N.Y.	5	33
Gudgeon, Robert B.	May 24, 1823	14	light	Providence, R.I.	4	27
Guild, William	Oct. 11, 1844	16	light	Dedham, Ma.	5	32
Gund, Alexander	July 1, 1803	29	dark	New London, Conn.	2	38
Gunn, George C.	Oct. 1, 1844	15	light	Providence, R.I.	5	32
Gurnett, Benjamin	June 12, 1835	30	black	Swansea, Ma.	5	31
Gurney, Benjamin	June 8, 1843	19	light	Hamstraw, N.Y.	5	32
Gurney, John	May 19, 1821	21	dark	Newport, R.I.	-	--
Sworn statement of Samuel Smith of Rehoboth in the Custom House Papers.						
Gurney, Nahum	May 2, 1825	28	light	Bridgewater, Ma.	4	28
Guthill, Peter	July 29, 1797	18	light	Charleston, S.C.	1	12
Hacker, Caleb	Apr. 15, 1809	22	light	Providence, R.I.	4	29
Hacker, William	Mar. 20, 1822	19	yellow	Providence, R.I.	4	32
Hackstone, James	Aug. 13, 1806	18	dark	Warwick, R.I.	3	79
Hackstone, James	Oct. 24, 1809	21	dark	Warwick, R.I.	4	29
Hackstone, John	Jan. 14, 1802	20	light	Warwick, R.I.	2	39
Hacker, Samuel	Apr. 15, 1797	32	dark	Providence, R.I.	1	13
Hackett, William	Aug. 1, 1801	19	light	Queens Anns Co., Md.	2	28
Hackett, William	Apr. 21, 1806	26	brown	Centreville, Md.	3	77
Hadley, Joseph	June 1, 1835	22	light	Boston, Ma.	5	36
Haffenden, Alfred	Jan. 5, 1858	20	light	New Haven, Conn.	6	8
Hail, George Gibbs	Apr. 26, 1842	16	light	Providence, R.I.	5	37
Hail, George G.	Nov. 30, 1849	24	light	Providence, R.I.	5	39
Hail, John	Dec. 17, 1821	18	light	Swansea, Ma.	4	32
Haile, Charles, M.	Dec. 23, 1870	20	light	Brooklyn, Me.	6	8
Haile, John	Oct. 5, 1854	30	light	New York, N.Y.	5	40
Haile, John, Jr.	Mar. 1, 1849	27	light	Warren, R.I.	5	39

REGISTER OF SEAMEN'S PROTECTION

NAME	DATE OF CERTIFICATION	AGE	COMPLEXION	PLACE OF BIRTH	BOOK	PAGE
Hale, Darius	1798-1799	Oct. 8, 1777		Malbrough, Ma.	* -	--
Hale, Edward	Apr. 10, 1821	17	light	Swansea, Ma.	4	31
Hale, Henry	May 15, 1840	26	dark	Boston, Ma.	5	37
Hale, Joseph S.	Sept. 10, 1849	30	light	Providence, R.I.	5	39
Hall, Aaron	Nov. 15, 1811	18	yellow	Exeter, N.H.	4	30
Hall, Amos	Mar. 18, 1815	26	yellow	E. Greenwich, R.I.	4	30
Hall, Benjamian	1798-1799	Mar. 17, 1775		Rayham, Ma.	* -	--
Hall, Cesar	Oct. 28, 1796	31	black	No. Kingstown, R.I.	1	13&5
Hall, David	Feb. 1805	16	light	Harwich, Ma.	3	54
Hall, Francis	Nov. 2, 1840	21	light	Newport, R.I.	5	37
Hall, George	Oct. 6, 1841	17	light	Charlestown, Ma.	5	37
Hall, George	Feb. 22, 1845	23	light	No. Prov., R.I.	5	38
Hall, George	June 8, 1855	17	light	New York, N.Y.	5	45
Hall, George W.	Mar. 9, 1858	31	fair	England	6	8
Hall, Henry	Dec. 17, 1813	23	light	E. Greenwich, R.I.	4	30
Hall, Henry H.	Nov. 11, 1835	21	light	Providence, R.I.	5	36
Hall, Isaac	Nov. 14, 1831	21	mulatto	Plainfield, Conn.	5	35
Hall, Jesse	Feb. 26, 1805	22	light	Wrentham, Ma.	3	54
Hall, John	Oct. 26, 1799	24	dark	Springfield, Ma.	2	8
Hall, John	Apr. 21, 1853	24	light	Bath, Me.	5	40
Hall, John J.	Jan. 12, 1867	17	medium	Providence, R.I.	6	8
Hall, John Mortimer	Feb. 9, 1849	27	dark	No. Kingston, R.I.	5	39
Hall, Joseph F.	Apr. 29, 1815	25	dark	No. Kingstown, R.I.	4	31
Hall, Levi	Aug. 3, 1799	21	light	Providence, R.I.	2	8
Hall, Metcalf	July 11, 1799	24	light	Providence, R.I.	2	8
Hall, Milton	Apr. 24, 1849	45	dark	Norton, Ma.	5	39
Hall, Moses	May 3, 1823	19	mulatto	E. Greenwich, R.I.	4	32
Hall, Nathan	Apr. 3, 1812	22	light	Providence, R.I.	4	30
Hall, Nathan F.	July 12, 1805	16	light	Providence, R.I.	3	55
Hall, Nicholas	Mar. 25, 1809	23	light	Albany, N.Y.	4	29
Hall, Robert	Aug. 15, 1823	22	light	New Brunswick, Me.	4	32
Hall, Samuel	Oct. 26, 1799	25	dark	Springfield, Ma.	2	8
Hall, Samuel	Sept. 8, 1821	24	brown	Deer Isle, Me.	4	31

*Newport, R. I.

NAME	DATE OF CERTIFICATION	AGE	COMPLEXION	PLACE OF BIRTH	BOOK	PAGE
Hall, Samuel	Jan. 31, 1832	36	dark	Northbridge, Ma.	5	35
Hall, Samuel H.	Aug. 20, 1845	17	light	So. Kingston, R.I.	5	38
Hall, Stephen	June 16, 1806	18	black	E. Greenwich, R.I.	3	79
Hall, Stephen	July 13, 1863	34	light	Dennis, Ma.	6	8
Hall, Thomas	Sept. 15, 1804	28	dark	New York, N.Y.	3	16
Hall, Thomas H.	Sept. 17, 1858	23	fair	Boston, Ma.	6	8
Hall, William	1798-1799	July 16, 1781		Newport, R.I.	*-	--
Hall, William	June 29, 1835	43	light	E. Greenwich, R.I.	5	36
Hall, William	Nov. 1, 1852	22	light	Harwich, Ma.	5	40
Hallen, John P., Jr.	June 3, 1811	18	light	Somerset, Ma.	4	30
Hallett, Freeman	July 1, 1844	16	light	Falmouth, Ma.	5	38
Hallett, Robert W.	Feb. 27, 1843	27	light	West Farms, N.Y.	5	37
Hallowell, John D.	Nov. 29, 1816	18	light	Providence, R.I.	4	31
Hallowell, Simon Whipple	Dec. 13, 1822	18	light	Providence, R.I.	4	32
Halsy, James	Jan. 22, 1836	18	light	Boston, Ma.	5	36
Halsey, Pocup?	Jan. 26, 1799	25	black	Cape Francoia, St. Domingo	2	8
Halsey, Pompey	Jan. 4, 1804	32	black	Angola, Africa	3	15
Ham, James	June 16, 1797	19	light	Providence, R.I.	1	13
Ham, William	Jan. 4, 1800	16	light	Providence, R.I.	2	8
Hamblem, Grafton	Oct. 9, 1818	21	light	Falmouth, Ma.	4	31
Hamblin, Leonard	Sept. 11, 1861	48	light	Topsham, Me.	6	8
Hamilton, Charles	Nov. 24, 1826	25	yellow	Providence, R.I.	4	32
Hamilton, James	Aug. 5, 1837	46	dark	Phila., Pa.	5	36
Hamilton, Samuel	Mar. 2, 1811	37	dark	Chatham, Ma.	4	30
Hamilton, Stephen	June 7, 1816	21	dark	Portsmouth, N.H.	4	31
Hamilton, Thomas	Oct. 9, 1835	20	black	Boston, Ma.	5	36
Hamilton, William	Sept. 3, 1834	55	black	Phila., Pa.	5	36
Hamilton, William	Dec. 26, 1851	22	light	Boston, Ma.	5	40
Hamlin, George B.	May 24, 1838	26	light	Boston, Ma.	5	36
Hamlin, Nathan E.	Sept. 7, 1857	24	light	Falmouth, Ma.	6	8
Hammatt, John	July 14, 1810	35	florid	Nantucket, Ma.	4	30
Hammett, William	Dec. 12, 1797	27	light	Warwick, R.I.	1	27
Hammond, Charles	Noc. 23, 1840	40	light	Rochester, Ma.	5	37
Hammond, George	Aug. 21, 1857	21	dark	Salem, Ma.	6	8
Hammond, George W.	Sept. 12, 1800	20	dark	Providence, R.I.	2	28
Hammond, George W.	June 27, 1806	24	brown	Providence, R.I	3	79

*Newport, R. I.

NAME	DATE OF CERTIFICATION	AGE	COMPLEXION	PLACE OF BIRTH	BOOK	PAGE
Hammond, Jacob	Dec. 2, 1835	24	black	Green Castle, Pa.	5	36
Hammond, James, Jr.	June 3, 1805	18	light	Providence, R.I.	3	54
Hammond, James, Jr.	Jan. 12, 1807	19	light	Providence, R.I.	4	29
Hammond, Jeremiah	Dec. 14, 1800	22	light	Providence, R.I.	2	28
Hammond, John	1798-1799	Mar. 16, 1790		Jamestown, R.I.	*-	--
Hammond, John	Nov. 2, 1810	22	dark	Wareham, Ma.	4	30
Hammond, Robert	Oct. 13, 1803	18	light	Falmouth, Ma.	2	39
Hammond, Thomas	Dec. 17, 1803	17	yellow*	So. Kingstown, R.I.	2	49
Hammond, Thomas	Feb. 22, 1805	18	yellow*	So. Kingstown, R.I.	3	54
Hammond, Thomas	May 6, 1806	19	yellow*	So. Kingstown, R.I.	3	77
Hammond, Thomas	May 31, 1800	22	light	Brookhaven, N.Y.	2	28
Hammond, Tunbridge	Oct. 6, 1803	25	black	Newport, R.I.	2	39
Hammond, Tunbridge	Oct. 27, 1803	25	black	Newport, R.I.	2	39
Hammond, William	Nov. 3, 1826	19	light	NO. Kingstown, R.I.	4	32
Hammond, William	Aug. 31, 1849	21	light	Killingly, Conn.	5	39
Hammond, William F.	Aug. 29, 1849	43	light	Providence R.I.	5	39
Hamor, George R.	Mar. 15, 1853	21	light	Eden, Me.	5	40
Hampson, Henry	Nov. 13, 1847	20	fair	Fall River, Ma.	5	38
Hampton, Henry	Sept. 27, 1854	19	light	Eastport, Me.	5	40
Hancock, John	1798-1799	Mar. 2, 1775		Brooklyn, N.Y.	*-	--
Handly, Thos. M.	Mar. 16, 1852	25	dark	Boston, Ma.	5	40
Handy, Charles P.	Aug. 22, 1862	19	light	Sandwich, Ma.	6	8
Handy, Job	Jan. 14, 1801	27	light	Swansea, Ma.	2	28
Handy, Job	Mar. 23, 1812	21	black	Newport, R.I.	4	30
Handy, Peter	Mar. 11, 1799	16	dark	Providence, R.I.	2	8
Handy, Peter	July 12, 1800	17	dark	Providence, R.I.	2	28
Handy, Peter	Sept. 10, 1804	21	dark	Providence, R.I.	3	16
Handy, Raymond B.	Mar. 1, 1849	22	dark	Seekonk, Ma.	5	39
Handy, Richmond	June 12, 1839	22	light	Swansea, Ma.	5	36
Handy, Samuel J.	July 19, 1839	20	light	Northbridge, Ma.	5	36
Handy, Thomas Franklin	Sept. 7, 1801	18	light	Mendon, Ma.	2	28
Handy, Thomas F.	Apr. 17, 1807	24	light	Mendon, Ma.	4	29
Handy, William	Mar. 20, 1837	26	dark	Mendon, Ma.	5	36

*Newport, R. I.

REGISTER OF SEAMEN'S PROTECTION

NAME	DATE OF CERTIFICATION	AGE	COMPLEXION	PLACE OF BIRTH	BOOK	PAGE
Handy, William	July 11, 1854	49	mulatto	Virginia	5	40
Hanes, George	Dec. 4, 1833	18	light	Uxbridge, Ma.	5	35
Hanford, William	Aug. 23, 1822	21	light	Norwalk, Conn.	4	32
Hanibald, Thomas	Nov. 30, 1805	20	yellow*	New London, Conn.	2	49
Hankens, Peter F.	Mar. 19, 1844	24	dark	E. Greenwich, R.I.	5	38
Hanks, Dwight	May 20, 1825	19	light	Mansfield, Conn.	4	32
Hanks, Willard	Sept. 30, 1828	19	light	Mansfield, Conn.	4	32
Hanlon, John	Jan. 30, 1860	22	dark	Portland, Me.	6	8
Hanly, James	July 23, 1852	21	light	Fall River, Ma.	5	40
Hannam, Joseph	Oct. 24, 1850	23	light	Bangor, Me.	5	40
Hanney, Henry	Nov. 5, 1855	26	fair	Providence, R.I.	5	45
Hansen, Samuel	Apr. 11, 1859	24	light	Chicago, Ill.	6	8
Hanson, John A.	Mar. 3, 1849	34	sandy	Brookfield, N.Y.	5	39
Haradon, Jeremiah	Mar. 14, 1818	28	light	Providence, R.I.	4	31
Haradon, John	Aug. 26, 1801	14	light	Providence, R.I.	2	28
Haradon, John, Jr.	Aug. 19, 1805	18	light	Providence, R.I.	3	55
Haradon, John, Jr.	Oct. 5, 1807	20	light	Providence, R.I.	4	29
Haradon, John, Jr.	Oct. 1, 1813	25	light	Providence, R.I.	4	30
Harden, Robert	Feb. 22, 1821	23	yellow	Taunton, Ma.	4	31
Harden, William Nov	Nov. 12, 1822	20	light	New York, N.Y.	4	32
Hardenbergh, John C.	Nov. 14, 1812	20	brown	Providence, R.I.	4	30
Hardey, John	Aug. 15, 1845	32	dark	Portland, Me.	5	38
**Harding, Charles	1798-1799	about 1780		Warren, R.I.	*** --	--
Harding, Elias	Mar. 24, 1807	23	light	Mansfield, Ma.	4	29
Harding, Ezekiel	May 30, 1818	48	light	Chatham, Ma.	4	31
Hardin[g], Henry	Sept. 23, 1801	18	light	Providence, P.I.	-	--
Harding, James	Dec. 4, 1812	31	yellow	Bridgewater, Ma.	4	30
Harding, James	May 25, 1816	21	brown	Warren, R.I.	4	31
Hardy, Albert	Oct. 31, 1854	23	light	New Bedford, Ma.	5	40
Hardy, John I.	May 2, 1855	25	light	New York, N.Y.	5	40
Hardy, Joseph	Feb. 25, 1857	18	light	Newburyport, Ma.	5	45
**Hardey, Thomas	Dec. 9, 1822	45	light	Johnston, R.I.	4	32
Hardy, Thomas W.	Apr. 26, 1839	38	dark	Hollis, N.H.	5	36

*mulatto
**out of order
***Newport, R. I.

NAME	DATE OF CERTIFICATION	AGE	COMPLEXION	PLACE OF BIRTH	BOOK	PAGE
Hare, Levi	Oct. 26, 1805	20	light	Worcester, Ma.	3	55
Harel, John	Oct. 9, 1834	19	dark	Charleston, S.C.	5	36
Hargood, John	May 19, 1798	22	light	Micoleston, Pa.	2	8
Hargreaves,James	May 5, 1850	22	light	Fall River, Ma.	5	39
Harkins, James	June 15, 1855	26	light	Liberty Co., Tx.	5	45
Harlow, Pelham	Dec. 5, 1806	17	light	Plympton, Ma.	4	29
Harman, Elisha	May 6, 1839	25	black	Warwick, R.I.	5	36
Harman, Elisha	July 20, 1841	35	black	Warwick, R.I.	5	37
Harnes, Richard	Nov. 10, 1860	21	fair	New York, N.Y.	6	8
Harren, William	Apr. 5, 1850	19	light	Brooklyn, N.Y.	5	39
Harriman, Caleb	July 17, 1835	26	light	Boston, Ma.	5	36
Harrington, Abiel B.	Jan. 2, 1805	24	light	Norwich, Conn.	3	16
Harrington, Charles, Jr.	Nov. 12, 1807	23	light	Watertown, Ma.	4	29
Harrington, Charles R.	Dec. 22, 1858	24	light	Middletown, Conn.	6	8
Harrington, Crawford A.	Nov. 26, 1849	19	light	Cranston, R.I.	5	39
**Herrington, David	Jan. 14, 1824	23	light	Foster, R.I.	4	32
Harrington, David	Sept. 9, 1865	28	light	New York, N.Y.	6	8
Harrington, Nathan	June 21, 1845	19	light	Providence, R.I.	5	38
Harrington, William	Sept. 7, 1805	21	light	Foster, R.I.	3	55
Harris, Almond B.	May 20, 1844	16	light	Smithfield, R.I.	5	38
Harris, Caleb	May 23, 1815	17	light	Johnston, R.I.	4	31
Harris, Charles	July 8, 1819	22	light	Boston, Ma.	4	31
Harris, Charles E.	Mar. 16, 1839	19	dark	New London, Conn.	5	36
Harris, Daniel	Aug. 3, 1854	18	light	Providence, R.I.	5	40
Harris, Daniel	Oct. 15, 1855	21	dark	Providence, R.I.	5	45
Harris, Daniel T.	Apr. 28, 1864	29	light	Providence, R.I.	6	8
Harris, David	Dec. 14, 1805	22	dark	Glocester, R.I.	3	77
Harris, Edwin H.	Dec. 13, 1815	17	light	Providence, R.I.	4	31
Harris, Elisha R.	June 2, 1837	19	light	Burrillville, R.I.	5	36
Harris, Gideon	Mar. 17, 1835	26	yellow	Chalestown, R.I.	5	36
Harris, Griffith	May 25, 1797	57	light	Carmathan, Wales	1	13
Citizenship acquired by residence before Sept. 3, 1783.						
Harris, Henry	May 23, 1801	20	black	Charlestown, R.I.	2	28
Harris, James R.	July 10, 1839	25	dark	Providence, R.I.	5	36

**name is being placed in correct order.

NAME	DATE OF CERTIFICATION	AGE	COMPLEXION	PLACE OF BIRTH	BOOK	PAGE
Harris, Jeremiah, Jr.	Jan. 7, 1851	25	light	Burrillville, R.I.	5	40
Harris, John	1798-1799	Oct. 25, 1768		Somerset, Ma.	* _	--
Harris, John	June 5, 1804	27	dark	Bristol, Pa.	3	15
Harris, John	Nov. 20, 1804	36	dark	Somerset, Ma.	3	16
Harris, John	Feb. 24, 1852	24	dark	New York, N.Y.	5	40
Harris, Joseph	Mar. 29, 1800	21	light	Ipswitch, Ma.	2	28
Harris, Manton	Mar. 24, 1846	21	dark	Smithfield, R.I.	5	38
Harris, Nathaniel C.	Aug. 29, 1836	16	light	Providence, R.I.	5	36
Harris, Samuel	Dec. 24, 1822	21	light	Worcester, Ma.	4	32
Harris, Seamans M.F.	Nov. 21, 1809	17	dark	Cheshire, Ma.	4	30
Harris, Smith	Apr. 23, 1849	28	dark	Smithfield, R.I.	5	39
Harris, Stephen	Dec. 10, 1838	19	dark	Scituate, R.I.	5	36
Harris, Stephen, Jr.	Nov. 7, 1803	19	light	Providence, R.I.	2	49
Harris, Stephen M.	Mar. 23, 1805	20	light	Providence, R.I.	3	54
Harris, Thomas Naturalized in Providence in 1809.	Apr. 26, 1803	21	light	Great Britain	2	39
Harris, Thomas J.	Sept. 7, 1835	34	dark	Smithfield, R.I.	5	36
Harris, Thomas N.	Sept. 28, 1829	22	dark	Providence, R.I.	5	35
Harris, Warren	June 24, 1844	21	light	Cumberland, R.I.	5	38
Harris, Westcott	Dec. 3, 1827	22	light	Smithfield, R.I.	4	32
Harris, William	Mar. 2, 1804	19	light	Cranston, R.I.	3	15
Harris, William	Sept. 16, 1809	25	brown	Warwick, R.I.	4	29
Harris, William	Nov. 15, 1830	22	black	Smithfield, R.I.	5	35
Harris, William	Dec. 16, 1841	30	dark	Newburyport, Ma.	5	37
Harris, William A.	May 17, 1841	17	light	Cranston, R.I.	5	37
Harris, William B.	Nov. 14, 1803	19	light	Scituate, R.I.	2	49
Harris, William F.	Apr. 10, 1834	18	light	Cumberland, R.I.	5	35
Harrison, John	Nov. 7, 1833	24	light	Bellhaven, Va.	5	35
Harrison, John	June 13, 1850	23	light	New York, N.Y.	5	39
Harrison, Mathew	Apr. 25, 1857	30	light	Providence, R.I.	5	45
Harrison, Richard	Nov. 12, 1796	23	dark	Charleston, S.C.	1	13&5
Harrison, William	Oct. 11, 1797	16	dark	Providence, R.I.	1	27
Harrison, William	Nov. 3, 1800	31	dark	Boston, Ma.	2	28
Harrison, William	Oct. 13, 1843	18	light	New York, N.Y.	5	38
Harrison, William	Oct. 18, 1844	31	dark	Baltimore, Md.	5	38
Harrison, Wm. H.	Sept. 30, 1851	20	light	Phila., Pa.	5	40
Harry, Solomon	Aug. 24, 1824	20	Indian	Charlestown, R.I.	4	32
Hart, Farrington W. *Newport, R. I.	Mar. 30, 1864	16	light	St. George, Me.	6	8

REGISTER OF SEAMEN'S PROTECTION

NAME	DATE OF CERTIFICATION	AGE	COMPLEXION	PLACE OF BIRTH	BOOK	PAGE
Hart, James	1798-1799	Sept. 13, 1786		Newport, R.I.	-	--
Nicholas Hart of Newport swears the above to be true.						
Hart, John	Nov. 7, 1845	20	fair	New York, N.Y.	5	38
Hart, John C.	Dec. 23, 1851	21	fair	Needham, Ma.	5	40
Hart, Loring	Aug. 6, 1823	18	dark	East Greenwich, R.I.	4	32
Hart, Manly B.	Sept. 9, 1822	19	light	E. Greenwich, R.I.	4	32
Hart, Reuben	Nov. 14, 1801	21	dark	Taunton, Ma.	2	39
Hart, Samuel	July 4, 1819	40	light	W. George, Ma.	4	31
Hart, Thomas	May 14, 1800	30	light	Portsmouth, N.H.	2	28
Hartford, Alexander	Nov. 8, 1844	21	light	Abington, Me.	5	38
Hartshorn, Leander	Nov. 13, 1815	19	light	Johnstown, N.Y.	4	31
Hartshorn, Stephen	Nov. 14, 1809	17	dark	Johnstown, N.Y.	4	30
Hartwell, Daniel	Mar. 18, 1819	28	black	Dracut, Ma.	4	31
Hartwill, Reuben	Feb. 21, 1854	25	fair	Providence, R.I.	5	40
Harvey, Edward M.	Mar. 22, 1836	23	dark	No. Kingstown, R.I.	5	36
Harvey, George	Mar. 22, 1852	24	dark	Boston, Ma.	5	40
Harvey, James	Oct. 1, 1804	25	light	Baltimore, Md.	3	16
Harvey, James	June 17, 1806	22	light	Phila., Pa.	3	79
Harvey, Jonathan	Jan. 8, 1807	20	light	Holliston, Ma.	4	29
Harvey, Noah	Mar. 12, 1853	21	dark	Eastport, Me.	5	40
Harvey, Thomas	1798-1799	Mar. 18, 1773		New York	-	--
Harwood, Jonathan	Apr. 3, 1804	19	black	Providence, R.I.	3	15
Harword, Jonathan	Mar. 30, 1809	24	black	Charlestown, Ma.	4	29
Hascall, Elijah N.	Oct. 16, 1811	24	dark	Thompson, Conn.	4	30
Haskell, Benjamin	Nov. 19, 1796	25	black	Bristol, R.I.	1	13
Haskell, Benjamin	Feb. 29, 1804	33	black	Bristol, R.I.	3	15
Haskell, Benjamin	Oct. 25, 1820	20	black	Providence,R.I.	4	31
[Haskell]Harskell, Charles	Oct. 5, 1821	24	black	No. Prov., R.I.	4	31
Haskell, George	Mar. 11, 1815	22	black	No. Prov., R.I.	4	30
Haskell, George T. or J?	Aug. 19, 1845	26	fair	Newburyport, Ma.	5	38
Haskell, Moses, Jr.	May 1, 1829	21	dark	Providence, R.I.	5	35
Haskell, Song	Dec. 6, 1797	28	black	Bristol, R.I.	1	27
Hasker, James	May 28, 1799	21	black	Phila., Pa.	2	8
Haskill, Benjamin	Sept. 14, 1816	28	black	Swansea, MA.	4	31
Haskins, George	Sept. 5, 1842	21	dark	Rehoboth, Ma.	5	37

REGISTER OF SEAMEN'S PROTECTION

NAME	DATE OF CERTIFICATION	AGE	COMPLEXION	PLACE OF BIRTH	BOOK	PAGE
Haskins, George	Oct. 2, 1849	29	light	Rehoboth, Ma.	5	39
Haskins, Joseph B.	Jan. 25, 1847	36	fair	Portland, Me.	5	38
Hassen, Mathew	Oct. 29, 1849	24	light	Boston, Ma.	5	39
Hastings, Eleazer H.	Nov. 21, 1796	22	light	Warren, R.I.	1	13
Hastings, Thomas	Nov. 9, 1812	35	light	Newton, Ma.	4	30
Hatch, Henry	Oct. 19, 1797	16	light	E. Greenwich, R.I.	1	27
Hatch, Leonard	June 14, 1830	18	light	Portland, Me.	5	35
Hatch, Loring	May 1, 1830	28	light	Falmouth, Ma.	5	35
Hatch, Razel	Aug. 26, 1807	35	brown	Falmouth, Ma.	4	29
Hatch, Samuel	Nov. 25, 1805	21	light	E. Greenwich, R.I.	3	77
Hatch, Samuel B.	Aug. 6, 1864	28	light	E. Greenwich, R.I.	6	8
Hatch, Silvenus	Oct. 13, 1803	16	light	Falmouth, Ma.	2	39
Hatch, Theodore S.	Nov. 20, 1841	18	dark	Hanson, Ma.	5	37
Hatch, Theodore S.	Jan. 5, 1853	29	light	Hanson, Ma.	5	40
?Haterly, Frederick	Mar. 21, 1815	25	dark	So. Hampton, N.Y.	4	30
Hathaway, Anthony	Jan. 7, 1807	22	brown	E. Greenwich, R.I.	4	29
Hathaway, Clother	Oct. 29, 1803	37	light	Freetown, Ma.	2	49
Hathaway, Clother	Nov. 20, 1804	38	light	Freetown, Ma.	3	16
Hathaway, Elias	June 22, 1841	19	light	Freetown, Ma.	5	37
Hathaway, Fuller	Oct. 29, 1803	28	black	Freetown, Ma.	2	49
Hathaway, James	July 24, 1833	27	dark	Taunton, Ma.	5	35
Hathaway, Jerome	June 22, 1841	23	light	Freetown, Ma.	5	37
Hathaway, John C.	Feb. 29, 1848	32	light	New Bedford, Ma.	5	39
Hatnaway, Jonathan	Nov. 11, 1818	16	light	Wareham, Ma.	4	31
Hathaway, Leonard	Mar. 12, 1833	27	black	Taunton, Ma.	5	35
Hathaway, Leonard	July 23, 1841	36	black	Taunton, Ma.	5	37
Hathaway, Simon	Oct. 12, 1807	16	light	Wareham, Ma.	4	29
Hathaway, Stephen K.	Nov. 12, 1849	26	dark	Exeter, R.I.	5	39
Hathaway, Thomas	Sept. 30, 1820	23	light	Newport, R.I.	4	31
Hathaway, Thomas Z.	Oct. 26, 1849	25	light	Providence, R.I.	5	39
Hathaway, William	May 2, 1799	21	dark	Newport, R.I.	2	8
Hatten, John W.	Apr. 2, 1855	20	light	Smithfield, R.I.	5	40
Hatten, John W.	Sept. 10, 1855	20	light	Smithfield, R.I.	5	45
Hattan, Wilson	May 19, 1826	25	light	Thompson, Conn.	4	32
Havens, John Campbell	Mar. 20, 1821	21	dark	No. Kingstown,	* -	--

Birth certificate in The Custom House Papers. July 22, 1799.

*Newport, R. I.

NAME	DATE OF CERTIFICATION	AGE	COMPLEXION	PLACE OF BIRTH	BOOK	PAGE
Havens, Samuel	Mar. 27, 1823	25	black	So. Kingstown, R.I.	4	32
Havens, Sylvester	1798-1799	Dec. 13, 1760		No. Kingstown,	* -	--
Havens, Thomas	Aug. 30, 1796	16	light	Warwick, R.I.	1	2
Havens, William	Aug. 4, 1803	32	dark	Warwick, R.I.	2	39
Haword, L.W.J.M.	May 13, 1853	39	dark	Montgomery, Pa.	5	40
Hawes, James E.	Oct. 6, 1851	27	light	Wrentham, Ma.	5	40
Hawes, Jonathan	Aug. 27, 1831	39	light	Barnstable, Ma.	5	35
Hawes, Russell	May 1, 1830	19	light	Yarmouth, Ma.	5	35
Hawes, Thomas	Oct. 29, 1849	22	light	Providence, R.I.	5	39
Hawkes, Augustus C.	July 5, 1855	17	light	Manilius, N.Y.	5	45
Hawkes, Thomas J.	Aug. 31, 1849	39	light	Smithfield, R.I.	5	39
Hawkins, Edward	Apr. 27, 1797	20	light	No. Prov., R.I.	1	13
Hawkins, Francis	Sept. 3, 1842	29	dark	No. Prov., R.I.	5	37
Hawkins, George	Aug. 5, 1834	22	light	Providence, R.I.	5	35
Hawkins, Geo. B.	Mar. 2, 1849	22	light	Griswold, Conn.	5	39
Hawkins, George W.	Nov. 30, 1849	18	light	Smithfield, R.I.	5	39
Hawkins, Jabez	May 1, 1797	34	light	No. Prov., R.I.	1	13
Hawkins, James	July 20, 1798	24	light	No. Prov., R.I.	2	8
Hawkins, Joseph	Sept. 23, 1801	22	light	Providence, R.I.	2	39
Hawkins, Joseph	Apr. 17, 1809	28	light	Providence, R.I.	4	29
Hawkins, Luther	Sept. 28, 1847	37	light	Providence,R.I.	5	38
Hawkins, Newbury	Apr. 27, 1829	23	black	So. Kingston, R.I.	5	35
Hawkins, Oliver C.	Mar. 3, 1849	18	light	No. Prov., R.I.	5	39
Hawkins, Pardon	Oct. 29, 1799	22	light	Providence, R.I.	2	8
Hawkins, Pardon	Dec. 1, 1806	28	light	Scituate, R.I.	4	29
Hawkins, Sheldon	June 17, 1797	23	light	No. Prov., R.I.	1	13
Hawkins, Stephen	June 11, 1849	38	light	Sterling, Conn.	5	39
Hawkins, William	Dec. 3, 1810	23	yellow	So. Kingstown, R.I.	4	30
Hawly, Morris	Nov. 28, 1849	23	light	Dover, N.Y.	5	39
Hawley, William	Apr. 20, 1846	41	dark	Hanson, Ma.	5	38
Hay, John J.	July 8, 1839	18	light	New Bedford, Ma.	5	36
Hayden, John	Mar. 28, 1842	24	light	Wiscasset, Me.	5	37
Hayden, Michale	Nov. 15, 1799	20	dark	Cumberland, R.I.	2	8

*Newport, R. I.

NAME	DATE OF CERTIFICATION	AGE	COMPLEXION	PLACE OF BIRTH	BOOK	PAGE
Hayden, Nahum	Nov. 27, 1830	26	dark	Fitzwilliam, N.H.	5	35
Hayes, Cornelius	Mar. 24, 1848	18	fair	Phila,, Pa.	5	39
Hays, Edward	Sept. 8, 1843	25	light	New Shoreham, R.I.	5	38
Hayes, Henry	Nov. 28, 1834	26	light	New York, N.Y.	5	36
Hayes, Henry	Mar. 10, 1848	18	light	Boston, Ma.	5	39
Hayes, James	Aug. 26, 1857	28	fair	Newburyport, Ma.	6	8
Hayes, Henry B.	Oct. 17, 1803	20	light	Rehoboth, Ma.	2	39
Hayes, James	Sept. 9, 1857	20	light	Phila., Pa.	6	8
Hayes, John	Dec. 3, 1804	21	light	Westchester Co., N.Y.	3	16
Hays, Edward	Nov. 7, 1845	26	fair	New York, N.Y.	5	38
Hays, Henry	Apr. 6,,1850	19	light	Boston, Ma.	5	39
Hayford, Charles	Apr. 24, 1838	18	dark	Providence, R.I.	5	36
Hayford, Charles F.	May 31, 1815	18	brown	Providence, R.I.	4	31
Hayford, Garner	May 9, 1807	17	dark	Dighton, Ma.	4	29
Haynes, Stephen	Oct. 30, 1852	50	light	Bowdoin, Me.	5	40
Haynes, William	Aug. 20,	22	dark	Bridgehampton, N.Y.	5	38
Hayward, Adin	Mar. 9, 1838	30	dark	Easton, Ma.	5	36
Hayward, Augustus	Oct. 16, 1801	21	light	Pomfret, Conn.	4	30
Hayward, Leonard H.	July 27, 1864	24	medium	Providence, R.I.	6	8
Hayward, William, 2nd.	June 12, 1804	21	dark	Raynham, Ma.	3	15
Hazzard, Abraham	Apr. 2, 1841	23	dark	So. Kingston, R.I.	5	37
Hazard, Adam	Dec. 8, 1825	23	black	No. Kingstown, R.I.	4	32
Hazard, Bowdoin	May 2, 1799	24	dark	Scituate, R.I.	2	8
Hazard, Charles	May 15, 1809	19	black	Charlestown, R.I.	4	29
Hazard[Hazzard], Ephraim	Jan. 12, 1802	25	black	So. Kingstown, R.I.	2	39
Hazard, Ephraim	Oct. 31, 1804	27	black	Charlestown, R.I.	3	16
Hazard, Ephraim	Nov. 23, 1807	29	black	Charlestown, R.I.	4	29
Hazard, Frederick	Jan. 13, 1830	20	black	So. Kingston, R.I.	5	35
Hazard, George	July 12, 1805	18	black	Providence, R.I.	3	55
Hazard, George P.	Dec. 22, 1826	17	light	Warwick, R.I.	4	32
Hazard, Henry S.	Oct. 19, 1811	20	light	So. Kingstown, R.I.	4	30
Hazard, Isaac	Aug. 11, 1835	20	black	No. Kingston, R.I.	5	36
Hazard, James	May 31, 1826	32	black	So. Kingstown, R.I.	4	32
Hazard, James	Mar. 9, 1852	28	black	So. Kingston, R.I.	5	40
Hazard, James	June 6, 1852	28	black	So. Kingston, R.I.	5	40
Hazard, Job G.	Apr. 4, 1818	18	light	So. Kingstown, R.I.	4	31

REGISTER OF SEAMEN'S PROTECTION

NAME	DATE OF CERTIFICATION	AGE	COMPLEXION	PLACE OF BIRTH	BOOK	PAGE
Hazard, John	May 7, 1835	17	black	Charlestown, R.I.	5	36
Hazard, John B.	May 10, 1821	42	light	No. Kingstown, R.I.	4	31
Hazard, John H.	June 24, 1854	18	mulatto	Providence, R.I.	5	40
Hazard, Joseph S.	Oct. 27, 1849	33	light	So. Kingston, R.I.	5	39
Hazard, Luke	Oct. 15, 1817	22	light	So. Kingstown, R.I.	4	31
Hazard, Nathaniel	Dec. 25, 1818	28	yellow	No. Kingstown. R.I.	4	31
Hazard, Newport	Sept. 19, 1803	22	black	Jamestown, R.I.	2	39
Hazard, Peyton R.	Oct. 4, 1831	21	dark	Newport, R.I.	5	35
Hazard, Scipio	May 23, 1810	22	black	Colchester, Conn.	4	30
Hazard, Scipio	Dec. 22, 1819	28	black	So. Kingstown, R.I.	4	31
Hazard, Thomas	Aug. 7, 1812	23	black	So. Kingstown, R.I.	4	30
Hazard, Thomas E.	Mar. 16, 1842	17	light	So. Kingstown, R.I.	5	37
Hazard, William C.	Aug. 31, 1849	22	dark	No. Kingston, R.I.	5	39
Hazzard, Henry S., Jr.	June 1, 1843	21	dark	Warwick, R.I.	5	38
Hazzard, Isaac	Dec. 25, 1843	23	copper	No. Kingston, R.I.	5	38
Hazzard, Joseph	Aug. 1, 1842	20	black	New York, N.Y.	5	37
[Hassard]Hazzard, William	Mar. 30, 1857	22	light	Balitmore, Md.	5	45
Hazelhurst, Edward	Oct. 4, 1853	22	light	Providence, R.I.	5	40
Head, John	Sept. 16, 1847	29	light	New York	5	38
Head, Nathaniel	Sept. 26, 1810	18	yellow	Little Compton, R.I.	4	30
Head, Nathaniel	Jan. 23, 1818	25	yellow	Little Compton, R.I.	4	31
Head, Samuel	Dec. 24, 1832	16	yellow	Newport, R.I.	5	35
Headen, James	Sept. 13, 1851	21	dark	New York, N.Y.	5	40
Headley, William	1798-1799	June 15, 1781		No. Kingston,	* -	--
Healy, Rowland G.	Feb. 11, 1842	18	light	Hopkinton, R.I.	5	37
Healy, Thomas	Sept. 23, 1805	21	light	Providence,R.I.	3	55
Heap, George P.	Oct. 23, 1849	21	light	Hudson, N.Y.	5	39
Heard, Thomas	May 13, 1797	15	light	Plainfield, Conn.	1	13
Hearn, John	May 25, 1861	28	dark	Kennebunk, Me.	6	8
Heath, Benjamin	Dec. 9, 1829	22	light	Barrington, R.I.	5	25
Heath, Henry A.	Aug. 7, 1841	22	light	Gorton, Conn.	5	37
Heath, Isaac	Oct. 13, 1828	23	ruddy	Stoddard, N.H.	4	32
Heath, Nathaniel	Nov. 9, 1796	21	light	Barrington, R.I.	1	13&5

*Newport, R. I.

NAME	DATE OF CERTIFICATION	AGE	COMPLEXION	PLACE OF BIRTH	BOOK	PAGE
Heath, Olney	Nov. 9, 1826	22	light	Rehoboth, Ma.	4	32
Heath, Robert	Mar. 29, 1799	18	light	Newport, R.I.	2	8
Heath, Robert	Mar. 28, 1809	28	light	Newport, R.I.	4	29
Hedges, Jason	1798-1799	Mar. 11, 1775		Sag Harbor, N.Y.	* -	--
Hedger, William	Apr. 21, 1846	23	fair	Baltimore, Md.	5	38
Hefron, Joseph	Mar. 29, 1851	30	dark	No. Prov., R.I.	5	40
Helen, William	Dec. 21, 1837	34	light	No. Prov., R.I.	5	36
Helme, David	Dec. 30, 1818	22	yellow	So. Kingstown, R.I.	4	31
Helms, James	Jan. 9, 1798	25	black	So. Kingstown, R.I.	1	27
Hemenway, Alanson	Dec. 30, 1823	19	ruddy	Holliston, Ma.	4	32
Hender, Geo. A.	Aug. 30, 1853	18	light	Camden, Me.	5	40
Henderson, James	June 18, 1855	22	light	Providence, R.I.	5	45
Henderson, Thomas	Dec. 9, 1799	23	light	Chatham, Ma.	2	8
Henderson, Warren	Oct. 20, 1856	20	light	St. George, Me.	5	45
Hendrick, Charles	July 29, 1853	29	light	Phila., Pa.	5	40
Hendrick, Otis	Nov. 11, 1841	32	light	Smithfield, R.I.	5	37
Hendrick, Samuel	Jan. 6, 1804	24	light	Norwalk, Conn.	3	15
Hanry, Caleb	May 21, 1847	25	dark	Cranston, R.I.	5	38
Henry, Charles	July 9, 1819	23	black	Flatbush, N.Y.	4	31
Henry, Charles F.	Oct. 5, 1849	21	light	New Bedford, Ma.	5	39
Henry, Hardin[g]	Sept. 23, 1801	18	light	Providence, R.I.	2	39
Henry, Harding	Aug. 16, 1803	20	light	Cranston, R.I.	2	39
Henry, James T.	Nov. 29, 1832	17	yellow	Norwich, Conn.	5	35
Henry, John C.	Apr. 16, 1863	23	dark	Cumberland, N.J.	6	8
Henry, Joseph	Jan. 21, 1832	21	black	New York, N.Y.	5	35
Henry, Sheldon	Feb. 22, 1805	18	light	Cranston, R.I.	3	54
Henry, Sheldon	July 2, 1810	22	florid	Cranston, R.I.	4	30
Henry, Stephen	Nov. 22, 1805	33	light	Cranston, R.I.	3	77
Henry, Thomas	Dec. 21, 1807	19	yellow	New York, N.Y.	4	29
Henry, William	Oct. 7, 1831	19	light	Phila., Pa.	5	35
Henrys, Caleb	Dec. 4, 1833	21	light	Cranston, R.I.	5	35
Henryx, James	Mar. 18, 1797	28	dark	Providence, R.I.	1	13
Hensey, William	May 30, 1806	16	light	Plainfield, Conn.	3	79

*Newport, R. I.

REGISTER OF SEAMEN'S PROTECTION

Page 129

NAME	DATE OF CERTIFICATION	AGE	COMPLEXION	PLACE OF BIRTH	BOOK	PAGE
Henson, Jason	June 16, 1798	23	black	Norwich, Conn.	2	8
Henson, Jason	Mar. 31, 1800	23	black	E. Hampton, N.Y.	2	28
Henson, Jason	Aug. 11, 1804	27	black	Stonington, Conn.	3	15
Hensey, William R.	May 9, 1810	19	dark	Plainfield, Conn.	4	30
Henyon, Elias	Oct. 2, 1801	18	dark	Redhook, N.Y.	2	39
Hermans, Halsted	Nov. 29, 1830	22	light	Albany, N.Y.	5	35
Heron, Calvin	May 18, 1807	22	light	Killingsworth, Conn.	4	29
Herrington, David	Jan. 14, 1824	23	light	Foster, R.I.	4	32
Herrington, James	Oct. 24, 1806	20	brown	Wiscasset, Me.	4	29
Herrington, James R.	May 14, 1842	16	light	Woodstock, Conn.	5	37
Herrington, Thomas	Oct. 27, 1801	27	dark	Smithfield, R.I.	2	39
Hersey, Israel	Mar. 18, 1851	20	light	Eastport, Me.	5	40
Heston, Alfred J.	Aug. 19, 1822	19	light	Phila., Pa.	4	32
Hewes, William	Apr. 29, 1797	27	dark	Providence, R.I.	1	13
Hewins, Joseph D.	Nov. 7, 1820	18	light	Sharon, Ma.	4	31
Hewitt, George	Mar. 27, 1863	17	light	Newport, R.I.	6	8
Hewlett, James	June 19, 1810	41	fresh	New London, Conn.	4	30
Hewson, Richard	Oct. 15, 1830	19	light	Roxbury, Ma.	5	35
Heyliger, Benjamin	Oct. 8, 1808	22	dark	Christienstead, St. Croix	4	29
Hicker, John	Nov. 9, 1810	21	black	Newport, R.I.	4	30
Hicks, Benjamin	June 15, 1801	23	light	Little Compton, R.I.	2	28
Hicks, David	May 3, 1797	23	light	Swansey, Ma.	1	13
Hicks, James	JUNE 16, 1842	38	dark	Phila., Pa.	5	37
Hicks, John	1797	37	black	Roxbury, Ma.	1	13
Hicks, Oliver	1798-1799	Mar. 11, 1776		Westport, Ma.	*_	--
Hicks, Stephen P.	Mar. 29, 1827	29	ruddy	Glocester, R.I.	4	32
Hicks, Stephen P.	Mar. 25, 1841	42	ruddy	Glocester, R.I.	5	37
Hide, Joseph	Apr. 10, 1824	25	yellow	Dighton, Ma.	4	32
Higbee, John	Dec. 26, 1806	27	light	New York, N.Y.	4	29
Higgins, Daniel	Jan. 18, 1813	22	light	Boston, Ma.	4	30
Higgins, Hiram Henry	Apr. 22, 1830	26	dark	No. Prov., R.I.	5	35
Higgens, John	Aug. 28, 1807	21	black	Boston, Ma.	4	29
Higgins, Henry	July 26, 1797	25	light	Haddam, Conn.	1	27

*Newport, R. I.

NAME	DATE OF CERTIFICATION	AGE	COMPLEXION	PLACE OF BIRTH	BOOK	PAGE
Higgins, William	Sept. 24, 1846	23	fair	Plymouth, England	5	38
Higgins, William S.	Nov. 4. 1846	19	fair	Hampden, Me.	5	38
Hilborn, Chas. S.	Jan. 5, 1843	22	light	Portland, Me.	5	37
Hildreth, W.F.	Jan. 27, 1854	30	light	Dracutt, Ma.	5	40
Hill, Albert T.	Nov. 19, 1846	34	light	No. Prov., R.I.	5	38
Hill, Benjamin M.	July 3, 1810	17	dark	Newport, R.I ,	4	30
Hill, David	June 24, 1818	20	black	Swansea, Ma.	4	31
Hill, George	Mar. 31, 1797	19	light	Newport, R.I.	1	13
Hill, George	Dec. 23, 1800	28	light	Smithfield, R.I.	2	28
Hill, George W.	Oct. 6, 1852	30	dark	East Hartford, Conn.	5	40
Hill, Harris	Feb. 2, 1821	20	dark	E. Hartford, Conn.	-	--
Sworn statement of Normand Hill of Hartford in Custom House Papers. Feb. 25, 1800.						
Hill, Jacob	June 7, 1849	54	black	Dover, Del.	5	39
Hill, James	Jan. 4, 1805	28	black	Wilmington, Pa.	3	54
Hill, John D.	Feb. 21, 1867	25	dark	Boston, Ma.	6	8
Hill, Jonathan	Dec. 29, 1825	17	light	Warren, R.I.	4	32
Hill, Samuel M.	May 5, 1852	36	dark	Bristol, N.Y.	5	40
Hill, Stephen	Mar. 4, 1797	30	dark	Cumberland, R.I.	1	13
Hill, Thomas	Feb. 14, 1843	19	light	Sullivan, Me.	5	37
Hill, Thomas	June 11, 1849	60	light	Scituate, R.I.	5	39
Hill, William	Aug. 5, 1796	24	light	Swansea, Ma.	1	1
Hill, William	Mar. 28, 1815	21	light	Newport, R.I.	4	31
Hill, William	Sept. 22, 1858	35	dark	Plymouth, Ma.	6	8
Hillman, Charles	Oct. 12, 1825	15	dark	Boston, Ma.	4	32
Hillman, George G.	Feb. 24, 1859	33	light	Wilton, Me.	6	8
Hilton, Charles	Oct. 4, 1850	42	black	Egg Harbor, N.J.	5	39
Hilton, William	Aug. 20, 1803	16	light	Norfolk, Va.	2	39
Hilton, William	July 20, 1804	18	light	Richmond, Va.	3	15
Himes, George	Feb. 14, 1806	15	light	No. Kingstown, R.I.	3	77
Himes, James	Apr. 20, 1846	18	dark	Newport, R.I.	5	38
Himes, Joshua	Aug. 26, 1845	15	dark	Boston, Ma.	5	38
Himes, Palmer	Aug. 11, 1817	18	light	No. Kingstown, R.I.	4	31
Himes, William, Jr.	Aug. 29, 1845	23	dark	No. Kingston, R.I.	5	38
Hinckly, James F.	Aug. 12, 1834	34	light	Boston, Ma.	5	36
Hinds, James	Oct. 5, 1838	23	dark	No. Prov., R.I.	5	36
Hines, Lawrence	Mar. 10, 1852	23	sandy	Eastport, Me.	5	40
Hinkley, George	Oct. 8, 1856	21	light	Providence, R.I.	5	45

NAME	DATE OF CERTIFICATION	AGE	COMPLEXION	PLACE OF BIRTH	BOOK	PAGE
Hinkly, John	Oct. 9, 1855	41	light	Georgetown, Me.	5	45
Hinman, George	Sept. 12, 1801	21	dark	Providence, R.I.	2	28
Hinman, Sidney	July 29, 1837	17	light	Farmington, Conn.	5	36
Hitch, James	May 30, 1799	15	black	Providence, R.I.	2	8
Hitch, James	Feb. 13, 1806	22	yellow*	Providence, R.I.	3	77
Hitchins, Henry	July 25, 1797	28	dark	New York, N.Y.	1	27
Hoar, Albert N.	July 19, 1841	14	light	Attleboro, Ma.	5	37
Hoar, Charles	July 20, 1841	20	light	Warren, R.I.	5	37
Hoar, Davniel	July 12, 1824	21	ruddy	Warren, R.I.	4	32
Hoard, Gilbert	Oct. 29, 1804	19	dark	Somerset, Ma.	3	16
Hoban, John J.	Sept. 26, 1843	21	light	New York, N.Y.	5	38
Hobbs, John	Mar. 12, 1844	16	dark	Hampden, Me.	5	38
Hobbs, Timothy	July 11, 1839	21	light	Spencer, Ma.	5	36
HOdgdon, Alexander	May 2, 1840	19	light	Mount Desert, Me.	5	37
Hodges, Ephraim	Sept. 18, 1823	25	ruddy	Belgrade, Me.	4	32
Hodges, Harford B.	Nov. 24, 1828	28	light	Norton, Ma.	4	32
Hodges, John	Mar. 23, 1821	19	light	Belgrade, Me.	4	31
Hodges, William G.	Mar. 13, 1835	18	light	Providence, R.I.	5	36
Hodgin, Thomas	Oct. 6, 1800	26	dark	Phila., Pa.	2	28
Hodgins, Frank	Dec. 8, 1865	17	light	Calais, Me.	6	8
Hogan, George	June 22, 1836	21	mulatto	Phila., Pa.	5	36
Hoke, Newman E.	Apr. 12, 1854	20	dark	Rockland, Me.	5	40
Holbrook, Henry	Sept. 15, 1851	20	dark	Mendon, Ma.	5	40
Holbrook, James	Oct. 6, 1806	18	light	Sherburn, Ma.	4&3**	29&79**
Holbrook, John E.	Nov. 8, 1839	17	light	Swansea, Ma.	5	37
Holcomb, Francis	Feb. 8, 1847	25	black	Paterson, N.J.	5	38
Holden, Alfred	July 7, 1840	33	black	Warwick, R.I	5	37
Holden, Alfred	Jan. 11, 1847	42	black	Warwick, R.I.	5	38
Holden, Andrew	July 14, 1806	21	light	Copenhagen, Denmark	3	79
Holden, Benjamin	Mar. 25, 1805	19	dark	Warwick, R.I.	3	54
Holden, Caleb	July 15, 1805	21	light	Warwick, R.I.	3	55
Holden, Caleb	Nov. 20, 1804	21	light	Warwick, R.I.	3	16

*mulatto
**Book 4, page 29; book 3, page79.

NAME		DATE OF CERTIFICATION	AGE	COMPLEXION	PLACE OF BIRTH	BOOK	PAGE
Holden,	Caleb	June 4, 1832	17	dark	Warwick, R.I.	5	35
Holden,	Cato	Dec. 7, 1821	18	black	Warwick, R.I.	4	31
Holden,	Charles	Feb. 27, 1800	21	light	Providence, R.I.	2	8
Holden,	Charles	Oct. 16, 1821	19	dk. yellow	Canterbury, Conn.	4	31
Holden,	David	July 0, 1798	29	black	Warwick, R.I.	2	8
Holden,	Freeman	May 13, 1797	23	black	Warwick, R.I.	1	13
Holden,	Freeman	Aug. 26, 1817	41	black	Warwick, R.I.	4	31
Holden,	Henry	June 17, 1806	22	brown	Warwick, R.I.	3	79
Holden,	Henry	Feb. 22, 1842	52	dark	Providence, R.I.	5	37
Holden,	Jacob	Oct. 26, 1826	16	mulatto	Warwick, R.I.	4	32
Holden,	James W.	Aug. 11, 1803	18	dark	Providence, R.I.	2	39
Holden,	James W.	Sept. 20, 1801	17	dark	Providence, R.I.	2	39
Holden,	Job	Sept. 30, 1835	22	black	Warwick, R.I.	5	36
Holden,	John	Nov. 25, 1797	23	dark	Providence, R.I.	1	27
Holden,	John	Sept. 9, 1844	42	light	Warwick, R.I.	5	38
Holden,	John Pierce	Nov. 13, 1847	14	fair	Providence, R.I.	5	38
Holden,	Joseph M.	Apr. 18, 1833	18	light	Warwick, R.I.	5	35
Holden,	Randall	Sept. 6, 1796	16	dark	Providence, R.I.	1	2
Holden,	Randall	Oct. 19, 1797	17	dark	Providence, R.I.	1	27
Holden,	Samuel	Nov. 19, 1821	19	dk. yellow	Warwick, R.I.	4	31
Holden,	Thomas, Jr.	Sept. 9, 1822	19	light	Warwick, R.I.	4	32
Holden,	Thomas R.	Nov. 29, 1822	16	light	Warwick, R.I.	4	32
Holden,	Ulysses	May 2, 1809	20	light	Providence, R.I.	4	29
Holden,	Wanton	July 20, 1816	23	black	Providence, R.I.	4	31
Holden,	William A.	Sept. 7, 1799	22	dark	Warwick, R.I.	2	8
Holden,	William A.	June 12, 1800	23	dark	Warwick, R.I.	2	28
Holden,	William D.	Dec. 4, 1833	15	light	Providence, R.I.	5	35
Holdref,	John	Dec. 19, 1818	14	light	Providence, R.I.	4	31
Holdoff,	Joseph	June 26, 1830	21	light	Palmer, Ma.	5	35
Holland,	Joseph	May 7, 1856	22	black	Philadelphia, Pa.	5	45
Holligan,	Dennis	July 14, 1863	25	light	Providence, R.I.	6	8
Holly,	Edward	Jan. 18, 1850	24	dark	New York, N.Y.	5	39
Holley,	James	June 12, 1810	19	black	Charlestown, R.I.	4	30

REGISTER OF SEAMEN'S PROTECTION

NAME	DATE OF CERTIFICATION	AGE	COMPLEXION	PLACE OF BIRTH	BOOK	PAGE
Hollingsworth, JOHN	Oct. 4, 1805	24	dark	York Town, Va.	3	55
Holloway, Guilderoy	Dec. 4, 1833	21	light	Richmond, R.I.	5	35
Holloway, William R.	May 22, 1839	23	light	No. Prov., R.I.	5	36
Hollowell, Benjamin G.	Nov. 16, 1796	24	light	So, Kingstown, R.I.	1	13
Holkins, Philip	June 22, 1840	27	light	Albany, N.Y.	5	37
Holloway, Christopher	1798-1799	Dec. 19, 1769		Exeter, R.I.	** -	--
Holman, Alexander	Aug. 14, 1852	22	light	Rochester, N.Y.	5	40
Holmes, Allen	Oct. 18, 1834	33	black	Phila., Pa.	5	36
Holmes, George C.	July 29, 1864	20	light	Boston, Ma.	6	8
Holmes, Henry A.	July 28, 1819	15	light	Providence, R.I.	4	31
Holmes, Jacob	Dec. 9, 1826	23	black	Warwick, R.I.	4	32
Holmes, John	1798-1799	Mar. 6, 1784		Newport, R.I.	** -	--
Holmes, Joseph	Mar. 20, 1815	18	light	Raynham, Ma.	4	30
Holmes, Joseph J.	Mar. 5, 1849	32	light	Easton, Ma.	5	39
Holmes, Peter B.	Nov. 11, 1850	21	dark	Providence, R.I.	5	40
Holmes, Robert	Oct. 16, 1833	34	sallow	Providence, R.I.	5	35
Holmes, Robert	Aug. 26, 1845	20	dark	Lubeck, Me.	5	38
Holmes, Samuel	1798-1799	June 14, 1753		New York	** -	--
Holmes, Stephen B.	Nov. 27, 1839	22	dark	Boston, Ma.	5	37
Holmes, William	Mar. 22, 1848	25	light	New Bedford, Ma.	5	39
Holmes, William F.	Jan. 9, 1816	32	light	Warwick, R.I.	4	31
Holroyd, Samuel J.	Aug. 22, 1806	16	light	Providence, R.I.	3	79
Holt, James	Jan. 5, 1798	23	dark	Newport, R.I.	1	27
Holt, Joseph H.	Jan. 26, 1828	19	dark	Mansfield, Conn.	4	32
Holt, Saluf?	June 28, 1836	18	light	New London, Conn.	5	36
Homer, Michael	July 23, 1833	32	light	Boston, Ma.	5	35
Homer, Samuel	Jan. 18, 1805	20	yellow*	Trenton, N.J.	3	54
Homes, Isaac H.	July 14, 1856	18	light	Bucksport, Me.	5	45
Honeywell, Elliot	Mar. 27, 1834	20	light	New Shoreham, R.I.	5	35
Hood, Augustus L.	Nov. 11, 1842	17	dark	Salem, Ma.	5	37
Hood, Barton Quincy	June 22, 1825	17	light	Somerset, Ma.	4	32
Hood, Joseph L.	June 14, 1850	39	dark	Salem, Ma.	5	39
Hooker, Edward, Jr.	July 22, 1841	18	light	Farmington, Conn.	5	37
Hooker, John	June 10, 1799	23	light	Medfield, Ma.	2	8
Hooker, Pardon	Mar. 16, 1810	17	light	Woodstock, Conn.	4	30
Hooper, Charles	July 10, 1805	23	dark	Baltimore, Md.	3	55

*mulatto

*Newport. R. I.

NAME	DATE OF CERTIFICATION	AGE	COMPLEXION	PLACE OF BIRTH	BOOK	PAGE
Hooper, Linus	Sept. 6, 1811	22	light	Bridgewater, Ma.	4	30
Hope, Caesar	Nov. 9, 1810	20	yellow	Rockaway, N.Y.	4	30
Hope, Eldridge	Apr. 9, 1812	19	dark	East Hartford, Conn.	4	30
Hopewell, Nelson	Mar. 21, 1857	40	black	Georgetown, D.C.	5	45
Hopkins, Abel	Mar. 7, 1812	25	florid	Scituate, R.I.	4	30
Hopkins, Abial	May 30, 1797	23	dark	W. Greenwich, R.I.	1	13
Hopkins, Arnold	June 7, 1799	21	dark	Newport, R.I.	2	8
Hopkins, Clvin	June 23, 1832	19	sandy	Harwich, Ma.	5	35
Hopkins, David	June 17, 1800	20	light	Coventry, R.I.	2	28
Hopkins, Davis	Dec. 13, 1839	21	light	Vareham, MA.	5	37
Hopkins, Edmond	Aug. 1, 1804	22	light	?Brewster, Ma.	3	15
Hopkins, Franklin	Nov. 11, 1800	16	light	Providence, R.I.	2	28
Hopkins, George	Aug. 5, 1796	21	dark	Scituate, R.I.	1	1
Hopkins, George	Dec. 3, 1839	29	dark	Scituate. R.I.	5	37
Hopkins, John	July 29, 1815	24	light	Providence, R.I.	4	31
Hopkins, John	Sept. 11, 1850	44	dark	So. Kingston, R.I.	5	39
Hopkins, Joshua	Nov. 17, 1847	41	dark	Bucksport, Me.	5	39
Hopkins, Lewis	Mar. 10, 1804	20	black	Providence, R.I.	3	15
Hopkins, Lewis	Sept. 5, 1812	28	black	Providence, R.I.	4	30
Hopkins, Nathan G.	Apr. 4, 1839	34	light	Foster, R.I.	5	36
Hopkins, Nicholas	June 20, 1797	20	dark	Providence, R.I.	1	13
Hopkins, Perez, Jr.	Nov. 4, 1829	21	light	Yarmoutn, Ma.	5	35
Hopkins, Reuben	Apr. 2, 1805	22	dark	W. Greenwich, R.I.	3	54
Hopkins, Reuben	Dec. 27, 1823	21	light	Yarmouth, Ma.	4	32
Hopkins, Rowland	Dec. 17, 1800	21	light	W. Greenwich, R.I.	2	28
Hopkins, Rufus	Sept. 26, 1805	17	light	Providence, R.I.	3	55
Hopkins, Rufus	Oct. 1, 1807	18	light	Providence, R.I.	4	29
Hopkins, Samuel	Sept. 26, 1796	20	dark	Glocester, R.I.	1	3
Hopkins, Samuel	July 16, 1804	28	light	Scituate, R.I.	3	15
Hopkins, Samuel	July 20, 1818	26	black	Providence, R.I.	4	.31
Hopkins, Samuel	Jan. 12, 1831	39	black	Providence, R.I.	5	35
Hopkins, Samuel S.	Aug. 11, 1815	16	dark	Scituate, R.I.	4	31
Hopkins, Samuel Stevens?	Nov. 2, 1805	19	black	Newport, R.I.	3	77
Hopkins, Stephen	June 20, 1797	20	dark	Providence, R.I.	1	13
Hopkins, Stephen	Sept. 10, 1803	27	dark	Providence, R.I.	2	39
Hopkins, Thomas	Oct. 29, 1803	34	light	Providence, R.I.	2	39

REGISTER OF SEAMEN'S PROTECTION

NAME	DATE OF CERTIFICATION	AGE	COMPLEXION	PLACE OF BIRTH	BOOK	PAGE
Hopkins, Thomas	Aug. 9, 1808	38	light	Providence, R.I	4	29
Hopkins, Thomas	Apr. 1, 1809	16	brown	Providence, R.I.	4	29
Hopkins, Thomas, Jr.	Feb. 27, 1810	17	brown	Providence, R.I.	4	30
Hopkins, Thos. Henry	Apr. 12, 1852	21	light	Eastport, Me.	5	40
Hopkins, Uriah	Nov. 21, 1822	16	light	Providence, R I.	4	32
Hopkins, Zelotes	Nov. 9, 1843	33	light	Yarmouth, Ma.	5	38
Hopkins, Zelotus W.	Nov. 24, 1829	19	light	Barnstable, Ma.	5	35
Hopkins, Zelotes	Nov. 9, 1843	33	light	Yarmouth, Ma.	5	38
Hopkins, Zelotus W.	Nov. 24, 1829	19	light	Barnstable, Ma.	5	35
Hoppin, Davis	Sept. 21, 1796	24	light	Providence, R.I.	1	3
Hoppin, Edward D.	Oct. 2, 1811	14	light	Providence, R.I.	4	30
Hoppin, John	Mar. 25, 1800	22	light	Providence, R.I.	2	8
Hoppin, John L.	July 8, 1797	21	light	Salem, Ma.	1	27
Horan, Tintin	Nov. 17, 1841	22	light	New York, N.Y.	5	37
Horkins, Joseph	Nov. 30, 1796	16	light	Providence, R.I.	1	13
Horn, Jacob E.	Jan. 8, 1852	25	dark	New York. N.Y.	5	40
Horn, John	Feb. 17, 1824	20	light	Barrington, R.I.	4	32
Horswell, Nathaniel	Nov. 11, 1800	19	light	Providence, R.I.	2	28
Horswell, Nathaniel	May 31, 1805	24	light	Providence, R.I.	3	54
Horton, Earnest	Apr. 22, 1859	24	dark	New Bedford, Ma.	6	8
Horton, James H.	June 8, 1849	22	light	Providence, R.I.	5	39
Horton, Jarvis G.	Oct. 13, 1856	16	fair	Bristol, R.I.	5	45
Horton, John	July 21, 1801	27	dark	Baltimore, Md.	2	28
Horton, John	July 10, 1835	19	dark	Providence, R.I.	5	36
Horton, John C.	July 29, 1809	23	dark	Smithfield, R.I.	4	29
Horton, Nathaniel B.	June 19, 1843	23	light	Providence, R.I.	5	38
Horton, Sanford	Sept. 14, 1812	27	dark	Providence, R.I.	4	30
Horton, Seth Luther	Nov. 8, 1850	15	light	Bristol, R.I.	5	40
Horton, Stephen A.	May 19, 1858	15	light	Dillen, Ill.	6	8
Hoswell, Peter	July 13, 1799	14	light	Providence, R.I.	2	8
Hotchkiss, Joel P.	Nov. 5, 1831	22	light	Guildford, Conn.	5	35
Hotsopple, Jacob	1798-1799	July 16, 1776		New York	* -	--
House, JOhn	1798-1799	Sept. 3, 1783		Settled in New York City -		--*
House, John	1798-1799	Sept. 13, 1775		Norfolk, Va.	* -	--

*Newport, R. I.

NAME	DATE OF CERTIFICATION	AGE	COMPLEXION	PLACE OF BIRTH	BOOK	PAGE
Hovewater, Henry	Oct. 8, 1806	20	black	New York, N.Y.	3&4*	79&29
Howard, Albert	Apr. 1, 1865	28	light	Boston , Ma.	6	8
Howard, Amos	Nov. 5, 1800	18	black	Boston, Ma.	2	28
Howard, Benjamin	Dec. 5, 1811	17	light	Cranston, R.I.	4	30
Howard, Burby	Mar. 23, 1821	25	dark	Cumberland, R.I.	4	31
Howard, Caesar	Nov. 18, 1809	21	black	Newport, R.I.	4	30
Howard, Caleb	Aug. 21, 1804	18	light	Stoughton, Ma.	3	16
Howard, Charles	Dec. 6, 1830	24	dark	Philadelphia, Pa.	5	35
Howard, Daniel	June 9, 1815	20	light	Westerly, R.I.	4	31
Howard, George F.	Apr. 13, 1835	22	light	Smithfield, R.I.	5	36
Howard, Harvey	Nov. 14, 1815	23	dark	Pembroke, Ma.	4	31
Howard, Henry	Dec. 5, 1801	18	light	Cranston, R.I.	2	39
Howard, Henry	Mar. 30, 1836	23	mulatto	New Bedford, Ma.	5	36
Howard, Hiram	Nov. 21, 1806	14	light	Wrentham, Ma.	4	29
Howard, Hiram	June 5, 1807	14	light	Bennington, Vt.	4	29
Howard, Holder	1798-1799	Mar. 19, 1779		New Bedford, Ma.	* * -	--
Howard, Isaac	Apr. 7, 1797	21	light	Middleborough, Ma.	1	13
Howard, Isaac	Nov. 20, 1811	27	light	Stoughton, Ma.	4	30
Howard, Isaac	Aug. 23, 1841	22	dark	Foster, R.I.	5	37
Howard, Jacob	Sept. 2, 1842	20	black	Providence, R.I.	5	37
Howard, James	Sept. 10, 1796	23	dark	Warwick, R.I.	1	2
Howard, James	Nov. 20, 1803	30	dark	Warwick, R.I.	2	49
Howard, James	May 31, 1804	31	dark	Warwick, R.I.	3	15
Howard, James W.	Nov. 10, 1846	18	fair	Providence, R.I.	5	38
Howard, John	Aug. 15, 1832	24	sandy	Nantucket, Ma.	5	35
Howard, John	Sept. 18, 1858	22	fair	Skancatales, N.Y.	6	8
Howard, Nathan	Dec. 1, 1800	22	light	Sturbridge, Ma.	2	28
Howard, Oliver	Dec. 21, 1844	24	light	Bloomingburgh, N.Y.	5	38
Howard, Richard	June 22, 1807	15	brown	Bridgewater, Ma.	4	29
Howard, Rufus	Oct. 22, 1803	21	light	Raynham, Ma.	2	39
Howard, Seth F.	July 19, 1841	15	dark	No. Prov., R.I.	5	37
Howard, Seth F.	July 24, 1845	19	dark	Providence, R.I.	5	38
Howard, Thomas	Dec. 19, 1804	14	light	Providence, R I.	3	16
Howard, Thomas	Mar. 14, 1809	19	light	Providence, R.I.	4	29
Howard, Welcome	Dec. 2, 1811	17	light	Wrentham, Ma.	4	30

*Book 3, page 79; book 4, page 29.
**Newport, R. I.

REGISTER OF SEAMEN'S PROTECTION

NAME	DATE OF CERTIFICATION	AGE	COMPLEXION	PLACE OF BIRTH	BOOK	PAGE
Howard, William	1798-1799	Jan. 22, 1768		Newport, R.I.	** -	--
Howard, William Henry	May 11, 1855	17	mulatto	Providence, R,I.	5	40
Howe, Joel A.	Dec. 28, 1849	37	light	Prospect, Me.	5	39
Howe, John K.	Feb. 25, 1846	25	dark	Wiscasset, Me.	5	38
Howe, Mark Anthony DeWolf	1798-1799	Apr. 29, 1777		Bristol, R.I.	** -	--
Howe, William	July 16, 1849	19	black	Brooklyn, N.Y.	5	39
Howes, Abner	Dec. 4, 1823	21	light	Bucksport, Me.	4	32
Howit, Calvin	May 7, 1855	21	light	Portsmouth, R.I.	5	45
Howland, Benjamin, Jr.	Sept. 25, 1817	39	light	E. Greenwich, R.I.	4	31
Howland, George	June 6, 1809	12	light	Providence, R.I.	4	29
Howland, Israel	Dec. 14, 1826	19	mulatto	Jamestown, R.I.	4	32
Howland, Jacob	May 31, 1806	19	black	Taunton, Ma.	3	79
Howland, Job	1798-1799	Jan. 8, 1779		Taunton, Ma.	** -	--
Joseph Howland swears the above to be true.						
Howland, John	1798-1799	Year 1777		Dartmouth, Ma.	** -	--
Howland, Lefavour	1798-1799	June 6, 1778		Bristol, R.I.	** -	--
Howland, Peckham	Apr. 3, 1797	30	dark	Dartmouth, Ma.	1	13
Howland, Robert	May 23, 1821	32	black	Jamestown, R.I.	4	31
Howland, Shubael, Jr.	June 25, 1827	18	light	Yarmouth, Ma.	4	32
Howland, Thomas H.	Apr. 3, 1844	29	black	Newport, R.I.	5	38
Hoxsie, Asa	Mar. 12, 1833	29	black	Charlestown, R.I.	5	35
Hoxsie, Charles	Dec. 23, 1809	18	yellow	Charlestown, R.I.	4	30
Hoxsie, Charles	Aug. 6, 1812	20	yellow	Charlestown, R.I.	4	30
Hoxie, Thomas	Sept. 16, 1803	26	black	Charleston, R.I.	2	39
Hoxsie, Thomas	Mar. 1, 1806	29	yellow*	Charlestown, R.I.	3	77
Hoyle, Samuel	May 21, 1803	19	light	Providence, R.I.	2	39
Hoyt, Henry	May 2, 1835	17	light	Danbury, Conn.	5	36
Hoyt, William	Aug. 25, 1825	20	light	Boston, Ma.	5	36
Hubbard, Benj. C.	Nov. 3, 1849	42	Light	Newport, R.I.	5	39
Hubbard, Elihu	May 31, 1798	53	dark	Hartford, CONN.	2	8
Hubbard, Henry	May 29, 1835	25	yellow	Winsor, N.C.	5	36
Hubbard, Henry	Aug. 31, 1849	26	light	Killingly, Conn.	5	39
Hubbard, William B.	Nov. 3, 1849	32	light	Newport, R.I.	5	39
[Hubbard]Hubbert, Wm.	Dec. 8, 1804	26	light	Frankford, Pa.	3	16
Hudson, Benjamin	July 20, 1841	27	dark	Boston, Ma.	5	37
Hudson, Caleb B.	Aug. 26, 1819	15	brown	Providence, R.I.	4	31
Hudson, Calvin S.	Oct. 7, 1831	16	black	Smithfield, R.I.	5	35

*mulatto
**Newport, R. I.

NAME	DATE OF CERTIFICATION	AGE	COMPLEXION	PLACE OF BIRTH	BOOK	PAGE
Hudson, Henry	Aug. 27, 1796	20	light	Newport, R.I.	1	1
Hudson, James	Oct. 4, 1800	22	dark	Providence, R.I.	2	28
Hudson, James	Feb. 25, 1853	24	light	Boston, Ma.	5	40
Hudson, Jonathan	Oct. 24, 1803	21	light	Rehoboth, Ma.	2	39
Hudson, Robert, Jr.	Dec. 16, 1800	18	dark	Providence, R.I.	2	28
Hudson, Samuel Thomas Hudson his brother swears the above to be true.	1796-1799	Jan. 18, 1775		Newport, R.I.	** -	--
Hudson, Thomas	May 8, 1799	18	light	Providence, R.I.	2	8
Hughes, Christopher Greene	May 18, 1803	18	light	Freetown, Ma.	2	39
Hughes, John	June 28, 1845	29	dark	New York, N.Y.	5	38
Hughes, William	Nov. 10, 1841	15	light	Providence, R.I.	5	37
Hugins, James	Dec. 5, 1797	18	dark	No. Prov., R.I.	1	27
Huggins, James	Dec. 21, 1804	23	dark	Phila., Pa.	3	16
Huggins, James	Dec. 8, 1804	23	dark	Phila., Pa.	3	16
Hughes, Wilson	Aug. 19, 1836	28	ruddy	Elizabeth City, N.C.	5	36
Hughs, Thomas	Feb. 20, 1845	24	light	Providence, R.I.	5	38
Hulbert, Seth	Nov. 10, 1803	29	dark	Chatham, Conn.	2	49
Huling, Christ'r D.	Oct. 26, 1849	24	light	No. Kingston, R.I.	5	39
Hull, Daniel	Aug. 8, 1814	21	light	Providence, R.I.	4	30
Hull, Frederick L.	May 22, 1847	22	fair	Providence, R.I.	5	38
Hull, George	Aug. 24, 1805	18	dark	Newport, R.I.	3	55
Hull, George A.	July 8, 1864	23	light	New Shoreham, R.I.	6	8
Hull, George B.	Oct. 15, 1858	23	dark	Providence, R.I.	6	8
Hull, Gideon	July 8, 1951	25	dark	Providence, R.I.	4	31
Hull, Henry	Oct. 10, 1839	20	light	Troy, N.Y.	5	37
Hull, Henry F.	Mar. 29, 1807	25	black	Fairfield, Conn.	4	29
Hull, Jacob	Nov. 19, 1800	25	black	Jamestown, R.I.	2	28
Hull, John	Feb. 21, 1839	21	yellow	Providence, R.I.	5	36
Hull, John T.	Oct. 1, 1841	22	black	New Shoreham, R.I.	5	37
Hull, Nathaniel	June 4, 1805	12	yellow*	Providence, R.I.	3	54
Hull, Robert	Nov. 24, 1848	20	yellow	So. Kingston, R.I.	5	39
Hull, Samuel	June 23, 1832	19	dark	Providence, R.I.	5	35
Hull, Thomas	May 30, 1822	15	dark	Providence, R.I.	4	32
Hull, William	Oct. 24, 1827	15	light	Providence, R.I.	4	32

*mulatto

**Newport, R. I.

REGISTER OF SEAMEN'S PROTECTION

Page 139

NAME	DATE OF CERTIFICATION	AGE	COMPLEXION	PLACE OF BIRTH	BOOK	PAGE
Hull, William	July 11, 1835	25	black	New Shoreham, R.I.	5	36
Human, Barzila	Mar. 8, 1799	42	black	Prince George, Md.	2	8
Human, William	Mar. 7, 1806	18	black	Providence, R.I.	3	77
Humphrey, Abel	Feb. 3, 1801	19	light	Providence, R.I.	2	28
Humphrey, Eben. G.	Aug. 18, 1846	37	fair	Bristol, Me.	5	38
Humphrey, John	Mar. 29, 1852	24	light	New York, N.Y.	5	40
Humphrey, Joseph	July 17, 1804	28	black	Stockbridge, Ma.	3	15
Humphrey, Josiah	Mar. 6, 1815	18	light	Brookfield, Vt.	4	30
Humphrey, William J.	July 27, 1847	20	fair	Providence, R.I.	5	38
Humphrey, Simon	Sept. 22, 1796	26	light	Barrington, R.I.	1	3
Humphy, Lewis	Aug. 31, 1805	29	dark	Barrington, R.I.	3	55
Hungerford, John	Sept. 7, 1803	17	light	Phila., Pa.	2	39
Hunt, Alva	July 7, 1831	21	light	Bridgewater, Ma.	5	35
Hunt, Clifford	Dec. 3, 1806	22	light	Attleboro, Ma.	4	29
Hunt, Dudley	Nov. 16, 1799	19	light	Providence, R.I.	2	8
Hunt, Dudley	Dec. 12, 1803	23	light	Providence, R.I.	2	49
Hunt, Dudley	Aug. 13, 1806	26	light	Providence,R.I.	3	79
Hunt, Ethan	Nov. 29, 1806	22	light	Sudbury, Ma.	4	29
Hunt, Henry	Dec. 12, 1822	20	yellow	Providence,R.I.	4	32
Hunt, Henry Hall	June 9, 1830	26	light	Cranston, R.I.	5	35
Hunt, James A.	Oct. 17, 1849	17	light	Providence, R.I.	5	39
Hunt, John	Oct. 13, 1810	49	black	Petersburgh, Va.	4	30
Hunt, John	Nov. 18, 1803	48	dark	Providence,R.I.	2	49
Hunt, Joseph	Aug. 29, 1815	17	brown	Cranston, R.I.	4	31
Hunt, Joshua	Sept. 5, 1796	22	light	Cranston, R.I.	1	2
Hunt, Josiah	Sept. 29, 1797	19	light	Cranston, R.I.	1	27
Hunt, Josiah A.	May 17, 1819	17	light	Cranston, R.I.	4	31
Hunt, Oliver	Sept. 2, 1842	19	light	Hunter, N.Y.	5	37
Hunt, Stephen	July 11, 1840	21	light	Cranston, R.I.	5	37
Hunt, Sylvester	Feb. 8, 1799	17	dark	Rehoboth, Ma.	2	8
Hunt, Thomas	Mar. 28, 1800	21	dark	Providence, R.I.	2	8
Hunt, Thomas	July 8, 1797	19	dark	Providence,R.I.	1	13
Hunt, William	May 17, 1798	35	black	New York, N.Y.	2	8
Hunt, William R.	July 24, 1841	12	light	Providence, R.I.	5	37

REGISTER OF SEAMEN'S PROTECTION

NAME	DATE OF CERTIFICATION	AGE	COMPLEXION	PLACE OF BIRTH	BOOK	PAGE
Hunt, Zebedee	Dec. 13, 1817	18	light	Cranston, R.I.	4	31
Hunter, Abraham	Sept. 24, 1823	23	yellow	Tiverton, R.I.	4	32
Hunter, Andrew	1798-1799	Aug. 25, 1782		Newport, R.I.	* -	--
Hunter, Barney	Sept. 3, 1832	19	light	Dartmouth, Ma.	5	35
Hunter, David	Jan. 17, 1854	21	light	Morristown, N.J.	5	40
Hunter, Ebenezer Oct	Oct. 15, 1821	23	dark	Tiverton, R.I.	4	31
Hunter, John	Apr. 4, 1805	21	black	Newport, R.I.	3	54
Hunter, John N.	Mar. 15, 1852	17	light	So. Dartmouth, Ma.	5	40
Hunter, Thomas	July 30, 1839	23	dark	New York, N.Y.	5	37
Hunter, Walter F.	Aug. 5, 1853	35	dark	Providence, R.I.	5	40
Huntly, Thomas	Jan. 18, 1826	28	dark	Groton, Conn.	4	32
Huntley, James	Oct. 9, 1848	21	dark	Eastport, Me.	5	39
Huntley, Nelson	Mar. 14, 1855	22	dark	Colchester, Conn.	5	40
Hupper, Nathaniel	Oct. 20, 1856	18	dark	St. George, Me.	5	45
Hurd, Alvan	Oct. 15, 1827	38	light	Orleans, Ma.	4	32
Hurd, Freeman	Dec. 11, 1844	19	light	Framingham, Ma.	5	38
Hurd, Henry W.	Apr. 30, 1806	26	brown	E. Haddam, Conn.	3	77
Hurd, Henry W.	Dec. 11, 1807	28	brown	E. Haddam, Conn.	4	29
Hurd, Henry W.	Apr. 22, 1809	29	brown	E. Haddam, Conn.	4	29
Hurd, John	Dec. 26, 1812	15	light	Greenfield, N.Y.	4	30
Hurd, Joseph	Mar. 16, 1842	26	light	Boston, Ma.	5	37
Hurlbert, James H.	June 10, 1841	23	light	Guiford, N.Y.	5	37
Huse, John	June 9, 1809	27	dark	Newburyport, Ma.	4	29
Hussey, Amos T.	Mar. 29, 1833	29	black	Salem, Ma.	5	35
Hussey, Joseph	Dec. 29, 1810	26	black	Warwick, Ma.	4	30
Huston, David	May 9, 1838	19	dark	Bristol, Me.	5	36
Huston, James	July 11, 1849	21	light	Chester, Pa.	5	39
Hutchins, Arthur	Mar. 13, 1798	48	dark	Boston, Ma.	1	27
Hutchins, John	June 20, 1854	21	light	Lowell, Ma.	5	40
Hutchins, John M.	April 29, 1835	18	dark	Providence, R.I.	5	36
Hutchins, Richard	June 20, 1797	30	light	York, Me.	1	13
Hutchinson, Cyrus B.	Sept. 27, 1844	16	light	Smithfield, R.I.	5	38
Hutchinson, Francis	Jan. 14, 1834	28	ruddy	Milford, N.H.	5	35
Hutchinson, James D.	Oct. 11, 1844	22	light	Woodstock, Vt.	5	38

*Newport, R. I.

NAME	DATE OF CERTIFICATION	AGE	COMPLEXION	PLACE OF BIRTH	BOOK	PAGE
Hutson, William, Jr.	Feb. 20, 1832	28	mulatto	New York, N.Y.	5	35
Huttleston, Simeon P.	May 21, 1851	33	dark	Fairhaven, Ma.	5	40
Huttleston, Simeon P.	Aug. 17, 1857	38	light	Fairhaven, Ma.	6	8
Hyath, Richard C.	Oct. 12, 1830	14	light	Providence, R.I.	5	35
Hyatt, Charles, Leonard	Nov. 24, 1798	22	light	Bedford, Gr. Britain	2	8
Hyde, Theodore W.	May 18, 1867	18	black	Boston, Ma.	6	8
Ide, Alfred	Apr. 26, 1811	22	brown	Rehoboth, Ma.	4	36
Ide, Calvin	Mar. 2, 1815	17	light	Seekonk, Ma.	4	36
Ide, David	Nov. 1, 1803	23	light	Rehoboth, Ma.	2	47
Ide, Welcome	Dec. 9, 1819	21	light	Glocester, R.I.	4	36
Ingalls, Royall	May 7, 1803	24	light	Rehoboth, Ma.	2	9
Ingals, Royal	Sept. 3, 1811	32	light	Rehoboth, Ma.	4	36
Ingham, Edward	Nov. 17, 1797	22	light	Wilminton, Del.	1	14
Ingraham, James	Jan. 16, 1821		light	Barrington, R.I.	-	--

Son of James Ingraham of Barrington, deceased. Birth certificate in Custom House Papers. May 30, 1802

Ingraham, John	June 23, 1834	37	dark	Windham, Conn.	5	41
Ingraham, Mason	Oct. 20, 1829	29	light	Glocester, R.I.	5	41
Ingraham, William A.	Dec. 10, 1824	18	light	Seekonk, Ma.	4	37
Ingraham, William Gladding	Nov. 22,[1821]	20	dark	Barrington, R.I.	-	--

Son of Watson Ingraham. Birth Certificate in the Custom House Papers. Oct. 2, 1801

Ingram, William	Nov. 21, 1796	24	light	Providence, R.I.	1	14
Inman, Benjamin	Apr. 2, 1821	23	dark	Smithfield, R.I.	4	36
Inman, Harris	Aug. 10, 1827	16	light	Glocester, R.I.	4	37
Innis, Benjamin	June 24, 1816	19	light	Nantucket, Ma.	4	36
Innis, Goodwin	July 23, 1821	23	dark	Bath, Me.	4	36
Innis, William	Oct. 6, 1818	28	light	Nantucket, Ma.	4	36
Irons, Arnold T.	Sept. 23, 1847	26	light	Burrillville, R.I.	5	42
Irons, Asa	May 10, 1813	31	light	Burrillville, R.I.	4	36
Irons, Nelson A.	Oct. 10, 1850	24	light	No. Prov., R.I.	5	42
Irons, Nicholas	Mar. 14, 1806	31	light	Glocester, R.I.	3	18
Irons, Richard	July 15, 1818	18	light	Providence, R.I.	4	36
Irons, Stephen	Oct. 28, 1819	17	light	Providence, R.I.	4	36
Irving, William	Feb. 28, 1800	20	light	Cumberland, R.I.	2	9
?Irwin, Michael	Nov. 1, 1799	27	dark	Ireland	2	9
Jackson, Abner	Dec. 15, 1852	38	black	Dutchess Co., N.Y.	5	42

REGISTER OF SEAMEN'S PROTECTION

NAME	DATE OF CERTIFICATION	AGE	COMPLEXION	PLACE OF BIRTH	BOOK	PAGE
Jackson, Alfred	Oct. 9, 1819	18	yellow	Providence, R.I.	4	36
Jackson, Anthony	Oct. 7, 1801	25	black	New York, N.Y.	2	9
Jackson, Aaron	July 17, 1804	25	yellow*	Monmouth, N.J.	3	17
Jackson, Benjamin	Sept. 29, 1821	16	black	Killingly, Conn.	4	36
Jackson, Benjamin B.	Dec. 29, 1810	21	dark	Newburyport, Ma.	4	36
Jackson, Calver	Jan. 8, 1819	26	black	Ashburnham, Ma.	4	36
Jackson, Charles	Dec. 23, 1826	17	black	Providence, R.I.	4	37
Jackson, Daniel	July 7, 1824	16	dark	Providence, R.I.	4	37
Jackson, Edmund	Apr. 4, 1831	20	dark	Portland, Me.	5	41
Jackson, Edward	June 2, 1831	21	light	Providence, R.I.	5	41
Jackson, Elisha	Dec. 16, 1797	22	light	Nixonton, N.C.	1	14
Jackson, Francis	Mar. 31, 1807	33	black	Albany, N.Y.	4	35
Jackson, George J.	Oct. 8, 1849	31	light	Woodstock, Conn.	5	42
Jackson, Henry	Oct. 9, 1818	19	black	Johnston, R.I.	4	36
Jackson, Henry	May 4, 1844	32	mulatto	Cumberland, N.J.	5	42
Jackson, Henry	May 16, 1857	24	dark	Alexandria, Va.	5	43
Jackson, Isaac	Jan. 10, 1829	23	yellow	Newport, R.I.	5	41
Jackson, Isaac	Dec. 27, 1836	21	light	Newport, R.I.	5	41
Jackson, Isaac, Jr.	Oct. 7, 1844	29	dark	Belford, Me.	5	42
Jackson, James	May 15, 1811	28	yellow	New Bedford, Ma.	4	36
Jackson, James	June 29, 1841	25	light	Baltimore, Md.	5	41
Jackson, James A.	Sept. 27, 1830	24	light	Providence, R.I.	5	41
Jackson, Jeremiah	Nov. 4, 1799	14	light	Providence, R.I.	2	9
Jackson, John	Aug. 22, 1800	20	light	New York, N.Y.	2	9
Jackson, John	Apr. 20, 1810	24	black	Salem, Ma.	4	35
Jackson, John	Oct. 31, 1836	31	black	Boston, Ma.	5	41
Jackson, JOhn	Apr. 12, 1852	22	light	Natchidotes, Tx.	5	42
Jackson, Joseph	1798-1799	Apr. 29, 1778		Plymouth, Ma.	**_	--
Jackson, Joseph	May 11, 1802	23	dark	Plymouth, Ma.	2	9
Jackson, Norris	Mar. 8, 1855	31	black	Burlington, N.J.	5	43
Jackson, Peter	July 13, 1805	26	black	Charlestown, R.I.	3	18
Jackson, Richard	Apr. 16, 1808	23	black	Catskill, N.Y.	4	35
Jackson, Richard	Apr. 6, 1809	22	black	Catskill, N.Y.	4	35
Jackson, Richard M.	Nov. 22, 1854	52	mulatto	Flatbush, N.Y.	5	43

*mulatto

**Newport, R. I.

NAME	DATE OF CERTIFICATION	AGE	COMPLEXION	PLACE OF BIRTH	BOOK	PAGE
Jackson, Robert	Aug. 13, 1806	23	black	New York, N.Y.	3	22
Jackson, Samuel	June 3, 1797	19	dark	Providence, R.I.	1	14
Jackson, Samuel	Dec. 15, 1803	24	black	Phila., Pa.	2	47
Jackson, Samuel	Mar. 27, 1806	32	black	Norfolk, Va.	3	18
Jackson, Stephen	Dec. 19, 1800	22	dark	New York, N.Y.	2	9
Jackson, Stephen	Dec. 12, 1797	34	dark	Providence, R.I.	1	14
Jackson, Thomas	Mar. 28, 1797	28	black	Trenton, N.J.	1	14
Jackson, Thomas	Jan. 14, 1801	23	black	Montgomery, N.Y.	2	9
Jackson, Thomas	Mar. 1, 1805	31	black	Bergen, N.J.	3	18
Jackson, Thomas	Aug. 21, 1809	40	black	Bergen, N.J.	4	35
Jackson, Thomas	June 27, 1810	28	black	Taunton, Ma.	4	35
Jackson, Thomas	July 10, 1810	25	black	Woodbridge, N.J.	4	35
Jackson, Thomas	May 17, 1828	19	black	Providence, R.I.	4	37
Jackson, Thomas	June 10, 1843	22	black	New York, N.Y.	5	41
Jackson, Thomas	Feb. 28, 1849	34	light	Bridgewater, Ma.	5	42
Jackson, Thomas	Apr. 0, 1860	20	dark	Portland, Me.	6	10
Jackson, Walter	Nov. 20, 1843	18	black	Masshipee, Ma.	5	41
Jackson, William	June 3, 1797	22	light	Newburyport, Ma.	1	14
Jackson, William	Mar. 14, 1815	26	black	Albany, N.Y.	4	36
Jackson, William	Apr. 13, 1841	21	light	Phila., Pa.	5	41
Jackson, William	May 11, 1852	22	light	Calais, Me.	5	42
Jackson, William	Oct. 9, 1854	27	light	Wankesha, Wis.	5	43
Jackson, William, Jr.	Oct. 5, 1829	21	black	Killingly, Conn.	5	41
Jacobs, Edward W. Rees	Oct. 29, 1803	18	black	Hartford, Conn.	2	47
Jacobs, Isaac	Nov. 16, 1810	22	light	Rehoboth, Ma.	4	36
Jacobs, John	Aug. 7, 1812	49	light	Rehoboth, Ma.	4	36
Jacobs, John, Jr.	Dec. 13, 1806	18	brown	Rehoboth, Ma.	4	35
Jacobs, Linus	Oct. 6, 1812	21	brown	No. Haven, Conn.	4	36
Jacobs, Rees	Mar. 1, 1805	19	black	Hartford, Conn.	3	18
Jacobs, Rees	Dec. 10, 1811	25	black	Hartford, Conn.	4	36
Jacobs, Samuel	Jan. 18, 1805	18	light	Rehoboth, Ma.	3	18
Jacobs, Thomas	Mar. 27, 1810	23	black	No. Prov., R.I.	4	35
Jacobs, William	Mar. 25, 1836	17	mulatto	Providence, R.I.	5	41
Jacobs, Wilson, Jr.	Dec. 9, 1797	19	light	Killingly, Conn.	1	14

REGISTER OF SEAMEN'S PROTECTION

NAME	DATE OF CERTIFICATION	AGE	COMPLEXION	PLACE OF BIRTH	BOOK	PAGE
Jacques, Bengin	Oct. 15, 1855	25	fair	So. Kingston, R.I.	5	43
Jaquays, Elisha C.	Aug. 14, 1839	19	light	So. Kingston, R.I.	5	41
Jacquays, Nathan	Dec. 5, 1797	57	light	So. Kingstown, R.I.	1	14
James, Aaron	Dec. 4, 1805	36	black	Providence, R.I.	3	18
James, Aaron	Apr. 12, 1808	36	black	Newport, R.I.	4	35
James, Benjamin	Mar. 22, 1797	20	dark	Newport, R.I.	1	14
James, Benjamin	Apr. 22, 1809	32	dark	Newport, R.I.	4	35
James, Clark W.	July 22, 1803	22	light	Richmond, R.I.	2	9
James, David R.	May 16, 1807	18	brown	Liverpool, England	4	35
James, David R.	July 20, 1810	21	brown	Liverpool, England	4	35
James, Francis	Nov. 20, 1813	19	light	Sherburne, Ma.	4	36
James, Frederick	May 4, 1844	17	mulatto	Glastonbury, Conn.	5	41
James, George	Nov. 14, 1803	23	light	Brooklyn, N.Y.	2	47
James, George	Dec. 27, 1797	43	light	New York, N.Y.	1	14
James, Isaac	June 18, 1800	29	black	Albany, N.Y.	2	9
James, Isaac	Sept. 17, 1803	22	yellow*	Newport, R.I.	2	47
James, Isaac	June 12, 1804	38	black	Albany, N.Y.	3	17
James, Jonathan	1798-1799		June 30, 1788	Richmond, R.I.	** _	--
Son of Robert James and his wife Ann or Anna.						
James, Robert	Sept. 16, 1803	15	dark	New York, N.Y.	2	47
James, Thomas	Feb. 3, 1804	30	light	Groton, Conn.	3	17
James, Thomas	Jan. 10, 1834	21	light	Boston, Ma.	5	41
James, Walter	May 5, 1863	19	dark	Newburyport, Ma.	6	10
James, William	Dec. 17, 1855	23	black	Providence, R.I.	5	43
Jane, Benjamin	May 17, 1799	16	light	Providence, R.I.	2	9
Jane, Joseph	June 17, 1806	14	light	Providence, R.I.	3	22
Jane, Joseph	Oct. 14, 1806	15	light	Providence, R.I.	4	35
Jane, Joseph	Mar. 31, 1809	17	light	Providence, R.I.	4	35
Jane, William	Dec. 13, 1803	17	light	Providence, R.I.	2	47
Janifer, John H.	Dec. 4, 1849	32	yellow	Prince George, Md.	5	42
Janson, Hogan	Mar. 15, 1809	29	light	Frederickstadt, Denmark	4	35
Jarvis, Jeremiah	Mar. 14, 1809	27	yellow	Preston, Conn.	4	35
Jarvis, William	Mar. 17, 1809	17	light	Salem, Ma.	4	35
Jarvis, William	June 20, 1850	38	sandy	New York, N.Y.	5	42

*mulatto
**Newport, R. I.

REGISTER OF SEAMEN'S PROTECTION

NAME	DATE OF CERTIFICATION	AGE	COMPLEXION	PLACE OF BIRTH	BOOK	PAGE
Jasper, John	June 9, 1806	35	yellow*	Charles City, Va.	3	22
Jastram, Joseph	Apr. 30, 1803	17	light	Providence, R.I.	2	9
Jastram, Joseph	July 22, 1805	18	light	Providence, R.I.	3	18
Jay, Gilbert	July 22, 1817	16	dark	Nantucket, Ma.	4	36
Jay, Isaac R.	Nov. 15, 1834	44	black	New York, N.Y.	5	41
Jay, John	Aug. 1, 1797	22	light	New York, N.Y.	1	14
Jeffers, Thomas	Dec. 19, 1800	20	light	Newport, R.I.	2	9
Jeffers, Thomas	May 31, 1805	24	light	Newport, R.I.	3	18
Jefferson, Anthony	May 24, 1841	24	black	Hoboken, N.J.	5	41
Jeffrey, Henry G.	Mar. 7, 1831	30	light	Groton, Conn.	5	41
Jelly, John	Jan. 24, 1854	25	light	New York, N.Y.	5	43
Jemerson, Abraham	Aug. 22, 1846	23	black	Shresbury, N.J.	5	42
Jemison, Samuel	Nov. 6, 1855	22	light	Johnston, R.I.	5	43
Jenckes, Amos Throop	Nov. 15, 1803	25	light	No. Prov., R.I.	2	47
Jenckes, Bucklin	July 15, 1806	19	dark	No. Prov., R.I.	3	22
Jenckes, Daniel	May 1, 1810	16	light	No. Prov., R.I.	4	35
Jenckes, Ephraim	Mar. 9, 1797	24	dark	Smithfield, R.I.	1	14
Jenckes, George	Aug. 20, 1836	23	dark	Providence, R.I.	5	41
Jenckes, George B.	Aug. 22, 1838	20	dark	Smithfield, R.I.	5	41
Jenckes, Israel	Aug. 29, 1815	34	light	No. Prov., R.I.	4	36
Jenckes, John	Apr. 16, 1808	23	black	Providence, R.I.	4	35
Jenckes, John	Nov. 6, 1828	17	light	Smithfield, R.I.	4	37
Jenckes, Rufus	June 17, 1815	17	light	Smithfield, R.I.	4	36
Jenckes, Samuel	Mar. 16, 1797	17	dark	No. Prov., R.I.	1	14
Jenckes, 'Thomas	May 30, 1806	18	light	No. Prov., R.I.	3	22
Jenckes, Thomas W.	Sept 28, 1811	22	light	No. Prov., R.I.	4	36
Jenckes, Washington	Nov. 22, 1804	30	light	Smithfield, R.I.	3	17
Jenckes, William	Nov. 27, 1797	19	dark	Providence, R.I.	1	14
Jencks, Almoran	May 24, 1811	16	light	Providence, R.I.	4	36
Jencks, Jabez	Sept. 12, 1801	18	dark	Cumberland, R.I.	2	9
Jencks, Jabez W.	Aug. 24, 1849	34	light	Cumberland, R.I.	5	42
Jencks, Rufus 2nd	Mar. 7, 1848	20	light	Smithfield, R.I.	5	42

*mulatto

NAME	DATE OF CERTIFICATION	AGE	COMPLEXION	PLACE OF BIRTH	BOOK	PAGE
Jenkes, John A.	Dec. 12, 1853	24	dark	Smithfield, R.I.	5	42
Jenkins, Albert	Oct. 5, 1833	20	light	Hardwick, Ma.	5	41
Jenkins, Benjamin S.	Oct. 25, 1796	22	light	Falmouth, Ma.	1	14&5
Jenkins, David	Feb. 9, 1835	21	light	Chrleston, S.C.	5	44
Jenkins, George G.	Aug. 21, 1806	19	light	Providence, R.I.	3	22
Jenkins, Ivory	Oct. 14, 1803	22	light	Falmouth, Ma.	2	47
Jenkins, James	Apr. 22, 1820	22	black	Kingston, Ulster Co., N.Y.	4	36
Jenkins, John	June 13, 1832	17	ruddy	Phila., Pa.	5	41
Jenkins, John J.	Feb. 20, 1845	24	light	Charleston, S.C.	5	42
Jenkins, Joseph M.	Nov. 16, 1804	21	light	Newburyport, Ma.	3	17
Jenkins, William	Apr. 19, 1867	42	medium	Richmond, Me.	6	10
Jenkinson, Richard S.	Dec. 11, 1834	18	light	Woodstock, Conn.	5	41
Jenks, Edward B.B.	Nov. 16, 1821	18	dark	No. Prov., R.I.	-	--
Sworn statement of Caleb Miller in the Custom House Papers. DOB: June 6, 1803.						
Jenks, Joseph	July 12, 1826	20	light	Warwick, R.I.	4	37
Jenks, Joseph H.	Jan. 29, 1828	17	light	No. Prov., R.I.	4	37
Jenks, Robert W.	Jan. 23, 1858	27	dark	Chepachet, R.I.	6	10
Jenks, Samuel	Aug. 30, 1815	41	dark	No. Prov., R.I.	4	36
Jenks, Vaneasen[Vaneaston]	Nov. 16, 1848	29	light	No. Prov., R.I.	5	42
Jennings, David	Oct. 8, 1806	21	yellow*	Swansea, Ma.	3&4**	22&35
Jennings, Edward	May 11, 1829	27	light	Troy, Ma.	5	41
Jennings, Gideon	1798-1799	May 5, 1780		Tiverton, R.I.	***-	--
Jennings, Gurden	Dec. 8, 1803	21	dark	Windham, Conn.	2	47
Jennings, Isaac	1798-1799	Nov. 5, 1777		Tiverton, R.I.	***-	--
Jennings, Timothy	Sept. 17, 1803	24	light	New Bedford, Ma.	2	47
Jennison, Nathaniel	Dec. 6, 1803	24	light	Barrie, Ma.	2	47
Jennison, William	June 20, 1854	17	fair	Brooklyn, N.Y.	5	43
Jepson, Nicholas	Dec. 1, 1846	20	fair	Sag Harbor, N.Y.	5	42
Jepson, William	Oct. 5, 1808	16	light	Newport, R.I.	4	35
Jerauld, John, Jr.	June 23, 1826	20	dark	Warwick, R.I.	4	37
Jillson, Albert	Jan. 16, 1846	20	fair	Providence, R.I.	5	42
Jillson, Arnold	May 9, 1806	18	brown	Attleboro, Ma.	3	22
Jillson, Franklin	Dec. 11, 1847	24	light	Providence, R.I.	5	42
Jillson, Oliver	Nov. 2, 1814	19	dark	Johnston, R.I.	4	36
Jilson, Samuel	July 25, 1815	40	dark	Attleboro, Ma.	4	36
Jillson, Thomas	Apr. 21, 1809	17	dark	Providence, R.I.	4	35
Jillson, William	Dec. 22, 1817	17	ruddy	Providence, R.I.	4	36

*mulatto **Book 3, page 22; book 4, page 35.
***Newport, R. I.

REGISTER OF SEAMEN'S PROTECTION

NAME	DATE OF CERTIFICATION	AGE	COMPLEXION	PLACE OF BIRTH	BOOK	PAGE
Jipson, Edward R.M.	Aug. 31, 1849	31	dark	Providence, R.I.	5	42
Joffes, Frank	May 21, 1855	21	light	No. Prov., R.I.	5	43
Johnson, Alfred J.	Oct. 3, 1849	24	light	E. Greenwich, R.I.	5	42
Johnson, Andrew	Nov. 12, 1796	22	black	Taunton, Ma.	1	14&5
Johnson, Benjamin	Mar. 14, 1798	14	light	E. Greenwich, R.I.	1	14
Johnson, Benjamin	Feb. 28, 1810	28	light	Exeter, N.H.	4	35
Johnson, Benjamin	May 4, 1820	32	dark	Providence, R.I.	4	36
Johnson, Benjamin	Oct. 12, 1847	28	dark	Boston, Ma.	5	42
Johnson, Benj. G.	Oct. 9, 1849	17	light	Warwick, R.I.	5	42
Johnson, Cato	Mar. 3, 1815	25	black	Newport, R.I.	4	36
Johnson, Charles	Oct. 27, 1803	22	black	New York, N.Y.	2	47
Johnson, Charles	Mar. 16, 1840	26	black	Portland, Me.	5	41
Johnson, Charles	Oct. 25, 1849	24	black	Warren, R.I.	5	42
Johnson, Charles A.	Aug. 20, 1853	49	black	Hartford, Conn.	5	42
Johnson, Eber	Aug. 10, 1808	17	light	Cumberland, R.I.	4	35
Johnson, Edward	Oct. 24, 1821	18	black	No. Prov., R.I.	4	36
Johnson, Edward	Nov. 1, 1837	31	black	So. Kingston, R.I.	5	41
Johnson, Frederick A.	Mar. 15, 1851	37	dark	Malden, Ma.	5	42
Johnson, George	June 12, 1804	27	black	Providence, R.I.	3	17
Johnson, George	Oct. 28, 1817	21	dark	Providence, R.I.	4	36
Johnson, George	Sept. 8, 1857	20	black	Phila., Pa.	6	10
Johnson, George	Dec. 29, 1857	20	black	Phila,. Pa.	6	10
Johnson, George	Dec. 26, 1866	37	light	Portland, Me.	6	10
Johnson, George W.	Sept. 14, 1815	21	brown	Providence, R.I.	4	36
Johnson, 'Gideon	Nov. 10, 1796	17	light	E. Greenwich, R.I.	1	14&5
Johnson, Harrison	Sept. 28, 1858	25	yellow	Camden, Me.	6	10
Johnson, Henry	Sept. 26, 1815	15	black	Hartford, Conn.	4	36
Johnson, Henry	Apr. 20, 1832	25	mulatto	Phila., Pa.	5	41
Johnson, Henry	Oct. 11, 1842	25	black	Baltimore, Md.	5	41
Johnson, Henry	Dec. 10, 1851	24	light	New York, N.Y.	5	42
Johnson, Henry C.	Feb. 28, 1849	30	florid	Coventry, R.I.	5	42
Johnson, James	Mar. 20, 1810	21	light	Providence, R.I.	4	35
Johnson, James	Aug. 20, 1811	16	light	No. Kingstown, R.I.	4	36

NAME	DATE OF CERTIFICATION	AGE	COMPLEXION	PLACE OF BIRTH	BOOK	PAGE
Johnson, James	July 8, 1815	17	dark	Providence, R.I.	4	36
Johnson, James C.	Sept. 5, 1842	18	light	E. Greenwich, R.I.	5	41
Johnson, James P.	Apr. 29, 1815	21	black	Troy, N.Y.	4	36
Johnson, Joel	Nov. 30, 1829	37	light	Chester, Vt.	5	41
Johnson, John	Oct. 10, 1801	23	black	New York, N.Y.	2	9
Johnson, John	Aug. 5, 1805	25	black	Bedford, N.Y. (Long Island)	3	
Johnson, John	Nov. 14, 1807	13	light	Providence, R.I.	4	35
Johnson, John	May 10, 1811	22	yellowish	New York, N.Y.	4	36
Johnson, John	July 13, 1811	29	black	New York, N.Y.	4	36
Johnson, John	June 8, 1843	22	light	Boston, Ma.	5	41
Johnson, John	Aug. 25, 1849	32	dark	New London, Conn.	5	42
Johnson, John C.	Nov. 11, 1806	21	light	Scituate, R.I.	4	35
Johnson, John C.	May 18, 1807	22	brown	Old Guilford, Conn.	4	35
Johnson, Joseph	July 3, 1858	20	light	Baltimore, Md.	6	10
Johnson, Joseph J.	Jan. 9, 1832	16	black	Providence, R.I.	5	41
Johnson, Marcus J.	Oct. 7, 1807	21	light	Grafton, Ma.	4	35
Johnson, Michel	June 17, 1805	28	dark	Boston, Ma.	3	18
Johnson, Peter	Jan. 2, 1804	16	yellow*	Newport, R.I.	3	17
Johnson, Peter	June 17, 1859	22	light	New York, N.Y.	6	10
Johnson, Philip	May 22, 1834	29	black	Baltimore, Md.	5	41
Johnson, Richard	Sept. 22, 1838	37	black	Providence, R.I.	5	41
Johnson, Samuel	May 29, 1807	54	dark	Providence, R.I.	4	35
Johnson, Samuel dead Jan. 1824.	Sept. 29, 1820	41	black	New York, N.Y.	4	36
Johnson, Stephen	Aug. 9, 1808	19	dark	Providence, R.I.	4	35
Johnson, Thomas	Nov. 10, 1804	22	black	New York, N.Y.	3	17
Johnson, Thomas	Apr. 15, 1818	28	black	Hartford, Conn.	4	36
Johnson, Thomas	Sept. 24, 1834	20	black	Providence, R.I.	5	41
Johnson, Thomas	Aug. 19, 1836	19	light	New York, N.Y.	5	41
Johnson, Thomas	May 3, 1844	27	light	New Bedford, Ma.	5	41
Johnson, Thomas	Mar. 10, 1853	20	light	New York, N.Y.	5	42
Johnson, William	Jan. 2, 1798	18	dark	Newport, R.I.	1	14
Johnson, William	Nov. 7, 1804	24	black	New York, N.Y.	3	17
Johnson, William	Dec. 21, 1809	19	light	No. Kingstown R.I.	4	35

*mulatto

REGISTER OF SEAMEN'S PROTECTION

Page 149

NAME	DATE OF CERTIFICATION	AGE	COMPLEXION	PLACE OF BIRTH	BOOK	PAGE
Johnson, William	Jan. 8, 1852	22	light	New York, N.Y.	5	42
Johnson, William	Feb. 26, 1853	34	dark	Baltimore, Md.	5	42
Johnson, William H.	May 25, 1831	21	black	Phila., Pa.	5	41
Johnson, William S.	Sept. 25, 1850	19	light	Oxford, Ma.	5	42
Johnston Benjamin	Nov. 18, 1809	19	black	Newport, R.I.	4	35
Johnston Edward	July 3, 1822	16	dk/yellow	No. Kingstown, R.I.	4	37
Johnston, George	June 13, 1842	39	dark	Salem, N.J.	5	41
Johnston, John	Sept. 30, 1796	52	dark	Newport, R.I.	2	4
Johnston, John	June 10, 1797	20	light	Pasquotank, N.C.	1	14
Johnston, John	July 10, 1807	26	black	New York, N.Y.	4	35
Johnston, John B.	June 6, 1853	20	light	Marblehead, Ma.	5	42
Johnston, Mark Anthony	Aug. 27, 1806	20	dark	Boston, Ma.	3	22
Johnston, Robert	Nov. 9, 1803	21	light	Providence, R.I.	2	47
Johnston, Robert	June 19, 1798	19	light	Phila., Pa.	2	9
Johnston, Robert A.	Oct. 10, 1810	23	light	New York, N.Y.	4	36
Jolle, Haile	1798-1799	1726		Holden Ma.	* -	--
Jones, Alfred	Aug. 29, 1848	21	dark	Bennington, Vt.	5	42
Jones, Benjamin Dunn	Feb. 26, 1806	22	light	Providence, R.I.	3	18
Jones, Daniel	Sept. 28, 1804	26	black	Frederickton, Md.	3	17
Jones, David A.	May 22, 1845	28	light	Somerset, Ma.	5	42
Jones, David B.	Oct. 7, 1865	27	light	Hartford, Conn.	6	10
Jones, Edward	Sept. 16, 1822	42	brown	Bristol, R.I.	4	37
Jones, Edward H.	Nov. 28, 1832	27	light	Providence, R.I.	5	41
Jones, Freancis H.	May 11, 1848	27	light	Charleston, S.C.	5	42
JOnes, George	July 13, 1847	22	dark	Baltimore, Md.	5	42
Jones, George B.	May 31, 1843	18	light	Providence, R.I.	5	41
Jones, Geo. W.	Oct. 16, 1855	31	black	Anne Arundel Co., Md.	5	43
Jones, Henry	Sept. 2, 1826	17	light	Swansea, Ma.	4	37
Jones, Henry	July 3, 1850	27	black	Suffolk, Va.	5	42
Jones, Isaac	Dec. 15, 1830	23	black	Phila., Pa.	5	41
Jones, Isaac	Mar. 15, 1838	31	black	Taunton, Ma.	5	41
Jones, James	Oct. 6, 1836	21	light	Providence, R.I.	5	41
Jones, James T.	Sept. 17, 1847	22	dark	Arcadia, N.Y.	5	42
Jones, Jenkins	Oct. 31, 1807	23	light	Tiverton, R.I.	4	35
Jones, Jeremiah	Apr. 4, 1797	20	dark	Providence, R.I.	1	14

*Newport, R. I.

NAME	DATE OF CERTIFICATION	AGE	COMPLEXION	PLACE OF BIRTH	BOOK	PAGE
Jones, John	Apr. 7, 1797	35	light	Newburyport, Ma.	1	14
Jones, John	Nov. 14, 1804	23	dark	Baltimore, Md.	3	17
Jones, John	Nov. 25, 1811	20	light	New York, N.Y.	4	36
Jones, John P.	Oct. 3, 1806	19	light	Providence, R.I.	3&4*	22&3
Jones, LeRoy	Aug. 9, 1821	18	light	Swansea, Ma.	DOB: May 17-18
Sworn statement of Peleg G. Jones of Bristol, in the Custom House Papers.
Jones, Nathan	Feb. 6, 1807	28	light	Concord, Ma.	4	35
Jones, Peter	Aug. 1, 1801	29	dark	Tiverton, R.I.	2	9
JOnes, Robert	Sept. 15, 1799	22	black	New London, Conn.	2	9
Jones, Samuel B.	Apr. 21, 1809	17	light	Providence, R.I.	4	35
Jones, Samuel B.	May 18, 1811	20	light	Providence, R.I.	4	36
Jones, Simpson	Aug. 8, 1808	18	light	Rehoboth, Ma.	4	35
Jones, Simpson	Aug. 16, 1809	18	light	Rehoboth, Ma.	4	35
Jones, Stephen	Apr. 19, 1854	24	black	Baltimore, Md.	5	42
Jones, Thomas	Sept. 10, 1803	21	light	Providence, R.I.	2	9
Jones, Thomas	Nov. 2, 1803	23	black	Norfolk, Va.	2	47
Jones, Thomas	Jan. 8, 1807	22	yellow	Middletown, Conn.	4	35
Jones, Thomas	Mar. 28, 1809	21	yellow	Catskill, N.Y.	4	35
Jones, Thomas	Aug. 10, 1810	25	yellow	Middletown, Conn.	4	36
Jones, Timothy	July 16, 1810	18	light	E. Greenwich, R.I.	4	35
Jones, William	Nov. 15, 1803	23	light	New York, N.Y.	2	47
Jones, William	May 2, 1799	18	light	Providence,R.I.	2	9
Jones, William	Aug. 4, 1803	22	light	Providence, R.I.	2	9
Jones, William	Dec. 5, 1838	22	dark	Brookhaven, N.Y.	5	41
Jones, William	Dec. 7, 1842	22	light	Swedesboro, N.J.	5	41
Jones, William	Nov. 24, 1843	20	light	New York, N.Y.	5	41
Jones, William	Apr. 24, 1849	23	dark	Providence, R.I.	5	42
Jones, William	Mar. 23, 1853	23	black	Elizabeth City, N.C.	5	42
Jones, William	Mar. 17, 1857	28	dark	New York, N.Y.	5	43
Jones, Wm. A.	Feb. 26, 1856	32	light	Jefferson, Ga.	5	43
Jones, William O.	Dec. 19, 1804	16	light	Providence, R.I.	3	17
Jones, William O.	Oct. 7, 1808	20	light	Providence, R.I.	4	35
Jordan, Ezekiel	Dec. 5, 1823	18	light	Thomaston, Me.	4	37
Jordan, George	June 20, 1844	22	dark	Scituate, R.I.	5	42
Jorden, Nathaniel S.	Dec. 23, 1870	24	dark	Ellsworth, Me.	6	10
Jordon, Solomon	Aug. 1, 1825	18	light	Surry, Me.	4	37

*Book 3, page 22; book 4, page 35.

REGISTER OF SEAMEN'S PROTECTION

NAME	DATE OF CERTIFICATION	AGE	COMPLEXION	PLACE OF BIRTH	BOOK	PAGE
Joseph, John	June 14, 1848	23	dark	New Bedford, Ma.	5	42
Joseph, Manuel	Nov. 3, 1847	28	dark	Warren, R.I.	5	42
Joseph, George E.	Dec. 14, 1849	26	dark	New Orleans, La.	5	42
Joseph, Isaac	Jan. 21, 1851	22	light	Warren, R.I.	5	42
Joseph, Leander	Dec. 24, 1852	21	dark	New Orleans, La.	5	42
Joslin, Charles C.	Feb. 5, 1849	21	light	Providence, R.I.	5	42
Joslyn, John	Mar. 4, 1797	20	dark	Marlborough, Ma.	1	14
Joslin, John	Nov. 5, 1822	14	ruddy	Charlestown, Ma.	4	37
Joslin, Leonard	June 2, 1831	22	light	Cumberland, R.I.	5	41
Joslin, Rufus	Dec. 3, 1850	21	light	Cumberland, R.I.	5	42
Joslin, Thomas, 2nd.	Dec. 16, 1825	18	light	Cumberland, R.I.	4	37
Joslin[Josselin], Willard	Jan. 2, 1804	17	light	Cumberland, R.I.	3	17
Jouret, Peter	1798-1799	Jan. 15, 1786		Newport, R.I.	** -	--
Joy, Peter	May 29, 1823	24	light	Cranston, R.I.	4	37
Joy, Thomas	Nov. 8, 1799	23	dark	Thompson, Conn.	2	9
Joyce, John G.	Sept. 19, 1836	27	light	Warren, R.I.	5	41
Justin, Charles	June 23, 1804	20	dark	Providence, R.I.	3	17
Justin, Joshua H.	June 8, 1825	29	light	Providence, R.I.	4	37
Justin, Philip	Nov. 17, 1817	14	dark	Newport, R.I.	4	36
Joyce, John	Nov. 19, 1841	26	dark	Boston, Ma.	5	41
Jubilee, Thomas R.	Mar. 17, 1849	24	black	Bell Haven, Md.	5	42
Justin, Samuel	July 20, 1797	16	dark	Providence, R.I.	1	14
Justin, Samuel	Aug. 13, 1798	17	light	Providence, R.I.	2	9
Justin, Samuel	Nov. 19, 1803	22	dark	Providence, R.I.	2	47
Justin, Samuel	May 20, 1803	22	dark	Providence, R.I.	2	9
Justin, William	Feb. 8, 1799	19	light	Providence, R.I.	2	9
Justin, William	June 3, 1818	19	light	Newport, R.I.	4	36
Kailley, Michael F.	Sept. 28, 1846	26	fair	Boston, Ma.	5	46
Kaine, Joseph	July 30, 1844	45	black	Dorchester Co., Md.	5	46
Kane, James	Apr. 8, 1805	28	yellow*	New York, N.Y.	3	19
Kane, James	Nov. 8, 1805	29	black	New York, N.Y.	3	19
Kane, John	Mar. 28, 1863	25	light	Worcester, Ma.	6	11
Kannady, William	Apr. 15, 1854	21	fair	New York, N.Y.	5	47
Keach, Wm. Henry	Aug. 2, 1848	18	dark	Cranston, R.I.	5	46
Kean, John M.	Feb. 29, 1856	29	light	Warren, R.I.	5	47
Kearne, Patrick	Sept. 5, 1863	24	dark	Ireland	6	11

*mulatto
**Newport, R.I.

NAME	DATE OF CERTIFICATION	AGE	COMPLEXION	PLACE OF BIRTH	BOOK	PAGE
Keef, John	Nov. 25, 1824	19	light	St. George, Me.	4	38
Keegan, William E.	Feb. 26, 1856	27	light	Cranston, R.I.	5	47
Keene, Charles	Oct. 23, 1799	23	light	Providence, R.I.	2	10
Keen, John	Feb. 6, 1804	21	light	Providence, R.I.	3	19
Keen, (?Keean), Robert	Mar. 29, 1800	19	light	Providence, R.I.	2	10
Keen, Robert	Mar. 6, 1805	23	light	Warren, R.I.	3	19
Keene, William P.	Sept. 4, 1813	20	light	Providence, R.I.	4	38
Keith, George W.	Sept. 7, 1861	17	dark	Providence, R.I.	6	11
Keiting, John	May 17, 1855	21	fair	Johnston, R.I.	5	47
Keller, John W.	Aug. 18, 1819	15	brown	Barnstable, Ma.	4	38
Kelley, Beers	Mar. 1, 1805	20	light	Warren, R.I.	3	19
Kelley, Edward	Jan. 9, 1826	18	light	Warren, R.I.	4	38
Kelley, James	May 6, 1854	22	light	New York, N.Y.	5	47
Kelley, Jesse E.	Aug. 18, 1856	25	light	Providence, R.I.	5	47
Kelley, Jetson	Mar. 24, 1863	22	dark	Clayville, R.I.	6	11
Kelley, Nathaniel	Mar. 5, 1849	19	light	Providence, R.I.	5	46
Kelley, William	Dec. 27, 1854	19	light	New York, N.Y.	5	47
Kelly, Charles H.	Aug. 31, 1849	24	light	Johnston, R.I.	5	47
Kelly, Ezra	May 5, 1823	23	light	Dennis, Ma.	4	38
Kelly, George	Sept. 9, 1844	20	dark	Boston, Ma.	5	46
Kelly, Henry	Sept. 7, 1855	19	light	Little Falls, N.Y.	5	47
Kelly, James H.	Oct. 16, 1841	19	light	Boston, Ma.	5	46
Kelly, John	Mar. 29, 1850	26	light	New York, N.Y.	5	47
Kelly, John	Oct. 8, 1858	29	dark	New York, N.Y.	6	11
Kelly, Martin	Sept. 13, 1796	23	dark	Warren, R.I.	1	2
Kelly, Robert L.	Apr. 26, 1842	17	light	Providence, R.I.	5	46
Kelly, Wilbur	Aug. 24, 1799	18	dark	Yarmouth, Ma.	2	10
Kelshaw, James	Oct. 7, 1834	32	black	Jamaica, N.Y.	5	46
Kempt, Henry	Feb. 23, 1852	35	dark	New York, N.Y.	5	47
[Kempton], Kimpton, Thomas	June 27, 1801	23	dark	Mendon, Ma.	2	10
Kendall, Andrew J.	Nov. 21, 1854	17	light	Providence, R.I.	5	47
Kendall, Duane	May 17, 1830	36	light	Concord, N.H.	5	46
Kendall, Thomas	Oct. 10, 1806	32	dark	New York, N.Y.	4	38
Kendall, Thomas	Aug. 21, 1858	18	florid	New York, N.Y.	6	11
Kendrick, Doan S.	Jan. 3, 1827	18	light	Chatham, Mass.	4	38

REGISTER OF SEAMEN'S PROTECTION

NAME	DATE OF CERTIFICATION	AGE	COMPLEXION	PLACE OF BIRTH	BOOK	PAGE
Kennedy, Alcesta	Baptism of Dec. 8, 1822		Rev. Benedict Record.			
Kennedy, David	Sept. 25, 1799	19	black	Rehoboth, Ma.	2	10
Kennedy, Duncan	Apr. 10, 1834	25	light	No. Prov., R.I.	5	46
Kennedy, James	Sept. 22, 1801	23	light	Johnston, R.I.	2	10
Kennedy, John	1798-1799	Apr. 12, 1774		Boston, Ma.	*-	--
Kenney, William S.	Mar. 6, 1834	21	freckled	Gardiner, Me.	5	46
Kenniff, Sam'l	Nov. 8, 1856	17	dark	Eastport, Me.	5	47
Kensil, Christopher	Aug. 26, 1807	21	brown	Phila., Pa.	4	38
Kent, Bosworth	Nov. 19, 1796	25	dark	Rehoboth, Ma.	1	15
Kent, Olney	Nov. 8, 1843	31	light	Seekonk, Ma.	5	46
Kent, Pherez	Dec. 12, 1797	21	light	Rehoboth, Ma.	1	15
Kent, Sylvester	Mar. 18, 1850	19	light	Waterford, Vt.	5	47
Kent, Wilson	Mar. 14, 1801	22	light	Barrington, R.I.	2	10
Kenyon [Kinyon] James	June 24, 1841	20	dark	Charlestown, R.I.	5	46
Kenyon, Robert	Aug. 21, 1845	20	dark	Cranston, R.I.	5	46
Kennyon, Sylvester	1798-1799	June 5, 1772		E. Greenwich, R.I.	*-	--
Kenyon, Thomas G.	Dec. 24, 1855	19	light	Charlestown, R.I.	5	47
Kerr, Robert	Aug. 29, 1848	23	light	Eastport, Me.	5	46
Kettell, John H.	Mar. 2, 1848	25	light	Boston, Ma.	5	46
Kidd, Thomas	May 1, 1807	30	yellow	Westfield, N.J.	4	38
Kiff, William H.	Mar. 22, 1855	22	light	St. George, Me.	5	47
Kilbey, Ephraim	June 2, 1804	27	dark	Monson, Ma.	3	19
Kilborn, Noah	July 13, 1805	17	light	Hartford, Conn.	3	19
Kilburn [Kilborn],	Staunton Nov. 14, 1803	28	light	Newport, R.I.	2	10
Kilburn, William	1798-1799	Mar. 15, 1782		Newport, R.I.	*-	--
Katherine Kilburn swears the above to be true.						
Kilburn [Kilborn], Wm.	Aug. 5, 1803	20	light	Newport, R.I.	2	10
Killing, John	May 18, 1867	34	dark	Eastport, Me.	6	11
Kim, Samuel	Jan. 4, 1831	28	dk/yel.	Bristol, R.I.	5	46
Kimball, Benjamin, Jr.	Nov. 15, 1804	29	dark	Johnston, R.I.	3	19
Kimball, Benjamin, S.	Mar. 22, 1845	20	light	Portland, Me.	5	46
Kimball, Charles	Mar. 21, 1836	22	black	Phila., Pa.	5	46
Kimball, Charles T.	Aug. 23, 1848	23	dark	New York, N.Y.	5	46
Kimball, George W.	Feb. 5, 1801	16	dark	Glocester, R.I.	2	10
Kimball, James	July 15, 1848	22	dark	Salem, Ma.	5	46
Kimball, Moody	June 21, 1827	22	light	Newburyport, Ma.	4	38
Kimball, Sanford	June 2, 1831	24	light	Amherst, N.H.	5	46

*Newport, R.I.

NAME	DATE OF CERTIFICATION	AGE	COMPLEXION	PLACE OF BIRTH	BOOK	PAGE
Kimball, Samuel	Nov. 17, 1804	14	light	Providence, R.I.	3	19
Kimball, Samuel	May 8, 1807	16	light	Providence, R.I.	4	38
Kimball, William	Jan. 6, 1823	16	light	Randolph, Ma.	4	38
Kimberly, Orin	Nov. 14, 1855	20	light	Binghampton, N.Y.	5	47
Kindred, Henry E.	Apr. 21, 1854	21	light	Providence, R.I.	5	47
King, Asa	Nov. 20, 1847	18	light	Cumberland, R.I.	5	46
King, Charles A.	July 3, 1839	27	dark	Providence, R.I.	5	46
King, Charles J.	June 13, 1849	17	light	Roxbury, Pa.	5	46
King, Charles J.	Dec. 8, 1851	20	light	Roxbury, Pa.	5	47
King, Elijah	Aug. 20, 1800	27	dark	Dighton, Ma.	2	10
King, George	Sept. 2, 1852	25	light	Phila., Pa.	5	47
King, George D.	Mar. 10, 1831	18	light	Johnston, R.I.	5	46
King, Geo. F.	Nov. 25, 1848	18	dark	Providence, R.I.	5	46
King, Holden	Dec. 20, 1806	17	light	Cranston, R.I.	4	38
King, Horatio	July 3, 1839	17	dark	Providence, R.I.	5	46
King, James	Jan. 21, 1851	24	light	Providence, R.I.	5	47
King, James S.	Dec. 4, 1834	23	ruddy	Johnston, R.I.	5	46
King, John	Nov. 6, 1799	25	light	Dighton, Ma.	2	10
King, John	July 22, 1803	37	light	Newport, R.I.	2	10
King, John	Jan. 6, 1804	21	light	Cranston, R.I.	3	19
King, John	Apr. 9, 1811	23	brown	Scituate, R.I.	4	38
King, John	Oct. 4, 1844	26	light	Tiverton, R.I.	5	46
King, John Asa	Oct. 5, 1824	29	light	Cranston, R.I.	4	38
King, John W.	Aug. 20, 1845	19	dark	Warwick, R.I.	5	46
King, John W.	Oct. 4, 1849	22	light	Warwick, R.I.	5	47
King, Jonathan	Mar. 21, 1805	21	light	Cranston, R.I.	3	19
King, Joseph	Jan. 4, 1833	33	light	Attleboro, Ma.	5	46
King, Josiah	Nov. 20, 1821	19	light	Cumberland, R.I.	4	38
King, Manuel	Oct. 2, 1848	24	dark	New Orleans, La.	5	46
King, Richard G.	Mar. 15, 1847	21	fair	Foster, R.I.	5	46
King, Richard H.	July 11, 1849	19	light	Johnston, R.I.	5	47
King, Rufus	July 3, 1815	16	dark	Cranston, R.I.	4	38
King, Samuel	Mar. 21, 1828	21	light	Little Compton, R.I.	4	38
King, Samuel W.	Aug. 11, 1812	26	light	Johnston, R.I	4	38

NAME	DATE OF CERTIFICATION	AGE	COMPLEXION	PLACE OF BIRTH	BOOK	PAGE
King, Samuel W.P.	Oct. 25, 1844	20	light	Providence, R.I.	5	46
King, Thomas S.	Aug. 19, 1846	18	fair	Roxborough, Pa.	5	46
King, William	Dec. 19, 1800	18	light	Barrie, Ma.	2	10
King, William	Jan. 27, 1800	22	light	Nantucket, Ma.	2	10
King, William P.	Oct. 10, 1808	24	light	Rutland, Ma.	4	38
King, Wilson	Mar. 4, 1797	27	light	No. Prov., R.I.	1	15
Kingsley, Benjamin, Jr.	July 4, 1798	21	light	Rehoboth, Ma.	2	10
Kinney, Daniel S.	Apr. 25, 1864	23	dark	Mattapoisett, Ma.	6	11
Kinnicut, Christopher	Nov. 10, 1813	36	black	Providence, R.I.	4	38
Kinnicutt, George Gorham	Apr. 21, 1801	21	dark	Warren, R.I.	2	10
Kinnicutt, John C.	Jan. 14, 1804	28	light	Providence, R.I.	3	19
Kinnicutt, William	Apr. 22, 1801	24	light	Warren, R.I.	2	10
Kirby, John A.	May 17, 1859	31	fair	New York, N.Y.	6	11
Kitchen, Jospeh	May 17, 1800	19	light	Boston, Ma.	2	10
Kitchen, Joseph	Oct. 12, 1803	23	light	Boston, Ma.	2	10
Kittle, Henry G.	May 30, 1859	17	fair	Coventry, R.I.	6	11
Knapp, David	Apr. 6, 1849	17	light	Providence, R.I.	5	46
Knapp, George W.	Mar. 30, 1835	21	light	Boston, Ma.	5	46
Knapp, John	Mar. 24, 1813	21	brown	Chatham, Ma.	4	38
Knapp, Noah	Apr. 4, 1799	18	dark	Stamford, Conn.	2	10
Kneeland, William	Nov. 2, 1841	22	light	Prospect, Me.	5	46
Knight, Aborn	Dec. 6, 1805	19	dark	Cranston, R.I.	3	19
Knight, Albert H.	Sept. 30, 1851	21	dark	Cranston, R.I.	5	47
Knight, Benjamin	Nov. 18, 1822	19	light	Cranston, R.I.	4	38
Knight, Benjamin	Sept. 4, 1849	46	light	Johnston, R.I.	5	47
Knight, Esek	Sept. 25, 1806	21	light	Glocester, R.I.	3	26
Knight, James	Sept. 3, 1832	21	dark	Alexandria, D. of C.	5	46
Knight, Jere	June 5, 1849	25	light	Cranston, R.I.	5	46
Knight, Jeremiah	June 5, 1838	17	light	Cranston, R.I.	5	46
Knight, John	July 12, 1811	19	light	Cranston, R.I.	4	38
Knight, Joseph	Nov. 1, 1844	34	dark	Boston, Ma.	5	46
Knight, Joseph W.	Feb. 28, 1849	52	light	Cranston, R.I.	5	46
Knight, Moses	July 29, 1835	21	dark	Boston, Ma.	5	46
Knight, Obadial Matthewson	Sept. 4, 1849	21	light	Providence, R.I.	5	47

NAME	DATE OF CERTIFICATION	AGE	COMPLEXION	PLACE OF BIRTH	BOOK	PAGE
Knight, Sanford	Apr. 21, 1807	19	florid	Cranston, R.I.	4	38
Knight, Seril N.	Apr. 28, 1854	28	dark	Cranston, R.I.	5	47
Knight, Sheldon	May 30, 1849	28	light	Cranston, R.I.	5	46
Knight, Silvester	May 26, 1802	16	light	Cranston, R.I.	2	10
Knight, Solomon	Dec. 13, 1845	24	fair	Rockport, Ma.	5	46
Knight, Stephen A.	Feb. 27, 1849	32	dark	Haverhill, Ma.	5	46
Knight, William	Mar. 6, 1857	23	fair	Wayne, Michigan	5	47
Knowles, Daniel S.	Oct. 29, 1849	27	dark	So. Kingston, R.I.	5	47
Knowles, Horatio N., Jr.	Dec. 24, 1855	18	light	So. Kingston, R.I.	5	47
Knowles, James D.	Mar. 26, 1849	16	light	Boston, Ma.	5	46
Knowles, John G.	Sept. 20, 1866	28	light	New York, N.Y.	6	11
Knowles, Thomas H.	Sept. 27, 1844	15	light	Kingston, R.I.	5	46
Knowlton, Stephen	Nov. 2, 1858	35	dark	Islesboro, Me.	6	11
Knox, Henry L.	Jan. 13, 1852	22	light	Lowell, Ma.	5	47
Knox, Peter	Sept. 30, 1797	24	light	Boston, Ma.	1	15
Knox, Sullivan	Oct. 1, 1831	17	light	Pembroke, N.H.	5	46
Kyer, Philip	Aug. 22, 1829	34	black	Exeter, N.H.	5	46
Labell, Sidney	Apr. 7, 1851	18	dark	Prospect, Me.	5	50
Labers, Charles C.	Mar. 14, 1853	20	light	Portland, Me.	5	50
Lacey, Thomas	1798-1799	May 25, 1777		New York, N.Y.	*-	--
Lackey, William	June 7, 1833	18	light	No. Prov., R.I.	5	48
Lacosta, Joseph	Mar 16, 1849	25	dark	Concord, N.H.	5	49
Lacount, William	Feb. 8, 1832	25	light	Smyrna, Del.	5	48
Ladd, Joseph	Oct. 9, 1855	21	dark	Coventry, R.I.	5	50
La Due, Crumline	Feb. 27, 1849	40	light	Fishkill, New York	5	49
Ladue, Curtis	Dec. 3, 1796	33	light	Barrington, R.I.	1	16
Ladue, Samuel	Oct. 29, 1804	16	dark	Barrington, R.I.	3	21
La Due, Wm. J.	Jan. 1, 1856	20	light	Warren, R.I.	5	50
Lafong, John	Aug. 22, 1836	54	light	Edenton, N.C.	5	48
Lafort, John B.	June 6, 1853	38	dark	New York, N.Y.	5	50
Lahey, John	Aug. 27, 1845	14	dark	Providence, R.I.	5	49
Lake, Amos	Dec. 7, 1811	18	light	Rehoboth, Ma.	4	40
Lake, Benjamin	Oct. 12, 1805	19	light	Rehoboth, Ma.	3	56
Lake, Borden	Dec. 15, 1825	21	light	Tiverton, R.I.	4	41
Lake, Edward	1798-1799	Mar. 12, 1765		Tiverton, R.I.	*-	--

*Newport, R.I.

NAME	DATE OF CERTIFICATION	AGE	COMPLEXION	PLACE OF BIRTH	BOOK	PAGE
Lake, Joseph	1798-1799	Aug. 25, 1781		Tiverton, R.I.	* -	--
Lake, Joseph	June 14, 1817	15	dark	Tiverton, R.I.	4	46
Lake, Noah	Jan. 1, 1806	19	light	Tiverton, R.I.	3	57
Lake, Richard	Aug. 11, 1808	17	light	Rehoboth, Ma.	4	40
Lake, Thurston H.	Oct. 23, 1849	28	light	Newport, R.I.	5	50
Lamb, Charles	Dec. 22, 1845	19	black	Boston, Ma.	5	49
Lamb, Henry	Jan. 2, 1861	16	light	Fall River, Ma.	6	12
Lamb, Isaac	Oct. 13, 1830	15	light	Camden, N.C.	5	48
Lambert, Charles	Feb. 10, 1846	16	fair	Cranston, R.I.	5	49
Lamphier, Champlin	Jan. 3, 1850	19	light	Prospect, Me.	5	50
Landerkin, William N.	Nov. 8, 1833	18	light	Bath, Me.	5	48
Landy, Thomas	July 7, 1847	19	fair	Providence, R.I.	5	49
Lane, Adam	Nov. 13, 1835	26	light	Charlestown, N.Y.	5	48
Lane, Alfred	Feb. 13, 1849	27	dark	Providence, R.I.	5	49
Lane, Amos	Aug. 7, 1815	24	light	Rehoboth, Ma.	4	40
Lane, Benjamin F.	June 13, 1832	26	light	New York, N.Y.	5	48
Lane, Charles W.	Nov. 5, 1844	25	light	Jamaica, N.Y.	5	49
Lane, George W.	May 3, 1843	18	dark	Foster, R.I.	5	49
Lane, George W.	Nov. 27, 1844	20	dark	Foster, R.I.	5	49
Lane, John B.	Dec. 28, 1858	26	mulatto	Philadelphia, Pa.	6	12
Lane, John E. T.	Jan. 19, 1856	25	dark	Phila., Pa.	5	50
Lane, Joseph	Oct. 3, 1818	21	light	Dorchester, Ma.	4	40
Lane, Lyman	Sept. 20, 1866	32	light	Somerset, Ma.	6	12
Lane, William	Aug. 27, 1840	20	dark	Killingly, Conn.	5	48
Lane, Wm. R.	Nov. 27, 1844	24	dark	Killingly, Conn.	5	49
Lang, John	Aug. 15, 1865	27	light	Providence, R.I.	6	12
Langford, John P.	Sept. 11, 1804	26	dark	E. Greenwich, R.I.	3	21
Langford, John P.	Oct. 10, 1806	30	dark	E. Greenwich, R.I.	4	40
Langley, Lee	Aug. 4, 1801	18	dark	Newport, R.I.	2	11
Langley, Lee, Jr.	Sept. 30, 1820	15	dark	Providence, R.I.	4	40
Langley, Richard	Sept. 10, 1838	21	light	Newport, R.I.	5	48
Langley, Samuel	Oct. 26, 1829	15	light	Providence, R.I.	5	48
Lapham, Edward G.	Mar. 25, 1867	19	light	Providence, R.I.	6	12
Lapham, James	Nov. 14, 1803	16	light	Cumberland, R.I.	2	43
Lapham, William	Feb. 19, 1805	17	light	Cumberland, R.I.	3	21

*Newport, R. I.

NAME	DATE OF CERTIFICATION	AGE	COMPLEXION	PLACE OF BIRTH	BOOK	PAGE
Laranour, David W.	Sept. 4, 1845	32	dark	Tarrytown, N.Y.	5	49
Larchar, Lewis	Aug. 3, 1809	17	light	Providence, R.I.	4	40
Lark, Josiah	Nov. 2, 1827	17	light	Bristol, R.I.	4	41
Larkham, David L.	Oct. 27, 1849	25	light	Voluntown, Conn.	5	50
Larkin, Ephraim	June 29, 1830	35	black	Dorset, Md.	5	48
Larkin, Francis	Aug. 2, 1849	29	dark	St. George, Me.	5	50
Larkin, George	Sept. 17, 1803	24	black	Richmond, R.I.	2	43
Larkin, George	Feb. 17, 1806	27	black	Richmond, R.I.	3	57
Larkin, John G.	Nov. 7, 1845	23	dark	So. Kingston, R.I.	5	49
Larkin, Thomas S.	Aug. 26, 1845	21	light	So. Kingston, R.I.	5	49
Larned, William	June 27, 1800	18	light	Thompson, Conn.	2	11
Larry, Dennis	Feb. 1, 1854	17	light	Roxbury, Ma.	5	50
Latham, Jeremiah	Jan. 16, 1818	18	dark	New London, Conn.	4	40
Lathrop, Cyrus	Aug. 17, 1853	27	black	Plainfield, Conn.	5	50
Langhran, John	Mar. 2, 1846	18	fair	Portland, Me.	5	49
Law, John	July 14, 1845	17	dark	Henniker, N.H.	5	49
Lawrence, Alexander	Apr. 22, 1797	21	light	Providence, R.I.	1	16
Lawrence, Archibald S.	Oct. 12, 1821	15	light	Providence, R.I.	4	41
Lawrence, Charles	Mar. 15, 1852	19	mulatto	Hartford, Conn.	5	50
Lawrence, John	June 18, 1845	17	light	Providence, R.I.	5	49
Lawrence, John H.	Nov. 11, 1841	23	light	Kinderhook, N.Y.	5	49
Lawrence, Levin	Apr. 9, 1834	20	light	Dogsborough, Del.	5	48
[Lawrence]Lawrance, Walter	June 7, 1799	18	light	Providence, R.I.	2	11
Laws, Dennis	June 16, 1852	48	black	Concord, Del.	5	50
Laws, James	June 9, 1854	32	black	Snow Hill, Md.	5	50
Laws, Smith	July 12, 1839	26	black	Snow Hill, Md.	5	48
Lawton, George	Mar. 10, 1810	19	brown	Rehoboth, Ma.	4	40
Lawton, George	June 5, 1835	18	light	Warwick, R.I.	5	48
Lawton, Isaac E.	Mar. 25, 1863	32	light	Exeter, R.I.	6	12
Lawton, Job	1798-1799	Aug. 9, 1782		Portsmouth, R.I.	*-	--
George Lawton swears the above to be true.						
Lawton, Jonathan	Dec. 27, 1826	32	dark	Troy, Ma.	4	41
Lawton, Joseph	1798-1799	Jan. 15, 1776		Swansey	*-	--
Lawton, Joseph S.	June 17, 1836	39	light	Uxbridge, Ma.	5	48
Lawton, Lorenso	Jan. 2, 1830	13	dark	Freetown, Ma.	5	48
Lawton, Peleg	Aug. 13, 1803	18	light	E. Greenwich, R.I.	2	43
Lawton, Peleg	June 16, 1800	16	light	E. Greenwich, R.I.	2	11

*Newport, R.I.

REGISTER OF SEAMEN'S PROTECTION

NAME	DATE OF CERTIFICATION	AGE	COMPLEXION	PLACE OF BIRTH	BOOK	PAGE
Lawton, Samuel	1798-1799	Jan. 18, 1744		Newport, R.I.	* _	--
Lawton, Samuel	Oct. 17, 1818	18	dark	Uxbridge, Ma.	4	40
Lawton, Thomas	Nov. 4, 1805	45	light	Tiverton, R.I.	3	57
Lawton, Thomas	Oct. 15, 1855	28	light	Dover, N.H.	5	50
Lawton, Thomas J.	Oct. 22, 1849	24	light	Dover, N.H.	5	50
Lawton, William	Oct. 13, 1807	28	dark	Providence, R.I.	4	40
Lawton, William B.	Sept. 4, 1828	24	light	No. Kingstown, R.I.	4	41
Lawton, William Wilson	Dec. 4, 1805	19	black	Newport, R.I.	3	57
Lawton, William Wilson	Aug. 31, 1805	19	black	Portsmouth, R.I.	3	56
Layman, Jacob	Jan. 1, 1835	31	light	New York, N.Y.	5	48
Leach, Almond L.	May 31, 1837	26	dark	Providence, R.I.	5	48
Leach, Asa	Apr. 24, 1809	29	brown	Scituate, R.I.	4	40
Leach, Edmund	Aug. 19, 1839	17	light	Scituate, R.I.	5	48
Leach, John	Dec. 15, 1824	17	light	Easton, Ma.	4	41
Leach, John	Apr. 27, 1849	33	light	Portland, Me.	5	49
Leach, William	Oct. 17, 1838	18	light	Scituate, R.I.	5	48
Leach, William H.	Aug. 20, 1841	10	light	Providence, R.I.	5	49
Learning, Aaron	Aug. 2, 1806	26	brown	Middletown, Conn.	3	57
Learned, George N.	Feb. 27, 1843	17	dark	Providence, R.I.	5	49
Leary, Daniel	Sept. 20, 1856	22	dark	New York, N.Y.	5	82
Leary, Daniel	?Sept. 1857	23	dark	New York, N.Y.	5	82
Leary, Daniel	Sept. 9, 1857	22	dark	New York, N.Y.	6	12
Leary, Jeremiah	Feb. 25, 1857	22	fair	Lowell, Ma.	5	82
Leary, John	Nov. 3, 1862	31	light	Bucksport, Me.	6	12
Leavens, Jesse S.	June 9, 1826	19	light	Killingly, Conn.	4	41
Leavitt, Joshua	Dec. 8, 1832	19	light	Suffield, Conn.	5	48
Lecount, James	Jan. 25, 1858	22	black	Newcastle, Del.	6	12
Leddy, Peter	May 11, 1858	26	light	Providence, R.I.	6	12
Ledger, Joseph	Apr. 26, 1832	32	light	Phila., Pa.	5	48
Lee, Edwin	Oct. 7, 1844	20	light	No. Prov., R.I.	5	49
Lee, Isaac O.	Nov. 28, 1832	35	dark	Cumberland, R.I.	5	48
Lee, James	Mar. 16, 1799	36	black	Phila., Pa.	2	11
Lee, James	Apr. 1, 1797	23	dark	Portsmouth, N.H.	1	16
Lee, John	Sept. 3, 1834	35	dark	Cumberland, R.I.	5	48
Lee, John	Mar. 19, 1849	32	light	Eastport, Me.	5	49
Lee, John G.	Feb. 21, 1834	21	black	Providence, R.I.	5	48

*Newport, R.I.

NAME	DATE OF CERTIFICATION	AGE	COMPLEXION	PLACE OF BIRTH	BOOK	PAG
Lee, John H.	May 22, 1816	18	light	Providence, R.I.	4	40
Lee, Joseph	June 12, 1809	16	light	Cumberland, R.I.	4	40
Lee, Joseph	Feb. 15, 1854	27	light	Berwick, Me.	5	50
Lee, Joseph B.	Apr. 12, 1815	19	ruddy	Providence, R.I.	4	40
Lee, Otis	May 30, 1818	19	dark	Cumberland, R.I.	4	40
Lee, Robert H.	Mar. 16, 1842	28	dark	Boston, Ma.	5	49
Lee, Samuel	1798-1799	Oct. 2, 1782		Swansey, Ma.	*-	--
Lee, Stephen	Nov. 8, 1852	30	light	Dighton, Ma.	5	50
Lee, Thomas	Dec. 4, 1837	23	light	Warren, R.I.	5	48
Lee, William	Mar. 6, 1805	25	light	Thompson, Conn.	3	56
Lee, William	Aug. 9, 1828	19	light	Woodstock, Conn.	4	41
Leek, Josiah H.	Oct. 9, 1834	19	dark	Sag Harbor, N.Y.	5	48
Leeland, Simeon	Mar. 28, 1863	53	light	Gardiner, Ma.	6	12
Leet, Alexander T. or Y.	Dec. 1, 1848	22	light	Guilford, Conn.	5	49
Leet, James A.	Sept. 13, 1838	21	light	Guilford, Conn.	5	48
Leman, John	Oct. 30, 1856	24	light	Boston, Ma.	5	82
Lennan, John	Dec. 10, 1851	42	dark	New Orleans, La.	5	50
Lent, Jacob	Jan. 5, 1843	20	dark	New York, N.Y.	5	49
Leonard, Andrew	Mar. 13, 1847	22	freckled	Albany, N.Y.	5	49
Leonard, David C.	Sept. 10, 1834	22	light	Raynham, Ma.	5	48
Leonard, Ephraim	Sept. 21, 1803	25	dark	Mansfield, Ma.	2	43
Leonard, Galanthus	May 6, 1805	19	black	Dighton, Ma.	3	56
Leonard, Galanthus	Dec. 13, 1809	23	black	Dighton, Ma.	4	40
Leonard, George	Mar. 10, 1843	22	light	Monroe Co., N.Y.	5	49
Leonard, George E.	July 26, 1864	27	light	Valley, Falls, R.I.	6	12
Leonard, Henry M.	Dec. 23, 1861	26	dark	Bristol, R.I.	6	12
Leonard, John	July 15, 1854	19	light	Smithfield, R.I.	5	50
Leonard, Samuel	Mar. 15, 1850	33	light	Taunton, Ma.	5	50
Leonard, Simeon	Sept. 21, 1803	20	light	Mansfield, Ma.	2	43
Leonard, Wright	Apr. 5, 1837	17	light	Taunton, Ma.	5	48
Lescomb, Henry R.	May 2, 1855	17	fair	Salem, Ma.	5	50
Leslie, Joseph H.	Mar. 7, 1853	29	dark	New Orleans, La.	5	50
Leslie, Thomas C.	Mar. 12, 1851	30	dark	St. Louis, Missouri	5	50
Letherbee, George	Nov. 22, 1824	16	light	Providence, R.I.	4	41
Levalley, Christopher	Apr. 9, 1834	18	freckled	Warwick, R.I.	5	48
Leverett, George	May 26, 1823	21	light	Windsor, Vt.	4	41
Leverts, Robert, Jr.	Dec. 13, 1844	26	dark	Worcester, Ma.	5	49

*Newport, R.I.

NAME	DATE OF CERTIFICATION	AGE	COMPLEXION	PLACE OF BIRTH	BOOK	PAGE
Levett, Charles	May 9, 1825	22	light	Hallowell, Me.	4	41
Lewin, Haile	1798-1799	Sept. 2, 1778		Swansey	** _	--
Lewis, Allen	May 15, 1823	20	dark	Yarmouth, Ma.	4	41
Lewis, Asa	Feb. 12, 1799	24	light	Cambridge, Ma.	2	11
Lewis, Charles	Aug. 4, 1821	22	light	Swansea, Ma.	4	41
Lewis, Charles H.	May 4, 1865	27	light	Nantucket, Ma.	6	12
Lewis, David	Mar. 27, 1837	23	light	New London, Conn.	5	48
Lewis, Edward B.	Oct. 24, 1837	25	black	So. Berwick, Me.	5	48
Lewis, George	June 2, 1831	21	light	Glastonbury, Conn.	5	48
Lewis, George	Dec. 19, 1849	31	light	Nantucket, Ma.	5	50
Lewis, George A.	Feb. 27, 1856	18	light	Cumberland, R.I.	5	82
Lewis, George D.	July 6, 1858	22	dark	Milford, Ma.	6	12
Lewis, Higgins	Jan. 4, 1821	16	dark	Yarmouth, Ma.	** _	--
Sworn statement of Benjamin Lewis of Warren in Custom House Papers. DOB : July 11, 1804.						
Lewis, James	Feb. 29, 1804	26	black	Hartford, Conn.	3	21
Lewis, James W.	Apr. 5, 1856	22	light	Cornwall, Conn.	5	82
Lewis, Jeremiah	Sept. 30, 1820	24	light	Swansea, Ma.	4	40
Lewis, John	June 27, 1806	19	light	Germantown, Pa.	3	57
Lewis, John	Dec. 8, 1827	26	light	Marblehead, Ma.	4	41
Lewis, John	Apr. 3, 1849	23	light	New Orleans, La.	5	49
Lewis, Joseph	Jan. 10, 1850	18	dark	Newport, R.I.	5	50
Lewis, Peter	Jan. 31, 1804	24	black	Newport, R.I.	3	21
Lewis, Peter	July 17, 1804	23	yellow*	New York, N.Y.	3	21
Lewis, Peter	July 13, 1805	30	black	Newport, R.I.	3	56
Lewis, Peter	Sept. 27, 1836	34	black	Newport, R.I.	5	48
Lewis, Phineas	June 19, 1822	46	light	Stonnington, Conn.	4	41
Lewis, Richard	Nov. 18, 1806	23	dark	Yarmouth, Ma.	4	40
Lewis, Robert	May 18, 1867	26	black	Greensboro, Ala.	6	12
Lewis, Samuel	Jan. 16, 1804	27	black	Baltimore, Md.	3	21
Lewis, Sam'l A.	Feb. 26, 1849	19	light	No. Prov., R.I.	5	49
Lewis, Simeon	Dec. 10, 1811	19	yellow	Hopkinton, R.I.	4	40
Lewis, Thomas	Aug. 15, 1839	27	light	Rochester, Ma.	5	48
Lewis, Thomas	Sept. 4. 1856	22	dark	Warwick, R.I.	5	82
Lewis, Timothy	Nov. 24, 1821	28	light	Swansea, Ma.	4	41
Lewis, William	Apr. 23, 1857	21	fair	Providence, R.I.	5	82
Lewis, William	Apr. 9, 1860	26	light	New York, N.Y.	6	12
Lewis, William F.	Mar. 20, 1850	30	light	Calais, Me.	5	50
Lewis, William J.	Feb. 3, 1840	24	black	Johnston, R.I.	5	48

*mulatto **Newport, R.I.

NAME	DATE OF CERTIFICATION	AGE	COMPLEXION	PLACE OF BIRTH	BOOK	PAGE
Levy, Pomp	Jan. 3, 1806	20	black	Newport, R.I.	3	57
Libby, John	Feb. 27, 1852	21	light	Richmond Co., N.Y.	5	50
Lillibridge, David	1798-1799	Apr. 7, 1780		So. Kingston,	** -	--
Lillibridge, Liman	Nov. 23, 1861	30	light	Hartford, Conn.	6	12
Lillibridge, Wm.	1798-1799	Mar. 27, 1778		So. Kingston	-	--
Lilly, George	June 8, 1855	24	fair	Burlington, Vt.	5	50
Lilly, Henry	Apr. 11, 1859	20	light	Providence, R.I.	6	12
Limas, Benjamin	Feb. 15, 1805	23	yellow*	Newport, R.I.	3	21
Limehouse, Richard	Dec. 8, 1804	24	yellow*	Newtown, Pa.	3	21
Limehouse, Richard	Aug. 3, 1805	24	yellow*	Newtown, Pa.	3	56
Linch, John	Feb. 3, 1834	19	light	Beauport, N.C.	5	48
Lincoln, Charles	Sept. 9, 1806	18	light	Windham, Conn.	3	57
Linde, George	Aug. 21, 1858	22	dark	Nantucket, Ma.	6	12
Lind, John P.	Oct.. 15, 1849	49	light	Providence, R.I.	5	50
Lindley, George	Mar. 11, 1797	26	dark	Rehoboth, Ma.	1	16
Lindley, Thomas	Mar. 3, 1804	22	light	Providence, R.I.	3	21
Lindon, Robert	Sept. 26, 1805	19	black	Providence, R.I.	3	56
Lindsey, George	Apr. 23, 1852	20	light	Providence, R.I.	5	50
Lindsey, James	Oct. 25, 1805	35	dark	Newburgh, N.Y.	3	56
Lindsey, Wm.	1798-1799	Aug. 23, 1780		Bristol, R.I.	** -	--
Lindsley, Sam'l A.	Mar. 5, 1849	26	light	Seekonk, Ma.	5	49
Linell, George	May 8, 1819	20	light	Yarmouth, Ma.	4	40
Linn, Joseph	Dec. 30, 1845	35	yellow	Phila., Pa.	5	49
Lion, John	July 10, 1837	33	light	Hyannis, Ma.	5	48
Lippincott, Wm.	Dec. 10, 1853	18	dark	Morristown, N.J.	5	50
Lippincott, Stephen	Jan. 9, 1855	22	light	Phila., Pa.	5	50
Lippitt, Affrica	Nov. 30, 1803	19	yellow*	Warwick, R.I.	2	43
Lippitt, Africa	July 19, 1802	18	black	Warwick, R.I.	2	11
Lippitt, Andrew	Dec. 7, 1796	18	black	Warwick, R.I.	1	16
Lippitt, Cesar	Jan. 2, 1800	18	black	Warwick, R.I.	2	11
Lippitt, Seasar	May 30, 1803	20	black	Warwick, R.I.	2	11
Lippitt, Caesar	Dec. 25, 1805	23	black	Warwick, R.I.	3	21
Lippitt, Caesar	Nov. 25, 1817	33	black	Warwick, R.I.	4	40
Lippitt, George	Mar. 17, 1819	15	black	Warwick, R.I.	4	40
Lippitt, George	Apr. 21, 1835	21	black	Warwick, R.I.	5	48
Lippitt, George A.	Oct. 24, 1826	19	black	Sandwich, Ma.	4	41
Lippitt, George G.	Mar. 17, 1827	29	mulatto	Warwick, R.I.	4	41

*mulatto   **Newport, RI

NAME	DATE OF CERTIFICATION	AGE	COMPLEXION	PLACE OF BIRTH	BOOK	PAGE
Lippitt, James	Sept. 25, 1821	16	black	Sandwich, Ma.	4	41
Lippitt, Jeremiah	May 18, 1807	17	yellowish	Warwick, R.I.	4	40
Lippitt, Jeremiah	Oct. 13, 1827	19	yellow native	Providence, R.I.	4	41
Lippitt, Jeremiah	Jan. 9, 1845	35	black	Providence, R.I.	5	49
Lippitt, John	Mar. 2, 1849	25	dark	Cranston, R.I.	5	49
Lippitt, Joseph	Nov. 20, 1800	14	black	Warwick, R.I.	2	11
Lippitt, Joseph	May 30, 1803	18	black	Warwick, R.I.	2	43
Lippitt, Joseph	Nov. 28, 1825	26	black	Warwick, R.I.	4	41
Lippitt, Joseph W.	Dec. 19, 1849	27	black	Warwick, R.I.	5	50
Lippitt, Juba	June 12, 1804	16	black	Warwick, R.I.	3	21
Lippitt, Peter	Aug. 22, 1803	21	yellow*	New York, N.Y.	2	43
Lippitt, Prince	Oct. 6, 1798	26	black	Providence, R.I.	2	11
Lippitt, Richard	Aug. 12, 1803	18	light	Providence, R.I.	2	43
Lippitt, Richard	May 4, 1799	14	light	Providence, R.I.	2	11
Lippitt, Samuel	Nov. 19, 1800	16	black	Warwick, R.I.	2	11
Lippitt, Samuel	Dec. 9, 1817	20	black	Warwick, R.I.	4	40
Lippitt, Simon	June 1, 1820	24	black	Warwick, R.I.	4	40
Lippitt, Stephen	Apr. 21, 1835	16	black	Warwick, R.I.	5	48
Lippitt, Walter	Dec. 17, 1799	16	black	Greenwich, R.I.	2	11
Lippitt, Warren	July 14, 1803	17	light	Providence, R.I.	2	43
Lippold, William	Apr. 6, 1850	23	light	New York, N.Y.	5	50
Liscomb, Joseph D.	Aug. 18, 1821	16	dark	Bristol, R.I.	-	--

Sworn statement of Sanford Pearse of Bristol in the Custom House Papers. DOB: Feb. 3, 1805

NAME	DATE OF CERTIFICATION	AGE	COMPLEXION	PLACE OF BIRTH	BOOK	PAGE
Litchfield, Richard	Sept. 10, 1861	54	fair	Drumerstown, Va.	6	12
Little, Amos H.	Mar. 22, 1855	51	fair	Windham, Conn.	5	50
Little, Philip F.	Nov. 21, 1855	18	light	Little Compton, R.I.	5	50
Little, William G.	July 12, 1849	20	light	Augusta, Me.	5	49
Littlefield, Frederick	Sept. 11, 1856	17	light	New Shoreham, R.I.	5	82
Littlefield, George	Nov. 20, 1821	15	fair	Bristol, R.I.	-	--

Sworn statement of Nathaniel Wardwell in The Custom House Papers.

NAME	DATE OF CERTIFICATION	AGE	COMPLEXION	PLACE OF BIRTH	BOOK	PAGE
Littlefield, John	Mar. 23, 1848	24	mulatto	Sag Harbor, N.Y.	5	49
Littlefield, John B.F.	May 26, 1851	17	dark	Warwick, R.I.	5	50
Littlefield, Luther	Mar. 23, 1848	27	mulatto	New Shoreham, R.I.	5	49
Littlefield, Nathaniel 3rd.	Mar. 7, 1815	23	light	New Shoreham, R.I.	4	40
Littlefield, Sylvester H.	Apr. 17, 1849	22	dark	So. Kingston, R.I.	5	49

*mulatto

NAME	DATE OF CERTIFICATION	AGE	COMPLEXION	PLACE OF BIRTH	BOOK	PAGE
Littlefield, Sylvester H.	Sept. 11, 1849	23	dark	So. Kingston, R.I.	5	50
Littlefield, Theodore	Mar. 14, 1842	34	light	Kennebunkport, Me.	5	49
Lively, Richard	Oct. 14, 1846	32	black	Petersburg, Va.	5	49
Livermore, Braddy C.	Dec. 1, 1809	21	dark	Augusta, Me.	4	40
Livingston, James	June 18, 1833	23	black	Albany, N.Y.	5	48
Livsey, Milton	Oct. 10, 1862	19	dark	Providence, R.I.	6	12
Lloyd, Thomas	Apr. 1, 1850	19	light	Portsmouth, R.I.	5	50
Lobson, John	May 29, 1844	26	light	Newport, R.I.	5	49
Locke, Henry	1798-1799	Jan. 28, 1779		So. Kingston, R.I.	* -	--
Locke, Jeremiah	1798-1799	Sept. 4, 1780		So. Kingston, R.I.	-	--
Lockwood, Adam	Aug. 26, 1831	19	light	Warwick, R.I.	5	48
Lockwood, Benoni	Oct. 18, 1809	20	light	Warwick, R.I.	4	40
Lockwood, Benoni	June 4, 1811	22	light	Warwick, R.I.	4	40
Lockwood, Benoni, Jr.	Apr. 19, 1821	16	dark	Cranston, R.I.	4	41
Lockwood, Caleb	July 2, 1810	17	black	Warwick, R.I.	4	40
Lockwood, Charles M.	Dec. 5, 1849	22	dark	Warwick, R.I.	5	50
Lockwood, Nathaniel	Sept. 26, 1796	35	dark	Warwick, R.I.	1	3
Lockwood, Oliver	Aug. 15, 1817	19	light	Warwick, R.I.	4	40
Lodford, John	June 11, 1855	23	light	Troy, N.Y.	5	50
Lofty, Thomas J.	Apr. 7, 1851	18	light	No. Prov., R.I.	5	50
Logan, Benjamin	Apr. 16, 1797	18	light	Providence, R.I.	1	16
Logan, James	Oct. 20, 1858	39	fair	Providence, R.I.	6	12
Logan, William	Nov. 19, 1806	28	light	Providence, R.I.	4	40
Lomey, William	June 8, 1857	22	fair	Brooklyn, N.Y.	5	82
Long, George	Mar. 14, 1815	17	light	Nantucket, Ma.	4	40
Long, Pearl	Aug. -- 1864	16	light	Blue Hill, Me.	6	12
Longworth, George	Oct. 26, 1844	24	light	New York, N.Y.	5	26
Loper, Sylvester L.	Apr. 1, 1850	19	light	Greene, N.Y.	5	50
Lopez, Jacob	Apr. 13, 1816	15	dark	Providence, R.I.	4	40
Lopez, Samuel	Oct. 23, 1819	21	dark	Providence, R.I.	4	40
Lord, Geo. W.	Feb. 16, 1854	13	light	So. Berwick, Me.	5	50
Lord, Richard	May 8, 1826	19	light	Seekonk, Ma.	4	41
Lorimer, William	Oct. 20, 1849	15	light	Eastport, Me.	5	50
Loring, Cyrus	Dec. 11, 1810	19	light	Rehoboth, Ma.	4	40

*Newport, R. I.

NAME	DATE OF CERTIFICATION	AGE	COMPLEXION	PLACE OF BIRTH	BOOK	PAGE
Lothrop, Cyrus	Nov. 14, 1803	22	black	Canterbury, Conn.	2	43
Lothrop, Rodman	Feb. 24, 1810	19	yellowish	Canterbury, Conn.	4	40
Lothrop, William H.	June 20, 1822	17	light	Cranston, R.I.	4	41
Lott, Abraham	July 7, 1798	19	light	New York, N.Y.	2	11
Loud, Ebenezer	Dec. 15, 1809	16	dark	Weymouth, Ma.	4	40
Loud, Ebenezer	Nov. 7, 1810	18	dark	Weymouth, Ma.	4	40
Loud, Hiram	Dec. 23, 1823	23	light	Weymouth, Ma.	4	41
Loughlan, John Mc.	June 28, 1806	25	light	Phila., Pa.	3	57
Love, Arthur	Nov. 15, 1803	21	dark	Sterling, Conn.	2	43
Love, Arthur	May 20, 1803	20	dark	Sterling, Conn.	2	11
Love, James	June 23, 1806	29	brown	Coventry, R.I.	3	57
Loveland, Horace	Oct. 29, 1810	18	light	Glastonbury, Conn.	4	40
Lovell, Albert	Apr. 18, 1855	20	fair	Scituate, R.I.	5	50
Lovell, Alexander	Aug. 28, 1799	24	light	Scituate, R.I.	2	11
Lovett, Ezeck	May 6, 1801	22	dark	Cumberland, .R.I.	2	11
Lovett, Samuel	July 21, 1841	32	dark	Falmouth, Me.	5	48
Lovitt, Thomas	Oct. 10, 1797	20	dark	Cumberland, RiI.	1	16
Lovitt, William	Sept. 8, 1856	23	light	Boston, Ma.	5	82
Low, Benjamin	Mar. 29, 1805	21	dark	Providence, R.I.	3	56
Low, Charles H.	Sept. 10, 1822	15	light	Providence, R.I.	4	41
Low, John	Aug. 15, 1803	20	light	Warwick, R.I.	2	43
Low, John H.	July 21, 1815	15	light	Warwick, R.I.	4	40

[Low Papers: Deeds and correspondence of Anthony Low and his descendants, Samuel Joseph
Anthony and Joseph H. Low of Warwick 1725-1854.   Misc. Mss. L-95.

Lowe, Levi¸.	Aug. 5, 1837	22	light	Baltimore, Md.	5	48
Low, Nathaniel	Oct. 2, 1854	20	mulatto	New York, N.Y.	5	50
Low, Samuel	Dec. 12, 1797	26	dark	Warwick, R.I.	1	16
Low, Samuel, Jr.	Aug. 6, 1823	18	light	Providence, R.I.	4	41
Low, Thomas	Apr. 24, 1798	29	light	Somerset, Ma.	1&2*	16&11*
Lowd, John D.	Mar. 18, 1825	22	dark	Portsmouth, N.H.	4	41
Lowry, James	Sept. 15, 1841	40	light	Portsmouth, N.H.	5	49
Lucas, John	Mar. 29, 1844	17	light	New York, N.Y.	5	49
Lucas, John	Jan. 8, 1845	20	dark	Providence, R.I.	5	49

*Book 1, page 16; book 2, page 11.

REGISTER OF SEAMEN'S PROTECTION

NAME	DATE OF CERTIFICATION	AGE	COMPLEXION	PLACE OF BIRTH	BOOK	PA
Luckey, John	Mar. 25, 1801	36	black	Tinboo, Africa	2	1
Ludden, William A.	Aug. 14, 1837	19	light	So. Hampton, Ma.	5	4
*Ludlow, John	1798-1799	Apr. 1787		New York	* * -	-
Lum, Gibson	July 10, 1821	20	dark	Derby, Conn.	4	4
Lum, John	July 10, 1821	22	light	Derby, Conn.	4	4
Lunt, James	1798-1799	June 1, 1780		Stillwater, Ma.	* * -	-
Lunt, Stephen	Mar. 22, 1852	23	sandy	Baltimore, Md.	5	5
Luscomb, George	Nov. 26, 1849	20	light	Salem, Ma.	5	5
Luscomb, William	Dec. 21, 1825	17	light	Providence, R.I.	4	4
Luscombe, Robert	Mar. 17, 1809	26	light	Whitingham, Vt.	4	4
Lusk, George	Jan. 8, 1839	20	light	Cairo, N.Y.	5	4
Luther, Alading	July 3, 1822	18	light	Glocester, R.I.	4	4
Luther, Allen	Dec. 12, 1821	24	light	Warren, R.I.	-	-
Son of Frederick and Parmelea Luther. Birth certificate in Custom House Papers. March 7.						
Luther, Aroin	Mar. 21, 1815	22	dark	Glocester, R.I.	4	4
Luther, Benjamin	Apr. 22, 1809	16	light	Providence, R.I.	4	4
Luther, Benjamin T.	June 16, 1798	30	light	Newport, R.I.	2	1
Luther, Calvin	Nov. 14, 1801	18	light	Johnston, R.I.	2	1
Luther, Charles	Dec. 24, 1845	48	dark	Seekonk, Ma.	5	4
Luther, Dan'l W.	Mar. 5, 1849	36	light	Warren, R.I.	5	4
Luther, Eber C.	Mar. 1, 1849	39	fair	Somerset, Ma.	5	4
Luther, Edward	Aug. 21, 1840	34	dark	Somerset, Ma.	5	4
Luther, Edward	July 10, 1841	36	light	Somerset, Ma.	5	4
Luther, George	Mar. 5, 1849	32	light	Dighton, Ma.	5	4
Luther, George A.	Oct. 9, 1857	17	light	Providence, R.I.	6	1
Luther, George W.	June 14, 1826	15	light	Providence, R.I.	4	4
Luther, Henry	June 29, 1819	20	light	Providence, R.I.	4	4
Luther, Hezekiah E.	May 19, 1821	--	dark	Swansea, Ma.	-	-
Sworn statement of Jonathan W. Lindsey in the Custom House Papers. DOB: May 13, 1797						
Luther, James	Aug. 21, 1799	17	light	Swansea, Ma.	2	1
Luther, James	Apr. 17, 1810	17	brown	Swansea, Ma.	4	4
Luther, John	Dec. 16, 1797	22	light	Newport, R.I.	1	1
Luther, John H.	Oct. 2, 1805	14	dark	Swansea, Ma.	3	5
Luther, Joseph	1798-1799	Mar. 1, 1782		Freetown	* * -	-
Luther, Joseph S.	Aug. 21, 1845	17	dark	Warren, R.I.	5	4
Luther, Nathaniel	Oct. 17, 1803	20	light	Providence, R.I.	2	4
Luther, Nathaniel	Sept. 12, 1796	22	light	Providence, R.I.	1	1
Luther, Pearce	Aug. 23, 1805	23	light	Swansea, Ma.	3	5

*Of Block Island.   **Newport, R. I.

NAME	DATE OF CERTIFICATION	AGE	COMPLEXION	PLACE OF BIRTH	BOOK	PAGE
Luther, Stephen	Mar. 30, 1806	17	light	Johnston, R.I.	3	57
Luther, Thomas	May 29, 1815	19	light	Johnston, R.I.	4	40
Luther, Thomas, Jr.	June 19, 1807	21	brown	Providence, R.I.	4	40
Luther, William	Dec. 2, 1805	18	dark	Swansea, Ma.	3	57
Luzmore, Jonathan	Dec. 5, 1797	39	dark	Charleston, N.H.	1	16
Lymas, Benjamin	Oct. 27, 1801	18	black	E. Greenwich, R.I.	2	11
Lynch, Thomas	Nov. 22, 1797	26	dark	Hillsborough, N.H.	1	16
Lynch, William [Linch]	Sept. 22, 1804	30	dark	Marblehead, Ma.	3	21
Lynch, William .	May 21, 1805	31	dark	Marblehead, Ma.	3	56
Lynch, William	Feb. 10, 1835	35	light	Snow Hill, Md.	5	48
Lyndon, Henry D.	Dec. 28, 1811	18	light	Providence, R.I.	4	40
Lynes, William	Oct. 7, 1841	20	copper	Eastport, Me.	5	49
Lyon, Albert	July 8, 1845	17	dark	Foster, R.I.	5	49
Lyon, Amos	Oct. 12, 1804	31	light	Woodstock, Conn.	3	21
Lyon, Charles	Sept. 3, 1830	21	light	Lancaster [Worcester Co.] Ma.	5	48
Lyons, Dennis	Feb. 24, 1852	24	dark	Barnstable, Ma.	5	50
Lyon, Elisha	June 7, 1799	26	light	Woodstock, Conn.	2	11
Lyons, James	May 7, 1832	17	light	Yarmouth, Ma.	5	48
Lyons, John	Mar. 25, 1835	18	light	Baltimore, Md.	5	48
Lyons, John	Aug. 7, 1854	21	light	New York, N.Y.	5	50
Lyons, John	July 11, 1856	22	dark	Lisbon, N.H.	5	82
Lyons, Morris	Mar. 29, 1850	27	light	New York, N.Y.	5	50
Lyons, William	Aug. 22, 1845	27	dark	Phila., Pa.	5	49
McAlester, DeWitt	Aug. 1, 1854	18	fair	Lincolnville, Me.	5	5
McArthur, Neil	Aug. 7, 1846	20	fair	Brooklyn, N.Y.	5	54
McCall, Daniel	1798-1799	Oct. 27, 1769		Lebanon, Conn.	* _	--
McCallester, John	Apr. 24, 1850	27	light	Baltimore, Md.	5	55
McCartney, Sam'l	May 26, 1853	34	light	No. Prov., R.I.	5	5
McCarty, James	Feb. 25, 1861	18	dark	Nantucket, Ma.	6	13
McCarty, John	Apr. 13, 1853	46	dark	Boston, Ma.	5	5
McCarty, John	Apr. 4, 1855	23	dark	Stonington, Conn.	5	5
McCauley, William	Oct. 31, 1834	21	light	New York, N.Y.	5	51
McClain, Chadwick	Oct. 12, 1820	18	light	Falmouth, Ma.	4	46
McClain, Nathan	Oct. 12, 1820	16	light	Falmouth, Ma.	4	46
McClaran, Peter	Sept. 27, 1849	61	light	Boston, Ma.	5	55
McClellan, James	May 9, 1807	16	light	Smithfield, R.I.	4	44
McClellan, Kitt	June 14, 1804	22	black	Woodstock, Conn.	3	23

*Newport, R. I.

NAME	DATE OF CERTIFICATION	AGE	COMPLEXION	PLACE OF BIRTH	BOOK	PAGE
McClellan, Kitt	Aug. 19, 1806	25	black	Woodstock, Conn.	3	76
McClellan, Simon	Oct. 4, 1800	24	black	Woodstock, Conn.	2	30
McClemens, Alexander	June 22, 1836	25	black	Phila., Pa.	5	52
McCoach, William	Dec. 5, 1849	21	dark	Charlton, Ma.	5	55
McColly, George	Oct. 11, 1813	18	dark	Phila., Pa.	4	45
McCoon, James	June 20, 1844	21	dark	Tiverton, R.I.	5	53
McCormick, William	Sept. 4, 1855	19	fair	New York, N.Y.	5	5
McCoy, Thomas	Apr. 4, 1856	25	dark	Williamsport, Pa.	5	5
McCrea, Robert	Apr. 13, 1853	23	light	Boston, Ma.	5	5
McCullum, Peter	Sept. 21, 1846	20	light	Brookhaven, N.Y.	5	54
McCune, William	Dec. 5, 1849	22	light	Providence, R.I.	5	55
McCurdy, Richard	Nov. 13, 1797	24	dark	Plainfield, Conn.	1	17
McCusker, James	Apr. 24, 1856	20	fair	Providence, R.I.	5	90
McDaniel, John	June 10, 1811	17	light	Cranston, R.I.	4	45
McDermot, James	Mar. 17, 1852	23	light	New York, N.Y.	5	5
McDine, John	June 10, 1867	33	dark	New York, N.Y.	6	13
McDonald, Abraham I.	May 8, 1854	22	fair	Clayton, N.Y.	5	5
McDonald, Bartlett	Dec. 4, 1841	51	light	Portland, Me.	5	53
McDonald, David	Oct. 1, 1849	21	light	Cranston, R.I.	5	55
McDonald, Harley	Jan. 15, 1849 (1/1?)	23	light	Scituate, R.I.	5	54
McDonald, James	Apr. 6, 1797	22	light	Voluntown, Conn.	1	9
McDonald, Jeremiah	Oct. 24, 1855	49	dark	Johnston, R.I.	5	5
McDonald, John	July 20, 1841	20	light	Richfield, Conn.	5	52
McDonald, Peter	Mar. 15, 1845	19	light	Calais, Me.	5	53
*McDonall, James	Nov. 3, 1848	18	dark	Staten Island, N.J.	5	54
McFoy, Daniel	May 31, 1805	23	dark	Providence, R.I.	3	64
McFoy, Edward Melony	Nov. 30, 1796	17	light	Providence, R.I.	1	11
MacFoy, John	Aug. 26, 1801	17	light	Providence, R.I.	2	30
McFoy, John	Sept. 26, 1804	20	light	Providence, R.I.	3	23
[McFoy]MacFoy, Maloney John	Sept. 14, 1799	15	light	Providence, R.I.	2	12
McGee, George	Oct. 9, 1843	22	dark	Dighton, Ma.	5	53
McGee, William	Apr. 14, 1856	21	light	New York, N.Y.	5	90
McGilvery, Duncan	Dec. 13, 1850	19	light	Bristol, Me.	5	55
McGinney, James	Aug. 1, 1842	17	light	Boston, Ma.	5	53
McGlauson, Joseph	July 6, 1838	30	dark	Somerset, Ma.	5	52
McGrath, John	Sept. 6, 1856	22	light	Boston, Ma.	5	90

*see page 168a

NAME	DATE OF CERTIFICATION	AGE	COMPLEXION	PLACE OF BIRTH	BOOK	PAGE
McDonnough, Wm.	Aug. 19, 1852	19	light	Newport, R.I.	5	5
McDougall, Thomas	Apr. 1, 1805	21	light	Bristol, R.I.	3	8
McDormand, John M.	March 19, 1851	20	light	Eastport, Me.	5	55
McDounough, John	Nov. 20, 1851	20	light	Roxbury, Mass.	5	55
McDuff, Thomas	Dec. 27, 1854	23	light	Boston, Mass.	5	5
Mace, Daniel J.	June 7, 1839	33	light	Newburyport, Mass.	5	52
Mace, Eliphalet	Nov. 21, 1805	21	light	Pomfret, Conn.	3	75
McFarland, Frederick W.	July 19, 1845	15	dark	Ashfield, Mass.	5	53
McFarland, John	Aug 5, 1864	24	light	Coventry, R. I.	6	13
McFarland, Thomas	May 25, 1853	21	light	Providence, R. I.	5	5
McFoy, Daniel [Mack Foy]	July 17, 1798	15	light	Providence, R. I.	2	12
McFoy, Daniel	May 2, 1799	17	light	Providence, R. I.	2	12

REGISTER OF SEAMEN'S PROTECTION

NAME	DATE OF CERTIFICATION	AGE	COMPLEXION	PLACE OF BIRTH	BOOK	PAGE
McGregor, James	Mar. 27, 1835	21	dark	Newburyport, Ma.	5	52
McIntire, Joseph	Feb. 24, 1849	17	light	No. Providence, R.I.	5	54
McIntosh, Christ'r	Oct. 4, 1852	21	light	Belfast, Me.	5	5
McIntosh, Robert	Dec. 27, 1854	23	light	Boston, Ma.	5	5
McIsaacs, Angus	Feb. 29, 1848	20	light	Portsmouth, N.H.	5	54
McKay, Charles B.	July 15, 1835	15	light	Providence, R.I.	5	52
MacKay, George F.	Feb. 24, 1819	17	light	Providence, R.I.	4	45
McKay, William	Apr. 22, 1800	22	light	Phila., Pa.	2	12
McKay, William W.	Feb. 23, 1859	21	dark	Salem, Ma.	6	13
McKee, John	Apr. 3, 1861	28	dark	Fall River, Ma.	6	13
McKeinew, Patrick	July 27, 1857	21	light	Providence, R.I.	6	13
McKenna, John	May 3, 1860	22	fair	Providence, R.I.	6	13
McKenzie, Thomas	1798-1799	July 26, 1784		---------	-	--
Mary Gravell swears the above to be true.						
McKenzie, John	Oct. 19, 1858	22	fair	New York, N.Y.	6	13
McKenzie, John	May 24, 1860	20	fair	Bangor, Me.	6	13
McKewan, Wm.	Nov. 28, 1851	21	light	New York, N.Y.	5	55
McKibbin, George	Oct. 27, 1834	24	light	Phila., Pa.	5	51
McKilroy, Cornelius	May 1, 1810	19	light	Canterbury, N.Y.	4	44
McKinny, Loring	Dec. 18, 1848	41	dark	Bath, Me.	5	54
McLane, Charles A.	Oct. 29, 1833	13	light	Providence, R.I.	5	51
McLane, Horace A.	Sept. 1, 1852	21	dark	Providence, R.I.	5	5
McLane, John	Apr. 6, 1810	21	light	Providence, R.I.	4	44
McLane, John	Jan. 13, 1852	23	dark	Baltimore, Md.	5	55
McLane, William D.	May 2, 1839	14	light	Providence, R.I.	5	52
McLane, William D.	Oct. 16, 1841	16	light	Providence, R.I.	5	53
McLaughlin, Timothy	May 6, 1801	28	dark	Hudson, N.Y.	2	30
McLeduff, Thomas	Jan. 23, 1849	19	light	Boston, Ma.	5	54
McLerren, Thomas	May 12, 1856	21	light	Johnston, R.I.	5	90
McLoughlan, John	June 28, 1806	25	light	Phila., Pa.	3	57
McMahon, James	Apr. 20, 1860	21	dark	Providence, R.I.	6	13
McMillen, William	Dec. 13, 1847	34	light	New York, N.Y.	5	54
McNabb, Owen	May 19, 1857	21	dark	Lowell, Ma.	5	90
McNamara, Ephraim	Sept. 1, 1809	20	light	Northbridge, Ma.	4	44

NAME	DATE OF CERTIFICATION	AGE	COMPLEXION	PLACE OF BIRTH	BOOK	PAGE
[McNamara]MacNemara, Moses	Aug. 9, 1799	20	light	Smithfield, R.I.	2	12
McNatt, Robert	July 24, 1845	21	dark	Eastport, Me.	5	53
McNeal, Henry	Oct. 14, 1842	25	light	Providence, R.I.	5	53
McNeal, Hopestill P.	Oct. 2, 1830	17	light	Providence, R.I.	5	51
McNeal, William	Mar. 3, 1835	25	light	Hudson, N.Y.	5	52
McNot, John	Dec. 23, 1803	22	dark	BelAir, Md.	2	16
McPherson, Henry	Oct. 18, 1841	24	black	Leonardtown, Md.	5	53
McQuade, James	May 31, 1859	15	light	Providence, R.I.	6	13
McQuade, Michael	May 25, 1858	22	dark	Cranston, R.I.	6	13
McQuilton, John	Apr. 24, 1856	25	light	Warren, R.I.	5	90
Macklin, Billy	Nov. 1, 1809	14	yellow	Raleigh, N.C.	4	44
Macklin, Peter	Mar. 14, 1801	30	light	Providence, R.I.	2	30
Macomber, Ebenezer, Jr.	Mar. 29, 1815	17	light	Providence, R.I.	4	45
*Macomber, George	Apr. 15, 1800	14	dark	Providence, R.I.	2	12
*Macamber, George	Sept. 15, 1803	17	dark	Providence, R.I.	2	42
*Macumber, George	June 25, 1805	19	dark	Providence, R.I.	3	64
Macomber, James	July 10, 1850	22	light	Providence, R.I.	5	55
Macomber, Jesse	1798-1799	May 13, 1779		Tiverton, R.I.	*** -	--
Macomber, Samuel	July 14, 1806	16	light	Providence, R.I.	3	76
Macomber, Samuel C.	Mar. 22, 1841	27	light	Rehoboth, Ma.	5	52
Macomber, Seth	Sept. 18, 1811	20	dark	Taunton, Ma.	4	45
Macomber, Stephen	July 17, 1855	19	fair	Calais, Me.	5	5
Madden, John	Sept. 3, 1832	18	dark	Providence, R.I.	5	51
Maddan, William	June 5, 1839	22	dark	Cranston, R.I.	5	52
Madison, Alexander	Mar. 3, 1820	20	light	Newport, R.I.	4	45
Madison, Alexander	July 15, 1854	22	dark	Taunton, Ma.	5	5
Magee, Charles	Feb. 21, 1854	28	dark	New York, N.Y.	5	5
Magee, James	July 16, 1803	20	dark	Boston, Ma.	2	42
Magee, Peter	June 14, 1805	19	dark	Cumberland, R.I.	3	64
Magers, William	Oct. 1, 1806	22	black	New London, Conn.	3&4**	76&44*
Maginnis, Edward	Sept. 26, 1850	20	dark	Phila., Pa.	5	55

*Not sure which spelling of name is right.
**Book 3, page 76; book 4, page 44.
***Newport, R. I.

NAME	DATE OF CERTIFICATION	AGE	COMPLEXION	PLACE OF BIRTH	BOOK	PAG
Magoon, William	Dec. 14, 1847	24	light	Calais, Me.	5	54
Maguire, Eusebin	Nov. 19, 1796	18	light	Bucks Co., Pa.	1	17
Maguire, Francis	Oct. 27, 1845	20	light	Providence, R.I.	5	54
Mahaffey, James	Feb. 26, 1852	33	dark	Richmond Co., N.Y.	5	55
Mahan, John	Dec. 21, 1843	17	light	Cazenoria, N.Y.	5	53
Mahon, Francis	Mar. 13, 1856	20	dark	New Orleans, La.	5	5
Mahon, Michael	Mar. 13, 1856	20	dark	New Orleans, La.	5	5
Mahony, Cornelius	Oct. 27, 1810	21	light	Uxbridge, Ma.	4	44
Mahony, Cornelius, Jr.	Aug. 19, 1845	17	fair	Providence, R.I.	5	53
Mahoney, Timothy	Mar. 7, 1801	18	light	Spencer, Ma.	2	30
Mahuy, John	Dec. 8, 1797	22	black	Providence, R.I.	1	17
Mailllard, Henry	Nov. 28, 1834	24	dark	Albany, N.Y.	5	51
Maine, Asahel Jarvis	Nov. 17, 1819	15	light	Hartford, Conn.	4	45
Maines, Owen	Aug. 17, 1855	19	fair	Providence, R.I.	5	5
Major, John	Apr. 2, 1852	23	light	Poughkeepsie, N.Y.	5	5
Makin, John	June 15, 1853	24	florid	New York, N.Y.	5	5
Malbone, Amos	Dec. 21, 1842	23	black	Brooklyn, Conn.	5	53
Malbone, Evan	May 1, 1799	17	light	Pomfret, Conn.	2	12
Malbone, Evan, Jr.	Nov. 17, 1803	22	dark	Pomfret, Conn.	2	42
Malbone, Frances	------	--		May 12, 1759 Newport, R.I.	*-	--
Malbone, Henry	1798-1799			Aug. 19, 1783 Newport, R.I.	*-	--
Malbone, Henry	Jan. 5, 1853	16	light	Eastport, Me.	5	5
Malbone, Othello	Nov. 7, 1809	26	black	Brookline, Conn.	4	44
Mallett, James Fenner	Feb. 10, 1843	20	light	Providence, R.I.	5	53
Mallet, Joseph	Nov. 19, 1839	34	dark	New Orleans, La.	5	52
Mallory, Nathaniel	Dec. 26, 1845	20	light	Bridgeport, Conn.	5	54
Malony, John	Dec. 13, 1853	17	light	Hudson, N.Y.	5	5
Manchester, Albert	Apr. 23, 1857	47	light	Bristol, R.I.	5	90
Manchester, Alexander	Aug. 5, 1840	16	light	Tiverton, R.I.	5	52
Manchester, Benjamin	1798-1799			Sept. 11, 1785 Tiverton, R.I.	*-	--
Manchester, Benjamin B.	Dec. 21, 1844	14	light	Westport, Ma.	5	53
Manchester, Cyrus B.	Mar. 29, 1817	15	dark	Providence, R.I.	4	45
Manchester, Ellery	Feb. 21, 1824	21	light	Tiverton, R.I.	4	46
Manchester, Henry	Apr. 28, 1800	13	dark	Cranston, R.I.	2	12
Manchester, Ira	July 23, 1803	23	light	Cranston, R.I.	2	42

*Newport, R. I.

NAME	DATE OF CERTIFICATION	AGE	COMPLEXION	PLACE OF BIRTH	BOOK	PAGE
Manchester, Jesse	Nov. 24, 1827	23	light	Springfield, Ma.	4	46
Manchester, John	Aug. 30, 1796	17	light	Cranston, R.I.	1	2
Manchester, John	Apr. 24, 1798	18	dark	Cranston, R.I.	1&2*	17&12*
Manchester, John	Mar. 21, 1806	54	dark	Providence, R.I.	3	75
Manchester, John	July 22, 1836	27	light	Tiverton, R.I.	5	52
Manchester, Knight	Dec. 25, 1800	18	light	Cranston, R.I.	2	30
Manchester, Philip	1798-1799		Jan. 9, 1773	Little Compton	** -	--

Rebecca Zebedee swears the above to be true.

NAME	DATE OF CERTIFICATION	AGE	COMPLEXION	PLACE OF BIRTH	BOOK	PAGE
Manchester, Philip	1798-1799		Jan. 3, 1774 or 1	Tiverton, R.I.	** -	--

Manchester, Saloma Ann m. Ebeneser Young Bassen Mar. 9, 1826 both of this place (Pawtucket) Rev. Benedict Record.

NAME	DATE OF CERTIFICATION	AGE	COMPLEXION	PLACE OF BIRTH	BOOK	PAGE
Manchester, Samuel	1798-1799		Mar. 25, 1775	Tiverton, R.I.	** -	--
Manchester, Samuel S.	Feb. 11, 1841	28	dark	Tiverton, R.I.	5	52
Manchester, Simeon	July 14, 1819	22	light	Bristol, R.I.	4	45
Manchester, Simon	1798-1799		Dec. 28, 1782	Little Compton, R.I.	** -	--

Philip Manchester swears the above to be true.

NAME	DATE OF CERTIFICATION	AGE	COMPLEXION	PLACE OF BIRTH	BOOK	PAGE
Manchester, Stephen	Oct. 12, 1822	29	light	Scituate, R.I.	4	46
Manchester, William	-----		May 29, 1778	Tiverton, R.I.	** -	--

Wm. Manchester of Tiverton, R.I. swears the above to be true.

NAME	DATE OF CERTIFICATION	AGE	COMPLEXION	PLACE OF BIRTH	BOOK	PAGE
Manchester, William C.	Dec. 22, 1825	31	light	Tiverton, R.I.	4	46
Manett, Robert	June 18, 1845	28	dark	Salem, Ma.	5	53
Mange, Henry	May 3, 1843	32	light	Portland, Me.	5	53
Manimon, James F.	Aug. 27, 1853	20	light	Wareham, Ma.	5	5
Manley, James	Apr. 18, 1806	26	light	Baltimore, Md.	3	76
Man, Barzilla	May 4, 1810	22	yellow	No. Prov., R.I.	4	44
Mann, Daniel	Nov. 12, 1796	24	light	Providence, R.I.	1	17&5
Man, Daniel	Sept. 17, 1796	18	light	Cambridge, Ma.	1	3
Mann, Geo. N.	Feb. 19, 1857	24	fair	Blackstone, Ma.	5	90
Mann, George N.	Jan. 4, 1865	33	light	Blackstone, Ma.	6	13
Man, Sherman S.	Dec. 10, 1841	51	black	Litchfield, Conn.	5	53
Mann, William	May 7, 1806	23	light	Dedham, Ma.	3	76
Manning, John	Aug. 2, 1854	28	dark	New York, N.Y.	5	5
Manning, John	July 6, 1861	25	dark	Providence, R.I.	6	13
Mannington, Isaac	Nov. 29, 1848	20	fair	Warren, R.I.	5	54
Mansfield, Wm.	Dec. 4, 1851	22	light	Smithfield, R.I.	5	55
Manton, Benj. D.	Jan. 9, 1849	19	fair	Providence, R.I.	5	54
Manton, Joseph	Oct. 13, 1807	24	light	Johnston, R.I.	4	44
Manton, Joseph R.	Dec. 24, 1844	23	light	Providence, R.I.	5	53
Manton, Shadrach	Oct. 13, 1807	18	light	Johnston, R.I.	4	44

*Book 1, page 17; book 2, page 12.   **Newport, R. I.

NAME	DATE OF CERTIFICATION	AGE	COMPLEXION	PLACE OF BIRTH	BOOK	PAG
Manton, William	Aug. 2, 1799	19	light	Johnston, R.I.	2	12
Manuel, John	June 7, 1849	26	yellow	New York , N.Y.	5	55
Manuel, Marcus	Feb. 24, 1852	35	dark	New Orleans, La.	5	55
Marbel, Andrew F.	Dec. 15, 1830	16	dark	Providence, R.I.	5	51
Marble, Bradford E.	Nov. 17, 1849	19	light	Somerset, Ma.	5	55
Marble, David	1798-1799		Jan. 6, 1779	Somerset, Ma.	* -	--
Jonathan Marble of Newport swears the above to be true.						
Marble, George R., Jr.	Aug. 11, 1840	17	dark	Warren, R.I.	5	52
Marble, James	June 5, 1835	15	dark	Warwick, R.I.	5	52
March, Dick	Aug. 9, 1803	26	black	Cumberland, R.I.	2	42
Marchant, Abraham	Mar. 27, 1810	45	black	Charlestown, R.I.	4	44
Marchant, Nathaniel N.	Mar. 27, 1822	22	light	Yarmouth, Ma.	4	46
Marchant, Samuel	Feb. 27, 1834	26	light	Yarmouth, Ma.	5	51
Marchant, Sherburn, Jr.	Nov. 12, 1833	21	light	Yarmouth, Ma.	5	51
Mardenbrough, Jack	Dec. 4, 1805	32	black	Baltimore, Md.	3	75
Mark, Edward	Nov. 21, 1803	34	light	Lynn, Ma.	2	16
Markmon, Joseph	1798-1799		Sept. 20, 1777	Bristol, R.I.	* -	--
Mars, Michael	Nov. 7, 1849	22	light	Boston, Ma.	5	55
Marschalk, Edwin	Nov. 25, 1822	20	light	New York, N.Y.	4	46
Marsh, John Cahoone	Mar. 22, 1821	14	dark	Newport, R.I.	* -	--
Sworn statement of Josias Lawton of Newport in Custom House Papers. 1807.						
Marsh, Richard	Jan. 2, 1800	23	black	Cumberland, R.I.	2	12
Marsh, William	Mar. 5, 1805	22	light	Baltimore, Md.	3	24
Marshall, Charles	June 2, 1838	21	light	Providence, R.I.	5	52
Marshall, Charles R.	Dec. 22, 1849	22	light	Islesboro, Me.	5	55
Marshall, Christopher	Oct. 16, 1805	26	light	Savannah, Ga.	3	64
Marshall, Edwin	Sept. 30, 1864	23	dark	Sag Habor, N.Y.	6	13
Marshall, Elot	Oct. 12, 1803	18	light	Providence, R.I.	2	42
Marshall[Marchall], Eliot	Sept. 18, 1805	19	light	Providence, R.I.	3	64
Marshall, Elliott	June 6, 1818	32	light	Providence, R.I.	4	45
Marshall, Francis	July 30, 1805	19	light	Albany, N.Y.	3	64
Marshall, George	Dec. 30, 1850	27	light	Providence, R.I.	5	55
Marshall, Jesse	Nov. 13, 1849	25	light	No. Prov., R.I.	5	55
Marshall, John	1798-1799		Aug. 17, 1783	Newport, R.I.	* -	--
Green Marshall swears the above to be true.						
Marshall, Peter	1798-1799		May 14, 1781	Newport, R.I.	* -	--

*Newport, R. I.

NAME	DATE OF CERTIFICATION	AGE	COMPLEXION	PLACE OF BIRTH	BOOK	PAGE
Marshall, Reuben	Dec. 16, 1800	27	light	Northampton, Ma.	2	30
Marshall, Robert	July 10, 1851	21	light	Providence, R.I.	5	55
Marshall, Thomas P.	Aug. 13, 1849	27	light	Vassalboro, Me.	5	55
Marshall, William	Mar. 25, 1835	22	dark	New York, N.Y.	5	52
Marshall, William	Aug. 22, 1851	32	dark	New Orleans, La.	5	55
Marshall, Wm. H.	Nov. 10, 1848	23	light	Mendon, Ma.	5	54
Martin, Abraham	Aug. 28, 1804	40	black	Jamestown, R.I.	3	23
Martin, Calvin	Jan. 17, 1801	31	light	Barrington, R.I.	2	30
Martin, Cato	Nov. 28, 1796	17	black	Dutchess Co., N.Y.	1	17
Martin, Charles	Apr. 26, 1822	19	ruddy	Providence, R.I.	4	46
Martin, Charles B.	Dec. 2, 1841	13	light	Providence, R.I.	5	53
Martin, Edward	Dec. 15, 1798	26	black	New York, N.Y.	2	12
Martin, Edward D.	Mar. 9, 1815	16	light	Providence, R.I.	4	45
Martin, Edward J.	Aug. 15, 1865	40	light	New Haven, Conn.	6	13
Martin, Ephraim	Aug. 13, 1800	17	dark	Rehoboth, Ma.	2	30
Martin, Esek H.	Aug. 17, 1810	14	light	Troy, N.Y.	4	44
Martin, Esek Hopkins	Dec. 11, 1848	52	light	Troy, N.Y.	5	54
Martin, Francis	Aug. 20, 1853	27	light	Warren, R.I.	5	5
Martin, Francis	Feb. 26, 1856	27	dark	Boston, Ma.	5	5
Martin, Francis T.	July 23, 1841	23	light	Providence, R.I.	5	52
Martin, Frank	July 1, 1811	25	black	Southington, Conn.	4	44
Martin, Henry	Oct. 11, 1831	23	light	Norfolk, Va.	5	51
Martin, Hezekiah	Nov. 7, 1838	17	dark	Rehoboth, Ma.	5	52
Martin, James	Dec. 14, 1797	21	dark	Providence, R.I.	1	17
Maritn, James	Oct. 1, 1804	25	light	Newport, R.I.	3	24
Martin, James B.	Aug. 27, 1838	17	dark	Eastport, Me.	5	52
Martin, Jeremiah	May 15, 1800	27	light	Providence, R.I.	2	30
Martin, Jeremiah, Jr.	June 30, 1821	20	light	Providence, R.I.	4	46
Martin, John	1798-1799	July 5, 1780		Swansey	* -	--
Martin, John	June 19, 1801	19	dark	New York, N.Y.	2	30
Martin, John	July 16, 1834	27	dark	New London, Conn.	5	51
Martin, John	Dec. 1, 1848	30	dark	New York, N.Y.	5	54
Martin, John R.	Dec. 21, 1818	15	light	Rehoboth, Ma. ".I.	4	45
Martin, John W.	June 12, 1849	21	light	New York, N.Y.	5	55
Martin, Jonathan	Dec. 25, 1820 m. Nancy Claflin of Swansay and Milleboro but now residing here (Pawtucket) Rev. Benedict Record.					
Martin, Joseph	June 20, 1797	17	dark	Providence, R.I.	1	17

*Newport, R. I.

NAME	DATE OF CERTIFICATION	AGE	COMPLEXION	PLACE OF BIRTH	BOOK	PAGE
Martin, Joseph	Mar. 23, 1816	19	dark	Seekonk, Ma.	4	45
Martin, Josiah	Oct. 29, 1821	23	light	Barrington, R.I.	4	46
Martin, Luther	May 21, 1800	18	light	Barrington, R.I.	2	30
Martin, Luther	Nov. 16, 1829	18	light	Barrington, R.I.	5	51
Martin, Manuel	Feb. 25, 1836	24	dark	-- Portugal	5	5
Martin, Peter	Oct. 24, 1842	30	light	Nantucket, Ma.	5	53
Martin, Peter	Mar. 30, 1857	23	fair	New Orleans, La.	5	90
Martin, Robert H.	Apr. 27, 1846	44	fair	Newark, N.J.	5	54
Martins, Robert H.	Sept. 23, 1847	42	light	New York, N.Y.	5	54
Martin, Samuel B.	May 31, 1806	18	light	Providence, R.I.	3	76
Martin, Samuel B.	May 29, 1807	19	light	Providence, R.I..	4	44
Martin, Sylvanus Perry	July 27, 1799	24	light	Rehoboth, Ma.	2	12
Martin, Thomas	Mar. 25, 1853	30	dark	Otswego, N.Y.	5	5
Martin, Welcome C.	Dec. 4, 1838	31	dark	Swansey, Ma.	5	52
Martin, William	Mar. 27, 1810	15	dark	Rehoboth, Ma.	4	44
Martin, William	Nov. 17, 1818	21	light	Salem, Ma.	4	45
Martin, William	Nov. 4, 1835	17	light	Baltimore, Md.	5	52
Martin, William H.	Oct. 15, 1830	27	light	Providence, R.I.	5	51
Martin, William P.	Oct. 8, 1829	14	light	Providence, R.I.	5	51
Martinborough, Franeses	Feb. 27, 1804	28	yellow*	Phila., Pa.	3	23
Martinear, Henry	Mar. 24, 1835	26	light	Baltimore, Md.	5	52
Martinez, Ambrosia	Jan. 7, 1853	29	dark	-----Spain	5	5
Marvel, Packer	Aug. 20, 1847	31	dark	Milton, Del.	5	54
Marvil, William	Apr. 9, 1834	19	light	Warwick, R.I.	5	51
Marvin, Daniel	Nov. 11, 1852	21	light	Brookhaven near Brooklyn, N.Y.	5	5
Maservey, Levi	June 24, 1863	14	light	St. George, Me.	6	13
Mashar, Joseph H.	Oct. 8, 1847	23	dark	New Orleans, La.	5	54
Mason, Aaron	Oct. 20, 1804	12	dark	Providence, R.I.	3	24
Mason, Aaron	Oct. 10, 1812	20	dark	Providence, R.I.	4	45
Mason, Alexander	Nov. 9, 1797	17	dark	Swansey, Ma.	1	17
Mason, Ceasar	Dec. 17, 1799	30	black	Groton, Conn.	2	12
Mason, Daniel	Nov. 5, 1805	27	dark	Swansea, Ma.	3	75
Mason, Daniel	Jan. 16, 1807	16	light	Newport, R.I.	4	44

*mulatto

REGISTER OF SEAMEN'S PROTECTION

NAME	DATE OF CERTIFICATION	AGE	COMPLEXION	PLACE OF BIRTH	BOOK	PAGE
Mason, Edward	Nov. 5, 1805	15	light	Sawansea, Ma.	3	75
Mason, George	Nov. 15, 1806	17	yellow	Millington, Conn.	4	44
Mason, George W.	Sept. 13, 1823	23	light	Providence, R.I.	4	46
Mason, Homer	Dec. 19, 1822	19	light	Attleboro, Ma.	4	46
Mason, Isaac	Dec. 29, 1817	23	light	Hartford, Conn.	4	45
Mason, Israel	May 10, 1802	17	light	Swansea, Ma.	2	30
Mason, James	July 23, 1804	21	light	Grafton, N.H.	3	23
Mason, James B.	July 19, 1820	18	light	Providence, R.I.	4	46
Mason, John A.	July 1, 1829	24	light	No. Prov., R.I.	5	51
Mason, Joseph M.	Mar. 28, 1846	15	dark	Swansea, Ma.	5	54
Mason, May D.	Aug. 10, 1812	25	light	Swansea, Ma.	4	45
Mason, Miller	Apr. 30, 1835	22	light	Rehoboth, Ma.	5	52
Mason, Obadiah	Jan. 5, 1830	16	light	Providence, R.I.	5	51
Mason, Pardon	Dec. 4, 1848	18	light	No. Prov., R.I.	5	54
Mason, Pardon	Sept. 2, 1856	26	light	No. Prov., R.I.	5	90
Mason, Richard	Nov. 11, 1803	38	black	Baltimore, Md.	2	42
Mason, Richard	Apr. 2, 1841	53	dark	Flatbush L.I., N.Y.	5	52
Mason, Roderick	Mar. 23, 1801	19	dark	Swansea, Ma.	2	30
Mason, Samuel P.	Mar. 6, 1815	19	light	Cranston, R.I.	4	45
Mason, William	Dec. 7, 1804	20	dark	Boston, Ma.	3	24
Mason, William	Sept. 18, 1805	21	light	Boston, Ma.	3	64
Mason, William	June 18, 1842	45	light	New York, N.Y.	5	53
Mason, William B.	Dec. 24, 1818	19	brown	Providence, R.I.	4	45
Mason, William C.	Sept. 11, 1815	19	light	Seekonk, Ma.	4	45
Mason, William Hail	Dec. 27, 1800	22	light	Thompson, Conn.	2	30
Masury, Josep S.	Nov. 2, 1803	15	light	Providence, R.I.	2	42
Masury, Samuel	Dec. 28, 1815	20	brown	Providence, R.I.	4	45
Mathews, Benajah	Feb. 21, 1801	24	light	Rehoboth, Ma.	2	30
Mathews, Caleb Medbury	Nov. 2, 1797	51	light	Rehoboth, Ma.	1	17
Mathews, Edward B.	Dec. 16, 1844	21	light	Providence, R.I.	5	53
Mathews, Joseph	June 22, 1804	20	light	Rehoboth, Ma.	3	32
Mathews, Joseph	Nov. 29, 1806	23	light	Rehoboth, Ma.	4	44
Mathews, Michal	Nov. 14, 1803	40	dark	Boston, Ma.	2	42
Mathews, Michael	May 10, 1864	23	light	New York, N.Y.	6	13
Mathews, William D.	Jan. 22, 1847	34	black	Laurel, Del.	5	54
Mathews, William	May 12, 1845	24	dark	Staten Island, N.Y.	5	53
Mathewson, Alfred	Apr. 24, 1839	32	light	W. Greenwich, R.I.	5	52

REGISTER OF SEAMEN'S PROTECTION

NAME	DATE OF CERTIFICATION	AGE	COMPLEXION	PLACE OF BIRTH	BOOK	PAGE
Mathewson, Benjamin E.	Oct. 12, 1844	17	dark	Coventry, R.I.	5	53
Mathewson, Daniel	Feb. 26, 1831	18	light	Scituate, R.I.	5	51
Mathewson, Daniel	Apr. 7, 1837	18	light	Johnston, R.I.	5	52
Mathewson, Daniel T.	Nov. 28, 1849	20	light	Glocester, R.I.	5	55
Mathewson, Ebenezer	Oct. 18, 1820	22	light	Barrington, R.I.	4	46
Mathewson, Ezra J.	May 22, 1855	21	dark	Killingly, Conn.	5	5
Mathewson, George	Sept. 20, 1831	15	light	Cranston, R.I.	5	51
Mathewson, Henry	Nov. 5, 1796	19	dark	Warwick, R.I.	1	17&
Mathewson, Henry B.	Mar. 17, 1851	19	light	Smithfield, R.I.	5	55
Mathewson, Hiram	Dec. 6, 1849	39	light	W. Greenwich, R.I.	5	55
Mathewson, James	Nov. 30, 1841	19	dark	Warren, R.I.	5	53
Mathewson, John	Jan. 10, 1834	26	light	Portland, Me.	5	51
Mathewson, Jube	June 25, 1799	17	black	Providence, R.I.	2	12
Mathewson, Nathan	Aug. 10, 1829	19	dark	Scituate, R.I.	5	51
Mathewson, Philip	Nov. 6, 1818	24	dark	Scituate, R.I.	4	45
Mathewson, Silas C.	June 23, 1798	24	dark	Warwick, R.I.	2	12
Mathewson, Silas	Sept. 21, 1796	22	dark	Warwick, R.I.	1	3
Mathewson, Thomas	Aug. 26, 1799	21	dark	Providence, R.I.	2	12
Mathewson, Thomas	Nov. 28, 1849	45	light	Wheelock, Vt.	5	55
Mathewson, Zachary	Nov. 10, 1797	14	light	Providence, R.I.	1	17
Matterson, Daniel	1798-1799	May 22, 1770		Warren, R.I.	* -	--
Matterson, Noel	1798-1799	June 7, 1774		Warren, R.I.	* -	--
Matterson, Edwin H.	Nov. 5, 1849	17	light	Scituate, R.I.	5	55
Matthews, Isaac N.	Mar. 9, 1838	19	light	Providence, R.I.	5	52
Matthews, Peter	Apr. 20, 1818	17	light	Tewksbury, Ma.	4	45
Mauly, John	Dec. 26, 1851	30	light	Dorchester, Ma.	5	55
Mauran, Ira	Aug. 1, 1804	18	light	Barrington, R.I.	3	23
Mauran, James J.	Oct. 8, 1842	24	light	Roxbury, Ma.	5	53
Mauran, Nathaniel S.	Oct. 19, 1822	17	light	Providence, R.I.	4	46
Mauran, Suchet	Nov. 9, 1810	17	light	Barrington, R.I.	4	44
Mauran, Sucket, Jr.	Oct. 19, 1848	27	light	Barrington, R.I.	5	54
Mavis, John A.	July 26, 1805	22	light	Newport, R.I.	3	64
Mavis, John F.	Apr. 10, 1810	26	light	Berlin, Prussia	4	44
Mavis, John Frederick	Oct. 18, 1803	20	light	Phila., Pa.	2	42
Mawney, Moses	Feb. 3, 1804	23	light	E. Greenwich, R.I.	3	23
Mawney, Peter L.	Dec. 15, 1797	24	dark	E. Greenwich, R.I.	1	17
Mawney, Robert G.	Feb. 21, 1810	22	dark	E. Greenwich, R.I.	4	44

*Newport, R. I.

NAME	DATE OF CERTIFICATION	AGE	COMPLEXION	PLACE OF BIRTH	BOOK	PAGE
Mawney, Samuel A.	Oct. 20, 1809	17	light	E. Greenwich, R.I.	4	44
Maxfield, Benjamin	Dec. 23, 1817	21	ruddy	No. Prov., R.I.	4	45
Maxwell, Abner	Nov. 18, 1797	27	dark	Providence, R.I.	1	17
Maxwell, Francis J.	Mar. 31, 1862	21	fair	Westport, Ma.	6	13
Maxwell, Jenckes	May 28, 1810	21	light	No. Prov., R.I.	4	44
Maxwell, Jenks	Nov. 19, 1819	26	light	No. Prov., R.I.	4	45
Maxwell, Stephen	Apr. 2, 1847	29	fair	Wells, Me.	5	54
Maxwell, William	Jan. 22, 1851	33	light	Hudson, N.Y.	5	55
Maxwell, William	Dec. 8, 1815	30	light	Warren, R.I.	4	45
Maxwell, Wm. K.	Mar. 15, 1852	23	light	Bowdoinham, Me.	5	55
May, James	1798-1799		July 28, 1780	So. Kingston, R.I.	* -	--
John Franklin Gardner of So. Kingston, R.I. swears the above to be true.						
May, James	Apr. 25, 1818	20	light	Newport, R.I.	4	45
May, John	July 25, 1805	28	light	Johnston, Vt.	3	64
May, Samuel	1798-1799		Oct. 18, 1777	So. Kingston, R.I.	* -	--
John Franklin Gardner of S. Kingston, R.I. swears the above to be true.						
May, William	Mar. 14, 1815	18	light	Newport, R.I.	4	45
May, William H.	Mar. 3, 1849	31	light	Cumberland, R.I.	5	54
Mayden, George	Aug. 7, 1835	38	black	Richmond, Va.	5	52
Meads, James	Oct. 22, 1834	25	black	Baltimore, Md.	5	51
Mead, William H.	Dec. 15, 1843	27	light	Westchester, N.Y.	5	53
Mecanger, Michael	Sept. 28, 1804	24	light	Dunkirk, France	3	24
Medbury, Edwin R.	Mar. 1, 1849	30	fair	Seekonk, Ma.	5	54
Medbury, John	June 11, 1844	21	dark	No. Prov., R.I.	5	53
Medbury, Matthew	May 20, 1822	19	light	Rehoboth, Ma.	4	46
Medbury, Nathaniel	Dec. 24, 1825	22	dark	Barrington, R.I.	4	46
Medbury, Samuel B.	Dec. 18, 1829	22	light	Providence, R.I.	5	51
Medbury, Thomas	Feb. 21, 1801	27	dark	Rehoboth, Ma.	2	30
Medbury, Thomas	Mar. 29, 1820	19	dark	Seekonk, Ma.	4	45
Megee, Charles Elliot	July 16, 1803	17	light	Boston, Ma.	2	42
Megee, William F.	May 2, 1799	38	dark	Newport, R.I.	2	12
Megee, William F., Jr.	Sept. 12, 1807	15	light	Providence, R.I.	4	44
Meigs, Alfred F.	Mar. 11, 1846	33	dark	New Haven, Conn.	5	54
Meker, Lewis	Dec. 30, 1836	33	mulatto	New York, N.Y.	5	52
Mellen, Daniel C.	Dec. 27, 1822	26	light	Yarmouth, Ma.	4	46
Melville, Mathew	Sept. 30, 1796	15	light	Baltimore, Md.	2	4

*Newport, R. I.

NAME	DATE OF CERTIFICATION	AGE	COMPLEXION	PLACE OF BIRTH	BOOK	PAGE
Melwaine, James	Apr. 29, 1840	24	light	Alexandria, D.C.	5	52
Mendall, Elihu B.	Dec. 5, 1833	31	light	New Bedford, Ma.	5	51
Mendell, David, Jr.	Oct. 19, 1821	21	light	Rochester, Ma.	4	46
Mensetter, John O.	Sept. 14, 1846	20	fair	Phila., Pa.	5	54
Merceran, Augustus W.	Sept. 29, 1826	12	dark	New York, N.Y.	4	46
Merchant, Alexander	Feb. 24, 1834	21	light	Yarmouth, Ma.	5	51
Merchant, Alexander	Apr. 19, 1855	37	light	New York, N.Y.	5	5
Merchant, Edmond E.	Apr. 23, 1849	29	dark	Yarmouth, Ma.	5	54
Merchant, Joel	May 21, 1829	22	light	Yarmouth, Ma.	5	51
Merchant, Leander	Apr. 5, 1819	17	light	Yarmouth, Ma.	4	45
Merrick, Billings	Aug. 10, 1821	20	light	Stonington, Conn.	-	--
Sworn statement of Elof Benson of Stonington in the Custom House Papers. DOB: Apr. 6, 1801.						
?Merrie, John	Dec. 22, 1797	35	dark	Wilmington, Del.	1	17
Merrihew[Meryhew] James	Dec. 20, 1800	22	dark	Cranston, R.I.	2	30
Merrill, Almon	July 11, 1856	18	light	Portland, Me.	5	90
Merrill, Henry	Feb. 15, 1851	21	light	Bath, Me.	5	55
Merrill, John	June 8, 1838	34	dark	Bristol, Me.	5	52
Merrill, Lewis Chandler	Sept. 1, 1849	36	light	Warwick, R.I.	5	55
Merrill, Nathan	Mar. 7, 1806	19	light	Providence, R.I.	3	75
Merrill, Peter	Oct. 17, 1833	30	sandy	Windsor, Conn.	5	51
Merrill, Stephen	July 31, 1843	48	light	Wiscasset, Me.	5	53
Merritt, Billings	Dec. 18, 1822	22	light	Stonington, Conn.	4	46
Merritt, James	May 6, 1800	22	black	New York, N.Y.	2	12
Merritt, Mike	Aug. 2, 1804	26	dark	Marblehead, Ma.	3	23
Merritt, Robert G.	Aug. 31, 1805	29	light	New York, N.Y.	3	64
Merry, Barney	Nov. 18, 1800	17	dark	Providence, R.I.	2	30
Merry, Benjamin	Apr. 27, 1797	21	light	Swansey, Ma.	1	17
Merry, Hauson	Aug. 16, 1831	26	light	No. Prov., R.I.	5	51
Merry, Samuel	June 26, 1798	18	light	Scituate, R.I.	2	12
Merry, Samuel	May 20, 1805	25	light	Scituate, R.I.	3	24
Merry, Stewart	Nov. 18, 1800	19	light	Providence, R.I.	2	30
Merryfield, George W.	Aug. 31, 1832	25	light	Norwich, Conn.	5	51
[Merryweather]Merewether, Wm.	Sept. 24, 1798	17	light	Bristol, R.I.	2	12
[Merryweather]Merewether, Wm.	Dec. 16, 1799	19	light	Bristol, R.I.	2	12
Merryweather, Wm.	May 6, 1801	20	light	Bristol, R.I.	2	30
Merryweather, Wm.	Feb. 23, 1805	25	light	Bristól, Eng.	3	24

NAME	DATE OF CERTIFICATION	AGE	COMPLEXION	PLACE OF BIRTH	BOOK	PAGE
Baptism of Messenger, Capt. Eli May 3, 1807 Rev. Benedict Record.						
Messenger, Jason	May 1, 1799	25	dark	Wretham, Ma.	2	12
Messer, Charles J.	Mar. 28, 1828	21	light	Nottingham West, N.H.	4	46
Messer, Thomas	Jan. 11, 1821	17	dark	Newport, R.I.	-	--
Sworn statement of Charles S. Rawlings of Bristol in Custom House Papers. DOB: Apr. 4, 1804.						
?Mesury, Rufus	Dec. 6, 1853	45	dark	Columbia, Me.	5	5
Metcalf, George	June 1, 1842	16	light	Providence, R.I.	5	53
Metcalf, Levi	Nov. 30, 1810	16	light	Providence, R.I.	4	44
Metcalf, Samuel	1798-1799	Nov. 26, 1769		Ipswich, Ma.	*-	--
Metcalf, Thomas	Sept. 26, 1796	45	light	Ann Arundle Co., Md.	1	3
Metcalf, William M.	Apr. 12, 1810	20	light	Providenc, R.I.	4	44
Mew, John	Feb. 24, 1801	18	black	No. Kingstown, R.I.	2	30
Mew, John	Feb. 24, 1832	49	dark	So. Kingston, R.I.	5	51
Middleton, Henry C.	Jan. 13, 1852	23	light	Phila., Pa.	5	55
Middleton, Thomas	Nov. 19, 1803	19	light	New York, N.Y.	2	16
Middleton, Wm. F.	Dec. 11, 1844	21	light	Portland, Me.	5	53
Midgett, Abner	Mar. 12, 1812	15	dark	Carrebuck Co., N.C.	4	45
Mildrum, David	May 11, 1803	28	light	Phila., Pa.	2	42
Mill, Charles	Aug. 11, 1798	21	black	New York, N.Y.	2	12
Millard, Benjamin	May 30, 1799	17	dark	Warwick, R.I.	2	12
Millens, Lovett	Oct. 29, 1799	22	light	Hopkinton, Ma.	2	12
Miller, Albert	Dec. 17, 1849	25	light	Cumberland, R.I.	5	55
Miller, Alexander J.	Oct. 5, 1818	20	light	Rehoboth, Ma.	4	45
Millar, Amos	Nov. 7, 1801	23	black	New London, Conn.	2	30
Miller, Caleb	July 31, 1843	20	light	Bristol, R.I.	5	53
Miller, Charles	Apr. 19, 1859	41	fair	Gloucester, Ma.	6	13
Miller, Christian	Mar. 23, 1848	26	light	Denmark, Europe	5	54
Miller, Daniel	Mar. 31, 1820	26	light	E. Greenwich, R.I.	4	45
Miller, Daniel	June 8, 1857	26	light	Providence, R.I.	5	90
Miller, Daniel F.	Mar. 6, 1848	20	fair	Providence, R.I.	5	54
Miller, Francis	Mar. 28, 1848	26	dark	Phila., Pa.	5	54
Miller, Francis	Mar. 20, 1856	34	light	Memel, Prussia	5	5
Miller, George	July 18, 1804	27	black	Baltimore, Md.	3	23
Miller, George B.	Oct. 27, 1818	20	light	Rehoboth, Ma.	4	45
Miller, Howard Allen	Oct. 22, 1830	23	light	Seekonk, Ma.	5	51
Miller, Jabez	June 9, 1804	30	black	Stonington, Conn.	3	23

*Newport, R. I.

NAME	DATE OF CERTIFICATION	AGE	COMPLEXION	PLACE OF BIRTH	BOOK	PAGE
Miller, Jabez	Dec. 26, 1804	33	yellow*	Stonington, Conn.	3	24
Miller, James	Aug. 20, 1803	20	dark	Wilmington, N.C.	2	42
Miller, James W.	Feb. 18, 1841	27	light	Providence, R.I.	5	52
Miller, John	Dec. 8, 1804	23	light	Chester, Pa.	3	24
Miller, John	Nov. 25, 1805	25	dark	Boston, Ma.	3	75
Miller, John	Jan. 9, 1810	25	black	Westchester, Pa.	4	44
Miller, John	Sept. 11, 1866	19	light	New York, N.Y.	6	13
Miller, John L.	Mar. 17, 1845	20	light	E. Greenwich, R.I.	5	53
Miller, John William	Dec. 6, 1849	24	light	Eastport, Me.	5	55
Miller, Joseph	June 15, 1853	24	dark	Bridgetown, N.J.	5	5
Miller, Josiah	Apr. 23, 1832	27	light	Westbury, Ma.	5	51
Miller, Josiah	July 31, 1834	29	dark	Westboro, Ma.	5	51
Miller, Pardon	Apr. 3, 1822	23	light	Glocester, R.I.	4	46
Miller, Richard	Mar. 8, 1853	23	light	Provincetown, Ma.	5	5
Millar, Robert	Mar. 22, 1837	21	light	Phila., Pa.	5	52
Miller, Rufus	June 26, 1845	16	dark	Cumberland, R.I.	5	53
Miller, Seth, Jr.[or J.]	Apr. 7, 1819	17	light	Rehoboth, Ma.	4	45
Miller, Seth J.	Nov. 22, 1828	26	light	Rehoboth, Ma.	4	46
Miller, Thomas	June 19, 1798	35	light	Charleston, S.C.	2	12
Miller, Thomas	Sept. 17, 1845	26	fair	Newark, Ohio	5	54
Miller, Timothy	Mar. 5, 1851	32	mulatto	Bucks Co., Pa.	5	55
Miller, Volney	June 8, 1838	21	dark	Troy, N.Y.	5	52
Miller, William	Oct. 15, 1828	20	mulatto	Cranston, R.I.	4	46
Miller, William	Apr. 4, 1844	17	light	Boston, Ma.	5	53
Miller, William	July 15, 1854	23	light	Cumberland, R.I.	5	5
Miller, William A.	Sept. 26, 1826	20	light	E. Greenwich, R.I.	4	46
Miller, Zadok H.	June 10, 1833	17	freckled	Medway, Ma.	5	51
Millikin, Elias	1798-1799	Nov. 6, 1780		Mass.	**	--
Millin, Andrew	Mar. 20, 1809	29	light	Lancaster, Pa.	4	44
Millington, William	Apr. 1, 1805	20	light	New York, N.Y.	3	24
Mills, Abraham A.	Dec. 28, 1844	25	light	Southport, Conn.	5	53
Mills, Frederick	Nov. 18, 1831	25	light	Baltimore, Md.	5	51
Mills, George	Oct. 22, 1798	25	black	White Plains, N.Y.	2	12

*mulatto

**Newport, R. I.

NAME	DATE OF CERTIFICATION	AGE	COMPLEXION	PLACE OF BIRTH	BOOK	PAGE
Mills, Henry	Oct. 29, 1806	32	black	Portsmouth, Ma.	4	44
Mills, Henry C.	Oct. 1, 1844	17	dark	Savannah, Ga.	5	53
Mills, Joseph	Apr. 16, 1863	25	dark	G.[?] Egg Harbour	6	13
Mills, Wm. E.	May 12, 1852	35	dark	Boston, Ma.	5	5
Milly, John	May 10, 1864	22	dark	Eastport, Me.	6	13
Milner, Thomas	Nov. 13, 1840	28	dark	Phila., Pa.	5	52
Miner, Edward A.	Dec. 11, 1847	21	light	Calais, Me.	5	54
Miner, James	Apr. 4, 1849	22	light	New York, N.Y.	5	54
Miner, Peleg	Mar. 22, 1825	41	ruddy	Stonington, Conn.	4	46
Miner, Peter	Jan. 24, 1849	23	fair	Augusta, Me.	5	54
Mingo, John	July 13, 1819	25	black	Tiverton, R.I.	4	45
Mingo, William	Nov. 25, 1809	16	black	Glocester, R.I.	4	44
Mitchell, Charles	May 13, 1853	21	dark	Balden Oswego Co., N.Y.	5	5
Mitchel, George	Oct. 6, 1846	23	black	Milton, Del.	5	54
Mitchel, Henry	Apr. 8, 1809	20	dark	Newport, R.I.	4	44
Mitchell, Henry	Sept. 11, 1866	22	dark	Boston, Ma.	6	13
Mitchell, James	May 16, 1810	13	fair	Providence, R.I.	4	44
Mitchell, John	May 2, 1855	22	dark	New York, N.Y.	5	5
Mitchell, Martin	Dec. 7, 1835	19	dark	Norfolk, Va.	5	52
Mitchell, Nicholas	Sept. 13, 1819	19	light	Warwick, R.I.	4	45
Mitchell, Peter	Nov. 25, 1797	29	dark	Providence, R.I.	1	17
[Mitchell]Mitchel, Silas B.	June 9, 1800	27	light	Block Island, R'I.	2	30
Mitchell, Thomas	June 10, 1797	21	light	Sherburne or Nantucket,[1]Ma.		17
Mitchell, Wm.	Mar. 10, 1853	23	dark	Portland, Me.	5	5
Mix, James[?]	Nov. 7, 1809	34	yellow	Hartford, Conn.	4	44
Moffatt, George	Jan. 13, 1846	23	fair	New York, N.Y.	5	54
Moffitt, John M.	Jan. 19, 1838	21	dark	Smithfield, R.I.	5	52
Moffott, Piercen	July 23, 1853	23	florid	Providence, R.I.	5	5
Moll, William	Jan. 8, 1839	19	dark	New York, N.Y.	5	52
Molony, Edmond	July 13, 1805	23	dark	Norfolk, Va.	3	64
Munroe, Alfred H.	Oct. 2, 1829	15	light	Providence, R.I.	5	51
Munroe, Allen	1798-1799	Oct. 3, 1773		Bristol, R.I.	-	--
Munro, Amos	May 30, 1844	17	black	Schenectady, N.Y.	5	53
Munro, Amos	June 18, 1845	19	black	Little Egg Harbor, N.J.	5	53
Munro, Edward	Aug. 21, 1807	16	light	Providence, R.I.	4	44
Munro, Edward	Aug. 8, 1808	17	light	Providence, R.I.	4	44
Munro, Edward	Nov. 11, 1813	21	light	Providence, R.I.	4	45

*Newport, R. I.

NAME	DATE OF CERTIFICATION	AGE	COMPLEXION	PLACE OF BIRTH	BOOK	PAG
Munro, Hail	Dec. 19, 1821	22	light	Bristol, R.I.	-	--
Sworn statement of David Munro of Bristol in the Custom House Papers. DOB: June 24, 1799.						
Munro, John	July 12, 1804	38	light	Providence, R.I.	3	23
Munro, John, Jr.	May 24, 1805	21	light	Providence, R.I.	3	24
Munro, Joseph S.	Sept. 15, 1807	20	light	Providence, R.I.	4	44
Munro, Ralph K.	Oct. 20, 1856	18	light	Providence, R.I.	5	90
Munro, Russell	Apr. 23, 1832	24	light	Bristol, R.I.	5	51
Munro, Sanford	Nov. 17, 1827	29	light	Bristol, R.I.	4	46
Munro, Thomas	July 3, 1798	20	dark	Pomfret, Conn.	2	12
Munro, Thomas, Jr.	Mar. 25, 1800	21	dark	Pomfret, Conn.	2	12
Munro, Thomas, Jr.	July 16, 1804	25	dark	Providence, R.I.	3	23
Munroe, Caleb B.	May 18, 1840	37	light	Boston, Ma.	5	52
Munroe, Charles	Mar. 11, 1844	21	light	Boston, Ma.	5	53
Munroe, Frank C.	July 23, 1868	23	light	Providence, R.I.	6	13
Monroe, George	Dec. 20, 1834	33	light	New York, N.Y.	5	51
Monroe, George	Nov. 22, 1854	25	black	Burlington, N.J.	5	5
Monroe, Henry R.	Oct. 8, 1856	20	dark	Providence, R.I.	5	90
Munroe, James	Nov. 13, 1819	15	light	Providence, R.I.	4	45
Munroe, James M., Jr.	Nov. 14, 1859	16	dark	Bristol, R.I.	6	13
Monroe, John J.	Oct. 1, 1856	22	fair	Brooklyn, N.Y.	5	90
Munroe, John L.	Dec. 9, 1818	16	light	Providence, R.I.	4	45
Munroe, Joseph, Jr.	May 31, 1851	32	light	Bristol, R.I.	5	55
Munroe, William	Apr. 17, 1807	22	yellow	Bristol, R.I.	4	44
Munroe, William	Sept. 4, 1849	32	light	Coventry, R.I.	5	55
Monroe, William C.	May 28, 1858	17	light	Providence, R.I.	6	13
Monsear, John	Oct. 18, 1832	22	mulatto	Brooklyn, N.Y.	5	51
Montgomery, Hugh	Oct. 7, 1811	21	light	Windham, N.H.	4	45
Montgomery, John	Oct. 18, 1832	22	dark	Phila., Pa.	5	51
[Moody]Moodey, Edward	Oct. 4, 1800	18	light	Newport, R.I.	2	30
Moody, Jedediah	July 10, 1807	23	yellowish	Preston, Conn.	4	44
Moody, Jedediah	Feb. 19, 1812	28	yellow	Norwich, Conn.	4	45
Moody, Nicholson S.	May 17, 1867	39	light	Pittston, Me.	6	13
Moon, William S.	Sept. 17, 1847	28	dark	Savannah, Ga.	5	54
Moore, Ezra	Aug. 17, 1811	18	light	Worcester, Ma.	4	45
Moore, Francis	May 29, 1827	19	light	Bristol, R.I.	4	46
Moore, Francis	Apr. 19, 1864	23	light	Boston, Ma.	6	13

NAME	DATE OF CERTIFICATION	AGE	COMPLEXION	PLACE OF BIRTH	BOOK	PAGE
Moore, Jacob	July 15, 1809	27	black	New York, N.Y.	4	44
Moore, James	Mar. 13, 1818	17	light	Newport, R.I.	4	45
Moore, James	Sept. 20, 1837	24	dark	Portsmouth, N.H.	5	52
Moore, James	Jan. 12, 1846	24	dark	New York, N.Y.	5	54
Moore[More],Jeremiah	May 20, 1803	30	dark	Norwich, Conn.	2	42
Moore, John	Sept. 14, 1803	22	light	Phila., Pa.	2	42
Moore, John	Nov. 1, 1805	23	dark	Hampton, Va.	3	75
Moore, Nahum	Aug. 1, 1825	19	light	Trenton, Me.	4	46
Moore, Simeon	Nov. 27, 1797	33	black	Baltimore, Md.	1	17
Moore, William	May 8, 1845	35	dark	Norfolk, Va.	5	53
Moore, William	June 2, 1849	40	dark	New Bedford, Ma.	5	55
Moors, John	Oct. 22, 1849	20	dark	Providence, R.I.	5	55
Moran, James T.	Jan. 25, 1860	19	dark	Providence, R.I.	6	13
Moran, Michael	July 28, 1797	20	light	Boston, Ma.	1	17
Moran, William	July 3, 1822	26	dark	New London, Conn.	4	46
Moren, Patrick	Feb. 20, 1847	21	fair	Boston, Ma.	5	54
Morey, William	Aug. 27, 1838	30	light	Providence, R.I.	5	52
Morgan, Joseph	Oct. 20, 1797	27	dark	Baltimore, Md.	1	17
Morgan, Joseph C.	Nov. 14, 1803	16	light	Morristown, N.J.	2	42
Morgan, Samuel	Apr. 20, 1797	20	light	Providence, R.I.	1	17
Morgan, William	Aug. 17, 1850	20	black	New London, Conn.	5	55
Morgan, Joseph	Aug. 14, 1841	21	dark	Marblehead, Ma.	5	52
Morgan, Peleg R.	Nov. 22, 1841	22	light	Coventry, R.I.	5	53
Morgan, William	May 4, 1844	20	mulatto	Stonington, Conn.	5	53
Morris, Alonzo L.	Nov. 9, 1848	23	light	Groton, Conn.	5	54
Morris, Archable	Dec. 23, 1805	35	dark	New York, N.Y.	3	75
Morris, Benjamin	June 5, 1807	22	dark	Barcelona, Spain	4	44
Morris, Benjamin	Aug. 21, 1809	20	dark	Scituate, Ma.	4	44
Morriss, Bradley	Feb. 16, 1847	21	fair	Bucksport, Me.	5	54
Morris, Elisha	Oct. 22, 1804	16	light	Phila., Pa.	3	24
Morris, Francis	Feb. 24, 1845	21	light	New York, N.Y.	5	53
Morris, Frank	Nov. 11, 1803	24	dark	New York, N.Y.	2	42
Morris, Frederick G.	Apr. 2, 1830	26	dark	Groton, Conn.	5	51
Morriss, George	Nov. 20, 1833	32	dark	Chillicothe, Ohio	5	51
Morris, George	Dec. 13, 1850	30	light	Buffalo, N.Y.	5	55
Morris, George W.	July 7, 1845	17	light	Bucksport, Me.	5	53

REGISTER OF SEAMEN'S PROTECTION

NAME	DATE OF CERTIFICATION	AGE	COMPLEXION	PLACE OF BIRTH	BOOK	PAGE
Morris, Horace	Nov. 9, 1815	27	dark	Woodstock, R.I.	4	45
Morris, Jack	Aug. 16, 1803	25	black	Phila., Pa.	2	42
Morris, James	Oct. 16, 1841	30	black	Frederick, Md.	5	52
Morris, James M.	May 16, 1820	18	light	Newport, R.I.	4	46
Morris, John	Dec. 13, 1797	27	black	So. Kingtown, R.I.	1	17
Morris, John	Sept. 27, 1805	15	light	New York, N.Y.	3	64
Morris, John	Apr. 2, 1853	23	light	Providence, R.I.	5	5
Morris, John	Nov. 7, 1849	22	black	Providence, R.I.	5	55
Morris, Nathaniel	June 22, 1804	21	light	Morristown, N.J.	3	23
Morris, Robert	Nov. 20, 1796	23	light	New York, N.Y.	1	17
Morris, Samuel	Mar. 7, 1825	28	light	Cumberland, R.I.	4	46
Morris, Thomas	Oct. 5, 1813	25	florid	Phila., Pa.	4	45
Morris, William	Aug. 17, 1844	27	dark	Scituate, Ma.	5	53
Morrisa, Timothy	Nov. 22, 1832	18	light	Boston, Ma.	5	51
Morrison, Charles	Nov. 3, 1862	35	light	Belfast, Me.	6	13
Morrison, John	Apr. 11, 1835	22	dark	Newark, N.J.	5	52
Morrison, John B.	Nov. 8, 1849	42	light	Bath, Me.	5	55
Morrison, Robert	Mar. 6,,1838	28	dark	Lubec, Me.	5	52
Morrison, William	Feb. 13, 1851	38	dark	Providence, R.I.	5	55
Morse, Benjamin	May 10, 1800	21	light	Providence,R.I.	2	30
Morse, Christopher	Mar. 25, 1825	21	light	Coventry, R.I.	4	46
Morse, Edward	Dec. 15, 1809	34	brown	Chester, N.H.	4	44
Morse, Edward T.	Sept. 23, 1818	22	light	Foxboro, Ma.	4	45
Morse, George S.	Sept. 22, 1818	22	yellow	Rehoboth, Ma.	4	45
Morse, Isaac S.	Oct. 20, 1856	29	light	Coventry, R.I.	5	90
Morse, Joseph L.	Dec. 23, 1861	25	brown	New Bedford, Ma.	6	13
Morse, Ladie	Dec. 21, 1818	22	black	Hartford, Conn.	4	45
Morse, Lewis	Jan. 8, 1833	23	dark	Foxboro, Ma.	5	51
Morse, Otis	July 26, 1824	20	dark	Foxboro, Ma.	4	46
Morse, Pero	Dec. 13, 1796	27	yellow*	Newport, R.I.	1	17
Morse, Rufus K.	Feb. 18, 1840	19	dark	Providence, R.I.	5	52
Morse, Spencer	Jan. 4, 1817	22	dark	Foxboro, Ma.	4	45
?Morse, William	June 5, 1797	23	dark	Worcester, Ma.	1	17
Mortis, William	Nov. 25, 1809	24	black	Bridgewater, Ma.	4	44
Morton, Charles	Apr. 10, 1854	20	dark	New Orleans, La.	5	5
Mosely, Gustuous	May 20, 1833	26	light	Westfield, Ma.	5	51

*mulatto

NAME	DATE OF CERTIFICATION	AGE	COMPLEXION	PLACE OF BIRTH	BOOK	PAGE
MOseley, Harvey	May 24, 1831	22	light	Hampton, Conn.	5	51
Mosely, John	June 17, 1826	20	dark	Hampton, Conn.	4	46
Moseley, John H.	Oct. 17, 1849	16	light	Providence, R.I.	5	55
Moseley, Lemuel H.	Jan. 3, 1856	19	dark	Providence, R.I.	5	5
Moses, Benjamin H.	Jan. 8, 1834	21	black	Plainfield, Conn.	5	51
Moses, Edward L.	Dec. 3, 1825	21	light	Newport, R.I.	4	46
Mott, Charles	May 1, 1799	27	yellow*	Chaleston, S.C.	2	12
Mott, Charles	Feb. 16, 1805	31	yellow*	Charlestown, S.C.	3	24
Mott, Charles	Mar. 7, 1806	32	yellow*	Charleston, S.C.	3	75
Mott, Charles, Jr.	Mar. 13, 1812	15	yellow*	Providence, R.I.	4	45
Moulton, William	Nov. 27, 1797	18	light	Scituate, R.I.	1	17
Molton, William	July 19, 1803	24	light	Scituate, R.I.	2	42
[Moulton]Molton, William	Aug. 8, 1800	21	light	Providence, R.I.	2	30
Mount, Charles	Apr. 23, 1863	22	light	New York, N.Y.	6	13
Mowatt, John	May 11, 1803	25	black	Newport, R.I.	2	42
Mower, Charles C.	July 17, 1845	19	light	No. Hampton, Ma.	5	53
Mowry, Arnold	Dec. 6, 1827	23	light	Smithfield, R.I.	4	46
Mowry, Bradford	July 10, 1818	18	black	Norton, Ma.	4	45
Mowry, Charles E.	Mar. 15, 1843	14	light	Providence, R.I.	5	53
Mowry, Charles E.	May 23, 1845	17	light	Providence, R.I.	5	53
Mowry, Daniel A.	Apr. 21, 1849	20	light	Providence, R.I.	5	54
Mowry, Daniel C.	Aug. 6, 1847	19	light	Smithfield, R.I.	5	54
Mowry, Demarcus	July 17, 1811	19	yellow	Norton, Ma.	4	45
Mowry, Erastus R.	Oct. 1, 1830	16	dark	Providence, R.I.	5	51
Mowry, Ezckiel F.	Mar. 2, 1849	29	light	Smithfield, R.I.	5	54
Mowry, Gamaliel	Dec. 2, 1854	30	black	Taunton, Ma.	5	5
Mowry, Gideon, Jr.	Mar. 15, 1808	24	light	Smithfield, R.I.	4	44
Mowry, John	May 29, 1827	23	light	Smithfield, R.I.	4	46
Mowry, John A.	Nov. 9, 1827	22	ruddy	Smithfield, R.I.	4	46
Mowry, Nelson	Nov. 6, 1828	20	ruddy	Smithfield, R.I.	4	46
Mowry, Nelson H.	Dec. 24, 1829	21	light	Smithfield, R.I.	5	51
Mowry, Ovin	May 30, 1849	24	light	Johnston, R.I.	5	55
Mowry, Richard	Nov. 9, 1820	21	light	Smithfield, R.I.	4	46
Mowry, Smith	Dec. 20, 1848	23	light	Smithfield, R.I.	5	54
Muenscher, John	July 18, 1803	17	light	Newport, R.I.	2	42

*mulatto

NAME	DATE OF CERTIFICATION	AGE	COMPLEXION	PLACE OF BIRTH	BOOK	PAGE
Muldoon Charles	Aug. 20, 1853	23	light	Charlestown, Ma.	5	5
Mulhurn, Peter	Sept. 19, 1849	21	light	Albany, N.Y.	5	55
Mulligan, Steuben	May 28, 1831	31	light	New York, N.Y.	5	51
Mulliner, Robert	Oct. 6, 1834	28	light	New York, N.Y.	5	51
Mumford, Amos W.	Dec. 8, 1823	14	light	Providence, R.I.	4	46
Mumford, Henry	Oct. 12, 1801	19	light	Providence, R.I.	2	30
Mumford, Pomp	Nov. 14, 1803	39	black	Newport, R.I.	2	42
Mumford, Samuel	Oct. 25, 1815	21	black	Providence, R.I.	4	45
Mumford, Samuel B.	Nov. 19, 1806	16	light	Wickford, R.I.	4	44
Mumford, William	Dec. 12, 1803	15	dark	Providence, R.I.	2	16
Mumford, William	July 6, 1804	15	light	No. Kingstown, R.I.	3	23
Mundain, Ephraim	Sept. 21, 1830	26	light	Westminster, Ma.	5	51
Munday, Zacheus	Dec. 14, 1803	31	black	Windham, Conn.	2	16
Munro, Munroe see Monroe.						
Murphy, Barney	Oct. 5, 1847	24	dark	Providence, R.I.	5	54
Murphy, David	Oct. 29, 1849	20	light	Boston, Ma.	5	55
Murphey, Edward	Oct. 1, 1805	25	light	Newport, R.I.	3	64
Murphey, John	1798-1799		June 10, 1776	Newport, R.I.	* -	--
Benjamian Billings swears the above to be true.						
Murphy, John	1798-1799		Oct. 1, 1784	Westerly, R.I.	* -	--
Amos Briggs of Newport swears the above to be true.						
Murphy, John L.	June 1, 1837	39	light	Kennibunk, Me.	5	52
Murphy, Samuel	1798-1799		Oct. 27, 1775	Newport, R.I.	* -	--
Edward Murphy swears the above to be true.						
Murphyson, John D.	Sept. 18, 1839	31	black	New York, N.Y.	5	52
Murry, Alexander	Nov. 3, 1842	23	light	Buffalo, N.Y.	5	53
Murray, Anthony	Apr. 14, 1821	32	dark	Bristol, R.I.	-	--
Sworn statement of Aaron Eastabrooks in the Custom House Papers. DOB: 1789.						
Murray, Anthony	May 31, 1798	20	dark	Providence, R.I.	2	12
Murray, Anthony	Oct. 9, 1807	29	dark	Providence, R.I.	4	44
Murray, David	June 11, 1855	26	dark	Westchester, N.Y.	5	5
Murray, George W.	Dec. 25, 1826	18	light	Providence, R.I.	4	46
Murry, Israel	July 13, 1849	20	black	Camden, N.J.	5	55
Murray, John	Nov. 12, 1841	22	Indian	Phila., Pa.	5	53
Murray, John	Mar. 3, 1848	25	dark	New York, N.Y.	5	54
Murray, John	Dec. 2, 1848	21	dark	Boston, Ma.	5	54
Murray, John	May 6, 1867	31	black	New York, N.Y.	6	13

*Newport, R. I.

REGISTER OF SEAMEN'S PROTECTION

NAME	DATE OF CERTIFICATION	AGE	COMPLEXION	PLACE OF BIRTH	BOOK	PAGE
Murray, Richard	Aug. 29, 1804	?22	dark	Charlestown, Ma.	3	23
Murray, Robert	Dec. 21, 1805	20	light	Providence, R.I.	3	75
Murray, William	Aug. 12, 1834	38	dark	Bangor, Me.	5	51
Muzzy, William	May 8, 1826	18	ruddy	Needham, Ma.	4	46
Myers, Abraham	Dec. 23, 1837	24	light	New York, N.Y.	5	52
Myers, Henry	Aug. 29, 1848	29	light	Castine, Me.	5	54
Myers, Perry	May 7, 1810	24	black	Phila., Pa.	4	44
Nage, John	June 16, 1862	22	light	Greenport, L.I., N.Y.	6	14
Nahan, Charles E.	July 15, 1854	16	yellow	Providence, R.I.	5	56
Nash, Adolphus	July 5, 1855	17	light	Williamsburg, N.J.	5	57
Nash, Christopher	Nov. 17, 1797	22	light	Wilmington, Del.	1	18
Nash, Joseph C.	Dec. 18, 1822	23	light	Westerly, R.I.	4	49
Nason, Alfred	Oct. 23, 1855	25	light	Mansfield, Conn.	5	57
Nason, William G.	Apr. 7, 1837	22	light	Warwick, R.I.	5	56
Natisa, Samuel M.	Mar. 15, 1852	24	black	Wilmington, Del.	5	56
Nava, George	Sept. 3, 1796	23	black	Providence, R.I.	1	2
Navey, George	Aug. 10, 1804	29	black	Providence, R.I.	3	25
Navey, George	Sept. 18, 1805	30	black	Providence, R.I.	3	25
Navey, George	May 12, 1806	33	black	Providence, R.I.	3	26
Negus, Isaac	1798-1799		Oct. 12, 1775	Tiverton, R.I.	*-	--
Ezekiel Wilborn of Little Compton swears the above to be true.						
Neil, George F.	Oct. 15, 1841	23	dark	Fairhaven, Ma.	5	56
Neil, Mathew	July 30, 1832	16	light	Baltimore, Md.	5	56
Neill, William	Nov. 14, 1812	21	dark	Frederickstown, Md.	4	49
Neal, William O.	Nov. 10, 1853	28	dark	Yarmouth, Ma.	5	56
Nedson, Joseph	Mar. 30, 1849	21	black	Stonington, Conn.	5	56
Needham, William G.	Nov. 11, 1845	17	fair	Providence, R.I.	5	56
Nelson, Benjamin	May 5, 1846	24	fair	Cranston, R.I.	5	56
Nelson, Calvin	Nov. 22, 1807	22	florid	Newfane, Vt.	4	49
Nelson, Charles	July 7, 1818	21	light	Smithfield, R.I.	4	49
Nelson, Charles	Aug. 25, 1854	24	light	Phila., Pa.	5	57
Nelson, Francis	Feb. 14, 1844	29	mulatto	Providence, R.I.	5	56
Nelson, George	Sept. 10, 1836	40	dark	New Orleans, La.	5	56
Nelson, Jack	Apr. 4, 1855	18	light	Danville, Pa.	5	57
Nelson, John	Mar. 27, 1851	24	light	Providence, R.I.	5	56

Newport, R. I.

NAME	DATE OF CERTIFICATION	AGE	COMPLEXION	PLACE OF BIRTH	BOOK	PAG
Nelson, Robert	Sept. 25, 1855	31	light	Portland, Me.	5	57
Nelson, Thomas	Apr. 17, 1821	20	light	Boston, Ma.	4	49
Nelson, William	Apr. 4, 1855	28	light	Danville, Pa.	5	57
Neville, John	July 11, 1856	23	fair	New Shoreham, R.I.	5	57
Newcomb, Ebenezer	Feb. 2, 1828	21	dark	Charlestown, Ma.	4	49
Newell, Franklin	Apr. 24, 1807	19	light	Providence, R.I.	4	49
Newell, Henry H.	Mar. 24, 1825	18	dark	Attleboro, Ma.	4	49
Newell, James	Sept. 22, 1807	22	light	Berkley, Ma.	4	49
Newell, James	Oct. 23, 1812	26	dark	Berkley, Ma.	4	49
Newell, Jabez, 2d.	June 17, 1819	25	dark	Attleboro, Ma.	4	49
Newell, William	Jan. 5, 1797	21	light	No. Providence, R.I	1	18
Newman, Almon	July 3, 1847	21	fair	Eastport, Me.	5	56
Newman, Henry	May 22, 1809	23	dark	Washington, N.C.	4	49
Newman, John	Oct. 15, 1855	22	light	Providence, R.I.	5	57
Newman, Paschal	Dec. 9, 1830	21	light	Seekonk, Ma.	5	56
Newman, Peter	Aug. 26, 1822	26	light	Wilmington, Del.	4	49
Newman, Timothy	Feb. 11, 1855	25	fair	Providence, R.I.	5	57
Newton, Amos	Sept. 30, 1831	20	light	Newport, R.I.	5	56
Newton, Charles	July 31, 1837	18	light	Phila., Pa.	5	56
Newton, Elbridge G.	June 23, 1835	25	light	Westboro, Ma.	5	56
Nicholas, Christopher	Aug. 16, 1809	20	dark	Cranston, R.I.	4	49
Nicholas, Christopher	Apr. 29, 1811	22	dark	Cranston, R.I.	4	49
Nicholas, Emanuel	June 25, 1810	18	brown	Cranston, R.I.	4	49
Nicholas, Henry D.	Mar. 18, 1852	21	light	Cranston, R.I.	5	56
Nicholas, Jesse	Nov. 11, 1803	18	light	Warwick, R.I.	2	13
Nicholas, John	July 18, 1803	21	light	Cranston, R.I.	2	13
Nicholas, Larry	Jan. 3, 1816	22	brown	Cranston, R.I.	4	49
Nicholas, Thomas	Feb. 1, 1811	24	dark	Cranston, R.I.	4	49
Nicholas, William	Mar. 11, 1815	17	black	Providence, R.I.	4	49
Nichols, Asa	Nov. 2, 1825	30	dark	Rochester, Ma.	4	49
Nichols, Benjamin	Apr. 6, 1799	17	light	So. Kingstown, R.I.	2	13
Nichols, Benjamin D.	Aug. 5, 1850	19	light	Bristol, R.I.	5	56
Nichols, Christopher	Feb. 18, 1804	19	light	Cranston, R.I.	3	25
Nichols, Christopher	Mar. 5, 1805	20	light	Cranston, R.I.	3	25
Nichols, George	June 22, 1807	32	light	Haverhill, Ma.	4	49
Nichols, James	Dec. 16, 1799	28	light	E. Greenwich, R.I.	2	13
Nichols, James	Oct. 31, 1866	61	light	Rehoboth, Ma.	6	14

NAME	DATE OF CERTIFICATION	AGE	COMPLEXION	PLACE OF BIRTH	BOOK	PAGE
Nichols, James Hiram	June 17, 1821	16	light	Rehoboth, Ma. -	-	--
Son of James Nichols. Birth ceritficat in the Custom House Papers. DOB: Feb. 8, 1805						
Nichols, James H.	Aug. 16, 1836	14	light	Groton, Conn.	5	56
Nichols, James H.	Oct. 17, 1849	27	light	Groton, Conn.	5	56
Nichols, Jesse	May 16, 1811	25	light	Woodstock, Conn.	4	49
Nichols, John	Sept. 26, 1805	13	light	Portsmouth, N.H.	3	25
Nichols, John	Feb. 7, 1807	23	brown	Woodstock, Conn.	4	49
Nichols, John	Mar. 4, 1815	31	dark	Woodstock, Conn.	4	49
Nichols, John	Mar. 10, 1852	21	sandy	Baltimore, Md.	5	56
Nichols, John	Aug. 1, 1854	21	light	Fall River, Ma.	5	56
Nichols, Joseph	Jan. 9, 1804	29	black	New York, N.Y.	3	25
Nichols, Lafayette G.	Aug. 31, 1849	24	light	Sterling, Conn.	5	56
Nichols, Moses	Aug. 26, 1846	21	fair	Plymouth, Ma.	5	56
Nichols, Samuel	Feb. 29, 1816	21	black	So. Kingstown, R.I.	4	49
Nichols, Silas	July 27, 1819	42	dark	Fairfield, Conn.	4	49
Nichols, Sylranus B.	July 7, 1845	26	dark	Rehoboth, Ma.	5	56
Nichols, Thomas M.	Mar. 28, 1863	17	light	Wickford, R.I.	6	14
Nichols, William	June 2, 1849	26	light	No. Kingston, R.I.	5	56
Nichols, Wm. H.	Nov. 30, 1849	26	light	Nantucket, Ma.	5	56
Nicholson, John	Nov. 11, 1803	33	black	Boston, Ma.	2	13
Nickel, Joseph	May 25, 1860	26	light	Eastport, Me.	6	14
Nickerson, Alfred	Oct. 16, 1855	27	light	So. Dennis, Ma.	5	57
Baptism of Nickerson, Almyra April 13, 1823 Rev. Benedict Record.						
Nickerson, Cork	1798-1799	Apr. 10, 1776		Portsmouth, R.I.	*-	--
Nickerson, Dean	May 23, 1839	51	dark	Harwich, Ma.	5	56
Nickerson, Eli	Aug. 1, 1845	45	dark	Chatham, Ma.	5	56
Nickerson, Freeman	Nov. 15, 1799	21	dark	Dennis, Ma.	2	13
Nickerson, Isaac	April 7, 1851	20	light	Yarmouth, Ma.	5	56
Nickerson, Jacob	Aug. 28, 1838	23	black	Phila., Pa.	5	56
Nickerson, Nehemiah	Nov. 15, 1799	17	dark	Harwich, Ma.	2	13
Nickerson, Stephen	July 28, 1836	20	dark	New Bedford, Ma.	5	56
Nickerson, Voxanus	June 23, 1832	26	light	Harwich, Ma.	5	56
Nickle, Lewis	Mar. 16, 1853	21	light	Delaware City, Del.	5	56
Nightingale, Brister	Dec. 17, 1807	23	black	Providence, R.I.	4	49
Nightingale, Joseph	June 10, 1811	16	yellow	Providence, R.I.	4	49
Nightingale, Joshua	July 19, 1803	18	black	Providence, R.I.	2	13

*Newport, R. I.

Page 191

REGISTER OF SEAMEN'S PROTECTION

NAME	DATE OF CERTIFICATION	AGE	COMPLEXION	PLACE OF BIRTH	BOOK	PAGE
Nightingale, Randall	Dec. 24, 1806	19	yellow	Providence, R.I.	4	49
Nightingale, Randall	Apr. 7, 1809	21	yellow	Providence, R.I.	4	49
Nightingale, Randall	Nov. 20, 1813	26	black	Providence, R.I.	4	49
Nightingale, Samuel, Jr.	Nov. 14, 1803	21	dark	Providence, R.I.	2	13
Nightingale, William	July 5, 1804	20	dark	Providence, R.I.	3	25
Nightingale, William	Oct. 1, 1805	21	dark	Providence, R.I.	3	25
Nightingale, William	Nov. 5, 1807	23	dark	Providence, R.I.	4	49
Niles, George F.	Aug. 7, 1815	15	light	Norwich, Conn.	4	49
Niles, Quash	Jan. 29, 1798	20	black	So. Kingstown, R.I.	1	18
Niles, Silas	July 9, 1839	29	light	Charlestown, Ma.	5	56
Nisbith, Thomas	Aug. 28, 1835	28	mulatto	New York, N.Y.	5	56
[Nixon]Nickson, George	Nov. 19, 1803	30	black	Swansea, Ma.	2	13
Nixon, William	June 22, 1833	26	dark	Pittsburg, Pa.	5	56
Nobles, Stephen	Sept. 2, 1803	18	light	Cranston, R.I.	2	13
Nocake, Peter	Nov. 29, 1836	23	Indian	Charlestown, R.I.	5	56
Nolan, James A.	Sept. 21, 1858	28	florid	Boston, Ma.	6	14
Nolan, W.P.	Feb. 15, 1862	23	light	Brooklyn, N.Y.	6	14
Norris, Jeremiah	Aug. 21, 1837	38	light	Salem, Ma.	5	56
Norris, John	Sept. 1, 1860	23	fair	Jersey City, N.J.	6	14
North, Norton	Feb. 3, 1846	21	fair	Middlebury, Ohio	5	56
Northup, Alexander	Aug. 10, 1803	16	black	No. Kingstown, R.I.	2	13
Northup, Alexander	July 20, 1805	17	black	No. Kingstown, R.I.	3	25
Northup, Alexander	Sept. 20, 1811	27	black	No. Kingstown. R.I.	4	49
Northup, Benj. R.	Nov. 11, 1850	17	light	Portsmouth, R.I.	5	56
Northup, Cato	Dec. 21, 1819	36	black	No. Kingstown, R.I.	4	49
Northup, Charles	June 9, 1855	20	mulatto	Providence, R.I.	5	57
Northup, Cyrus	Jan. 25, 1799	27	dark	No. Kingstown, R.I.	2	13
Northup, Cyrus H.	June 20, 1828	16	light	Newport, R.I.	4	49
Northup, Daniel	Mar. 30, 1798	17	light	No. Kingstown, R.I.	1	18
Northup, David	June 18, 1826	21	dark	No. Kingstown, R.I.	4	49
Northup, Ebenezer	1798-1799	Dec. 25, 1774		No. Kingston, R.I.	* -	--
Northup, Ebenezer G.	Jan. 14, 1812	37	light	No. Kingstown, R.I.	4	49
Northup, Frederick	May 17, 1797	18	dark	No. Kingstown, R.I.	1	18
Northup, Frederick B.	Nov. 13, 1828	23	light	Newport, R.I.	4	49
Northup, Harvey	June 29, 1819	20	dark	New Haven, Conn.	4	49
Northup, Henry	Sept. 23, 1864	19	dark	So. Kingston, R.I.	6	14
Northup, Ichabod, Jr.	Mar. 23, 1815	24	black	E. Greenwich, R.I.	4	49

*Newport, R. I.

NAME	DATE OF CERTIFICATION	AGE	COMPLEXION	PLACE OF BIRTH	BOOK	PAGE
Northup, James	May 9, 1809	16	yellowish	E. Greenwich, R.I.	4	49
Northup, John	June 10, 1825	27	dark	No. Kingstown, R.I.	4	49
Northup, Joseph C.	Dec. 14, 1826	23	light	So. Kingstown, R.I.	4	49
Northup, JOseph H.	Nov. 26, 1830	21	light	Newport, R.I.	5	56
Northup, Rufus, Jr.	Mar. 10, 1832	20	dark	No. Kingston, R.I.	5	56
Northup, Smith	Mar. 1, 1805	22	light	So. Kingstown, R.I.	3	25
Northup, Stephen	Dec. 5, 1797	23	light	So. Kingstown, R.I.	1	18
Northup, Stephen H.	Apr. 18, 1855	25	fair	Warwick, R.I.	5	57
Northup, Sylvester	Nov. 14, 1804	23	light	So. Kingstown, R.I.	3	25
Northup, Wm. D.	Nov. 11, 1850	22	light	No. Kingston, R.I.	5	56
Norton, John	May 13, 1828	17	dark	Lincolnville, Me.	4	49
Norton, Joseph	May 23, 1818	27	dark	Somerset, Ma.	4	49
Norton, Peter	Dec. 22, 1803	33	black	Providence, R.I.	2	13
Nottage, Edward W.	Aug. 9, 1837	18	light	Boston, Ma.	5	56
Nottage William S.	Dec. 21, 1829	21	light	Boston, Ma.	5	56
Nourse, Abner J.	May 13, 1842	26	light	Danvers, Ma.	5	56
Noyes, John, Jr.	June 14, 1849	36	light	Newburyport, Ma.	5	56
Noyes, John U. [pdike]	Sept. 13, 1821	14	light	Providence, R.I.	4	49
Noyes, Joshua	July 12, 1825	17	light	Westerly, R.I.	4	49
Nutt, William	June 26, 1839	20	light	Camden, Me.	5	56
Nutter, John A.	Sept. 8, 1840	17	light	Barnstead, N.H.	5	56
Nye, Bartlett	1798-1799	Mar. 10, 1778		Sandwich, Ma.	* -	--
Nye, Ezekiel D.	May 12, 1818	21	dark	Rochester, Ma.	4	49
Nye, Henry A.	Oct. 9, 1849	31	light	Braintree, Ma.	5	56
Nye, Philip	Nov. 5, 1819	30	light	New Braintree, Ma.	4	49
Nyles, James	Dec. 13, 1806	25	yellow	So. Kingstown, R.I.	4	49
Oatley, William	June 3, 1839	35	light	Newport, R.I.	5	58
Oakes, Ebenezer	Nov. 14, 1840	18	light	Berlin, Me.	5	58
Oatley, William	Dec. 10, 1839	26	light	Newport, R.I.	5	58
O'Brian, John	June 16, 1855	20	fair	Providence, R.I.	5	91
O'Brien, Patrick	July 15, 1854	19	light	So. Kingston, R.I.	5	58
Obus, Jack	July 31, 1806	25	black	Weathersfield, Conn.	3	27
O'Connor, Daniel	June 13, 1851	30	light	New York, N.Y.	5	58
O'Connor, John	Jan. 6, 1853	25	light	New York, N.Y.	5	58
Odekirk, Calvin F.	Feb. 27, 1857	23	dark	Albany, N.Y.	5	58

*Newport, R.I.

NAME	DATE OF CERTIFICATION	AGE	COMPLEXION	PLACE OF BIRTH	BOOK	PAS
Odell, Samuel H.	July 18, 1833	23	light	Poughkeepsie, N.Y.	5	58
O'Donnell, George	Oct. 5, 1864	32	light	New York, N.Y.	6	15
Ogilvie, Henry	July 14, 1863	21	light	New York, N.Y.	6	15
Ogilvie, James	Feb. 23, 1852	20	sandy	Charleston, S.C.	5	58
Ogilvie, John	July 12, 1806	17	light	New York, N.Y.	3	27
Ohanley, James	Jan. 13, 1855	21	fair	Bangor, Me.	5	58
Oldham, Daniel	Dec. 18, 1800	26	dark	Newport, R.I.	2	14
Oldridge, Benjamin	June 14, 1809	19	dark	Rehoboth, Ma.	4	50
Oldridge, Samuel	Mar. 14, 1801	19	dark	Rehoboth, Ma.	2	14
Oldridge, Samuel	July 20, 1803	22	dark	Rehoboth, Ma.	2	14
Oldridge, William	Sept. 23, 1796	21	dark	Rehoboth, Ma.	1	3
Oldridge, William	Nov. 25, 1807	33	dark	Bristol, R.I.	4	50
Olin, John G.	June 12, 1800	17	dark	Warwick, R.I.	2	7
Oliver, Robert	Aug. 2, 1854	22	light	Ogdensburg, N.Y.	5	58
Olney, Amasa	Sept. 13, 1837	19	light	Johnston, R.I.	5	58
Olney, Amos	July 24, 1807	18	yellow	Charlestown, R.I.	4	50
Olney, Augustus	Nov. 30, 1849	23	light	No. Prov., R.I.	5	58
Olney, Benjamin	Aug. 27, 1796	22	light	Providence, R.I.	1	1
Olney, Benjamin	Jan. 13, 1844	17	black	New Shoreham, R.I.	5	58
Olney, Benjamin S.	Aug. 8, 1810	19	light	Providence, R.I.	4	50
Olney, Charles C.P.	July 24, 1820	23	light	Smithfield, R.I.	4	50
Olney, Christopher	Mar. 16, 1825	15	light	Providence, R.I.	4	50
Olney, Frederick A.	Mar. 16, 1831	14	dark	Providence, R.I.	5	58
Olney, Henry N.	Aug. 20, 1818	15	light	Providence, R.I.	4	50
Olney, Hezekiah	Mar. 2, 1849	26	ruddy	Plainfield, Conn.	5	58
Olney, James	m. Elisabeth Wood, Nov. 1815			Rev. Benedict Record.		
Olney, Jeremiah	Sept. 26, 1817	20	light	Providence, R.I.	4	50
Olney, John B.	Nov. 24, 1838	18	dark	Boston, Ma.	5	58
Olney, Joseph	July 14, 1797	22	black	Providence, R.I.	1	19
Olney, Joseph	Jan. 9, 1798	22	black	Providence, R.I.	1	19
Olney, Peter	May 17, 1805	21	light	Providence, R.I.	3	27
Olney, Richard	Oct. 5, 1849	48	dark	Scituate, R.I.	5	58
Olney, Samuel	Aug. 11, 1796	20	light	Providence, R.I.	1	1
Olney, Samuel	Nov. 25, 1797	22	light	Providence, R.I.	1	19
Olney, Samuel S	Oct. 23, 1829	18	light	Providence, R.I.	5	58
Olney, Solomon	Jan. 9, 1798	27	black	Providence, R.I.	1	19
Olney, Stephen	Dec. 22, 1800	16	light	No. Prov., R.I.	2	14
Olney, William	Sept. 14, 1803	17	dark	Providence, R.I.	2	14

NAME	DATE OF CERTIFICATION	AGE	COMPLEXION	PLACE OF BIRTH	BOOK	PAGE
Olney, William	July 16, 1804	18	dark	Providence, R.I.	3	27
O'Neil, Andrew	Oct. 3, 1844	16	light	Newport, R.I.	5	58
O'Neil, Patrick	July 20, 1852	25	light	Fall River, Ma.	5	58
Onsley, Thomas	June 16, 1809	25	yellow	No. Prov., R.I.	4	50
Onsley, Willis A.K.	Aug. 25, 1838	24	black	Burrillville, R.I.	5	58
Ormsbee, Alfred	Sept. 29, 1831	18	freckled	Providence, R.I.	5	58
Ormsbee, Charles A.	Oct. 29, 1830	20	light	Providence, R.I.	5	58
Ormsbee, David C.	July 17, 1815	19	light	Providence, R.I.	4	50
Ormsbee, Edward D.	May 10, 1815	17	light	Providence, R.I.	4	50
Ormsbee, Jesse	Oct. 13, 1819	27	light	Rehoboth, Ma.	4	50
Ormsbee, John	Sept. 21, 1796	20	dark	Providence, R.I.	1	3
Ormsbee, John H.	Aug. 2, 1799	19	dark	Pomfret, Conn.	2	14
Ormsbee, John S.	Mar. 21, 1833	16	light	Providence, R.I.	5	58
Ormsbee, Royal	July 21, 1809	16	light	Rehoboth, Ma.	4	50
Ormsbee, Samuel P.	Apr. 25, 1809	24	dark	Rehoboth, Ma.	4	50
Ormsbee, Seneca	Sept. 26, 1805	20	dark	Providence, R.I.	3	27
Ormsbee, William	Apr. 2, 1811	14	light	Providence, R.I.	4	50
Ormsbee, William	Sept. 14, 1836	20	light	Providence, R.I.	5	58
Ormsbee, William P.	Sept. 25, 1811	17	dark	Rehoboth, Ma.	4	50
Ormsbee, William W.	Oct. 4, 1806	15	brown	Providence, R.I.	3	27
Ormsbee, William W.	Oct. 4, 1809	15	brown	Providence, R.I.	4	50
Ormsbee, William W.	May 15, 1811	20	dark	Providence, R.I.	4	50
Orr, James	July 13, 1812	21	brown	Harpswell, Ma. [Me.]	4	50
Orrell, David	Feb. 26, 1851	21	light	Gloucester, N.J.	5	58
Ormsby, George	June 28, 1833	27	light	Baltimore, Md.	5	58
Osborne, Nathaniel	Mar. 9, 1798	27	light	Danvers, Ma.	1	19
Otis, Alanson	July 10, 1807	14	light	Bellingham, Ma.	4	50
Otis, Amos	Oct. 9, 1834	36	light	New Castle, Me.	5	58
Otis, Isaac	Oct. 29, 1801	16	light	Cumberland, R.I.	2	14
Otterson, Samuel	Dec. 5, 1800	27	dark	Barrington, R.I.	2	14
Oughten, William E.	Nov. 27, 1849	19	light	New York, N.Y.	5	58
Overing, Jack	Sept. 10, 1796	20	black	Newport, R.I.	1	2
Owen, Almond	July 3, 1807	18	light	Cranston, R.I.	4	50
Owen, Brown	July 17, 1805	16	light	Glocester, R.I.	3	27
Owen, James	Sept. 10, 1864	27	light	Warwick, R.I.	6	15
Owen, Samuel	Aug. 5, 1850	28	mulatto	Northampton, N.Y.	5	58
Owen, W. Henry	Aug. 7, 1852	23	mulatto	Phila., Pa.	5	58

Page 195

NAME	DATE OF CERTIFICATION	AGE	COMPLEXION	PLACE OF BIRTH	BOOK	PAG
Owen, William	Dec. 24, 1817	23	light	Providence, R.I.	4	50
Owen, William	Apr. 25, 1849	44	dark	No. Prov., R.I.	5	58
Owens, John	Feb. 6, 1847	19	fair	New York, N.Y.	5	58
Owens, Michael	June 10, 1797	33	light	Rehoboth, Ma.	1	19
Owens, Thomas [Owans]	Aug. 23, 1800	14	light	Providence, R.I.	2	14
Oxx, Benjamin	Aug. 29, 1822	24	light	Bristol, R.I.	4	50
Oxx, George	1798-1799	Feb. 3, 1783		Bristol, R.I.	-	--
Oxx, Samuel H.	Oct. 29, 1849	40	light	Newport, R.I.	5	58
Pabodie, Benjamin	July 13, 1799	17	light	Providence, R.I.	2	15
Pabodie, Joseph	May 10, 1800	20	dark	Providence, R.I.	2	15
Pabody, Stephen	Apr. 1, 1800	27	dark	Boxford, Ma.	2	15
Packard, Albert	Oct. 14, 1834	14	light	Providence, R.I.	5	59
Packard, George	Oct. 16, 1805	17	light	Providence, R.I.	3	73
Packard, John C.	Sept. 17, 1810	16	light	Providence, R.I.	4	51
Packard, John C.	Apr. 11, 1815	21	light	Providence, R.I.	4	52
Packard, Samuel	July 24, 1820	16	light	Providence, R.I.	4	53
Packard, Stephen H.	Dec. 16, 1805	22	light	Providence, R.I.	3	73
Packard, Stephen H.	Aug. 8, 1803	20	light	Providence, R.I.	2	31
Paddock, Francis	Jan. 9, 1798	27	light	Sherburne, Ma.	1	20
Padelford, Abraham H.	Oct. 8, 1819	20	light	Taunton, Ma.	4	53
Padelford, Frederick	Apr. 4, 1855	28	fair	Taunton, Ma.	5	63
Page, Henry	July 22, 1829	29	black	Providence, R.I.	5	59
Page, James B.	Mar. 8, 1805	13	light	Providence, R.I.	3	30
Page, James B.	Aug. 20, 1810	20	light	Providence, R.I.	4	51
Page, James B.	May 9, 1815	23	light	Providence, R.I.	4	52
Page, John	June 16, 1800	17	light	Providence, R.I.	2	15
Page, John Little	Mar. 6, 1805	20	light	Newport, R.I.	3	30
Page, Michael	Oct. 11, 1839	54	dark	Smithfield, R.I.	5	60
Page, Richard	Sept. 14, 1803	18	light	Providence, R.I.	2	46
Page, Stephen Philip	Dec. 1, 1849	21	light	Glocester, R.I.	5	62
Page, Thomas	Oct. 16, 1819	20	yellow	Providence, R.I.	4	53
Page, Thomas B.	Nov. 30, 1815	16	light	Providence, R.I.	4	52
Page, William	June 27, 1806	18	light	Providence, R.I.	3	65
Page, William	Sept. 22, 1797	23	dark	Providence, R.I.	1	20
Paine, Aldrich	Mar. 5, 1849	22	light	Glocester, R.I.	5	61
Paine, Daniel	Feb. 23, 1805	22	dark	Mansfield, Ma.	3	30
Pain, Daniel	Apr. 27, 1809	25	dark	Mansfield, Ma.	4	5

NAME	DATE OF CERTIFICATION	AGE	COMPLEXION	PLACE OF BIRTH	BOOK	PAGE
Pain, John D.	Apr. 4, 1855	32	light	Johnston, R.I.	5	63
Pain, Philip	Nov. 5, 1811	19	light	Cranston, R.I.	4	52
Paine, Daniel S.	Jan. 18, 1828	21	dark	Providence, R.I.	4	53
Paine, Dennis	Nov. 15, 1841	29	Indian	Newport, R.I.	5	60
Paine, Dutee S.	Aug. 16, 1849	19	light	Burrillville, R.I.	5	61
Paine, Henry	June 1, 1836	24	black	New Shoreham, R.I.	5	60
Paine, Henry J.	June 18, 1864	24	light	No. Prov., R.I.	6	16
Paine, James D.	Oct. 30, 1805	20	dark	Rehoboth, Ma.	3	73
[Paine]Pain, John	Dec. 9, 1799	18	light	Rehoboth, Ma.	2	15
Paine, John	Nov. 27, 1839	46	sandy	Harwich, Ma.	5	60
Paine, John C.	Sept. 12, 1842	18	light	Providence, R.I.	5	60
Paine, John F.	Aug. 5, 1841	21	dark	Providence, R.I.	5	60
Paine, Jonathan, Jr.	Apr. 19, 1815	20	ruddy	Seekonk, Ma.	4	52
Paine, Joseph	Mar. 3, 1849	26	light	Augusta, Me.	5	61
Paine, Nathan	Apr. 14, 1853	33	light	Burrillville, R.I.	5	62
[Paine]Pain, Olney	Nov. 18, 1796	16	light	No. Prov., R.I.	1	20
Paine, Thomas	June 22, 1838	16	dark	Calais, Me.	5	60
Paine, William	Mar. 14, 1809	21	light	Rehoboth, Ma.	4	51
Painter, Peter	May 16, 1834	24	black	Lewiston, Del.	5	59
Palmer, Benjamin G.	Aug. 25, 1831	16	light	Newport, R.I.	5	59
Palmer, Dudley	1798-1799	Dec. 5, 1771		Westport, Ma.	* -	--
Palmer, Francis	Nov. 9, 1831	33	black	Charlestown, R.I.	5	59
Palmer, George H.	Mar. 16, 1811	21	light	Lennox, Ma.	4	52
Palmer, Jabez	Nov. 22, 1796	23	dark	No. Prov., R.I.	1	20
Palmer, James N.	Mar. 26, 1838	26	dark	Medford, Ma.	5	60
Palmer, John	Nov. 6, 1835	23	light	Poughkeepsie, N.Y.	5	59
Palmer, John P.	Mar. 8, 1827	52	light	Dighton, Ma.	4	53
Palmer, Jonas G.	Aug. 14, 1837	23	light	Woodstock, Vt.	5	60
Palmer, Richard	Mar. 20, 1837	36	mulatto	Brooklyn, N.Y.	5	60
Palmer, Robert C.	Sept. 12, 1828	35	light	Stonington, Conn.	4	54
Palmer, Sam'l J.	Mar. 15, 1855	21	light	New York, N.Y.	5	63
Palsor, Jacob	May 20, 1805	21	light	Cumberland, R.I.	3	30
Pannel, James	Apr. 4, 1806	23	light	New York, N.Y.	3	73
Park, Joshua	June 4, 1844	16	light	Dixfield, Me.	5	60
Park, Thomas	May 31, 1803	22	light	Boston, Ma.	2	31
Parker, Abijah	Oct. 20, 1797	19	light	Boston, Ma.	1	20
Parker, Andrew	Mar. 6, 1848	26	black	Fredericksburg, Va.	5	61

*Newport, R. I.

REGISTER OF SEAMEN'S PROTECTION

NAME	DATE OF CERTIFICATION	AGE	COMPLEXION	PLACE OF BIRTH	BOOK	PAG
Parker, Benjamin	May 23, 1806	21	light	Providence, R.I.	3	69
Parker, Franklin	Feb. 28, 1849	22	light	Boston, Ma.	5	61
Parker, George	Sept. 12, 1796	19	dark	Providence, R.I.	1	2
Parker, Groves A.	June 12, 1851	18	light	Sedgwick, Me.	5	62
Parker, Henry	Nov. 19, 1813	16	light	Falmouth, Ma.	4	52
Parker, Henry	Mar. 21, 1815	18	light	Falmouth, Ma.	4	52
Parker, James	Mar. 22, 1806	23	light	Northbridge, Ma.	3	73
Parker, James	Apr. 23, 1841	21	black	Lewistown, Del.	5	60
Parker, James	July 15, 1850	25	light	Boston, Ma.	5	62
Parker, John	Dec. 24, 1830	35	light	Bucksport, Me.	5	59
Parker, John D.	Dec. 30, 1811	21	light	Boston, Ma.	4	52
Parker, Jonas	Mar. 6, 1828	28	light	Shirley, Ma.	4	53
Parker, Jonathan	1798-1799	Sept. 20, 1767		Andover, Ma.	* -	--
Parker, Joseph	Sept. 18, 1805	20	dark	Northcumberland Co., Va.	3	31
Parker, Josiah	Feb. 23, 1824	28	light	Falmouth, Ma.	4	53
Parker, Lewis W.	Sept. 17, 1857	25	light	Fall River, Ma.	6	16
Parker, Simeon	Dec. 18, 1850	33	light	Blue Hill, Me.	5	62
Parker, Theodore	Nov. 20, 1849	26	light	Boston, Ma.	5	62
Parker, Thomas	Aug. 25, 1800	22	light	Phila., Pa.	2	31
Parker, Thomas	July 7, 1845	31	ruddy	Portland, Me.	5	61
Parker, William	Dec. 4, 1823	16	light	Bucksport, Me.	4	53
Parker, William	Apr. 25, 1842	26	light	Dighton, Ma.	5	60
Parkes, Joseph	Oct. 3, 1801	38	dark	Warren, R.I.	2	31
Parkis, Stephen F.	June 8, 1821	14	yellow	Brooklyn, Conn.	4	53
Parlow, William	Sept. 20, 1832	21	dark	Rochester, Ma.	5	59
Parmenter, John A.	July 10, 1839	25	light	Providence, R.I.	5	60
Parris, Elisha P.	June 4, 1831	27	light	Middleboro, Ma.	5	59
Parrish, Gideon M.	June 23, 1804	17	light	Wickford, R.I.	3	29
Parrish, Gideon M.	Mar. 18, 1806	17	light	E. Greenwich, R.I.	3	73
Parrish, Gideon M.	June 9, 1807	19	light	E. Greenwich, R.I.	4	51
Parroth, David	-----	18	light	Charleston, S.C.	1	3
Parsons, Richard	Dec. 12, 1834	23	light	Hampton, Va.	5	59
Parsons, William	Aug. 8, 1846	30	fair	Machias, Me.	5	61
Parsons, Wm. H.	June 23, 1841	22	light	Woodstock, Conn.	5	60
Partridge, Welcome L.	Dec. 22, 1825	19	light	Bristol, R.I.	4	53
Parum, Mansfield	July 26, 1853	50	black	Phila., Pa.	5	62

*Newport, R. I.

REGISTER OF SEAMEN'S PROTECTION

NAME	DATE OF CERTIFICATION	AGE	COMPLEXION	PLACE OF BIRTH	BOOK	PAGE
Patchey, Samuel	July 25, 1804	28	light	New York, N.Y.	3	29
Paton, Andrew	Mar. 26, 1835	18	light	Baltimore, Md.	5	59
Paton, John	Feb. 23, 1852	19	light	Charleston, S.C.	5	62
Patt, Alfred A.	Oct. 10, 1850	33	dark	No. Prov., R.I.	5	62
Patten, John H.	July 29, 1836	22	light	Boston, Ma.	5	60
Patten, Welcome	July 27, 1844	21	light	Mendon, Ma.	5	60
Patten, William W.	Apr. 19, 1860	25	fair	Richmond, Va.	6	16
Patterson, Frederick	July 28, 1840	28	light	Phila., Pa.	5	60
Patterson, George	Dec. 15, 1847	40	light	Saco, Me.	5	61
Patterson, Horatio	Oct. 27, 1849	28	florid	Manchester, Great Britain	5	62
Patterson, John	Oct. 27, 1849	25	florid	Manchester, Great Britain	5	62
Patterson, Rufus, Jr.	Dec. 17, 1856	20	dark	Northport, Me.	5	63
Paul, Henry	Oct. 8, 1819	22	light	Providence, R.I.	4	53
Paul, Joseph	Jan. 13, 1852	23	dark	Brooklyn, N.Y.	5	62
Paun, John	Apr. 23, 1811	17	dark	So. Kingstown, R.I.	4	52
Parson, John	Apr. 14, 1856	27	sandy	Bordentown, N.J.	5	63
Pay, Charles	Mar. 16, 1848	24	dark	Boston, Ma.	5	61
Payerne, John	Apr. 17, 1818	18	dark	Phila., Pa.	4	52
Payne, Enos B.	Nov. 8, 1831	14	dark	Freetown, Ma.	5	59
Payne, Freeborn	June 2, 1830	29	dark	Freetown, Ma.	5	59
Payne, Solomon	Oct. 26, 1805	17	light	Freetown, Ma.	3	73
Payne, Wm. H.C.	Apr. 27, 1848	19	dark	Taunton, Ma.	5	61
Payson, Ebenezer W.	Apr. 18, 1846	25	fair	New Bedford, Ma.	5	61
Peach, John	Mar. 14, 1850	45	dark	Marblehead, Ma.	5	62
Peach, John	Feb. 18, 1851	24	light	Marblehead, Ma.	5	62
Peach, John	June 13, 1857	52	dark	Marblehead, Ma.	5	63

Pearce Regardless of Spelling (Pearce, Pierce, Peirce) all are filed here according to first or given name.

Pearce, Abraham	Mar. 21, 1806	30	black	Warwick, R.I.	3	73
Pearce, Abraham	Dec. 17, 1804	28	black	Prudence, R.I.	3	30
Pearce, Abraham B.	May 16, 1820	14	light	Rehoboth, Ma.	4	53
In Rehoboth Vital Records: Abram Blanding Pearce, b. 12/29/1805						
Pearce, Benjamin M.	June 12, 1835	25	dark	Rehoboth, Ma.	5	59
Pearce[Pierce],Bethuel	Mar. 6, 1807	24	light	Freetown, Ma.	4	51
Pearce[Peirce], Caleb	Nov. 7, 1807	20	light	Rochester, Ma.	4	51
Peirce, Christopher B.	Dec. 19, 1815	17	light	East Greenwich, R.I.	4	52
Pierce, Daniel	May 28, 1863	34	light	E. Greenwich, R.I.	6	16
Pearce, Daniel B.	Dec. 1, 1829	21	light	Warwick, R.I.	5	59

NAME	DATE OF CERTIFICATION	AGE	COMPLEXION	PLACE OF BIRTH	BOOK	PAGE
Pearce[Peirce], Darius	Jan. 4, 1849	23	light	No. Kingstown, R.I.	5	61
Pearce, Elijah L.	Dec. 12, 1817	21	light	E. Greenwich, R.I.	4	52
Pearce[peirce],Enos	Nov. 17, 1810	22	light	Middleborough, Conn.	4	51
Pearce, George	Mar. 15, 1815	15	light	Providence, R.I.	4	52
Pearce, Jacob	June 27, 1806	37	black	Providence, R.I.	3	69
Pearce, Jacob	Mar. 1, 1805	35	yellow*	Providence, R.I.	3	30
Peirce, James	Apr. 2, 1860	19	fair	Phila., Pa.	6	16
Pearce, James Leonard	Nov. 7, 1796	18	light	E. Greenwich, R.I.	1	20&5
Pearce[Pierce], James M.	Mar. 5, 1849	27	light	Swansea, Ma.	5	61
Pearce, James S.	Nov. 8, 1856	26	black	Plymouth, Ma.	5	63
Pearce, Jerauld	Sept. 25, 1804	23	light	Warwick, R.I.	3	29
Pearse, Jeremiah	1798-1799	Jan. 25, 1779		Bristol, R.I.	* -	--
Pearce[Peirce], Job	Dec. 19, 1801	20	dark	E. Greenwich, R.I.	2	31
Pearce, John	Jan. 19, 1801	21	dark	Portsmouth, R.I.	2	31
Peirce, John	May 1, 1866	20	light	Goshen, Ma.	6	16
Pearce, John, Jr.	Dec. 4, 1826	15	black	Providence, R.I.	4	53
Pearce, John A.	June 20, 1804	22	light	Newport, R.I.	3	29
Pearce[Peirce],John B.	Jan. 15, 1849	21	light	No. Kingston, R.I.	5	61
Pearce[Peirce], John H.	Oct. 2, 1826	21	light	Providence, R.I.	4	53
Pearce, John M.	Dec. 4, 1826	29	yellow	Providence, R.I.	4	53
Pearce, John W.	Dec. 16, 1844	18	light	Johnston, R.I.	5	61
Pearce[Pierse], John W.	Aug. 7, 1852	25	light	Providence, R.I.	5	62
Peirce, Jonathan	1798-1799	Sept. 17, 1771		Somerset, Ma.	* -	--
Pearce, Joseph	Mar. 20, 1809	17	light	Franklin, Ma.	4	51
Pearse, Joshua	1798-1799	Aug. 28, 1779		No. Kingstown	* -	--
Pearce, Joseph G.	Dec. 20, 1847	13	light	Seekonk, Ma.	5	61
Pearce, Martin	Nov. 2, 1805	22	dark	E. Greenwich, R.I.	3	73
Pearce, Pardon S.	Sept. 20, 1815	23	fresh	Little Compton, R.I.	4	52
Pearce, Robert	Oct. 11, 1799	22	dark	Killingly, Conn.	2	15
Pearce, Samuel	Oct. 19, 1797	20	light	No. Kingstown, R.I.	1	20
Pearce, Samuel W.	Nov. 7, 1809	21	florid	Warwick, R.I.	4	51
Pearce, Sam'l R.	Aug. 28, 1854	19	light	Providence, R.I.	5	63
Pierce, Stephen	1798-1799	Apr. 6, 1781		Newport, R.I.	-	--
Pearce, Stephen	Dec. 17, 1800	18	light	E. Greenwich, R.I.	2	31
Pearce[Pierce], Stephen W.	Sept. 4, 1849	21	light	Scituate, R.I.	5	61
Pearce, Thomas	Oct. 21, 1812	20	light	Providence, R.I.	4	52

*mulatto

REGISTER OF SEAMEN'S PROTECTION

NAME	DATE OF CERTIFICATION	AGE	COMPLEXION	PLACE OF BIRTH	BOOK	PAGE
Pearce[Pierce], Thomas A.	Oct. 5, 1849	34	light	Providence, R.I.	5	62
Pearce[Peirce], Thomas C.	Jan. 9, 1849	19	light	No. Kingston, R.I.	5	61
Pearce, Timothy	1798-1799	Apr. 23, 1786		Newport, R.I.	* -	--
Pearce[Peirce], William	Oct. 31, 1797	17	light	E. Greenwich, R.I.	1	20
Pearce[Pierce], William	Sept. 29, 1809	17	dark	New York, N.Y.	4	51
Pearce, William	Dec. 27, 1811	23	dark	No. Kingstown, R.I.	4	52
Pearce, William H.	Mar. 4, 1812	13	light	Providence, R.I.	4	52
Pearce, Wm. J.	Feb. 26, 1849	27	light	Providence, R.I.	5	61
Pearce[Peirce], Wm. R.	Feb. 15, 1853	22	fair	Gardiner, Me.	5	62
Pearce, William T.	July 24, 1805	20	light	Portsmouth, R.I.	3	31
Pearce, William T.	Aug. 8, 1804	20	dark	Portsmouth, R.I.	3	29
Pearson, Daniel C.	June 15, 1815	17	light	Providence, R.I.	4	52
Pearson, George	July 3, 1839	23	light	No. Prov., R.I.	5	60
Pearson, Henry A.	Dec. 16, 1825	15	dark	Providence, R.I.	4	53
Pearson, Samuel A.	Mar. 14, 1843	16	light	Providence, R.I.	5	60
Pease, Cornelius	Mar. 30, 1819	33	dark	Rochester, Ma.	4	52
Pease, Peter	1798-1799	Mar. 6, 1772		Hartford, Conn.	* -	--
Pease, Shubael	Mar. 19, 1827	21	light	Hallowell, Me.	4	53
Peatchey, Samuel	May 18, 1799	26	dark	Cranston, R.I.	2	15
Pebbles, John	Mar. 5, 1810	22	light	Rochester, Ma.	4	51
Peck, Arnold	Dec. 23, 1817	21	dark	Rehoboth, Ma.	4	52
Peck, Benjamin	Nov. 10, 1800	19	light	Rehoboth, Ma.	2	31
Peck, Benjamin S.	June 28, 1805	20	light	Providence, R.I.	3	31
Peck, Benjamin S.	Mar. 25, 1867	40	light	Pawtucket, R.I.	6	16
Peck, Charles H.	Feb. 15, 1828	13	light	Providence, R.I.	4	53
Peck, Cyrus	Aug. 25, 1804	19	light	Providence, R.I.	3	29
Peck, Cyrus	Aug. 6, 1807	21	light	Providence, R.I.	4	51
Peck, David, Jr.	Mar. 2, 1815	16	light	Sutton, Ma.	4	52
Peck, Edwin	May 5, 1815	19	brown	Rehoboth, Ma.	4	52
Peck, Ezra	Dec. 16, 1799	20	light	Rehoboth, Ma.	2	15
Peck, Foster S.	Nov. 22, 1833	18	light	No. Prov., R.I.	5	59
Peck, George	Jan. 12, 1824	15	light	Warwick, R.I.	4	53
Peck, George A.	May 13, 1853	19	light	Cumberland, R.I.	5	62
Peck, Henry C.	Aug. 31, 1849	22	light	Providence, R.I.	5	61
Peck, Horace	Apr. 25, 1806	21	light	Providence, R.I.	3	69

*Newport, R. I.

NAME	DATE OF CERTIFICATION	AGE	COMPLEXION	PLACE OF BIRTH	BOOK	PAGE
Peck, Israel	Apr. 14, 1807	18	light	Rehoboth, Ma.	4	51
Peck, John	Dec. 20, 1811	19	dark	No. Providence, R.I.	4	52
Peck, John S.	Sept. 12, 1806	18	light	Providence, R.I.	3	69
Peck, Joseph B.	Apr. 3, 1813	12	light	Providence, R.I.	4	52
Peck, Joshua, Jr.	Sept. 5, 1796	23	light	Rehoboth, Ma.	1	2
Peck, Lyman	Nov. 13, 1810	18	light	Sutton, Ma.	4	51
Peck, Menzo W.	Feb. 4, 1853	20	light	Cumberland, R.I.	5	62
Peck, Paschal P.	June 1, 1806	19	dark	Providence, R.I.	3	69
Peck, Peleg	Nov. 30, 1849	33	light	Swansea, Ma.	5	62
Peck, Titus	Jan. 8, 1807	21	yellow	Bristol, R.I.	4	51
Peck, William	Oct. 17, 1801	21	dark	Rehoboth, Ma.	2	31
Peck, Wm. F.	Feb. 24, 1851	19	light	Warren, R.I.	5	62
Peck, William K.	June 29, 1819	16	dark	Providence, R.I.	4	52
Peck, William W.	Oct. 26, 1814	18	light	Providence, R.I.	4	52
Peckham, Asa	1798-1799	Aug. 6, 1774		New Bedford, Ma.	* -	--
Peckham, Charles J.	Sept. 22, 1851	18	dark	Providence, R.I.	5	62
Peckham, Henry	June 15, 1810	18	black	So. Kingstown, R.I.	4	51
Peckham, Joseph	Sept. 12, 1796	18	light	Middletown, R.I.	1	2
Peckham, Joseph	Oct. 16, 1819	16	brown	Providence, R.I.	4	53
Peckham, Peleg	May 16, 1809	19	dark	Newport, R.I.	4	51
Peckham, Philip	1798-1799	Oct. 8, 1771		Newport, R.I.	* -	--
Peckham, Philip	Dec. 8, 1819	18	light	Providence, R.I.	4	53
Peckham, Philip	Sept. 27, 1843	19	light	Kingston, R.I.	5	60
Peckham, Thomas	Sept. 12, 1796	20	light	Newport, R.I.	1	2
Peckham, Thomas C.	Nov. 4, 1836	19	light	Providence, R.I.	5	60
Peckham, Thomas C.	Aug. 6, 1841	23	light	Providence, R.T.	5	60
Peckham, William	July 10, 1821	23	dark	Rehoboth, Ma.	-	--

Sworn statement of Aaron Peckham of Rehoboth, in the Custom House Papers. DOB: Sept. 23, 17

Pecot, John	June 10, 1867	36	dark	Calais, Me.	6	16
Peets, James C.	May 20, 1859	23	dark	Fall River, Ma.	6	16

Peirce   Filed according to first name under Pearce.

Pendergast, James	Oct. 29, 1849	19	light	Providence, R.I.	5	62
Pendleton, Anderson	Jan. 10, 1856	20	light	Perry, Me.	5	63
Pendleton, Cambridge	Apr. 12, 1820	44	black	Newport, R.I.	4	53
Pendleton, Charles B.	Dec. 7, 1836	21	light	Dighton, Ma.	5	60
Pendleton, John	Oct. 15, 1822	21	ruddy	Exeter, R.I.	4	53
Pennell, Ira	Mar. 22, 1859	34	light	Providence, R.I.	6	16

NAME	DATE OF CERTIFICATION	AGE	COMPLEXION	PLACE OF BIRTH	BOOK	PAGE
Penniger, Isaac A.	June 15, 1819	21	dark	E. Greenwich, R.I.	4	52
Pepall, George	Apr. 26, 1850	28	dark	Tiverton, R.I.	5	62
Percivall, Charles L.	Oct. 21, 1833	26	dark	Dorchester, Ma.	5	59
Percival, Ebenezer W.	Oct. 25, 1838	19	dark	Providence, R.I.	5	60
Percival, Joseph	Oct. 14, 1803	26	light	Sandwich, Ma.	2	46
Percival, Thomas	June 1, 1835	21	light	Boston, Ma.	5	59
Perigo, Norman W.	Apr. 18, 1855	27	fair	Windham, Conn.	5	63
Penn, Thomas	1798-1799	Dec. 25, 1771		Hudson, N.Y.	* -	--
Perkins, Barnebas	Nov. 30, 1838	23	light	Chester, N.H.	5	60
Perkins, Eben	June 9, 1841	22	light	Salem, Ma.	5	60
Perkins, Erastus T.	Sept. 11, 1810	24	light	Lyme, Conn.	4	51
Perkins, George W.	Mar. 8, 1799	22	dark	Bridgewater, Ma.	2	15
Perkins, Joseph H.	June 2, 1849	20	light	Woodstock, Me.	5	61
Perkins, Richard	June 12, 1818	19	yellow	New York, N.Y.	4	52
Perkins, William	June 7, 1809	22	dark	New York, N.Y.	4	51
Pero, Nathaniel	Nov. 19, 1803	18	dark	Johnston, R.I.	2	46
Perot, Jacob	May 7, 1810	19	light	Warwick, R.I.	4	51
Perrin, Jesse	Feb. 14, 1843	18	dark	Goldsbury, Me.	5	60
Perrin, Lewis	Sept. 11, 1860	17	fair	Wiscasset, Me.	6	16
Perrin, Otis, Jr.	Mar. 3, 1849	22	light	Mansfield, Ma.	5	61
Perry, Blake	Dec. 21, 1825	16	light	Tiverton, R.I.	4	53
Perry, Charles	1798-1799	Aug. 7, 1781		Newport, R.I.	* -	--
Perry, Daniel	Sept. 24, 1850	20	black	Norfolk, Va.	5	62
Perry, Dan'l D.	June 9, 1855	25	mulatto	Providence, R.I.	5	63
Perry, Edward	Mar. 15, 1864	31	dark	Providence, R.I	6	16
Perry, Elijah	Jan. 2, 1801	21	light	Rehoboht, Ma.	2	31
Perry, Franklin	Apr. 2, 1849	25	dark	New Orleans, La.	5	61
Perry, Gideon	Mar. 20, 1818	26	black	So. Kingstown, R.I.	4	52
Perry, Hiram A.	Dec. 8, 1827	26	light	Holland, Ma.	4	53
Perry, Howard C.	Dec. 14, 1844	19	light	Dighton, Ma.	5	61
Perry, Isaac	Oct. 11, 1815	22	black	So. Kingstown, R.I.	4	52
Perry, John L.	Sept. 27, 1823	23	light	Belfast, Ireland	4	53
Naturalized at Sept. term Superior Court, Prov.						
Perry, Joseph	Oct. 17, 1803	18	light	No. Prov., R.I.	2	46
Perry, Milton	Mar. 25, 1825	23	black	So. Kingstown, R.I.	4	53
Perry, Orion	July 25, 1820	18	dark	Bristol, R.I.	4	53

*Newport, R. I.

NAME	DATE OF CERTIFICATION	AGE	COMPLEXION	PLACE OF BIRTH	BOOK	PAGE
Perry, Robert A.	Mar. 2, 1849	26	light	So. Kingston, R.I.	5	61
Perry, Samuel	Mar. 21, 1840	22	dark	Bridgeton, N.J.	5	60
Perry, Samuel R.	Dec. 18, 1821	21	light	Nantucket, Ma.	4	53
Perry, Theodore A.	July 10, 1854	22	mulatto	Warwick, R.I.	5	63
Perry, William	Nov. 29, 1848	19	dark	Montipelier, Vt.	5	61
Persons, William	Sept. 22, 1826	34	light	Northbridge, Ma.	4	53
Peters, Aaron	Feb. 7, 1812	18	yellow	Narragansett, R.I.	4	52
Peters, Albert G.	Nov. 8, 1839	21	dark	Johnston, R.I.	5	60
Peters, Benjamin	Dec. 12, 1803	20	light	Clavick, N.Y.	2	23
Peters, Benjamin	Mar. 18, 1848	21	yellow	Warren, Me.	5	61
Peters, Charles	May 21, 1858	21	dark	Norwick, Conn.	6	16
Peters, Gardner	1798-1799	Sept. 17, 1777		Somerset, Ma.	*_	--
Peters, George	Aug. 13, 1840	20	dark	New York, N.Y.	5	60
Peters, James	June 5, 1843	17	dark	Providence, R.I.	5	60
Peters, James	May 15, 1834	26	black	Portland, Me.	5	59
Peters, John	July 6, 1801	20	light	Bristol, R.I.	2	31
Peters, John	Dec. 9, 1852	21	black	Hebron, Conn.	5	62
Peters, Joseph	Feb. 26, 1810	17	yellow	Sterling, Conn.	4	51
Peters, Joseph	July 10, 1810	19	yellow	Sterling, Conn.	4	51
Peter, Nicholas C.	May 6, 1846	22	dark	Providence, R.I.	5	61
Peters, Smith	Oct. 31, 1831	18	light	Providence, R.I.	5	59
Peters, William H.	July 20, 1841	19	light	Boston, Ma.	5	60
Petersen, Benjamin	May 26, 1846	19	dark	New Bedford, Ma.	5	61
Peterson, Charles	Aug. 12, 1806	26	black	Phila., Pa.	3	69
Peterson, Henry	Jan. 31, 1849	22	mulatto	W. Bridgewater, Ma.	5	61
Peterson, James	Sept. 19, 1843	23	black	New Bedford, Ma.	5	60
Peterson, John	Nov. 8, 1803	20	light	Salem, Ma.	2	46
Peterson, John	Jan. 10, 1812	34	black	Woodbridge, N.J.	4	52
Peterson, John	Sept. 26, 1843	21	light	Baltimore, Md.	5	60
Peterson, John P.	Apr. 7, 1809	20	light	Copenhagen, Denmark	4	51
Naturalized. Providence, R.I. Apr. 6, 1809.						
Peterson, Noah	Jan. 1, 1835	32	black	Sharon, Conn.	5	59
Peterson, Peter	Oct. 12, 1804	25	yellow*	New York, N.Y.	3	29
Peterson, Thomas	Nov. 8, 1805	37	black	Bargaintown, N.J.	3	73

*mulatto

*Newport, R.I.

NAME	DATE OF CERTIFICATION	AGE	COMPLEXION	PLACE OF BIRTH	BOOK	PAGE
Peterson, William	Dec. 13, 1849	38	black	New York, N.Y.	5	62
Pettey, Joseph	May 9, 1822	20	light	Providence, R.I.	4	53
Pettis, James	Sept. 26, 1817	22	light	Brookline, Conn.	4	52
Phelan, James	May 5, 1853	27	dark	Watertown, Ma.	5	62
Phelps, Henry	Aug. 18, 1803	29	light	Andover, Ma.	2	31
Phelps, Jeremiah	June 12, 1807	28	light	Edenton, N.C.	4	51
Phelps, Joseph W.	Mar. 8, 1853	42	dark	New Haven, Conn.	5	62
Phelps, Seth	Apr. 19, 1822	20	light	Suffield, Conn.	4	53
Phillamon, Isaac	July 21, 1819	33	black	Johnston, R.I.	4	53
Phillips, Albert A.	Nov. 1, 1851	24	dark	Scituate, R.I.	5	62
Philips, Amos	Nov. 17, 1810	19	dark	Warwick, R.I.	4	51
Phillips, Augustus E.	Sept. 10, 1838	16	light	Providence, R.I.	5	60
Phillips, Benjamin	Jan. 7, 1800	20	dark	Warwick, R.I.	2	15
Phillips, Benjamin	Oct. 27, 1804	25	dark	Warwick, R.I.	3	29
Philips, Benjamin	Apr. 2, 1810	18	dark	Taunton, Ma.	4	51
Philips, Benjamin	May 9, 1812	20	dark	Taunton, Ma.	4	52
Phillips, Benoin	May 11, 1818	30	dark	Foster, R.I.	4	52
Phillips, David	Dec. 21, 1825	22	yellow	Charlestown, R.I.	4	53
Phillips, Edward J.	Feb. 27, 1843	28	dark	Boston, Ma.	5	60
Phillips, Francis	Nov. 17, 1823	18	light	Provincetown, Ma.	4	53
Phillips, George	Aug. 29, 1803	17	light	Providence, R.I.	2	31
Phillips, George	May 31, 1805	19	dark	Providence, R.I.	3	31
Phillips, George	Juy 8, 1808	22	dark	Providence, R.I.	4	51
Philips, George	June 17, 1828	23	light	Grafton, Ma.	4	54
Phillips, James	Jan. 9, 1798	19	dark	Providence, R.I.	1	20
Phillips, James	Feb. 8, 1800	20	dark	Providence, R.I.	2	15
Phillips, James	Mar. 30, 1805	25	dark	Providence, R.I.	3	30
Phillips, James	Feb. 23, 1852	28	light	New York, N.Y.	5	62
Phillips, James	July 15, 1854	22	fair	Lynn, Ma.	5	63
Phillips, Job	Oct. 29, 1849	45	dark	Coventry, R.I.	5	62
Phillips, John	July 10, 1801	24	light	Washington, N.C.	2	31
Phillips, John	Oct. 22, 1804	20	light	Tiverton, R.I.	3	29
Philips, John	May 17, 1811	23	brown	Newport, R.I.	4	52
Phillips, John W.	Aug. 29, 1825	20	light	Taunton, Ma.	4	53
Phillips, Joseph	Oct. 11, 1799	17	light	Harwich, Ma.	2	15
Phillips, Joseph	June 30, 1832	20	dark	Newport, R.I.	5	59

NAME	DATE OF CERTIFICATION	AGE	COMPLEXION	PLACE OF BIRTH	BOOK	PAGE
Phillips, Joseph	May 21, 1833	47	light	Warwick, R.I.	5	59
Phillips, Lewis	Apr. 26, 1838	20	light	Foster, R.I.	5	60
Phillips, Nathan I.	Jan. 23, 1850	25	fair	No. Prov., R.I.	5	62
Phillips, Otis	Aug. 31, 1849	38	light	Scituate, R.I.	5	61
Phillips, Reuben	Nov. 11, 1825	20	light	Yarmouth, Ma.	4	53
Phillips, Richard	June 13, 1801	19	dark	Providence, R.I.	2	31
Phillips, Richard	Apr. 15, 1835	27	light	Portsmouth, N.H.	5	59
Phillips, Richard C.	Apr. 14, 1818	35	light	Dartmouth, Ma.	4	52
Phillips, Robert	Nov. 9, 1831	24	light	Taunton, Ma.	5	59
Phillips, Silas	Oct. 30, 1852	21	light	Pittsfield, Me.	5	62
Phillips, William	May 2, 1835	21	dark	Charleston, S.C.	5	59
Phillips, William	Dec. 6, 1849	25	dark	Ten Droghe, Ireland	5	62
Phillips, William	Oct. 13, 1860	38	dark	Brooklyn, N.Y.	6	16
Phillips, Wm. Jr.	1798-1799	Year 1781		Tiverton, R.I.	* -	--
Phillips, Zenos	Oct. 11, 1799	19	light	Harwich, Ma.	2	15
Phiney, Benjamin H.	Nov. 24, 1818	14	light	Brewster, Ma.	4	52
Phinney, Horatio	Feb. 26, 1849	18	light	Montpelier, Vt.	5	61
Phipps, Samuel	May 2, 1853	41	dark	Providence, R.I.	5	62
Pibbles, John	Oct. 20, 1804	16	light	Rochester, Ma.	3	29
Pickens, George W.	Dec. 10, 1836	17	light	Freetown, Ma.	5	60
Pickens, George W.	June 22, 1841	21	light	Freetown, Ma.	5	60
Pickett, Charles W.	Aug. 6, 1847	22	fair	Plainfield, Conn.	5	61
Pickett, Thomas	May 24, 1838	44	light	Hartford, Conn.	5	60
Pidge, Nathaniel M.	May 25, 1825	16	light	Providence, R.I.	4	53
Pierce Filed according to the first name under Pearce.						
Pierpout, Evelyn	Aug. 7, 1811	21	dark	New Haven, Conn.	4	52
Piggins, Robert	Feb. 27, 1819	24	yellow	Gray [Ma.], Me.	4	52
Pike, Henry	Aug. 13, 1806	16	dark	Providence, R.I.	3	69
Pike, James	Sept. 4, 1810	22	light	Providence, R.I.	4	51
Pike, John, Jr.	1798-1799	Dec. 8, 1814		Newport, R.I.	* -	--
John Pike of Newport swears for him.						
Pike, Stephen C.	Aug. 10, 1810	20	light	Providence, R.I.	4	51
Pilcher, Edmund	Apr. 15, 1851	20	light	Charleston, S.C.	5	62
Pineo, George	Nov. 14, 1800	25	light	?Machias, [Me.] Ma.	2	31
Pinkham, Alexander	Apr. 20, 1859	35	light	Hudson, N.Y.	6	16
Pinneger, John	1798-1799	Nov. ?, 1784		Newport, R.I.	* -	--
Wm. Pinneger swears fo him. Newport R.I.						
Pinneger, Thomas	Jan. 3, 1826	20	light	E. Greenwich, R.I.	4	53

Page 206

NAME	DATE OF CERTIFICATION	AGE	COMPLEXION	PLACE OF BIRTH	BOOK	PAGE
Pinneger, Wm.	1798-1799		Jan. 26, 1771	Portsmouth, R.I.	* -	--
Rebecca Pinneger a widow swears for him.						
Pinkher, Alexander	Dec. 6, 1849	27	light	Philadelphia, Pa.	5	62
Pinnegar, James M.	June 12, 1832	14	light	E. Greenwich, R.I.	5	59
Pitcher, Benjamin	Nov. 9, 1797	17	dark	Providence, R.I.	1	20
Pitcher, Benjamin	Dec. 9, 1803	23	dark	Providence, R.I.	2	46
Pitcher, Ezra	Dec. 7, 1825	36	light	Barnstable, Ma.	4	53
Pitcher, George F.	Dec. 3, 1806	21	brown	No. Prov., R.I.	4	51
Pitcher, John	Oct. 22, 1803	16	dark	Rochester, Ma.	2	46
Pitcher, John	Mar. 25, 1815	22	dark	Cranston, R.I.	4	52
Pitcher, Peleg	Oct. 30, 1807	13	light	Rochester, Ma.	4	51
Pitcher, Peleg S.	Nov. 2, 1810	16	dark	Rochester, Ma.	4	51
Pitcher, Samuel	Dec. 5, 1832	13	light	Barnstable, Ma.	5	59
Pitman, George	Mar. 12, 1821	--	light	Bristol, R.I.	-	--
Sworn statement of Nicholas Peck, Jr. of Bristol in Custom House Papers. DOB: Dec. 6, 1805.						
Pitman, John	1798-1799		Oct. 20, 1778	Newport, R.I.	* -	--
Pitman, John O.	May 10, 1797	22	light	Providence, R.I.	1	20
Pitman, Nathaniel	1798-1799		Oct. 15, 1782	Newport, R.I.	* -	--
Samuel Pitman of Bristol, R.I. swears for him.						
Pitty [Pittey], William	July 23, 1805	18	light	Boston, Ma.	3	31
Pitts, Daniel	Feb. 7, 1798	39	light	Providence, R.I.	1	20
Pitts, James	July 21, 1807	14	brown	Providence, R.I.	4	51
Pitts, William	Mar. 28, 1809	33	dark	Providence, R.I.	4	51
Pitts, William	Jan. 11, 1826	24	light	Falmouth, Ma.	4	53
Place, Benjamin	Mar. 31, 1810	14	light	Foster, R.I.	4	51
Place, Elihu	Dec. 1, 1810	28	light	Foster, R.I.	4	51
Place, George	Oct. 31, 1803	29	dark	Glocester, R.I.	2	46
Place, James W.	May 12, 1809	18	light	Foster, R.I.	4	51
Place, Samuel	Oct. 12, 1804	17	light	Providence, R.I.	3	29
Place, Sylvester	June 24, 1847	16	light	Douglas, Ma.	5	61
Plaisted, Charles	Mar. 17, 1857	22	dark	Bath, Me.	5	63
Platt, George	Sept. 11, 1811	24	black	Sag Harbor, N.Y.	4	52
Plummer, Edward	Mar. 1, 1867	27	light	Fairhaven, Ma.	6	16
Plumer, Goin Wilson (or) [Plummer], [Gowen] Wilson	May 6, 1824	18	light	Addison, Me.	4	53

Page 207

NAME	DATE OF CERTIFICATION	AGE	COMPLEXION	PLACE OF BIRTH	BOOK	PAGE
Plummer, John	Sept. 15, 1832	27	black	Somerset, Md.	5	59
Plummer, William	Nov. 27, 1835	26	light	Castine, Me.	5	59
Plunkett, John H.	Jan. 30, 1849	30	light	Brunswick, Me.	5	61
Polk, Jacob	Jan. 23, 1858	25	black	Milton, Del.	6	16
Pollock, James	July 20, 1799	31	dark	So. Kingstown, R.I.	2	15
Pollock, Robert A.	Nov. 3, 1835	17	light	So. Kingston, R.I.	5	59
Pollys, Henry W.	July 14, 1848	15	light	Canton, Ma.	5	61
Pomroy, Daniel K.	Nov. 3, 1856	24	light	Bangor, Me.	5	63
Pomroy, Elijah	July 15, 1848	31	dark	Providence, R.I.	5	61
Pond, John C.	April 7, 1853	15	fair	Salem, Ma.	5	62
*Pond, Joseph W.	July 24, 1845	25	dark	Sardinia	5	61
Ponicitowski, R.A.	Feb. 21, 1853	44	dark	Philadelphia, Pa.	5	62
Pool, Isaac R.	Feb. 26, 1853	24	light	Portland, Me.	5	62
Poole, John	Oct. 9, 1818	24	light	Hallowell, Ma. [Me.]	4	52
Poole, William	Oct. 9, 1818	18	light	Hallowell, Ma. [Me.]	4	52
Poor, Albert W.	Mar. 12, 1846	26	dark	Fitchburg, Ma.	5	61
Pope, Elnathan	Oct. 8, 1806	15	light	Middleborough, Ma.	3&4**	69&51
Porter, Benjamin	July 20, 1836	35	dark	Freetown, Ma.	5	60
Porter, Frederic C.	Oct. 23, 1840	15	dark	Freetown, Ma.	5	60
Portland, Israel	Aug. 26, 1819	23	black	New York, N.Y.	4	53
Post, Arthur	Oct. 4, 1806	21	light	Tappan, N.Y.	3&4**	69&51
Pothin, Alphonse	Mar. 9, 1859	26	dark	New Orleans, La.	6	16
Pothin, Richard	Mar. 2, 1859	23	light	New Orleans, La.	6	16
Potter, Abraham	Aug. 27, 1796	29	black	So. Kingstown, R.I.	1	2
Potter, Abraham	Jan. 14, 1800	36	black	Warwick, R.I.	2	15
Potter, Abraham	Aug. 28, 1804	36	black	So. Kingstown, R.I.	3	29
Potter, Aldrich	Dec. 21, 1825	28	light	Charlestown, R.I.	4	53
Potter, Alfred	Aug. 13, 1834	25	black	Fishkill, N.Y.	5	59
Potter, Allen	Feb. 13, 1801	19	light	W. Greenwich, R.I.	2	31
Potter, Anson	June 7, 1799	15	light	Providence, R.I.	2	15
Potter, Arthur M.	Dec. 16, 1797	24	light	Providence, R.I.	1	20
Potter, Benj. G.	Sept. 16, 1852	24	dark	Warwick, R.I.	5	62
Potter, Charles H.	Sept. 26, 1849	21	light	Richmond, R.I.	5	61
Potter, Charles S.	Oct. 11, 1827	17	light	Providence, R.I.	4	53

*naturalized.

** Book 3, page 69; book 4, page 51.

REGISTER OF SEAMEN'S PROTECTION

NAME	DATE OF CERTIFICATION	AGE	COMPLEXION	PLACE OF BIRTH	BOOK	PAGE
Potter, Cyrus	June 8, 1799	17	light	Providence, R.I.	2	15
Potter, Cyrus	Oct. 11, 1806	25	light	Providence, R.I.	4	51
Potter, Edward H.	Oct. 15, 1834	21	light	Providence, R.I.	5	59
Potter, George G.	Apr. 22, 1820	18	black	Swansea, Ma.	4	53
Potter, George H.	Nov. 15, 1825	18	light	Warwick, R.I.	4	53
Potter, George W.	Mar. 28, 1848	30	light	Newport, R.I.	5	61
Potter, Gilbert	Oct. 4, 1796	23	light	Rehoboth, Ma.	1	20&4
Potter, Hanan	Aug. 13, 1834	26	dark	Scituate, R.I.	5	59
Potter, Henry	Mar. 10, 1801	12	black	E. Greenwich, R.I.	2	31
Potter, Henry	May 2, 1805	24	dark	Warwick, R.I.	3	30
Potter, Henry	May 31, 1805	16	yellow*	E. Greenwich, R.I.	3	31
Potter, Hezekiah	June 7, 1836	21	light	Providence, R.I.	5	60
Potter, Ichabod	Jan. 7, 1804	22	light	Newport, R.I.	3	29
Potter, Isaac	June 4, 1833	21	mulatto	So. Kingston, R.I.	5	59
Potter, Isaac	Apr. 21, 1835	18	mulatto	Providence, R.I.	5	59
Potter, James	Aug. 16, 1800	20	dark	Coventry, R.I.	2	31
Potter, James	Mar. 12, 1805	22	dark	Westerly, R.I.	3	30
Potter, James	Sept. 7, 1810	23	light	Cheshire, Ma.	4	51
Potter, James	July 29, 1814	25	light	Providence, R.I.	4	52
Potter, James	Dec. 12, 1818	27	yellow	No. Kingstown, R.I.	4	52
Potter, James B.	Mar. 29, 1805	18	dark	Providence, R.I.	3	30
Potter, James P.	Jan. 29, 1839	23	black	No. Kingston, R.I.	5	60
Potter, John	Oct. 4, 1796	22	light	Rehoboth, Ma.	1	20&4
Potter, John	Nov. 24, 1801	18	black	Cranston, R.I.	2	31
Potter, John	Aug. 26, 1806	19	black	So. Kingstown, R.I.	3	69
Potter, John	Dec. 19, 1800	30	black	So. Kingstown, R.I.	2	31
Potter, John A.	June 5, 1838	24	light	Scituate, R.I.	5	60
Potter, John Carr	Dec. 14, 1822	20	light	Providence, R.I.	4	53
Potter, John D.	Dec. 8, 1815	19	light	Providence, R.I.	4	52
Potter, John H.A.	Feb. 6, 1847	18	yellow	New York, N.Y.	5	61
Potter, John H.A.	Nov. 29, 1848	21	yellow	Penn Yan, N.Y.	5	61
Potter, Joseph	Nov. 29, 1796	17	dark	No. Providence, R.I.	1	20
Potter, Joseph	1798-1799	Dec. 13, 1781		Middletown, R.I.	** -	--
Potter, Joseph A.	Nov. 24, 1829	23	light	Cranston, R.I.	5	59
Potter, Joseph G.	May 1, 1852	23	black	No. Kingston, R.I.	5	62

*mulatto
**Newport

NAME	DATE OF CERTIFICATION	AGE	COMPLEXION	PLACE OF BIRTH	BOOK	PAGE
Potter, Joseph H.	Jan. 22, 1851	19	light	Providence, R.I.	5	62
Potter, Joseph K.	Mar. 29, 1809	17	brown	Providence, R.I.	4	51
Potter, Joseph W.	Dec. 11, 1799	20	light	Warwick, R.I.	2	15
Potter, Knight	Apr. 2, 1805	22	dark	Coventry, R.I.	3	30
Potter, Lucius B.	Aug. 31, 1831	30	light	Providence, R.I.	5	59
Potter, Nicholas	1798-1799	May 27, 1777		So. Kingston, R.I.	*-	--
Potter, Nicholas	June 17, 1799	14	black	Providence, R.I.	2	15
Potter, Pardon	Feb. 17, 1800	17	light	Dartmouth, Ma.	2	15
Potter, Peter	Oct. 23, 1820	21	black	So. Kingstown, R.I.	4	53
Potter, Peter	Apr. 21, 1840	18	light	Scituate, R.I.	5	60
Potter, Phinelus	Nov. 11, 1803	23	light	Providence, R.I.	2	46
Potter, Phineas	Mar. 11, 1801	20	dark	Providence, R.I.	2	31
Potter, Robert	Mar. 28, 1797	20	light	E. Greenwich, R.I.	1	20
Potter, Robinson	1798-1799	May 19, 1768		S. Kingston, R.I.	*-	--
Potter, Rowland	1798-1799	June 3, 1780		S. Kingston, R.I.	*-	--
Potter, Samuel	May 17, 1804	13	black	W. Greenwich, R.I.	3	29
Potter, Samuel	Aug. 16, 1805	14	black	Warwick, R.I.	3	31
Potter, Samuel	June 11, 1855	25	light	New York, N.Y.	5	63
Potter, Sam'l	Feb. 27, 1857	26	light	Newport, R.I.	5	63
Potter, Samuel, Jr.	Sept. 1, 1849	34	light	Glocester, R.I.	5	61
Potter, Samuel F.	Mar. 28, 1851	21	mulatto	Taunton, Ma.	5	62
Potter, Thomas	Nov. 25, 1805	22	black	Charlestown, R.I.	3	73
Potter, Thomas	Apr. 21, 1855	21	light	Spencer, N.Y.	5	63
Potter, Thomas C.	July 10, 1820	27	light	Newport, R.I.	4	53
Potter, William	June 25, 1800	28	black	?Monmouth, N.J.	2	15
Potter, William H.	Mar. 13, 1815	21	dark	Providence, R.I.	4	52
Potter, William M.	May 30, 1849	19	light	Scituate, R.I.	5	61
Potter, Wm. O.	Dec. 1, 1848	24	light	Cranston, R.I.	5	61
Potter, Zelous	Aug. 26, 1806	23	black	So. Kingstown, R.I.	3	69
Pottle, Charles	Oct. 18, 1852	25	light	Marblehead, Ma.	5	62
Potts, John H.	Oct. 1, 1803	32	light	Phila., Pa.	2	46
Potts, John H.	Dec. 28, 1826	21	light	Providence, R.I.	4	53
Potts, Samuel	May 23, 1809	26	florid	Phila., Pa.	4	51
Powell, Henry	April 21, 1853	22	light	Phila., Pa.	5	62
Powell, James	July 19, 1821	30	dark	New York, N.Y.	-	--

Sworn statement of Lucritin James of Bristol in the Custom House Papers.b.Jan. 22, 1791

Powell, Thomas	Nov. 17, 1834	19	dark	Louisville, Ky.	5	59

*Newport, RI

NAME	DATE OF CERTIFICATION	AGE	COMPLEXION	PLACE OF BIRTH	BOOK	PAGE
Power, James	Mar. 11, 1853	20	light	New York, N.Y.	5	62
Powers, Ephraim	Dec. 5, 1800	24	black	Washington, N.C.	2	31
Powes, Benjamin	Aug. 1, 1850	19	light	Plattsburg, N.Y.	5	62
Poyer, James N.	Mar. 1, 1848	17	dark	Providence, R.I.	5	61
Pratt, Alfred U.	Jan. 16, 1849	42	light	Newport, R.I.	5	61
Pratt, Charles	Mar. 17, 1809	17	light	Cranston, R.I.	4	51
Pratt, Edwin C.	Mar. 18, 1840	19	light	Cranston, R.I.	5	60
Pratt, Greenleaf S.	Mar. 24, 1863	23	light	Harwich, Ma.	6	16
Pratt, James	Nov. 6, 1799	19	dark	Cranston, R.I.	2	15
Pratt, John	Dec. 8, 1804	21	light	Worcester, Ma.	3	30
Pratt, John	Nov. 28, 1828	19	dark	New Bedford, Ma.	4	54
Pratt, John	Oct. 3, 1846	42	dark	Needham, Ma.	5	61
Pratt, Nathan	Sept. 21, 1803	26	light	Easton, Ma.	2	46
Pratt, Nathan	Sept. 15, 1832	25	dark	Needham, Ma.	5	59
Pratt, Olney	Mar. 31, 1800	23	light	Cranston, R.I.	2	15
Pratt, Seth	Aug. 22, 1801	34	light	Barnstable, Ma.	2	31
Pratt, Thomas	Oct. 28, 1800	40	light	New York, N.Y.	2	31
Pratt, William	Oct. 10, 1860	33	dark	Charleston, S.C.	6	16
Prebble, John R.	Nov. 9, 1813	25	light	Rochester, Ma.	4	52
Prentice, Asa	July 7, 1798	22	light	Alstead, N.H.	2	15
Prentiss, Joshua	Apr. 13, 1859	38	fair	Marblehead, Ma.	6	16
Prentiss, Joshua C.	May 22, 1827	17	brown	Marblehead, Ma.	4	53
Prentice, Richard	Dec. 22, 1818	16	light	Providence, R.I.	4	52
Prentice, Samuel	Jan. 21, 1824	24	light	Mendon, Ma.	4	53
Prentiss, Thomas, Jr.	Dec. 11, 1821	16	dark	Marblehead, Ma.	4	53
Presham, Joseph	Mar. 19, 1859	27	dark	Conneaut, Ohio	6	16
Pressey, [Chase] Chace	Aug. 11, 1821	20	light	Deer Isle, Me.	4	53
Price, Constant W.	Feb. 7, 1812	22	dark	Newport, R.I.	4	52
Price, David	June 10, 1841	26	light	Columbus, Ohio	5	60
Price, James	Dec. 20, 1799	21	light	Warwick, R.I.	2	15
Price, James	Apr. 19, 1811	32	light	Warwick, R.I.	4	52
Price, John	Dec. 20, 1796	26	light	Newport, R.I.	1	20
Price, Simeon	May 1, 1799	19	light	Newport, R.I.	2	15
Price, William	Dec. 20, 1799	22	light	Warwick, R.I.	2	15

REGISTER OF SEAMEN'S PROTECTION

Page 211

NAME	DATE OF CERTIFICATION	AGE	COMPLEXION	PLACE OF BIRTH	BOOK	PAGE
Price, William	Aug. 9, 1800	22	light	Warwick, R.I.	2	15
Price, William S.	Feb. 5, 1801	21	dark	Providence, R.I.	2	31
Prichard, Albert	June 20, 1844	23	light	Suffolk, Ma.	5	60
Priest, Aaron	Apr. 13, 1852	23	light	Thomaston, Me.	5	62
Priest, John	Nov. 14, 1831	38	light	Fitchburg, Ma.	5	59
Priggrem, ----	Oct. 10, 1866	33	light	Boston, Ma.	6	16
Primroze, Lamdrel	Dec. 8, 1841	53	black	Milford, Del.	5	60
Prince, Harlan	Mar. 18, 1853	16	light	No. Yarmouth, Me.	5	62
Prince, Samuel	June 13, 1855	27	light	Dudley, Ma.	5	63
Prince, Thomas	Nov. 12, 1803	30	black	Worcester, Ma.	2	46
Prince, Thomas	Jan. 11, 1805	34	black	Worcester, Ma.	3	30
Prince, Thomas	Mar. 31, 1800	32	black	Stratford, Conn.	2	15
Pringle, George	Nov. 20, 1821	45	light	Middleboro, Ma.	4	53

His name is crossed out and the word Englisham written above it in red.

NAME	DATE OF CERTIFICATION	AGE	COMPLEXION	PLACE OF BIRTH	BOOK	PAGE
Printer, Edward	1798-1799	Dec. 6, 1765		Somerset, Ma.	**-	--
Pritchard, William	Dec. 31, 1834	25	black	New York, N.Y.	5	59
Pritchett, Daniel	Nov. 10, 1860	28	dark	Vincent, N.J.	6	16
Proctor, Daniel	Nov. 16, 1825	17	light	Cambridge, Ma.	4	53
Proctor, Martin	May 26, 1830	19	light	Providence, R.I.	5	58
Proffit, Ansel	Oct. 29, 1845	18	sallow	Homer, N.Y.	5	61
Proffit, Franklin G.	Mar. 27, 1857	19	black	E. Greenwich, R.I.	5	63
Prophet, Henry	Nov. 19, 1834	20	yellow	Warwick, R.I.	5	59
Prophet, Henry R.	Mar. 12, 1828	18	black	Warwick, R.I.	4	53
Prophet, John	Apr. 6, 1801	18	black	Warwick, R.I.	2	31
[Prophet] Profit, John	Nov. 11, 1803	20	black	Warwick, R.I.	2	46
Prophet, John	Nov. 18, 1831	22	mulatto	Warwick, R.I.	5	59
Prophet, Moses	Mar. 21, 1832	45	Indian	Cranston, R.I.	5	59
Prophet, Peter	Oct. 26, 1835	17	mixed	Warwick, R.I.	5	59
Profit, Peter	Aug. 12, 1836	20	yellow	Warwick, R.I.	5	60
Prophet, Rowland	Aug. 16, 1805	19	yellow*	Warwick, R.I.	3	31
Proffit, Rowland	Mar. 12, 1863	32	dark	Warwick, R.I.	6	16
Prophet, Summersut	Oct. 5, 1810	27	yellow	Warwick, R.I.	4	51
Prophet, Thomas W.	Oct. 1, 1844	28	mulatto	Warwick, R.I.	5	61
Proud, Pratt Robert	1798-1799	Oct. 12, 1777		Newport, R.I.	**-	--

*mulatto
**Newport

NAME	DATE OF CERTIFICATION	AGE	COMPLEXION	PLACE OF BIRTH	BOOK	PAGE
Prout, Joseph P.	May 6, 1831	15	light	Portland, Me.	5	59
Provost, B. Benjamin	Feb. 3, 1801	25	light	Columbia, N.Y.	2	31
Prudden, John	Nov. 17, 1797	44	dark	Suffolk, Va.	1	20
Pullen, Henry	Mar. 3, 1849	33	light	Phila., Pa.	5	61
Pulver, Albert	Aug. 19, 1852	26	dark	Kinderhook, N.Y.	5	62
Pulsipher, Charles H.	Aug. 27, 1849	21	light	Providence, R.I.	5	61
Pulsipher, Joseph J.	Mar. 7, 1827	21	light	Ackworth, N.H.	4	53
Purdy, Abijah	Dec. 12, 1805	23	light	New Rochelle, N.Y.	3	73
Purdy, John	Nov. 26, 1841	16	light	Harrisburg, Va.	5	60
Purinton, Joseph	Sept. 11, 1823	23	light	Somerset, Ma.	4	53
After his name is the word dead in red.						
Purintor, Joseph B.	Nov. 28, 1832	22	light	Somerset, Ma.	5	59
Purkis, John H.	March 1, 1830	15	light	Providence, R.I.	5	59
Purkis, Robert	Oct. 6, 1807	21	light	Newport, R.I.	4	51
Purkis, Robert	Sept. 30, 1809	23	light	Newport, R.I.	4	51
Purkis, Robert, Jr.	Jan. 31, 1829	12	light	Providence, R.I.	5	59
Purkis, William E.	Nov. 18, 1835	15	light	Providence, R.I.	5	59
Purnall, Rufus	July 26, 1853	38	black	Kent, Pa.	5	62
Putnam, James	Oct. 29, 1818	30	dark	Stow, Ma.	4	52
Putnam, Mark	June 3, 1797	22	black	Pomfret, Conn.	1	20
Putnam, William	May 1, 1799	17	light	Windham, Conn.	2	15
Quam, Joshua	Feb. 12, 1799	25	black	Barrington, R.I.	2	16
Quarman, James I.	Nov. 28, 1800	20	light	Bristol, R.I.	2	16
Queen, John	Aug. 2, 1833	36	black	Phila., Pa.	5	64
Quimby, Benjamin	Aug. 2, 1848	20	dark	Greene, Me.	5	64
Quinby, Daniel	Aug. 9, 1832	30	dark	Shapleigh, Me.	5	64
Quindley, George	Aug. 18, 1804	17	light	Attleboro, Ma.	3	31
Quindley, George	May 31, 1805	18	light	Attleboro, Ma.	3	31
Quincy, Samuel D.	Feb. 24, 1834	21	light	Yarmouth, Ma.	5	64
Quiner, Benjamin	Aug. 27, 1825	20	light	Boston, Ma.	4	56
Quinn, Leonard	June 9, 1856	17	light	Foster, R.I.	5	64
Quinn, Thomas	Dec. 21, 1858	32	fair	Providence, R.I.	6	17
Quinnell, Henry	Oct. 15, 1841	27	light	Philadelphia, Pa.	5	64
Quint, Oran	Apr. 28, 1846	27	fair	Sanford, Me.	5	64
Radcliffe, Thomas	Nov. 19, 1832	19	dark	Phila., Pa.	5	65
Radlof[f], Charles	May 23, 1804	21	dark	Rehoboth, Ma.	3	33
Radney, Joshua	Mar. 4, 1837	21	black	Phila., Pa.	5	65

Page 213

NAME	DATE OF CERTIFICATION	AGE	COMPLEXION	PLACE OF BIRTH	BOOK	PAGE
Rafferty, Michael	Feb. 27, 1866	21	dark	Pawtucket, R.I.	6	19
Ralph, Nathan	Apr. 28, 1800	17	light	Coventry, R.I.	2	17
Rament, Cornelius	Oct. 19, 1805	19	dark	Middleborough, Ma.	3	63
Ramsdell, Phineas B.	June 7, 1816	23	brown	Mendon, Ma.	4	58
Rand, Samuel	May 5, 1800	23	light	Charlestown, Ma.	2	17
Randall, Asa	Aug. 31, 1849	19	light	Cranston, R.I.	5	67
Randall, Benjamin F.	June 7, 1816	15	light	Cranston, R.I.	4	58
Randall, Charles	Apr. 10, 1798	16	light	Providence, R.I.	1&2*	22&)
Randal[1], Charles	July 27, 1803	22	light	Providence, R.I.	2	34
Randall, Charles	May 20, 1809	26	light	Providence, R.I.	4	57
Randall, Daniel A.	Mar. 29, 1817	24	dark	Cranston, R.I.	4	58
Randall, Ebenezer	Nov. 1, 1806	15	light	Rochester, Ma.	4	57
Randall, George	Mar. 30, 1811	15	dark	Rochester, Ma.	4	57
Randall, George W.	June 19, 1862	17	dark	Johnston, R.I.	6	19
Randall, Henry	Nov. 15, 1841	20	dark	Sictuate, R.I.	5	66
Randall, Hiram M.	Oct. 29, 1849	26	light	Foster, R.I.	5	67
Randall, James	Oct. 23, 1812	20	light	Tiverton, R.I.	4	58
Randall, James B.	Aug. 25, 1846	17	dark	Providence, R.I.	5	67
Randall, Jeremiah	May 8, 1802	40	dark	Providence, R.I.	2	34
Randal[1], Jeremiah	Nov. 9, 1803	18	light	No. Prov., R.I.	2	34
Randall, Jeremiah	Mar. 9, 1805	18	light	No. Prov., R.I.	3	34
Randall, Job	June 8, 1815	21	brown	Cranston, R.I.	4	58
Randall, John	May 14, 1800	17	dark	Providence, R.I.	2	17
Randall, Josiah	Aug. 10, 1827	18	light	Coventry, R.I.	4	59
Randall, Nehemiah	Oct. 29, 1849	24	dark	Johnston, R.I.	5	67
Randall, Noah	Oct. 7, 1807	21	brown	Rochester, Ma.	4	57
Randall, Rufus I.	Mar. 18, 1853	22	light	Freeport, Me.	5	68
Randall, Seth	Apr. 28, 1821	18	light	Rochester, Ma.	4	58
Randall, Silas	Oct. 28, 1819	14	yellow	Cranston, R.I.	4	58
Randall, Warren	Apr. 29, 1853	17	light	Eastport, Me.	5	68
Randall, William	July 29, 1805	13	light	Providence, R.I.	3	62
Randall, William A.	Feb. 14, 1828	17	light	Providence, R.I.	4	59
Randolph, Anthony	Feb. 5, 1810	28	black	Woodbridge, N.J.	4	57

* Book 1, page 22; Book 2, page17.

NAME	DATE OF CERTIFICATION	AGE	COMPLEXION	PLACE OF BIRTH	BOOK	PAGE
Randolph, Horace	Oct. 1, 1811	17	light	Stockbridge, Ma.	4	57
Randolph, Richard	Sept. 3, 1811	23	light	Hobshole, Va.	4	57
Rankin, Collins	Aug. 3, 1853	21	fair	Warren, R.I.	5	68
Rankin, Thomas	Aug. 3, 1853	22	light	Warren, R.I.	5	68
Raphel, Joseph R.	Sept. 2, 1863	18	dark	Taunton, Ma.	6	19
Rates, George A.	June 1, 1837	21	dark	Easton, Pa.	5	66
Rathbone, Anthony A.	Jan. 22, 1849	20	fair	Johnston, R.I.	5	67
Rathbone, George N.	Aug. 25, 1845	23	dark	Providence, R.I.	5	66
Rathbone, Henry	Feb. 14,1806	18	light	No. Kingstown, R.I.	3	63
Rathbone, James	Oct. 9, 1810	24	light	Lisbon, Conn.	4	57
[Rathbone] Rathbun, Joshua	Oct. 29, 1803	36	dark	Westerly, R.I.	2	34
Rathbun, Sam'l J.	June 12, 1852	27	black	So. Kingston, R.I.	5	68
Rathbun, Simeon	Oct. 1, 1844	18	light	Foster, R.I.	5	66
Rathbon[e], Thomas	Sept. 5, 1801	26	light	Exeter, R.I.	2	34
Rathbone, William	June 5, 1815	19	light	Newport, R.I.	4	58
Rattle, Charles	June 13, 1834	24	dark	New Orleans, La.	5	65
Rawls, Aaron	Nov. 14, 1803	18	dark	New York, N.Y.	2	34
Rawcliffe, Daniel	Feb. 8, 1847	29	fair	Hartford, Conn.	5	67
Rawson, Elijah	Dec. 8, 1818	33	dark	Worcester, Ma.	4	58
Rawson, Ethan Allen	Sept. 12, 1815	17	light	Bristol, R.I.	4	58
Rawson, Grindall	June 14, 1803	40	dark	Providence, R.I.	2	34
Rawson, Joseph W.	Oct. 26, 1831	21	light	Barrington, R.I.	5	65
Ray, Amos	Dec. 8, 1800	22	dark	Wretham, Ma.	2	17
Ray, David	Feb. 20, 1807	26	black	County of Sussex, N.J.	4	57
Ray, Halsey	Nov. 6, 1828	28	light	Cumberland, R.I.	4	59
Ray, John	May 7, 1832	18	light	Yarmouth, Ma.	5	65
Ray, Joel R.	June 9, 1849	33	light	Providence, R.I.	5	67
Ray, Uriah	July 29, 1820	37	light	Nantucket, Ma.	4	58
[Ray] Rea, Uriel, Jr.	Dec. 17, 1800	21	light	Dartmouth, Ma.	2	17
[Ray] Rea, William	Sept. 17, 1806	16	light	Providence, R.I.	3	20
Raymo, John	June 12, 1833	22	black	New York, N.Y.	5	65
Raymond, Horace	Sept. 20, 1830	19	dark	Taunton, Ma.	5	65
Raymond, Jacob	Aug. 12, 1847	26	black	Phila., Pa.	5	67
Raymond, Stephen	Mar. 7, 1827	32	dark	Nantucket, Ma.	4	59
Raymont, James	Nov. 20, 1805	31	dark	Preston, Conn.	3	63
Raymond, James	July 10, 1803	19	light	Portland, Me.	2	34

NAME	DATE OF CERTIFICATION	AGE	COMPLEXION	PLACE OF BIRTH	BOOK	PAGE
Raymond, James	Dec. 21, 1804	21	light	Portland, Me.	3	34
Raymond, John W.	Jan. 6, 1858	35	light	Boston, Ma.	6	19
Raymond, William [Remmends]	Oct. 27, 1834	18	light	Salem, Ma.	5	65
Raynes, John	Aug. 11, 1821	17	light	Deer Island, Me.	4	58
Rea, William	Mar. 29, 1809	18	brown	Providence, R.I.	4	57
Read, Abijah	July 13, 1819	21	black	Boston, Ma.	4	58
Read, George E.	Oct. 31, 1861	24	dark	Newport, R.I.	6	19
Read, James	Dec. 19, 1821	17	dark	Troy [Fall River], Ma. -	--
Sworn statement of Oliver Whitwell of Troy in the Custom House Papers.b.Aug. 24, 1804.						
Read, Benjamin, Jr.	1798-1799	Apr. 5, 1775		Freetown, Ma.	*_	--
Read, Daniel	June 7, 1805	22	dark	Mathews County, Va.	3	62
Read, Edward	May 3, 1844	21	light	New Orleans, La.	5	66
Read, Ezra	Nov. 9, 1797	20	dark	Rehoboth, Ma.	1	22
Read, George W.	Nov. 17, 1828	20	light	Troy, Ma.	4	59
Read, Gilbert	Nov. 15, 1844	24	light	Woolwich, Me.	5	66
Read, Henry	June 19, 1805	15	light	Boston, Ma.	3	62
[Read] Reed, Henry	Nov. 14, 1803	20	light	Newport, R.I.	2	34
Read, James	Nov. 20, 1827	25	dark	Troy, Ma.	4	59
Read, John	1798-1799	Dec. 16, 1773		Newport, R.I.	*--	--
Read, John	Nov. 18, 1796	21	black	Vassalboro, Me.	1	22
Read, John	Jan. 4, 1827	27	light	Troy, Ma.	4	59
Read, John N.	Mar. 17, 1829	22	light	Rehoboth, Ma.	5	65
Read, John W.	July 2, 1817	21	brown	Sharon, Conn.	4	58
Read, Jonathan	Mar. 22, 1845	27	light	Albany, N.Y.	5	66
Read, Martin	Apr. 8, 1805	36	dark	No. Kingstown, R.I.	3	34
Read, Mathew	June 26, 1847	18	dark	Rutland, Vt.	5	67
Read, Nathan D.	Dec. 7, 1803	22	light	Sharon, Conn.	2	24
Read, Scipio	Dec. 31, 1811	24	black	Swansea, Ma.	4	58
Read, Silas	Mar. 19, 1840	32	light	Newport, R.I.	5	66
Read, Washington	Oct. 1, 1831	18	light	Freetown,.Ma.	5	65
Read, William	Apr. 7, 1827	16	black	Troy, Ma.	4	59
Reed, Bela	Dec. 16, 1805	36	light	Abington, Ma.	3	63
Reed, Charles C.	Nov. 29, 1819	24	light	New Haven, Conn.	4	58
Reed, Charles S.	Dec. 14, 1824	19	light	Providence, R.I.	4	59
Reed, Hanson A.	Oct. 11, 1844	21	light	No. Providence, R.I.	5	66

*Newport

REGISTER OF SEAMEN'S PROTECTION

NAME	DATE OF CERTIFICATION	AGE	COMPLEXION	PLACE OF BIRTH	BOOK	PAGE
Reed, John	Apr. 5, 1832	22	light	No. Kingston, R.I.	5	65
Reed, John	Jan. 31, 1849	25	light	Phila., Pa.	5	67
Reed, John B.F.	Mar. 31, 1863	32	dark	No. Kingstown, R.I.	6	19
Reed, Joseph	Dec. 3, 1796	25	yellow*	Vassalboro, Me.	1	22
Reed, Peter	Apr. 2, 1841	17	light	Derby, Conn.	5	66
Reed, Robert	June 15, 1827	27	light	No. Kingstown, R.I.	4	59
Reed, Thomas	Aug. 24, 1831	27	light	Freeport, Me.	5	65
Reed, William	May 17, 1825	48	dark	Norwich, Conn.	4	59
Reid, Enoch P.	Aug. 7, 1845	23	dark	Phila., Pa.	5	66
Reid, John	Feb. 23, 1852	23	dark	New York, N.Y.	5	68
** Reardon?, Peter	Nov. 8, 1851	21	light	Eastport, Me.	5	68
** Reardon?, William S.	Mar. 16, 1839	34	ruddy	Georgetown, Me.	5	66
Reaves, Henry S.	Oct. 5, 1838	21	light	W. Greenwich, R.I.	5	66
Redding, Thomas R.	Apr. 15, 1850	39	light	Boston, Ma.	5	67
Redford, Samuel	May 20, 1851	21	light	Buffalo, N.Y.	5	67
Redwood, Francis B.	June 23, 1841	19	black	Attleboro, Ma.	5	66
Redwood, Henry Alexander	Jan. 13, 1844	18	black	Attleboro, Ma.	5	66
Redwood, Lyman A.	July 9, 1841	17	black	Attleboro, Ma.	5	66
Reese, Adam	Aug. 30, 1809	26	brown	Baltimore, Md.	4	57
Reeves, Abraham	Mar. 23, 1867	28	medium	Millville, N.J.	6	19
Relph, Ezekiel	Dec. 6, 1805	19	dark	Scituate, R.I.	3	63
Remick, Edmund	Mar. 2, 1859	22	dark	Eden, Me.	6	19
Remington, Benjamin John Remington swears	1798-1799 for him.	June 4, 1777		Exeter, R.I.	*** -	--
Remington, Caleb, Jr.	Mar. 3, 1849	23	dark	Dedham, Ma.	5	67
Remington, Enoch	Oct. 2, 1809	17	light	Barrington, R.I.	4	57
Remington, George	Apr. 9, 1822	36	light	Providence, R.I.	4	58
Remington, James	Nov. 10, 1797	18	light	Warwick, R.I.	1	22
Remington, James	May 27, 1799	21	light	Coventry, R.I.	2	17
Remington, James M.V.	Mar. 11, 1812	22	dark	Cheshire, Ma.	4	58
Remington, John	Aug. 9, 1800	19	light	Johnston, R.I.	2	17
Remington, John	Apr. 7, 1827	22	light	Warwick, R.I.	5	65
Remington, John C.	Aug. 2, 1809	23	light	Johnston, R.I.	4	57
Remington, John P.	Feb. 24, 1797	23	light	Newport, R.I.	1	22
Remington, Peleg	May 15, 1811	46	light	Cranston, R.I.	4	57
Remington, Samuel	June 16, 1801	18	light	Johnston, R.I.	2	34

*mulatto

**Radden [Reardon?], Peter.   Rairdan [Reardon?], William S.
***Newport

NAME	DATE OF CERTIFICATION	AGE	COMPLEXION	PLACE OF BIRTH	BOOK	PAGE
Remington, Samuel	Nov. 25, 1820	23	light	Warwick, R.I.	4	58
Remington, Stephen	Feb. 22, 1805	49	light	Johnston, R.I.	3	34
Remington, Stephen W.	Dec. 4, 1833	34	light	Johnston, R.I.	5	65
Renches, Henry	Aug. 31, 1849	25	light	Providence, R.I.	5	67
Reston, John R.	Nov. 4, 1843	27	light	Wilmington, N.C.	5	66
Reynolds, Albert A.	Oct. 16, 1841	18	light	Providence, R.I.	5	66
Reynolds, Anthony	June 25, 1823	29	light	E. Greenwich, R.I.	4	58
Reynolds, Daniel M.	Mar. 17, 1825	17	dark	Warwick, R.I.	4	59
Reynolds, Edward	Sept. 26, 1857	26	light	New York, N.Y.	6	19
Reynolds, George	Nov. 27, 1818	24	black	Exeter, R.I.	4	58
Reynolds, Geo. B.	Apr. 21, 1853	23	light	Lyme, Conn.	5	68
Reynolds, Geo. W.	Feb. 6, 1849	24	light	Richmond, R.I.	5	67
Reynolds, Geo. W.	June 6, 1857	22	black	Providence, R.I.	5	68
Reynolds, Hazard A.	Aug. 18, 1856	20	light	Providence, R.I.	5	68
Reynolds, Henry H.	July 20, 1841	21	light	Barrington, N.H.	5	66
Reynolds, Henry J.	Nov. 15, 1865	23	light	New York, N.Y.	6	19
Reynolds, Isaac, Jr.	May 21, 1832	21	light	No. Kingston, R.I.	5	65
Reynolds, John	Nov. 14, 1796	24	light	Exeter, R.I.	1	22
Reynolds, John	Apr. 20, 1846	27	dark	Pomfret, Conn.	5	67
Reynolds, John L.	Dec. 16, 1819	39	light	Warwick, R.I.	4	58
Reynolds, Nicholas P.	Jan. 22, 1849	26	fair	Exeter, R.I.	5	67
Reynolds, Oliver F.	Mar. 12, 1851	21	light	Gardiner, Me.	5	67
Reynolds, Perley R.	Dec. 21, 1859	26	fair	Stockton, Me.	6	19
Reynolds, Peter	Jan. 4, 1819	26	black	Exeter, R.I.	4	58
Reynolds, Robert T.	Jan. 16, 1849	22	fair	Richmond, R.I.	5	67
Reynolds, Spencer	1798-1799	Feb. 14, 1782		E. Greenwich, R.I.	-	--
Reynolds, Stephen B.	Oct. 26, 1838	26	dark	No. Kingston, R.I.	5	66
Reynolds, Thomas	Dec. 10, 1800	21	light	Warwick, R.I.	2	17
Reynolds, Thomas	Nov. 10, 1804	25	dark	Warwick, R.I.	3	34
Reynolds, Thomas Andrew	Dec. 18, 1800	22	light	W. Greenwich, R.I.	2	17
Reynolds, Thomas D.	July 26, 1816	23	light	E. Greenwich, R.I.	4	58
Reynolds, Tibbits	Oct. 8, 1824	20	dark	No. Kingstown, R.I.	4	59
Reynolds, William	July 13, 1805	21	light	No. Kingstown, R.I.	3	62
Reynolds, William	Oct. 24, 1806	22	light	No. Kingstown, R.I.	4	57

NAME	DATE OF CERTIFICATION	AGE	COMPLEXION	PLACE OF BIRTH	BOOK	PAGE
Reynolds, William	June 18, 1808	24	light	Wickford, R.I.	4	57
Reynolds, William	Feb. 6, 1849	29	light	Richmond, R.I.	5	67
Reynolds, William H.	May 21, 1839	39	light	No. Kingston, R.I.	5	66
Reynolds, William H.	July 17, 1839	26	light	No. Kingston, R.I.	5	66
Reynolds, William H.	June 25, 1849	20	light	Richmond, R.I.	5	67
Rhodes, Arnold	May 8, 1797	21	light	Warwick, R.I.	1	22
Rhodes, Arnold	July 25, 1809	33	light	Cranston, R.I.	4	57
Rhodes, Benjamin	July 31, 1804	15	light	Warwick, R.I.	3	33
Rhodes, Benjamin N.	Oct. 23, 1830	13	light	Warwick, R.I.	5	65
Rhodes, Bonnah?	Nov. 11, 1803	18	black	Cranston, R.I.	2	34
Rhodes, Bonner	Nov. 24, 1804	18	black	Cranston, R.I.	3	34
Rhodes, Bonner	May 24, 1804	19	black	Warwick, R.I.	3	33
Rhodes, Charles	July 24, 1797	16	light	Warwick, R.I.	1	22
Rhodes, Charles R.	July 30, 1841	28	dark	Dorchester, Ma.	5	66
Rhodes, Christopher C.	Apr. 14, 1855	24	light	Warwick, R.I.	5	68
Rhodes, Cyrus	July 14, 1804	19	black	Cranston, R.I.	3	33
Rhodes, Daniel A.	May 29, 1841	18	light	No. Prov., R.I.	5	66
Rhodes, Edward	Oct. 22, 1829	17	light	Providence, R.I.	5	65
Rhodes, Geo. C.	Aug. 8, 1853	15	light	Providence, R.I.	5	68
Rhodes, George W.	Feb. 13, 1798	22	light	Cranston, R.I.	1	22
Rhodes, James A.	June 10, 1841	16	light	Providence, R.I.	5	66
Rhodes, James B.	May 8, 1800	18	light	Johnston, R.I.	2	17
Rhodes, Holden	Dec. 8, 1796	46	light	Warwick, R.I.	1	22
Rhodes, Isaac	Dec. 7, 1796	20	light	Warwick, R.I.	1	22
Rhodes, Jacob C.	Apr. 5, 1845	19	light	Ma.	5	66
Rhodes, James	Sept. 30, 1796	23	light	Warwick, R.I.	2	4
Rhodes, John	June 15, 1811	14	light	Cranston, R.I.	4	57
Rhodes, John	Oct. 21, 1822	21	black	Stonington, Conn.	4	58
Rhodes, Peleg	July 13, 1810	18	light	Warwick, R.I.	4	57
Rhodes, Peleg R.	July 8, 1818	24	light	Warwick, R.I.	4	58
Rhodes, Perry	Mar. 21, 1812	20	light	Warwick, R.I.	4	58
Rhodes, Prince	Jan. 7, 1804	46	black	Cranston, R.I.	3	33
Rhodes, Richard	Oct. 20, 1804	40	black	Cromintee, Africa	3	33
Rhodes, Robert	Apr. 6, 1854	18	fair	Warwick, R.I.	5	68
Rhodes, Samuel R.	July 28, 1809	21	light	Warwick, R.I.	4	57

NAME	DATE OF CERTIFICATION	AGE	COMPLEXION	PLACE OF BIRTH	BOOK	PAGE
Rhodes, Sylvester	Apr. 1, 1806	26	light	Warwick, R.I.	3	63
Rhodes, Sylvester	Jan. 5, 1798	18	light	Warwick, R.I.	1	22
Rhodes, William	Apr. 13, 1832	28	ruddy	Kennebunk, Me.	5	65
Rhodes, William	Feb. 23, 1844	22	light	Lowell, Ma.	5	66
Rhodes, William H.	Sept. 1, 1860	21	fair	Cranston, R.I.	6	19
Rhodes, William N., Jr.?	Aug. 1, 1817	15	dark	Providence, R.I.	4	58
Rice, Augustus	May 18, 1822	22	ruddy	Brookfield, Ma.	4	58
Rice, Amnon	Dec. 4, 1823	19	light	Bucksport, Me.	4	58
Rice, Benjamin	Dec. 17, 1800	22	light	Warwick, R.I.	2	17
Rice, Dutee	Apr. 8, 1797	17	dark	Coventry, R.I.	1	22
Rice, Henry	June 10, 1801	18	light	E. Greenwich, R.I.	2	17
Rice, Henry, Jr.	June 6, 1806	28	light	Providence, R.I.	3	63
Rice, Henry, Jr.	Mar. 26, 1805	26	light	Sudbury, Ma.	3	34
Rice, Isaac	Nov. 15, 1799	25	dark	Boston, Ma.	2	17
Rice, John	Nov. 16, 1804	16	light	Warwick, R.I.	3	34
Rice, Joseph	1798-1799	July 15, 1779		Hardwick, Ma.	*_	--
Rice, Joseph H.	Dec. 2, 1820	17	light	Warwick, R.I.	4	58
Rice, Nahum P.	Nov. 29, 1830	22	light	Bolton, Ma.	5	65
Rice, Randall	Apr. 7, 1809	22	light	Warwick, R.I.	4	57
Rice, Tibbetts	Oct. 12, 1804	27	dark	Warwick, R.I.	3	33
Rice, Thomas	May 28, 1799	17	dark	Warwick, R.I.	2	17
Rice, Samuel	July 29, 1797	40	light	E. Greenwich, R.I.	1	22
Rice, Whipple	Nov. 1, 1817	23	dark	Warwick, R.I.	4	58
Rich, Charles E.	June 15, 1853	18	light	Saco, Me.	5	68
Richards, Henry C.	Dec. 13, 1853	30	light	Franklin, Ma.	5	68
Richards, Samuel	Jan. 23, 1822	22	light	Camden, Me.	4	58
Richards, Thomas	July 23, 1830	26	black	No. Kingston, R.I.	5	65
Richards, Willard	Nov. 2, 1818	18	light	Sherburne, Ma.	4	58
Richards, William	Jan. 3, 1806	24	black	Newport, R.I.	3	63
Richardson, Charles	Nov. 22, 1832	22	light	Providence, R.I.	5	65
Richardson, Ebenezer	Feb. 25, 1804	20	light	Leominster, Ma.	3	33
Richardson, Ebenezer G.	June 5, 1823	17	brown	Dearing, N.H.	4	58
Richardson, Henry	Sept. 26, 1849	23	light	Attleboro, Ma.	5	67
Richardson, James	Mar. 23, 1857	23	light	Eden, Me.	5	68

*Newport, R. I.

NAME	DATE OF CERTIFICATION	AGE	COMPLEXION	PLACE OF BIRTH	BOOK	PAGE
Richardson, James A.	Dec. 1, 1856	26	dark	Augusta, Me.	5	68
Richardson, Joel	Oct. 22, 1804	28	light	Attleboro, Ma.	3	34
Richardson, John	Aug. 16, 1805	35	black	Smithfield, R.I.	3	62
Richardson, John	Mar. 22, 1805	22	yellow*	New York, N.Y.	3	34
Richardson, Jonas	Apr. 17, 1807	28	light	Attleboro, Ma.	4	57
Richardson, Robert	June 6, 1833	55	black	Boston, Ma.	5	65
Richardson, William	July 14, 1798	19	light	Providence, R.I.	2	17
Richardson, William	July 8, 1846	18	dark	Eastport, Me.	5	67
Richmond, Caleb	Oct. 3, 1807	19	black	Dighton, Ma.	4	57
Richmond, Charles	Dec. 2, 1800	27	dark	Little Compton, R.I.	2	17
Richmond, Ezra	Dec. 5, 1800	21	light	Swansea, Ma.	2	17
Richmond, George A.	Oct. 15, 1834	17	light	Providence, R.I.	5	65
Richmond, Jack	June 17, 1805	36	black	Swansea, Ma.	3	62
Richmond, Jacob	Oct. 29, 1835	25	black	Barrington, R.I.	5	65
Richmond, James G.	June 5, 1807	15	light	Providence, R.I.	4	57
Richmond, James H.	Oct. 14, 1826	18	light	Providence, R.I.	4	59
Richmond, John	Dec. 23, 1800	24	dark	Dighton, Ma.	2	17
Richmond, John R.	Dec. 16, 1825	23	light	Seekonk, Ma.	4	59
Richmond, John Rogers	Oct. 15, 1796	27	dark	Rehoboth, Ma.	1	22&4
Richmond, William	Nov. 10, 1796	20	light	New Haven, Conn.	1	22&5
Richmond, William F..	May 4, 1826	18	light	Providence, R.I.	4	59
Richmond, Zephaniah	Aug. 11, 1810	22	black	Tiverton, R.I.	4	57
Richmond, Zephaniah	June 12, 1811	23	black	Tiverton, R.I.	4	57
Rickard, Joseph	May 22, 1809	26	light	Phila., Pa.	4	57
Ricker, Eli R.	June 18, 1864	18	light	Searsport, Me.	6	19
Ricker, Hiram B.	Mar. 10, 1854	20	dark	Vassalboro, Me.	5	68
Ricker, Hiram B.	Nov. 26, 1856	22	light	Vassalboro, Me.	5	68
Ricketson, Frederick A.	Aug. 27, 1859	27	light	New Bedford, Ma.	6	19
Ricketson, Jonathan	Dec. 21, 1819	25	light	New Bedford, Ma.	4	58
Riddle, Levin	July 20, 1797	27	light	Baltimore, Md.	1	22
Riddle, Thomas	Mar. 13, 1812	16	dark	Bridgewater, Ma.	4	58
Rideout, Robert	Mar. 21, 1840	27	light	Augusta, Me.	5	66
Rider, James	Nov. 14, 1801	19	light	No. Prov., R.I.	2	34
Rider, Job P.	Nov. 17, 1827	17	light	Vinal Haven, Me.	4	59
Rider, William	Aug. 24, 1805	20	light	Newport, R.I.	3	62
Ridgeway Elihu	Mar. 15, 1852	23	mulatto	Phila., Pa. .	5	68

*mulatto

NAME	DATE OF CERTIFICATION	AGE	COMPLEXION	PLACE OF BIRTH	BOOK	PAG
Riggs, William	Nov. 23, 1805	22	light	Baltimore, Md.	3	63
Riley, Charles F.	Sept. 4, 1854	22	fair	Providence, R.I.	5	68
Riley, George	Nov. 19, 1846	39	dark	Lisbon, N.H.	5	67
Riley, James	Feb. 27, 1843	15	dark	Newport, R.I.	5	66
Riley, John B.	July 25, 1836	22	light	Westerly, R.I.	5	65
Riley, Johnson M.	Aug. 4, 1834	20	light	Tiverton, R.I.	5	65
Riley, Wm. B.	Oct. 16, 1855	19	fair	Lowell, Ma.	5	68
Rimmen, John T.	May 26, 1842	26	dark	New Bedford, Ma.	5	66
Rimmer, Richard	July 10, 1803	18	dark	Portland, Me.	2	34
Ring, David	Nov. 4, 1846	40	fair	Freeport, Me.	5	67
Ripley, Herebiah, Jr.	Nov. 12, 1822	16	light	Fairfield, Conn.	4	58
Ripley, Oliver	Apr. 22, 1809	20	brown	Windham, Conn.	4	57
Ripley, Simon	July 25, 1864	28	light	Providence, R.I.	6	19
Rittal, Philip H.	Dec. 6, 1849	22	light	Dresden, Me.	5	67
Rix, James	Jan. 18, 1836	40	dark	Norwich, Conn.	5	65
Roach, John	June 16, 1855	22	light	Providence, R.I.	5	68
Roach, Peter	April 12, 1854	21	florid	Williamsburg, N.Y.	5	68
Roach, Matheas	Sept. 16, 1839	33	black	New York, N.Y.	5	66
Roach, Samuel	Oct. 19, 1858	19	fair	New York, N.Y.	6	19
Roane, William	Jan. 11, 1853	25	mulatto	Boston, Ma.	5	68
Roath, Ebenezer	June 19, 1797	33	dark	Norwich, Conn.	1	22
Robbins, Charles D.	Apr. 29, 1865	34	fair	Tremont, Me.	6	19
Robbins, Charles H.	Oct. 16, 1841	18	black	Canaan, Conn.	5	66
Robbins, David T.	May 17, 1853	27	black	Dedham, Ma.	5	65
Robbins, Edward	Sept. 9, 1825	22	light	Roxbury, Ma.	4	59
Robbins, Isaiah	Dec. 13, 1814	25	light	Westford, Ma.	4	58
Roberts, Abraham	Jan. 11, 1853	22	black	New York, N.Y.	5	68
Roberts, Benjamin	June 22, 1841	19	black	Cranston, R.I.	5	66
Roberts, Charles	Aug. 30, 1853	24	dark	Hartford, Conn.	5	68
Roberts, Eleaser	May 9, 1829	18	light	East Hartford, Conn.	5	65
Roberts, Ephraim	Aug. 2, 1848	21	dark	Cranston, R.I.	5	67
Roberts, Griffith	Mar. 14, 1851	24	dark	New York, N.Y.	5	67
Roberts, Henry	Oct. 27, 1818	23	brown	Cranston, R.I.	4	58
Roberts, Henry	Apr. 23, 1830	22	light	Norfolk, Va.	5	65
Roberts, James	Dec. 8, 1817	16	light	Scituate, R.I.	4	58
Roberts, John	Jan. 11, 1811	26	black	Charleston, S.C.	4	57
Roberts, John F.	Aug. 27, 1859	36	dark	Baltimore, Md.	6	19

NAME	DATE OF CERTIFICATION	AGE	COMPLEXION	PLACE OF BIRTH	BOOK	PAGE
Roberts, John R.	Aug. 31, 1844	23	black	Baltimore, Md.	5	66
Roberts, Richard	Jan. 17, 1817	22	light	Cranston, R.I.	4	58
Roberts, Samuel	July 20, 1841	15	light	Warwick, R.I.	5	66
Roberts, Thomas	Nov. 11, 1803	17	dark	Scituate, R.I.	2	34
Roberts, William	Nov. 11, 1830	21	light	Bucksport, Me.	5	65
Robertson, Alexander	Apr. 16, 1849	22	light	New York, N.Y.	5	67
Robertson, Bristol	Dec. 5, 1804	22	black	So. Kingstown, R.I.	3	34
Robertson, James	Nov. 27, 1849	22	light	New York, N.Y.	5	67
Robertson, Robert	Oct. 30, 1856	23	fair	Boston, Ma.	5	68
Rober[t]son, William	Jan. 12, 1804	29	black	New York, N.Y.	3	33
Robertson, William	Sept. 9, 1865	31	light	Portland, Me.	6	19
Robinson, Benjamin	Dec. 17, 1800	17	light	Providence, R.I.	2	17
Robinson, Benjamin	Sept. 14, 1801	26	black	Middletown, W. Jersey	2	34
Robinson, Cato	July 19, 1820	22	black	So. Kingstown, R.I.	4	58
Robinson, Charles B.	Mar. 24, 1820	21	light	Plainfield, Conn.	4	58
Robinson, Charles F.	Mar. 8, 1850	33	light	Providence, R.I.	5	67
Robinson, Daniel	Dec. 22, 1842	39	black	New York, N.Y.	5	66
Robinson, David	July 3, 1809	22	black	Grainger, N.Y.	4	57
Robinson, Eli K.	Jan. 6, 1843	21	mulatto	Wilmington, Del.	5	66
Robinson, George	Sept. 2, 1805	14	light	Attleboro, Ma.	3	62
Robinson, George	Sept. 4, 1849	22	light	Providence, R.I.	5	67
Robinson, Henry	May 13, 1806	19	yellow*	So. Kingstown, R.I.	3	63
Robinson, Henry	May 15, 1805	17	yellow*	So. Kingstown, R.I.	3	62
Robinson, Henry	Dec. 10, 1849	26	black	Phila., Pa.	5	67
Robinson, Henry C.	Jan. 1, 1855	17	light	Smithfield, R.I.	5	68
Robinson, Hiram	Jan. 10, 1831	21	light	Portland, Me.	5	65
Robinson, Isaac	Apr. 20, 1832	19	mulatto	So. Kingston, R.I.	5	65
Robinson, James	June 8, 1805	21	dark	New York, N.Y.	3	62
Robinson, James	Feb. 22, 1805	18	black	So. Kingstown, R.I.	3	34
Robinson, James	Aug. 2, 1830	19	black	So. Kingston, R.I.	5	65
Robinson, John	July 27, 1799	37	black	Dorchester, Ma.	2	17
Robinson, John	May 18, 1804	29	dark	Boston, Ma.	3	33
Robinson, John	July 28, 1806	21	light	Phila., Pa.	3	63
Robinson, John	May 8, 1807	22	black	New York, N.Y.	4	57
Robinson, John	June 16, 1807	33	brown	Havre de Grace, Md.	4	57
Robinson, John	Aug. 29, 1831	21	yellow	So. Kingston, R.I.	5	65
Robinson, John	Mar. 28, 1834	28	black	Baltimore, Md.	5	65

*mulatto

NAME	DATE OF CERTIFICATION	AGE	COMPLEXION	PLACE OF BIRTH	BOOK	PA
Robinson, John G.	July 3, 1850	38	mulatto	So. Kingstown, R.I.	5	67
Robinson, John J.	Apr. 29, 1831	34	light	Greenbush, N.Y.	5	65
Robinson, Joseph	Mar. 24, 1799	20	black	So. Kingstown, R.I.	2	17
Robinson, Joseph	Nov. 14, 1803	22	black	No. Kingstown, R.I.	2	34
Robinson, Joseph	Jan. 3, 1810	23	dark	Lexington, Ma.	4	57
Robinson, Joseph	Oct. 7, 1834	37	black	Jamaica, N.Y.	5	65
Robinson, Joseph	Mar. 14, 1842	32	black	Providence, R.I.	5	66
Robinson, Kinyon	Dec. 20, 1810	21	black	So. Kingstown, R.I.	4	57
Robinson, Marcellus L.	Nov. 1, 1837	19	light	Providence, R.I.	5	66
Robinson, Mathew	Aug. 27, 1796	25	black	Charleston, R.I.	1	2
Robinson, Nathaniel C.	Oct. 22, 1822	16	light	Concord, N.H.	4	58
Robinson, Peter	June 7, 1810	25	black	So. Kingstown, R.I.	4	57
Robinson, Richard	July 5, 1810	16	light	Providence, R.I.	4	57
Robinson, Robert	1798-1799	May 10, 1768		So. Kingston, R.I.	** -	--
Robinson, Samuel	Apr. 12, 1799	19	light	Franklin, Ma.	2	17
Robinson, Samuel	Aug. 23, 1800	20	dark	Charleston, S.C.	2	17
Robinson, Samuel	Nov. 18, 1803	24	dark	Providence, R.I.	2	34
Robinson, Samuel	June 18, 1845	23	black	Phila., Pa.	5	66
Robinson, Samuel	Oct. 28, 1858	39	black	Phila., Pa.	6	19
Robinson, Thomas	May 15, 1801	35	light	Charleston, S.C.	2	17
Robinson, Thomas	Nov. 12, 1806	21	black	Newport, R.I.	4	57
Robinson, Thomas	May 23, 1834	30	light	Phila., Pa.	5	65
Robinson, Thomas	Mar. 25, 1853	25	light	Otswego, N.Y.	5	68
Robinson, William	Dec. 15, 1843	32	light	New Bedford, Ma.	5	66
Robinson, William	Nov. 30, 1846	23	fair	New Bedford, Ma.	5	67
Robinson, William	July 27, 1853	39	black	Penn.	5	68
Robinson, C. Wm.	1798-1799	Oct. 20, 1773		So. Kingston, R.I.	** -	--
Robinson, William H.J.	Aug. 24, 1849	21	light	New York, N.Y.	5	67
Robinson, William S.	Nov. 6, 1849	18	light	Cranston, R.I.	5	67
Robinson, Zephaniah	Oct. 14, 1805	13	light	Falmouth, Ma.	3	62
Robley, George W.	Dec. 22, 1847	28	light	Providence, R.I.	5	67
Roddock, William	Apr. 30, 1835	23	light	New York, N.Y.	5	65
Rodman, Aaron	July 23, 1803	36	black	So. Kingstown, R.I.	2	34
Rodman, Benjamin F.	July 29, 1805	19	black	Newport, R.I.	3	62
Rodman, Daniel	Nov. 23, 1797	22	yellow*	So. Kingstown, R.I.	1	22

*mulatto

**Newport

NAME	DATE OF CERTIFICATION	AGE	COMPLEXION	PLACE OF BIRTH	BOOK	PAGE
Rodman, Isaac	July 15, 1800	24	black	So. Kingstown, R.I.	2	17
Rodman, Isaac	Feb. 22, 1805	29	black	So. Kingstown, R.I.	3	34
Rodman, Moses	Aug. 31, 1818	24	black	Newport, R.I.	4	58
Rodman, Timothy	Apr. 23, 1805	20	black	So. Kingstown, R.I.	3	62
Rodman, Timothy	May 12, 1806	21	black	So. Kingstown, R.I.	3	63
Rodman, William	Mar. 27, 1805	21	light	Providence, R.I.	3	34
Rodrig[u]ez, Custodio	Mar. 21, 1804	34	dark	Belzar, Portugal	3	33
Rofee, Christopher	May 10, 1815	19	light	Providence, R.I.	4	58
Rogers, Calvin	Dec. 12, 1823	23	dark	Yarmouth, Ma.	4	58
Rogers, Charles	Nov. 6, 1855	20	light	Warwick, R.I.	5	68
Rogers, Elias	Jan. 3, 1806	41	light	New London, Conn.	3	63
Rogers, Ezekiel	Aug. 27, 1810	17	light	Warwick, R.I.	4	57
Rogers, Ezekiel	Apr. 29, 1811	18	light	Warwick, R.I.	4	57
Rogers, Francis	Nov. 30, 1835	17	dark	Charleston, S.C.	5	65
Rogers, Henry	Nov. 20, 1807	18	black	So. Kingstown, R.I.	4	57
Rogers, James	Aug. 22, 1805	21	black	Newport, R.I.	3	62
Rogers, James	April 7, 1852	21	light	Boston, Ma.	5	68
Rogers, James	Mar. 30, 1857	22	fair	Boston, Ma.	5	68
Rogers, John	Dec. 3, 1810	23	light	W. Greenwich, R.I.	4	57
Rogers, Joseph H.	Mar. 8, 1839	18	light	Boston, Ma.	5	66
Rogers, Laban T.	Aug. 27, 1831	26	light	Dartmouth, Ma.	5	65
Rogers, Levi	May 13, 1837	23	black	New York, N.Y.	5	65
Rogers, Peter	Sept. 6, 1804	37	yellow*	Weston, Ma.	3	33
Rogers, Richard	Nov. 19, 1828	16	light	Newburyport, Ma.	4	59
Rogers, Samuel F.	Aug. 7, 1829	22	light	Vernon Sussex Co., N.J.	5	65
Rogers, Jr., Smith	Dec. 21, 1858	31	dark	Harwich, Ma.	6	19
Rogers, Spencer	Apr. 20, 1836	33	dark	Portland, Me.	5	65
Rogers, William	July 28, 1840	18	light	New York, N.Y.	5	66
Rogers, William H.	Nov. 10, 1826	20	ruddy	E. Greenwich, R.I.	4	59
Rolf, Ephraim	Jan. 4, 1819	32	light	Rochester, N.H.	4	58
Rollins, Albert	Sept. 10, 1858	19	fair	Gardiner, Me.	6	19
Romes, John	Nov. 30, 1805	21	black	No. Kingstown, R.I.	3	63
Romes, William	Nov. 27, 1818	21	black	No. Kingstown, R.I.	4	58
Roning, Henry M.	June 10, 1841	16	light	Providence, R.I.	5	66
Ronning, Frederick	Sept. 13, 1841	19	light	Providence, R.I.	5	66
Rooms, Abraham	Oct. 8, 1806	19	yellowish*	No. Kingstown, R.I.	3	20

*mulatto

NAME	DATE OF CERTIFICATION	AGE	COMPLEXION	PLACE OF BIRTH	BOOK	P
Rooms, Abraham	Oct. 8, 1806	19	yellowish	No. Kingstown, R.I.	4	5
Rophey, James	Mar. 28, 1797	21	light	Providence, R.I.	1	2
Ropke, Christian	Nov. 23, 1861	23	light	Baltimore, Md.	6	1
Rose, Antone	Sept. 5, 1861	20	dark	Stonington, Conn.	6	1
Rose, Cesar	Dec. 14, 1798	23	black	Providence, R.I.	2	1
Rose, Daniel	Apr. 7, 1851	25	light	So. Kingston, R.I.	5	6
Rose, Gideon	Mar. 27, 1834	20	light	New Shoreham, R.I.	5	6
Rose, Giles P.	Dec. 24, 1818	21	light	No. Kingstown, R.I.	4	58
Rose, Godfrey	Sept. 26, 1823	22	light	No. Kingstown, R.I.	4	58
Rose, Jesse	Apr. 11, 1848	25	light	New Shoreham, R.I.	5	6
Rose, John	Mar. 27, 1834	20	light	New Shoreham, R.I.	5	6
Rose, Levi	Dec. 3, 1825	24	light	Providence, R.I.	4	59
Rose, Moses	Oct. 2, 1809	16	brown	No. Kingstown, R.I.	4	57
Rose, Oliver	Dec. 4, 1850	29	light	New Shoreham, R.I.	5	67
Rose, Perry	Feb. 27, 1796	19	light	Norfolk, Va.	1	3
Rose, Peter	Aug. 19, 1811	20	black	So. Kingstown, R.I.	4	57
Rose, Robert B.	Sept. 12, 1837	14	dark	Poughkeepie, N.Y.	5	66
Rose, Rufus M.	Nov. 23, 1832	20	light	So. Kingston, R.I.	5	65
Rose, Varnum S.	June 2, 1849	28	dark	Islesboro, Me.	5	67
Rose, William H.	Sept. 18, 1850	26	light	No. Prov., R.I.	5	67
Rosetta, Augustus	June 14, 1832	29	light	Copenhagan, Denmark	5	65
Ross, Alexander	Nov. 22, 1854	36	light	Boston, Ma.	5	68
Ross, Benjamin	Apr. 16, 1807	19	light	Cumberland, R.I.	4	57
Ross, George	Jan. 16, 1836	25	fair	Perry, Me.	5	68
Ross, George	Oct. 21, 1839	19	light	Hampton, Conn.	5	66
Ross, James	Feb. 19, 1959	29	fair	New York, N.Y.	6	19
Ross, John S.	Aug. 2, 1854	30	dark	Camden, Me.	5	68
Ross, Spaulding N.	June 13, 1849	34	light	Cumberland, R.I.	5	67
Ross, William	Mar. 14, 1851	24	light	New York, N.Y.	5	67
Rounds, Ambrose	June 9, 1818	19	dark	Seekonk, Ma.	4	58
Round, George	Oct. 31, 1811	33	dark	Rehoboth, Ma.	4	57
Rounds, James	Aug. 26, 1837	18	dark	Providence, R.I.	5	66
Rounds, Luther	May 16, 1818	18	light	Smithfield, R.I.	4	58
Rotch, Joseph	Nov. 3, 1847	26	dark	New Bedford, Ma.	5	67
Rounds, James	Jan. 4, 1798	33	?dark?	Rehoboth, Ma.	1	22

NAME	DATE OF CERTIFICATION	AGE	COMPLEXION	PLACE OF BIRTH	BOOK	PAGE
Rousmaniere, Wm. E.	Nov. 22, 1839	30	light	Newport, R.I.	5	66
Rover, John	May 2, 1855	22	light	Southport, N.Y.	5	68
Rowand, David	Oct. 29, 1849	23	light	Pomfret, Conn.	5	67
Rowe, James	Nov. 14, 1803	38	dark	New York, N.Y.	2	34
Rowe, Julius	Feb. 10, 1808	28	light	Amherst, Ma.	4	57
Rowe, William	Aug. 31, 1849	22	light	Colchester, Conn.	5	67
Rowell, John	June 23, 1848	18	dark	Houlton, Me.	5	67
Ruggles, Spooner	Nov. 28, 1803	22	light	Rutland, Ma.	2	34
Ruggles, Timothy	May 31, 1809	24	light	Rutland, Ma.	4	57
Ruggles, William A.	Dec. 7, 1830	17	light	Providence, R.I.	5	65
Rumsey, Benjamin	Apr. 5, 1797	20	light	Fairfield, Conn.	1	22
Rumsey, James	Oct. 11, 1854	27	light	Bloomingrove, N.Y.	5	68
Runnels, Charles H.	July 12, 1845	21	dark*	Portsmouth, R.I.	5	66
Rupp, William	Oct. 24, 1849	28	dark	Boston, Ma.	5	67
Ruscoe, John	June 24, 1826	19	light	Thomaston, Me.	4	59
Russell, Charles S.	Sept. 18, 1834	19	dark	Dartmouth, Ma.	5	65
Russell, Henry	July 30, 1839	18	light	Portsmouth, Va.	5	66
Russel, John	July 22, 1841	27	dark	Medway, Ma.	5	66
Russell, Joseph	June 10, 1804	16	light	Woodstock, Conn.	3	33
Russel, Samuel	Jan. 12, 1854	21	light	Providence, R.I.	5	68
Russell, Seth	June 13, 1832	37	dark	Nantucket, Ma.	5	65
Russell, Thomas	July 15, 1854	22	light	E. Thomaston, Me.	5	68
Russell, William	May 1, 1799	14	light	Providence, R.I.	2	17
Russell, William	Nov. 14, 1803	19	light	Providence, R.I.	2	34
Russell, William	Jan. 11, 1847	28	fair	Warren, R.I.	5	67
Russell, William G.	Oct. 22, 1829	20	light	Providence, R.I.	5	65
Russell, William H.	Apr. 12, 1815	16	light	Newport, R.I.	4	58
Ryan, John	Oct. 30, 1849	22	light	No. Prov., R.I.	5	67
Ryan, Joseph	Mar. 16, 1852	21	sandy	Albany, N.Y.	5	68
Ryan, Maurice	Dec. 7, 1838	31	light	Bangor, Me.	5	66
Ryan, Patrick H.	Mar. 9, 1860	33	light	Taunton, Ma.	6	19
Sabin, Henry	Dec. 15, 1798	15	light	Providence, R.I.	2	18
Sabin, James	Dec. 23, 1800	18	light	New Haven, Conn.	2	26
Sabin, James	Sept. 9, 1803	21	light	New Haven, Conn.	2	36

*mulatto

NAME	DATE OF CERTIFICATION	AGE	COMPLEXION	PLACE OF BIRTH	BOOK	PAGE
Sabin, James	Aug. 2, 1809	27	light	New Haven, Conn.	4	63
Sabins, James M.	Oct. 21, 1809	21	dark	Providence, R.I.	4	63
Sabin, Jesse	Mar. 9, 1798	36	dark	Providence, R.I.	1	30
Sabins, Jonathan	July 31, 1805	16	dark	Rehoboth, Ma.	3	51&51
Sabin, Jonathan	Oct. 29, 1806	17	brown	Rehoboth, Ma.	4	62
Sabins, Joshua	Nov. 29, 1809	21	light	Providence, R.I.	4	63
Sabins, Joshua A.	Feb. 24, 1812	23	light	Providence, R.I.	4	64
Sabin, Mefcalf	May 23, 1798	16	dark	Providence, R.I.	2	18
Sabin, Samuel	1798-1799	Aug. 10, 1780		New Haven, Conn.	*-	--
Sabin, William A.	Jan. 26, 1838	22	light	Providence, R.I.	5	70
Sabine, George C.	July 2, 1858	20	dark	Eddington, Me.	6	18
Safford, Jabez E.	Oct. 23, 1816	19	light	Canterbury, Conn.	4	64
Salisbury, Alpheus	June 17, 1854	22	light	Scituate, R.I.	5	75
Salisbury, Barnard	1798-1799	Certificate		Warren, R.I.	*-	--
Salisbury, Charles H.	Oct. 30, 1833	26	Dark	Baltimore, Md.	5	70
Salisbury, Daniel G.	Aug. 27, 1810	20	light	Cranston, R.I.	4	63
Salisbury, Daniel W.	May 21, 1851	45	black	Catskil, N.Y.	5	74
Salesbury, George [Salisbury]	Sept. 28, 1803	21	light	Foster, R.I.	2	36
Sal[i]sbury, George	Sept. 7, 1804	22	light	Foster, R.I.	3	36
Salisbury, George L.	July 3, 1839	17	light	Providence, R.I.	5	71
Salisbury, George W.	Nov. 22, 1800	22	dark	Barrington, R.I.	2	26
Salisbury, Henry	June 1, 1836	22	black	Providence, R.I.	5	70
Salisbury, Hezekiah	Oct. 12, 1804	31	light	Barrington, R.I.	3	51
Salisbury, Hezekiah	Nov. 9, 1796	23	light	Barrington, R.I.	1	23&
Salisbury, John	Aug. 14, 1806	21	light	E. Greenwich, R.I.	3	67
Salisbury, John	Dec. 13, 1815	30	dark	E. Greenwich, R.I.	4	64
Salisbury, Joseph	July 17, 1823	23	light	No. Providence, R.I.	4	66
Salisbury, Joseph M.	July 13, 1799	19	light	Cranston, R.I.	2	18
Salisbury, Joshua	June 9, 1826	19	light	Providence, R.I.	4	66
Salisbury, Marinus	Jan. 14, 1834	19	dark	Scituate, R.I.	5	70
Salisbury, Moses	July 17, 1830	19	black	Providence, R.I.	5	69
Salisbury, Peleg	July 11, 1806	18	light	Cranston, R.I.	3	67
Salisbury, Samuel O.	Sept. 12, 1806	16	light	Providence, R.I.	3	67
Salisbury, Smith	June 7, 1820	21	light	No. Prov., R.I.	4	65
Salisbury, Spencer	Sept. 28, 1805	19	light	Cranston, R.I.	3	70

*Newport, R. I.

NAME	DATE OF CERTIFICATION	AGE	COMPLEXION	PLACE OF BIRTH	BOOK	PAGE
Salisbury, William H.	Aug. 16, 1836	21	dark	Trenton, Me.	5	70
Salisbury, William M.	Oct. 8, 1858	18	fair	Nantucket, Ma.	6	18
Sallisbury, William P.	Mar. 13, 1811	17	brown	E. Greenwich, R.I.	4	63
Salisbury, William P.	Nov. 24, 1837	18	light	Providence, R.I.	5	70
Salisbury, William P. 2nd	Oct. 13, 1828	14	light	E. Greenwich, R.I.	4	67
Salley, John	May 1, 1809	24	light	Woolwich,[Me.] Ma.	4	62
Suspected to be a foreigner.						
Salook, John	Dec. 28, 1841	16	dark	New Orleans, La.	5	71
Saltonstall, Breton	Dec. 20, 1797	38	black	New London, Conn.	1	30
Sambo, David	Oct. 26, 1829	20	yellow	E. Greenwich, R.I.	5	69
Sambo, Francis L.	July 2, 1852	17	mulatto	E. Greenwich, R.I.	5	75
Sambo, Henry	Dec. 28, 1818	22	black	E. Greenwich, R.I.	4	65
Sambo, Samuel	Mar. 30, 1818	24	yellow	No. Kingstown, R.I.	4	65
Sambo, William	Oct. 26, 1820	16	black	No. Kingstown, R.I.	4	65
Samborn, Jacob	May 19, 1826	26	dark	Canaan, N.H.	4	66
Samendike, Lewis	May 9, 1810	25	black	Norwalk, Conn.	4	63
Samendike, Lewis	Mar. 1, 1813	28	black	Norwalk, Conn.	4	64
Sampson, Daniel	May 30, 1822	19	black	Richmond, R.I.	4	65
Sampson, Enoch	Mar. 29, 1811	26	dark	Old Chester, N.H.	4	63
Sampson, George	Nov. 24, 1848	19	black	Providence, R.I.	5	73
Sampson, George P.	Sept. 16, 1847	25	black	Newport, R.I.	5	73
Sampson, Henry	Oct. 25, 1831	21	black	Richmond, R.I.	5	69
Sampson, James	Jan. 16, 1804	22	black	Baltimore, Md.	3	35
Sampson, John	Aug. 10, 1830	26	black	Middleboro, Ma.	5	69
Sampson, Thomas	Apr. 5, 1809	31	black	New York, N.Y.	4	62
Sanders interfiled with Saunders.						
Sanderson, Charles W.	Apr. 4, 1844	21	light	Charlestown, Ma.	5	72
Sanderson, Marshall	Apr. 23, 1824	21	light	Waltham, Ma.	4	66
Sands, George	Mar. 15, 1852	26	mulatto	Springfield, Ma.	5	75
Sands, James	Aug. 1, 1825	25	mulatto	New Shoreham, R.I.	4	66
Sands, James	Aug. 7, 1830	30	yellow	New Shoreham, R.I.	5	69
Sands, James	Dec. 26, 1859	25	fair	Northfield, N.Y.	6	18
Sands, William A.	Dec. 20, 1832	20	light	Newport, R.I.	5	69
Sandydale, John	Sept. 13, 1796	20	black	Savannah, Ga.	1	2
Sanford, Alphonso	Mar. 10, 1852	20	light	Charlestown, Ma.	5	75
Sanford, George	1798-1799	Feb. 18, 1781		Tiverton, R.I.	* -	--

*Newport, R. I.

NAME	DATE OF CERTIFICATION	AGE	COMPLEXION	PLACE OF BIRTH	BOOK	P/
Sanford, James	Dec. 13, 1833	18	light	Goshen, Conn.	5	7
Sanford, John	Oct. 3, 1843	26	light	New Hamburg, N.Y.	5	7
Sanford, John W.	Nov. 9, 1813	16	light	Hartford, Conn.	4	6
Sanford, Joseph Mary Sanford, his mother swears for him.	1798-1799		Oct. 25, 1775	Newport, R.I.	* -	-
Sanford, Richard or Richmond Giles Sanford his father, swears for him.	1798-1799		Oct. 9, 1765	Middletown, R.I.	* -	-
Sanford, Thomas	May 16, 1797	25	dark	Westport, Ma.	1	2
Sanford, William	Oct. 30, 1835	40	yellow	Providence, R.I.	5	7
Sank, Winder	Feb. 25, 1846	20	black	Northumberland, Va.	5	7
Santee, George W.	Oct. 8, 1830	22	black	Sutton, Ma.	5	6
Sargant, Charles P.	Oct. 30, 1849	20	light	Webster, Ma.	5	74
Sargent, James M.	June 6, 1843	21	light	Londen, N.H.	5	7
Sargeant, Thomas	Sept. 9, 1815	17	light	Springfield, Ma.	4	64
Sarle, Benjamin Greene	Sept. 2, 1797	17	dark	Warwick, R.I.	1	30
Sarle, Richard	Mar. 22, 1797	16	light	Cranston, R.I.	1	23
Sarle, Thomas A.	Feb. 17, 1834	28	dark	Cranston, R.I.	5	70
Saunders, Charles H.	Oct. 18, 1858	18	dark	Providence, R.I.	6	18
Saunders, Dutee	Dec. 16, 1797	27	light	Smithfield, R.I.	1	30
Saunders, Horace	Nov. 1, 1825	19	light	Tiverton, R.I.	4	66
Saunders, Jackson	Apr. 6, 1854	17	fair	Gloucester, Ma.	5	75
Sanders, James	Oct. 27, 1834	18	light	Augusta, Me.	5	70
Saunders, James	Mar. 2, 1859	22	light	New Orleans, La.	6	18
Saunders, Job or Sanders	Oct. 7, 1796	20	dark	Swansea, Ma.	1	23
Sanders, Job	Oct. 1, 1811	35	dark	Swansea, Ma.	4	64
[Saunders] Sanders, John	Aug. 4, 1803	19	light	Providence, R.I.	2	36
Saunders, John	Dec. 7, 1804	21	light	Providence, R.I.	3	51
Saunders, John Justin Hacher	Jan. 4, 1824	20	light	Providence, R.I.	4	66
Saunders, John R.	July 19, 1843	19	light	Oswego, N.Y.	5	72
Saunders, Jonathan	Dec. 15, 1847	46	light	Islesboro, Me.	5	73
[Saunders] Sanders, Jos.	Mar. 2, 1798	26	dark	Swansea, Ma.	1	30
Sanders, Oliver W.	Feb. 2, 1848	22	light	Woodstock, Conn.	5	73
Saunders, Peter	June 4, 1803	22	black	Wickford, R.I.	2	36
[Saunders] Sanders, Robert	Aug. 20, 1803	22	light	Hampton, Va.	2	36
Saunders, Samuel	June 10, 1797	25	dark	Boston, Ma.	1	23
Saunders, Samuel	Mar. 20, 1822	22	light	Providence, R.I.	4	65

*Newport, R. I.

NAME	DATE OF CERTIFICATION	AGE	COMPLEXION	PLACE OF BIRTH	BOOK	PAGE
Saunders, William	Oct. 26, 1797	22	light	Providence, R.I.	1	30
Saunders, William	Feb. 15, 1812	33	light	Providence, R.I.	4	64
Saunders, William H.	Nov. 7, 1844	19	dark	Glocester, R.I.	5	72
Sanders, William H.	Aug. 18, 1847	17	light	Warren, R.I.	5	73
Savage, James	May 15, 1811	21	light	Norwich, Conn.	4	63
Savage, William	Aug. 15, 1801	17	light	Sharon, Ma.	2	36
Sawyer, Barzilleel	Dec. 14, 1810	43	light	Lancaster, Ma.	4	63
Sawyer, Hugh N.	May 13, 1840	30	dark	Portland, Me.	5	71
Sawyer, Jacob	May 29, 1806	21	black	Taunton, Ma.	3	67
Sawyer, James	1798-1799	Oct. 31, 1779		Little Compton, R.I. *	-	--
Sawyer, Peter B.	Nov. 27, 1849	36	light	New York, N.Y.	5	74
Sax, Joseph	May 7, 1810	18	light	Providence, R.I.	4	63
Sayer, Benjamin	Oct. 17, 1806	21	light	Little Compton, R.I.	4	62
Sayers, Hugh	Aug. 13, 1849	25	dark	Norwich, Conn.	5	73
Sayer, Robert C.	June 10, 1831	15	dark	Newport, R.I.	5	69
Sayer, Thomas W.	Aug. 9, 1847	33	fair	Boston, Ma.	5	73
Sayles, Arnold	Dec. 30, 1816	23	dark	Providence, R.I.	4	64
Sayles, Daniel	Nov. 29, 1851	19	dark	Smithfield, R.I.	5	75
Sayles, George W.	Dec. 2, 1841	19	dark	Southbridge,Ma.	5	71
Sayles, Horace K.	Nov. 23, 1841	19	light	Cumberland, R.I.	5	71
Sayles, MOwry	Nov. 12, 1849	19	light	Smithfield, R.I.	5	74
Sayles, Nahum	July 10, 1810	20	light	Franklin, Ma.	4	63
Sayles, Seth ·	Aug. 25, 1832	18	light	Smithfield, R.I.	5	69
Scanlen, William A.	Sept. 6, 1856	26	light	Boston, Ma.	5	76
Scarborough, John H.	Feb. 3, 1834	33	light	Currituck, N.C.	5	70
Schappen, George F.	Aug. 14, 1832	14	dark	Providence,R.I.	5	69
Schifflin, Adolph	Aug. 18, 1846	21	dark	New York, N.Y.	5	73
Scott, Albert	Mar. 15, 1836	16	mulatto	Providence,R.I.	5	70
Scott, Alexander	Apr. 13, 1853	21	light	Boston, Ma.	5	75
Scott, Edmund	Sept. 13, 1830	21	light	Cumberland, R.I.	5	69
Scott, Hiram	Nov. 16, 1815	17	fresh	Bellingham, Ma.	4	64
Scott, James	Nov. 16, 1796	20	light	Smithfield, R.I.	1	23
Scott, James	Feb. 28, 1849	46	black	New York, N.Y.	5	73
Scott, Thomas	Mar. 9, 1837	18	light	Thomaston, Me.	5	70
Scott, Walter	Aug. 17, 1357	37	light	Baltimore, Md.	6	18
Scott, William	Sept. 26, 1843	35	black	Portland, Me.	5	72

*Newport, R.I.

NAME	DATE OF CERTIFICATION	AGE	COMPLEXION	PLACE OF BIRTH	BOOK	P.
Scott, William	May 22, 1855	24	light	Boston, Ma.	5	7
[Scoville], Scovil, Peter	Nov. 10, 1797	37	dark	Providence, R.I.	1	3
[Scoville] Scoval, Peter	Dec. 18, 1799	40	dark	Windham, Conn.	2	2
Scranton, Robert	May 30, 1842	27	light	Griswold, Conn.	5	7
Scrymgeour, David	Feb. 27, 1857	22	light	Boston, Ma.	5	7
Scudden, Henry	Apr. 6, 1849	25	yellow	Smith Town, N.Y.	5	7
Seabury, Andrew E.	May 12, 1834	27	light	Little Compton, R.I.	5	7
Seabury, Cornelius, Jr.	Oct. 28, 1824	17	ruddy	Tiverton, R.I.	4	6
Seabury, George W.	Dec. 16, 1824	24	light	Little Compton, R.I.	4	6
Seabury, Frederick	1798-1799		Nov. 2, 1789	Little Compton, R.I.	*-	-
Seabury, Lemuel	Jan. 11, 1798	23	black	Islip, N.Y.	1	3
Seabury, Lemuel	Sept. 13, 1796	25	dark	Long Island, N.Y.	1	3
Seabury, Peleg	1798-1799		Feb. 19, 1757	Newport, R.I.	*-	-
George Seabury of Tiverton, R.I. swears for him.						
Seah, Peleg	1798-1799		Feb. 19, 1757	Newport, R.I.	*-	-
George Seabury swears for him.						
Seamans, Benjamin	June 20, 1809	18	light	Providence, R.I.	4	62
Seamans, Benjamin	May 12, 1810	19	light	Providence, R.I.	4	63
Seamans, Benjamin M.	Nov. 23, 1797	23	light	So. Kingstown, R.I.	1	3
Seamans, Charles	Mar. 14, 1815	28	dark	Providence, R.I.	4	64
Seamans, Daniel T.	Nov. 9, 1831	26	light	Providence, R.I.	5	69
Seamans, George	Dec. 14, 1815	19	light	Providence, R.I.	4	64
Seamans, Gilbert	May 30, 1806	40	light	No. Prov., R.I.	3	67
Seamans, James	Aug. 30, 1809	20	light	Providence, R.I.	4	63
Seamans, James A.	Apr. 12, 1859	22	dark	Springfield, Ma.	6	18
Seamans, John L.	July 27, 1821	24	light	Providence, R.I.	4	65
Seamans, Obed	Jan. 17, 1810	13	light	Providence, R.I.	4	63
Seamans, Prince	May 4, 1810	19	black	Jericho, N.Y.	4	63
Seamans, Samuel Y.	Oct. 12, 1810	17	light	Providence, R.I.	4	63
Seamans, William S.	Mar. 7, 1861	25	fair	Providence, R.I.	6	18
Seamore, William F.	Oct. 29, 1849	21	light	Barrington, R.I.	5	74
Searle, Benjamin	Oct. 9, 1799	20	dark	Providence, R.I.	2	18
Searle, Charles F.	Aug. 26, 1822	15	light	Providence, R.I.	4	66
Searle, William	June 10, 1801	18	dark	Warwick, R.I.	2	26

*Newport, R. I.

NAME	DATE OF CERTIFICATION	AGE	COMPLEXION	PLACE OF BIRTH	BOOK	PAGE
Sears, Edward	Nov. 5, 1805	26	light	Yarmouth, Ma.	3	70
Sears, Hammond	June 21, 1825	29	light	New York, N.Y.	4	66
Sears, Warren L.	Aug. 17, 1857	26	light	Wiscasset, Me.	6	18
Seekel, Apollos	June 7, 1843	18	dark	Providence, R.I.	5	72
Seely, Isaac .	May 11, 1858	26	dark	Waltham, N.Y.	6	18
Seibs, John	Feb. 25, 1851	25	light	New York, N.Y.	5	74
Seixas, Peter	Dec. 13, 1806	29	yellow	Newport, R.I.	4	62
Seixas, Peter	Dec. 21, 1825	21	black	Newport, R.I.	4 .	66
Seketer, Daniel	June 16, 1810	19	yellow	Charlestown, R.I.	4	63
Selkick, James M.	Aug. 9, 1841	21	light	Boston, Ma.	5	71
Selsey, Eli	May 17, 1848	22	mulatto	Burlington, N.J.	5	73
?Septon, Gilbert	June 20, 1818	22	light	Warwick, R.I.	4	65
Sessions, Robert	Sept. 25, 1804	23	yellow*	Boston, Ma.	3	51
Sesson, William	Feb. 18, 1854	21	yellow	Syracuse, N.Y.	5	76
Setler, Francis	Apr. 10, 1837	23	dark	New York, N.Y.	5	70
Sevien, James	Apr. 9, 1840	42	dark	Salem, Ma.	5	71
Sewall, Parker D.	Aug. 22, 1843	21	light	Bath, Me.	5	72
Sewall, Zolmony	Apr. 3, 1844	20	dark	Kennibeck, Me.	5	72
Sewards, John	Dec. 12, 1838	32	dark	Ipswich, Ma.	5	71
Seybert, William	Nov. 1, 1826	34	light	Phila., Pa.	4	66
Seymour, George S.	Oct. 9, 1810	23	light	Hartford, Conn.	4	63
Seymour, Robert	Sept. 17, 1853	21	light	New York, N.Y.	5	75
Seymour, Samuel	1798-1799	Mar. 24, 1779		Litchfield, Conn.	** -	--
Shannon, William R.	Oct. 8, 1833	25	light	Powell's Point, N.C.	5	70
Sharp, Henry	June 25, 1835	23	black	New Castle, Del.	5	70
Sharp, James S.	Feb. 26, 1828	25	black	Providence, R.I.	4	66
Sharp, John	May 14, 1851	30	light	New York, N.Y.	5	74
Sharpe, Liberty	Apr. 21, 1815	24	ruddy	Pomfret, Conn.	4	64
Sharp, Peter	Nov. 8, 1805	14	black	Providence, R.I.	3	70
Sharp, Samuel	Oct. 25, 1799	50	black	Warwick, R.I.	2	18
Sharp, Samuel	May 21, 1803	52	black	Warwick, R.I.	2	36
Sharpley, Henry	July 1, 1846	19	dark	Woodbury, N.J.	5	72
Shattuck, Warrell	June 26, 1849	23	dark	Boston, Ma.	5	73
Shaw, Anthony	Sept. 12, 1796	21	light	Dartmouth, Ma.	1	2

*mulatto
**Newport, R.I.

NAME	DATE OF CERTIFICATION	AGE	COMPLEXION	PLACE OF BIRTH	BOOK	PAGE
Shaw, Byron	Nov. 24, 1849	19	light	Warwick, R.I.	5	74
Shaw, Charles	May 6, 1818	22	black	Boston, Ma.	4	65
Shaw, David	Aug. 1, 1844	29	dark	Boston, Ma.	5	72
Shaw, Elias	Aug. 10, 1804	18	light	Warwick, R.I.	3	36
Shaw, Hiram	Nov. 18, 1826	23	light	Dighton, Ma.	4	66
Shaw, James	June 20, 1797	25	light	Norfolk, Va.	1	23
Shaw, James	Dec. 1, 1800	34	light	Providence, R.I.	2	26
Shaw, James H.	Oct. 6, 1830	18	dark	Providence, R.I.	5	69
Shaw, John	Jan. 12, 1798	35	dark	Raynham, Ma.	1	30
Shaw, John	Dec. 11, 1819	17	light	Providence, R.I.	4	65
Shaw, William	Oct. 8, 1797	15	light	Cranston, R.I.	1	30
Shaw, William	Apr. 21, 1797	15	light	Cranston, R.I.	1	23
Shaw, William E.	Dec. 11, 1849	22	Indian	Brookhaven, N.Y.	5	74
Shawnessey, Michael O.	Sept. 6, 1842	19	light	New York, N.Y.	5	72
Shea, Timothy	Jan. 5, 1853	19	light	Manchester, N.H.	5	75
Shea, William	June 19, 1801	19	light	New York, N.Y.	2	26
Sheany, John	Apr. 12, 1798	24	light	Baltimore, Md.	1&2*	31&18
Shedd, John W.	Dec. 1, 1848	17	light	Providence, R.I.	5	73
Sheehen, Thomas	Apr. 21, 1854	18	fair	Cabbotville, Ma.	5	75
Sheehen, Thomas	Feb. 16, 1857	21	fair	Springfield, Ma.	5	76
Sheffield, Cuff	Jan. 16, 1804	21	black	Newport, R.I.	3	35
Sheffield, Edmund	Oct. 29, 1821	22	light	Waterford, Conn.	4	65
Sheffield, Lewis	Nov. 25, 1817	28	black	Newport, R.I.	4	65
Sheffield, Prince	Oct. 31, 1804	29	black	Newport, R.I.	3	51
Sheffield, Primus	July 17, 1806	29	black	Newport, R.I.	3	67
Sheffield, Samuel	Apr. 27, 1815	22	black	Newport, R.I.	4	64
Sheffield, Titus	Aug. 13, 1807	22	black	New Shoreham, R.I.	4	62
Sheldon, Christopher	May 15, 1807	23	brown	Cranston, R.I.	4	62
Sheldon, Christopher	May 2, 1809	18	brown	Providence, R.I.	4	62
Smith, Richard	Sept. 2, 1864	21	black	Kinderhook, N.Y.	6	18
Smith, Richardson	Apr. 21, 1854	22	light	Burlington, Vt.	5	75
Smith, Robert	Feb. 13, 1805	22	yellow**	New York, N.Y.	3	51
Smith, Robert	Nov. 11, 1847	21	fair	New York, N.Y	5	73

*Book 1, page 31; book 2, page 18.

**mulatto

NAME	DATE OF CERTIFICATION	AGE	COMPLEXION	PLACE OF BIRTH	BOOK	PAGE
Smith, Robert	Apr. 23, 1852	23	light	Providence, R.I.	5	75
Smith, Rufus	Mar. 9, 1837	21	dark	Thomaston, Me.	5	70
Sheldon, Edward	June 17, 1797	34	dark	Johnston, R.I.	1	23
Sheldon, Edward L.	June 10, 1807	19	light	Providence, R.I.	4	62
Sheldon, George	Apr. 17, 1806	17	light	Cranston, R.I.	3	71
Sheldon, George	Mar. 16, 1805	15	light	Cranston, R.I.	3	51A
Sheldon, George J.W.	May 30, 1851	17	light	Glocester, R.I.	5	74
Sheldon, Jamse M.	Dec. 15, 1806	15	light	Cumberland, R.I.	4	62
Sheldon, John F., Jr.	Jan. 27, 1830	18	light	Providence, R.I.	5	69
Sheldon, John J.	Jan. 20, 1800	26	dark	Providence, R.I.	2	26
Sheldon, Joseph	Aug. 1, 1799	18	light	Cranston, R.I.	2	18
Sheldon, Joseph	Sept. 26, 1818	22	dark	Providence, R.I.	4	65
Sheldon, Palmer	May 1, 1807	22	light	Woodstock, Conn.	4	62
Sheldon, Pardon	Aug. 17, 1820	19	light	Cranston, R.I.	4	65
Sheldon, Simon W.	Aug. 23, 1821	21	light	Cumberland, R.I.	4	65
Sheldon, Stephen R.	Apr. 7, 1804	17	dark	Cranston, R.I.	3	35
Sheldon, Stephen R.	Aug. 13, 1833	18	light	Cranston, R.I.	5	70
Sheldon, Thomas	Mar. 13, 1805	14	dark	Cranston, R.I.	3	51
Sheldon, Thomas	Apr. 7, 1806	15	light	Cranston, R.I.	3	71
Sheldon, Thomas	Apr. 5, 1809	18	brown	Cranston, R.I.	4	62
Sheldon, Tyra	Apr. 20, 1860	24	light	Thompson, Conn.	6	18
Shelly, William	Nov. 11, 1847	18	fair	Thompson, Conn.	5	73
Shelly, William	Sept. 5, 1857	37	light	Taunton, Ma.	6	18
Shepherd, Albert H.	Aug. 18, 1853	18	light	Cranston, R.I.	5	75
Shepard, Alfred R.	June 27, 1839	15	light	Foxboro, Ma.	5	71
[Shepard]Shephard, Elijah	Nov. 1, 1799	13	light	Providence, R.I.	2	18
[Shepard]Shepherd, Jacob	July 17, 1804	23	black	New York, N.Y.	3	36
Shepard, James	May 20, 1851	20	light	Providence, R.I.	5	74
Shepherd, Joseph H.	Mar. 8, 1826	18	light	Barnstable, Ma.	4	66
Shepard, Joseph R.	Aug. 28, 1854	15	light	Cranston, R.I.	5	76
Shepherd, Rossel	Apr. 8, 1826	18	dark	Barnstable, Ma.	4	66
Shepard, Thomas	Sept. 1, 1860	25	fair	Harpswell, Me.	6	18
Shepard, Wm. L.	Feb. 1, 1849	28	light	Brooklyn, Conn.	5	73
Sherburne, Henry W.	Nov. 7, 1854	18	light	Providence, R.I.	5	76

NAME	DATE OF CERTIFICATION	AGE	COMPLEXION	PLACE OF BIRTH	BOOK	PAG
Sherden, John	1798-1799	Oct. 11, 1777		Somerset, Ma.	* -	--
Sherdon, Joseph	Apr. 7, 1812	17	dark	Somerset, Ma.	4	64
Sherden, William, Jr.	Oct. 21, 1818	20	light	Somerset, Ma.	4	65
Sheridon, Ellison	Sept. 28, 1826	32	light	Somerset, Ma.	4	66
Sheriff, John	Apr. 10, 1854	25	fair	New York, N.Y.	5	75
Sherman, Albert	Nov. 6, 1848	15	dark	Providence, R.I.	5	73
Shearman, Benjamin	Nov. 5, 1818	16	yellow	Providence, R.I.	4	65
Sherman, Benj. F.	Feb. 17, 1852	23	light	Providence, R.I.	5	75
Shearman, Caleb	June 25, 1810	13	dark	Cranston, R.I.	4	63
Shearman, Caleb	June 24, 1811	15	dark	Cranston, R.I.	4	63
Shearman, Charles	Apr. 8, 1807	27	yellow	Newport, R.I.	4	62
Shearman, Charles H.	Nov. 9, 1820	24	dark	So. Kingstown, R.I.	4	65
Shearman, Clark	Oct. 13, 1826	33	light	Tiverton, R.I.	4	66
[Sherman] Shearman, Cuff	June 17, 1801	19	black	Exeter, R.I.	2	26
Shearman, Easton	Dec. 16, 1825	20	ruddy	No. Kingstown, R.I.	4	66
Shearman, Elisha	Nov. 11, 1820	22	dark	Cranston, R.I.	4	65
Sherman, George	Apr. 4, 1797	20	dark	Warwick, R.I.	1	23
Sherman, George	June 13, 1836	24	light	Exeter, R.I.	5	70
Shearman, Henry O.	June 15, 1825	18	dark	Cranston, R.I.	4	66
Sherman, Horace D.	Dec. 14, 1844	20	light	So. Kingston, R.I.	5	72
Shearman, James	[1821]	22	light	No. Kingstown	-	--
Sworn statement of John C. Havens of No. Kingstown in the Custom House Papers.					b. Dec. 30, 1
Shearman, James	Oct. 8, 1823	25	light.	No. Kingstown, R.I.	4	66
Sherman, Job	1798-1799	May 10, 1779		Portsmouth, R.I.	* -	--
Shearman, John	Mar. 6, 1815	20	light	No. Kingstown, R.I.	4	64
Shearman, John H.	Nov. 15, 1841	17	light	Derby, Conn.	5	71
Sherman, Levi	1798-1799	Certificate		------	* -	--
Shearman, Nathaniel	Oct. 6, 1821	29	light	So. Kingstown, R.I.	4	65
Sherman, Orin W.	June 26, 1841	25	light	Canterbury, Conn.	5	71
Sherman, Peleg	Apr. 6, 1815	28	dark	Newport, R.I.	4	64
Sherman, Robert	Mar. 8, 1805	16	light	Swansea, Ma.	3	51
Sherman, Robert	Oct. 19, 1805	16	light	Swansea, Ma.	3	70
Sherman, Robert	June 23, 1854	24	dark	Smithfield, R.I.	5	75
Shearman, Robert, Jr.	Nov. 20, 1811	21	dark	Exeter, R.I.	4	64
Shearman, Royal	Sept. 2, 1842	36	dark	No. Kingston, R.I.	5	72

*Newport, R. I.

REGISTER OF SEAMEN'S PROTECTION

NAME	DATE OF CERTIFICATION	AGE	COMPLEXION	PLACE OF BIRTH	BOOK	PAGE
Shearman, Silas G.	Dec. 12, 1829	22	light	Tiverton, Ma.	5	69
Shearman, Thomas	Oct. 29, 1849	19	light	So. Kingston, R.I.	5	74
Sherman, William	1798-1799	May 26, 1780		Swansea, Ma.	*-	--
Shearman, William	July 23, 1829	17	light	Warwick, R.I.	5	69
Shearman, Wm. E.	Nov. 11, 1841	27	light	Tiverton, R.I.	5	71
Sherman, Wm. H. Harrison	Apr. 7, 1854	20	light	Portsmouth, R.I.	5	75
Sheredan, John	Apr. 18, 1855	26	dark	New York, N.Y.	5	76
Sheridan, Thomas P.	June 19, 1840	30	dark	Bristol, R.I.	5	71
Sherritt, William	Feb. 14, 1862	23	dark	Savannah, Ga.	6	18
Shields, John	Apr. 13, 1860	25	dark	Providence, R.I.	6	18
Shippey, Henry	Nov. 1, 1826	19	light	Richmond, Va.	4	66
Shiverick, Nathaniel	Oct. 25, 1796	26	dark	Falmouth, Ma.	1	23&4
Shores, Abel P.	Mar. 6, 1827	28	light	Taunton, Ma.	4	66
Shoers, , Nathaniel	Sept. 29, 1796	18	light	Rehoboth, Ma.	1	3
Shores, Nathaniel	Nov. 18, 1809	30	light	Rehoboth, Ma.	4	63
Shorkley, Elisha	Dec. 9, 1819	21	brown	New Bedford, Ma.	4	65
Short, Abraham	Jan. 12, 1832	31	black	New York, N.Y.	5	69
Short, Daniel Cooke	Sept. 10, 1799	17	light	Barrington, R.I.	2	18
Short, Daniel C.	Sept. 26, 1826	20	light	Warwick, R.I.	4	66
Short, John	Apr. 25, 1844	33	dark	Boston, Ma.	5	72
Short, John, Jr.	Oct. 31, 1801	20	light	Barrington, R.I.	2	36
Shorta, W. N.	Mar. 30, 1852	14	black	Boston, Ma.	5	75
Shorter, Isaac	Aug. 25, 1832	23	black	Washington, D.C.	5	69
Shortle, Charles	Mar. 10, 1853	16	light	Boston, Ma.	5	75
Shore, Stephen G.	Dec. 20, 1843	20	dark	Berkley, Ma.	5	72
Shreve, Samuel	Sept. 14, 1803	24	dark	Portsmouth, N.H.	2	36
Shumway, William	Apr. 3, 1820	17	light	Middletown, Conn.	4	65
Shundell, William	1798-1799	Nov. 28, 1770		Somerset, Ma.	*-	--
Shute, Johnston	July 31, 1811	21	yellow	New Haven, Conn.	4	63
Shute, Thomas	Nov. 20, 1846	23	dark	Prospect, Me.	5	73
Sibley, Osborn	July 27, 1844	22	light	Mendon, Ma.	5	72
Sieman, Frank	Apr. 13, 1865	24	dark	Newport, R.I.	6	18
Silver, Caleb	June 28, 1836	23	light	Dunbarton, N.H.	5	70
Silver, Joseph	May 13, 1867	25	dark	Boston, Ma.	6	18
Silver, Wm. J.	Jan. 19, 1849	28	sandy	Salem, Ma.	5	73
Silvia, Antone	Sept. 5, 1861	25	dark	New London, Conn.	6	18

*Newport, R. I.

NAME	DATE OF CERTIFICATION	AGE	COMPLEXION	PLACE OF BIRTH	BOOK	PA
Silvia, Lewis	Nov. 4, 1861	15	dark	New Bedford, Ma.	6	18
Simkin, Thomas H.	Oct. 1, 1844	17	light	Bath, Me.	5	72
Simmons, Charles	Dec. 31, 1799	16	light	Barrington, R.I.	2	26
Simmons, Charles	May 9, 1806	22	light	Barrington, R.I.	3	67
Simmons, Charles	June 26, 1801	17	light	Barrington, R.I.	2	26
Simmons, Charles	Feb. 25, 1804	21	light	Providence, R.I.	3	3
Simmons, Charles	Dec. 5, 1818	34	light	Barrington, R.I.	4	6
Simmons, Charles	Aug. 26, 1824	20	light	Providence, R.I.	4	66
Simmons, Charles J.[or Jr.]	July 26, 1826	22	light	Providence, R.I.	4	66
Simmons, Clark T.	March 10, 1840	29	light	Tiverton, R.I.	5	7
Simons, Daniel	March 8, 1815	23	black	Wrentham, Mass.	4	6
Simmons, Eben	Dec. 17, 1800	32	dark	Somerset, Mass.	2	26
Simmons, Eben	Aug. 3, 1804	35	dark	Swansea, Mass.	3	36
Simmons, Ebenezer	Nov. 14, 1839	19	dark	Chatham, Mass.	5	7
Simmons, Francis M.	Dec. 2, 1834	21	light	Charleston, So.Car.	5	70
Simmons, George	Nov. 24, 1851	20	dark	Portland, Me.	5	75
Simmons, George H.	March 29, 1852	23	light	Providence, R.I.	5	75
Simmons, Gilbert	May 1, 1799	32	dark	Providence, R.I.	2	18
Simmons, Henry	Sept. 27, 1804	12	light	Freetown, Mass.	3	52
Simmons, Henry	Feb. 28, 1810	16	light	Freetown, Mass.	4	63
Simmons, Henry B.	Sept. 30, 1806	23	light	East Greenwich,R.I.	3	67
Simmons, Isaac	Nov. 20, 1840	22	dark	Dartmouth, Mass.	5	7
Simmons, James	March 12, 1833	31	black	Providence, R.I.	5	69
Simmons, James H.	Aug. 26, 1845	17	dark	Smithfield, R.I.	5	72
Simmons, James	July 17, 1834	28	dark	Dover, N.H.	5	70
Simmons, Job	March 9, 1805	35	light	Freetown, Mass.	3	5
Simmons, Job	June 9, 1804	27	dark	Swansea, Mass.	3	36
Simmons, John	1798-1799	b. Aug. 29, 1779		Dighton, Mass.	*-	--

Simmons, John of Providence. M. Betsey Allen of Bristol, Nov. 30, 1828.
Rev. Benedict Record

Simmons, Nathan	Oct. 19, 1803	16	light	Dighton, Mass.	2	36
Simmons, Nathan	Nov. 10, 1849	37	light	Providence, R.I.	5	74
Simmons, Nathan B.	April 29, 1806	19	light	Dighton, Mass.	3	7
Simmons, Pardon	Oct. 31, 1821	24	light	Little Compton, R.I.	4	65
Simmons, Robert	Jan. 24, 1811	23	black	Jerusalem, N.Y.	4	63

+Newport, R. I.

NAME	DATE OF CERTIFICATION	AGE	COMPLEXION	PLACE OF BIRTH	BOOK	PAGE
Simmons, Seth	Jan. 12, 1798	17	dark	Tolland, Conn.	1	30
Simmons, Seth	Aug. 3, 1804	23	light	Tolland, Conn.	3	36
Simmons, Seth, Jr.	Nov. 12, 1849	34	light	Providence, R.I.	5	74
Simmons, Stephen	July 3, 1804	19	light	Dighton, Mass.	3	36
Simons, Stephen	Sept. 1, 1863	18	dark	Norwich, Conn.	6	18
Simmons, Thomas	March 16, 1799	27	light	Providence, R.I.	2	18
Simmons, Thomas	May 3, 1831	21	light	Warwick, R. I.	5	69
Simmons, Thomas, Jr.	1798-1799	b.Oct. 23, 1813		Tiverton, R.I.	*-	--
Simmons, William	Aug. 29, 1800	16	light	Philadelphia, Pa.	2	26
Simmons, William	Aug. 3, 1801	16	dark	Providence, R.I.	2	26
Simmons, William	July 20, 1803	19	dark	Providence, R.I.	2	36
Simmons, William	May 20, 1833	19	light	Plainfield, Conn.	5	69
Simmons, William	May 17, 1811	24	light	Newburyport, Mass.	4	63
Simpson, Charles	Nov. 20, 1856	20	light	Hampden, Me.	5	76
Simpson, Edward	Dec. 13, 1803	30	light	Derby, Pa.	2	20
Simpson, William	Oct. 8, 1834	27	light	Boston, Ma.	5	70
Simpson, William	Nov. 15, 1841	17	light	New York, N.Y.	5	71
Simpsn, William A.	Dec. 4, 1833	26	light	Providence, R.I.	5	70
Sims, Edmund	March 6, 1840	18	light	Pompey, N.Y.	5	71
Sinclair, Joseph	1798-1799	b.Aug. 6, 1776		Bowdin, Mass.	*-	--
Sirrkins, George	Aug. 2, 1797	24	light	Providence, R.I.	1	30
Sirrkins, James	Aug. 11, 1796	26	light	Providence, R. I.	1	1
Sirass, James	March 19, 1827	20	black	South Kingstown, R.I.	4	66
Sisk, David	Oct. 10, 1851	23	light	Providence, R.I.	5	75
Sisson, David, Jr.	May 29, 1826	17	light	Middletown, R.I.	4	66
Sisson, Daniel W.	March 31, 1821	22	light	Tiverton, R.I.		

Sworn statement of Joseph Rounds of Tiverton in the Custom House Papers. b.June 1, 1799

NAME	DATE OF CERTIFICATION	AGE	COMPLEXION	PLACE OF BIRTH	BOOK	PAGE
Sisson, Fantee	June 15, 1820	25	black	Warren, R.I.	4	65
Sisson, Freeborn	May 19, 1840	24	light	Warren, R.I.	5	71
Sisson, Henry	1798-1799	b.Oct. 12, 1770		Swansea, Mass.	*-	--
Sisson, Jabez	1798-1799	b.Aug. 28, 1774		Portsmouth, R.I.	*-	--
Sisson, James L.	Feb. 19, 1857	19	dark	Fall River, Mass.	5	76
Sisson, Job. J.	Sept. 16, 1863	20	dark	New Bedford, Mass.	6	18
Sisson, Richard	March 30, 1805	22	light	East Greenwich, R.I.	3	51A
Sisson, Richard	March 7, 1815	26	light	East Greenwich, R.I.	4	64
Sisson, Silas	May 21, 1821	19	light	Middletown, R.I.	4	65
Sisson, Truman B.	July 15, 1854	17	light	So. Kingston, R.I.	5	75

*Newport, R.I.

NAME	DATE OF CERTIFICATION	AGE	COMPLEXION	PLACE OF BIRTH	BOOK	PAGE
Sisson, Zebulon N.	Sept. 16, 1863	21	dark	New Bedford, Mass.	6	18
Sivow, Andrew	Aug. 24, 1849	24	yellow	Salem, New Jersey	5	73
Skinfull, Richard	Nov. 16, 1807	16	florid	Dighton, Mass.	4	62
Skinner, Elijah	Nov. 2, 1819	19	fresh	Norton, Mass.	4	65
Skinner, Isaac	July 27, 1820	27	light	Royalton, Vt.	4	65
Skinner, Joseph B.	June 2, 1831	18	light	Norton, Mass.	5	69
Slade, Cuff	Dec. 30, 1800	42	black	Somerset, Mass.	2	26
[Slade], William	Nov. 17, 1803	15	black	Somerset, Mass.	2	45
Slater, Robert	July 15, 1854	17	light	Smithfield, R. I.	5	75
Sloan, John	Dec. 5, 1796	18	dark	Providence, R.I.	1	23
Sloan, Phillip	Dec. 16, 1797	30	light	Cranston, R.I.	1	30
Slocum, Amasa	June 16, 1809	21	light	Providence, R.I.	4	62
Slocum, Amasa K., Jr.	Aug. 14, 1837	21	light	Providence, R.I.	5	70
Slocum, Benjamin	Feb. 21, 1812	19	light	Warwick, R.I.	4	64
Slocum, Charles	July 14, 1854	21	light	Staten Island, N.Y.	5	75
Slocum, Charles G.	Nov. 29, 1848	29	sallow	Seekonk, Mass.	5	73
Slocum, Clarke	1798-1799	b.Mar. 6, 1778		Tiverton, R.I.	*-	--
Samuel Slocum of Newport swears for him.						
Slocum, David	Oct. 13, 1797	24	dark	Newport, R.I.	1	30
Slocum, James	March 5, 1849	20	light	Seekonk, Mass.	5	73
Slocum, James Edwin	June 30, 1852	16	dark	Westport, Mass.	5	75
Slocum, John P.	Sept. 28, 1837	17	light	Providence, R. I.	5	70
Slocum, Joshua	Dec. 17, 1803	26	dark	Rehoboth, Mass.	2	20
Slocum, Lyman	Apr. 6, 1824	18	light	Tiverton, R. I.	4	66
Slocum, Oliver W.	Oct. 26, 1849	22	light	South Kingston, R.I.	5	74
Slocum, Robert	April 21, 1854	54	yellow	New York, NY	5	75
Slocum, Samuel	1798-1799	b. Nov. 16, 1785		Portsmouth, R.I.	*-	--
Samuel Slocum of Newport swears for him.						
Slocum, Sissero[Cicero]	Dec. 2, 1823	18	black	Tiverton, R. I.	4	66
Slocum, Smith	Feb. 21, 1812	18	light	Warwick, R.I.	4	64
Slocum, Varnum	Aug. 19, 1811	26	light	Newport, R.I.	4	63
Slocum, William	July 14, 1806	22	light	Newport, R.I.	3	67
Sly, Amasa	June 27, 1801	19	black	Smithfield, R.I.	2	26
Small, Gamaliel	April 27, 1849	22	light	Richmond, Me.	5	73
Small, John	June 30, 1851	48	dark	Prospect, Me.	5	74
Small, John	Sept. 1, 1863	32	dark	Sommerset, Mass.	6	18
Small, Thomas	Oct. 11, 1803	18	light	Harwich, Mass.	2	36
Smart, Anthony	June 6, 1810	30	dark	East Greenwich, R.I.	4	63
Smart, Henry	March 29, 1853	21	dark	Stamford, Vt.	5	75

*Newport, R.I.

NAME	DATE OF CERTIFICATION	AGE	COMPLEXION	PLACE OF BIRTH	BOOK	PAGE
Smart, John J.	July 16, 1850	28	black	Providence, R.I.	5	74
Smee, Thomas	March 25, 1835	22	light	Philadelphia, Penn.	5	70
Smellage, James	Sept. 2, 1797	27	dark	Boston, Mass.	1	30
Smiley, James	Oct. 19, 1858(?)	28	fair	New York, N.Y.	6	18
Smith, Alonzo	Oct. 18, 1858	39	dark	Greenport, N.Y.	6	18
Smith, Alpheus	Apr. 19, 1822	19	light	Cranston, R.I.	4	65
Smith, Amos	Jan. 2, 1934	23	black	North Kingston, R.I.	5	70
Smith, Andrew C.	Jan. 23, 1849	23	yellow	Montgomery Co., Penn.	5	73
Smith, Archer	July 29, 1864	26	dark	Providence, R.I.	6	18
Smith, Archibald	March 28, 1804	21	dark	Scituate, R.I.	3	35
Smith, Arnold M. (written Smith, M. Arnold)	August 24, 1799	20	dark	Smithfield, R.I.	2	18
Smith, Arnold	March 28, 1804	22	light	Scituate, R.I.	3	35
Smith, Arnold	May 9, 1807	14	light	Cranston, R.I.	4	62
Smith, Augustus C.	Apr. 13, 1827	16	dark	Sandwich, Mass.	4	66
Smith, Benajah	Aug. 6, 1832	26	light	North Kingston, R.I.	5	69
Smith, Benjamin	Apr. 27, 1797	16	dark	Providence, R.I.	1	23
Smith, Benjamin	Aug. 26, 1797	21	light	Rehoboth, Mass.	1	30
Smith, Benjamin	May 1, 1799	30	light	Providence, R.I.	2	18
Smith, Benjamin	Apr. 12, 1805	19	light	Cranston, R.I.	3	51A
Smith, Benjamin	Aug. 2, 1817	16	dark	Warwick, R. I.	4	65
Smith Benjamin	July 11, 1821	16	light	Warren, R.I., Aug. 29, 1804		
Son of James and Salley Smith; birth certificate in the Custom House Papers						
Smith, Benjamin, Jr.	May 18, 1813	27	light	Cranston, R.I.	4	64
Smith, Benjamin M.	Nov. 17, 1809	34	dark	Rehoboth, Mass.	4	63
Smith, Caesar	Aug. 6, 1805	36	black	Barrington, R.I.	3	70
Smith, Canton	Oct. 7, 1831	27	dark	Scituate, R.I.	5	69
Smith, Charles	March 1, 1825	21	light	Taunton, Mass.	4	66
Smith, Charles	August 28, 1845	28	dark	New Orleans, La.	5	72
Smith, Charles	March 18, 1847	22	fair	Islip, N. Y.	5	73
Smith, Charles	Dec. 8, 1852	28	light	Albany, N. Y.	5	75
Smith, Charles	June 11, 1855	19	light	New York, N. Y.	5	76
Smith, Charles	Feb. 28, 1857	24	black	Long Island, N.Y.	5	76
Smith, Charles C.	Nov. 19, 1828	19	light	North Kingstown, R.I.	4	67
Smith, Charles D.	Sept. 20, 1856	19	dark	Columbia, Maine	5	76
Smith, Charles F.	Feb. 2, 1854	20	florid	Orrington, Maine	5	76
Smith, Charles J.	Feb. 23, 1859	25	fair	Philadelphia, Pa.	6	18

NAME	DATE OF CERTIFICATION	AGE	COMPLEXION	PLACE OF BIRTH	BOOK	PA.
Smith, Chas. M.	July 17, 1855	16	fair	Providence, R.I.	5	76
Smith, Christopher	Oct. 29, 1830	18	light	Cranston, R.I.	5	69
Smith, Christopher	Sept. 2, 1842	16	light	Paterson, N.J.	5	72
Smith, Daniel	June 7, 1800	22	dark	Smithfield, R.I.	2	26
Smith, David	Aug. 5, 1840	22	light	Bath, N.H.	5	71
Smith, Domanay	Apr. 28, 1813	26	black	North Kingstown, R.I.	4	64
Smith, Edward	March 11, 1797	16	dark	Providence, R.I.	1	23
Smith, Edward	April 28, 1797	19	light	Providence, R.I.	1	23
Smith, Edward	April 14, 1804	16	dark	Foster, R.I.	3	36
Smith, Edward	April 1, 1805	17	light	Foster, R.I.	3	51
Smith, Edward	May 17, 1823	19	light	Cranston, R.I.	4	66
Smith, Edward	April 29, 1853	25	light	New York, N.Y.	5	75
Smith, Elijah	April 15, 1835	30	black	Philadelphia, Penn.	5	70
Smith, Elisha P. 2nd	Nov. 4, 1829	21	light	Cranston, R.I.	5	69
Smith, Esek	Oct. 16, 1828	19	light	Providence, R.I.	4	67
Smith, Ezekiel P.	Dec. 13, 1817	18	light	Warwick, R.I.	4	65
Smith, Francis	Oct. 20, 1849	28	dark	Boston, Mass.	5	74
Smith, Francis	June 16, 1852	19	mulatto	Boston, Mass.	5	75
Smith, Frederick	April 10, 1854	26	light	Williamsburg, N.Y.	5	75
Smith, Frederick	Dec. 1, 1856	22	light	Chelsea, Mass.	5	76
Smith, Frederick H.	June 7, 1830	19	light	Providence, R.I.	5	69
Smith, Gardner	Jan. 31, 1807	14	yellowish	Barrington, R.I.	4	62
Smith, Gardner	Jan. 16, 1811	18	black	Barrington, R.I.	4	63
Smith, Garner	Oct. 14, 1803	24	light	Scituate, R.I.	2	36
Smith, George	May 17, 1831	18	light	North Kingston, R.I.	5	69
Smith, George	Aug. 6, 1844	21	dark	Boston, Mass.	5	72
Smith, George	Oct. 9, 1856	30	light	Providence, R.I.	5	76
Smith, George A.	Oct. 18, 1849	46	light	East Greenwich, R.I.	5	74
Smith, George B.	Aug. 26, 1815	17	light	Warwick, R.I.	4	64
Smith, George B.	Oct. 7, 1836	28	light	Charlotte Vermont	5	70
Smith, George H.	Sept. 18, 1839	24	black	North Hempstead, N.Y.	5	71
Smith, George H.	Jan. 15, 1849	23	light	Marlboro, Mass.	5	73
Smith, George H.	March 9, 1860	20	fair	Buffalo, N.Y.	6	18
Smith, Gideon W.	Nov. 21, 1826	20	light native	Sandwich, Mass.	4	66
Smith, Gilbert	Dec. 26, 1856	17	light	Gouldsboro, Maine	5	76
Smith, Gustavus	Apr. 19, 1822	14	light	Cranston, R.I.	4	65
Smith, Henry	Aug. 1, 1805	18	light	Boston, Mass.	3	51

NAME	DATE OF CERTIFICATION	AGE	COMPLEXION	PLACE OF BIRTH	BOOK	PAGE
Smith, Henry	Dec. 10, 1817	43	light	Middleboro, Mass.	4	65
Smith, Henry	March 9, 1818	20	light	Cranston, R.I.	4	65
Smith, Henry	July 22, 1839	24	dark	Charleston, S. C.	5	71
Smith, Henry	Sept. 26, 1843	27	light	Boston, Mass.	5	72
Smith, Henry, 2nd	July 18, 1805	17	light	Providence, R.I.	3	51A
Smith, Henry, 2nd	March 27, 1809	21	light	Providence, R.I.	4	62
Smith, Henry F.	Feb. 27, 1854	23	light	Boston, Mass.	5	76
Smith, Henry T.	Dec. 14, 1841	24	dark	Dartmouth, Mass.	5	71
Smith, Israel, Jr.	July 19, 1810	18	light	Cranston, R.I.	4	63
Smith, Jacob	Feb. 23, 1852	29	light	New Orleans, La.	5	75
Smith, Jacob, Jr.	Nov. 30, 1821	15	light	Newport, R.I.	4	65
Smith, James	Mar. 31, 1800	17	light	Barrington, R.I.	2	26
Smith, James	May 24, 1805	22	light	Salem, Mass.	3	51A
Smith, James	Nov. 9, 1820	25	light	Smithfield, R.I.	4	65
Smith, James	April 23, 1830	21	light	Chester, Maryland	5	69
Smith, James	Jan. 1, 1833	25	light	Smithtown, N.Y.	5	69
Smith, James	Dec. 11, 1838	20	light	Brooklyn, N.Y.	5	71
Smlith, James	Oct. 9, 1843	23	dark	Baltimore, Md.	5	72
Smith, James	Aug. 24, 1849	18	light	Eastport, Me.	5	73
Smith, James	Aug. 28, 1849	36	dark	Sherborn, Mass.	5	74
Smith, James	Aug. 14, 1854	35	light	Killingly, Conn.	5	76
Smith, James	Aug. 15, 1857	28	dark	Mystic, Conn.	6	18
Smith, James	June 10, 1858	28	light	Providence, R.I.	6	18
Smith, James	Feb. 4, 1861	31	fair	New Orleans, La.	6	18
Smith, James H.	Nov. 14, 1812	24	dark	Wilmington, Del.	4	64
Smith, James H.	Nov. 21, 1849	22	light	Glocester, R.I.	5	74
Smith, John, 2nd	April 24, 1807	15	brown	Providence, R. I.	4	62
Smith, Jeremiah L.	March 5, 1849	26	light	Smithfield, R. I.	5	73
Smlith, John	April 12, 1798	21	dark	Cranston, R.I.	(1 (2	31 18
Smith, John	1798-1799	b. Dec. 7, 1777		N. Kingston, R.I.	Newport, R.I.	
Smith, John	Aug. 17, 1803	16	dark	Newport, R.I.	2	36
Smith, John	Apr. 5, 1809	21	black	Wilmington, N. C.	4	62
Smith, John	July 9, 1811	25	yellow	Baltimore, Md.	4	63
Smith, John	Dec. 7, 1811	26	yellow	Baltimore, Md.	4	64
Smith, John	March 27, 1823	20	light	Yarmouth, Mass.	4	66
Smith, John	Dec. 7, 1832	15	light	Bristol, R. I.	5	69
Smith, John	May 18, 1833	23	mulatto	Biddeford, Maine	5	69

NAME	DATE OF CERTIFICATION	AGE	COMPLEXION	PLACE OF BIRTH	BOOK	PAGE
Smith, John	Aug. 27, 1839	49	light	Alexandria, D.C.	5	71
Smith, JOhn	July 24, 1842	31	light	Eastport, Maine	5	71
Smith, John	July 15, 1843	17	light	Great Egg Harbor, N.J.	5	72
Smith, John	Oct. 26, 1843	26	dark	Coventry, R. I.	5	72
Smith, John	Aug. 26, 1845	26	fair	Philadelphia, Pa.	5	72
Smith, John	May 17, 1848	32	dark	New York, N.Y.	5	73
Smith, John	June 23, 1848	25	light	Hudson, N.Y.	5	73
Smith, John	Feb. 14, 1850	30	light	New York, N. Y.	5	74
Smith, John	June 13, 1850	20	light	New York, N. Y.	5	74
Smith, John	July 24, 1850	21	light	Albany, N. Y.	5	74
Smith, John	March 15, 1852	28	light	New York, N. Y.	5	75
Smith, John	October 4, 1854	24	dark	New York, N. Y.	5	76
Smith, John	April 19, 1855	23	mulatto	Monmouth, N. J.	5	76
Smith, John	Sept. 7, 1855	29	light	Charleston, S. C.	5	76
Smith, John, 2nd.	March 2, 1812	19	light	Providence, R. I.	4	64
Smith, John	Jan. 1, 1858	20	light	Woodstock, Conn.	6	18
Smith, John A.	Jan. 18, 1828	25	florid	Hartford, Conn.	4	66
Smith, John B.	Dec. 2, 1806	11	light	Hudson, N. Y.	4	62
Smith, John C.	Oct. 22, 1817	22	dark	Baltimore, Md.	4	65
Smith, John K.	June 23, 1809	20	brown	Glocester, R. I.	4	63
Smith, John W.	June 29, 1805	18	light	Cranston, R. I.	3	51A
Smith, John W.	Nov. 2, 1812	25	light	Cranston, R. I.	4	64
Smith, John W.	Oct. 17, 1832	32	light	Haverhill, Mass.	5	69
Smith, Jonathan	March 28, 1804	17	light	Foster, R. I.	3	35
Smith, Joseph	June 4, 1805	42	dark	Charleston, S. C.	3	51A
Smith, Joseph	Nov. 15, 1811	17	light	Barrington, R. I.	4	64
Smith, Joseph	June 13, 1815	20	black	Seekonk, Mass.	4	64
Smith, Joseph	July 8, 1818	19	light	Cranston, R. I.	4	65
Smith, Joseph	April 23, 1849	25	light	New York, N.Y.	5	73
Smith, Joseph B.	Apr. 18, 1810	18	dark	Scituate, R. I.	4	63
Smith, Joseph C.	July 29, 1839	21	mulatto	Providence, R.I.	5	71
Smith, Joseph W.	March 28, 1863	30	light	South Kingstown, R. I.	6	18
Smith, Joshua	July 5, 1823	16	light	Providence, R.I.	4	66
Smith, Josiah Gibbs	Aug. 29, 1849	21	light	Cranston, R. I.	5	74
Smith, Joshua C.	Sept. 8, 1843	20	dark	New Shoreham, R. I.	5	72
Smith, Lewis	March 5, 1806	23	black	New York, N. Y.	3	71
Smith, M. Arnold (also filed under Smith, Arnold M.)	Aug. 24, 1799	20	dark	Smithfield, R. I.	2	18

NAME	DATE OF CERTIFICATION	AGE	COMPLEXION	PLACE OF BIRTH	BOOK	PAGE
Smith, Melbornen	Feb. 2, 1854	14	light	Orrington, Me.	5	76
Smith, Mory	Dec. 18, 1799	36	light	Smithfield, R.I.	2	18
Smith, Moses	Mar. 4, 1811	17	light	Warwick, R.I.	4	63
Smith, Mowry W.	Nov. 28, 1849	32	light	Smithfield, R.I.	5	74
Smith, Nathan	March 2, 1839	22	dark	Providence, R.I.	5	71
Smith, Nathan H.	Dec. 24, 1852	21	light	Orrington, Me.	5	75
Smith, Nathaniel	April 10, 1848	37	light	Providence, R.I.	5	73
Smith, Nelson	May 23, 1821	20	dark	Canterbury, Conn.	4	65
Smith, Nicholas	March 16, 1811	24	light	Warwick, R.I.	4	63
Smith, Nicholas	Oct. 11, 1831	20	light	Portland, Me.	5	69
Smith, Orin	March 3, 1849	45	light	Smithfield, R.I.	5	73
Smith, Peter	Apr. 14, 1804	29	dark	New York, N. Y.	3	35
Smith, Remington	June 14, 1800	18	light	Warwick, R. I.	2	26
Smith, Remington	Nov. 16, 1807	25	light	Warwick, R.I.	4	62
Smith, Remington	Oct. 12, 1825	24	light	Cranston, R. I.	4	66
Smith, Reuben	Nov. 20, 1804	14	light	Cranston, R.I.	3	51
Smith, Ruben	June 9, 1797	38	light	Cranston, R.I.	1	23
Smith, Reuben	Oct. 22, 1803	17	black	Rochester, Mass.	2	36
Smith, Reuben, Jr.	May 8, 1805	14	light	Cranston, R. I.	3	51A
Smith, Reuben, Jr.	Oct. 24, 1809	18	light	Cranston, R. I.	4	63
Smith, Richard	Aug. 12, 1846	31	dark	Fishkill, N. Y.	5	73
Smith, Samuel	Sept. 26, 1796	18	dark	Providence, R. I.	1	3
Smith, Samuel	May 19, 1821	23	light b.3/18/1794 Rehoboth, Mass.	-	--
Sworn statement of John Gorney of Newport, in the Custom House Papers.						
Smith, Samuel	Dec. 11, 1838	26	black	Brooklyn, N. Y.	5	71
Smith, Samuel	March 3, 1843	20	dark	Portsmouth, N. H.	5	72
Smith, Samuel C.	Feb. 19, 1810	17	dark	Rehoboth, Mass.	4	63
Smith, Simeon, Jr.	May 15, 1807	28	light	Cranston, R. I.	4	62
Smith, Simon	Apr. 26, 1808	16	light	Cranston, R. I.	4	62
Smith, Simon	July 16, 1813	22	light	Cranston, R. I.	4	64
Smith, Stephen	Aug. 1, 1799	17	light	Warwick, R. I.	2	18
Smith, Stephen	Feb. 14, 1805	22	light	Warwick, R. I.	3	51
Smith, Theodore	Feb. 27, 1857	22	dark	Milford, N. H.	5	76
Smith, Thomas	May 18, 1799	17	dark	Cranston, R. I.	2	18
Smith, Thomas	Feb. 15, 1806	23	light	Cranston, R. I.	3	71
Smith, Thomas	Jan. 4, 1819	27	dark	Harwich, Mass.	4	65
Smith, Thomas	July 26, 1833	18	light	Norfolk, Va.	5	70

NAME	DATE OF CERTIFICATION	AGE	COMPLEXION	PLACE OF BIRTH	BOOK	PAGE
Smith, Thomas	Nov. 20, 1837	22	dark	Newport, R. I.	5	70
Smith, Thomas	Sept. 30, 1844	20	black	Philadelphia, Pa.	5	72
Smith, Thomas	Sept. 30, 1844	20	black	Philadelphia, Pa.	5	72
Smith, Thomas	March 3, 1849	22	florid	New York, N. Y.	5	73
Smith, Thomas	Feb. 15, 1860	25	fair	New Haven, Conn.	6	18
Smith, Turpin, Jr.	Sept. 13, 1804	17	light	Providence, R.I.	3	36
Smith, William	Aug. 18, 1796	23	light	Rehoboth, Mass.	1	1
Smith, William	Sept. 23, 1796	26	light	Providence, R. I.	1	3
Smith, William Newport, R. I.	1798 to 1799 Samuel Smith swears for him.	b. 2/5/1773		Newport, R. I.	-	--
Smith, William	Apr. 24, 1799	27	black	Warwick, R. I.	2	18
Smith, William	May 6, 1801	25	dark	Bristol, R. I.	2	26
Smith, William	July 30, 1803	16	light	Scituate, R. I.	2	36
Smith, William	Sept. 6, 1803	22	light	Philadelphia, Pa.	2	36
Smith, William	Apr. 24, 1804	25	dark	Harwich, Mass.	3	36
Smith, William	Aug. 12, 1806	20	dark	New York, N. Y.	3	67
Smith, William	May 20, 1809	22	dark	Newport, R. I.	4	62
Smith, William	May 13, 1811	24	dark	Newport, R. I.	4	63
Smith, William	Nov. 13, 1811	19	dark	New York, N. Y.	4	64
Smith, William	Nov. 19, 1827	25	dark	Middletown, R. I.	4	66
Smith, William	May 21, 1834	22	black	Boston, Mass.	5	70
Smith, William	Oct. 22, 1834	20	light	New York, N. Y.	5	70
Smith, William	July 7, 1835	26	light.	New York, N. Y.	5	70
Smith, William	Oct. 14, 1836	22	light	Philadelphia, Pa.	5	70
Smith, William	Aug. 5, 1839	22	dark	New York, N. Y.	5	71
Smith, William	Dec. 10, 1841	20	light	Baltimore, Md.	5	71
Smith, William	Sept. 2, 1846	27	black	Wilmington, Del.	5	73
Smith, William	Aug. 24, 1849	32	light	Eastport, Me.	5	73
Smith, William	Aug. 13, 1853	25	light	New London, Conn.	5	75
Smith, William	May 4, 1859	25	fair	Sussex Co., Del.	6	18
Smith, William	Sept. 1, 1860	32	fair	Philadelphia, Pa.	6	18
Smith, William, Jr.	Apr. 7, 1815	18	light	Warwick, R. I.	4	64
Smith, William, Jr.(?)	Dec. 22, 1826	26	light native	Sandwich, Mass.	4	66
Smith, Wm. B.	Sept. 10, 1850	26	florid	Weymouth, Mass.	5	74
Smith, William G.	May 19, 1813	34	light	Cranston, R. I.	4	64
Smith, William H.	Apr. 2, 1806	25	dark	Providence, R. I.	3	71

REGISTER OF SEAMEN'S PROTECTION

NAME	DATE OF CERTIFICATION	AGE	COMPLEXION	PLACE OF BIRTH	BOOK	PAGE
Smith, Wm. H. H.	Oct. 2, 1856	15	dark	Seekonk, Mass.	5	76
Smith, William W.	June 5, 1835	22	light	Wareham, Mass.	5	70
Smith, Winthrop	Oct. 19, 1826	30	light	Brookfield, Conn.	4	66
Smith, Ziba	Dec. 18, 1799	27	light	Glocester, R.I.	2	26
Smithwick, Wm.	1798 to 1799	b. Mar. 15, 1780		Edenton, N. C.	Newport, R.I.	
Snare, James M.	Aug. 6, 1864	27	light	Robbinstown, Me.	6	18
Snell, Asa	Nov. 8, 1809	25	light	Hopkinton, Mass.	4	63
Snell, Moses	1798 to 1799	b. Apr. 7, 1780		Little Compton, R.I.	Newport, R.I.	
Snell, Nathan	Oct. 13, 1809	33	florid	Bridgewater, Mass.	4	63
Snell, William	Dec. 22, 1796	23	light	Warren, R.I.	1	23
Snow, Azel	July 28, 1821	20	light	Easton, Mass.	4	65
Snow, Charles	Aug. 15, 1840	23	light	Providence, R.I.	5	71
Snow, Charles Knox	July 29, 1823	26	light	Norwich, Conn.	4	66
Snow, David	Apr. 21, 1804	30	light	Harwich, Mass.	3	36
Snow, Elisha	Oct. 26, 1803	18	dark	Rochester, Mass.	2	36
Snow, Enos	Jan. 7, 1818	15	light	Chatham, Mass.	4	65
Snow, George W.	May 12, 1825	16	light	Rochester, Mass.	4	66
Snow, John L.	Nov. 3, 1819	24	brown	Providence, R. I.	4	65
Snow, Joseph	Mar. 28, 1807	19	light	Providence, R. I.	4	62
Snow, Joseph	Apr. 19, 1811	23	light	Providence, R. I.	4	63
Snow, Thomas	June 7, 1834	20	light	Harwich, Mass.	5	70
Snow, Thomas A.	Oct. 16, 1829	19	light	Providence, R. I.	5	69
Snow, Washington	Mar. 29, 1815	19	brown	Harwich, Mass.	4	64
Snow, William, Jr.	Oct. 16, 1805	23	light	Providence, R. I.	3	70
Snow, William C.	Nov. 30, 1806	19	dark	Scituate, R. I.	3	71
Sohlgren, Olaf	Oct. 25, 1803	28	light	Albany, N. Y.	2	36
Solomon, James M.	April 25, 1831	20	mulatto	Seekonk, Mass.	5	69
[Soule][Sowle], Abner	Aug. 3, 1801	18	dark	Tiverton, R. I.	2	26
[Soule][Sowle], Christopher	Aug. 3, 1801	27	dark	Tiverton, R. I.	2	26
Sowle, George L.	July 20, 1841	22	light	Westport, Mass.	5	71
Soule, Peleg	Oct. 9, 1798	18	light	Tiverton, R. I.	2	18
[Soule][Sowle, Peleg	Mar. 9, 1804	23	light	Tiverton, R. I.	3	35
Soule, William	Apr. 29, 1809	25	light	Providence, R.I.	4	62
Sowle, William C.	June 8, 1843	21	light	New Bedford, Mass.	5	72
Southerland, James	Nov. 26, 1849	22	light	Boston, Mass.	5	74
Southwait, James	Dec. 30, 1865	21	light	Chicago, Il.	6	18

NAME	DATE OF CERTIFICATION	AGE	COMPLEXION	PLACE OF BIRTH	BOOK	PAGE
Southwick, Benjamin	Apr. 30, 1821	18	light	Mendon, Mass.	4	65
Southwick, Francis M.	March 12, 1844	28	light	Newport, R.I.	5	72
Southwick, George F.	Dec. 12, 1853	30	fair	Smithfield, R.I.	5	75
Southwick, George F.	Aug. 15, 1865	40	dark	Pawtucket, R. I.	6	18
Southwick, John	1798-1799	b. Oct. 17, 1777		Dartmouth, Mass.	Newport, R.	
Silas Southwick of Newport swears for his brother.						
Southwick, Lyman	Mar. 26, 1824	21	brown	Richmond, R. I.	4	66
Southwick, Silas	1798-1799	b. Oct. 17, 1777		Dartmouth, Mass.	Newport, R.	
Southwick, Silas L.	July 8, 1845	21	light	Newport, R.I.	5	72
Southworth, Eleazer	Mar. 26, 1804	22	light	Mansfield, Conn.	3	35
Southworth, Isaac	Mar. 14, 1812	19	dark	Franklin, Mass.	4	64
Sowens, Henry	March 30, 1857	22	light	New York, N. Y.	5	76
Sowle, John	Sept. 25, 1818	19	light	Tiverton, R. I.	4	65
Spalding, Henry	April 8, 1854	22	dark	Providence, R.I.	5	75
Spaulding, Joseph	July 2, 1861	28	dark	Lowell, Mass.	6	18
Sparks, Aaron	May 10, 1813	23	dark	Killingly, Conn.	4	64
Speakman, John Thomas	July 27, 1848	25	light	Eastern Shore, Va.	5	73
Spear, Edwin	July 9, 1855	26	light	Utica, N. Y.	5	76
Spear, Nathan	July 8, 1809	18	black	Providence, R. I.	4	63
Spear, William R.	Sept. 12, 1837	25	light	Newport, R. I.	5	70
Spears, Charles	Jan. 9, 1845	23	light	Mendon, Mass.	5	72
Spelman, Daniel	Dec. 14, 1803	48	light	Durham, Conn.	2	20
Spellman, Elihu	July 15, 1797	27	light	Middletown, Conn.	1	23
Spelman, James E.	March 1, 1830	16	dark	Providence, R. I.	5	69
Spellman, JOhn	Oct. 3, 1806	21	light	Providence, R. I.	3	67
Spellman, JOhn	Nov. 25, 1805	20	light	Providence, R. I.	3	70
Spellman, John	Oct. 3, 1806	21	light	Providence, R. I.	4	62
Spelman, Joseph	Dec. 19, 1807	19	light	Providence, R. I.	4	62
Spelman, Lemuel	Sept. 2, 1863	20	dark	Elizabeth City, N.C.	6	18
Spellman, Oliver	Mar. 30, 1805	15	light	Providence, R. I.	3	51A
Spellman, Oliver	May 13, 1807	16	light	Providence, R. I.	4	62
Spence, Horace	June 5, 1843	22	light	New York, N. Y.	5	72
Spencer, Aaron	July 21, 1803	17	black	East Greenwich, R. I.	2	36
Spencer, Abraham	Mar. 7, 1857	28	light	Warwick, R.I.	5	76
Spencer, Albert C.	March 19, 1844	28	dark	East Greenwich, R.I.	5	72
Spencer, Albert J.	Sept. 4, 1849	19	florid	East Greenwich, R.I.	5	74
Spencer, Caleb	Aug. 6, 1796	22	light	East Greenwich, R. I.	1	1

REGISTER OF SEAMEN'S PROTECTION

NAME	DATE OF CERTIFICATION	AGE	COMPLEXION	PLACE OF BIRTH	BOOK	PAGE
Spencer, David	Nov. 12, 1796	28	black	East Greenwich, RI	1	23 & 5
Spencer, David	May 9, 1809	23	black	Warwick, R.I.	4	62
Spencer, Dexter	Feb. 24, 1797	19	dark	Providence, RI	1	23
Spencer, E. A.	April 21, 1855	22	dark	Annapolis, Md.	5	76
Spencer, Edwin	Jan. 16, 1849	25	fair	Warwick, R. I.	5	73
Spencer, George W.	Oct. 4, 1841	22	light	East Machias, Me.	5	71
Spencer, Gorton	Oct. 29, 1849	45	dark	Warwick, R. I.	5	74
Spencer, Horace	Dec. 3, 1849	23	light	East Greenwich, R.I.	5	74
Spencer, Horace	May 3, 1855	28	light	East Greenwich, R. I.	5	76
Spencer, Jacob	Nov. 2, 1797	16	light	East Greenwich, R. I.	1	30
Spencer, Job	Feb. 1, 1799	19	black	East Greenwich, R. I.	2	18
Spencer, Joseph S.	Oct. 17, 1805	32	dark	East Hartford, Conn.	3	70
Spencer, Julius	Oct. 11, 1797	25	black	Warwick, R. I.	1	30
Spencer, Julius	June 29, 1798	26	black	East Greenwich, R.I.	2	18
Spencer, Oliver C.	Aug. 29, 1846	17	fair	Warwick, R. I.	5	73
Spencer, Pardon	March 7, 1857	22	light	East Greenwich, R. I.	5	76
Spencer, Peleg	July 27, 1798	18	light	East Greenwich, R. I.	2	18
Spencer, Rhodes G.	Aug. 10, 1850	31	light	East Greenwich, R.I.	5	74
Spencer, Richmond	Feb. 27, 1849	25	light	Providence, R. I.	5	73
Spencer, Stephen	Apr. 25, 1801	19	light	East Greenwich, R.I.	2	26
Spencer, Thomas	Sept. 10, 1796	21	light	Coventry, R. I.	1	2
Spencer, Thomas L.	Dec. 17, 1816	25	light	East Greenwich, R.I.	4	64
Spencer, Varnum	Oct. 18, 1849	36	light	East Greenwich, R.I.	5	74
Spencer, William J.	Nov. 5, 1849	39	light	East Greeniwch, R. I.	5	74
Spink, Anthony	June 6, 1809	25	dark	East Greenwich, R.I.	4	62
Spink, Job W.	June 2, 1849	32	light	West Greenwich, R. I.	5	73
Spink, Michael	Sept. 13, 1796	26	dark	Providence, R. I.	1	2
Spink, Rufus S.	Sept. 26, 1808	16	brown	East Greenwich, R. I.	4	62
Spink, Rufus S.	Oct. 6, 1821	28	dark	East Greenwich, R. I.	4	65
Spinney, John	Nov. 1, 1844	24	light	Boston, Mass.	5	72
Spoffard, Samuel	Aug. 17, 1807	18	light	Peterborough, N.H.	4	62
Spooner, Charles	Nov. 25, 1796	23	light	Newport, R.I.	1	23
Spooner, Gardner	Nov. 18, 1839	18	light	East Haddam, Conn.	5	71
Spooner, Henry	Apr. 28, 1806	21	yellow*	East Greenwich, R. I.	3	71

*mulatto

NAME	DATE OF CERTIFICATION	AGE	COMPLEXION	PLACE OF BIRTH	BOOK	PAGE
Spooner, Henry	Sept. 16, 1806	20	yellow	East Greenwich, R.I.	3	67
Spooner, Henry	April 27, 1809	22	yellow	East Greenwich, R.I.	4	62
Spooner, John W.	Aug. 9, 1821	25	ruddy	[Newport?] Sept. 16, 1796		
Sworn statement of Nathaniel G. Bourne of Bristol in the Custom House Papers						
Spooner, Joseph B.	Dec. 15, 1815	16	light	Providence, R.I.	4	64
Spooner, Joseph B.	Dec. 1, 1849	45	dark	Providence, R.I.	5	74
Spooner, Milton W.	Aug. 22, 1855	25	light	Wrentham, Mass.	5	76
Spooner, Richard C. G.	Nov. 12, 1849	36	light	Kinderhook, N. Y.	5	74
Spooner, Stephen D.	Dec. 22, 1842	19	light	Jewett City, Conn.	5	72
Spooner, Thomas	1798-1799	b. 1/15/1774		Newport, R. I.		Newport,
Wing Spooner, Jr. swears for him.						
Spooner, Thomas	Feb. 2, 1804	18	light	Providence, R.I.	3	35
Spooner, William	1798-1799	b. 1/25/1782		Newport, R. I.		Newport, R.
Spooner, Wing	1798-1799	b. 4/27/1797		Newport, R. I.		Newport, R.
Son of Charles Spooner.						
Spragg, Edward	April 12, 1834	27	light	Oyster Bay, N. Y.	5	70
Sprague, Benjamin	May 3, 1806	22	light	Cranston, R. I.	3	67
Sprague, Daniel	May 23, 1800	16	light	New York, N.Y.	2	26
Sprague, George	April 18, 1855	17	fair	Warwick, R. I.	5	76
Sprague, George K.	Aug 2, 1854	22	dark	New Shoreham, R.I.	5	76
Sprague, Humphrey	Mar. 10, 1815	21	light	Portsmouth, R. I.	4	64
Sprague, John	May 27, 1818	19	light	Providence, R. I.	4	65
Sprague, John	Sept 17, 1835	36	light	Providence, R. I.	5	70
Sprague, John, Jr.	Apr. 15, 1802	18	light	East Greenwich, R. I.	2	36
Sprague, Jonathan	July 27, 1799	23	dark	Smithfield, R. I.	2	18
Sprague, Nathan	Dec. 9, 1797	18	light	Smithfield, R. I.	1	30
Sprague, Nathaniel Anthony,	Apr. 2, 1798	17	light	Providence, R. I.	1	30
					2	18
Sprague, Nathaniel A.	March 1, 1805	23	light	Providence, R. I.	3	51

REGISTER OF SEAMEN'S PROTECTION

NAME	DATE OF CERTIFICATION	AGE	COMPLEXION	PLACE OF BIRTH	BOOK	PAGE
Sprague, Pierce Giles	1798-1799	b. June 17, 1798		Block Island, R. I.	Newport, R.I.	
Sprague, Record	Oct. 2, 1801	17	dark	Scituate, R. I.	2	36
Sprague, Richard	Aug. 31, 1804	20	light	scituate, R. I.	3	36
Sprague, Samuel	Sept. 22, 1797	22	light	Providence, R.I.	1	30
Sprague, Sylvester	July 15, 1805	21	light	Providence, R. I.	3	51A
Sprague, William Jr.	July 8, 1839	22	light	Derby, VT	5	71
Springer, Isaac	Jan. 9, 1797	19	light	Tiverton, R.I.	1	30
Springer, Isaac	May 7, 1832	15	light	Providence, R.I.	5	69
Springer, John	1798-1799	b. Dec. 11, 1759		Little Compton, R.I.	Newport, RI	
Springer, Richmond	Oct. 17, 1809	18	light	Providence, R.I.	4	63
Springer, Richmond	March 11, 1812	21	light	Cranston, R.I.	4	64
Springer, Stephen T.	July 7, 1831	17	light	Providence, R. I.	5	69
Spywood, Anson	Oct. 24, 1818	17	black	Warwick, R.I.	4	65
Spywood, Ezekiel	Dec. 7, 1805	14	black	Sandwich, Mass.	3	70
Spywood, Ezekiel	March 11, 1809	18	yellow	Sandwich, Mass.	4	62
Spywood, Sampson	Dec. 27, 1809	21	yellow	Warwick, R.I.	4	63
Spywood, Samuel	Oct. 6, 1801	27	black	Providence, R.I.	2	36
Spywood, Wm.	March 14, 1842	24	copper-colored	Cranston, R.I.	5	71
Spywood, Stephen	Jan. 3, 1849	29	dark	Providence, R. I.	5	73
Spywood, Wanton	Aug. 27, 1799	30	black	Warwick, R. I.	2	18
Spywort, Samuel	June 16, 1815	17	yellow	Providence, R. I.	4	64
Squeen, Benjamin	Dec. 20, 1796	23	dark	Middleboro, Mass.	1	23
Stacey, Ambrose	May 2, 1806	47	brown	Marblehead, Mass.	3	71
Stack, John	Nov. 14, 1828	19	sallow	Dorchester, MD.	4	67
Stacy, Sylvester	Dec. 5, 1809	19	dark	Sterling, Conn.	4	63
Stafford, Edward	1798-1799	b. July 19, 1754		Tiverton, R. I.	Newport,R.I.	
Stafford, John	1798-1799	b. June 8, 1778		Portsmouth, R.I.	Newport,R.I.	

NAME	DATE OF CERTIFICATION	AGE	COMPLEXION	PLACE OF BIRTH	BOOK	PAGE
Stafford, Nicholas	April 2, 1828	24	dark	Cranston, R.I.	4	66
Stafford, Samuel	May 13, 1811	18	light	Warwick, R.I.	4	63
Stafford, Stephen	1798-1799 b. on or abt. 7.19.1754			Tiverton, R. I.		Newport,R
Stafford, Stephen	Sept. 18, 1834	24	light	Tiverton, R.I.	5	70
Stafford, Thomas?Darious	Sept. 12, 1801	21	light	Coventry, R. I.	2	36
Stafford, Thomas D.	Nov. 26, 1805	25	light	Coventry, R. I.	3	70
Stall, James A.	Nov. 7, 1844	25	light	Newport, R. I.	5	72
Standfield, William	May 30, 1849	32	light	Burrillville, R.I.	5	73
Standish, Thomas D.	Nov. 29, 1830	21	light	Dighton, Mass.	5	69
Standley, John	May 3, 1797	22	light	Newport, R. I.	1	23
Stanley, Jacob P.	July 10, 1815	17	light	Attleboro, Mass.	4	64
Stanley, John H.	Oct. 23, 1832	21	light	Attleboro, Mass.	5	69
Stanton, Charles	June 29, 1835	22	light	Lubec, Maine	5	70
Stanton, Lewis	Nov. 7, 1826	24	yellow	Providence, R. I.	4	66
Stanton, Oscar C.	Dec. 29, 1857	23	light	Sag Harbor, N. Y.	6	18
Stanton, Thomas	Dec. 13, 1826	17	mulatto	Providence, R. I.	4	66
Stapleford, William H.	Jan. 14, 1848	27	light	Abington, Md.	5	73
Staples, Cornelius S.	Nov. 2, 1841	31	dark	Prospect, Maine	5	71
Staples, Henry H.	Nov. 2, 1841	17	light	Prospect, Maine	5	71
Staples, John D.	March 9, 1846	28	dark	Raymond, Maine	5	72
Staples, Jonah G.	Nov. 2, 1841	24	light	Prospect, Maine	5	71
Staples, Nathan, 2nd	Dec. 16, 1825	21	light	Cumberland, R. I.	4	66
Staples, Richard	Nov. 8, 1844	22	light	Swansea, Maine	5	72
Staples, Samuel	Jan. 2, 1798	27	light	Rutland, Mass.	1	30
Starkweather, Jonathan	Nov. 17, 1803	18	light	Charlton, N. Y.	2	45
Starr, Abel	Aug. 19, 1836	46	black	Fairfield, Conn.	5	70
Stateman, David	Aug. 29, 1848 ·	19	dark	Boston, Mass.	5	73

REGISTER OF SEAMEN'S PROTECTION

NAME	DATE OF CERTIFICATION	AGE	COMPLEXION	PLACE OF BIRTH	BOOK	PAGE
Stead, John	Nov. 17, 1828	17	light	Hartford, Vt.	4	67
Stead, John F.	June 14, 1856	22	fair	Providence, R. I.	5	76
Steadman, Enoch, Jr.	Nov. 28, 1820	24	light	South Kingstown, R. I.	4	65
Stedman, Simeon	May 1, 1840	33	light	Simsbury, Conn.	5	71
Steel, Robert	Aug. 7, 1845	25	light	Eastport, Maine	5	72
Steele, Thomas	Aug. 26, 1831	25	black	Queen Annes Co., Md.	5	69
Steen, Joab	Apr. 17, 1819	19	dark	Boston, Mass.	4	65
Steere, David	Aug. 9, 1808	33	brown	Scituate, R. I.	4	62
Steere, Hosea	Jan. 10, 1807	23	florid	Glocester, R. I.	4	62
Steere, John	June 9, 1809	18	dark	Glocester, R. I.	4	62
Steere, Noah, Jr.	Jan. 10, 1807	18	brown	Glocester, R. I.	4	62
Steere, Thomas	Dec. 28, 1805	16	light	Glocester, R. I.	3	71
Steib, John	Dec. 10, 1803	24	light	New York, N. Y.	2	24
Steib, John Jr.	Nov. 12, 1831	17	light	Providence, R. I.	5	69
Steinhauer, George W.	June 24, 1840	18	light	Providence, R. I.	5	71
Stennerd, Francis	April 16, 1853	18	light	New Haven, Conn.	5	75
Stephens, Hervey	July 26, 1820	21	light	Boston, Mass.	4	65
Stephens, Hiram	Nov. 12, 1853	45	dark	Smithfield, R. I.	5	75
Stephenson, Lucius C.	Feb. 28, 1851	32	light	Belfast, Maine	5	74
Sterling, Hiram	Apr. 20, 1860	24	fair	New York, NY	6	18
Sterling, James	Jan. 16, 1851	20	mulatto	Mobile, Alabama	5	74
Sterny, Joseph	Aug. 15, 1797	20	dark	Providence, R. I.	1	30
Stetson, Albert	Jan. 27, 1860	24	fair	Pawtucket, Mass.	6	18
Studson[Stetson],David	Nov. 16, 1822	37	light	East Greenwich, R. I.	4	66
Studson[Stetson],Daniel S.	Dec. 8, 1838	14	light	Providence, R. I.	5	71
Stutson[Stetson],George	Jan. 26, 1854	37	fair	Bristol, R. I.	5	75
Stutson[Stetson],Moses J.	June 7, 1816	17	light	Warwick, R. I.	4	64
Stetson, Stephen C.	April 23, 1857	24	fair	Pownal, Maine	5	94

NAME	DATE OF CERTIFICATION	AGE	COMPLEXION	PLACE OF BIRTH	BOOK	PAG
Stetson, William	July 28, 1854	25	light	Westport, Conn.	5	76
Studson[Stetson],William H.	June 6, 1838	16	light	Providence, R.I.	5	71
Stevens, Archibald	March 9, 1811	16	dark	Addington, Conn.	4	63
Stevens, David	Oct. 1, 1844	18	light	Bellville, N. J.	5	72
Stevens, James	Feb. 15, 1832	44	mulatto	Norwalk, Conn.	5	69
Stevens, James H.	June 27, 1854	26	fair	Chelmsford, Mass	5	75
Stevens, Henry	Nov. 16, 1847	19	black	Westerly, R. I.	5	73
Stevens, Henry	Apr. 16, 1860	17	light	Middlesex, Mass.	6	18
Stevens, Hiram	Sept. 20, 1855	45	dark	Smithfield, R. I.	5	76
Stevens, Hiram H.	Oct. 29, 1835	23	dark	Templeton, Mass.	5	70
Stephens, John, Jr.	June 28, 1809	19	yellow	Stonington, Conn.	4	63
Stephens, John R.	March 2, 1811	29	light	Norton, Mass.	4	63
Stevens, Nathaniel	Nov. 20, 1811	15	light	Providence, R. I.	4	64
Stevens, Lyman S.	May 7, 1856	28	light	New Canaan, Conn.	5	76
Stevens, Samuel	June 11, 1844	23	yellow	Charlestown, R. I.	5	72
Stevens, Samuel H.	Sept. 21, 1804	18	black	Newport, R. I.	3	36
Stevens, William	May 29, 1848	21	light	Taunton, Mass.	5	73
Stevens, William	March 4, 1852	38	light	New York, N.Y.	5	75
Stevens, William	Nov. 22, 1854	21	light	New York, N.Y.	5	76
Stevenson Peter	Aug. 24, 1848	32	black	Hartford, Conn.	5	73
Stewart, Anthony	June 19, 1809	18	light	Chatham, Conn.	4	62
Stewart, Charles	Sept. 23, 1796	17	dark	Providence, R. I.	1	3
Stewart, Charles,2nd	Oct. 30, 1805	20	light	Providence, R.I.	3	70
Stewart, George	Aug. 3, 1808	23	light	Boston, Mass.	4	62
Stewart, Henry	June 1, 1839	23	florid	Caroline, N.Y.	5	71
Stewart, Henry	July 9, 1839	21	light	Homer, N. Y.	5	71
Stewart, James	Dec. 13, 1850	22	light	Boston, Mass.	5	74
Stewart, Samuel	Nov. 6, 1805 ·	25	black	Philadelphia, Pa.	3	70

REGISTER OF SEAMEN'S PROTECTION

NAME	DATE OF CERTIFICATION	AGE	COMPLEXION	PLACE OF BIRTH	BOOK	PAGE
Stewart, Samuel	Oct. 14, 1811	39	black	Nausemond Co., Va.	4	64
Stewart, Thomas	Aug. 12, 1854	27	fair	Boston, Mass.	5	76
Stewart, William	Aug. 6, 1844	39	light	Boston, Mass.	5	72
Stickney, Charles E.	Jan. 5, 1858	21	light	Newport, Me.	6	18
Stickney, Isaac	Dec. 8, 1827	16	light	Andover, Mass.	4	66
Still, Henry	Feb. 3, 1853	29	light	Brookhaven, N. Y.	5	75
Stillwell, Aron	1798-1799	b. Feb. 14, 1781		Freetown, Mass.	Newport,R.I.	
Stillwell, Caleb W.	Oct. 8, 1856	18	fair	Providence, R. I.	5	76
Stillwell, Nicholas	Oct. 18, 1798	21	light	Milford, Mass.	2	18
Stilwell, Stephen	July 5, 1825	27	light	Albany, N. Y.	4	66
Stilphen, John	May 21, 1833	48	dark	Dresden, Maine	5	69
Stiness, John J.	Oct. 18, 1844	44	dark	Marblehead, Mass.	5	72
Stiles[Stites],Israel	Oct. 5, 1838	25	dark	Cape May, N. J.	5	71
Stivers, Robert	Dec. 5, 1845	21	yellow	Jamaica, N. Y.	5	72
Stober, William	Apr. 6, 1799	41	black	Charleston, S.C.	2	18
Stober, William	June 16, 1804	43	black	Charleston, S. C.	3	36
Stockhouse, Amos	July 3, 1847	33	fair	Eastport, Maine	5	73
Stockman, Charles	Nov. 11, 1803	14	dark	New London, Conn.	2	45
Stockman, Charles S.	May 6, 1806	17	dark	New London, Conn.	3	67
Stockton, William	Sept. 7, 1853	29	dark	Gloucester, Mass.	5	75
Stockwell, Jeriah	Nov. 22, 1800	24	light	Hadley, Mass.	2	26
Stoddard, Albert G.	Oct. 15, 1833	30	dark	Litchfield, Conn.	5	70
Stoddard, Ichabod	May 25, 1799	17	dark	Providence, R.I.	2	18
Stoddard, Luther	Dec. 11, 1838	23	light	Hingham, Mass.	5	71
Stoddard, Miles	1798-1799	b.July 12, 1775		Taunton, Mass.	Newport,R.I.	
Stoddard, William H.	May 19, 1847	29	florid	Providence, R.I.	5	73
Stokely, Arthur	Feb. 7, 1829	23	black	Warwick, R. I.	5	69
Stokely, Lorenzo	Nov. 8, 1836	25	black	Somerset Co., Md.	5	70

NAME	DATE OF CERTIFICATION	AGE	COMPLEXION	PLACE OF BIRTH	BOOK	PAG
Stoker, James	July 20, 1804	17	light	Norfolk, Va.	3	36
Stone, Albert W.	Oct. 10, 1833	18	dark	Cranston, R.I.	5	7C
Stone, Charles	July 24, 1850	21	light	Lowell, Mass.	5	74
Stone, Dutee	Jan. 31, 1804	17	light	Cranston, R. I.	3	35
Stone, Dutee	May 22, 1806	19	light	Cranston, R. I.	3	67
Stone, Elias S.	Sept. 2, 1842	16	dark	Coventry, R. I.	5	72
Stone, Foster	Nov. 8, 1803	23	dark	Warwick, R. I.	2	45
Stone, George	Feb. 23, 1852	26	dark	Providence, R. I.	5	75
Stone, Henry	March 1, 1804	20	dark	Cranston, R. I.	3	35
Stone, Henry	Aug. 21, 1845	17	light	Cranston, R. I.	5	72
Stone, John S.	March 12, 1812	24	fresh	Framingham, Mass.	4	64
Stone, Robert	March 30, 1798	17	light	Cranston, R. I.	1	3C
Stone, Stephen	June 26, 1798	27	dark	Woodstock, Conn.	2	18
Stone, Thomas C.	May 18, 1833	19	dark	Cranston, R. I.	5	69
Stone, William A.	March 13, 1805	20	light	Cranston, R. I.	3	51
Stone, William J.[or Jr.]	Nov. 20, 1822	19	light	Cranston, R. I.	4	66
Stormes, John	Oct. 15, 1841	23	light	New York, N. Y.	5	71
Story, John	June 3, 1797	22	light	County Suffolk, Mass.	1	23
Stow, William D.	April 10, 1854	23	dark	Camden, Maine	5	75
Strahan, William	March 10, 1853	25	light	Eastport, Maine	5	75
Straight, Henry	March 6, 1805	21	light	Warwick, R. I.	3	51
Straite, William M.	Nov. 20, 1839	18	freckled	" "	5	71
Strang, Cyrus D.	March 18, 1864	26	light	New Brunswick	6	18
Strange, Job D.	March 5, 1827	22	light	Berkley, Mass.	4	66
Stratton, Joseph A.	July 11, 1845	21	dark	Simsbury, Conn.	5	72
Streeter, Benoin	May 4, 1810	28	dark	Cumberland, R. I.	4	63
Streeter, Ebenezer	Sept. 4, 1813	15	dark	Chesterfield, N. H.	4	64
Streeter, George P.	March 20, 1850	18	light	Scituate, R. I.	5	74
Streeter, Randall	Dec. 23, 1809	24	light	Chesterfield, N. H.	4	63
Streeter, Rufus	June 5, 1857	28	light	Smithfield, R. I.	5	94
Streets, Thomas	June 4, 1846	24	dark	Fall River, Mass.	5	72
Stretch, Samuel	Sept. 3, 1851	33	light	Salem, N. J.	5	74
Strong, Samuel	May 16, 1797	16	light	Norfolk, Va.	1	23
Strong, Samuel	Dec. 18, 1799	19	light	Norfolk, Va.	2	26
Strong, William	Feb. 20, 1867	20	light	Sedgwick, Me.	6	18
Stuart, Charles	March 30, 1836	19	dark	Burlington, Vt.	5	7C

Page 256

NAME	DATE OF CERTIFICATION	AGE	COMPLEXION	PLACE OF BIRTH	BOOK	PAGE
Stubbs, Ephraim	Oct. 29, 1799	25	dark	Wellfleet, Mass.	2	18
Stubs, Henry	March 10, 1852	17	light	Milford, Del.	5	75
Stubbs, James	May 2, 1825	22	light	Nantucket, Mass.	4	66
Studley, Abraham	Nov. 9, 1798	22	dark	Yarmouth, Mass.	2	18
Studley, Abraham	June 23, 1820	47	dark	Yarmouth, Mass.	4	65
Studley, Edward	May 26, 1831	18	light	Dennis, Mass.	5	69
Studley, Henry	Oct. 7, 1834	21	light	Yarmouth, Mass.	5	70
Studley, John	April 1, 1850	32	light	Providence, R. I.	5	74
Studley, Jonathan	May 15, 1823	20	light	Yarmouth, Mass.	4	66
Studley, Simeon	Jan 4, 1817	27	light	Yarmouth, Mass.	4	65
Sturges, Burr	April 26, 1858	44	light	Westport, Conn.	6	18
Sturtevant, Joseph	1798 to 1799 b.Feb. 26, 1772			Pembroke, Mass.	Newport,R.I.	
Sturtevant, Perry	Nov. 22, 1805	19	light	Wareham, Mass.	3	70
Sturtevant, Thomas D.	May 30, 1849	30	light	Hebron, Maine	5	73
Studson see Stetson						
Stutson see Stetson						
Styran, Francis	Oct. 10, 1825	21	light	Newbern, N.C.	4	66
Suesman, Emanuel	Aug. 31, 1849	31	light	Providence, R. I.	5	74
Sullivan, Cornelius	Sept. 12, 1821	28	light	Kerry, Ireland	4	65
Naturalized court C. C. Prov. Dec. 20, 1820						
[Sullivan]Sullivan, Daniel	Oct. 7, 1808	32	brown	Torneo, Sweeden	4	62
Naturalized at a Supreme Judicial Court in Providence, Sept, 1808.						
Sullivan, Daniel	Dec. 28, 1849	22	light	Boston, Mass.	5	74
Sullivan, Daniel	March 26, 1851	20	light	Fall River, Mass.	5	74
Sullivan, Dennis	Sept. 4, 1855	20	light	Lockport, N. Y.	5	76
Sullivan, James	Sept. 9, 1865	24	light	Fall River, Mass.	6	18
Sullivan, James M.	Feb. 25, 1853	29	mulatto	Hartford, Conn.	5	75
Sullivan, John	Dec. 19, 1797	32	dark	Providence, R. I.	1	30
Sullivan, John	Feb. 5, 1855	24	fair	Rome, Penn.	5	76
Sullivan, John	Sept. 11, 1855	17	light	Pawtucket, R. I.	5	76
Sullivan, Martin O.	March 24, 1856	26	dark	Boston, Mass.	5	76
Sullivan, Michael	Sept. 4, 1855	21	fair	Fall River, Mass.	5	76
Sullivan, Michael	Sept. 6, 1864	19	light	Fall River, Mass.	6	18
Sullivan, Michael E.	April 26, 1855	20	fair	Prov., R. I.	5	76
Sullivan, Patrick	Nov. 15, 1862	22	light	Providence, R. I.	6	18
Sutherland, Angus	Sept. 11, 1866	22	dark	Providence, R. I.	6	18
Sunderland, John	Feb. 5, 1855	25	fair	Exeter, R. I.	5	76

NAME	DATE OF CERTIFICATION	AGE	COMPLEXION	PLACE OF BIRTH	BOOK	PAGE
[Sunsiman] John Suncemun	August 16, 1800	23	black	Woodstock, Conn.	2	26
Surgens, Charles	October 20, 1853	21	light	Warren, R. I.	5	75
Sutton, Oliver	April 14, 1819	22	light	Providence, R.I.	4	65
Sutton, Robert, Jr.	Oct. 24, 1809	38	light	Rehoboth, Mass.	4	63
Sutton, William	March 4, 1797	18	light	Providence, R.I.	1	23
Sutton, William	Oct. 13, 1801	21	light	Rehoboth, Mass.	2	36
Swain, Benjamin	Jan. 13, 1855	21	fair	Bucksport, Maine	5	76
Swain, John G.	Nov. 17, 1851	25	dark	Nantucket, Mass.	5	75
Swain, Peter H.	March 27, 1815	23	light	Westfield, N. Y.	4	64
Swain, Thomas	Dec. 18, 1822	25	dark	Nantucket, Mass.	4	66
Swan, George T.	Jan. 21, 1851	30	light	Alexandria, VA	5	74
Swan, William	Dec. 8, 1804	27	light	Colchester, Conn.	3	51
Swarts, John	Nov. 11, 1822	21	light	Newport, R. I.	4	66
Swazey, Ayres	March 15, 1815	22	light	Somerset, Mass.	4	64
Sweeney, Benjamin	Oct. 12, 1819	31	dark	Newport, R.I.	4	65
Sweeney, Charles	Jan. 9, 1855	19	fair	Philadelphia, Penn.	5	76
Sweeney, Theodore	Jan. 21, 1859	19	florid	Providence, R.I.	6	18
Sweet, Alanson	Oct. 7, 1811	26	dark	Attleboro, Mass.	4	64
Sweet, Angell	Sept. 1, 1809	19	dark	Oxford, Mass.	4	63
Sweet, Cuffe	Oct. 31, 1796	28	black	North Kingstown, R.I.	1	23
Sweet, Daniel, Jr.	Oct. 6, 1828	22	dark	Exeter, R. I.	4	67
Sweet, Daniel H.	April 21, 1809	16	brown	Providence, R.I.	4	62
Sweet, Eldredge	Dec. 24, 1822	19	light	East Greenwich, R. I.	4	66
Sweet, Elisha W.	Nov. 10, 1830	25	light	East Greenwich, R. I.	5	69
Sweet, Elkanah C.	Nov. 12, 1841	15	light	Providence, R. I.	5	71
Sweet, Gideon R.	April 21, 1829	22	ruddy	Seekonk, Mass.	5	69
Sweet, Isaac M.	May 20, 1844	18	light	Smithfield, R. I.	5	72
Sweet, James	August 30, 1797	20	light	East Greenwich, R. I.	1	30
Sweet, James F.	Sept. 4, 1849	20	light	Glocester, R. I.	5	74
Sweet, John Clark	Oct. 19, 1803	20	light	East Greenwich, R.I.	2	36
Sweet, Luther	Dec. 20, 1800	18	dark	East Greenwich, R. I.	2	26
Sweet, Manly	Sept. 15, 1803	18	dark	Providence, R. I.	2	36
Sweet, Manley	March 9, 1804	18	light	Providence, R. I.	3	35
Sweet, Manly	July 13, 1808	21	light	Providence, R. I.	4	62
Sweet, Michael	Aug. 26, 1846	31	fair	Taunton, Mass.	5	73
Sweet, Nathaniel	Jan. 5, 1830	19	light	Providence, R. I.	5	69
Sweet, Peleg	Aug. 20, 1798	27	light	East Greenwich, R. I.	2	18

REGISTER OF SEAMEN'S PROTECTION

NAME	DATE OF CERTIFICATION	AGE	COMPLEXION	PLACE OF BIRTH	BOOK	PAGE
Sweet, Stephen	July 3, 1815	33	dark	Warwick, R. I.	4	64
Sweet, Willard J.	Feb. 27, 1854	17	dark	Providence, R.I.	5	76
Sweet, William	1798-1799 b. Dec. 23, 1778			N. Kingston, R. I.	Newport,R.I.	
Sweet, William	Aug. 4, 1796	18	light	East Greenwich, R.I.	1	1
Sweet, William C.	Aug. 27, 1838	27	dark	Coventry, R. I.	5	71
Sweeten, Moses	Sept. 3, 1851	22	dark	Scituate, R. I.	5	74
Sweeting, Ambrose	June 16, 1856	24	fair	Pomfret, Conn.	5	76
Sweetland, Daniel	Sept. 29, 1803	19	dark	Providence, R. I.	2	36
Sweetland, Daniel	Jan. 15, 1830	48	dark	Providence, R. I.	5	69
Sweetland, Joseph	Dec. 5, 1823	21	ruddy	Thomaston, Maine	4	66
Sweetland, Virgil S.	July 15, 1831	25	dark	Attleboro, Mass.	5	69
[Sweetland] William Sweatland	Mar. 29, 1800	19	light	North Providence, R. I.	2	26
Sweetland, Gabriel	Mar. 31, 1797	23	dark	Attleboro, Mass.	1	23
Sweetland, Gabriel	Nov. 25, 1803	29	dark	Attleboro, Mass.	2	45
Sweetland, Nathan (Swetland)	May 30, 1797	18	dark	Attleboro, Mass.	1	23
Swett, Frank G.	Feb. 14, 1866	32	light	Belfast, Maine	6	18
Swett, Isaac J. [or Jr.]	Oct. 9, 1824	11	light	Arland, Maine	4	66
Swift, Francis	Apr. 2, 1822	27	brown	Dalton, Mass.	4	65
Swift, William	Nov. 11, 1818	17	light	Wareham, Mass.	4	65
Swinburne, Joseph	Feb. 23, 1824	35	light	Newport, R. I.	4	66
Swinburne, William J.	Nov. 14, 1835	14	light	Newport, R. I.	5	70
Swift, Robert	March 15, 1851	24	dark	Detroit, MI	5	74
Sylvester, Amos	Oct. 22, 1833	29	dark	Freeport, Maine	5	70
Sylvester, Benjamin	Nov. 4, 1813	15	dark	Hanover, Mass.	4	64
Sylvester, Lewis W.	Aug. 5, 1857	18	Red,Sandy	Freeport, Maine	6	18
Sylvester, Manuel	Oct. 10, 1849	26	dark	New Bedford, Mass.	5	74
Sylvia, Antone	Oct. 7, 1854	27	dark	New York, N. Y.	5	76
Sylvia, John	Dec. 24, 1849	25	dark	New York, N.Y.	5	74
Sylvia, Minwell	Sept. 20, 1850	20	light	New London, Conn.	5	74
Synja, Jacob	Oct. 6, 1818	30	light	Collum, Netherlands	4	65
Naturalized Sept. 1818. Providence Sup. Jud. Court.						
Taalman, John	Dec. 21, 1807	19	brown	Hackinsack, N.Y.[sic]	4	68
Taber, Abraham	Oct. 20, 1825	19	light	Tiverton, R. I.	4	69
Taber, Charles	Jan. 25, 1830	32	light	New Bedford, Mass.	5	77
Taber, Cornelius G.	Sept. 23, 1864	34	light	New Bedford, Mass.	6	20
Taber, Henry	Dec. 2, 1833	17	light	Chesterfield, Mass.	5	77

NAME	DATE OF CERTIFICATION	AGE	COMPLEXION	PLACE OF BIRTH	BOOK	PAGE
Taber, Henry W.	July 5, 1855	25	light	Killingly, Conn.	5	80
Taber, Jacob	March 29, 1800	21	light	Tiverton, R. I.	2	19
Taber, John	July 21, 1820	23	light	Providence, R.I.	4	69
Taber, Joseph	July 27, 1809	17	dark	Providence, R. I.	4	68
Tabor, Lawton	Aug. 30, 1796	20	light	Tiverton, R. I.	1	2
Tabor, Peter Son of Eseck and Roby	1798 to 1799	b. Dec. 10, 1780		Westport, Mass.	Newport, R
Taber, Ruben Abner Tabor swears for him	1798 to 1799	b. July 9, 1770		Westport, Mass.	Newport,
Taber, Thomas	Nov. 22, 1813	45	light	Little Compton, R.I.	4	69
Taber, Thomas, Jr.	April 13, 1831	20	light	Providence, R. I.	5	77
Taber, William H.	Jan. 4, 1865	34	light	Hopkinton, R. I.	6	20
Taft, David H.	May 30, 1849	25	light	Mendon, Mass.	5	79
Taft, Royal	Oct. 13, 1807	21	brown	Mendon, Mass.	4	68
Taft, William	July 22, 1825	22	light	Shrewsbury, Mass.	4	69
Talbot, Boston	Sept. 27, 1805	23	black	Warwick, R. I.	3	46
Talbot, Charles	May 27, 1853	32	black	Providence, R. I.	5	79
Talbot, Charles	May 8, 1856	33	yellowish black	Cranston, R.I.	5	80
Talbot, Daniel	May 31, 1804	18	light	Peterborough, N.H.	3	37
Talbot, Edward A.	Nov. 11, 1822	17	dark	Providence, R. I.	4	69
Talbot, George	March 12, 1853	29	dark	Killingly, Conn.	5	79
Talbot, George W.	Oct. 14, 1833	20	light	Dighton, Mass.	5	77
Talbot, Jared	Aug. 24, 1846	18	fair	Uxbridge, Mass.	5	78
Talbot, James? Jared?	June 26, 1852	23	dark	Smithfield, R. I.	5	79
Talbot, Jared W.	Nov. 12, 1855	28	dark	Smithfield, R. I.	5	80
Talbut, Silas	Nov. 2, 1827	25	light	Killingly, Conn.	4	70
Talbot, Thomas	May 25, 1805	22	black	Warwick, R. I.	3	38
Talbot, William G.	June 12, 1818	22	dark	Providence, R. I.	4	69
Talbury, Benja[min]	July 20, 1810	15	black	Coventry, R. I.	4	68
Tall, William	Oct. 1, 1827	29	light	Barnstable, Mass	4	70
Tallison, George	Sept. 5, 1853	18	light	Belfast, Maine	5	80
Tal[l]man, Benjamin		36	light	Providence, R. I.	3	38
Tallman, Edward	July 9, 1822	20	light	Providence, R. I.	4	69
Tallman, Esek	Aug. 31, 1849	39	light	Providence, R. I.	5	79
Tallman, James	Dec. 21, 1810	18	light	Newport, R. I.	4	68
Tal[l]man, John	Oct. 6, 1804	24	dark	Bridgewater, Mass.	3	38

NAME	DATE OF CERTIFICATION	AGE	COMPLEXION	PLACE OF BIRTH	BOOK	PAGE
Tal[l]man, Moses	Dec. 7, 1804	24	dark	Norwich, Conn.	3	38
Tallman, William	March 16, 1811	16	light	Providence, R. I.	4	68
Tallman, William F.	Oct. 15, 1860	17	light	Providence, R. I.	6	20
Talmadge, Abijah	Oct. 15, 1841	20	light	Goshen, N.Y.	5	78
Tanner, Benjamin	Aug. 9, 1796	18	light	North Kingstown, R.I	1	1
Tanner, Isaac W.	Aug. 4, 1848	34	dark	Stonington, Conn.	5	79
Tanner, James A.	June 3, 1815	18	ruddy	North Kingstown, R.I.	4	69
Tanner, John	1798 to 1799		b. July 4, 1770	Newport, R. I.		Newport,R.I.
Tanner, John	Jan. 2, 1836	27	mulatto	Springfield, Mass.	5	77
Tanner, John B.	March 5, 1844	17	light	Providence, R. I.	5	78
Tanner, Palmér, Jr.	March 17, 1815	19	light	North Kingstown, R.I.	4	69
Tardiff, Nicholas	Oct. 9, 1857	31	dark	Staten Island, N. Y.	6	20
Tarp, George	Oct. 26, 1811	17	light	Providence, R. I.	4	68
Tarr, Aaron D.	Feb. 20, 1833	32	dark	Newburyport, Mass.	5	77
Tasker, Thomas	Oct. 27, 1849	45	light	Lancashire, Gr. Britain	5	79
Tasker, William H.	Feb. 27, 1866	26	light	Providence, R. I.	6	20
Tate, William	Nov. 8, 1813	12	light	New London, Conn.	4	69
Tavener, Abraham	April 24, 1827	21	light	Newton, Mass.	4	70
Tavenner, Jacob	June 13, 1836	17	freckled	Newton, Mass.	5	77
Tayer, Paul	1798 to 1799		b. April 7, 1780	Newport, R. I.		Newport,R.I.
Benjamin Tayer swears for him						
Tayer, Thomas	May 9, 1815	20	light	Newport, R. I.	4	69
Taylor, Abraham	Nov. 8, 1836	33	black	Buckingham, Penn.	5	77
Taylor, Ambrose, Jr.	Aug. 11, 1810	18	light	Warwick, R. I.	4	68
Taylor, Ambrose N.	Sept. 6, 1849	27	dark	Warwick, R. I.	5	79
Taylor, Barton	Jan. 11, 1821	19	dark	Newport, R. I.		
Sworn statement of Charles S. Rowlings of Bristol in the Custom House Papers (b. July 4, 1801)						
Taylor, Benjamin	Sept. 4, 1797	21	light	Providence, R. I.	1	24
Taylor, Benjamin F.	May 30, 1844	15	light	Freetown, Mass.	5	78
Taylor, Charles	Feb. 28, 1849	23	light	Philadelphia, Penn.	5	79
Taylor, Charles	Dec. 22, 1855	21	light	Lowell, Mass.	5	80
Taylor, Charles A.	March 23, 1827	25	light	Providence, R. I.	4	70
Taylor, Charles N.	Aug. 5, 1849	18	dark	Cumberland, R. I.	5	79
Taylor, Crispin	Aug. 31, 1849	27	light	Yorkshire, Gr.Britain	5	79
Taylor, Daniel	June 21, 1845	18	light	Scituate, R. I.	5	78
Taylor, Daniel P.	Dec. 13, 1809	18	yellow	South Kingstown, R. I.	4	68

NAME	DATE OF CERTIFICATION	AGE	COMPLEXION	PLACE OF BIRTH	BOOK	PAGE
Taylor, Freeman	Dec. 8, 1852	23	light	Calais, Vermont	5	79
Taylor, George	Nov. 20, 1805	26	black	Newport, R. I.	3	46
Taylor, George	Oct. 20, 1809	30	black	Newport, R. I.	4	68
Taylor, George	Jan. 21, 1829	42	light	Yarmouth, Mass.	5	77
Taylor, George	May 3, 1836	26	black	Baltimore, Md.	5	77
Taylor, George W.	Sept. 29, 1849	22	light	Warwick, R. I.	5	79
Taylor, Havilla	Dec. 19, 1865	22	dark	Warwick, R. I.	6	20
Taylor, Henry	May 19, 1841	20	dark	Providence, R. I.	5	78
Taylor, Humphrey Peter Taylor swears for him.	1798 to 1799 b. Oct. 6, 1772			Portsmouth, R. I.	Newport, R.	
Taylor, James	Jan. 9, 1798	25	black	Providence, R. I.	1	24
Taylor, James	Nov. 18, 1803	21	black	Swansea, Mass.	2	35
Taylor, James	June 22, 1805	26	dark	Dedham, Mass.	3	45
Taylor, James	July 28, 1807	24	black	Wickford, R. I.	4	68
Taylor, Jeremiah	Sept. 5, 1818	22	light	Yarmouth, Mass.	4	69
Taylor, John	Nov. 20, 1805	22	black	Newport, R. I.	3	46
Taylor, John	April 5, 1810	16	yellow	South Kingstown, R. I.	4	68
Taylor (Tayler) John S.	Oct. 28, 1803	17	dark	Providence, R. I.	2	35
Taylor, Joseph	Aug. 25, 1796	21	light	Newport, R. I.	1	1
Taylor, Peter Mary, wife of James Taylor, swears for him.	1798 to 1799 b. Jan. 26, 1770			Newport, R. I.	Newport, R.	
Taylor, Peter	Nov. 17, 1806	27	light	Smithfield, R. I.	4	68
Taylor, Peter	June 6, 1810	15	light	Providence, R. I.	4	68
Taylor, Rowland	March 22, 1799	21	dark	Providence, R. I.	2	19
Taylor, Samuel	1798 to 1799 b. Nov. 9, 1782			Newport, R. I.	Newport, R.	
Taylor, Stephen	April 15, 1829	20	dark	Havre de Grace, Md.	5	77
Taylor, William	April 7, 1797	20	light	Providence, R.I.	1	24
Taylor, William James Taylor swears for him.	1798 to 1799 ·b. April 11, 1780			Newport, R. I.	Newport, R.	

REGISTER OF SEAMEN'S PROTECTION

NAME	DATE OF CERTIFICATION	AGE	COMPLEXION	PLACE OF BIRTH	BOOK	PAGE
Taylor, William	April 1, 1800	26	light	Warwick, R. I.	2	19
Taylor, William	Mar. 9, 1804	30	light	Warwick, R. I.	3	37
Taylor, William	June 7, 1816	16	light	Providence, R. I.	4	69
Taylor, William	April 26, 1844	18	light	Scituate, R. I.	5	78
Taylor, William	March 5, 1849	39	dark	Warwick, R. I.	5	79
Taylor, William H.	Jan. 15, 1846	16	fair	Providence, R. I.	5	78
Teel, George W.	June 8, 1819	18	light	Providence, R. I.	4	69
Teel, Nathan .R.	March 3, 1810	21	dark	Providence, R. I.	4	68
Teel, .Thomas A.	Sept. 1, 1821	21	light	Providence, R. I.	4	69
Teal, William	Sept. 24, 1798	19	light	Providence, R. I.	2	19
Tears, Benjamin	Aug. 18, 1797	36	light	Newport, R. I.	1	24
Teft, Daniel	Aug. 31, 1849	27	dark	Providence, R. I.	5	79
Tefft, David	July 11, 1809	21	brown	Providence, R. I.	4	68
Tefft, Obediah	Oct. 1, 1804	34	dark	Providence, R. I.	3	38
Tefft, Peter	Nov. 14, 1803	22	dark	Scituate, R. I.	2	35
Tift, Ransom	March 6, 1849	36	fair	Smithfield, R. I.	5	79
Tefft, Smauel H.	Oct. 29, 1849	28	light	Richmond, R. I.	5	79
Tefft, Thomas T.	March 13, 1809	24	light	Providence, R. I.	4	68
Teft, Whitman	Jan. 18, 1849	24	light	Richmond, R. I.	5	79
Tefft, William	April 7, 1817	17	light	Sharon, N. Y.	4	69
Temina, Peter	Nov. 23, 1797	36	black	Hartford, Conn.	1	24
Tennant, John R.	Aug. 21, 1858	25	dark	East Greenwich, R. I.	6	20
Tennant, Ray	Oct. 28, 1833	17	light	North Kingston, R. I.	5	77
Terrell, Edward M.	Jan. 20, 1860	23	fair	Northport, Me.	6	20
Terrell, Eugene	June 14, 1842	32	light	Philadelphia, Penn.	5	78
Terrill, John	May 17, 1804	22	dark	Weymouth, Mass.	3	37
Terry, Ebenezer, Jr.	May 20, 1809 ·	22	light	Troy, Mass.	4	68

REGISTER OF SEAMEN'S PROTECTION

NAME	DATE OF CERTIFICATION	AGE	COMPLEXION	PLACE OF BIRTH	BOOK	PAGE
Terry, Seth W.	Sept. 27, 1804	33	dark	Freetown, Mass.	3	38
Tew, David	Sept. 13, 1804	20	light	Berkley, Mass.	3	37
Tew, Elisha	June 29, 1836	21	light	Charlestown, R. I.	5	77
Tew, Elisha	Oct. 10, 1849	34	light	Charlestown, R. I.	5	79
Tew, George	1798 to 1799 b. Nov. 6, 1781			Newport, R. I.		Newport, R.
Henry Tew of Portsmouth swears for him.						
Tew, George	Nov. 14, 1812	24	florid	Stonington, Conn.	4	69
Tew, Jack	August 11, 1836	24	light	Charlestown, R. I.	5	77
Tew, James	1798 to 1799 b. June 28, 1786			Newport, R. I.		Newport, R.
Wm. Tew of Newport swears for him.						
Tew, James	Dec. 12, 1809	17	black	South Kingstown, R.I.	4	68
Tew, John	Dec. 12, 1809	19	black	South Kingstown, R.I.	4	68
Tew, Phillip	July 11, 1804	19	light	Freetown, Mass.	3	37
Tew, William	1798 to 1799 b. Dec. 19, 1782			Newport, R. I.		Newport, R.
Wm. Tew of Newport swears for him.						
Tew, William, 3d.	Oct. 27, 1803	21	light	Newport, R. I.	2	35
Thacher, Edwin	June 16, 1856	20	fair	Yarmouth, Mass.	5	80
Thatcher, Edwin	Dec. 21, 1842	29	light	Plymouth, Mass.	5	78
Thaxter, John	July 1, 1844	16	light	Edgartown, Mass.	5	78
Thaxter, John	June 24, 1841	13	light	Edgarton, Mass.	5	78
Thayer, Benjamin D.	Oct. 29, 1849	18	dark	Boston, Mass.	5	79

Thayer, Cyrena of Smithfield. m. Willis Cook of Cumberland July 3, 1828 at Woonsocket Falls
Rev. Benedict Record

Thayer, George H.	Dec. 15, 1845	37	fair	Boston, Mass.	5	78
Thayer, Henry W.	Oct. 17, 1796	14	light	Providence, R. I.	1	24
On p. 4 his age is given as 13.						4
Thayer, James Horace	March 21, 1804	18	light	Killingly, Conn.	3	37

Thayer, Lillis. m. John Lewis June 29, 1823, Valley Falls.
Rev. Benedict Record

Thayer, Miss. m._____ Taft 1832. Both of Bellingham, Mass.
Rev. Benedict Record.

REGISTER OF SEAMEN'S PROTECTION

NAME	DATE OF CERTIFICATION	AGE	COMPLEXION	PLACE OF BIRTH	BOOK	PAGE
Thayer, Squire W.	June 9, 1819	21	light	Easton, Mass.	4	69
Thayer, Stephen	July 30, 1803	18	dark	Providence, R. I.	2	35
Thayer, Thomas	June 24, 1800	20	light	Providence, R. I.	2	19
Thayer, Thomas, Jr.	May 24, 1805	24	light	Providence, R. I.	3	38
Thayer, William	May 24, 1798	23	dark	Providence, R. I.	2	19
Thayer, William C.	March 8, 1799	24	dark	Providence, R. I.	2	19
Thayer, William C.	Nov. 29, 1817	16	light	Providence, R. I.	4	69
Thayer, William Henry	Jan. 5, 1858	23	fair	Bucksport, Me.	6	20
Theall, Philemon	May 18, 1832	25	light	Newburgh, N.Y.	5	77
Thorn, James	Jan. 9, 1798	17	black	Bristol, Mass.	1	24
Thomas, Ausell	Dec. 5, 1801	30	dark	Barnstable, Mass.	2	35
Thomas, Asa	1798-1799 b. Dec. 2, 1781			Portsmouth, R. I.	Newport,	R.I.
Thomas, Benjamin	Oct. 21, 1803	17	light	Providence, R. I.	2	35
Thomas, Benjamin	Dec. 9, 1831	16	light	Providence, R. I.	5	77
Thomas, Charles S.	Oct. 4, 1833	32	light	New York, N. Y.	5	77
Thomas, Clifford	Sept. 24, 1806	20	light	Attleboro, Mass.	3	40
Thomas, George	May 5, 1806	25	black	Baltimore, Md.	3	46
Thomas, George	May 16, 1806	30	black	New London, Conn.	3	46
Thomas, George	Feb. 18, 1813	25	black	Baltimore, Md.	4	69
Thomas, Henry	Feb. 24, 1832	34	black	Washington, DC	5	77
Thomas, James	Feb. 28, 1812	28	black	Warwick, R. I.	4	68
Thomas, John	1798 to 1799 b. Nov. 5, 1779			Newport, R. I.	Newport,	R.I.
Thomas, John	Aug. 24, 1799	18	light	Providence, R. I.	2	19
Thomas, John	Sept. 19, 1803	35	black	Philadelphia, Pa.	2	35
Thomas, John	June 15, 1832	24	black	Boston, Mass.	5	77
Thomas, John	Dec. 27, 1832	21	mulatto	St. Mary's, Md	5	77
Thomas, John	Feb. 17, 1850	25	dark	Boston, Mass.	5	79

REGISTER OF SEAMEN'S PROTECTION

NAME	DATE OF CERTIFICATION	AGE	COMPLEXION	PLACE OF BIRTH	BOOK	PAG
Thomas, John	June 10, 1857	36	light	Staten Island, N. Y.	5	80
Thomas, John A.	April 11, 1801	19	light	Marshfield, Mass.	2	19
Thomas, Joseph	Nov. 1, 1803	27	light	Providence, R. I.	2	35
Thomas, Nathaniel	July 25, 1805	42	dark	Boston, Mass.	3	45
Thomas, Robert	June 5, 1843	45	black	Baltimore, Md	5	78
Thomas, Samuel	Aug. 6, 1830	28	black	Boston, Mass.	5	77
Thomas, Stephen	Oct. 15, 1860	17	dark brown	Baltimore, Md.	6	20
Thomas, Thaddeus	1798 to 1799 b. Mar 25, 1775 or '76			Woodbridge, Conn.		Newport,
Thomas, William	May 31, 1805	23	black	Elizabethtown, N. J.	3	45
Thomas, William	Jan. 23, 1807	18	light	Providence, R. I.	4	68
Thomas, William	Sept. 21, 1836	25	dark	New London, Conn.	5	77
Thomas, William	Dec. 7, 1838	29	light	Rome, N. Y.	5	77
Thomas, William	May 22, 1839	19	light	New York, N. Y.	5	77
Thomas, William	Sept. 20, 1856	22	dark	Lyonville, Penn.	5	80
Thomas, William H.	April 4, 1845	22	black	Baltimore, Md.	5	78
Thomas, William S.	Dec. 29, 1825	19	light	Boston, Mass.	4	69
[Thomas]Thornley, John	Dec. 17, 1844	31	black	Salem, Mass.	5	78
Thompson, Abel	May 12, 1806	24	light	Woodstock, Conn.	3	46
Thompson, Alexander	Sept. 29, 1831	17	light	Providence, R. I.	5	77
Thompson, Andrew	Jan. 6, 1807	13	light	Providence, R. I.	4	68
Thompson, Andrew	June 10, 1815	21	light	Providence, R. I.	4	69
Thompson, Benjamin	Dec. 27, 1826	20	light	Providence, R. I.	4	69
Thompson, Benjamin	July 3, 1798	25	light	Newport, R. I.	2	19
Thompson, Charles	July 10, 1841	23	light	Dartmouth, Mass.	5	78
Thomson(?) Charles E.	May 13, 1829	22	light	Mansfield, Conn.	5	77
Thompson, Christopher	Dec. 1, 1846	28	fair	Hudson, N. Y.	5	78
Thompson, Daniel S.	July 28, 1840	18	light	New York, N. Y.	5	78

NAME	DATE OF CERTIFICATION	AGE	COMPLEXION	PLACE OF BIRTH	BOOK	PAGE
Thompson, Ebenezer	October 18, 1811	42	brown	Uxbridge, Mass.	4	68
Thompson, Ebenezer	May 20, 1839	31	black	South Kingston, R. I.	5	77
Thompson, Henry	June 4, 1839	28	black	New York, N. Y.	5	78
Thompson, Jack	August 15, 1806	18	black	Boston, Mass.	3	40
Thompson, James	April 1, 1805	23	light	New York, N. Y.	3	38
Thompson, James	Nov. 11, 1841	23	light	Gainsville, N. Y.	5	78
Thompson, James	Jan. 10, 1850	25	light	New York, N. Y.	5	79
Thompson, John	Dec. 16, 1803	44	light	Ipswitch, Mass.	2	35
Thompson, John	Jan. 19, 1805	22	black	Middletown, N. J.	3	38
Thompson, John	Feb. 16, 1805	22	black	Middletown, N. J.	3	38
Thompson, John	Aug. 6, 1808	22	black	Newport, R. I.	4	68
Thompson, John	Feb. 20, 1812	21	yellow	Albany, N. Y.	4	68
Thompson, John	Dec. 19, 1817	25	light	Philadelphia, Pa.	4	69
Tomson, John	June 22, 1836	23	freckled	New Orleans, La.	5	77
Tompson, John	Sept. 29, 1837	21	dark	Bston, Mass.	5	77
Thompson, John	Oct. 7, 1842	28	dark	Boston, Mass.	5	78
Thompson, John	Jan. 7, 1847	25	black	Baltimore, Md.	5	79
Thompson, John	Jan. 13, 1852	24	light	Richmond, Maine	5	79
Thompson, John B.	June 15, 1821	16	light	Warren, R. I. b. Nov. 1, 1803		

son of William and Sarah Thompson; birth certificate in Custom House Papers.

Thompson, John B.	Aug. 18, 1856	18	light	Swansea, Mass.	5	80
Thompson, John G.	Sept. 2, 1842	21	light	Fairfield, Conn.	5	78
Thomson, Joseph, Jr.	March 31, 1821	19	light	Tiverton, R. I. b. Nov. 9, 1802		

Sworn statement of Joseph Rounds of Tiverton in the Custom House Papers.

Thompson, Lemuel	May 29, 1817	25	fresh	Walpole, Mass.	4	69
Thompson, Richard	April 14, 1841	25	light	Bristol, R. I.	5	78
Thompson, Robert	June 6, 1818	25	light	Portsmouth, N. H.	4	69
Thompson, Robert	Nov. 25, 1824 .	22	light	Sterling, Conn.	4	69

NAME	DATE OF CERTIFICATION	AGE	COMPLEXION	PLACE OF BIRTH	BOOK	PP
Thompson, Rufus	Jan. 3, 1856	15	light	Union, Maine	5	8
Thompson, Samuel	Feb. 19, 1796	20	dark	Portsmouth, N. H.	1	2
Thompson, Samuel	Nov. 26, 1825	45	dark	Marblehead, Mass.	4	6
Thompson, Samuel S.	Oct. 18, 1858	45	dark	Gay Head, Mass.	6	2
Thompson, Thomas	Sept. 25, 1804	17	light	Warwick, R. I.	3	3
Thompson, Thomas	Dec. 14, 1805	18	light	Warwick, R. I.	3	4
Thompson, Thomas	April 5, 1841	32	black	Patterson, N. J.	5	7
Thompson, Thomas	March 15, 1849	22	fair	Providence, R. I.	5	7
Thompson, Thomas	Oct. 10, 1860	40	dark	Providence, R. I.	6	2
Thompson, William	July 8, 1805	24	dark	Milford, Conn.	3	4
Thompson, William	Nov. 1, 1803	20	dark	Marblehead, Mass.	2	3
Thomson, William	Oct. 2, 1821	13	light	Bristol, R. I. b. July 31, 1808		

Sworn statement of his father, Samuel Thomson of Bristol in the Custom House Papers

NAME	DATE OF CERTIFICATION	AGE	COMPLEXION	PLACE OF BIRTH	BOOK	PP
Thompson, William	June 5, 1809	19	light	Bristol, R. I.	4	6
Thompson, William	July 5, 1809	17	light	New Bedford, Mass.	4	6
Thompson, William	May 5, 1842	21	light	Philadelphia, Penn.	5	7
Thompson, William	May 30, 1844	33	dark	Boston, Mass.	5	7
Thompson, William	Feb. 4, 1861	30	dark	New Orleans, La.	6	2
Thompson, William H.	Aug. 21, 1845	28	black	New York, N. Y.	5	7
Thompson, William W.	July 30, 1839	17	light	Newark, N. J.	5	7
Thorington, John	May 20, 1854	50	mulatto	Portland, Maine	5	8
Thormons, George	July 22, 1805	20	dark	New York, N. Y.	3	4
Thorn, Charles	Aug. 14, 1854	28	dark	Grafton, N. H.	5	8
Thornford, James E.	April 28, 1847	19	light	Boston, Mass.	5	7
Thornton, Asabel	Dec. 14, 1798	17	dark	Cranston, R. I.	2	1
Thornton, Ashel	April 30, 1799	18	dark	Cranston, R. I.	2	1
Thornton, Christopher	June 17, 1820	16	light	Cranston, R. I.	4	6

NAME	DATE OF CERTIFICATION	AGE	COMPLEXION	PLACE OF BIRTH	BOOK	PAGE
Thornton, Ezekiel	Oct. 2, 1801	18	dark	Cranston, R. I.	2	35
Thornton, Ezekiel	Feb. 3, 1804	20	light	North Prov., R. I.	3	37
Thornton, John	July 3, 1827	16	light	Cranston, R. I.	4	70
Thornton, John P. m. Emeline Frank, Aug. 17, 1828, both of this town (Pawtucket, R. I.) Rev. Benedict Record						
Thornton, Solomon, Jr.	March 2, 1811	45	light	Warwick, R. I.	4	68
Thornton, Thomas	July 13, 1839	25	freckled	Bath, Maine	5	78
Thornton, Thos. J.	July 13, 1849	19	light	Providence, R. I.	5	79
Thorp, David	Aug. 5, 1824	26	dark	Providence, R. I.	4	69
Thrift, William	Jan. 23, 1811	17	dark	Alexandria, Va.	4	68
Throop, Jonathan T.	Aug. 12, 1834	34	light	Lisbon, Conn.	5	77
Throop, Newport	Nov. 17, 1797	17	Black	Providence, R. I.	1	24
Thurber, Albert E.	May 30, 1849	20	light	Johnston, R. I.	5	79
Thurber, Charles	July 27, 1799	22	light	Providence, R. I.	2	19
Thurber, David	Apr. 20, 1805	15	light	Rehoboth, Mass.	3	38
Thurber, Edward	June 5, 1810	21	light	Providence, R. I.	4	68
Thurber, Edward M.	Dec. 4, 1823	16	light	Providence, R. I.	4	69
Thurber, Gardner	July 10, 1818	14	light	Providence, R. I.	4	69
Thurber, Ira M.	April 24, 1829	22	dark	Seekonk, Mass.	5	77
Thurber, James	Sept. 18, 1805	20	light	Providence, R. I.	3	45
Thurber, James W.	June 24, 1808	18	light	Providence, R. I.	4	68
Thurber, John A.	Oct. 18, 1849	26	light	Warren, Mass.	5	79
Thurber, John G.	June 27, 1854	49	light	Providence, R. I.	5	80
Thurber, John, Jr.	Oct. 29, 1799	25	light	Warren, R. I.	2	19
Thurber, Martin	May 2, 1799	18	light	Providence, R. I.	2	19
Thurber, Martin	July 27, 1807	24	light	Providence, R. I.	4	68
Thurber, Martin R.	Sept. 1, 1849	19	light	Johnston, R. I.	5	79
Thurber, Martin W.	June 16, 1858	28	light	Providence, R. I.	6	20

NAME	DATE OF CERTIFICATION	AGE	COMPLEXION	PLACE OF BIRTH	BOOK	PAGE
Thurber, Nath'l Dexter	June 5, 1843	17	light	Providence, R. I.	5	78
Turber, Paul	May 23, 1805	42	light	Providence, R. I.	3	38
Thurber, Relief, Jr.	April 15, 1819	18	light	Providence, R. I.	4	69
Thurber, Samuel	May 11, 1807	19	light	Providence, R. I.	4	68
Thurber, Samuel	Nov. 3, 1832	17	dark	Providence, R. I.	5	77
Thurber, Samuel	Oct. 16, 1833	18	dark	Providence, R. I.	5	77
Thurbet, Silas	June 26, 1801	35	light	Providence, R. I.	2	35
Thurber, Stephen, Jr.	Oct. 27, 1803	19	light	Providence, R. I.	2	35
Thurston, Anthony	Sept. 6, 1798	42	black	Newport, R. I.	2	19
Thurston, David	Feb. 15, 1834	28	light	Providence, R. I.	5	77
Thurston, Edward	July 31, 1797	16	light	Newport, R. I.	1	24
Thurston, Edward	Feb. 25, 1805	24	light	Newport, R. I.	3	38
Thurston, Edward	April 26, 1809	29	light	Newport, R. I.	4	68
Thurston, Harvey	July 22, 1809	19	light	Plainfield, Conn.	4	68
Thurston, James W.	Nov. 8, 1826	18	light	Newport, R. I.	4	69
Thurston, John	Nov. 27, 1837	29	light	Providence, R. I.	5	77
Thurston, Jonathan	1798 to 1799 b. Oct. 5, 1773			Newport, R. I.	Newport, R.
Thurston, Joseph	June 29, 1836	24	light	Coventry, R. I.	5	77
Thurston, Robt.	Jan. 10, 1853	21	mulatto	Williamsburgh, Va.	5	79
Thurston, Thomas	Oct. 7, 1834	23	dark	Newport, R. I.	5	77
Thurston, Thomas W.	March 9, 1842	16	light	Newport, R. I.	5	78
Thurston, Troy	Nov. 6, 1805	18	black	Hudson, N. Y.	3	46
Thurston, William	1798 to 1799 b. June 5, 1784			Newport, R. I.	Newport, R
Thurston, William H.	June 29, 1836	21	light	Cranston, R. I.	5	77
Tibbetts, Allen J.	Jan. 6, 1846	23	dark	West Greenwich, R. I.	5	78
Tibbits, Benjamin	Aug. 14, 1824	19	dark	East Greenwich, R. I.	4	69
Tippitts, Ebenezer	Nov. 8, 1805	21	light	Warwick, R. I.	3	46

REGISTER OF SEAMEN'S PROTECTION

NAME	DATE OF CERTIFICATION	AGE	COMPLEXION	PLACE OF BIRTH	BOOK	PAGE
Tilghanan, John	Aug. 13, 1855	42	dark	Philadelphia, Pa.	5	80
Tillinghast, Chas. H.	Sept. 6, 1856	17	light	Providence, R. I.	5	80
Tillinghast, Daniel Paris	Apr. 8, 1797	12	light	Providence, R. I.	1	24
Tillinghast, Daniel P.	Jan. 30, 1811	21	light	Providence, R. I.	4	68
Tillinghast, Fred A.	April 15, 1854	20	light	Cohoes, N. Y.	5	80
Tillinghast, James	Nov. 25, 1805	29	black	North R. I.	3	46
Tillinghast, James	Aug. 20, 1803	28	black	North Kingstown, R. I.	2	35
Tillinghast, Jeremiah	Oct. 31, 1842	23	dark	Cranston, R. I.	5	78
Tillinghast, Joseph, Jr.	Dec. 2, 1803	16	dark	Providence, R. I.	2	35
Tillinghast, Joseph H.	Oct. 19, 1830	16	light	Providence, R. I.	5	77
Tillinghast, Joseph R.	Oct. 19, 1801	18	dark	North Kingstown, R. I.	2	35
Tillinghast, Philip	Aug. 14, 1827	19	dark	North Kingstown, R. I.	4	70
Tillinghast, Richard R.	Oct. 30, 1846	15	fair	Providence, R. I.	5	78
Tillinghast, Richard R.	June 11, 1855	23	light	Providence, R. I.	5	80
Tillinghast, Samuel	Nov. 3, 1840	19	light	Exeter, R. I.	5	78
Tillinghast, Simon	Oct. 3, 1801	40	black	East Greenwich, R. I.	2	35
Tillinghast, Thomas H.	Sept. 27, 1826	21	light	Providence, R. I.	4	69
Tillinghast, William E.	Dec. 15, 1797	20	dark	Smithfield, R. I.	1	24
Tilman, John	March 25, 1863	35	dark	Milford, Del.	6	20
Tillman, William	Oct. 8, 1856	24	black	Philadelphia, Pa.	5	80
Tillmohn, Isaac H.	Sept. 19, 1843	42	black	Peterford, N. J.	5	78
Tilman, William	April 13, 1849	23	black	Philadelphia, Penn.	5	79
Timan, Christian	June 10, 1867	27	light	Boston, Mass.	6	20
Tims, John	Nov. 8, 1809	18	light	Augusta, Maine	4	68
Tindal, Benjamin, Jr.	March 13, 1818	19	yellow	Richmond, R. I.	4	69
Tindal, Benjamin	March 15, 1842	32	mulatto	Richmond, R. I.	5	78
Tinkham, Hilkiah	1798 to 1799	b. Middlebrough	Jan. 4, 1775		Newport, R.I.	

NAME	DATE OF CERTIFICATION	AGE	COMPLEXION	PLACE OF BIRTH	BOOK	PAGE
Tinkham, Silas	Oct. 26, 1849	33	light	Middleboro, Mass.	5	79
Tisdale, Alvin	July 12, 1817	18	fresh	Freetown, Mass.	4	69
Tisdale, John	June 13, 1801	16	light	Boston, Mass.	2	19
Titus, Albert O.	Dec. 27, 1850	24	light	Providence, R. I.	5	79
Tobey, Lawrence James	March 9, 1843	17	light	Savannah, Georgia	5	78
Tobias, Charles	Feb. 28, 1857	23	black	Long Island, N. Y.	5	80
Tobias, John	June 15, 1807	27	black	Flemington, N.J.	4	68
Tobin, John	July 31, 1840	23	light	Gouldsboro, Maine	5	78
Todd, Henry	June 3, 1843	21	dark	Philadelphia, Penn.	5	78
Tolman, John	June 23, 1825	21	dark	Newport, R. I.	4	69
Tomkinson, George	June 19,1805	23	dark	Philadelphia, Pa.	3	45
Tompkins, Ephraim	July 18, 1806	21	light	Little Compton, R. I.	3	40
Tompkins, Ephraim	Apr. 5, 1809	24	light	Little Compton, R. I.	4	68
Tompkins, Gideon	1798 to 1799	b. Apr. 13, 1783		Newport, R. I.	Newport, R
Tompkins, Ichabod	June 28, 1830	30	light	Little Compton, R. I.	5	77
Tompkins, Isaac	April 9, 1817	18	light	Little Compton, R. I.	4	69
Tompkins, John	1798 to 1799	b. June 10, 1778		Little Compton, R. I.	Newport, R
[Tompkins] John Tomkins	March 29, 1800	23	light	New Paltz, N. Y.	2	19
Tompon, Peter	Oct. 6, 1798	22	black	Sandwich, Mass.	2	19
Topliff, Calvin F.	May 22, 1855	18	fair	Providence, R. I.	5	80
Topliff, John W.	Sept. 24, 1861	21	light	Providence, R. I.	6	20
Topliff, Thomas	Feb. 6, 1861	20	light	Providence, R. I.	6	20
Topham, August	1798 to 1799	b. May 29, 1782		Newport, R. I.	Newport, R
Tophan, Franklin George (2) (1)	" "	b. Apr. 2, 1782		Jamestown, R. I.	"
Tophan, H. George (2) (1)	" "	b. Jan. 17, 1804		Newport, R. I.	"
Topham, George W.	Apr. 25, 1823	20	light	Newport, R. I.	4	69

NAME	DATE OF CERTIFICATION	AGE	COMPLEXION	PLACE OF BIRTH	BOOK	PAGE
Toshack, McGavin	Dec. 2, 1848	26	light	New York, N. Y.	5	79
Tourgee, Benjamin	Aug. 23, 1858	21	light	Natick, R. I.	6	20
Tourgee, George R.	Nov. 11, 1853	22	light	Warwick, R. I.	5	80
Tourgee, Philip	1798 to 1799 b. Sept. 22, 1786			S. Kingston, R. I.	Newport, R.I.	
Tourjee, Benjamin	Apr. 10, 1821	20	light	North Kingstown, R. I.	4	69
Tourjee, Jeremiah	Oct. 11, 1824	19	light	North Kingstown, R. I.	4	69
Tourjee, William	Nov. 1, 1826	20	light	North Kingstown, R. I.	4	69
Tourtellot, Jesse F.	July 16, 1853	17	light	Glocester, R. I.	5	80
Tourtellot, John	Nov. 1, 1805	25	light	Mendon, Mass.	3	46
Tourtellot, John	Apr. 23, 1800	19	light	Mendon, Mass.	2	19
Tourtellot, Samuel	Sept. 21, 1799	37	light	Glocester, Mass.	2	19
Tower, Samuel	June 29, 1801	19	dark	Cumberland, R. I.	2	35
Towne, Ransom	July 20, 1847	34	dark	Southbridge, Mass.	5	79
Townsend, Benjamin C.	July 17, 1846	19	fair	Providence, R. I.	5	78
Townsend, Edw. A.	Feb. 11, 1853	17	mulatto	Norwich, Conn.	5	79
Townsend, Edward Carrington	Dec. 8, 1841	18	light	Providence, R. I.	5	78
Townsend, George	July 16, 1846	17	fair	Newport, R. I.	5	78
Townsend, James	Nov. 3, 1845	21	black	Westchester, N. Y.	5	78
Townsend, John H.	Oct. 21, 1848	21	light	Newport, R. I.	5	79
Townsend, Soloman	March 1, 1797	18	light	Providence, R. I.	1	24
Tozer, Simon	May 31, 1806	20	light	Southboro, Mass.	3	46
Tracy, Samuel E.	Sept. 13, 1860	21	dark	Pawtucket, R. I.	6	20
Trafford, Bradford	Oct. 20, 1807	20	brown	Dartmouth, Mass.	4	68
Tranir, Richard Trainer ?	June 5, 1804	19	brown	Swansea, Mass.	3	37
Trask, Frederick A.	Dec. 8, 1826	18	light	Smithfield, R. I.	4	69
Trask, Richmond B.	Nov. 19, 1846	20	fair	Providence, R. I.	5	78
Trask, Samuel	Feb. 12, 1799	21	light	New Castle, Mass.	2	19

NAME	DATE OF CERTIFICATION	AGE	COMPLEXION	PLACE OF BIRTH	BOOK	PAGE
Travers, John H.	Oct. 17, 1837	30	black	Sandwich, Mass.	5	77
Traverse, Thomas	Sept. 13, 1796	14	dark	Providence, R. I.	1	2
(Traverse) Treavers, Thomas	Dec. 14, 1797	16	light	Providence, R. I.	1	24
Traverse, Thomas	May 10, 1799	18	dark	Providence, R. I.	2	19
Traverse, Vassell	March 16, 1799	19	light	Providence, R. I.	2	19
Traverse, Vassell S.	Nov. 10, 1797	17	dark	Providence, R. I.	1	24
Treadwell, Henry P.	July 23, 1823	18	ruddy	North Providence, R. I.	4	69
Treadwell, James	August 22, 1846	57	black	Providence, R. I.	5	78
Treavers, Thomas Traverse?	Dec. 14, 1797	16	light	Providence, R. I.	1	24
Tredway, Peter H.	April 26, 1838	23	light	Rutland, N. Y.	5	77
Trevaras, Charles	Oct. 2, 1852	35	dark	Mobile, Alabama	5	79
Treworgy, John P.	Dec. 23, 1870	22	dark	Blue Hill, Me.	6	20
Tripe, William Henry	July 16, 1804	19	dark	Portsmouth, N. H.	3	37
Tripp, Arthur	May 8, 1807	17	light	Providence, R. I.	4	68
Tripp, Charles	August 6, 1864	22	dark	Fall River, Mass.	6	20
Tripp, David	June 20, 1818	23	ruddy	Warwick, R. I.	4	69
Tripp, Ephirian	1798 to 1799	(certificate)		Portsmouth, R. I.	Newport,	
Tripp, George	Oct. 23, 1818	21	light	Warwick, R. I.	4	69
Tripp, James R.	Sept. 11, 1856	23	light	North Dartmouth, Mass.	5	80
Tripp, Jeremiah G.	July 30, 1839	21	light	Newport, R. I.	5	78
Tripp, John C.	March 30, 1861	30	light	New Bedford, Mass.	6	20
Tripp, Joseph	1798 to 1799	b. March 13, 1782		Portsmouth, R. I.	Newport,	
Tripp, Lilley	May 12, 1830	21	light	Little Compton, R. I.	5	77
Tripp, Samuel	Feb. 21, 1801	14	light	Providence, R. I.	2	19
Tripp, Samuel	Dec. 10, 1803	18	light	Providence, R. I.	2	35
Tripp, Samuel	April 24, 1804	35	dark	Harwich, Mass.	3	37

NAME	DATE OF CERTIFICATION	AGE	COMPLEXION	PLACE OF BIRTH	BOOK	PAGE
Tripp, Samuel	Oct. 9, 1809	21	brown	Rochester, Mass.	4	68
Tripp, Seth	Nov. 6, 1811	42	light	Johnston, R. I.	4	68
Tripp, Stephen	Oct. 23, 1805	30	dark	Warwick, R. I.	3	46
Tripp, Stephen	Oct. 20, 1797	22	dark	Warwick, R. I.	1	24
Tripp, Stephen	July 25, 1804	29	dark	Warwick, R. I.	3	37
Tripp, William	1798 to 1799	b. April 9, 1776		Tiverton, R. I.	Newport, R.I	
Tripp, William	March 3, 1820	36	light	Tiverton, R. I.	4	69
Tripp, William H.	Aug. 31, 1849	29	light	Johnston, R. I.	5	79
Tripp,. Wm. Stillman	Nov. 27, 1849	14	light	Providence, R. I.	5	79
Trott, Mason	April 13, 1831	26	light	Swansea, Mass.	5	77
Trott, Thomas	Nov. 14, 1803	23	black	Norfolk, Va.	2	35
Trowbridge, Benjamin, Jr.	Feb. 3, 1804	14	dark	Providence, R. I.	3	37
Trowbridge, William H.	May 20, 1839	17	light	New York, N. Y.	5	77
Trufant, Stephen	April 2, 1830	17	light	Bath, Maine	5	77
Trufatt, Peter	May 21, 1833	28	dark	New Orleans, La.	5	77
Trumbel, Henry	March 16, 1799	18	light	Norwich, Conn.	2	19
Truscott, Henry	July 28, 1854	19	light	Gouldsboro, Maine	5	80
Trute, Henry	June 22, 1854	22	light	Providence, R. I.	5	80
Tubbs, Elihu	Oct. 1, 1796	22	dark	Warwick, R. I.	1	24(4)
Tucker, Azel	Nov. 13, 1828	18	ruddy	So. Kingstown, R. I.	4	70
Tucker, Brightman	Oct. 27, 1849	23	light	So. Kingstown, R. I.	5	79
Tucker, Charles I.	July 5, 1855	34	light	New York, N. Y.	5	80
Tucker, Elisha	May 20, 1801	18	dark	Glocester, R. I.	2	19
Tucker, Elisha	Aug. 23, 1803	21	dark	Glocester, R. I.	2	35
Tucker, Israel	Oct. 16, 1819	22	light	Smithfield, R. I.	4	69
Tucker, John H.	July 6, 1858	23	fair	Philadelphia, Pa.	6	20
Tucker, Mason	April 11, 1834 ·	22	light	Dexter, Maine	5	77
Tucker, Newman	Nov. 26, 1849	25	dark	South Kingston, R. I.	5	79

NAME	DATE OF CERTIFICATION	AGE	COMPLEXION	PLACE OF BIRTH	BOOK	PAG
Tucker, Waldo	June 13, 1825	26	dark	Woodstock, Conn.	4	69
Tuckerman, John Tufton	Sept. 3, 1801	17	light	Boston, Mass.	2	35
Tuell, Bristol [Teuell]	Jan. 16, 1804	25	black	Newport, R. I.	3	37
Tuell, William P.	Sept. 26, 1827	20	light	Newport, R. I.	4	70
Turner, Amos	June 9, 1798	29	light	Rehoboth, Mass.	2	19
Turner, Daniel	Aug. 18, 1849	23	black	Bristol, R. I.	5	79
Turner, Gardner	Oct. 18, 1810	16	light	Tiverton, R. I.	4	68
Turner, George	1798 to 1799 b. Mar. 14, 1776			Whitman, Mass.	Newport, R
Turner, Henry	Oct. 4, 1798	18	light	North Kingstown, R. I.	2	19
Turner, Hilford	Sept. 21, 1866	23	light	Providence, R. I.	6	20
Turner, John	1798 to 1799 b. July 4, 1770			Newport, R. I.	Newport, R
Turner, John	Dec. 19, 1832	19	light	Wiscasset, Maine	5	77
Turner, John	Jan. 19, 1856	19	fair	Rinshead, N. Y.	5	80
Turner, John C.	Dec. 1, 1846	25	fair	Sandwich, Mass.	5	79
Turner, Joseph	July 3, 1821	18	light	Tiverton, R. I. b. April 17, 1803		
Sworn statement of William Richmond in the Custom House Papers.						
Turner, Joseph	Jan. 3, 1826	22	light	Tiverton, R. I.	4	69
Turner, Joseph	Jan. 9, 1845	21	light	New York, N. Y.	5	78
Turner, Samuel	June 13, 1825	16	light	Sandwich, Mass.	4	69
Turner, Thomas	Aug. 24, 1809	42	light	Tiverton, R. I.	4	68
Turner, William	June 4, 1799	23	dark	Barnstable, Mass.	2	19
Turner, William	Oct. 8, 1861	36	dark	Blackstone, Mass.	6	20
Turner, William Henry	Jan. 11, 1845	26	light	North Yarmouth, Maine	5	78
Tuttle, John	Aug. 14, 1839	26	dark	Boston, Mass.	5	78
Tweedy, Aaron C.	Aug. 10, 1849	18	light	Eastport, Maine	5	79
Tweedy, Samuel	Nov. 10, 1813	20	yellow	Newport, R. I.	4	69
Tweedy, Samuel	Feb. 25, 1823	29	black	Newport, R. I.	4	69

REGISTER OF SEAMEN'S PROTECTION

NAME	DATE OF CERTIFICATION	AGE	COMPLEXION	PLACE OF BIRTH	BOOK	PAGE
Twining, Abner	Aug. 16, 1831	30	light	Plymouth, Mass.	5	77
Tyler, Fernandes H.	Oct. 6, 1848	25	dark	Foster, R. I.	5	79
Tyler, Joseph	Nov. 3, 1800	28	light	Providence, R. I.	2	19
Tyler, Samuel	Nov. 20, 1846	18	light	Edgecomb, Maine	5	78
Tyler, Solomon	June 13, 1809	36	dark	Newport, R. I.	4	68
Tylor, Samuel	Jan. 7, 1826	27	light	Seekonk, Mass.	4	69
Tynes, George T.	Aug. 1, 1848	25	dark	Smithfield, Virginia	5	79
Tyng, Samuel.S.	March 21, 1860	26	fair	Smithfield, R. I.	6	20
Ulmer, Philip	May 23, 1835	42	light	Thomaston, Maine	5	81
Umford, Gaylord	Sept. 11, 1803	25	dark	Middle Haddam, Conn.	2	20
Underhill, William H.	March 1, 1867	26	dark	New York, N. Y.	6	21
Underwood, Bristol	Feb. 1, 1798	25	black	Jamestown, R. I.	1	25
Underwood, Ebenezer	June 1, 1805	19	black	Boston, Mass.	3	39
Underwood, Samuel	Oct. 24, 1849	22	light	South Kingston, R. I.	5	81
Updike, Alfred	Aug. 24, 1799	19	light	North Kingstown, R. I.	2	20
Updike, Caesar	April 15, 1825	24	yellow	North Kingstown, R. I.	4	73
Updike, Christopher	May 1, 1821	19	yellow	North Kingstown, R. I.	4	73
Updike, George	May 30, 1803	22	black	Newport, R. I.	2	20
Updike, George	Feb. 25, 1805	24	black	Newport, R. I.	3	39
Updike, George W.	June 16, 1819	16	black	North Kingstown, R. I.	4	73
Updike, Isaac	Feb. 13, 1805	20	yellow (mulatto)	Wickford, R. I.	3	39
Updike, James	April 3, 1810	18	yellow	North Kingstown, R. I.	4	73
Updike, John	July 29, 1805	18	yellow (mulatto)	North Kingstown, R. I.	3	39
Updike, John	Dec. 20, 1806	20	yellow	Wickford, R. I.	4	73
Updike, John	Jan. 7, 1812	24	yellow	North Kingstown, R. I.	4	73
Updike, John	March 5, 1818 ·	28	yellow	North Kingstown, R. I.	4	73

NAME	DATE OF CERTIFICATION	AGE	COMPLEXION	PLACE OF BIRTH	BOOK	PA(
Updike, Joseph	Oct. 13, 1806	27	yellow	North Kingstown, R. I.	4	73
Urann, Thomas	July 16, 1810	21	dark	Troy, N. Y.	4	73
Usher, John	1798 to 1799	b. May 5, 1771		Bristol, R. I.	Newport, R. I
Usher, Joseph E.	Aug. 31, 1821	15	light	Bristol, R. I. b. June 25, 1806		
Sworn statement of Edward Usher in the Custom House Papers.						
Utley, Dan	March 29, 1805	24	dark	Pomfret, Conn.	3	39
Valentine, Edmund	July 5, 1817	18	dark	Freetown, Mass.	4	73
Valentine, James	July 29, 1808	22	black	Wilmington, Del.	4	73
Van Arnam, Richard	March 30, 1805	23	light	Cumberland, R. I.	3	39
Van Beuren	Aug. 14, 1821	22	sandy	Albany, N. Y. b. Sept. 19, 1799		
Sworn statement of Peleg Slocum in the Custom House Papers.						
Vanderpool, John	Oct. 20, 1809	27	black	Hartford, Conn.	4	73
Van dyke, Richard	Oct. 8, 1805	31	dark	New York, N. Y.	3	39
Van Gilt, James	Jan. 23, 1818	27	black	North Kingstown, R. I.	4	73
Vankleak, John M.	July 31, 1837	31	dark	New York, N. Y.	5	81
Vanmetre, John	Dec. 24, 1849	25	black	Bangor, Maine	5	81
Van Ness, George	Mar. 26, 1855	32	black	Colwell, Essez Co., N.J.	5	81
Van Norden, John G.	Aug. 5, 1840	32	dark		5	81
Van Riper, William E.	June 2, 1849	32	light	New York City, New York	5	81
Varnsdale, Joseph	March 11, 1833	20	light	Philadelphia, Penn.	5	81
Varse, Pardon	Dec. 4, 1797	18	light	Middletown, R. I.	1	25
Vassal, Jonah L.	Feb. 29, 1812	25	light	Charlton, Mass.	4	73
Vaughan, Alexander	Oct. 7, 1796	24	light	East Greenwich, RI	1	25 / 4
Vaughn, Christopher	Jan. 8, 1849	18	light	Smithfield, R. I.	5	81
Vaughan, Daniel	Nov. 28, 1831	18	light	Charleston, S. C.	5	81
Vaughan, John	Dec. 22, 1797	28	light	Emerleaven, Scotland	1	25
Vaughan, Peter	Dec. 15, 1832	18	light	North Kingston, R. I.	5	81
Vaughan, Peter	Jan. 26, 1860	23	light	Eastport, Me.	6	22

NAME	DATE OF CERTIFICATION	AGE	COMPLEXION	PLACE OF BIRTH	BOOK	PAGE
Vaughn, Wilber	Sept. 24, 1849	39	light	East Greenwich, R. I.	5	81
[Vaughan]Vaughn, Prince	March 1, 1797	34	black	North Kingstown, R. I.	1	25
Verily, Charles	Sept. 30, 1809	18	brown	Falmouth, Mass.	4	73
Vernon, James	March 16, 1852	22	dark	Boston, Mass.	5	81
Viall, Benjamin F.	March 24, 1858	19	light	Providence, R. I.	6	22
Viall, Joshua	Dec. 30, 1796	17	light	Barrington, R. I.	1	25
Vickers, William	May 26, 1851	18	dark	Hamilton, Conn.	5	81
Vickery, Highland	May 19, 1809	25	light	Taunton, Mass.	4	73
Vickery, John, Jr.	Feb. 28, 1807	15	light	Scituate, R. I.	4	73
Vickery, John W.	Aug. 16, 1831	18	light	Bristol, R. I.	5	81
Vickery, Reuben C.	Dec. 30, 1808	26	light	Dighton, Mass.	4	73
Vickery, Samuel	Jan. 22, 1807	20	florid	Dighton, Mass.	4	73
Vickery, William	Oct. 29, 1803	41	light	Marblehead, Mass.	2	20
Vigus, John	April 10, 1854	52	light	New York, N. Y.	5	81
Vilson, Peter	May 16, 1836	33	dark	New Orleans, La.	5	81
Vincent, John	July 27, 1804	35	dark	Edgartown, Mass.	3	39
Vincent, Joseph W.	Oct. 29, 1849	18	light	Westerly, R. I.	5	81
Vincent, Thomas H.	July 8, 1806	36	light	Piscataway, Mass.	3	39
Vinnicum, John, Jr.	Apr. 12, 1821	22	light	Warren, R. I.	4	73
Vinton, Albert	May 10, 1833	22	dark	Providence, R. I.	5	81
Vinton, Ezra	March 20, 1812	21	brown	Dudley, Mass.	4	73
Voase, Timothy	Aug. 24, 1799	29	dark	Swansea, Mass.	2	20
Vose, Avery	Dec. 15, 1813	21	light	Norwich, Conn.	4	73
Vose, Edward	Oct. 30, 1823	20	yellow	Providence, R. I.	4	73
Vose, Timothy	Aug. 8, 1811	30	yellow	Somerset, Mass.	4	73
Vose, William	June 12, 1818	17	yellow	Providence, R. I.	4	73
Wade, Abel	Aug. 31, 1849.	32	light	Foster, R. I.	5	87
Wade, Benjamin	May 28, 1810	20	brown	Elizabethtown, N. J.	4	75

Page 277

NAME	DATE OF CERTIFICATION	AGE	COMPLEXION	PLACE OF BIRTH	BOOK	PAG
Wade, Charles	May 26, 1853	23	light	East Douglas, Mass.	5	88
Wade, Comfort	Nov. 21, 1804	19	light	Rehoboth, Mass.	3	42
Wade, Ebenezer	Apr. 5, 1800	24	dark	Rehoboth, Mass.	2	29
Wade, George	June 27, 1815	19	dark	Seekonk, Mass.	4	75
Wade(Waid), James	March 3, 1857	22	fair	Eastport, Maine	5	95
Wade, John L.	Jan. 4, 1798	18	light	Rehoboth, Mass.	1	28
Wadleigh, James M.	Nov. 12, 1835	28	light	Concord, N. H.	5	84
Waggoner, John	July 3, 1832	52	light	Bristol, Penn.	5	83
Waite, Beriah	1798 to 1799	b. Mar. 3, 1782		N. Kingston, R. I.	Newport,
Wait, David	Oct. 30, 1856	23	fair	Plymouth, Mass.	5	95
Waite, Fortune	Apr. 28, 1821	22	yellow	Exeter, R. I.	4	77
Waite, Hiram	Nov. 25, 1836	21	mulatto	East Greenwich, R. I.	5	84
Waite, James A.	June 5, 1857	17	dark	Providence, R. I.	5	95
Waite, Matthew	Apr. 15, 1805	24	light	So. Kingstown, R. I.	3	44
Waite, Stephen	1798 to 1799	b. Dec. 7, 1780		Westport, Mass.	Newport,
Wake, Matthew	1798 to 1799	b. Nov. 6, 1779		Boston, Mass.	Newport,
Wakefield, Benjamin, Jr.	June 13, 1832	27	dark	Saco, Maine	5	83
Walbridge, Henry	April 20, 1860	22	fair	Philadelphia, Pa.	6	23
Walcott, Charles S.	Oct. 13, 1845	19	light	Smithfield, R. I.	5	86
Walcott, Wm. Henry	Feb. 24, 1849	19	light	Smithfield, R. I.	5	87
Waldo, Frank	Nov. 11, 1803	21	light	Pomfret, Conn.	2	48
Waldron, Daniel	1798 to 1799	b. Nov. 24, 1781		Bristol, R. I.	Newport,
Waldron, George	1798 to 1799	b. Jan. 23, 1784		Bristol, R. I.	Newport,
Waldron, Isaac	1798 to 1799	b. Apr. 16, 1770		Bristol, R. I.	Newport,
Walker, Aaron	March 4, 1797	21	dark	Rehoboth, Mass.	1	26
Walker, Aaron	1798 to 1799			Bristol, R. I. certificate, Newport
Walker, Abiather	Oct. 27, 1801	21	dark	Dighton, Mass.	2	37

NAME	DATE OF CERTIFICATION	AGE	COMPLEXION	PLACE OF BIRTH	BOOK	PAGE
Walker, Calvin, Jr.	March 14, 1821	22	dark	Seekonk, Mass.	4	77
Walker, Ephraim	June 19, 1849	29	light	Seekonk, Mass.	5	87
Walker, Ezra	Oct. 26, 1803	23	light	Rehoboth, Mass.	2	37
Walker, Fred A.	June 11, 1855	20	fair	Medford, Mass.	5	95
Walker, George	Apr. 9, 1810	22	light	Rehoboth, Mass.	4	75
Walker, James	Sept. 30, 1805	26	light	Scituate, R. I.	3	47
Walker, James	Oct. 16, 1833	28	dark	Portland, Maine	5	83
Walker, James	Jan. 23, 1836	22	light	Yarmouth, Mass.	5	83
Walker, James M.	March 5, 1849	28	light	Seekonk, Mass.	5	87
Walker, Joel	Oct. 26, 1803	24	light	Rehoboth, Mass.	2	37
Walker, John	July 14, 1804	19	dark	Charleston, S. C.	3	41
Walker, John	March 5, 1849	30	light	Seekonk, Mass.	5	87
Walker, Joseph	Aug. 24, 1841	20	light	Johnston, R. I.	5	85
Walker, Peleg	Dec. 15, 1797	33	dark	Providence, R. I.	1	29
Walker, Simeon	Nov. 11, 1799	23	light	Rehoboth, Mass.	2	21
Walker, Stephen	Oct. 23, 1824	23	light	Rehoboth, Mass.	3	42
Walker, Thomas	Jan. 7, 1801	21	dark	Providence, R. I.	2	29
Walker, William	Nov. 8, 1851	26	light	Provincetown, Mass.	5	88
Wall, Benjamin	Nov. 3, 1818	21	light	North Kingstown, R. I.	4	77
Wall, Ezra	May 24, 1815	23	light	Pittstown, N. Y.	4	75
Wall, William	Jan. 2, 1835	27	light	North Kingston, R. I.	5	84
Wallace, Jack	Oct. 24, 1803	43	black	Ebo Coast, Africa	2	37
Wallis(Wallace)John	June 12, 1820	21	black	Providence, R. I.	4	77
Wallis (Wallace)John	June 8, 1843	17	light	Buffalo, N. Y.	5	85
Wallace, John	April 7, 1851	21	light	Prospect, Maine	5	88
Wallace, Newport	Oct. 19, 1812	14	black	Providence, R. I.	4	75
Wallis(Wallace),Newport	June 2, 1815.	15	black	Providence, R. I.	4	75

NAME	DATE OF CERTIFICATION	AGE	COMPLEXION	PLACE OF BIRTH	BOOK	PA(
Walling, Joseph	Jan. 19, 1854	48	light	Providence, R. I.	5	8(
Walmsley, Francis (Warmsley)	June 27, 1806	18	yellow(mulatto)	Cranston, R. I.	3	8(
Wamsley, George (Walmsley)	June 16, 1809	19	yellowish	North Prov., R. I.	4	7(
[Walmsley], Henry Wamsley	Feb. 24, 1801	37	black	Charleston, R. I.	2	2(
Wamsley, Stephen Walmsley	Dec. 11, 1809	22	yellow	North Providence, R. I.	4	7(
Walsh, John	May 10, 1845	30	light	Bristol, R. I.	5	8(
Walsh, Mark Walch	Aug. 21, 1804	12	light	Providence, R. I.	3	4.
Walsh, William	March 10, 1853	27	dark	Portsmouth, N. H.	5	8(
Walter, William	Aug. 8, 1803	17	light	Providence, R. I.	2	3(
Walters, John	Dec. 19, 1805	18	light	Providence, R. I.	3	4(
Walter, John	Jan. 2, 1804	17	light	Providence, R. I.	3	4(
Walters, Samuel	Sept. 25, 1811	26	dark	Providence, R. I.	4	7(
Walton, J. Blaver	Dec. 24, 1852	27	light	Lynn, Mass.	5	8(
Walton, John	Feb. 14, 1805	34	light	Norfolk, Va.	3	4(
Walton, Joshua	Aug. 24, 1799	17	dark	Cheshire, Conn.	2	2(
Walts, Charles	Oct. 26, 1862	19	dark	Waldoboro, Me.	6	2.
Warburton, Thomas	March 22, 1831	20	light	Scituate, R. I.	5	8
Ward, Charles	Jan. 22, 1859	21	dark	Philadelphia, Pa.	6	2
Ward, George	Oct. 25, 1833	27	light	Boston, Mass.	5	8.
Ward, George H.	Oct. 5, 1849	22	dark	Charlestown, R. I.	5	8
Ward, James	Nov. 19, 1832	23	light	Philadelphia, Penn.	5	8.
Ward, John	Oct. 22, 1804	19	light	New York, N.Y.	3	4.
Ward, John P.	Oct. 23, 1849	17	light	Charlestown, R. I.	5	8
Ward, Richard	Nov. 22, 1796	18	dark	So. Kingstown, R. I.	1	2(
Ward, Samuel	Sept. 1, 1804	17	black	Newport, R. I.	3	4(

NAME	DATE OF CERTIFICATION	AGE	COMPLEXION	PLACE OF BIRTH	BOOK	PAGE
Warner, Benajah C.	March 28, 1797	19	dark	Providence, R.I.	1	26
Warner, Elisha	May 22, 1809	18	dark	Providence, R. I.	4	74
Warner, James	July 29, 1797	18	light	Warwick, R. I.	1	26
Warner, John	Dec. 28, 1796	23	light	Warwick, R. I.	1	26
Warner, John	June 2, 1806	16	light	Warwick, R. I.	3	48
Warner, John	Oct. 3, 1849	23	light	Warwick, R. I.	5	87
Warner, Joseph	March 21, 1805	18	light	Glocester, R. I.	3	43
Warner, Nehemiah	July 7, 1798	18	dark	Glocester, R. I.	2	21
Warner, Samuel	Oct. 28, 1805	21	light	Providence, R. I.	3	47
Warner, Samuel	July 18, 1798	33	light	Providence, R. I.	2	21
Warner, Samuel	May 5, 1803	18	dark	Providence, R. I.	2	37
Warner, Samuel	Oct. 25, 1803	20	dark	New York, N. Y.	2	37
Warner, Stephen G.	Dec. 7, 1827	19	ruddy	Warwick, R. I.	4	78
Warner, Thomas	June 23, 1835	22	dark	Salem, Mass.	5	84
Warner, William	Dec. 23, 1815	19	light	Providence, R. I.	4	75
Warner, William	Sept. 10, 1866	31	dark	Boston, Mass.	6	23
Warner, William H.	May 2, 1809	19	dark	Providence, R. I.	4	74
Warren, Albigence	Dec. 29, 1815	24	light	Killingly, Conn.	4	75
Warren, Algernon	Aug. 13, 1825	26	dark	Killingly, Conn.	4	77
Warren, Benjamin W.	Dec. 12, 1827	23	light	Bristol, R. I.	4	78
Warren, Brom John	1798 to 1799			Warren, R. I. certificate	Newport, RI	
Warren, Elisha O.	April 16, 1832	27	dark	Plainfield, Conn.	5	83
Warren, Henry David	March 21, 1804	24	dark	East Haddam, Conn.	3	41
Warren, Osborn S.	March 19, 1849	36	light	Bristol, R. I.	5	87
Washburn, Wm. F.	May 30, 1850	29	dark	Nantucket, Mass.	5	88
Washington, William W.	March 19, 1859	18	Mulatto	Providence, R. I.	6	23
Wass, George	Aug. 11, 1840	18	light	Addison, Maine	5	85

NAME	DATE OF CERTIFICATION	AGE	COMPLEXION	PLACE OF BIRTH	BOOK	P.
Waterman, Alden	Jan. 6, 1808	17	light	Cranston, R. I.	4	
Waterman, Amaziah	March 4, 1797	17	dark	Cumberland, R. I.	1	
Waterman, Andrew	Oct. 29, 1849	35	dark	Scituate, R. I.	5	
Waterman, Anson	Sept. 16, 1801	22	light	Cranston, R. I.	2	
Waterman, Asa	July 12, 1806	21	brown	Norwich, Conn.	3	
Waterman, Cato	Nov. 25, 1805	21	black	Warwick, R. I.	3	
Waterman, John P.	Jan. 10, 1807	32	brown	Cranston, R. I.	4	
Waterman, Nathan	Nov. 7, 1854	17	light	Cranston, R. I.	5	
Waterman, Nero	Aug. 20, 1799	33	black	Providence, R. I.	2	
Waterman, Pardon	Oct. 11, 1806	17	light	Cranston, R. I.	4	
Waterman, Resolved	Oct. 28, 1819	20	light	Cranston, R. I.	4	
Waterman, Richard	Nov. 14, 1849	40	light	Warwick, R. I.	5	
Waterman, Richard M.	Dec. 6, 1826	18	light	Coventry, R. I.	4	
Waterman, Robert Sterry	Aug. 21, 1799	17	light	Norwich, Conn.	2	
Waterman, Timothy	Apr. 18, 1799	16	light	Norwich, Conn.	2	
Waterman, Townsend	June 1, 1826	31	light	Providence, R. I.	4	
Waterman, Walter	Nov. 8, 1810	19	light	Norwich, Conn.	4	
Waterman, Warren	March 23, 1810	27	black	Providence, R. I.	4	
Waterman, William F.	Oct. 14, 1806	16	light	Providence, R. I.	4	
Waters, Bryant	Oct. 5, 1818	20	dark	Branfort Court, N. C.	4	
Waters, Daniel	Apr. 6, 1802	24	light	Philadelphia, Pa.	2	
Waters, James	Oct. 23, 1837	28	black	Somerset Co., Maryland	5	
Waters, James	July 12, 1845	16	dark	Eastport, Maine	5	
Waters, John	June 8, 1838	31	dark	Philadelphia, Pa.	5	
Waters, Samuel	May 3, 1799	18	dark	Providence, R. I.	2	
Waters, Thomas Warters	Aug. 23, 1805	34	dark	Portsmouth, N. H.	3	
Watertown, Mathew	Aug. 31, 1849	30	light	Yorkshire, G. B.	5	

NAME	DATE OF CERTIFICATION	AGE	COMPLEXION	PLACE OF BIRTH	BOOK	PAGE
Wathby, Francis	May 19, 1838	17	dark	Providence, R. I.	5	85
Watkins, George	July 18, 1798	23	black	Newport, R. I.	2	21
Watkins, Peter	Feb. 24, 1845	36	light	Philadelphia, Penn.	5	86
Watkins, Thomas	1798 to 1799	b. Sept. 9, 1781		Westport, Mass.	Newport, R.I
Watkins, Thomas	June 13, 1809	31	dark	Dighton, Mass.	4	74
Watkins, William	Apr. 13, 1805	21	light	Canterbury, Conn.	3	43
Watson, Aaron	Dec. 10, 1841	29	dark	East Haddam, Conn.	5	85
Watson, Absalom	Jan 23, 1858	37	black	Milton, Del.	6	23
[Watson], Daniel Wattson	Dec. 17, 1798	28	black	South Kingstown, R. I.	2	21
[Watson] Daniel Wattson	May 3, 1799	29	black	South Kingstown, R. I.	2	21
Watson, Daniel	Oct. 12, 1803	32	black	South Kingstown, R. I.	2	37
Watson, Daniel	Nov. 13, 1812	45	yellow	South Kingstown, R. I.	4	75
Watson, Daniel, Jr.	March 14, 1809	19	yellow	North Kingstown, R. I.	4	74
Watson, Eugene W.	June 22, 1841	23	light	Poultney, Vermont	5	85
Watson, George	June 22, 1798	24	dark	Dundee, Scotland	2	21
Watson, George	July 10, 1833	20	yellow	North Providence, R. I.	5	83
Watson, George W.	June 10, 1841	35	light	New Bedford, Mass.	5	85
Watson, Harvey	Sept. 19, 1860	24	fair	Rockland, Me.	6	23
Watson, Hasard	March 10, 1852	22	light	Exeter, R. I.	5	88
Watson, James	March 1, 1805	19	black	South Kingstown, R. I.	3	43
Watson, James	May 31, 1805	19	black	South Kingstown, R. I.	3	44
Watson, James	March 15, 1809	17	yellow	North Kingstown, R. I.	4	74
Watson, James	April 23, 1807	16	yellowish	South Kingstown, R. I.	4	74
Watson, James	Sept. 25, 1834	31	light	Portland, Maine	5	84
Watson, James	May 21, 1847	23	dark	Argyle, N. Y.	5	86
Watson, John	Aug. 12, 1834	28	light	Bangor, Maine	5	84
Watson, John	June 6, 1838	21	dark	Philadelphia, Pa.	5	85

NAME	DATE OF CERTIFICATION	AGE	COMPLEXION	PLACE OF BIRTH	BOOK	PAGE
Watson, Joseph	March 27, 1810	27	yellowish	Nuant, Conn.(Noank?)	4	7
Watson, Moses H.	Nov. 15, 1831	21	black	Plainfield, Conn.	5	8
Watson, Robert	Nov. 1, 1839	24	light	Cumberland, R. I.	5	8
Watson, Thomas	March 25, 1853	19	black	Philadelphia, Penn.	5	8
Watson, Thomas B.	July 27, 1839	27	black	Providence, R. I.	5	8
Watson, Thomas C.	October 6, 1821	21	brown	Newport, R. I.	4	7
Watson, William	July 18, 1845	25	dark	New York City, N. Y.	5	8
Watt, Charles C.	Sept. 21, 1866	19	light	Pembroke, Me.	6	2
Watts, David	June 3, 1831	28	light	Arbroath, Scotland	5	8
Watts, James	May 28, 1855	28	light	Norfolk, N. H.	5	9
Watts, John	Dec. 13, 1803	33	dark	New York, N. Y.	2	2
Weamer, John	Dec. 9, 1803	15	dark	Schenectady, N. Y.	2	4
Weatherhead, Samuel	Apr. 1, 1797	21	dark	Cumberland, R. I.	1	2
Weaver, Benjamin	Dec. 29, 1810	24	black	No. Cumberland Co., Va.	4	7
Weaver, Caleb	Aug. 18, 1796	36	light	Warwick, R. I.	1	1
Weaver, Jerome N.	March 24, 1863	25	dark	Warwick, R. I.	6	2
Weaver, John	Feb. 23, 1797	20	light	Providence, R. I.	1	2
Weaver, John	April 1, 1807	30	light	Providence, R. I.	4	7
Weaver, John	October 8, 1819	18	light	Dennis, Mass.	4	7
Weaver, John	Feb. 2, 1854	28	mulatto	Providence, R. I.	5	8
Weaver, Jonathan R.	Jan. 2, 1835	16	light	Warwick, R. I.	5	8
Weaver, Samuel	1798 to 1799	b. 1775		Dartmouth, Mass.	Newport,	
Webb, Alfred	Oct. 15, 1850	15	light	Thomaston, Maine	5	8
Webb, James	July 12, 1803	18	light	Warwick, R. I.	2	3
Webb, James	Dec. 11, 1827	17	light	Smithfield, R. I.	4	7
Webb, James	July 10, 1837	24	light	Stamford, Conn.	5	8
Webb, Jeremiah	July 10, 1818.	22	light	Warwick, R. I.	4	7

NAME	DATE OF CERTIFICATION	AGE	COMPLEXION	PLACE OF BIRTH	BOOK	PAGE
Webber, Anthony	August 12, 1806	21	light	Albany, N. Y.	3	80
Webber, George	March 25, 1853	21	dark	Otswego, N. Y.	5	88
Webster, George M.	Aug. 31, 1849	26	light	Nantucket, Mass.	5	87
Webster, George W.	June 11, 1830	24	light	Portland, Maine	5	83
Weed, Lyman	Jan. 2, 1810	21	dark	Baskhamstead, Conn.	4	75
Weeden, Charles	Apr. 8, 1811	28	black	Jamestown, R. I.	4	75
Weeden, Charles	March 20, 1822	21	yellow	Charlestown, R. I.	4	77
Weeden, Charles W.	Nov. 19, 1846	19	fair	North Kingston, R. I.	5	86
Weeden, Daniel C.	April 27, 1837	33	light	Jamestown, R. I.	5	84
Weeden, Danuel D.	Sept. 1, 1849	18	light	North Kingston, R. I.	5	87
Weeden, David A.	Jan. 1, 1856	30	mulatto	Lisbon, Conn.	5	95
Weeden, George	Dec. 15, 1821	20	light	East Greenwich, R. I.	4	77
Weeden, George F.	Jan. 1, 1856	18	milatto	Griswold, Conn.	5	95
Weeden, Henry D.	March 21, 1815	20	light	Providence, R. I.	4	75
Weeden, James	June 23, 1854	23	light	Providence, R. I.	5	95
Weeden, Job, Jr.	Aug. 26, 1801	19	light	Boston, Mass.	2	29
Weeden, John	June 16, 1810	18	yellow	Charlestown, R. I.	4	75
Weeden, Joseph Jr.	Dec. 29, 1829	20	black	Newport, R. I.	5	83
Weeden, Samuel E.	June 23, 1852	21	light	East Greenwich, R. I.	5	88
Weeden, Samuel L.	July 1, 1817	17	light	East Greenwich, R. I.	4	75
Weeden, Thomas R.	July 8, 1815	18	light	East Greenwich, R. I.	4	75
Weeden, Wanton	Aug. 9, 1821	31	light	East Greenwich, R. I. b. Feb. 4, 1790

Sworn statement of Joseph F. Hall of North Kingstown in the Custom House Papers.

NAME	DATE OF CERTIFICATION	AGE	COMPLEXION	PLACE OF BIRTH	BOOK	PAGE
Weeden, William	March 31, 1797	16	dark	Newport, R. I.	1	26
Weeks, Alfred	Feb. 7, 1834	25	light	New York, N. Y.	5	83
Weeks, Charles Weekes	Dec. 5, 1801	19	dark	Falmouth, Mass.	2	37
Weeks, George	June 29, 1819	21	black	Providence, R. I.	4	77
Weeks, Henry	Nov. 4, 1853	31	light	New York, N. Y.	5	88

NAME	DATE OF CERTIFICATION	AGE	COMPLEXION	PLACE OF BIRTH	BOOK	PAG
Weeks, Hiram	March 3, 1849	26	light	Tisbury, Mass.	5	87
Weeks, James	Aug. 14, 1835	13	black	Warwick, R. I.	5	84
Weeks, Samuel	Apr. 1, 1806	23	*Yellow	Warwick, R. I.	3	48
Weeks, Samuel	Nov. 11, 1803	21	black	Warwick, R. I.	2	48
Weeks, William	April 12, 1834	20	light	Falmouth, Mass.	5	83
Weiss, Washington	July 5, 1855	22	light	Baltimore, Md.	5	95
Welch, Arthur	Sept. 10, 1821	19	light	Canterbury, Conn.	4	77
Welch, Edward	Jan. 30, 1860	24	fair	Portland, Me.	6	23
Welch, James	Nov. 1, 1800	13	light	Providence, R. I.	2	29
Welch, Stephen	Sept. 5, 1853	17	dark	Salem, Mass.	5	88
Welch, Thomas	July 17, 1844	22	dark	Seekonk, Mass.	5	86
Welch, Thomas	April 9, 1850	26	light	Providence, R. I.	5	88
Welch, Thomas	Feb. 2, 1854	27	light	Boston, Mass.	5	88
Welsh, Abraham [Welch]	April 12, 1852	19	light	Eastport, Maine	5	88
Welsh, William [Welch]	Aug. 26, 1803	18	light	Providence, R. I.	2	37
Weld, William W.	May 27, 1850	20	dark	North Providence, R. I.	5	88
Welden, Zenas	Dec. 4, 1818	38	light	Yarmouth, Mass.	4	77
Wells, Benoni	Oct. 22, 1832	23	light	Exeter, R. I.	5	83
Wells, Calvin	Nov. 9, 1848	20	light	Auburn, N. Y.	5	86
Wells, Erastus H.	Dec. 9, 1822	17	light	West Hartford, Conn.	4	77
Wells, Francis H.	June 13, 1851	22	dark	Hartford, Conn.	5	88
Wells, George	Sept. 2, 1805	18	black	Charleston, S. C.	3	44
Wells, Isaac	April 20, 1805	18	dark	Rehoboth, Mass.	3	44
Wells, John	March 17, 1815	21	black	New Shoreham, R. I.	4	75
Wells, John W.	May 29, 1857	28	fair	Cabotville, Mass.	5	95
Wells, Nathaniel	Aug. 21, 1800	51	dark	Scituate, R. I.	2	29
Wells, William	May 31, 1797	23	black	Hartford, Conn.	1	26

*mulatto

NAME	DATE OF CERTIFICATION	AGE	COMPLEXION	PLACE OF BIRTH	BOOK	PAGE
Wells, William	Aug. 15, 1804	15	light	Sudberry, Mass.	3	42
Wells, William	Jan. 13, 1798	24	black	Hartford, Conn.	1	28
Wells, William W.	July 28, 1823	20	light	Hartford, Conn.	4	77
Wesson, Daniel H.	Dec. 25, 1848	16	light	Providence, R. I.	5	86
Wesson, George T.	March 2, 1849	17	light	Providence, R. I.	5	87
Wesson, William	July 20, 1809	19	dark	Boston, Mass.	4	74
West, Abner	Oct. 19, 1805	27	light	Barnstable, Mass.	3	47
West, Chas. Enoch	Nov. 27, 1844	14	light	Seekonk, Mass.	5	86
West,. Daniel	April 14, 1854	22	light	Lyons, New York	5	95
West, Edward	Jan. 15, 1821	23	dark	New York City b. July 25, 1797		
Sworn statement of Joanna Fales of Swansea in Custom House Papers.						
West, H. H.	Aug. 17, 1864	22	medium	Waldo, Me.	6	23
West, Hiram	May 4, 1821	20	light	Scituate, R. I.	4	77
West, Hiram	Nov. 14, 1826	22	light	Providence, R. I.	4	77
West, Howell	Nov. 22, 1819	17	light	Scituate, R. I.	4	77
West, Job	Dec. 6, 1797	23	light	Newport, R. I.	1	28
West, Joseph	Apr. 20, 1799	29	black	Warwick, R. I.	2	21
West, Orrin S.	Aug. 5, 1840	20	light	Glocester, R. I.	5	85
West, Reuben	Oct. 29, 1803	13	light	Falmouth, Mass.	2	48
West, Simeon	March 4, 1797	17	light	West Greenwich, R. I.	1	26
West, Simeon	Jan. 30, 1798	18	light	East Greenwich, R. I.	1	28
West, Stephen	Oct. 31, 1805	20	light	East Greenwich, R. I.	3	47
West, Thomas	Oct. 28, 1803	21	light	Newport, R. I.	2	48
West, Thomas	Apr. 2, 1800	18	light	Newport, R. I.	2	29
West, Timothy	Jan. 2, 1798	16	yellow*	Warwick, R. I.	1	28
West, William	March 21, 1836	22	black	Philadelphia, Penn.	5	84
Westcott, Amasa	June 15, 1807	16	light	Warwick, R. I.	4	74
Westcott, Amasa	Nov. 8, 1813	23	light	Warwick, R. I.	4	75

*mulatto

NAME	DATE OF CERTIFICATION	AGE	COMPLEXION	PLACE OF BIRTH	BOOK	PAG
Westcott, Amos	May 16, 1804	25	light	Cranston, R. I.	3	41
Westcott, Arnold	Oct. 24, 1809	16	brown	Warwick, R. I.	4	74
Westcott, Charles	Oct. 13, 1803	24	dark	Cranston, R. I.	2	37
Westcott, Charles S.	Feb. 7, 1818	17	dark	Providence, R. I.	4	75
Westcott, David B.	June 12, 1849	18	light	Mendon, Mass.	5	87
Westcott, Eleazer	Aug. 23, 1798	19	dark	Cranston, R. I.	2	21
Westcott, George	Sept. 15, 1815	25	fresh	Cranston, R. I.	4	75
Westcott, George	Dec. 14, 1827	21	dark	Providence, R. I.	4	78
Westcott, James F.	June 5, 1843	17	dark	Providence, R. I.	5	85
Westcott, Jeremiah	May 17, 1797	25	dark	Cranston, R. I.	1	26
Westcott, John	March 26, 1805	39	dark	Warwick, R. I.	3	43
Westcott, John	Aug. 10, 1811	28	light	Cranston, R. I.	4	75
Westcott, John, Jr.	Nov. 7, 1797	19	dark	Providence, R. I.	1	29
Westcott, John, Jr.	Apr. 12, 1816	38	dark	Providence, R. I.	4	75
Westcott, Joseph	Dec. 22, 1797	21	light	Cranston, R. I.	1	29
Westcott, Josiah	Feb. 18, 1804	26	light	Cranston, R. I.	3	41
Westcott, Josiah	Aug. 20, 1800	22	dark	Cranston, R. I.	2	29
Westcott, Josiah	March 21, 1805	27	light	Cranston, R. I.	3	43
Westcott, Josias	Jan. 20, 1801	23	light	Cranston, R. I.	2	29
Westcott, Nathan	Oct. 30, 1805	15	light	Warwick, R. I.	3	47
Westcott, Reuben	March 2, 1804	20	dark	Cranston, R. I.	3	41
Westcott, Reuben	July 25, 1810	28	dark	Cranston, R. I.	4	75
Westcott, Samuel	Aug. 11, 1812	26	dark	Portsmouth, Va.	4	75
Westcott, Samuel, Jr.	July 12, 1815	17	dark	Providence, R. I.	4	75
Westcott, Thomas	March 1, 1805	20	light	Providence, R. I.	3	43
Westcott, Thomas	Nov. 12, 1803	17	light	Providence, R. I.	2	48
Westcott, Thomas	May 8, 1805 .	21	light	Providence, R. I.	3	44

REGISTER OF SEAMEN'S PROTECTION

NAME	DATE OF CERTIFICATION	AGE	COMPLEXION	PLACE OF BIRTH	BOOK	PAGE
Westcott, Thomas	Oct. 5, 1801	17	light	Providence, R. I.	2	37
Westcott, Valorus R.	Oct. 29, 1849	19	light	Scituate, R. I.	5	87
Westcott, William	June 17, 1797	25	light	Providence, R. I.	1	26
Westcott, William	Dec. 22, 1824	25	light	Warwick, R. I.	4	77
Westcott, William A.	Feb. 20, 1845	18	light	Penobscot, Maine	5	86
Westgate, Charles Wesgate	Aug. 23, 1800	20	dark	Cranston, R. I.	2	29
Westland, Charles	June 27, 1854	22	light	Manhattanville, NY	5	95
Weston, Frederick	Nov. 24, 1845	24	light	Saugerties, New York	5	86
Weston, Frederick	Aug. 2, 1850	26	light	East Greenwich, R. I.	5	88
Weston, William	Jan. 20, 1860	30	light	New York, N. Y.	6	23
Wethby, George W.	Nov. 13, 1821	16	light	Providence, R. I.	4	77
Wethby, Thomas W.	July 9, 1822	23	light	Providence, R. I.	4	77
Wetherell, Edward	Jan. 8, 1845	18	dark	Mansfield, Mass.	5	86
Weymouth, George	Feb. 14, 1866	20	dark	Portville, N. Y.	6	23
Whalen, Benjamin	Oct. 3, 1823	23	dark	Belfast, Mass.	4	77
Whaley, George W.	Dec. 9, 1836	22	light	So. Kingston, R. I.	5	84
Whally, Samuel	Sept. 25, 1855	25	florid	Philadelphia, Penn.	5	95
Wharff, Abraham	March 20, 1809	20	florid	Gloucester, Mass.	4	74
Wharton, Hiram	Dec. 2, 1854	21	light	Bangor, Maine	5	95
Wharton, John B.	July 13, 1863	23	dark	Sussex Co., Del.	6	23
Wheaton, Benjamin, Jr.	Aug. 29, 1801	14	dark	Providence, R. I.	2	29
Wheaton, Benjamin, Jr.	March 17, 1809	21	dark	Providence, R. I.	4	74
Wheaton, David Alexander	July 5, 1844	19	black	Lisbon, Conn.	5	86
Wheaton, George B.	May 9, 1845	15	light	Providence, R. I.	5	86
Wheaton, George H.	Feb. 10, 1849	39	dark	Seekonk, Mass.	5	86
Wheaton, Mason	Nov. 15, 1817	20	dark	Providence, R. I.	4	75
Wheaton, Sylvester	May 12, 1834	29	light	Smithfield, R. I.	5	83

NAME	DATE OF CERTIFICATION	AGE	COMPLEXION	PLACE OF BIRTH	BOOK	P.
Wheeler, Bristol	Dec. 24, 1810	33	black	Stonington, Conn.	4	7
Wheeler, Calvin	Nov. 4, 1799	17	light	Rehoboth, Mass.	2	2
Wheeler, Dennis	Dec. 24, 1805	17	light	Augusta, Maine	3	4
Wheeler, Edward R.	Oct. 31, 1849	23	florid	Seekonk, Mass.	5	8
Wheeler, Frederick A.	Nov. 23, 1849	28	light	Fall River, Mass.	5	8
Wheeler, Jencks	Aug. 17, 1797	25	dark	Rehoboth, Mass.	1	2
Wheeler, Jeroise	Nov. 28, 1806	32	florid	Rehoboth, Mass.	4	7
Wheeler, John .	Nov. 11, 1803	22	light	Providence, R. I.	2	4
Wheeler, Phillip	July 9, 1821	22	light	Rehoboth, Mass. b. June 21, 179		
Sworn statement of Israel Pearce of Rehoboth in Custom House Papers.						
Wheeler, Robert	July 10, 1846	27	fair	Baltimore, Md.	5	8
Wheeler, Samuel	May 26, 1809	20	dark	Brookline, Conn.	4	7
Wheeler, William H.	Feb. 10, 1816	15	brown	Glocester, R. I.	4	7
Wheelock, Calvin	Aug. 8, 1811	33	brown	Sturbridge, Mass.	4	7
Whelden, Charles C.	Sept. 1, 1854	19	light	Providence, R. I.	5	9
Whelden, Charles M.	Sept. 11, 1849	28	light	Boston, Mass.	5	8
Whelden, John T.	June 29, 1820	20	dark	Edgartown, Mass.	4	7
Whelden, Samuel	June 5, 1843	18	light	Boston, Mass.	5	8
Whelden, Seth	Jan. 26, 1829	21	light	Brewster, Mass.	5	8
Whipple, Albert A.	Sept. 4, 1849	20	light	North Providence, R. I.	5	8
Whipple, Amos	March 28, 1800	17	light	Cumberland, R. I.	2	2
Whipple, Caleb R.	Oct. 18, 1827	20	dark	Johnston, R. I.	4	7
Whipple, Charles	Sept. 30, 1796	22	dark	New London, Conn.	2	4
Whipple, Charles	March 18, 1811	14	light	North Providence, R. I.	4	7
Whipple, George	Nov. 22, 1849	25	light	Foster, R. I.	5	8
Whipple, George W.	Nov. 9, 1797	21	dark	Providence, R. I.	1	2
Whipple, George W.	Sept. 21, 1801	25	light	Smithfield, R. I.	2	3
Whipple, Henry	Oct. 28, 1803	19	light	Providence, R. I.	2	4

NAME	DATE OF CERTIFICATION	AGE	COMPLEXION	PLACE OF BIRTH	BOOK	PAGE
Whipple, Henry	Dec. 15, 1800	15	light	Providence, R. I.	2	29
Whipple, James	Feb. 24, 1806	19	dark	Cumberland, R. I.	3	48
Whipple, James L.	Sept. 22, 1818	20	yellow	Norwich, Conn.	4	77
Whipple, Jenckes	May 2, 1799	17	light	Providence, R. I.	2	21
Whipple, Jeremiah	July 7, 1798	21	light	Providence, R. I.	2	21
Whipple, Jeremiah	Jan. 4, 1805	24	light	Providence, R. I.	3	42
Whipple, John	March 27, 1805	27	light	Warwick, R. I.	3	43
Whipple, Joseph	May 16, 1803	17	light	Providence, R. I.	2	37
Whipple, Joseph	Nov. 6, 1805	20	light	Providence, R. I.	3	47
Whipple, Joseph B.	Oct. 13, 1845	19	light	Cumberland, R. I.	5	86
Whipple, Joseph C.	Nov. 12, 1805	25	light	Providence, R. I.	3	47
Whipple, Loury	Sept. 4, 1849	22	light	Warwick, R. I.	5	87
Whipple, Olney	April 23, 1811	23	light	Smithfield, R. I.	4	75
Whipple, Robert	Nov. 5, 1805	16	light	Cumberland, R. I.	3	47
Whipple, Smith	May 2, 1815	20	light	Glocester, R. I.	4	75
Whipple, Stephen	March 29, 1800	35	light	North Providence, R. I.	2	29
Whitaker, Thos. H.	Nov. 11, 1841	21	dark	Smithfield, R. I.	5	85
Whitaker, Asa Whillichur, Asa	Nov. 21, 1797	24	light	Rehoboth, Mass.	1	29
Whitaker, Asa	1798 to 1799	b. Apr. 14, 1779		Rehoboth, Mass.	Newport, R.I.	
Whitaker, Joseph	Dec. 16, 1800	18	light	Bristol, R. I.	2	29
Whitaker, Levi	Sept. 17, 1845	31	dark	Cape May, N. J.	5	86
White, Alfred	July 8, 1839	16	light	New Bedford, Mass.	5	85
White, Avery	Dec. 27, 1832	38	black	Bridgewater, Mass.	5	83
White, Charles	Dec. 10, 1841	16	light	Boston, Mass.	5	85
White, Dan	Dec. 19, 1800	15	light	Smithfield, R. I.	2	29
White, Dan	March 9, 1804	18	light	Smithfield, R. I.	3	41
White, Elisha	June 2, 1809	18	light	Windham, Conn.	4	74

NAME	DATE OF CERTIFICATION	AGE	COMPLEXION	PLACE OF BIRTH	BOOK	PAG
White, Enoch	Jan. 4, 1819	25	ruddy	Stoughton, Mass.	4	77
White, Francis	June 17, 1854	21	light	Ashford, Conn.	5	95
White, George	Sept. 6, 1803	21	light	Boston, Mass.	2	37
White, George N.	Feb. 14, 1850	24	light	South Kingston, R. I.	5	88
White, Geo. W.	June 28, 1841	20	light	Concord, N. H.	5	85
White, Henry	Aug. 21, 1837	31	dark	Baltimore, Md.	5	84
White, Herbert D.	Aug. 1, 1864	14	light	Boston, Mass.	6	23
White, James M. (Wight)	June 4, 1839	20	dark	Providence, R. I.	5	85
White, John	Oct. 11, 1834	42	black	Newport, R. I.	5	84
White, John W.	Nov. 18, 1803	19	light	Providence, R. I.	2	48
White, John W.	June 3, 1797	12	light	Providence, R. I.	1	26
White, Joseph	March 25, 1828	28	black	Smithfield, R. I.	4	78
White, Joseph	Nov. 21, 1835	30	black	Baltimore, Md.	5	84
White, Joseph	July 17, 1855	19	fair	Calais, Maine	5	95
White, Keith	Oct. 6, 1807	25	light	Uxbridge, Mass.	4	74
White, Lemuel	Nov. 4, 1818	25	dark	Wareham, Mass.	4	77
White, Nathan M.	Apr. 4, 1863	22	light	New Bedford, Mass.	6	23
White, Paul C.	March 1, 1849	25	fair	Berkley, Mass.	5	87
White, Stephen N.	Sept. 10, 1864	35	light	Woonsocket, R. I.	6	23
White, Thomas W.	Aug. 24, 1837	18	light	Boston, Mass.	5	85
White, Timothy	Dec. 12, 1831	24	light	Mansfield, Mass.	5	83
White, Welcome F.	July 3, 1850	19	light	Blackstone, Mass.	5	88
White, William	Dec. 15, 1800	13	light	Providence, R. I.	2	29
White, William	July 8, 1839	18	light	Lowell, Mass.	5	85
White, William F.	Sept. 5, 1842	17	light	Rochest, N. Y.	5	85
White, William H.	June 28, 1836	23	light	Bridgeville, Delaware	5	84
Whitehouse, Daniel	Dec. 7, 1826	21	light	North Kingstown, R. I.	4	78

REGISTER OF SEAMEN'S PROTECTION

NAME	DATE OF CERTIFICATION	AGE	COMPLEXION	PLACE OF BIRTH	BOOK	PAGE
Whitfield, Daniel C.	August 22, 1845	24	fair	Newark, N. J.	5	86
Whitfield, Thomas	Sept. 14, 1825	11	light	New York, N. Y.	4	77
Whitefield, Wm.	1798 to 1799	b.	1782	Nantucket, Mass.	Newport, R. I.	
Whitford, Casey	Feb. 7, 1797	25	light	Warwick, R. I.	1	26
Whiting, Benjamin	July 30, 1841	38	dark	Plymouth, Mass.	5	85
Whiting, Cyprian	June 29, 1837	20	light	Douglas, Mass.	5	84
Whiting, David	June 2, 1823	24	light	Providence, R. I.	4	77
Whiting, Gideon	Nov. 16, 1809	17	brown	Providence, R. I.	4	74
Whiting, James A.	Feb. 28, 1856	21	dark	North Kingston, R. I.	5	95
Whiting, Samuel C.	Oct. 10, 1810	20	dark	Providence, R. I.	4	75
Whiting, Samuel S.	Oct. 29, 1849	30	light	East Greenwich, R. I.	5	87
Whitman, George	July 22, 1809	17	light	Preston, Conn.	4	74
Whitman, Henry	May 21, 1829	23	black	Providence, R. I.	5	83
Whitman, Jacob, Jr.	June 7, 1810	15	dark	Providence, R. I.	4	75
Whitman, James	Aug. 30, 1826	30	light	Providence, R. I.	4	77
Whitman, Joseph	Apr. 8, 1805	22	light	So. Kingstown, R. I.	3	43
Whitman, Joseph	June 9, 1807	23	light	So. Kingstown, R. I.	4	74
Whitman, Prince	Dec. 28, 1796	22	black	Providence, R. I.	1	26
Whitmarsh, Holmes	Feb. 14, 1806	16	light	Dighton, Mass.	3	48
Whitmarsh, William	Oct. 13, 1841	36	light	Plymouth, Mass.	5	85
Whitney, Charles R.	Nov. 11, 1830	22	light	Lexington, Mass.	5	83
Whitney, Frederick A. L.	Nov. 30, 1841	18	dark	Boston, Mass.	5	85
Whitney, Henry	Jan. 10, 1801	19	dark	Warwick, R. I.	2	29
Whitney, Hercules	Nov. 25, 1797	20	light	Warwick, R. I.	1	29
Whitney, James	July 29, 1803	18	dark	Warwick, R. I.	2	37
Whitney, Joseph	Sept. 10, 1803	31	dark	Warwick, R. I.	2	37
Whitney, Lemuel	Aug. 7, 1800	22	dark	Providence, R. I.	2	29

REGISTER OF SEAMEN'S PROTECTION

NAME	DATE OF CERTIFICATION	AGE	COMPLEXION	PLACE OF BIRTH	BOOK	PAGE
Whitney, Thomas	Apr. 25, 1806	17	dark	Warwick, R. I.	3	48
Whittemore, Edward	Dec. 12, 1826	24	light	Dennis, Mass.	4	78
Whittey, James	Oct. 22, 1833	16	light	Philadelphia, Penn.	5	83
Whittekey, Stephen	1798 to 1799	b. Apr. 2, 1779		Saybrook, Conn.	Newport, R
Whittier, Joseph H.	July 19, 1841	20	light	Bangor, Maine	5	85
Whittington, William	Dec. 7, 1853	19	fair	New York, N. Y.	5	88
Wickes, Alvan	Dec. 25, 1830	19	light	Warwick, R. I.	5	83
Wicks, Charles	March 3, 1810	28	black	Philadelphia, Pa.	4	75
Wickes, Job. H.	Oct. 17, 1835	18	black	Warwick, R. I.	5	84
Wickes, Oliver A.	April 8, 1841	20	light	East Greenwich, R. I.	5	85
Wickes, Powers	Nov. 9, 1798	25	dark	Coventry, R. I.	1	26
Wickes, Samuel	Dec. 3, 1805	23	black	Warwick, R. I.	3	47
Wickes, William	Oct. 24, 1835	20	mulatto	Warwick, R. I.	5	84
Widger, Thomas	April 24, 1834	23	dark	Salem, Mass.	5	83
Wight, James M.	June 4, 1839	20	dark	Providence, R. I.	5	85
Wight, Moses	Sept. 30, 1796	27	dark	Cranston, R. I.	2	4
Wight, Timothy	March 6, 1838	29	light	Vienna, Maine	5	85
Wightman, Philip R.	Nov. 5, 1849	18	light	Warren, R. I.	5	87
Wightman, Samuel	Dec. 3, 1796	24	light	Rehoboth, Mass.	1	26
Wilber, Benjamin	July 5, 1810	20	light	Johnston, R. I.	4	75
Welbour, Benj.	Nov. 27, 1844	51	dark	Little Compton, R. I.	5	86
Wilbour, Charles	DEc. 21, 1843	22	dark	Taunton, Mass.	5	85
Wilbour, Ezekiel	1798 to 1799	(certificate)		Little Compton, R. I.	Newport,
Wilbour, James	Aug. 3, 1810	25	light	Freetown, Mass.	4	75
Wilbur, John	Feb. 7, 1801	17	dark	Providence, R. I.	2	29
Wilbur, John	Dec. 10, 1803	20	light	Providence, R. I.	2	20
Wilbur, Peleg N.	Jan. 1, 1835.	15	light	Warwick, R. I.	5	84

NAME	DATE OF CERTIFICATION	AGE	COMPLEXION	PLACE OF BIRTH	BOOK	PAGE
Welbour, Solomon	Jan. 18, 1848	31	light	Little Compton, R. I.	5	86
Wilbur, Thomas B.	Aug. 31, 1849	32	light	Warwick, R. I.	5	87
Wilber, Wanton	May 20, 1811	18	light	South Kingstown, R. I.	4	75
Wilbour, William	Oct. 1, 1819	28	light	Scituate, R. I.	4	77
Wilbur, William R.	Aug. 31, 1849	26	light	Warwick, R. I.	5	87
Wilcox, Bishop T.	Oct. 29, 1849	23	light	Griswold, Conn.	5	87
Wilcox, Christopher G.	Nov. 7, 1854	17	light	East Greenwich, R. I.	5	95
Wilcox, Daniel	1798 to 1799	b. Sept. 9, 1778		Westport, Mass.	Newport, R. I.	
Wilcox, Gardner	April 21, 1819	38	light	Exeter, R. I.	4	77
Willcox, George	Aug. 7, 1845	38	dark	Yonkers, New York	5	86
Wilcox, Isaac	Aug. 6, 1796	21	dark	Middlesex County, Va.	1	1
Wilcox, James L.	Nov. 27, 1832	22	light	Providence, R. I.	5	83
Wilcox, Jonathan B. S.	July 6, 1849	23	light	Exeter, R. I.	5	87
Wilcox, Leander	Nov. 5, 1849	24	light	So. Kingston, R. I.	5	87
Wilcox, Leonard	Oct. 10, 1797	22	light	Richmond, R. I.	1	28
Wilcox, Nathaniel	March 27, 1827	19	light	Tiverton, R. I.	4	78
Wilcox, Niel	Aug. 6, 1830	26	black	Charlestown, R. I.	5	83
Wilcox, Oliver	1798 to 1799	b. Sept. 9, 1798		Tiverton, R. I.	Newport, R. I.	
Wilcox, Samuel Son of Wm. and Mary	1798 to 1799			Tiverton, R. I.?	Newport, R. I.	
Wilcox, Samuel	Dec. 15, 1807	24	light	East Greenwich, R. I.	4	74
Wilcox, Samuel	Sept. 26, 1854	22	light	Uxbridge, Mass.	5	95
Wilcox, Stephen	1798 to 1799	b. July 4, 1771		Portsmouth, R. I.	Newport, R. I.	
Wilcox, Thomas O.	Nov. 20, 1863	33	light	Westerly, R. I.	6	23
Wilcox, William	Aug. 4, 1796	19	dark	East Greenwich, R. I.	1	1
Wilcox, William	May 15, 1849	35	light	Warwick, R. I.	5	87
Wilcox, William B.	Oct. 23, 1857	20	fair	Westerly, R. I.	6	23

NAME	DATE OF CERTIFICATION	AGE	COMPLEXION	PLACE OF BIRTH	BOOK	PAG
Wilcox, Wm. H.(Wilson?)	July 20, 1841	35	light	Providence, R. I.	5	8
Wilder, Stephen	Nov. 8, 1809	26	light	Glocester, R. I.	4	7
Wildman, Francis B.	Sept. 28, 1868	19	light	Providence, R. I.	6	2
Wiley, Charles	June 25, 1849	23	light	Savannah, Georgia	5	8
Wiley, Simon R.	Dec. 22, 1859	28	fair	Cushing, Me.	6	2
Wilkey, Henry B.	April 20, 1829	19	light	Newport, R. I.	5	8
Wilkins, Adrian W.	Oct. 11, 1856	23	light	Middleton, Mass.	5	9
Wilkins, John	Sept. 3, 1835	19	light	New York, N. Y.	5	8
Wilkinson, Alexander	July 24, 1849	21	light	North Stonington, Conn.	5	8
Wilkinson, David	April 7, 1804	24	light	Cumberland, R. I.	3	4
Wilkinson, Edward	Feb. 24, 1849	19	light	North Providence, R. I.	5	8
Wilkinson, William	Nov. 21, 1805	18	light	Providence, R. I.	3	4
Will, Jehn	Sept. 13, 1796	25	dark	Charleston, R. I.	1	3
Will, John	May 26, 1802	32	dark	Charleston, R. I.	2	3
Willard, Curtis E.	Feb. 28, 1849	26	light	Keene, N. H.	5	8
Willard, John	Aug. 22, 1845	25	black	New York, N. Y.	5	8
Willard, Luke	Feb. 22, 1805	25	light	Grafton, Mass.	3	4
Willard, Samuel	Nov. 10, 1825	24	dark	Worcester, Mass.	4	7
Willey, John Jr.	July 20, 1805	16	dark	Providence, R. I.	3	4
Willey, Josiah	Apr. 8, 1809	14	light	Boston, Mass.	4	7
Willey, Mathew K.	Oct. 24, 1856	22	fair	Friendship, Maine	5	9
Williams, Abel	Dec. 11, 1849	27	mulatto	Boston, Mass.	4	8
Williams, Alfred	Sept. 21, 1835	24	dark	Lynn, Mass.	5	8
Williams, Alfred	July 15, 1850	26	mulatto	Providence, R. I.	5	8
Williams, Alfred P.	Dec. 29, 1845	40	black	New London, Conn.	5	8
Williams, Amasa	Sept. 22, 1818	25	yellow	Canton, Mass.	4	7
Williams, Andrew	Aug. 13, 1806	28	light	Albany, N.Y.	3	8

NAME	DATE OF CERTIFICATION	AGE	COMPLEXION	PLACE OF BIRTH	BOOK	PAGE
Williams, Andrew	July 29, 1835	25	dark	Middlebury, Vermont	5	84
Williams, Anthony	March 26, 1849	28	dark	Mobile, Alabama	5	87
Williams, Arthur	March 11, 1799	22	light	Cranston, R. I.	2	21
Williams, Augustus	June 26, 1801	15	light	North Providence, R. I.	2	29
Williams, Caleb	May 4, 1805	21	light	Cranston, R. I.	3	44
Williams, Caleb	Apr. 3, 1817	20	light	Providence, R. I.	4	75
Williams, Casper	Feb. 1, 1804	34	dark	Flatbush, N. Y.	3	41
Williams, Charles John Williams swears for him.	1798 to 1799	b. Dec. 2, 1774		Newport, R. I.	Newport, R. I.	
Williams, Charles	March 18, 1809	22	yellow	New Brunswick, N. J.	4	74
Williams, Charles	Oct. 30, 1821	23	black	Providence, R. I.	4	77
Williams, Charles	Dec. 30, 1834	27	black	Boston, Mass.	5	84
Williams, Charles	July 20, 1835	22	yellow	Providence, R. I.	5	84
Williams, Charles	Dec. 4, 1835	15	black	Warren, R. I.	5	84
Williams, Charles	July 23, 1853	33	yellow	Providence, R. I.	5	88
Williams, Charles	June 17, 1862	30	black	Alabama	6	23
Williams, Chareles A.	June 9, 1856	31	dark	Edgecomb, Maine	5	95
Williams, Charles C.	July 1, 1861	19	brown	Providence, R. I.	6	23
Williams, Charles H.	Sept. 4, 1849	29	light	North Providence, R. I.	5	87
Williams, Cornelius	Jan. 9, 1839	19	dark	Boston, Mass.	5	85
Williams, Daniel	Oct. 9, 1810	27	yellow	Stoughton, Mass.	4	75
Williams, Daniel	Jan. 31, 1832	25	light	Weatherfield, Conn.	5	83
Williams, Edward	Dec. 14, 1798	17	light	Cranston, R. I.	2	21
Williams, Edward	Nov. 10, 1860	22	dark	Dennisville, N. J.	6	23
Williams, Edward B.	Feb. 27, 1849	26	light	Newport, R. I.	5	87
Williams, Edward M.	July 20, 1847	18	dark	Providence, R. I.	5	86
Williams, Elijah	Aug. 15, 1823	23	dark	Norwich, Conn.	4	77
Williams, Francis	Sept. 3, 1840	22	light	Alexandria, D. of C.	5	85

NAME	DATE OF CERTIFICATION	AGE	COMPLEXION	PLACE OF BIRTH	BOOK	PA
Williams, Frederick	March 18, 1864	22	light	Stonington, Conn.	6	2
Wioliams, Frederick W.	April 23, 1855	36	light	Norfork, N. H.	5	9
Williams, Gardner	June 16, 1809	23	black	Dighton, Mass.	4	7
Williams, Gaspart	Apr. 22, 1809	38	dark	Albany, N. Y.	4	7
Williams, George	1798 to 1799	b. June 1, 1775		Portsmouth, N. H.	Newport, R
Williams, George	June 22, 1798	22	dark	Moscow, Russia	2	2
Williams, George . having been settled in the United States prior to 3rd of Sept, 1803.	June 23, 1809	32	brown	Moscow, Russia	4	7
Williams, George	Feb. 29, 1820	20	black	East Greenwich, R. I.	4	7
Williams, George	May 13, 1840	22	light	Prospect, Maine	5	8
Williams, George	July 10, 1845	22	black	New York, New York	5	8
Williams, George H.	July 23, 1841	26	mulatto	New York, N. Y.	5	8
Williams, Henry	Oct. 29, 1800	16	light	Barre, Mass.	2	2
Williams, Henry	Jan. 4, 1805	20	light	Barre, Mass.	3	4
Williams, Henry	Aug. 13, 1833	19	yellow	Providence, R. I.	5	8
Williams, Henry	July 30, 1836	20	black	Philadelphia, Penn.	5	8
Williams, Henry	Nov. 5, 1838	23	dark	Boston, Mass.	5	8
Williams, Henry H.	Sept. 14, 1812	16	dark	Providence, R. I.	4	7
Williams, Isaac	Oct. 22, 1834	15	black	Providence, R. I.	5	8
Williams, Jacob	Jan. 22, 1800	25	black	New York, N. Y.	2	2
Williams, James	June 1, 1809	14	light	Brookline, Conn.	4	7
Williams, James	Sept. 12, 1835	27	dark	New London, Conn.	5	8
Williams, James	March 15, 1849	20	light	Hartford, Conn.	5	8
Williams, James Henry	Oct. 25, 1843	27	black	Boston, Mass.	5	8
Williams, Jeremiah	Sept. 4, 1797	35	dark	Cranston, R. I.	1	2
Williams, Jethniel	Oct. 6, 1824	22	dark	Wellington, Mass.	4	7
Williams, John	Aug. 24, 1798	19	light	East Greenwich, R. I.	2	2
Williams, John	Apr. 4, 1799	34	dark	Bucks County, Pa.	2	2

NAME	DATE OF CERTIFICATION	AGE	COMPLEXION	PLACE OF BIRTH	BOOK	PAGE
Williams, John	August 27, 1804	27	black	New York, N. Y.	3	42
Williams, John	May 19, 1806	13	light	Providence, R. I.	3	48
Williams, John	June 17, 1806	26	light	Worcester, Mass.	3	48
Williams, John	Sept. 18, 1809	16	light	Providence, R. I.	4	74
Williams, John	Dec. 6, 1819	24	yellow	Cranston, R. I.	4	77
Williams, John	Nov. 10, 1823	19	black	Providence, R. I.	4	77
Williams, John	June 24, 1830	23	dark	New York, N. Y.	5	83
Williams, John	May 5, 1830	15	light	Weathersfield, Conn.	5	83
Williams, John	Oct. 22, 1832	42	black	Scituate, R. I.	5	83
Williams, John	May 21, 1833	27	dark	Northfield, Conn.	5	83
Williams, John	May 21, 1833	25	ruddy	Boston, Mass.	5	83
William, John	Dec. 11, 1833	37	light	Middletown, Conn.	5	83
Williams, John	Oct. 7, 1834	35	dark	Boston, Mass.	5	84
Williams, John	Oct. 9, 1835	22	black	Boston, Mass.	5	84
Williams, John	June 1, 1837	37	dark	Baltimore, Maryland	5	84
Williams, John	June 29, 1837	23	light	Baltimore, Maryland	5	84
Williams, John	June 26, 1839	23	black	Brooklyn, New York	5	85
Williams, John	Aug. 5, 1839	25	dark	New York, New York	5	85
Williams, John	Oct. 18, 1841	21	light	Boston, Mass.	5	85
Williams, John	July 25, 1842	20	dark	Cranston, R. I.	5	85
Williams, John	Aug. 6, 1850	24	light	Eastport, Maine	5	88
Williams, John	Jan. 16, 1851	35	light	Reading, Penn.	5	88
Williams, John	April 12, 1852	23	dark	Weymouth, Mass.	5	88
Williams, John A.	Sept. 19, 1835	19	black	Providence, R. I.	5	84
Williams, John C.	April 17, 1854	25	light	New York, N. Y.	5	95
Williams, John G.	June 21, 1845	18	light	Providence, R. I.	5	86
Williams, John H.	March 12, 1833	19	black	Providence, R. I.	5	83

NAME	DATE OF CERTIFICATION	AGE	COMPLEXION	PLACE OF BIRTH	BOOK	PAG
Williams, Joseph	Aug. 30, 1836	60	dark	Newton, Mass.	5	8
Williams, Joseph	Oct. 15, 1849	27	dark	New Bedford, Mass.	5	8
Williams, Joseph	Oct. 22, 1849	20	dark	Warren, R. I.	5	8
Williams, Oliver C.	Nov. 17, 1849	27	light	North Providence, R. I.	5	8
Williams, Perry H.	Nov. 7, 1849	23	light	Johnston, R. I.	5	8
Williams, Peter	April 15, 1850	22	black	Norfolk, Va.	5	8
Williams, Philip	May 10, 1810	33	yellow	Smithfield, R. I.	4	7
Williams, Richard	July 21, 1809	30	black	New York, N. Y.	4	7
Williams, Samuel	Nov. 7, 1836	25	light	Bucksport, Maine	5	8
Williams, Sam'l R.	March 30, 1849	45	fair	Philadelphia, Penn.	5	8
Williams, Solomon S.	Dec. 18, 1824	21	light	Taunton, Mass.	4	7
Williams, Stephen	Oct. 15, 1805	30	black	Elk Forge, Del. (?)	3	4
Williams, Thomas	May 10, 1805	22	dark	Newport, R. I.	3	4
Williams, Thomas	Feb. 20, 1845	25	dark	New York, N. Y.	5	8
Williams, Thomas	Aug. 5, 1862	24	dark	Peacedale, R. I.	6	2
Williams, Timothy	Nov. 1, 1800	20	dark	Providence, R. I.	2	29
Williams, Waterman	Feb. 27, 1804	20	light	North Providence, R. I.	3	4
Williams, William	Feb. 5, 1800	21	black	Johnston, R. I.	2	2
Williams, William	Sept. 5, 1801	25	light	Barrington, R. I.	2	3
Williams, William	Oct. 2, 1801	22	dark	Providence, R. I.	2	3
Williams, William, Jr.	May 26, 1815	26	light	Wrentham, Mass.	4	75
Williams, William	Dec. 12, 1836	27	light	New Castle, Delaware	5	8
Williams, William	Aug. 1, 1844	28	dark	Boston, Mass.	5	8
Williams, William	April 9, 1849	21	black	Newton, Maryland	5	8
Williams, William	Dec. 7, 1853	20	light	Philadelphia, Penn.	5	88
Williamson, George	March 15, 1852	26	fair	Salem, New Jersey	5	88
Williamson, Gustavus	Jan. 31, 1829	27	light	Stockholm, Sweden	5	8
Williamson, William	Sept. 10, 1833	32	dark	Philadelphia, Penn.	5	83

REGISTER OF SEAMEN'S PROTECTION

NAME	DATE OF CERTIFICATION	AGE	COMPLEXION	PLACE OF BIRTH	BOOK	PAGE
Willis, Amasa, Jr.	March 5, 1849	25	light	Boston, Mass.	5	87
Willis, Daniel G.	Dec. 8, 1820	24	light	Lebanon, N. H.	4	77
Willis, Francis	March 16, 1843	17	light	New Shoreham, R. I.	5	85
Willis, George C.	April 24, 1809	23	black	New London, Conn.	4	74
Willis, Samuel	Dec. 4, 1850	21	dark	Philadelphia, Penn.	5	88
Willis, Solomon D.	July 18, 1835	19	dark	New Shoreham, R. I.	5	84
Williston, Darius	Oct. 19, 1827	18	light	Tiverton, R. I.	4	78
Willoby, Weston [Willoughby]	July 12, 1823	19	light	Windham, Conn.	4	77
Wills, Dublin	May 1, 1809	23	black	New York, N. Y.	4	74
Wills, William	Aug. 5, 1806	19	yellowish*	Wethersfield, Conn.	3	80
Wilmarth, Benoni	March 5, 1821	23	brown	Cumberland, R. I.	4	77
Willmarth, Nat	Feb. 8, 1804	19	light	Rehoboth, Mass.	3	41
[Wilmarth] Stephen Willmarth	Oct. 14, 1803	29	light	Glocester, R. I.	2	37
Wilmarth, Timothy, Jr.	Dec. 17, 1803	22	light	Glocester, R. I.	2	19A
Wilmarth, Wm. Henry	Nov. 18, 1848	13	light	Cincinnati, Ohio	5	86
Wilmarth, William H.	Oct. 20, 1855	20	light	Cincinnati, Ohio	5	95
Wilmot, Samuel	Apr. 17, 1820	16	light	Seekonk, Mass.	4	77
Wilson, Benjamin J.	June 14, 1832	28	black	New Haven, Conn.	5	83
Wilson, Casar	Nov. 17, 1836	23	black	Dorchester Co., Md.	5	84
Wilson, Charles	Nov. 9, 1846	26	fair	New York City, N. Y.	5	86
Wilson, Charles	June 4, 1851	20	light	East Greenwich, R. I.	5	88
Wilson, Charles	March 10, 1853	34	light	New York, N. Y.	5	88
Wilson, Charles	May 5, 1954	23	light	Baltimore, Md.	5	95
Wilson, Charles B.	June 6, 1844	17	black	Salem, Mass.	5	86
Wilson, Charles P.	Nov. 2, 1846	23	light	Portland, Maine	5	86
Wilson, Daniel	June 9, 1806	22	light	Boston, Mass.	3	48

*mulatto

NAME	DATE OF CERTIFICATION	AGE	COMPLEXION	PLACE OF BIRTH	BOOK	PAG
Wilson, Donald	Jan. 19, 1854	21	light	Warren, R. I.	5	88
Wilson, Edward	Sept. 7, 1832	23	dark	Boston, Mass.	5	83
Wilson, Francis	Feb. 15, 1855	23	fair	Warwick, R. I.	5	95
Wilson, Frederick	April 1, 1862	28	light	Milbury, Mass.	6	23
Wilson, George	May 1, 1806	21	light	Baltimore, Md.	3	48
Wilson, George	March 23, 1809	22	light	Providence, R. I.	4	74
Wilson, George	Oct. 12, 1829	50	dark	Portsmouth, N. H.	5	83
Wilson, George	March 25, 1835	24	dark	Bristol, R. I.	5	84
Wilson, George	Jan. 9, 1842	21	dark	Richmond, Virginia	5	85
Wilson, George	Dec. 4, 1851	31	light	Ashford, Conn.	5	88
Wilson, Henry	June 3, 1799	24	dark	Princeton, N. J.	2	21
Wilson, Henry	June 12, 1832	24	dark	Killingsworth, Conn.	5	83
Wilson, Henry	Feb. 25, 1845	36	light	New Haven, Conn.	5	86
Wilson, Hnery	Feb. 6, 1846	25	dark	New York City, N. Y.	5	86
Wilson, Henry	Jan. 22, 1847	20	fair	New York City, N. Y.	5	86
Wilson, Henry W.	Oct. 20, 1848	27	light	Reading, Penn.	5	86
Wilson, Hezekiah	Sept. 2, 1845	21	dark	New York, N. Y.	5	86
Wilson Horace	Jan. 11, 1853	27	mulatto	Swedesboro, New Jersey	5	88
Wilson, Jacobs	Sept. 13, 1796	18	light	Providence, R. I.	1	3
Wilson, James	Oct. 5, 1804	19	light	Wilmington, N. C.	3	42
Wilson, James	March 15, 1852	27	sandy	New York, N. Y.	5	88
Wilson, James	June 16, 1862	28	light	Bath, Me.	6	23
Wilson, John	Dec. 2, 1796	29	light	Philadelphia, Pa.	1	26
Wilson, John Willson	Dec. 12, 1800	34	light	Philadelphia, Pa.	2	29
Wilson, John	Oct. 1, 1811	20	light	New York, N. Y.	4	75
Wilson, John	March 30, 1825	22	light	South Kingstown, R. I.	4	77
Wilson, John	Oct. 4, 1833	19	dark	North Providence, R. I.	5	83

REGISTER OF SEAMEN'S PROTECTION

NAME	DATE OF CERTIFICATION	AGE	COMPLEXION	PLACE OF BIRTH	BOOK	PAGE
Wilson, John	March 21, 1840	38	freckled	Londonderry, N. H.	5	85
Wilson, JOhn	Sept. 10, 1844	31	dark	Belfast, Maine	5	86
Wilson, John	June 2, 1856	22	light	Providence, R. I.	5	95
Wilson, John	March 8, 1853	28	light	New York, N. Y.	5	88
Wilson, JOhn Jr.	Aug. 14, 1832	31	light	Boston, Mass.	5	83
Wilson, Josiah	Dec. 13, 1822	21	light	Mendon, Mass.	4	77
Wilson, Joseph	Nov. 28, 1857	26	dark	Fayal	5	95
Wilson, Joseph B.	April 10, 1858	27	dark	Great Britain	6	23
Wilson, Laurance	March 9, 1805	21	light	Providence, R. I.	3	43
Wilson, Matthew	1798 to 1799 b. Dec. 1 or 5, 1776			Bridgewater, Mass.	Newport, R. I.	
Wilson, Michal	July 13, 1805	28	dark	South Kingstown, R. I.	3	44
Wilson, Peter	Feb. 24, 1852	22	light	Charlestown, Mass.	5	88
Wilson, Robert	Dec. 5, 1836	49	black	Belfast, Penn.	5	84
Wilson, Robert Clark	June 6, 1799	15	light	New York, N. Y.	2	21
Wilson, Samuel	May 16, 1799	37	dark	Bristol, R. I.	2	21
Wilson, Sam'l	June 16, 1856	31	light	Calais, Maine	5	95
Wilson, Thomas	Nov. 18, 1831	22	light	POrtsmouth, N. H.	5	83
Wilson, Thomas	Sept. 12, 1836	24	sallow	Frederickville, Va.	5	84
Wilson, William	Dec. 16, 1803	26	dark	Weymouth, Mass.	2	20
Wilson, William	June 22, 1804	23	light	Providence, R. I.	3	41
Wilson, William	Jan. 10, 1806	25	dark	Providence, R. I.	3	48
Wilson, William	March 6, 1801	20	dark	Providence, R. I.	2	29
Wilson, William	March 4, 1797	33	dark	Swansea, Mass.	1	26
Wilson, William	Jan. 29, 1798	18	black	Baltimore, Md.	1	28
Wilson, William	Nov. 13, 1835	22	dark	Providence, R. I.	5	84
Wilson, William	March 31, 1836	21	dark	Dauphin Co., Penn.	5	84
Wilson, William	July 17, 1839	27	Indian	New York, N. Y.	5	85

NAME	DATE OF CERTIFICATION	AGE	COMPLEXION	PLACE OF BIRTH	BOOK	PAGE
Wilson, William	April 20, 1857	33	light	Boston, Mass.	5	95
Wilson, William	Nov. 10, 1860	22	light	New York, N. Y.	6	23
Willson, Wm. A.	Aug. 5, 1853	22	dark	South Kingston, R. I.	5	88
Wilson, Wm. D.	Nov. 22, 1851	24	dark	Apalachicola, Florida	5	88
Wilson, Wm. H. (or Wilcox)	July 20, 1841	35	light	Providence, R. I.	5	85
Wing, Benjamin	Nov. 11, 1818	17	dark	Rochester, Mass.	4	77
Wing, Clifton	Oct. 14, 1809	13	brown	Rochester, Mass.	4	74
Wing, Ebenezer	Oct. 25, 1803	13	light	Sandwich, Mass.	2	37
Wing, Ira	June 22, 1841	21	light	Lubec, Maine	5	85
Wing, Jerome Langley	June 4, 1824	13	light	Ware, N. H.	4	77
Wing, John	Nov. 1, 1803	26	light	Rehoboth, Mass.	2	48
Wing, Luin	Aug. 11, 1796	22	light	Rochester, Mass.	1	1
Wing, Paul	Oct. 28, 1807	15	light	Rochester, Mass.	4	74
Wing, Stephen	Oct. 11, 1806	23	light	Sandwich, Mass.	4	74
Wingate, John D.	Aug. 10, 1857	16	fair	Cheraw, S. C.	6	23
Winn, Michael	Nov. 20, 1800	20	dark	Sandwich, Mass.	2	29
Winman, Philip	June 4, 1805	44	light	West Greenwich, R. I.	3	44
Winman, Phillip	Feb. 17, 1797	36	light	West Greenwich, R. I.	1	26
Winn, Sam'l	Sept. 11, 1856	20	light	Brooklyn, N. Y.	5	95
Winslow, Asa	Apr. 27, 1804	16	light	North Providence, R. I.	3	41
Winslow, Assea	Dec. 19, 1821	21	fair	Troy [Fall River] Mass.b. July 25,18		
Sworn statement of Oliver Whitewell of Troy in the Custom House Papers.						
Winslow, Francis B.	Oct. 10, 1834	21	light	Swansea, Mass.	5	84
Winslow, Frederick	July 5, 1798	22	light	Freetown, Mass.	2	21
Winslow, George H.	Nov. 2, 1858	20	dark	Assonett, Mass.	6	23
Winslow, Gilbert	June 5, 1797	23	dark	Bristol, R. I.	1	26
Winslow, Godfrey	June 1, 1798	17	light	Freetown, Mass.	2	21

NAME	DATE OF CERTIFICATION	AGE	COMPLEXION	PLACE OF BIRTH	BOOK	PAGE
Winslow, Godfrey	July 20, 1803	22	light	Freeetown, Mass.	2	37
Winslow, Godfrey	May 7, 1810	29	light	Providence, R. I.	4	75
Winslow, Henry	Jan. 11, 1804	20	light	Swansea, Mass.	3	41
Winslow, Henry	Oct. 2, 1844	25	light	Livermore, Maine	5	86
Winslow, Henry B.	June 9, 1804	21	light	Swansea, Mass.	3	41
Winslow, Jeremiah	Nov. 23, 1798	21	light	Somerset, Mass.	2	21
Winslow, Jery	Sept. 13, 1800	23	light	Swansea, Mass.	2	29
Winslow, Job.	Jan. 12, 1801	18	light	Dighton, Mass.	2	29
Winslow, Richard H.	Jan. 18, 1826	17	light	Providence, R. I.	4	77
Winslow, Samuel	Nov. 23, 1798	16	dark	Pomfret, Conn.	2	21
Winslow, Samuel	July 23, 1803	21	dark	Pomfret, Conn.	2	37
Winslow, Thos. H.	June 18, 1852	29	light	Fall River, Mass.	5	88
Winslow, William	Jan. 17, 1838	21	light	Providence, R. I.	5	85
Winslow, Wm. S.	July 16, 1850	21	light	New York, N. Y.	5	88
Winsor, Emor [Enos?]	Nov. 16, 1803	30	light	Glocester, R. I.	2	48
Winsor, Emmor	July 31, 1799	24	light	Glocester, R. I.	2	21
Winsor, Ira B.	March 25, 1825	20	light	Providence, R. I.	-	-
Winsor, Obil A.	Dec. 7, 1810	19	light	Rehoboth, Mass.	4	75
Winsor, William B.	April 24, 1812	18	brown	Rehoboth, Mass.	4	75
Wirling, William	Jan. 12, 1831	25	dark	Salem, Mass.	5	83
Wirling, Wm. E.	June 20, 1855	18	dark	Providence, R. I.	5	95
Wirts, John P.	June 4, 1832	21	dark	Baltimore, Md.	5	83
Wise, George	Dec. 13, 1845	19	fair	New York City, N. Y.	5	86
Wise, John	Sept. 7, 1852	32	black	New York, N. Y.	5	88
Wise, Moses G.	Nov. 13, 1826	34	dark	Hebron, New Hampshire	4	77
Wisewell, James	1798 to 1799 [certificate]			Tiverton, R. I.	Newport, R. I.	
Witchlow, Charles	April 3, 1861	21	dark	New York, N. Y.	6	23

NAME	DATE OF CERTIFICATION	AGE	COMPLEXION	PLACE OF BIRTH	BOOK	PAG
Witherell, Edward	Dec. 6, 1853	27	fair	Providence, R. I.	5	8
Witherell, Russell	Aug. 22, 1845	19	dark	Mansfield, Mass.	5	8
Witter, John	Jan. 4, 1848	17	light	Woodstock, Conn.	5	8
Wood, Allen	March 10, 1797	23	light	Norwich, Conn.	1	2
Wood, Andrew	Sept. 4, 1849	61	light	East Greenwich, R. I.	5	8
Wood, Charles	Aug. 30, 1853	23	light	Providence, R. I.	5	8
Wood, Charles Henry	Aug. 2, 1848	20	dark	Mendon, Mass.	5	8
Wood, Ebenezer	Nov. 2, 1810	14	light	Rochester, Mass.	4	7
Wood, Edgar B.	April 13, 1854	16	light	Providence, R. I.	5	9
Wood, Edward S.	Oct. 28, 1834	24	dark	Westerly, R. I.	5	8
Wood, George	July 29, 1806	19	light	Swansea, Mass.	3	8
Wood, George D.	July 8, 1839	30	light	Chester, N. H.	5	8
Wood, George H.	Dec. 4, 1858	18	light	Providence, R. I.	6	2
Wood, Horatio N.	March 29, 1852	39	dark	Bridgewater, Mass.	5	8
Wood, Horatio N.	Aug. 26, 1857	47	dark	Bridgewater, Mass.	6	2
Wood, Isaac	June 14, 1820	20	yellow	Bridgewater, Mass.	4	7
Wood, James	March 9, 1805	15	dark	Warwick, R. I.	3	4
Wood, Joshua B.	Aug. 24, 1846	19	light	Coventry, R. I.	5	8
Wood, Liberty	May 28, 1810	19	light	Mendon, Mass.	4	7
Wood, Nathan	1798 to 1799 b. June 23, 1780			Rehoboth, Mass.	Newport, R.
Wood, Ralph	Feb. 17, 1800	17	light	Dartmouth, Mass.	2	21
Wood, Richard	Nov. 3, 1804	20	yellow*	Wallingford, Conn.	3	4
Wood, Robert	March 22, 1849	25	light	Eastport, Maine	5	8
Wood, Samuel	Jan. 21, 1832	22	dark	Woodstock, Vermont	5	8
Wood, Sylvanus A.	Oct. 29, 1849	21	light	North Providence, R. I.	5	8
Wood, Thomas P.	Oct. 25, 1796	11	light	Falmouth, Mass.	1	2
Wood, Washington A.	July 10, 1845	17	dark	Ludlow, Mass.	5	8

*mulatto

NAME	DATE OF CERTIFICATION	AGE	COMPLEXION	PLACE OF BIRTH	BOOK	PAGE
Wood, William	May 21, 1845	23	light	Ludlow, Mass.	5	86
Wood, William	Sept. 11, 1860	21	dark	Lowell, Mass.	6	23
Wood, William E.	Oct. 27, 1847	28	fair	New York, N. Y.	5	86
Wood, Wm. H.	Nov. 20, 1841	20	light	Warwick, R. I.	5	85
Wood, William Olney	Sept. 25, 1819	17	light	Warwick, R. I.	4	77
Wood, Zephaniah	Dec. 4, 1849	41	light	Swansea, Mass.	5	88
Woodberry, Andrew	Nov. 13, 1809	32	dark	Cranston, R. I.	4	74
Woodbridge, Charles	June 1, 1844	21	dark	Providence, R. I.	5	86
Wooding, William	1798 to 1799 b. June 2, 1779			Woodbridge, Conn.	Newport, R. I.	
Wooding, William	1798 to 1799 b. June 7, 1780			Woodbridge, Conn.	Newport, R. I.	
Woodland, Arthur	July 16, 1836	21	black	Laurel, Delaware	5	84
Woodley, William J.	Jan. 13, 1844	19	light	Bath, Maine	5	86
Woodley, William	Oct. 2, 1844	21	dark	Haverhill, Mass.	5	86
Woodmansee, George	July 8, 1806	26	dark	Dartmouth, Mass.	3	80
Woodmansee, George	May 20, 1808	28	dark	Smithfield, R. I.	4	74
Woodmansee, George	Jan. 3, 1812	31	dark	Smithfield, R. I.	4	75
Woodward, Elkanah M.	July 8, 1840	20	light	Taunton, Mass.	5	85
Woodward, John	Apr. 6, 1818	18	light	Providence, R. I.	4	77
Woodward, Robert B.	Feb. 24, 1849	26	light	Providence, R. I.	5	87
Wooster, Joseph D.	June 29, 1819	18	freckled	Derby, Conn.	4	77
Wooters, John	Aug. 25, 1831	25	light	Caroline Co., Maryland	5	83
Wordell, Abraham	1798 & 1799 b. Jan. 14, 1781			Tiverton, R. I.	Newport, R. I.	
Worden, Charles	1798 to 1799 b. Nov. 18, 1778			S. Kingston, R. I.	Newport, R. I.	
Work, Ezra M.	March 18, 1853	20	light	Providence, R. I.	5	88
Work, John	March 21, 1825	16	light	Newburyport, Mass.	4	77
Workman, Wm.	Nov. 30, 1857	24	fair	Baltimore, Maryland	5	95
Wormer, Henry	Sept. 14, 1842	18	dark	Salem, Mass.	5	85

NAME	DATE OF CERTIFICATION	AGE	COMPLEXION	PLACE OF BIRTH	BOOK	PAGE
Wormsley, Nelson	May 1, 1828	24	yellow	Providence, R. I.	4	78
Worrall, John	Nov. 1, 1836	21	light	Baltimore, Maryland	5	84
Worrell, John	Aug. 3, 1854	22	light	Mount Holly, N. J.	5	95
Worth, James	1798 to 1799	b. Feb. 9, 1783		Newport, R. I.	Newport, R.
Worthen, Amos	July 14, 1806	28	light	Chester, N. H.	3	80
Worthley, Moses	Aug. 14, 1829	23	dark	Amherst, N. H.	5	83
Wright, Adam	March 5, 1834	28	black	Philadelphia, Penn.	5	83
Wright, James D.	Nov. 10, 1849	27	light	Providence, R. I.	5	87
Wright, John	Aug. 7, 1854	22	light	Charlestown, Mass.	5	95
Wright, John	Dec. 8, 1804	22	dark	Boston, Mass.	3	42
Wright, Joseph	March 29, 1827	21	light	Rehoboth, Mass.	4	78
Wright, Orin	April 27, 1835	18	ruddy	Smithfield, R. I.	5	84
Wright, Prince	May 14, 1797	23	black	Swansea, Mass.	1	26
Wright, Reuben	Oct. 17, 1806	21	light	Providence, R. I.	4	74
Wright, Robert R.	March 6, 1827	21	light	South Kingstown, R. I.	4	78[7?
Wright, William	Dec. 21, 1842	31	dark	Albany, N. Y.	5	85
Wright, William	Jan. 3, 1856	45	light	Boston, Mass.	5	95
Wyatt, Constant B.	May 31, 1805	22	light	Rehoboth, Mass.	3	44
Wyatt, John L.	April 10, 1835	22	light	Norwich, Conn.	5	84
Wyatt, Lemuel	Aug. 29, 1804	23	light	Newport, R. I.	3	42
Wyatt, Lemuel	Feb. 21, 1801	20	light	Newport, R. I.	2	29
Wyatt, Robert	July 20, 1809	20	light	Rehoboth, Mass.	4	74
Wyatt, Seth	Feb. 10, 1852	45	light	Bellhaven, Virginia	5	88
Wyllys, Harold	Dec. 23, 1807	18	dark	Hartford, Conn.	4	74
Wyman, Daniel G.	March 6, 1834	20	light	Vassalboro, Maine	5	83

NAME	DATE OF CERTIFICATION	AGE	COMPLEXION	PLACE OF BIRTH	BOOK	PAGE
Yale, George	Feb. 16, 1821	21	dark	Norwich, Conn.	4	76
Yates, Alexander	May 9, 1838	22	light	Bristol, Maine	5	89
Yates, Chapin V.	June 8, 1838	20	light	Bristol, Maine	5	89
Yatses, Gideon	May 9, 1838	16	light	Bristol, Maine	5	89
Yates, Lorenzo D.	June 8, 1838	17	dark	Bristol, Maine	5	89
Yates, Samuel	July 31, 1819	16	light	Newport, R. I.	4	76
Yeaw, Henry	April 23, 1863	32	light	Sicutate, R. I.	6	24
Yeaw, James .	June 14, 1836	18	light	Foster, R. I.	5	89
Yeau, Leonard	July 15, 1854	21	light	Manchester, N. H.	5	89
Yerrington, Alonzo	Oct. 13, 1841	21	light	Newcastle, Delaware	5	89
York, Edward L.	July 19, 1841	20	light	Montpelier, Vermont	5	89
York, Goerge F.	Aug. 13, 1864	22	dark	Portland, Me.	6	24
Young, Benjamin E.	Dec. 16, 1841	16	light	Providence, R. I.	5	89
Young, Charles	May 20, 1811	22	dark	Cheshire, Mass.	4	76
Young, Charles C.	March 12, 1852	24	light	Boston, Mass.	5	89
Young, Columbia	Sept. 27, 1832	28	light	Harwich, Mass.	5	89
Young, Daniel	June 17, 1797	23	dark	North Providence, R. I.	1	28
Young, Ephraim	June 17, 1797	16	dark	North Providence, R. I.	1	28
Young, Ezekiel	March 7, 1815	21	light	Dennis, Mass.	4	76
Young, Francis	Oct. 12, 1857	18	fair	Lowell, Mass.	6	24
Young, Francis H.	Nov. 12, 1856	18	light	Cranston, R. I.	5	89
Young, Francis M.	March 1, 1849	22	fair	Scituate, R. I.	5	89
Young, George A.	June 2, 1849	19	light	Smithfield, R. I.	5	89
Young, Gideon	March 22, 1804	21	light	Providence, R. I.	3	45
Young, Henry	March 30, 1797	23	dark	Providence, R. I.	1	28
Young, Henry Olney	April 23, 1824	17	light	Providence, R. I.	4	76
Young, Horace	April 16, 1832	21	ruddy	Smithfield, R. I.	5	89

NAME	DATE OF CERTIFICATION	AGE	COMPLEXION	PLACE OF BIRTH	BOOK	PAG
Young, Hyram	Jan. 18, 1832	27	mulatto	Weathersfield, Conn.	5	89
Young, James	July 12, 1811	16	brown	Providence, R. I.	4	76
Young, James W.	Nov. 9, 1808	14	light	Providence, R. I.	4	76
Young, John	Aug. 1, 1825	24	light	Surry, Maine	4	76
Young, John, Jr.	Dec. 10, 1811	19	light	Foster, R. I.	4	76
Young, John J.	July 18, 1822	17	light	Providence, R. I.	4	76
Young, Joseph	March 22, 1845	30	light	Boston, Mass.	5	89
Young, Orville	Aug. 13, 1825	22	light	Scituate, R. I.	4	76
Young, Peter	Oct. 29, 1804	19	dark	Woodstock, Conn.	3	45
Young, Rufus K.	Dec. 30, 1811	17	light	Cranston, R. I.	4	76
Young, S. Samuel	May 13, 1818	18	light	Providence, R. I.	4	76
Young, Samuel	Nov. 19, 1796	23	light	Providence, R. I.	1	28
Young, Samuel	June 27, 1820	19	light	Providence, R. I.	4	76
Young, Samuel B.	Aug. 13, 1803	14	light	Providence, R.I.	2	23
Young, Stephen P.	Dec. 27, 1832	30	dark	Burlington, Vt.	5	89
Young, Thomas	Aug. 15, 1797	21	light	Providence, R. I.	1	28
Young, Thomas	Oct. 31, 1803	38	light	Providence, R. I.	2	23
Yuoung, Thomas, Jr.	Jan. 21, 1811	18	light	Providence, R. I.	4	76
Young, Thomas L. H.	July 29, 1820	18	light	Falmouth, Mass.	4	76
Young, William	Dec. 6, 1809	21	dark	Alexandria, Va.	4	76
Young, William	Nov. 30, 1816	15	light	Providence, R. I.	4	76
Young, William	July 3, 1820	18	light	Attleboro, Mass.	4	76
Young, William	Dec. 27, 1852	23	dark	New York, N. Y.	5	89
Young, Zenus	July 20, 1819	26	light	Chatham, Mass.	4	76
Yummy, Samuel	July 17, 1804	18	black	Providence, R. I.	3	45
Zado, Samuel	Oct. 16, 1837	26	black	New London, Conn.	5	94
Zanes, Elmer	June 7, 1843	23	light	Salem, New Jersey	5	94

www.ingramcontent.com/pod-product-compliance
Lightning Source LLC
Chambersburg PA
CBHW061002280326
41935CB00009B/801